THE BOOK OF MEMORY

Mary Carruthers's classic study of the training and uses of memory for a variety of purposes in European cultures during the Middle Ages has fundamentally changed the way scholars understand medieval culture. This fully revised and updated second edition considers afresh all the material and conclusions of the first. While responding to new directions in research inspired by the original, this new edition devotes much more attention to the role of trained memory in composition, whether of literature, music, architecture, or manuscript books. The new edition will reignite the debate on memory in medieval studies and, like the first, will be essential reading for scholars of history, music, the arts, and literature, as well as those interested in issues of orality and literacy (anthropology), in the working and design of memory (both neuropsychology and artificial memory), and in the disciplines of meditation (religion).

MARY CARRUTHERS is Remarque Professor of Literature at New York University and Fellow of All Souls College, Oxford. She is also the author of *The Craft of Thought: Meditation, Rhetoric, and the Making of Images, 400–1200* (Cambridge, 1998; paperback edition, 2000) and co-editor, with Jan M. Ziolkowski, of *The Medieval Craft of Memory: An Anthology of Texts and Pictures* (2002).

CAMBRIDGE STUDIES IN MEDIEVAL LITERATURE

GENERAL EDITOR
Alastair Minnis, *Yale University*

This series of critical books seeks to cover the whole area of literature written in the major medieval languages – the main European vernaculars, and medieval Latin and Greek – during the period *c.*1100–1500. Its chief aim is to publish and stimulate fresh scholarship and criticism on medieval literature, special emphasis being placed on understanding major works of poetry, prose, and drama in relation to the contemporary culture and learning which fostered them.

RECENT TITLES IN THE SERIES
Piers Plowman and the Medieval Discourse of Desire Nicolette Zeeman
The Jew in the Medieval Book: English Antisemitisms 1300–1500 Anthony Bale
Poets and Power from Chaucer to Wyatt Robert J. Meyer-Lee
Writing Masculinity in the Later Middle Ages Isabel Davis
Language and the Declining World in Chaucer, Dante and Jean de Meun
John M. Fyler
Parliament and Literature in Late Medieval England Matthew Giancarlo
Women Readers in the Middle Ages D. H. Green
The First English Bible: The Text and Context of the Wycliffite Versions
Mary Dove
The Creation of Lancastrian Kingship: Literature, Language and Politics in Late Medieval England Jenni Nuttall
Fiction and History in England, 1066–1200 Laura Ashe
The Poetry of Praise J. A. Burrow

A complete list of titles in the series can be found at the end of the volume.

THE BOOK OF MEMORY

A Study of Memory in Medieval Culture

Second Edition

MARY CARRUTHERS

New York University

and

All Souls College, Oxford

CAMBRIDGE
UNIVERSITY PRESS

CAMBRIDGE UNIVERSITY PRESS

Cambridge, New York, Melbourne, Madrid, Cape Town, Singapore, São Paulo,
Delhi, Dubai, Tokyo, Mexico City

Cambridge University Press
The Edinburgh Building, Cambridge CB2 8RU, UK

Published in the United States of America by Cambridge University Press, New York

www.cambridge.org
Information on this title: www.cambridge.org/9780521716314

First published 1990
First paperback edition 1992
Second edition 2008
3rd printing 2011

Printed in the United Kingdom at the University Press, Cambridge

A catalogue record for this publication is available from the British Library

ISBN 978-0-521-88820-2 hardback
ISBN 978-0-521-71631-4 paperback

Contents

List of illustrations   *page* vi
Preface to the second edition   ix
List of abbreviations   xv

Introduction   1

1   Models for the memory   18

2   Descriptions of the neuropsychology of memory   56

3   Elementary memory design   99

4   The arts of memory   153

5   Memory and the ethics of reading   195

6   Memory and authority   234

7   Memory and the book   274

Appendix A   339

Appendix B   345

Appendix C   361

Notes   369
Bibliography   458
Index of manuscripts   494
General index   496

Illustrations

1. New York, Pierpont Morgan Library MS. M. 917, p. 300.
   With permission of The Pierpont Morgan Library.   *page* 48
2. Paris, Bibliothèque nationale de France MS. n.a.l. 2334,
   fo. 9r. With permission of the Bibliothèque nationale de France.   52
3. Cambridge, University Library MS. Gg 1.1, fo. 490v.
   With permission of the University Library, Cambridge.   66
4. University of Oxford, Bodleian Library MS. Lat.th.b.4,
   fo. 21v. Reproduced by permission of the Bodleian Library,
   University of Oxford.   108
5. Paris, Bibliothèque nationale de France MS. lat. 15009,
   fo. 3v. With permission of the Bibliothèque nationale de France.   119
6. New York, Pierpont Morgan Library MS. M. 860,
   fo. 8v. With permission of The Pierpont Morgan Library.   120
7. Cambridge, Trinity College MS. B.5.4, fos. 146v–147r.
   Reproduced with permission of the Master and Fellows of
   Trinity College Cambridge.   266
8. University of Oxford, Bodleian Library, MS. Lat.th.b.4,
   fo. 23v. Reproduced by permission of the Bodleian Library,
   University of Oxford.   270
9. University of Oxford, Bodleian Library, MS. Bodley 717,
   fo. 287v. Reproduced by permission of the Bodleian Library,
   University of Oxford.   280
10. Utrecht, University Library MS. 32, fo. 82v. With
    permission of the University Library, Utrecht.   284
11. New York, Pierpont Morgan Library MS. M. 756,
    fo. 60r. With permission of The Pierpont Morgan Library.   286
12. New York, Pierpont Morgan Library MS. M. 756,
    fo. 105v. With permission of The Pierpont Morgan Library.   288
13. New York, Pierpont Morgan Library MS. M. 756,
    fo. 79r. With permission of The Pierpont Morgan Library.   289

14. University of Oxford, Bodleian Library, MS. Douce 104, fo. 79r. Reproduced by permission of the Bodleian Library, University of Oxford.   290

15. University of Oxford, Bodleian Library, MS. Lyell 71, fo. 3v. Reproduced by permission of the Bodleian Library, University of Oxford.   305

16. University of Oxford, Bodleian Library, MS. Lyell 71, fo. 4r. Reproduced by permission of the Bodleian Library, University of Oxford.   306

17. San Marino, California, Huntington Library MS. HM 19915, fo. 5r. Reproduced by permission of The Huntington Library.   311

18. San Marino, California, Huntington Library MS. HM 19915, fo. 36v. Reproduced by permission of The Huntington Library.   312

19. San Marino, California, Huntington Library MS. HM 19915, fo. 46r. Reproduced by permission of The Huntington Library.   313

20. London, British Library MS. Royal 10. E. IV, fo. 62r. © The British Library Board.   316

21. London, British Library MS. Royal 10. E. IV, fo. 62v. © The British Library Board.   316

22. London, British Library MS. Royal 10. E. IV, fo. 63r. © The British Library Board.   317

23. London, British Library MS. Royal 10. E. IV, fo. 63v. © The British Library Board.   317

24. London, British Library MS. Royal 10. E. IV, fo. 64r. © The British Library Board.   318

25. New York, Pierpont Morgan Library MS. M. 917, p. 240. With permission of The Pierpont Morgan Library.   319

26. New York, Pierpont Morgan Library MS. M. 945, fo. 20r. With permission of The Pierpont Morgan Library.   320

27. New York, Pierpont Morgan Library MS. M. 917, p. 247. With permission of The Pierpont Morgan Library.   321

28. New York, Pierpont Morgan Library MS. M. 917, p. 266. With permission of The Pierpont Morgan Library.   322

29. Cambridge, Corpus Christi College MS. 286, fo. 125r. With permission of the Master and Fellows of Corpus Christi College, Cambridge.   326

30. Dublin, Trinity College MS.A.1 (58), fo. 34r. With permission of The Board of Trinity College Dublin.   334

Preface to the second edition

Preparing a wholly new edition of work first undertaken more than twenty years ago has offered me an opportunity to rethink, recast, correct, and generally reassess the conclusions I offered in 1990. It is a task that carries mixed rewards. I have resisted my initial temptation to rewrite the entire thing from the beginning – this book cannot be started again. Published some eighteen years ago, translated entirely or in part into several other languages, and cited in many contexts by scholars with a great diversity of interests, it has a life of its own now and my control over it is limited. So the book begins as it did before, and the general ordering of the materials is unchanged. But each sentence and note has been reconsidered. I hope this has resulted in greater correctness in the translations and citations, increased felicity of style and clarity of presentation. I have also, however, updated the content when new scholarship has made old conclusions untenable. And I have added material to some of my analyses, reduced some discussions, and expanded others. The images selected for reproduction are somewhat different. I have also updated the notes and bibliography, to incorporate translations and editions that have appeared since I did my original research, and scholarly discussions that have matured over the past dozen years.

I wrote in 1989 that *The Book of Memory* was to be the first of three. It seemed an audacious promise at the time, but in fact it turned out to be truthful. *The Craft of Thought* (1998) examined an earlier medieval period, and focused even more particularly on the inventive and creative nature of recollection as it was cultivated in the practices of monastic reading and composition. An anthology of English translations of many of the medieval texts that had proved important in this history, *The Medieval Craft of Memory*, followed in 2002, prepared with my good friend Jan Ziolkowski, a consummate scholar of medieval Latin, and with the keen participation as translators and annotators of several members of his medieval Latin literature seminar.

Inevitably, as I have continued to work over the two decades intervening since *The Book of Memory* was first published, my own understanding of medieval memory culture (as it has come to be called) has changed and deepened. In this edition, I have adjusted and corrected more than just my Latin translations. I have come to understand far more clearly the place which the craft of memory training, *memoria artificialis*, had in medieval education, its perceived strengths, its accepted limitations, and most importantly its status as an instrument of thought, employing particular devices for specific goals and uses. *Ars memorativa* is not itself theoretical, though, like all crafts, it has its general principles. Two themes in particular stand out, which I did not focus on in the earlier edition, and it may be helpful to point them out now.

Though I did not know it at the time, *The Book of Memory* appeared just as interest was picking up in issues of memory and forgetting, particularly in relation to historical narratives of various sorts and to monuments. *The Book of Memory* was swept into this concern, although in fact the subject with which it dealt had little directly to do with monuments, and, while it certainly had a bearing on the construction of historical narratives, it was not directly illuminating of the issues of material selection and presentation that have most concerned historians like Pierre Nora, Patrick Geary, and Jean-Claude Schmitt. In rhetoric, memory craft is a stage in composing a work; presupposed is the axiom that recollection is an act of investigation and recreation in the service of conscious artifice. Its practitioners would not have been surprised to learn what was to them already obvious: that recollection is a kind of composition, and by its very nature is selective and formal.

Analysts of the postmodern have been particularly concerned for the past decade with issues of forgetting, which they often ally with issues of trauma and repression, as though remembering everything were the natural and desirable human condition, and forgetting was due to various psychic pathologies, if not to outright political immorality. In this postmodern presentation, the arts of memory have fared badly, the very idea of a memory art dismissed as a hoax or at best a chimerical quest. But the rush to condemn has itself created a historical illusion. For ancient and medieval writers supposed that human memories were by nature imperfect, and that humans recollected best by applying their reasoning abilities. These in turn could be aided by certain learned practices that build on some natural principles they had observed, concerning how people best learn and construct their thoughts and other artifacts.

St Augustine writes:[1]

I arrive in the fields and vast mansions of memory, where are treasured innumerable images brought in there from objects of every conceivable kind perceived by the senses. There too are hidden away the modified images we produce when by our thinking we magnify or diminish or in any way alter the information our senses have reported. There too is everything else that has been consigned and stored away and not yet engulfed and buried in oblivion . . . The huge repository of the memory, with its secret and unimaginable caverns, welcomes and keeps all these things, to be recalled and brought out for use when needed; and as all of them have their particular ways into it, so all are put back again in their proper places . . . This I do within myself in the immense court of my memory, for there sky and earth and sea are readily available to me, together with everything I have ever been able to perceive in them, apart from what I have forgotten.

"[A]part from what I have forgotten": in the cheerful admission of that phrase lies an essential difference between a modern and a medieval understanding of the cognitive function of memory. To have forgotten things is seen by us now as a failure of knowledge, however ordinary a failure it may be, and therefore a reason to distrust the power of memory altogether. Yet to have forgotten some things was understood in Augustine's culture as a necessary condition for remembering others. It is helpful to distinguish two sorts of forgetting, resulting from different causes. There is the kind that results from failing to imprint something in the first place – the sort Augustine seems to be talking about here. This should not even be called forgetting because, as Aristotle remarked in his discussion of memory and recollection, one cannot be properly said to have forgotten something that was never there in the first place.

On the other hand, there is deliberate or selective forgetting, the sort of forgetting that itself results from an activity of memory. In the passage I have just quoted, Augustine is certainly speaking of a consciously trained memory, one whose denizens, like prey (for he often speaks of memories as being like animals hunted from their lairs, whose tracks or vestiges are to be followed through their familiar pathways in the forest), can be rationally sought out via their particular paths when needed for use, and then returned to their proper places when finished with. But this edifice, this vast treasury, is chosen and constructed. It is a work of art, using the materials of nature as all arts do, but consciously crafted for some human use and purpose.

In his book on *Memory, History, Forgetting*, the French philosopher Paul Ricoeur, himself a profound student of Augustine, complained that arts of memory are "an outrageous denial of forgetfulness and . . . of the weaknesses inherent in both the preservation of [memory] traces and their evocation."[2] In a similar vein, Harald Weinrich in *Lethe*, a book that sweeps engagingly over the theme of forgetting in canonical Western literature, states that *ars memorativa* represents itself to be "an art that can serve to overcome forget-ting."[3] And he archly observes that in its celebrated advice about making multi-compartmental structures for a rich trove of remembered matters, "only forgetting has no place." But, as Augustine makes abundantly clear, Weinrich is wrong about that. Not only does forgetting have its honored place in an examination of *memoria* – indeed Augustine devotes a whole section of his discussion to the paradox that he can remember that he has forgotten something (*Confessions* X.16) – but forgetting, of a sort, is essential to constructing an art of memory in the first place.

Aristotle distinguishes clearly between the objects of memory and the investigative search, in his treatise "On memory and recollection" in the *Parva naturalia*, a matter I have dwelt on at some length in Chapter 2, and that is fundamental to all later analysis of the psychological processes of memory. This distinction is germane to the seeming lack of concern with forgetting in pre-modern teaching on memory, because the main focus of the arts of memory is on recollection – the search for stuff already there– and not on the representation of the object remembered. One can dem-onstrate this emphasis from the so-called *artes oblivionales* found in a few late humanist treatises on memory art. The "oblivion" discussed is to do with how to refresh one's search networks, not with worries about the accuracy or partialness of one's memories. As Lina Bolzoni has commented, "The techniques for forgetting handed down by the treatises are testimony to the persistence and power of the images," for they address the tasks of sorting out and reducing the number of memory places rather than with suppressing or otherwise editing content one has previously learned.[4]

Another matter to which the first edition gave much too short a shrift is the place of rote memorization – memorizing by heart – in the edifice of an ancient and medieval education. Most students of the arts of memory (including, when I began, me) have made a basic error when considering the relationship of memory craft to rote learning, by thinking both to be methods for initially memorizing the basic contents of educated memory. We have all been in good company in this confusion, for even the seventeenth-century Jesuit, Matteo Ricci, who practiced an art of memory, elided the two when he tried to teach his art as a helpful device for passing the content-based examinations of the Chinese imperial civil service.[5] Where this analysis went wrong was in supposing that learning an art for memory was intended as an alternative to rote learning, and in misunder-standing the ancient mnemotechnical term *memoria verborum* as a syno-nym for the verbatim memorization of long texts.

Matteo Ricci's Chinese hosts were on the right track when they complained that memorizing a scheme of memory places and cues added far too burdensome and confusing a task to the already difficult one of memorizing by rote – why memorize things twice? Why indeed. That simple question is the heart of the matter. In revising *The Book of Memory*, I have tried to set out the answer plainly in Chapter 3, during my discussion of Hugh of St Victor's preface to his elementary tables of the names and dates of Biblical history, addressed to the *pueri* or students of St. Victor in about 1135, after he had composed *Didascalicon*, his treatise on the goals and methods of education.[6]

It is with some chagrin that I realize now how wrong I was about this and for how long. When I first came across Hugh's preface in the early 1980s, I recognized that it offered the clearest presentation of an art of memory extant, much clearer than that in the *Rhetorica ad Herennium* – and also completely different in its details, though not in its basic principles. Seeking to understand it, I spent several months, while commuting to work in Chicago on the elevated train, memorizing psalms with the method Hugh described. I attached pieces of the texts I already knew by heart to the places I had created by using a mentally imposed grid system which was exactly that of the chapter and verse scheme of a modern printed Bible. I realized quickly that doing so gave me complete flexibility and security in finding the verses again in whatever order I chose. I could reverse the order, pull out all the odd-numbered verses, or all the even-numbered ones, or alternate reciting the odd verses in forward order and the even ones in reverse. I could also mentally interleave and recite the verses of one psalm with those of another. Bewitched by my new-found skill (I even once began a lecture by interleaving the verses of Psalm 1 in reverse order with those of psalm 23 in forward order), I overlooked the fact that I wasn't actually memorizing the words for the first time. I was instead imposing a divisional system onto something I already knew by heart.

This was a crucial ingredient of the method's success, though I failed to pay proper attention to it in my initial analysis. I did note that, for the quickest and most secure results, I needed to say the psalm text in English (and in the 1611 version which I learned as a child) and that I also needed to call up "The Lord is my shepherd" by its number in the Protestant Bible (23), not the Vulgate (22). What I was demonstrating was the power of such mental devices as finding tools rather than as retention devices. In fact, it was easy to impose such a scheme on material I already knew by heart (in King James English) because, with a bit of review and practice, the cues provided to my memory by just a few words of the texts I knew so securely brought out the whole quotation. Once started, my rote memory took over, and by conscious habit produced what I needed, very much in the manner of the Read-Only memory of a computer. The recollection devices of mnemonic art, like a Random-Access structure, took me where I wanted to go, in the order I had chosen and in the directions my mind had given to itself.

Many people have asked me over the years if memory arts really work. The answer to that is yes – if you know how to use them. They are not a pill or potion, and those who attempt to sell them as if they were are as fraudulent as any fake medicine purveyor. Nor can they be patented, or licensed to others like the secret recipe for a special sauce. All teachers of the subject, from the days of Cicero and his Greek masters, have made just these same points. It is amusing to me to read now in the science press some breathless accounts of how to improve memory by using the amazing Method of Loci, or to hear of efforts to introduce into schools a patented memory curriculum, guaranteeing improved learning for all. Some things never change . . .

Certainly, were I to begin *The Book of Memory* today, I would do it differently, but that is the way of scholarship. I have left the Introduction to the first edition unchanged, partly to measure just how much good work has been done in the subject since those words were first written in 1989. Most of this work has come from historians – of art and architecture, of music, of rhetoric, of law, of reading and of the book, of monasticism and religion, and of literature both in Latin and in vernaculars – but some as well has come, gratifyingly if astonishingly to me, from psychologists, anthropologists, neuroscientists, and computer designers. It did not occur to me when I began the project that it would resonate so broadly, nor that I would find myself keeping delightful intellectual company for so long a time with so wide a spectrum of scholar-scientists. Their friendship and collegiality towards me and my subsequent work has nourished and enriched me more than I could ever hope to acknowledge adequately. Most appear in my notes and bibliography, the site of our continuing conversations. One individual needs to be named: Linda Bree, literature editor at Cambridge University Press, who kept after me with unfailing good humor and gentle persistence until this work was done. Thank you. Three institutions also should be thanked: the University of Oxford and its unparalleled community of medievalists who have made me one of their own; the John Simon Guggenheim Memorial Foundation, with whose support I was able to continue this work and begin new projects; and New York University, my familiar base in the city that has been my home for so long.

Oxford and New York, 2007

Abbreviations

(Full citations for published titles are in the Bibliography.)

AASS	*Acta Sanctorum*
Ad Her.	[Cicero], *Rhetorica ad Herennium*
AMRS	Arizona Medieval and Renaissance Studies
Avi. Lat.	Avicenna (Ibn Sinna) latinus
CCCM	Corpus christianorum continuatio medievalis
CCSL	Corpus christianorum series latina
CHB	*The Cambridge History of the Bible*
Conf.	St. Augustine, *Confessiones*
CSEL	Corpus scriptorum ecclesiasticorum latinorum
DTC	*Dictionnaire de théologie catholique*
Du Cange	C. Du Cange *et al., Glossarium mediae et infimae latinitatis*
EETS	The Early English Text Society
Etym.	Isidore of Seville, *Etymologiarum libri*
Inst. orat.	Quintilian, *Institutio oratoria*
JMRS	*Journal of Medieval and Renaissance Studies* (now *Journal of Medieval and Early Modern Studies*)
JWCI	*Journal of the Warburg and Courtauld Institutes*
LCL	Loeb Classical Library
Lewis and Short	C. T. Lewis and C. Short, *A Latin Dictionary*
Liddell and Scott	H. G. Liddell and R. Scott, *A Greek–English Lexicon*
MED	*The Middle English Dictionary*
MGH	Monumenta Germaniae historica
MRTS	Medieval and Renaissance Texts Series
OED	*The Oxford English Dictionary*
Ox. Lat. Dict.	*The Oxford Latin Dictionary*
PG	Patrologia cursus completus series graeca. Compiled by J.-P. Migne. Paris, 1857–1866.
PIMS	Pontifical Institute of Medieval Studies (Toronto)

PL	Patrologia cursus completus series latina. Compiled by J.-P. Migne. Paris, 1841–1864.
SC	Sources chrétiennes
ST	St. Thomas Aquinas, *Summa theologiae*
STC	*A Short-Title Catalogue* (Pollard and Redgrave)
TLL	*Thesaurus linguae latinae*

Introduction

When we think of our highest creative power, we think invariably of the imagination. "Great imagination, profound intuition," we say: this is our highest accolade for intellectual achievement, even in the sciences. The memory, in contrast, is devoid of intellect: just memorization, not real thought or true learning. At best, for us, memory is a kind of photographic film, exposed (we imply) by an amateur and developed by a duffer, and so marred by scratches and inaccurate light-values.

We make such judgments (even those of us who are hard scientists) because we have been formed in a post-Romantic, post-Freudian world, in which imagination has been identified with a mental unconscious of great, even dangerous, creative power. Consequently, when they look at the Middle Ages, modern scholars are often disappointed by the apparently lowly, working-day status accorded to imagination in medieval psychology – a sort of draught-horse of the sensitive soul, not even given intellectual status. Ancient and medieval people reserved *their* awe for memory. Their greatest geniuses they describe as people of superior memories, they boast unashamedly of their prowess in that faculty, and they regard it as a mark of superior moral character as well as intellect.

Because of this great change in the relative status of imagination and memory, many moderns have concluded that medieval people did not value originality or creativity. We are simply looking in the wrong place. We should instead examine the role of memory in their intellectual and cultural lives, and the values which they attached to it, for there we will get a firmer sense of their understanding of what we now call creative activity.

The modern test of whether we really know something rests in our ability to use what we have been taught in a variety of situations (American pedagogy calls this "creative learning"). In this characterization of learning, we concur with medieval writers, who also believed that education meant the construction of experience and method (which they called "art") out of knowledge. They would not, however, have understood our separation of

I

memory from learning. In their understanding of the matter, it was memory that made knowledge into useful experience, and memory that combined these pieces of information-become-experience into what we call "ideas," what they were more likely to call "judgments."

A modern experimental psychologist has written that "some of the best 'memory crutches' we have are called laws of nature," for learning can be seen as a process of acquiring smarter and richer mnemonic devices to represent information, encoding similar information into patterns, organizational principles, and rules which represent even material we have never before encountered, but which is like what we do know, and thus can be recognized or remembered.[1] This is a position that older writers would have perfectly understood. It will be useful to begin my study by comparing descriptions of two men whom their contemporaries universally recognized to be men of remarkable scientific genius (assessments which time has proven correct, though that is only partly relevant to my discussion): Albert Einstein and Thomas Aquinas. Each description is the testimony (direct or reported) of men who knew and worked intimately with them over a long period of time. The first is by Leopold Infeld, a physicist who worked with Einstein at Princeton:

I was very much impressed by the ingenuity of Einstein's most recent paper. It was an intricate, most skillfully arranged chain of reasoning, leading to the conclusion that gravitational waves do not exist. If true, the result would be of great importance to relativity theory . . .

The greatness of Einstein lies in his tremendous imagination, in the unbelievable obstinacy with which he pursues his problems. Originality is the most essential factor in important scientific work. It is intuition which leads to unexplored regions, intuition as difficult to explain rationally as that by which the oil diviner locates the wealth hidden in the earth.

There is no great scientific achievement without wandering through the darkness of error. The more the imagination is restricted, the more a piece of work moves along a definite track – a process made up rather of additions than essentially new ideas – the safer the ground and the smaller the probability of error. There are no great achievements without error and no great man was always correct. This is well known to every scientist. Einstein's paper might be wrong and Einstein still be the greatest scientist of our generation . . .

The most amazing thing about Einstein was his tremendous vital force directed toward one and only one channel: that of original thinking, of doing research. Slowly I came to realize that in exactly this was his greatness. Nothing is as important as physics. No human relations, no personal life, are as essential as thought and the comprehension of how "God created the world." . . . one feels behind [his] external activity the calm, watchful contemplation of scientific problems, that the mechanism of his brain works without interruption. It is a constant motion which nothing can stop ... The clue to the understanding of Einstein's role in science lies in his loneliness and aloofness. In this respect he differs from all other scientists ... He had never studied physics at a famous university, he was not attached to any school; he worked as a clerk in a patent office ... For him the isolation was a blessing since it prevented his thought from wandering into conventional channels. This aloofness, this independent thought on problems which Einstein formulated for himself, not marching with the crowd but looking for his own lonely pathways, is the most essential feature of his creation. It is not only originality, it is not only imagination, it is something more.[2]

The following descriptions are excerpted from a life of St. Thomas Aquinas, written shortly after his death by Bernardo Gui, and from testimony taken at Thomas's canonization hearings from his close contemporary, Thomas of Celano, who also knew Reginald, Thomas's *socius*, or friar-companion.

Of the subtlety and brilliance of his intellect and the soundness of his judgment, sufficient proof is his vast literary output, his many original discoveries, his deep understanding of the Scriptures. His memory was extremely rich and retentive: whatever he had once read and grasped he never forgot; it was as if knowledge were ever increasing in his soul as page is added to page in the writing of a book. Consider, for example, that admirable compilation of Patristic texts on the four Gospels which he made for Pope Urban [the *Catena aurea* or "Golden Chain"] and which, for the most part, he seems to have put together from texts that he had read and committed to memory from time to time while staying in various religious houses. Still stronger is the testimony of Reginald his *socius* and of his pupils and of those who wrote to his dictation, who all declare that he used to dictate in his cell to three secretaries, and even occasionally to four, on different subjects at the same time ... No one could dictate simultaneously so much various material without a special grace. Nor did he seem to be searching for things as yet unknown to him; he seemed simply to let his memory pour out its treasures ...

He never set himself to study or argue a point, or lecture or write or dictate without first having recourse inwardly – but with tears – to prayer for the understanding and the words required by the subject. When perplexed by a difficulty he would kneel and pray and then, on returning to his writing or dictation, he was accustomed to find that his thought had become so clear that it seemed to show him inwardly, as in a book, the words he needed ...

Even at meal-times his recollection continued; dishes would be placed before him and taken away without his noticing; and when the brethren tried to get him into the garden for recreation, he would draw back swiftly and retire to his cell alone with his thoughts.[3]

It might be useful to isolate the qualities of genius enumerated in each of the above descriptions. Of Einstein: ingenuity, intricate reasoning, originality, imagination, essentially new ideas coupled with the notion that to achieve truth one must err of necessity, deep devotion to and understanding of physics, obstinacy, vital force, single-minded concentration, solitude. Of Thomas Aquinas: subtlety and brilliance of intellect, original discoveries coupled with deep understanding of Scripture, memory, nothing forgotten and knowledge ever-increasing, special grace, inward recourse, single-minded concentration, intense recollection, solitude.

As I compare these two lists I am struck first by the extent to which the qualities ascribed to each man's working habits are the same. In both, one gets a vivid sense of extraordinary concentration on problems to the exclusion of most daily routine. Infeld speaks of tremendous vital force, Bernardo of intense inner prayer, but both are describing a concentrated continuous energy that expresses itself in a profound singlemindedness, a remarkable solitude and aloofness. Each also praises the intricacy and brilliance of the reasoning, and its prolific character, its originality. It is important to appreciate that Bernardo values originality in Thomas's work – he praises its creativeness just as Infeld praises that in Einstein's.

What we have, in short, is a recognizable likeness between these two extraordinary intellects, in terms of what they needed for their compositional activity (the activity of thought), the social isolation required by each individual, and what is perceived to be the remarkable subtlety, originality, and understanding of the product of such reasoning. What is strikingly different is that in the one case this process and product are ascribed to intuition and imagination unfettered by "definite" tracks, in the other to a "rich and retentive memory," which never forgot anything and in which knowledge increased "as page is added to page in the writing of a book."

My point in setting these two descriptions up in this way is simply this: the nature of creative activity itself – what the brain does, and the social and psychic conditions needed for its nurture – has remained essentially the same between Thomas's time and our own. Human beings did not suddenly acquire imagination and intuition with Coleridge, having previously been poor clods. The difference is that whereas now geniuses are said to have creative imagination which they express in intricate reasoning and original discovery, in earlier times they were said to have richly retentive memories, which they expressed in intricate reasoning and original discovery.

We know a good deal about the actual procedures that Thomas Aquinas followed in composing his works, thanks in part to the full accounts we have from the hearings held for his canonization,[4] and in part to the remarkable survival of several pages of autograph drafts of certain of his early works. Both sources of material have received a thorough analysis from the paleographic scholar, Antoine Dondaine.[5] Dondaine's work confirmed the existence, alluded to many times in the contemporary accounts, of a group of three or four secretaries who took down Thomas's compositions in a fair hand from his own dictation. The autographs are written in *littera inintelligibilis*, a kind of shorthand that fully lives up to its name (Dondaine says that the great nineteenth-century editor, Uccelli, lost his eyesight scrutinizing these drafts) for it was not designed to be read by anyone other than the author himself. As Dondaine has reconstructed the process of composing the *Summa contra Gentiles*, an early work for which a number of autograph leaves exist, Thomas wrote first in *littera inintelligibilis* and then summoned one of his secretaries to take down the text in a legible hand while Thomas read his own autograph aloud. When one scribe tired, another took over.

But no autographs are found of the later major works. Dondaine remarks this fact as curious, because one would expect these autographs to have been treasured at least as carefully as those of earlier works. He suggests that their nonexistence is due not to loss but to there having been none in the first place to save. "Le fait qu'il n'y ait plus d'autographes des ouvrages postérieurs invite á penser que saint Thomas ne les a pas écrits, sinon peut-être sous forme de brouillons, et qu'il les a dictés en les composant."[6] Dondaine points out the tedium and waste of time involved for Thomas in writing out a complete text, even in shorthand, and then reading it aloud for it to be written again, this time in a fair hand.

There is good evidence in the remembrance of his peers that, certainly later in life, Thomas was not accustomed to writing his thoughts down himself, even in *inintelligibilis*. Two incidents in particular suggest this habit. There is the famous story of Thomas at dinner with Louis XI, Saint Louis. Though seated next to the king, Thomas was still preoccupied by an argument he was composing against the Manichees. Suddenly he struck the table, crying, "That settles the Manichees!" and called out to Reginald, his *socius*, "as though he were still at study in his cell . . . 'Reginald, get up and write!'"[7] This incident must have occurred between the springs of 1269 and 1270; the work in progress was the Second Part of the *Summa theologica*.[8]

The second incident occurred in conjunction with the writing of his commentary on Isaiah, a work for which an autograph of five chapters exists (Vatican lat. 9850).[9] Thomas became puzzled for days over the interpretation of a text:

At last, one night when he had stayed up to pray, his *socius* overheard him speaking, as it seemed, with other persons in the room; though what was being said the *socius* could not make out, nor did he recognize the other voices. Then these fell silent and he heard Thomas's voice calling: "Reginald, my son, get up and bring a light and the commentary on Isaiah; I want you to write for me." So Reginald rose and began to take down the dictation, which ran so clearly that it was as if the master were reading aloud from a book under his eyes.[10]

Pressed by Reginald for the names of his mysterious companions, Thomas finally replied that Peter and Paul had been sent to him, "and told me all I desired to know." This tale, among other things, suggests that some of Thomas's work was composed in a mixture of some parts written out in shorthand and then read to a secretary and some mentally composed and dictated. The contemporary sources suggest strongly that the entire *Summa theologica* was composed mentally and dictated from memory, with the aid at most of a few written notes, and there is no reason to disbelieve them.

Around 1263, Thomas wrote a compilation of patristic texts on the Gospels, the *Catena aurea*, which Gui describes, in the passage I just quoted, as "put together from texts that [Thomas] had read and committed to memory from time to time while staying in various religious houses."[11] Chenu accurately describes it as a "concatenation of patristic texts cleverly coordinated into a running commentary"; it includes a number of Greek authorities as well, which Thomas had had translated into Latin in order to add these extracts, "being careful to place the names of the authors before their testimonies" in the proper quotational style, whose purpose, as we will see in Chapter 3, was certainly to aid memorial retention.[12] The *catena* or chain is a very old medieval genre of scholarly commentary, used widely by the monastic scholars as part of *lectio divina*.[13] The authorities are chained, or hooked, together by a particular Biblical phrase. Thus the commentary entirely follows the sequence of the main text, each chapter division of the Gospel book forming a division of the *Catena*, and each verse (actually its unnumbered phrases and clauses) quoted separately with a string of relevant comments following it.

The written organization of the *catena* simply reproduces its memorial organization, as each bit of Biblical text calls up the authorities attached to it. For example, on Mt. 2:9, Thomas Aquinas first gives us a bit of Chrysostom on Matthew, then Augustine from two sources, then the ordinary gloss, then Ambrose on Luke, then Remigius, and then the gloss again. It is important to note that in writing this work Thomas did not look up each quotation in a manuscript tome as he composed; the accounts are specific on this point. The texts were already filed in his memory, in an ordered form that is one of the basics of mnemonic technique. And of course, once the texts were in his memory they stayed there for use on other occasions.

I am not suggesting that Thomas never made reference to manuscripts – on the contrary, we know that he did. We also know that one task of his secretaries was to copy manuscripts for his use.[14] But the picture we are often given of Thomas pausing while dictating in order to check a reference in a manuscript seems to me contrary to the evidence. For we are told over and over again that Thomas's flow to his secretaries was unceasing: it "ran so clearly that it was as if the master were reading aloud from a book under his eyes." He dictated "as if a great torrent of truth were pouring into him from God. Nor did he seem to be searching for things as yet unknown to him; he seemed simply to let his memory pour out its treasures." And again, "When perplexed by a difficulty he would kneel and pray and then, on returning to his writing or dictation, he was accustomed to find that his thought had become so clear that it seemed to show him inwardly, as in a book, the words he needed."[15]

That unceasing torrent, that clarity as though reading from a book before his eyes, that quality of retaining whatever he had read and grasped, can be understood if we are willing to give his trained memory its due. Thomas himself stresses the importance of concentration in memory, and we are told many times of his remarkable power of deep concentration, often approaching a trance-like state in which he did not feel physical pain. Thomas communed with his memory constantly, certainly before he dictated, and only when he clearly had "the understanding *and the words required*" (my emphasis) would he lecture or write or dictate.[16] (This, of course, is not to suggest that his works were dictated always in the absolutely final form in which we have them today; Dondaine gives much evidence of revision and reworking in the autographs and between the autographs and the fair texts. For some works, he left notes which were to be worked up later; the *Supplement* to the *Summa* is an example of such a practice.) I am even inclined to take somewhat seriously his comment to Reginald that Peter and Paul spoke with him and instructed him in his difficulties with the text of Isaiah. Their words were certainly intimately in his mind, among the many voices in his memory, intimate colleagues to his own thoughts. Moreover, subvocalization, a murmur, was a persistent and apparently necessary feature of memory work. One of his secretaries, a Breton called Evan, told how Thomas would sometimes sit down to rest from the work of dictating and, falling asleep, would continue to dictate in his sleep, Evan continuing to write just the same. What Evan took for sleep may have been an extreme form of Thomas's concentration. Or perhaps we should credit the story as told; since the matter had been worked out beforehand in

Thomas's memory, perhaps a kind of mental "automatic pilot" took over in times of extreme fatigue.

Most remarkable is the testimony of all his pupils and secretaries, including Reginald, that "he used to dictate in his cell to three secretaries, and even occasionally to four, on different subjects at the same time."[17] Gui comments, "No one could dictate simultaneously so much various material without a special grace." Dondaine is inclined to discount this story as the evidence of the single Breton secretary (are Bretons especially credulous?). Yet Gui ascribes the testimony to *all* those who wrote to Thomas's dictation.[18]

Moreover, as Dondaine himself notes, such stories have been told – though rarely – of other historical figures, notably Julius Caesar. Petrarch tells the story about Caesar, as an instance of trained memory ("ut memoria polleret eximia"), that he could dictate four letters on different subjects to others, while writing a fifth in his own hand.[19] Whether the tale is factual or not is less important for my analysis than that Petrarch understood it as evidence of the power of Caesar's *memory*, for Petrarch himself had a significant reputation as an authority on memory training. Thomas's biographer, too, understood a similar feat to be enabled by powerful memory. But it is not achieved by raw talent alone; indeed natural talent will not produce such facility or accuracy. Memory must be trained, in accordance with certain elementary techniques.

The nature of these techniques and how they were taught is the subject of much of my study. *Memoria* meant, at that time, trained memory, educated and disciplined according to a well-developed pedagogy that was part of the elementary language arts – grammar, logic, and rhetoric. The fundamental principle is to "divide" the material to be remembered into pieces short enough to be recalled in single units and to key these into some sort of rigid, easily reconstructable order. This provides one with a "random-access" memory system, by means of which one can immediately and securely find a particular bit of information, rather than having to start from the beginning each time in order laboriously to reconstruct the whole system, or – worse – relying on simple chance to fish what one wants out from the murky pool of one's undifferentiated and disorganized memory.

It is possible for one with a well-trained memory to compose clearly in an organized fashion on several different subjects. Once one has the all-important starting-place of the ordering scheme and the contents firmly in their places within it, it is quite possible to move back and forth from one distinct composition to another without losing one's place or becoming confused. As an experiment, I tried memorizing a few psalms (texts that come to us with a divisional system already in place) in accordance with an elementary scheme described by the twelfth-century teacher Hugh of St. Victor – a scheme that I analyze in detail in Chapter 3. That scheme enabled me to recall the texts in any order I pleased. If one so novice and unskilled as I am can recite without difficulty three psalms "at the same time" (that is, going easily from one psalm to another, verse to verse, backwards or forwards or skipping around at will), a memory as highly talented and trained as Thomas's could surely manage three *quaestiones* of his own composition at the same time. The key lies in the imposition of a rigid order to which clearly prepared pieces of textual content are attached. Both the initial laying down of the scheme and its recollection are accomplished in a state of profound concentration. Proper preparation of material, rigid order, and complete concentration are the requirements which Thomas Aquinas himself defines in his discourses on trained memory, and, as we will see, they are continuously emphasized in all ancient and medieval mnemonic practices.

Scholars have always recognized that memory necessarily played a crucial role in pre-modern Western civilization, for in a world of few books, and those mostly in communal libraries, one's education had to be remembered, for one could never depend on having continuing access to specific material. While acknowledging this, however, insufficient attention has been paid to the pedagogy of memory, to what memory was thought to be, and how and why it was trained. Nor can the immense value attached to trained memory be understood only in terms of differing technical applications, though these are basic.

It is my contention that medieval culture was fundamentally memorial, to the same profound degree that modern culture in the West is documentary. This distinction certainly involves technologies – mnemotechnique and printing – but it is not confined to them. For the valuing of *memoria* persisted long after book technology itself had changed. That is why the fact of books in themselves, which were much more available in the late Middle Ages than ever before, did not profoundly disturb the essential value of memory training until many centuries had passed. Indeed the very purpose of a book is differently understood in a memorial culture like that of the Middle Ages than it is today.

A book is not necessarily the same thing as a text. "Texts" are the material out of which human beings make "literature." For us, texts only come in books, and so the distinction between the two is blurred and even lost. But, in a memorial culture, a "book" is only one way among several to remember a "text," to provision and cue one's memory with "dicta et facta memorabilia." So a book is itself a mnemonic, among many other functions it can also have. Thomas Aquinas makes this assumption about books in a comment on Ps. 69:28 ("Let them be blotted from the book of life"):

A thing is said metaphorically to be written on the mind of anyone when it is firmly held in the memory ... For things are written down in material books to help the memory.[20]

Andrew of St. Victor, writing over a hundred years earlier, comments similarly on Is. 1:18 ("Though your sins be as scarlet, they shall be white as snow"):

According to Jewish tradition, the sins of all men are preserved in writing on a shining white substance ... Grievous sins are written in red and other colours which adhere more faithfully to the parchment and strike the reader's eye more readily ... When sins are said to be written in books, what else does it mean but that God remembers as though they were written?[21]

In the early twelfth century, Hugh of St. Victor, instructing some young students on how to remember, explains clearly the mnemonic utility of manuscript page layout and decoration. Repeating traditional advice about always memorizing from the same written source, lest a confusion of images caused by seeing different layouts make it impossible for the brain to impress a single image, he says:

it is a great value for fixing a memory-image that when we read books, we strive to impress on our memory ... the color, shape, position, and placement of the letters, ... in what location (at the top, the middle or bottom) we saw [something] positioned, in what color we observed the trace of the letter or the ornamented surface of the parchment. Indeed I consider nothing so useful for stimulating the memory as this.

Much later, in his *Archiloge sophie* (*c.* 1400), the humanist scholar Jacques Legrand gave similar advice to pay close attention to the color of lines and the appearance of the page in order to fix the text as a visual image in memory:

wherefore one best learns by studying from illuminated books, for the different colors bestow remembrance of the different lines and consequently of that thing which one wants to get by heart. And indeed, when they wanted to record and learn a matter by heart, the ancients placed various colors and figures in their books to the end that the diversity and difference would give [them] better recollection.[22]

Throughout this study, my concern is with educated memory. All my evidence comes from learned works, most of them written in Latin, from about the fourth through the fourteenth centuries; the few vernacular poets I cite are themselves learned, working within a highly educated group. *Memoria*, as these writers understood and practiced it, was a part of *litteratura*: indeed it was what literature, in a fundamental sense, was for. Memory is one of the five divisions of ancient and medieval rhetoric; it was regarded, moreover, by more than one writer on the subject as the "noblest" of all these, the basis for the rest. *Memoria* was also an integral part of the virtue of prudence, that which makes moral judgment possible. Training the memory was much more than a matter of providing oneself with the means to compose and converse intelligently when books were not readily to hand, for it was in trained memory that one built character, judgment, citizenship, and piety.

Memoria also signifies the process by which a work of literature becomes institutionalized – internalized within the language and pedagogy of a group. In describing the truth of Holy Scripture, John Wyclif argues that God's text is contained only in a sort of shorthand form in books, language, and other human artifacts "which are the memorial clues and traces of pre-existing truth"; because of this, the actual words are five times removed from Truth itself, and must therefore be continually interpreted and adapted to what he calls the *liber vitae*, the living book or book of life in the actual person of Christ.[23] This opinion is a commonplace; Wyclif attributes it to Augustine, but we find it earlier than that, for the idea that language, as a *sign* of something else, is always at a remove from reality is one of the cornerstones of ancient rhetoric. This idea gives to both books and language a subsidiary and derivative cultural role with respect to *memoria*, for they have no meaning except in relation to it. A work is not truly read until one has made it part of oneself – that process constitutes a necessary stage of its textualization. Merely running one's eyes over the written pages is not reading at all, for the writing must be transferred into memory, from graphemes on parchment or papyrus or paper to images written in one's brain by emotion and sense.

It should be clear from what I have said so far that I am not concerned with what has traditionally been the subject of studies of the rise of literacy during the Middle Ages, although I have, inevitably, run up against other scholars' distinctions between oral and literate societies in the course of my work. As a historian of literature, my emphasis is on the function of literature in particular societies – and "literature" is not the same thing as "literacy." The ability to write is not always the same thing as the ability to compose and comprehend in a fully textual way, for indeed one who writes (a scribe) may simply be a skilled practitioner, employed in a capacity akin to that of a professional typist today. The distinction of composing (or "making" in Middle English) from writing-down continued to be honored throughout the Middle Ages. Similarly, learning by hearing material and reciting aloud should not be confused with ignorance of reading. Especially in describing the Middle Ages, when the criterion of being *litteratus* was knowledge of Latin, one should be careful to remember that some degree of bilingualism (Latin and a vernacular) was a fact of every educated European's life, and not confuse apologies for "illiteracy," meaning "unable to compose fluently in Latin," with an apology for being unable to think or write clearly in any language.[24]

Historians of literacy have been concerned with normative channels of communication in societies. An oral society is thus one in which communication occurs in forms other than written documents, and in which law and government are conducted on the basis of orally preserved custom. For such a historian, much of the best evidence comes from studying the changing ways in which legally persuasive evidence was thought to be established.[25] In the medieval period, such studies have focused on the ways in which the tribal cultures of Germanic, northern Europe became acculturated to the literate norms of late Roman law and education, preserved primarily in Italy and in the institutions of the Roman church. Because oral cultures must obviously depend on memory, and hence value memory highly, such valorization has come to be seen as a hallmark of orality, as opposed to literacy. This has led to a further assumption that literacy and memory are per se incompatible, and that a "rise of literacy" will therefore bring with it a consequent devalorizing and disuse of memory.

It is this assumption that my study calls particularly into doubt. For the cultivation and training of memory was a basic aspect of the literate society of Rome as well as Greece, and continued to be necessary to literature and culture straight through the Middle Ages. This privileged cultural role of memory seems independent of "orality" and "literacy" as these terms have come to be defined in the social sciences, and it is dangerous to confuse those terms with a literary and ethical concept like medieval "memory."

Indeed, I think it is probably misleading to speak of literary culture as a version of "literacy" at all. The reason is simply this – as a concept, literacy privileges a physical artifact, the writing-support, over the social and rhetorical process that a text both records and generates, namely, the composition by an author and its reception by an audience. The institutions of literature, including education in the arts of language, the conventions of debate, and meditation, as well as oratory and poetry, are rhetorically conceived and fostered.

The valuing of memory training depends more, I think, on the role which rhetoric has in a culture than on whether its texts are presented in oral or written forms, or some combination of the two. For the sake of definition, I will distinguish here between fundamentalism and textualism as representing two polar views of what literature is and how it functions in society. These two extremes are always in tension with one another; one can analyze many changes in literary theory as efforts to redress an imbalance of one over the other. (For example, some Biblical scholars of the thirteenth century stressed the literal "intention" of the text in order to redress what they saw as an excess of interpretative commentary on the part of earlier exegetes – in my terms, this would be a dash of fundamentalism injected to offset too excessive a textualism.)

Fundamentalism regards a work of literature as essentially not requiring interpretation. It emphasizes its literal form as independent of circumstance, audience, author – of all those factors that are summed up in rhetorical analyses by the word "occasion." Legal scholars speak of "originalists," those who believe that the original intention of a written document is contained entirely in its words, and that all interpretation is unnecessary and distracting. The kinship of this position to religious fundamentalism is apparent. True fundamentalism understands words not as signs or clues but takes them as things in themselves. It also regards works exclusively as objects, which are therefore independent of institutions – perhaps that is why fundamentalism was so frequently a component of medieval heresies.[26]

Fundamentalism denies legitimacy to interpretation. Instead of interpreting, a reader is engaged at most only in rephrasing the meaning of the written document, a meaning which is really transparent, simple, and complete – but which the detritus of history and linguistic change have temporarily concealed. Fundamentalist translations are considered to be merely restatements of an inerrant truth that is clear and non-ambiguous – they are not adaptations or interpretive readings. Fundamentalism ideally should produce no gloss or commentary. Thus the role of scholarship is solely to identify the accumulations of interpretive debris and to polish up the original, simple meaning. It is reasonable, from a fundamentalist attitude, that God must be the direct author of the Bible. This belief holds true as well among secular fundamentalists writing about literature, who postulate a God-like author who plans, directs, and controls the meaning of his work.

But texts need not be confined to what is written down in a document. Where literature is valued for its social functions, works (especially certain

ones, of course) provide the sources of a group's memory. Societies of this
sort are "textual communities," in Stock's phrase, whether those texts exist
among them in oral or written form. The Latin word *textus* comes from the
verb meaning "to weave" and it is in the institutionalizing of a story
through *memoria* that textualizing occurs. Literary works become institutions as they weave a community together by providing it with shared
experience and a certain kind of language, the language of stories that can
be experienced over and over again through time and as occasion suggests.
Their meaning is thought to be implicit, hidden, polysemous, and complex, requiring continuing interpretation and adaptation. Taken to an
extreme, of course, textualism can bury the original work altogether in
purely solipsistic interpretation. Beryl Smalley, who spent her scholarly life
reading medieval commentaries, once remarked wryly that "choos[ing] the
most arbitrary interpreter of Biblical texts of the Middle Ages would be
rather like awarding a prize for the ugliest statue of Queen Victoria."[27]

In the process of textualizing, the original work acquires commentary
and gloss; this activity is not regarded as something other than the text, but
is the mark of textualization itself. *Textus* also means "texture," the layers of
meaning that attach as a text is woven into and through the historical and
institutional fabric of a society. Such "socializing" of literature is the work
of *memoria*, and this is as true of a literate as of an oral society. Whether the
words come through the sensory gateways of the eyes or the ears, they must
be processed and transformed in memory – they are made our own.
Thomas Aquinas was a highly literate man in a highly literate group, yet
his contemporaries reserved their greatest praise not for his books but for
his memory, for they understood that it was memory which allowed him to
weave together his astonishing works.

Memory also marked his superior moral character; it should not go
unnoticed that the praise heaped on his memory came at his canonization
trial. In fact, prodigious memory is almost a trope of saints' lives. One
thinks of St. Anthony, who learned the whole Bible by heart merely from
hearing it read aloud (the fact that he never saw the words written is what
astonished his contemporaries); of St. Francis of Assisi, reputed by his
followers to have a remarkably exact and copious memory. Tropes cannot
be dismissed as "mere" formulas, for they indicate the values of a society
and the way in which it conceives of its literature. The choice to train one's
memory or not, for the ancients and medievals, was not a choice dictated
by convenience: it was a matter of ethics. A person without a memory, if
such a thing could be, would be a person without moral character and, in a
basic sense, without humanity. *Memoria* refers not to how something is

communicated, but to what happens once one has received it, to the interactive process of familiarizing – or textualizing – which occurs between oneself and others' words in memory.

Many historians will wonder why I have avoided assigning Neoplatonist or Aristotelian labels in my discussion of memorial technique and practice, especially given the role of memory in Neoplatonist philosophy. But my decision is deliberate. A currently accepted picture of the intellectual history of the twelfth and thirteenth centuries is one of movement from a Neoplatonist matter/spirit dualism, influenced profoundly by Augustine (though not identical with his thought), to an Aristotelian hylemorphism articulated most successfully by Thomas Aquinas. But to associate an interest in memorial practice with one of these schools more than the other is misleading, as I discovered early in my study of the subject. While the Neoplatonist–Aristotelian distinction is crucial in some areas of medieval culture, it is not, I think, when it comes to this one. In fact, intellectual history, as traditionally practiced, is not the best way to go about studying the role of memory in medieval culture.

Memoria is better considered, in the context of my study, as *praxis* rather than as *doxis*. Practices are sometimes influenced by ideas (and vice versa) – Chapter 4 describes one major instance of this in later medieval mnemo-technique – but they are distinct, and follow different patterns and tempos of change. Historians of rhetoric have sometimes described Memory as one of the two "technical" parts of their subject, along with Delivery, distinguishing it thereby from the "philosophical" areas of Invention, Arrangement, and Style. This classification may well have contributed to the impression that *memoria*, being merely technical, was limited in its applicability to the conditions of oral debate, as was Delivery.[28] But as the practical technique of reading and meditation, *memoria* is fundamental in medieval paideia, having even greater importance in that context than it does as a "part" of rhetoric. If my study achieves nothing else, I hope it will prevent students from ever again dismissing mnemonics and mnemotech-nique with the adjective "mere," or from assuming that memory technique had no serious consequence just because it was useful and practical.

The historian Lawrence Stone has wisely remarked that all historical change is relative. Within any given period, we may stress differences or continuities. Most historians of the Middle Ages are now engaged in detailing the differences that existed among Western peoples during that immensely long stretch of time, geography, and linguistic and institutional developments that we hide within the blanket designation "the Middle Ages." In this study, I stress the continuities, though I am aware of the differing circumstances that separate the various scholars and poets whose work I discuss. I am concerned with elementary assumptions and the commonplaces which underlie the practices that are the subject of my study.

My method is, I hope, made legitimate by the nature of the topic I am studying: *memoria*, in the rich complex of practices and values that word acquired. It is also justified by the elementary nature of my subject, whose training began in one's earliest education and was basic to both reading and composition. And while this study lays some foundations, it is in fact the first of three. It must be complemented by a full study of how mnemo-technique changed over the medieval centuries (I glance at this aspect of my subject in Chapter 4). The third study would consider *memoria* not as a technique but as a cultural value or "modality" (in the sense developed by A. G. Greimas) of literature, and this aspect of it is touched upon especially in Chapters 5 and 6.[29]

I begin this book with an examination of two of the governing models for the operation of memory in respect to knowledge, expressed as two families of related metaphors: memory as a set of waxed tablets upon which material is inscribed; and memory as a storehouse or inventory. These models are complementary; they are also archetypal Western commonpla-ces. The next two chapters examine the workings of memory itself. Chapter 2 begins by considering memory's psychosomatic nature in clas-sical and medieval psychology, its intermediary relationship between sen-sory information and intellectual abstraction, and its identification with habit in the ethical realm. Chapter 2 next considers the ethical imperative attached to memory training, and ends by examining a parallel between the ancient memory system based upon placing images mentally in architec-tural places and the case history of a "memory artist" described by the Soviet psychologist A. R. Luria.

Chapter 3 describes several elementary schemes taught for designing a trained memory, which utilize the principle of a rigid order into which short pieces of material are placed and consciously supplied with a network of associations, the aim being to provide a securely accessible "library" (as it was often called) known by heart. In Chapter 4, I examine the circum-stances in which the ancient mnemotechnique described in the *Rhetorica ad Herennium*, attributed to Cicero, was revived in the scholastic setting of the universities and by the early humanists, and examine carefully three scholastic arts of memory that seem to show how an essentially medieval mnemotechnique was married (somewhat awkwardly) to principles of the ancient architectural scheme. I have provided, in appendices, English translations of three medieval texts that are not easily available now, but that are important descriptions of various memory techniques.[30]

The last part of this book turns from the theory and practice of mnemotechnique itself to examine why it was held in such esteem. Here I define in detail the important institutional role of *memoria*, first in relation to reading and then in the context of the activity of composition. These related discussions in Chapters 5 and 6 clarify how literature was thought to contribute to the ethical life of the individual and to the public memory of society. Finally, in Chapter 7, I examine how the memorial needs of readers and the memorial nature of literature affect the presentation and layout of the text in the physical book itself.

I would like to acknowledge at this point certain works whose influence on my opinions came as I was working out the earliest parts of this study, and is consequently more profound than may be entirely evident from my notes: Paul Ricoeur, *The Rule of Metaphor*; Jacques Derrida, "White Mythology"; Wesley Trimpi, *Muses of One Mind*; Gerald Bruns, *Inventions*; Richard Rorty, *Philosophy and the Mirror of Nature*; Clifford Geertz, *The Interpretation of Cultures*; A. J. Greimas, *On Meaning*; Jean Leclercq, *The Love of Learning and the Desire for God*; the studies of ancient and early medieval education by H.-I. Marrou and Pierre Riché; and Brian Stock, *The Implications of Literacy*. I have raided the footnotes of many scholarly studies, but none more fruitfully than those of Richard and Mary Rouse. Finally, and most importantly of all, any work on artificial memory systems must begin with the studies of Frances Yates and Paolo Rossi; though mine range far from theirs, I could not have done without them.

My subject is multifaceted. I have tried to keep my analysis adequate to it, though I know I have simplified some things, perhaps overly so. I must ask for some patience from my readers, as I follow out various strands of what is, actually, a skein. If I seem to be digressing unconscionably, I hope that they will bear with me until we come back to the main subject, enriched in understanding. (And perhaps some of the memory techniques described in my early chapters will help in remembering the parts of this discussion.) For this book can be read in at least two ways: as a history of a basic and greatly influential practice of medieval pedagogy, and as a reflection on the psychological and social value of the institution of *memoria* itself, which is in many ways the same as the institution of literature.

Models for the memory

Readers who are familiar with a current opinion that there are radical differences between oral culture (based upon memory) and literate culture (based upon writing) may be puzzled by the very title of this book, and even consider it self-contradictory. My source, however, is Dante,[1] who was newly articulating a very old observation. Even the earliest writers I discuss did not operate within a culture that could be described as fully oral. Yet for all these writers, memory is a central feature of knowledge – its very basis in fact – whether through recollection (as for Plato) or as the agent building experience (as for Aristotle). This emphasis upon memory persists, shared by societies varying widely in the availability of books to readers: that is, in their literacy. (I am adopting here Eric Havelock's useful definition of "literacy" as coterminous with "book-acquiring public.")[2]

In none of the evidence is the act of writing itself regarded as a supplanter of memory, not even in Plato's *Phaedrus*. Rather books are themselves memorial cues and aids, and memory is most like a book, a written page or a wax tablet upon which something is written. Cicero writes about the relationship of writing to memory in his elementary work, *Partitiones oratoriae*:

[M]emory ... is in a manner the twin sister of written speech [*litteratura*] and is completely similar to it [*persimilis*], [though] in a dissimilar medium. For just as script consists of marks indicating letters and of the material on which those marks are imprinted, so the structure of memory, like a wax tablet, employs places [*loci*] and in these gathers together [*collocat*] images like letters.[3]

This metaphor is so ancient and so persistent in all Western cultures that it must be seen as a governing model or "cognitive archetype," in Max Black's phrase.[4] In the passage most familiar to the later Middle Ages, the image is used by Aristotle in his treatise *De memoria et reminiscentia*. A memory is a mental picture (phantasm; Latin *simulacrum* or *imago*) of a sort which

Aristotle defines clearly in *De anima*, an "appearance" which is inscribed in a physical way upon that part of the body which constitutes memory. This phantasm is the final product of the entire process of sense perception, whether its origin be visual or auditory, tactile or olfactory. Every sort of sense perception ends up in the form of a phantasm in memory. And how is this "mental picture" produced? "The change that occurs marks [the body] in a sort of imprint, as it were, of the sense-image, *as people do who seal things with signet-rings*" (my emphasis).[5] In this particular passage, Aristotle uses, in addition to his usual word phantasm, the word *eikōn* or "copy," which he qualifies by calling it "a sort of *eikōn.*" His language here derives in turn from Plato, who uses several of the same words in his own descriptions of what constitutes the physiological process of memory. As Richard Sorabji notes, for Plato, too, recollection involved "the seeing of internal pictures" which are imprinted upon the memory as if with signet rings.[6]

The idea that the memory stores, sorts, and retrieves material through the use of some kind of mental image was not attacked until the eighteenth century.[7] It has recently been vigorously revived by certain cognitive psychologists, some of whose experimental work provides startling apparent corroboration of ancient observations concerning what is useful for recollection.[8] According to the early writers, retention and retrieval are stimulated best by visual means, and the visual form of sense perception is what gives stability and permanence to memory storage. They do not talk of "auditory memory" or "tactile memory" as distinct from "visual memory," the way some modern psychologists do.[9] The sources of what is in memory are diverse, but what happens to an impression or an idea once it gets into the brain is a single process resulting in the production of a phantasm that can be seen and scanned by "the eye of the mind." This sort of language is constant and pervasive in writings on the subject from earliest times. Albertus Magnus, for instance, writes that Isaiah's visionary experience "was not secured enough from hearing, but by seeing it was firmed up." And he quotes Horace to the effect that "things intrusted to the ear / Impress our minds less vividly than what is exposed / To our trustworthy eyes."[10]

A major source of confusion for proponents of the opinion that a "literate consciousness" replaced an earlier oral one lies in their frequent failure to distinguish this very matter, the generic cause from the physiological cause (if I may, on the verge of an Aristotelian analysis, freely adapt some Aristotelian categories). In discussing the acts of memory, we can be concerned with three quite separate matters: first, what is the actual origin of information entering the brain; second, how is that information encoded, and is it in a way that physically affects our brain tissue; and third, how is its recollection best stimulated and secured, or what kind of heuristic devices are necessary for us to find it again once it has been stored? According to the Greek tradition, all perceptions, however presented to the mind, are encoded as *phantasmata*, "representations" or a "kind of *eikōn*."[11] Because they are themselves "sort-of pictures," these representations were thought to be best retained for recollection by marking them in an order that was readable, a process the ancients thought to be most like the act of seeing.

Evidently, at least in the context of this metaphor, reading was considered to be essentially a visual act, despite the fact that most ordinary social reading, at least, was done aloud by someone to a group of listeners, throughout antiquity and the Middle Ages, and well into modernity. Nonetheless, as they understood the process, whatever enters the mind changes into a "see-able" form for storing in memory. Jerome describes it well and typically in his commentary on Ezekiel 40:4 ("And the man said unto me, Son of man, behold with thine eyes, and hear with thine ears, and set thine heart upon all that I shall shew thee; for to the intent that I might shew them unto thee art thou brought hither"). "Nothing," Jerome writes, "that you have seen or heard is useful, however, unless you deposit what you should see and hear in the treasury of your memory. When indeed he says, *all that I shall shew thee*, he makes his listener attentive, and also makes matters prepared for the eyes of his heart, so that he may hold in memory those things shown to him, *for to the intent that I might shew them unto thee art thou brought hither*."[12]

Material presented acoustically is turned into visual form so frequently and persistently, even when the subject is sound itself, that the phenomenon amounts to a recognizable trope. Guido d'Arezzo, the eleventh-century Benedictine music master whose annotation schemes profoundly influenced the writing of music, likens the values of the gamut to the letters of the alphabet – one writes with each: "Just as in all writing there are four-and- twenty letters, so in all melody we have seven notes."[13] A note is a cue recalling a *vox* or sound, as is a written letter. In his *Teseida*, Boccaccio describes how Palemone's prayer to Venus takes on human shape as his words rise up. This "shape" walks around the gardens and temple of Venus, and petitions the goddess, while the speaker himself remains corporeally below (Bk. 7, 50–69). And in Chaucer's *The House of Fame*, gossip-spread tales pass through the House of Rumor until, acquiring a feathered body, they creep through a window and fly away (*HF* III, 2081–2087).

One should distinguish very carefully between "pictorial" and "visual."[14] Memories could be marked by pictorial means; the ancient system described in *Rhetorica ad Herennium* was precisely that. But pictures are not the only sorts of objects we can see. We also see written words and numbers, punctuation marks, and blotches of color; if we read music, we hear it seen in notes on the staff; if we play the piano "by ear," we also see the music in the position of our fingers on the keys. Moreover, we can manipulate such information in ways that make it possible to bring it together or separate it in a variety of ways, to collate, classify, compose, and sort it in order to create new ideas or deconstruct old ones. In likening the notes of music to the letters of the alphabet, Guido d'Arezzo used a common trope of music theory. It always expresses admiration for how an abundance of material can be generated from a very few items. In other words, the trope articulates processes of recollection whose goals are to invent and compose in the present – not to reproduce a record of past events. This is a crucial distinction.

One accomplishment which seems always to have been greatly admired by both ancient and medieval writers was the ability to recite a text backwards as well as forwards, or to skip around in it in a systematic way, without becoming lost or confused. The ability to do this marked the difference between merely being able to imitate something (to reproduce it by rote) and really knowing it, being able to recall it in various ways. Such reports are common enough throughout the period of my study. For example, Augustine describes a school friend named Simplicius:

an excellent man of remarkable memory, who, when he might be asked by us for all the next-to-last verses in each book of Virgil, responded in order quickly and from memory. If we then asked him to recite the verse before each of those, he did. And we believed that he could recite Virgil backwards. If we desired a commonplace concerning any topic, we asked him to make one and he did. If we wanted even prose passages from whatever of Cicero's orations he had committed to memory, that also he could do; he followed in order however many divisions (*versus*) we wanted, backwards and forwards. When we wondered (about his abilities), he testified that he had not known God could do this before this proof from his experience.[15]

Notice that what is unusual to Augustine is not that Simplicius knew all of Virgil and much of Cicero, nor that he could manipulate these texts, but the *degree* to which he could do so – pulling single verses of Virgil out of context, composing commonplaces on any topic, running extensively backwards as well as forwards through various lengthy texts. The proof of a good memory lies not in the simple retention and regurgitation even of large amounts of material. Rather, it is the ability to move it about instantly, directly, and securely that is admired.

To produce this facility, memory must be trained as though it were a kind of calculative ability, manipulating letters, bits of texts, and commonplaces in addition to numbers. Such manipulation can only be accomplished if the materials can in some sense be internally read. Try the following two exercises. First, recite from memory the first verse of Psalm 23 ("The Lord is my shepherd; I shall not want") in normal order, and then backwards word by word. Next, whistle a short phrase from "Mary Had a Little Lamb" in normal order, and then backwards note by note. It is possible to scan both the words and the musical phrase backwards, but the music must be rendered in a form that makes the relations of pitch able to be read in a way similar mentally to reading the words backwards. For instance, if one assigns the pitches of the first phrase to the three joints of one finger, one will find that one is as easily able to perform the musical exercise as the recitational one. This is the principle of the so-called "Guidonian hand," associated with Guido d'Arezzo (though probably older), in which the tones of the gamut are assigned to various locations on the left hand. Drawings of it appear in many musical texts through the late Renaissance.[16] Visual coding, like writing, allows the memory to be organized securely for accurate recollection of a sort that permits not just reduplication of the original material, but sorting, analysis, and mixing as well – genuine learning, in short, rather than simple repetition.[17]

It might be useful to pause a moment here in order to clarify certain terms I have occasion to use throughout this work. First, I wish to clarify the distinction between memory understood as the ability to reproduce something exactly ("rote") and memory as recollection or reminiscence. Second, and related to the pre-modern understanding of reminiscence, I want to clarify the distinction I make between the adjectives "heuristic" and "hermeneutical."

Modern experimental psychology, focusing on the behavior and capacity of short-term or "working memory," has encouraged an understanding of memory that identifies it solely with the ability to reproduce exactly the items in a series, carefully excluding from its concerns the ability to reconstruct such information, whether logically or by a mnemonic scheme.[18] This is not at all what pre-modern writers meant by "memory." The distinction is clear in Albertus Magnus's commentary on Aristotle's *De memoria et reminiscentia*. Albertus says that the iteration, or rote repetition, of knowledge is not at all a task of *memorial* recollection or *memoria*. He defines reminiscence or recollection as the rational discovery (*investigatio*) of what has been set aside (*obliti*) through and by means of the memory. This process differs in nature from "rote repetition" (*iterata scientia*). Recollection occurs consciously through association: one finds or hunts out the stored memory-impressions by using other things associated with it either through a logical connection or through habit (*consuetudo*), the sort of associations taught by the various *artes memorativa*. Rote repetition, since it is not "found out" by any heuristic scheme, is not considered recollection or true memory (*memoria*).[19]

Chaucer's Summoner is a familiar example of mechanical, rote reiteration (*The Canterbury Tales*, I, 637–643); he can repeat a few Latin phrases heard in court, but Chaucer comments that a jay can cry "Wat" as well as the pope can – the Summoner's memory is of that sort. Notice that the Summoner is compared to a bird; animals were considered to have no true memory. It is also worth noticing that Chaucer does not use the word "rote" in connection with the Summoner's mimicry, in contrast to what he says about the trained legal memory of the Sergeant of Law (I, 323–327), who has every statute "pleyn by rote" in his memory, that is "habitually and systematically." This has made him formidable in "termes," or negotiations, because his mind "hadde" all cases and precedents from the time of King William ready for his immediate use.[20]

The "art of memory" is actually the "art of recollection," for this is the task which these schemes are designed to accomplish. They answer to principles that define and describe how reminiscence occurs, what it is, and what it is supposed to do. And among those tasks, iteration per se was not considered sufficient. The crucial task of recollection is *investigatio*, "tracking-down," a word related to *vestigia*, "tracks" or "footprints." All mnemonic organizational schemes are heuristic in nature. They are retrieval schemes, for the purpose of *inventio* or "finding." The word "heuristic" derives from a Greek verb meaning "to find," and I use it to mean any scheme or construct that is "valuable for stimulating or conducting empirical research but unproved or incapable of proof" itself (in the definition of Webster's *Third International Dictionary*).

Distinct from "heuristic" are the words "hermeneutic" and "iconographic." These latter two, as I use them, both refer to interpretation rather than retrieval. *Hermeneutic* refers to the methods and content of textual interpretation, especially of the Bible, and *iconographic* to the "illustration of a subject by pictures" (to quote Webster's *Third* again). The heuristic schemes might well take advantage of certain hermeneutic and/or iconographic conventions in constructing mnemonically valuable markers, but such meanings are not intrinsically necessary to mnemonic schemes. In fact, such received meanings can be more of a hindrance than not, and every writer on the subject urges students to form their own habitual schemes rather than relying on those of others. For the mnemonic scheme's basic function is only heuristic, to retrieve not to interpret.[21] Recollection can occur either naturally ("ex parte rei," as Albertus says, though we would probably use a word like "formally") or artificially ("ex parte consuetudinis," or as we more likely would say "associatively"). The latter sort is generally more useful because it can organize a mass of otherwise unrelated material, like texts or sermons. The former is restricted to material that is in itself formally congruent, like a logical proof. But both sorts of schemes are heuristic, inventive, and investigatory in the classical sense.

Thinking of memory as wax or a waxed surface on which "images of a sort" are inscribed involves us in two distinct, if related, questions: what is the physical nature of such "images" and in what sense do they "represent" that which they "copy?" In the discussion which follows, I am going to reverse the order of these questions and focus first on the representational character of the memory-likenesses and then on their physical nature. Directing my analysis is the ancient observation that I have just discussed, that memory is a process most like reading written characters.

The earliest explicit use of the seal-in-wax model for cognition is in Plato's *Theaetetus*, although the image is not original to Plato, who says that he was developing a metaphor already implicit in Homer. In fact, Socrates is at some pains to say that his way of describing the memory as being like seals (*sēmeia*) made by a signet ring is not new, but really very old. This is important because it is a model based upon how the eye sees in reading, not how the ear hears. In recollection, one *looks* at the contents of memory, rather than hearing or speaking them; the mediator is visual. Socrates says:

Imagine . . . that our minds contain a block of wax, which in this or that individual may be larger or smaller, and composed of wax that is comparatively pure or muddy, and harder in some, softer in others, and sometimes of just the right consistency . . . Let us call it the gift of the Muses' mother, Memory, and say that whenever we wish to remember something we see or hear or conceive in our own minds, we hold this wax under the perceptions or ideas and imprint them on it as we might stamp the impression of a seal ring. Whatever is so imprinted we remember and know so long as the image remains; whatever is rubbed out or has not succeeded in leaving an impression we have forgotten and do not know.[22]

Plato's choice of phrase, "kérinon ekmageion" (block of wax), is significant, for the noun *ekmageion* has a long career in philosophical writing.

Aristotle used it to mean "matter as a recipient of impressions" (for example, in *Metaphysics*, 988aI); it is used as a verb by Plato (in *Theaetetus*) and other philosophers to mean "mold" or "impress." It can also mean "model," and is so used by Plato in *Laws*, 800b.[23] The tablet on which the wax is spread, thickly or thinly or just right, is the pair (though sets of as many as ten have been found) of wooden slabs fastened together, familiar to every ancient student; it was one of the oldest surfaces for writing known to the Greeks, and representations of such tablets have been found in eighth-century BC reliefs from Western Asia.[24] They served for memoranda of all sorts – ephemeral and occasional writing, like school notes and exercises, sketches of compositions, bills and accounts.

The root Plato uses for "seal" is *sēme*-, which means "sign" or "a mark by which something is known"; it has several other more restricted meanings related to the basic one, like a "signal" as in battle, or a "badge."[25] It is significant, it seems to me, how emphatic Plato is about the "sign"-nature of his metaphor, for he repeats the idea three times in three words: the phrase translated "as we might stamp the impression of a seal ring" is in Greek "hōsper daktylion sēmeia ensēmainomenous." So the "seal in wax" is basically a model of inscription or incising, as writing is incised upon a clay or wax or stone surface. Moreover, the forms incised symbolize information and thus are representations that serve a cognitive purpose, as do the representations of words, whether by phoneme or syllable or unit of sense, used in writing systems. In other words, to borrow some terms from the cognitive psychologists, the "representation" in memory is "verbal" rather than "pictorial" in nature.

The underlying implication of the metaphor of the seal in wax receives one of its fullest expressions in Cicero's *De oratore*, one of the major vehicles through which the image came to later writers like Quintilian, St. Augustine, Martianus Capella, and others. Later still, writers of the scholastic Middle Ages found it anew in the *Rhetorica ad Herennium*, ascribed by them to Cicero, and in the Latin translations and commentaries on Aristotle's *De memoria* that became available during the thirteenth century.

In Book II of *De oratore*, Antonius discusses with his friends the value of memory training. He recounts how Simonides first discovered the principles of the mnemonic technique of placing images (*imagines*) in an orderly set of architectural backgrounds (*loci*) in his memory because one day he had just left a banquet hall when the roof collapsed on it, killing all who were still there. He was able to reconstruct the guest list by recalling the location of each person's seat (*sedes*) at the table. Antonius goes on to say that sight is the keenest of all our senses (*sensus vivendi*).[26] Therefore, perception received orally or by the other senses, or objects conceived through thought alone, "can be most easily retained in the mind if they are also conveyed to our minds by the mediation of the eyes." Of course, many things and events are of such a nature that we either have not seen or cannot see what we wish to remember. In these cases, we should make them visible by marking them with a sort of image or figure (*quasi et imago et figura*).

These mental images, the ancients say, are *sort of* figures and similitudes. The qualification is crucially important, for reasons well defined in modern philosophical discussions of the nature of mental images. Following suggestions of Wittgenstein, J. T. E. Richardson defines the representational aspect of mental images functionally rather than mimetically. What defines a mental image is not its pictorial qualities but whether its user understands it to represent a certain thing. As J. A. Fodor has written of this same subject, if asked to make a picture of a tiger I can paint a realistic portrait or I can draw a stick figure, but in both cases I understand the result to represent a tiger. "My images ... connect with my intentions ... I *take* them as tiger-pictures for the purposes of whatever task I have in mind."[27]

The mental image which an individual makes need have little to do with objective reality. Donald Norman reports on experiments with mental imaging which he has conducted, and notes that most people, when asked what city in North America is most directly across the Atlantic Ocean from Madrid, Spain, construct a mental map on which most of them say they "see" that Madrid is somewhere south of Washington, DC – Richmond, Virginia, or perhaps Cape Hatteras. In like manner, most place London on a line with Boston, and Paris with New York. A glance at a map shows that this mental image is clearly wrong as an accurate representation of the latitudinal relationship of these cities.[28] For my part, I cling to my "wrong" images no matter how often I am corrected, because the image functions cognitively for me not as a terrestrial map but as a cultural one. I know that Madrid is "south" in Europe, and so I place it "south" in the United States. Paris, London, and New York (lined up in a row in my mental image) are aligned because they are all three cultural capitals. Given its cognitive function for me, my cultural map is perfectly "correct," and I am right not to change it.

A functional definition understands the words "representation" and "image" in ways that I think are essentially compatible with ancient understanding embodied in words like *sēme-* and its derivatives, and in the subsequent, continuous development of the metaphor of mental image as writing. The likeness between the two terms of the metaphor is one of cognition (as a word "represents" a concept) rather than the replication of form. The structures which memory stores are not actual little pictures, but are *quasi*-pictures, "representations" in the sense that the information stored causes a change in the brain that encodes (the modern word) or molds (the ancient one) it in a certain way and in a particular "place" in the brain. This "sort-of" image is then used as the basis for thought by a process (intellection) which understands it to be a configuration standing in a certain relationship to something else – a "representation" in the cognitively functional sense, as writing represents language.

Such a distinction between objective and functional representation probably lies behind Aristotle's analysis, in 450b 11–20 of *De memoria*, of how a memory-image, which is "like an imprint or drawing in us," can also cause us to remember "what is not present." He likens the memory-drawing to a painted panel: "the figure drawn on a panel is both a figure and a copy ... And one can contemplate it both as a figure [*zōon*] and as a copy [*eikōn*]." As a figure or picture it is "an object of contemplation [*theorēma*] or an image [*phantasma*]. But, in so far as it is of another thing, it is a sort of copy [*oion eikon*] and a reminder [*mnēmoneuma*]."[29] If, for example, there should pop into my mind a delightful composition of the letters and numbers "Psalms 23:1," I may regard it simply as a picture that I can think about for its own sake. But if this "picture" also reminds me of the words, "The Lord is my shepherd; I shall not want," then it is a signal or cue for remembering, and it "stands for" those words as a "sort-of copy" of them.

The distinction between "figure" and "copy" continued to be emphasized in both Arabic and scholastic comment upon Aristotle's text. Avicenna and Averroës address it as the distinction between regarding an image as a picture or as a portrait. What is involved in remembering is the association and recollection of previously impressed material when the original is no longer present to us. If the object should become actually present to our senses again and we can compare our mental image to it for accuracy, we are engaged in a process of *recognizing* rather than of remembering or recollecting. We might, in such a situation, be momentarily embarrassed that our mental stick-figure bore so little resemblance to the actual lineaments of the tiger we see before us. At such a moment, we are regarding our mental image as a "picture," to be judged as good or bad according to whether it presents a *recognizable* likeness of the original we see. As portrait, however, the mental image calls to mind someone who, by definition, is not present; its function in such circumstances is to remind or recollect to us its original. As picture, the formal characteristics of the image itself are all-important; as portrait, its recollective or heuristic *function* is paramount to everything else.[30]

The distinction which philosophers of language are now making between "formal" and "functional" views of linguistic representation is useful also as a modern restatement of the ancient distinction between "philosophical" and "rhetorical" concerns.[31] The extreme idealist or formalist thinks of language in terms of how completely it represents the tiger, and since it can never fully get that right, would rather lapse into silence than speak. The rhetorician or pragmatist, having to speak, accepts that words are all more or less in the nature of crude stick-figures, but can be used meaningfully so long as speaker and audience share a common cultural and civic bond, whether that of *civitas Romana* or *civitas Dei*, a bond forged by the memories of people and their texts. Where classical and medieval rhetorical pragmatism diverges from modern, I think, is in assigning a crucial role to a notion of common memory, accessed by an individual through education, which acts to "complete" uninformed individual experience. This notion is basic to Aristotle's view of politics as the life of the individual completed in society. Such assumptions put the civic bond on a historically continuous basis, and make the notion of shared meaning less arbitrary and merely occasional than most modern "functional" theories of language tend to do.

If we, in Paul Ricoeur's phrase, unpack the metaphor incorporated in the scholastic dictum "veritas est adaequatio verbi et rei,"[32] we find that it embodies what is basically a rhetorical view of the representational relationship between word and thing (and we must always remember that the Latin word *res* is not confined to objects of our senses but includes notions, opinions, and feelings) – that is, a view based on the principle of decorum.[33] *Adaequatio* is a word of relationship, "adjustment," "fitting" a word to what one wants to say. The prefix is crucial to its meaning, not a dead metaphor. *Aequatio* and its adjective, *aequalis*, convey the notion of iteration, "equal," identity of a formal, quantifiable sort. But in this dictum, truth contained in words is always *ad-aequatio*, getting towards identity but never achieving it. Although *adaequatio* is sometimes applied even by medieval logicians to the sorts of mathematical identities one derives from truth-tables, that is a specialized use of the word which ignores its root metaphor. *Aequatio* conceptually admits only of true or false; *adaequatio*, being a matter of relationship and not identity, admits of many grades and degrees of approximation. *Aequalitas* is an absolute and necessary state of affairs; *adaequatio*, being a matter of more-or-less, requires human judgment. *Adaequatio* is a likeness between two non-identities, and it thus has more in common with a metaphor or a heuristic use of modelling than with an equal sign.[34]

Partialness is also a characteristic of memory. This is true not only because memory and recollection proceed by means of *imagines rerum* rather than the things-themselves, but because a part of the original experience is inevitably lost or "forgotten" when the memory impresses the *imago* of a *res*. This position is common to both Aristotelians and Platonists, those who believe the mind stores and makes use only of *phantasmata* derived from the sensory mediation of "objects," and those who believe the memory also has been truly stamped by divine Ideas, which humans have "forgotten" because of original sin or simply in the act of birth. Albertus Magnus writes that since recollection is of past experience, there is a "break" between the original action of memory that impresses the sensory image and its recollection. This break means that the original experience itself is lost, wholly or in part. Recollection thus becomes a reconstructive act, analogous to reading letters that "stand for" sounds (*voces*) that "represent" things in a more-or-less adequate, fitting way.[35] This is also to say that human understanding occurs in an occasional setting; it is not universally and eternally fixed. By their very nature signs are sensible, practical, worldly, belong to the traditional realm of rhetoric and must be understood within its procedures, most particularly the process of decorum, of fitting a word to a thing in terms that an audience will understand.[36]

Without getting too far into the intricacies of medieval signification theory, upon which much excellent work has been done,[37] I would stress that the assumption behind all the theory is that signs can be meaningfully judged and interpreted. Because it recalls signs, reminiscence is an act of interpretation, inference, investigation, and reconstruction, an act like reading. But in pre-modern thought, signs only have meaning as they refer to something else. A pre-modern memory phantasm is not a picture of what it represents, but neither is it "language," as modern philosophers use this term, for it has no inherent "grammar," no necessary structure of its own.[38] The task of the recollector who is composing (and, as we will see, recollection is commonly described as an act of composition, a gathering-up into a place) is to select the most fitting and adequate words to adapt what is in his memory-store to the present occasion. Language is shaped to thought, or, as Chaucer wrote, "The wordes moote be cosyn to the dede" (*The Canterbury Tales*, I. 742) – cousin, not parent.

This view of the matter, so characteristically different from our own, is well demonstrated in Augustine's notion of the "inner word" or understanding, "the word which shines within" illuminated by grace, and which then must find expression in words "spoken without" in human tongues conditioned by particular times and places. Because of its very nature, the relationship between the inner truth and its human expression in language will be inexact, unequal; like the pagan orator, the Christian will also have to seek a decorum, a mean or "adequacy" or plane of congruence between these two inequivalencies.[39]

Most pre-modern writers thought of knowledge as a collection of truths awaiting expression in human languages, and fitted, as appropriate, to various occasions. These truths are general but can never, with the exception of a limited set of mathematical axioms, be universally or singly expressed.[40] Ethical truths especially are expressed not singly but "copiously." When one examines a typical entry in a medieval florilegium one finds not generalized definitions, together with illustrative citations, as in a modern dictionary. One finds under a heading such as *justicia* dozens of *dicta* and often *facta* or exemplary stories as well, each of which is a definition, or, more precisely, a way-of-having-said (*dictum*) "justice." Copiousness, like decorum, is an essential part of a rhetorical understanding of the nature of human speech; indeed, copiousness and decorum are in a relationship analogous to symbiosis. The memory of an orator is like a storehouse of inventoried topics that ideally would contain all previous ways-of-saying ethical truths like "justice," "fortitude," "temperance," from which he draws in order to fit words to yet another occasion, requiring another way-of-saying. But this storehouse should be thought of as a set of bins that are empty when we are born and get filled up with a lot of "coins" or "flowers" or "nectar," whose aggregate is a meaningful if only partial "speaking" of "justice," or whatever. And each "speaking" of "justice" adds to the common store.

Thus "justice" has no single or simple meaning, but it is not thereby without meaning. It is a principle, a "starting-point," or a *res* (which in this context might best be translated "idea") one holds within oneself either through accrued experience, both individual and common, or through some combination of that and indwelling divine grace (to adopt Augustine's notion). This inner *res* needs to be spoken "without" in human language adjusted to occasions throughout time. Such occasional speaking will not coincide with or be fully extensive with (for a spatial notion is part of the root meaning of Latin *aequus*) the universal aggregate of "justice" that God alone knows, and in that sense it will be partial, lacking, and imperfect rather than complete. But, if its expression is "adequate," justice can be usefully, and in that sense truthfully, applied within a particular human situation. Words used by a wise speaker are the means of this application, words drawn from the copious inventory of *dicta et facta memorabilia* in the educated person's memorial *loci*.

The problem of how words "represent" *res* is related to but not identical with the question of what form the mental *imagines* or phantasmata take in the brain. In my next chapter I will discuss at greater length the physiological process by which such images were thought to be produced; this will get us closer still to understanding what they are, though not completely to an answer (indeed, the ancients themselves never completely defined their nature).[41] It is apparent from the metaphors they chose to model the processes of memory and perception that the *imagines* were thought in some way to occupy space. They are "incised" or "stamped" into matter, they are "stored" and can be recalled or reconstructed by means of memorial storage. And because each memorial phantasm is in some way physically present in the brain, it can be given a particular "address" during the process of memory storage, associations that will "send" recollection to it. Whatever else the memory-image may be, it is clearly in part material; as we shall see, the physical variations of individual brains were thought to be crucial to their "talent" for storing and recalling *phantasmata*.

This assumption concerning the material, and therefore spatial, nature of memory-images also helps to account for why the ancients persistently thought of *memoria* as a kind of eye-dependent reading, a visual process. There simply is no classical or Hebrew or medieval tradition regarding an "ear of the mind" equivalent to that of the "eye of the mind." The exception is the famous invocation to the monks which opens Benedict's Rule: "Ausculta, o fili, praecepta magistri, et inclina aurem cordis tui," "Listen, my son, to your master's precepts and incline the ear of your heart."[42] The image is not a general trope, however, but a specific literary recollection of Ps. 44:11, "Audi, filia, et vide, et inclina aurem tuam," "Listen, daughter, and behold, and incline your ear." The same verse was invoked by Jerome at the beginning of a famous letter on virginity (*Epist.* 22), and so Benedict was likely thinking of that association as well. The phrase "aurem cordis" seems to be his own; perhaps Benedict employed it because the Rule was to be read aloud to the monks during *collatio*, the occasion which combines eating, listening, and meditation. Elsewhere in the Rule, Benedict does not hesitate to use a meditational aid that is visual and spatial in character, the mnemonic trope of Jacob's ladder, to help recall the stages of humility.

Memory advice stresses the empirical observation that remembering what is aurally received is more difficult for most people than remembering what is visual, and the consequent need to secure the one by association with the other. Aural reception, as has often been remarked, is temporal not spatial, and yet, Aristotle says, even our ability to judge time-lapses depends on a mechanism of visual comparison like that by which we judge spatial magnitude. We must construct in our minds, he says, a kind of schematic diagram, by means of which we can judge relative durations just as we similarly use memory-images to judge relative size.[43]

Antonius says in Cicero's *De oratore* that we "employ the localities and images respectively as a wax tablet and the letters written on it."[44] Although his subject is an architectural *ars memorativa*, he yet understood the process not as one of viewing a picture or sculpture, but of reading letters. Even the most apparently pictorial of mnemonic systems are based on principles governing the nature of writing. Most require that the "picture" relate to the word or concept it marks for recollection via a pun or homophony. The earliest Greek memory text we possess, a pre-Socratic fragment called *Dialexeis*, relies upon a sort of visualized homophony in its advice about memorizing both words and things.[45] Thus to recall the name "Pyrilampes," we should "place it on" (i.e. connect it with) *pyr* "fire" and *lampein* "to shine." To remember things, we recall a significant figure to represent the particular theme; thus, to remember courage we fix it with a representation of Aries or Achilles. The connection between what is to be remembered and the device used to remember it is fundamentally through reading, through sign and not through mimicry. When the ancients use the word "visual" to refer to the nature of the phantasm, it is the act of reading words that they have in mind. The point is well made by John of Salisbury: "Letters however, that is their shapes [*figurae*], are in the first place signs of words [*vocum*, literally "sounds organized into words"]; then of things, which they bring to the mind through the windows of the eyes, and frequently they speak silently the sayings of those no longer present."[46]

Cicero uses the wax tablet image itself a bit later in Antonius's speech. Metrodorus of Scepsis, a man famous for his memory, said that he wrote down things to be remembered in particular places in his mind, as if he were writing letters on wax tablets.[47] The contemporaneous *Rhetorica ad Herennium*, which gives us the most detailed description of the ancient architectural mnemonic, also contains the fullest elaboration of the metaphor that likens writing on the memory to writing on wax or papyrus:

those who have learned mnemonics can set in backgrounds what they have heard, and from these backgrounds deliver it by memory. For the backgrounds are very much like wax tablets or papyrus, the images like the letters, the arrangement and disposition of images like the script, and the delivery is like the reading.[48]

The metaphor changes slightly over the centuries to reflect the most common form of writing materials, but its tenacity in Western thought is remarkable. Martianus Capella, writing in the early fifth century when the codex had supplanted the papyrus roll as the vehicle of choice for books, advises that "what is [sent] to memory is written into areas, as if in wax and on the written page."[49] Dante writes of "the book of my memory." Nor is the image exclusively Greco-Roman, nor only in rhetorical teaching, for there is a variant of it in Proverbs 3:3 (though Proverbs does show considerable Greek influence): "Let not mercy and truth forsake thee: bind them about thy neck; write them upon the table of thine heart."[50] The Hebrew words contain the metaphor, but of course it was the Latin that was known to the Middle Ages: *describere*, "write upon" or "incise," and *tabulae*, "wax tablets" of the sort used until paper tablets fully supplanted them in Europe sometime in the fifteenth century. The appearance of the metaphor in Biblical as well as classical tradition (so it would have seemed to medieval scholars) would have considerably enhanced its prestige as a governing archetype.

In addition to demonstrating that pre-modern scholars thought of remembering as a process of mentally visualizing signs both for sense objects and objects of thought, this metaphor also shows that the ancients and their medieval heirs thought that each "bit" of knowledge was remembered in a particular place in the memory, which it occupied as a letter occupies space on a writing surface. The words *topos*, *sedes*, and *locus*, used in writings on logic and rhetoric as well as on mnemonics, refer fundamentally to locations in the brain, which are made accessible by means of an ordering system that functions somewhat like the routing systems used by programs to retrieve, merge, and distinguish the information in a computer's "memory," and also postal addresses or library shelf-marks.[51] It is Cicero again who makes clear both the physiological nature and cognitive function of these words. In *Topica*, a work he composed from memory while on a voyage without his library, he writes:[52]

it is easy to find things that are hidden if the hiding place is pointed out and marked; similarly if we wish to track down some argument we ought to know the places or topics: for that is the name given by Aristotle to the "regions," as it were, from which arguments are drawn. Accordingly, we may define a topic as the region of an argument, and an argument as a course of reasoning which firmly establishes a matter about which there is some doubt.[53]

Aristotle did indeed think of his *topoi* as structured regions of the mind where arguments, either general or subject-particular, were stored. He advises students in his *Topica* (163b, a passage evidently known to

Cicero) to memorize these by number, for then they will be able to take a quick and sure mental look at them (the verb he uses is *blepein*) when composing their own discourse. Particularly in *De memoria*, Aristotle emphasizes the importance of order for storing the phantasmata in the memory, and recommends an alphabet-based mnemotechnique (evidently both number and alphabet were known to him as providing useful bases for mnemonic heuristics). In a crux that has proved very difficult for a number of commentators (partly because of a faulty text), but that has been considerably clarified by Richard Sorabji,[54] Aristotle describes the advantage of using the order of the alphabet to organize material in the memory. If one assigns a separate letter of the alphabet to distinct pieces of information, then one can move from one bit to the next using the rigid order of the letters to organize otherwise unrelated material. In recollecting, one can start with Alpha, if one wishes. But if one wants to remember something further on, one could begin instead at Theta. Or one could begin with Zeta and move easily to its "neighbors," Eta or Epsilon.[55] It is the interior orderliness of the places that makes it possible to read what is written in the shapes stored in memory.

Thus far, I have discussed this ancient metaphor of the waxed tablets as though its explanation of memory processes were modeled upon a previously familiar process of writing on a physical surface. In fact, however, both ancient and medieval authors reverse the direction of this metaphor. Ancient Greek had no verb meaning "to read" as such: the verb they used, *anagignōskō*, means "to know again," "to recollect." It refers to a memory procedure. Similarly, the Latin verb used for "to read" is *lego*, which means literally "to collect" or "to cull, pluck," referring also to a memory procedure (the re-collection or gathering up of material).[56]

Like reading, writing depends on and helps memory. The shapes of letters are memorial *cues*, direct stimuli to the memory. What is heard as well as what is seen is transformed into a mental signal that is "read" by the "eye of the mind." Thus Aeschylus speaks in *Prometheus* of "the unforgetting tablets of thy mind," and I have already mentioned the advice in Proverbs to "write upon the table of thy heart." It has been remarkable to me, and I will have occasion frequently to recall the phenomenon during this study, that none of the texts I have encountered makes the slightest distinction in kind between writing on the memory and writing on some other surface. Writing itself, the storing of information in symbolic "representations," is understood to be critical for knowing, but not its support (whether internal or external) or the implements with which it is performed. All these early writers are agreed that writing on the memory is the only writing truly valuable for one's education, literary style, reasoning ability, moral judgment, and (later) salvation, for in memorizing one writes upon a surface one has always with one. And the corollary assumption is that what one writes on the memory can be at least as orderly and accessible to thought as what is written upon a surface such as wax or parchment.

At the end of his *Phaedrus*, Plato gives one of the best statements of this assumption in antiquity. Written words, says Socrates, serve only to "remind one who knows that which the writing is concerned with."[57] The trouble with a written composition is that it becomes detached from its author, and goes off on its own, so to speak, falling into ignorant as well as learned hands. The educational value of writing thus depends upon the knowledge and quality of the person who reads it, for reading can only remind readers of what is already imprinted upon their memories, of what they alone "bring to the text," as we now say. To Socrates, "living discourse" is best; the wise man will write only "by way of pastime, collecting a store of refreshment both for his memory . . . and for all such as tread in his footsteps."[58] Two living minds can engage one another, whereas in the solitary reading of a written text the mind encounters, he implies, only itself. But Socrates allows value to writing as a way of storing experience for oneself and posterity (in a phrase which, incidentally, suggests strongly that he is thinking of something along the lines of a *florilegium*).[59]

It is in this context that Plato introduces the myth of Theuth (Thoth) and Thammuz (called Ammon in some versions). Theuth is the Egyptian god who invented calculation, number, geometry, dice – and script. He came to the king, Thammuz, to introduce his various arts, most of which were well received, but when he extolled writing, Thammuz expressed skepticism. Theuth claimed that writing was a "recipe for memory and wisdom." Thammuz replied that it hadn't anything to do with memory at all, but merely with reminding, and was thus clearly wisdom's semblance rather than the real thing. The danger in it was that men might begin to rely upon writing instead of truly learning things by imprinting them in memory first.[60] Socrates is concerned in the whole *Phaedrus* with distinguishing between true and apparent happiness, beauty, love, and – in the end of the dialogue – rhetoric. Full of finely crafted discourse itself, the dialogue is concerned to reveal the falseness of any teaching which suggests that rhetoric should be only a matter of knowing tropes, figures, and ornaments instead of having a firm conviction of truth and knowledge of philosophy as well. In context, Plato is specifically responding to the use of textbooks with a "cookbook" approach as a substitute for live teaching. So, Thammuz objects to Theuth's "recipe" for memory by saying that it is a mere gimmick which substitutes an appearance for the substance. Textbooks substitute writing "produced by external characters which are not part of [oneself]" for writing on the memory.[61]

The ancient observation that what we do in writing is itself a kind of memory, suggests an interesting correction to the popular idea that writing, defined as the use of an alphabet, and consequently literacy are essential human competencies (like the ability to add) rather than techniques (like digital computation) or technologies (like silicon chips). As M. T. Clanchy says of literacy, "It has different effects [on human societies] according to circumstances and *is not a civilizing force in itself*" (my emphasis).[62] The ancients began from the twin assumptions that the mind already writes when it stores up its experience in representations, and, as a corollary, that the graphic expression of such representations is not an event of particular importance, at least for "ways of thinking about things" – no more important than the sound of an individual's voice is to his or her ability to use language. From this viewpoint, the symbolic representations that we call writing are no more than cues or triggers for the memorial representations, also symbolic, upon which human cognition is based. And to mistake one sort of thing for the other would be a significant error. Writing something down cannot change in any significant way our mental representation of it, for it is the mental representation that gives birth to the written form, not vice versa.

From this viewpoint also anything that encodes information in order to stimulate the memory to store or retrieve information is "writing," whether it be alphabet, hieroglyph, ideogram, American Indian picture-writing, or Inca knot-writing. Writing is as fundamental to language as is speaking. We still habitually use "he said" to mean "he wrote"; though this idiom has been adduced as evidence of deeply buried "aural residue," it can equally well be interpreted as an acknowledgment that both writing and speaking are expressions of a more fundamental human competency.

Clearly various societies have felt variously a need to put systems of mental representation and organization down on some surface, but the impulse to do this, and the preserved form it may take, has more to do with the complexity of their social organization, the other groups with which they come into contact, the nature of materials used and their accessibility, than with the way in which a human being is able to form and organize mental representations for cognition, and to understand that they *are* representations (i.e. they "stand for" something). I will later discuss a case wherein a lag of well over a millennium demonstrably exists between the common use of a particular scheme of mental organization and its first appearance in written form. Similarly, neither the prevalence nor the form of written materials in a culture should, I think, be taken as any sure indication of those people's *ability* to think in rational categories, or of the structures those categories may take. I am not suggesting that technique and technology have no effect upon human culture; this study is concerned to identify and describe a number of distinctive features in medieval literary culture which are sometimes expressed in particular techniques, such as page layout. But I try not to reify technique, and in particular I think it very important to recognize that the form in which information is presented to the mind does not necessarily constrain the way in which such information is encoded by the brain nor the ways in which it can be found and sorted. The three are distinct.[63] Classical and medieval philosophers recognized this when they said that all information, whatever its source or form, becomes a phantasm in the brain. And those phantasmata are retrieved by heuristic schemes that need bear little resemblance to the form in which the information was originally received.

The idea that language is oral, that writing is not a fundamental part of it, is a modern one, enunciated by linguists like de Saussure and Leonard Bloomfield, and then generalized into a theory of culture and even of epistemology by the French Structuralists, chiefly Claude Lévi-Strauss. It has become a canon in this theory that Western culture can be divided into periods characterized by "pre-" and "post-Gutenberg man [sic]," and the dividing line is marked by a "veering toward the visual," to use Walter Ong's careening image.[64] My study will make it clear that from earliest times medieval educators had as visual and spatial an idea of *locus* as any Ramist had, which they inherited continuously from antiquity, and indeed that concern for the lay-out of memory governed much in medieval education designed to aid the mind in forming and maintaining heuristic formats that are both spatial and visualizable.

THESAURUS SAPIENTIAE

The second major metaphor used in ancient and medieval times for the educated memory was that of *thesaurus*, "storage-room," "treasury," and "strongbox." Whereas the metaphor of the seal-in-wax or written tablets was a model for the process of making the memorial phantasm and storing it in a place in the memory, this second metaphor refers both to the contents of such a memory and to its internal organization. An important ancient version of the storage-room metaphor occurs in Plato's *Theaetetus*, when Socrates, explaining how one is able to recall particular pieces of information, likens the things stored in memory to domestic pigeons housed in a pigeon-coop. This occurrence attests to the antiquity of the store-house; indeed, these metaphors, equally visual, equally spatial, seem to be equally ancient as well. But we should also take careful note of Plato's metaphor for memory's *contents*, namely domesticated birds. Pigeons have two salient characteristics for this model: they are raised for nourishment, and they naturally fly away. In his *Institutiones*, Cassiodorus uses a significant variant of Plato's pigeon-coop. He describes the structured memory, this *mirabile genus operis* or "remarkable piece of work," as a kind of inventoried set of coops or animal-pens. One should think of each stall or coop as a labeled "topic" or place, which not only keeps things, but informs the otherwise untrammeled brain, directs it, and makes it useful, in this case for the task of thinking.

Although the metaphor of animal-coops appears to be the same as the now-maligned filing-cabinet model for human memory, the reference of this pre-modern metaphor is considerably different, in a way that profoundly affects how we should understand it historically. The "filing-cabinet" model in Modernist psychology refers to the mind's success in finding unaltered, unculled material in memory, material that, like stored documents, remains unchangingly complete and accurate. In other words, the modern metaphor concerns memory's ability wholly to recapture a past, complete and unaltered, *for its own sake*. But the purpose of the metaphor in antiquity and the Middle Ages is not that. Treasuries and book-chests are not like twentieth-century filing-cabinets. They contain "riches," not documents. And their contents are valued for their richness in terms of their present usefulness, not their "accuracy" or their certification of "what really happened." When a medieval abbot wanted to authenticate the charters of his foundation, he sought out a written document in his monastery's library (or he forged one), he did not search for it in the *scrinium* of his well-structured memory.[65] This is a crucial difference between the pre-modern and modern notions of the goals of human *memoria*. Medieval abbots also cared deeply about authenticity, especially when the legal standing of their monasteries was at stake, but their own memory training served a different purpose, and its contents were imagined as alive (animals and birds) or as materials to be used richly in the commerce of creative thought (coins, jewels, foods).

In the medieval metaphor, memory's storage structures allow the mind its truly "liberal" essence, just as training a horse enables the animal to function at peak ability, to become what its nature intends. As Cassiodorus says, the inventory of *topica memoriae* at once structures and channels the untrammeled intellect ("conclusit liberum ac voluntarium intellectum"), because whatever notions ("cogitationes") the mind may have entered upon ("intraverit"), the intelligence ("humanum ingenium") drops into ("cadat") one or another of these places ("in aliquid eorum"), and having done this, then coherent thoughts can be formed out of the mobility and variety of the mind's experiences.[66]

The relationship which Cassiodorus conceives between the structures and their content is quite clear in this passage. Of first importance is the comprehensive form, laid out in *topica memoriae*, places of memory appropriate to rhetoric, dialectic, poetry, and jurisprudence – this structure (the trained memory) sorts and gathers the knowledge a person has gained. One is not born with this structure, nor is it passively gained; one constructs it oneself during one's education. And whatever experiences one has will be channeled by this previously laid-out inventory, and will find their appropriate place, each contributing its matter to the general store. Without the sorting structure, there is no invention, no inventory, no experience, and therefore no knowledge – there is only a useless heap, what is sometimes called *silva*, a pathless forest of chaotic material. Memory without conscious design is like an uncatalogued library, a useless contradiction in terms. For human memory should be most like a library of texts, made accessible and useful through various consciously applied heuristic schemes. St. Jerome wrote of a gifted young scholar that "by careful reading and daily meditation his heart [i.e. by means of his memory] constructed a library for Christ."[67] In order to understand something, we must first have a place to put it, something to attach it to in the inventory of all our previous experience.

Modern scholars usually translate *cogitatio* as "thought," but this conceals a crucial difference in how pre-moderns conceived of what that is from how we conceive of it. Cassiodorus says literally that "the mind enters into thoughts"; a modern would much more likely say "the mind thinks." *Cogitatio* (*con + agito*, "move, rouse") is defined in rhetoric (and in Greco-Arabic somatic psychology) as a combinative or compositional activity of the mind. It necessarily uses memory because it combines *imagines* from memory's store. One should therefore think of a single *cogitatio* or "thought" as a small-scale composition, a bringing-together (*con + pono*) of various pieces (as phantasmata) from one's inventory. The *topica* provide both content and structure for these *cogitationes*. Aristotle – and all succeeding writers – distinguishes between "general" *topica* and "particular" ones; basically, in this context, the general topics are structuring devices solely, such as comparison, contrast, and the like, while the particular topics are the collected expressions of an ethico-political concept, such as mercy, wisdom, justice, and so on. A commonplace is described as being "made" or "manufactured" – Augustine says that Simplicius, when asked for a *locus communis* on some subject, would "make" it ("de quocumque loco voluimus ... fecit"). One does not simply parrot forth some previously recorded *dictum* word for word by rote, but builds a "topic" or "commonplace" out of materials from one's memorial inventory.

The *topica* provide the construction materials for thoughts, for whether one takes a simple Aristotelian position that knowledge is composed of experience constructed from many memories, or whether one shares with the (Neo)Platonists the belief that knowledge is a process of remembering the imprints of hypostatized Ideas, thoughts cannot be made without the materials in memory. For whatever memory holds occupies a *topos* or place, by the very nature of what it is, and these *topica*, like bins in a storehouse, have both contents and structure. Every topic is in this sense a mnemonic, a structure of memory for recollection.

The image of the memorial store-house is a rich model of pre-modern mnemonic practice. It takes a number of related forms and gives rise to several allied metaphors for the activity of an educated mind, but all center upon the notion of a *designed* memory as the inventory of all experiential knowledge, and especially of those truths of ethics, polity, and law, which are copious and rich in their very nature. Synonyms of *thesaurus* which are also used for the memory include *cella* or *cellula*, *arca*, *sacculus*, *scrinium*, and the Middle English word *male* (carry-sack), used perhaps most famously in Harry Bailly's comment to the company in *The Canterbury Tales* just after the Knight has spoken: "This gooth aright; unbokeled is the male!" It occurs again, of course, at the end of the tale-telling, when Harry Bailly cautions the Parson to "unbokele and shew us what is in thy male."[68]

Zeno the Stoic (fourth–third century BC) defines memory as *thēsaurisma phantasiōn* or "storehouse of mental images."[69] *Thesaurus* is used metaphorically in both Romans (2:5) and the gospel of Matthew (6:19–20) in the sense of storing up intangible things for salvation, the Greek being translated by Jerome as a verb, *thesaurizare*, thus: "Nolite thesaurizare vobis thesauros in terra ... Thesaurizate autem vobis thesauros in caelo."[70] The *Rhetorica ad Herennium* calls memory the treasurehouse of invented things, "thesauru[s] inventorum" (III, 16), referring particularly to a memory trained by the artificial scheme which the author proceeds to recommend. Quintilian, also recommending a cultivated memory, calls it "thesaurus eloquentiae" (XI, 2, 2).

But these metaphorical uses, though they clearly demonstrate the pervasiveness and antiquity of the link between *thesaurus* and a trained memory, do not help us know how a medieval student, encountering the word, might visualize the object denoted. *Thesaurus* refers both to what is in the strongbox, the "treasures," as when Augustine speaks of the treasures of countless images in his memory, "ubi sunt thesauri innumerabilium imaginum" (*Conf.*, X, 8), and to the strongbox itself. When the wise men kneel before Jesus in Matthew's account (2:11), they bring out their offerings of gold, frankincense, and myrrh from opened *thesauri*: "et apertis thesauris suis obtulerunt ei munera, aurum, thus, et myrrham."[71] The *thesauri* of the wise men are portable strongboxes such as a merchant might carry.

Cella, the word used by Geoffrey of Vinsauf for the memory (which he calls a *cellula deliciarum*) also means "storeroom," as indeed its derivative form, *cellarium*, English "cellar," still indicates. When Chaucer's Monk threatens to tell numerous tragedies "Of whiche I have an hundred in my celle" (VII. 1972), he is more likely using the word to refer to his memory "cell" or store than to a cell in his monastery. After all, a hundred tragedies housed in books back home are not going to do him any good when having to tell a tale or two on the road to Canterbury, but stories in his memory-cell are a different matter. Therefore, though virtually every editor of Chaucer has thought the Middle English word needed no gloss, it does: the Monk is saying that he has a hundred stories tucked away in his memory. The gloss is underscored by the Monk's mention two lines later of the "memorie" of tragedies made to us by "olde bookes."

But the Latin word *cella* has a number of more specialized applications that link it complexly to several other common metaphors for both the stored memory and the study of books, as well as words like *arca* and *thesaurus. Cellae* are stalls or nesting-places for domestic animals and birds, and, by a transference of meaning, small rooms or huts for people (whence derives the word's monastic usage, invoked by Hugh of St. Victor as a metaphor for trained memory, which he likens in his *Chronicle* preface to the *cellae* of a cloister or *ambitus*). In classical Latin, a dove-cote was called a *cella columbarum*.[72] The compartments made by bees for their honey are called *cellae* (still called "cells" in English). So Virgil in his Fourth Georgic describes the various tasks of bees: "aliae purissima melle / stipant et liquido distendunt nectare cellas," "others pack the purest honey and distend the cells with liquid nectar."[73]

Bees and birds (which pre-modern natural history thought of as closely related creatures, "flying animals") are also linked by persistent associations with memory and ordered recollection. Indeed there is a long-standing chain or – a better word – a texture of metaphors that likens the placement of memory-images in a trained memory to the keeping of birds (especially pigeons) and to the honey-making of bees. Trained memory is also linked metaphorically to a library. And the chain is completed by a metaphoric connection of books in a library both to memories placed in orderly cells and to birds and bees in their celled coops and hives. These links are extensive and commonplace in Greek and Latin, as well as later languages. I hope I may be indulged for a few paragraphs while I trace some of them. My method of demonstrating these links, though hardly constituting proof in modern terms, may be justified its place in this study as an example of a basic memory technique called *collatio*, "gathering," which builds up a network, a texture, of associations to show a common theme.

First, pigeons. The first-century Roman writer, Junius Moderatus Columella, whose *De re rustica* is a guide to agricultural practices, calls the coop in which pigeons were kept a *cella* or *cellula*. He also uses the word *loculamenta*, and describes how such "tiers of pigeon-holes" are constructed of boards and pegs to make a structure divided into separate cells or compartments suitable for each pigeon to nest in. This structure he calls "columbis loculamenta vel cellulae."[74] The word *loculamenta* was also used at this time for bookcases. Seneca so uses it for personal bookcases; Martial uses the related word *nidus*, "nest" or "pigeon- hole," for the place where his book-seller kept copies of his work. In one of his epigrams, he says that his works can be bought easily from a book-seller: "Out of his first or second pigeon-hole [*nidus*], polished with pumice, smart in a purple covering, for five denarii he will give you Martial."[75] Another word for Roman bookcases was *forulus*, a diminutive of *forus*, meaning a "gallery" or "tier," and used by Virgil for the tiers of cells that make up a bee-hive.[76] J. W. Clark concludes that papyrus rolls were kept in shelving against a wall, in which the horizontal shelves were subdivided by verticals into pigeon-holes (*nidi, foruli, loculamenta*) "and it may be conjectured that the width of the pigeonholes would vary in accordance with the number of rolls included in a single work."[77] The English word "pigeon-holes," meaning compartments in a desk or cabinet into which papers are sorted and filed, is a recent imitation of classical usage (*OED*'s earliest citation is late eighteenth century).[78]

In the light of this ancient association between nesting birds and "nesting" scrolls, one might reconsider Plato's other metaphor in *Theaetetus* for memory, namely "pigeon-holes," *peristereon*. A *peristera* is the familiar domestic pigeon, *columba livia*, which inhabits buildings of every sort, whether especially designed for it or not.[79] The pigeons, Plato says, stand for bits of knowledge, some in flocks, some in small groups, some solitary. When we are infants, our coops are empty, and as we acquire pieces of information, we shut them up in our enclosure – this is called "knowing."[80]

Plato is clearly being partly playful, though *peristereon* certainly belongs to the large class of "store-room" images for the memory. Birds are a common image for souls, memories, and thoughts throughout the ancient world, both classical and Hebrew. Feathered thoughts and winged memories copiously flock in the Psalms, in Virgil, and many lesser texts, though one of the best and, in the Middle Ages, most remembered is that of Boethius, *The Consolation of Philosophy*, IV, prose and meter I.[81] But here Plato refers specifically to pigeons, not (more abstractly) souls with wings attached, like angels. Given the fundamental ancient assumption that written material in essence is an expression or extension of memory, I wonder if this *Theaetetus* image hasn't got something also to do with the use of words and phrases meaning "pigeon-holes" and "dove-boxes" for library-cases full of various sorts of written rolls. Perhaps Plato was fancifully playing with an established metaphor which the Romans later imitated, or perhaps this helped to establish later use. The point cannot be settled. There is, however, a curious use of the word *epistylion* in Aristotle's *Constitution of Athens*. The *epistylion* is the architrave on which, in the Doric architectural style, rested the characteristic entablature of metopes and triglyphs. In context, Aristotle's use of the word is a metaphoric transference, which John Edwin Sandys, the nineteenth-century classical scholar, explains as follows: "I should understand it to mean a shelf supporting a series of 'pigeon-holes,' and itself supported by wooden pedestals, in the office of the public clerk. The entablature in Doric architecture, with its originally open metopes alternating between the triglyphs, may well have suggested a metaphorical term for a shelf of 'pigeon-holes,' used for the preservation of public documents."[82] While I am engaged in this wild speculation concerning the foundations of the pigeon-hole metaphor, we might consider as well that open metopes make splendid pigeon-roosts, *columba livia* being no respecter of public buildings. I realize that these are slender reeds – but there they are.

The metaphoric relationship of birds, especially pigeons, to thoughts and memories persisted in the Middle Ages, aided by Boethius and the Holy Spirit, as well as the dove (*columba*) released by Noah from the Ark,[83] but medieval writers do not pick up the pigeon-hole/book/memory connections, probably because the idiom fell into disuse after the codex-book was generally adopted, for codices were kept flat on horizontal shelving without verticals, in a cupboard-like structure, free-standing or (more commonly) built into a recess in the thick medieval walls – called *arca, armarium, bibliotheca,* or *columna*.[84] Bees and honey-cells, however, are a different matter.

The earliest surviving occurrence of the trope is in Longinus, but Longinus himself suggests that he is using a well-established metaphor (as indeed the use of *loculamenta* and *forulus* for both "beehive" and "bookcase" would corroborate). Quintilian likens the orator, who makes eloquence from many arts and disciplines, to bees which "turn various kinds of flowers and juices into that flavour of honey which no human skill can imitate"; the trope is also used by Seneca, in a version I discuss at length in Chapter 6.[85] Richard de Bury, the fourteenth-century English humanist and Chancellor to Edward III, seems to have thought that the metaphor lay in some way behind Virgil's poem on bee-keeping, the Fourth Georgic, because of the mnemonic associations centering in the word *cella* and its synonyms, and the trope of readers as bees.

Richard de Bury's language (if it is his, though I see no reason to saddle Robert Holcot, in spite of that friar's own extreme inventiveness, with the preciosity of *Philobiblon*)[86] is allusive (several less kind adjectives also present themselves). He is inordinately fond, by modern taste, of elaborate allegories and learned conceits, obscure allusions, unattributed echoes, and other devices that test or flatter the learning of his readers, a style he characterizes as "stilo quidem levissimo modernorum," "in the very playful modern manner."[87] An example of it is the following description of how to read a book:

But the written truth of books, not transient but permanent, plainly offers itself to be observed, and through the translucent spheres of the eyes [*per sphaerulas pervias*],[88] passing through the vestibule of the common sense and the atriums of imagination, it enters the bed-chamber [*thalamum*] of the intellect, laying itself down in the beds [*cubili*] of memory, where it cogenerates [*congenerat*] the eternal truth of the mind.[89]

Bury is playing with a number of traditions here, among them the newly rediscovered ancient mnemonic based on architectural places of memory. Wisdom in books must be memorized to be useful and truth-producing – what more light-hearted modern way to state this old adage than by a witty play with the most learned and humanistic of mnemonic arts? Hence the process of turning a sense perception into a thought is imaged on the places of a classical house: *vestibulum, atrium, thalamus,* and *cubile*. But that is not all. Bury also seems to me to invoke here the Fourth Georgic particularly, for Virgil speaks of the bees' cells as "cubilia" (42, 243), and of the bees retiring for the night in their bed-chambers: "iam thalamis se composuere" (189). "Honeycombs," "bees," and "bee-hives" figure commonly as metaphors for books, book-collecting, memory, and scholarship elsewhere in *Philobiblon*, and to catch the allusion here to Virgil's bees in a discussion of memory and books would, I think, please Bury immensely. It's exactly the obscurely lumbering sort of pedantic play he found amusing.

But if Bury is being allusive, he is playing with one of the commonest medieval metaphors for study, that of a bee collecting nectar with which she makes honey to pack her *cella* or *thesaurus* with wisdom. Hrabanus Maurus, writing at the end of the ninth century, says that "Divine Scripture is a honeycomb filled with the honey of spiritual wisdom."[90] Ever alert to a bibliophilic cliché, Richard de Bury likens the labors of those who collect books to bees storing their cells with honey: "industrious bees constantly making cells of honey."[91] This association of bee-cells and honey with books whose wisdom is to be packed into the compartments, *cellae* or *loci*, of an ordered memory carries over also to the metaphors that liken books and memory to fields and gardens (*campi* and *prata*) full of flowers, which the reader must cull and digest in order to store the *cella* of his memory.

In other words, one should be alert in medieval discussions of honey-bees, for a trained memory may very well lurk within the gardens and flowers, chambers, treasure-hoards, and enclosures of the hives/books. The topic has a long history among people with a classical education. Francis Bacon likens a scholar–scientist to a bee in the first chapter of his *Novum organon*; in the eighteenth century, Jonathan Swift invokes the metaphor in his preface to *The Battle of the Books*, and Isaac Watts may also have been thinking of it, however dimly, in his poem "Against Idleness and Mischief," about the "busy little bee" improving "each shining hour." And it seems to me possible that the seventeenth-century Barberini pope, Urban VIII, was making a witty pun on this long-established trope when he fastened his family's insignia, bees, to the doors of the Vatican Library, that inventory filled with the gardens, flowers, and cloister-garths of memory.

Related to the concept of "treasure-hoard" is that of "money-pouch" or *sacculus*, the metaphor for trained memory used extensively by Hugh of St. Victor and other twelfth-century writers. In a variation of the seal-in-wax metaphor, Hugh likens the making of a memory-image to a coin stamped by the coiner with a likeness which gives it value and currency.[92] Coins were kept in coin-sacks. The *sacculus* was not a sack into which one dumped things any which way, but a leather moneybag with internal compartments which sorted coins by their type and size. Its outer shape is unclear from what Hugh says, though its compartmentalized nature is not; it may have been like a saddlebag or a leather-bound box tied onto a horse as such objects are described in Middle English, or it might have been a much smaller, wallet-like object, as the diminutive ending of the Latin suggests. In the *Dialogues Concerning the Lives and Miracles of the Italian Fathers*, the author (traditionally Pope Gregory the Great) tells how Abbot Equitius, in his frequent preaching journeys, mounted on a nag and humbly dressed, carried the sacred codices with him in leather saddle-bags ("in pelliciis sacculis") hung from left and right, and wherever he went he would tap the fountain of the scriptures and water the meadows of people's minds.[93] This suggests that a *sacculus* could be something rather larger than a purse, and was used sometimes to carry books as well as coin – very precious things, useful for nourishing minds.

The word *scrinium* in classical Latin denotes a letter-case or book-box, or any chest in which papers are kept. In the late Empire it came to mean the state archives; according to the sixth-century jurist, Julian Antecessor, who lived in the time of the younger Justinian, there were four state *scrinia* or repositories, the *scrinium libellorum*, the *scrinium epistolarum*, the *scrinium dispositionum*, and the *scrinium memoriae*.[94] Monasteries, churches, and the papacy had *scrinia* where documents relating to their rights and property were kept. More generally, *scrinium* was a synonym for *thesaurus* or *fiscus*, the treasury or mint, but in Christian usage it seems to have been associated with the keeping of all valuable ecclesiastical items, including records, books, and relics – things for remembering. These meanings are still present in the English word "shrine," which derives from the Latin. Spenser's historian, Eumnestes, "of infinite remembraunce," rightly lays what he records "in his immortall scrine," both his archive and his memory.[95]

The *scrinium* was presided over by an official called the *scrinarius*. The papal court had such an office, as did larger churches and monasteries. This person was an archivist, and he also wrote official documents; thus a document is authenticated, "scriptus per manum Petri Scrinarii sacri palati."[96] The close connection between writing and things laid in memory is evident – memory is not associated here with the oral, but with books. A *scrinarius* is often synonymous with a *secretarius*, as a *scrinium*, at least in the earlier Middle Ages, was also a *secretorium*; the words suggest a repository for (written) things that are closed away as well as precious, as treasure is laid or hidden away, most notably (for Christians) in Matthew 13:44, where the kingdom of heaven is likened to treasure hidden in a field.

The connotation of hidden treasure also links up with the common metaphor for memory as a cave or recess, which we see in Augustine and Hugh (*antrum, cavus*). I have already noted that Virgil calls the beehive, into which honey is closed, a *caveus*. Likening memory to an inner room or recess is also very common in antiquity, so much so that one cannot help speculating about its connection to the architectural mnemonic described in the *Rhetorica ad Herennium*. In meditational work, Quintilian says, one should withdraw both literally into a closed inner chamber (*cubiculum clausum*; x. iii. 25) and a mental inner chamber or *secretum* (x. iii. 30), where one can concentrate in intense communion with one's recollective and compositive faculties.

An early Christian *secretorium* is described by Paulinus of Nola. A part of the church, it contained at least the Bible, and these verses were inscribed: "Si quem sancta tenet meditanda in lege uoluntas / Hic poterit residens sacris intendere libris."[97] One notes the allusion to Psalm 1:2 in the invitation to meditate upon the holy law; the allusion seems to have been fairly commonly used when talking about the reading of Scripture. *Scrinium* maintained its association with books as well as saints through the Carolingian period at least. Isidore had some of his verses written on the book-cases of the episcopal palace at Seville; among them were these: "En multos libros gestant haec scrinia nostra; / Qui cupis, ecce lege, si tua vota libent," "Lo these our book-boxes breed many books; / You who wish, look [and] read, if they answer to your desires."[98] These books, he writes in verses on another wall, are really gardens full of thorns and flowers; if you haven't the strength to take up the thorns, take the roses instead. Take and read.[99] (Notice again the persistence of memorial gardens.) Around 794, Alcuin, complaining of the heat and politics in Rome where he had journeyed on business, wrote to a student, "O how sweet was life when we sat quietly among the shrines of wisdom, among the abundance of books, among the venerable wisdom of the Fathers."[100] Thus, as used by Isidore and Alcuin, *scrinia* has become a metaphor for books themselves, not only their repository.

Especially in the earlier Middle Ages, books were decorated in the same way as shrines, like reliquaries of saints, another memorial object. Book covers with jewels, ivory, and other precious material were used to bind Gospels and other precious books, the material making literal the book's function as a *scrinium* for its contents. The Book of Kells, for example, is said to have been originally covered with gold beaten over wood, which was wrenched from it after it was stolen in the eleventh century.[101] And it is recorded in the Book of Durrow that a silver case was made for it by Flann

1. New York, Pierpont Morgan Library MS. 917 ("The Hours of Catherine of Cleves," Netherlands, Utrecht, *c.* 1440) p. 300. Pearl and gold jewelry used as a border, as in the common trope of the precious jewels of memory, using as an example the "pearls" of Christian wisdom.

(d. 916), son of king Malochy of Ireland. Many jewelled book covers still exist, however, for the practice continued into the sixteenth century.[102] As a motif of illumination, jewels – often pearls, rubies, and other stones mentioned in the Bible – were commonly painted into the margins of Books of Hours at the end of the Middle Ages, an allusion to their nature as memorial shrines and *thesauri* (see figure 1).

The Middle English word *male* (Modern English "mail") is a "travelling-bag" or "pack" of leather, for leather-makers constructed them.[103] Its immediate origin is French, but it is not a Latin-derived word; cognates suggest its origin to be Germanic.[104] One could carry various items in a *male*, including clothing and other gear; in the *Romance of Sir Bevis of Hamptoun* someone takes bread and meat from his "male," and in the Towneley First Shepherds' play a shepherd takes a roasted oxtail from his "mayll."[105] But they also held valuables, especially gold; thus in *Havelock*, someone carries gold in his "male" on his back; Chaucer's Pardoner carries his relics in his "male"; in *Piers Plowman*, Avarice goes a-thieving in the night and riffles some pedlars' "males"; and in the earliest recorded occurrence of the word, in Layamon's *Brut*, Gordoille (Goneril) tells a servant that her father can have a "male riche" of a hundred pounds.[106]

Males also had at least some internal compartments. Thus a fifteenth-century cookbook instructs one to season with various powdered spices "of þe male," "from your bag"[107] – obviously powders that were kept separately. There is a leather-covered small box bound with a buckled belt and cylindrical locks in Holbein's portrait of the merchant, George Gisze, now in the Staatliche Museum, Berlin – his strongbox or *male*.[108] Such a *male* is like a *sacculus*, divided into internal compartments for ease of sorting and changing money.

When Chaucer uses the English word figuratively in *The Canterbury Tales*, he has in mind a *male* such as I have been describing, a leather strongbox bound with a buckle, rather than the "pedlar's pack" that Walter Skeat, and every subsequent annotator, gives as a gloss of this word. If it is understood in the sense I am suggesting, then the metaphor becomes an English-language version (indeed the first recorded) of an author opening the organized compartments of his memory to disclose its store of riches. Chaucer's metaphor seems to have been immediately and widely imitated. Thus in *The Tale of Beryn*, "Harry Bailly" asks, "Who shall be the first that shall vnlace his male / In comfort of vs all, & gyn som mery tale?"[109] (I don't claim that it was *well* imitated.)

But it is Stephen Hawes who most evidently understood this image of Chaucer's as I am suggesting it should be. In *The Pastime of Pleasure* (1517),

Dame Rhetoric, whose wise advice the narrator has carefully "marked in memory" (645)[110] (that is, "tagged" as well as "stored"), gives instructions on invention (composition), interesting for being among the earliest presentations in English of mnemonic teaching. Invention needs the five inward wits, Rhetoric says, the hindermost of which is "the retentyfe memory" (750), the agency that gathers together all thought. The orator hears various tales, encloses them "in due ordre" (1258) in his retentive memory, and, when he needs material, he brings forth both a tale and its moral from his store, "his closed male":

> Yf to the orature many a sundry tale
> One after other treatably be tolde
> Than sundry ymages in his closed male
> Eche for a mater he doth than well holde
> Lyke to the tale he doth than so beholde
> And inwarde a recapytulacyon
> Of eche ymage the moralyzacyon   (1247–1253)

There are a number of interesting matters in these lines, in addition to Hawes's use of *male* as an image of trained memory. The image which the orator makes for the sundry tales he hears is "Eche for a mater," that is, memory according to the *res*, the "matter." He holds these "One after other treatably," in orderly fashion; because the memorial imprinting is "in due ordre, maner and reson," everything comes forth "eche after other withouten varyaunce." These tales are held in memory according to both the subject matter (*ad res*) and their "moralyzacyon." Here Hawes means the moral category of virtue or vice under which inwardly one "recapitulates" each "image" – literally gives it a "re-chapter" (from Latin *capitula*, "heading"), or cross- reference. In other words, one stores the tale itself and also indexes it mentally under a subject classification, advice that also occurs in some of the early thirteenth-century *artes poeticae* (see Chapter 4).

This method of memory is learned in "the poetes scole" (1267), and Hawes calls it "the memoryall arte of rethoryke" (1269), which although at first obscure will be mastered "with exercyse" (1273). An art, for a medieval scholar, was a method and set of guidelines that added order and discipline to the pragmatic, natural activities of human beings. Hugh of St. Victor remarks in *Didascalicon* that while people certainly calculated and measured, wrote and spoke, reasoned and played music before the *artes* were introduced, the arts gave them order and enabled them to be systematically learned. Harkening back to Aristotle's definition, an art is a set of principles deduced from many experiences, which in turn result from many repeated memories: "All sciences, indeed, were matters of practice [*in usu*] before they became matters of art [*in arte*] . . . what was vague and subject to caprice . . . [was] brought into order by definite rules and precepts."[111]

The final member of the group of metaphors which I want to discuss is *arca*, the commonest and in some ways the most interesting of them all. An *arca* is basically a wooden "chest" or "box" for storage, and, like the other items, it came in several sizes and was used for varying purposes. Small *arcae* were used for transporting valuables, including books.[112] And the chests or cupboards in which books were kept in early monastic libraries were sometimes called *arcae*. So the *Regula Magistri* states that books should be brought for distribution from the "arca."[113] When Hugh of St. Victor says that wisdom is stored in the "archa" of the heart, and there are many compartments in this storage-chamber, he is taking advantage specifically of the long association of *arcae* with books. Memory is not just any strongbox or storage-chest – it is particularly one in which books are kept, a powerful portable library. Indeed, as John of Salisbury wrote, "the memory truly is a sort of mental bookcase, a sure and faithful custodian of perceptions."[114]

But there is another meaning of *arca* which is associated from earliest times with the process of Scriptural *lectio* and study. As *arca sapientiae*, one's memory is the ideal product of a medieval education, laid out in organized *loci*. One designs and builds one's own memory according to one's talent, opportunities, and energy. That makes it a construction, an *aedificatio*. As something to be built, the trained memory is an *arca* in the sense understood by the Biblical object called Noah's Ark, the construction of which occupies some detail in Genesis, and the Ark of the Covenant, into which the books of the Law were placed: "Take this book of the law, and put it in the side of the ark of the covenant of the Lord your God" (Deut. 31:26).[115]

The double understanding of *arca*, "chest," as both the Ark of Noah and the Ark of the Covenant, is clearly set out in a painting of the Deluge in the Ashburnham Pentateuch, shown in figure 2, a manuscript of the late sixth or early seventh century, possibly made in Rome (BnF MS. n.a.l. 2334). The Ark, floating above a sea full of drowned corpses, is shaped distinctly like a wooden chest with feet, its sides curved and bound with strips of red, pink, and brown, that are shown nailed to the surface boards, as leather strips were nailed to the frame of an actual chest. It has a wooden door and wooden-shuttered windows cut into it, and a wooden cover set over the box like the lid of a chest.[116]

By no means are architectural devices confined particularly to the Herennian mnemonic tradition. Philo speaks of Scriptural study as being

2. Paris, Bibliothèque nationale de France MS. n.a.l. 2334, fo. 9r. "The Ashburnham [or Tours] Pentateuch"; late sixth century or early seventh century, Italian [Rome?] or Spanish or North African [Carthage?]. Noah's Ark, in the shape of a four-legged wooden storage chest, floats atop a sea of drowned people, animals, and giants.

like constructing a building,[117] and the metaphor is a common one for the method of exegesis developed during the Middle Ages, whereby one builds layers of interpretation according to allegorical, moral, and mystical senses upon the foundation of the literal words. A well-known example of such analysis occurs in Gregory the Great's *Moralia in Job*: "For first we lay a secure foundation of history; next through typological signification we raise up in the citadel of faith a structure of our mind [*fabricam mentis*]; on the outside as well through the grace of the moral sense, we clothe as it were the superstructure of the edifice with color."[118] By *mens* Gregory meant the educated, trained memory; *mens* frequently is used by medieval writers to mean the whole complex of processes occuring in the brain, including memory, that precede understanding or intellection.[119] Hugh of St. Victor uses Gregory's description in *Didascalicon*, but his most original development of it is in his treatise on Noah's Ark, known in many manuscripts with varying titles including "De arca Noe pro arca sapientiae," "De archa intellectuali," and "De quatuor archis."[120]

It was also an exegetical commonplace to regard the development of the moral life of a Christian in terms of building a temple or church; Jerome's commentary on Ezekiel's vision of the Temple contains an elaborate example of such exegesis.[121] Hugh of St. Victor's particular genius in *De archa Noe* is to bring together the processes of Scriptural reading, moral development, and memory training in the single image of Noah's ark. "I give you," he writes, "the ark of Noah as a model of spiritual building, which your eye may see outwardly so that your soul may be built inwardly in its likeness."[122] His exegesis is on three levels, though the major part of the treatise is devoted to the third: first, the historical ark built by Noah; second, the ark of the Church which Christ built; and third, the *arca sapientiae*, which "every day wisdom builds in our hearts from continuous meditation on the law of God."[123] Hugh's words make it clear that it is memory he means by this last "ark"; *meditatio* is the stage at which reading is memorized and changed into personal experience, and "in our hearts" was understood throughout the Middle Ages to be an adequate synonym for "in our memories," as the injunction to "write upon the tables of thy heart" makes clear. Jerome, for instance, glosses the Biblical phrase *in corde tui* as "in memoriae thesauro."[124] Jerome's comments on Ezekiel 3:2–5, when the prophet is instructed to "eat the book," are also of interest: "Consumption of the book is the foundation of reading and the basis of history. When, by diligent meditation, we store away the book of the Lord in our memorial treasury, our belly is filled spiritually and our guts are satisfied that we may have, with the apostle Paul [Col. 3:12], the bowels of mercy."[125]

Jerome then links this action of eating the book to the story of Samson finding honey in the lion's mouth (Judges 14:8) and to Proverbs 6:8 ("Go to the bee"), read as an admonition to store the honey of Scripture in one's own memory/heart. In this way, he concludes, one imitates the prudence of the serpent and the innocence of the dove (a verse usually understood as an exegetical emblem of Ethica). The passage is an astonishingly compact memorial gathering-up or chain (*catena*) of many of the major themes which I have discussed in this chapter.

The *arca sapientiae* is constructed in the mind of each student. Hugh compares it to the *arca* of the Church, built in the eternal mind of God. In human minds, time exists, and yet by disciplined thought we can withdraw from it and in some way imitate the eternal present of God. "Thus, indeed, in our mind past, present, and future exist in thought at the same time. If therefore by a difficult program of meditation we begin to dwell in our heart, then in a certain way we withdraw from time, and, as though made dead to the world, we live within God."[126] It is clear that Hugh specifically means memory here, for in his Augustinian-influenced psychology, it is memory that makes time. Moreover, through disciplined training of and communion with our memory, we build the ark/chest/library of wisdom which allows us to dwell inwardly with God, "per studium meditationis assidue," "through the hard discipline of *meditatio*." "This," Hugh concludes, "is the ark you ought to build."[127]

The *arca sapientiae* is thus the process and product of a medieval education, both the construction process and the finished structure. The ark of full understanding (*arca intellectualis*) has three compartments in it (*mansiones*), and Hugh proceeds to detail at some length the characteristics of these rooms/way-stations. The ark is, on a grand scale, the compartmentalized, thoroughly filed, labelled, and addressed mental storage-chest described by Cassiodorus, which every scholar could carry to a library, store with a *summa* of commentary and texts, and take away with him.

At the very end of Hugh's treatise, it is clear that the Ark, as an organizing metaphor for education, has become a book itself, indeed The Book, together with the whole program of study undertaken to comprehend its wisdom and mysteries:

This ark is like to an apothecary's shop, filled with a variety of all delights. You will seek nothing in it which you will not find, and when you find one thing, you will see many more disclosed to you. Here are bountifully contained the universal works of our salvation from the beginning of the world until the end, and here is contained the condition of the universal Church. Here the narrative of historical events is woven together, here the mysteries of the sacraments are found, here are laid out the successive stages of responses, judgments, meditations, contemplations, of good works, virtues, and rewards.[128]

The triple-tiered ark is the triple mnemonic of medieval Scriptural study: *historia, allegoria, moralia*. Within its compartments are placed in orderly fashion all the gloss and commentary, the many *interpretationes*, together with the literal texts upon which they build, so that as one pulls forth one thing, a great many others are disclosed, in a systematic concordance and index. This book/ark, constructed by each student, is an apothecary of diverse, yet orderly, material. The word *apotheca* means "store-house," originally for wine, but extended, by Hugh's time, to mean something like a "shop," a store full of precious things laid away in order, any of which the *apothecarius* can bring forth immediately in response to a request, and, indeed, bring forth a host of related things too.[129] Hugh's *arca* is both a memory and a book, the common metaphor of store-house collapsing the two objects to which it simultaneously refers, as so many other ancient and medieval metaphors of this type also do.

CHAPTER 2

Descriptions of the neuropsychology of memory

All accounts of the workings of memory written after Aristotle separate its
activities into two processes: that of storage (in a strict definition, the
activity to which the words *memoria* and *mnesis* are applied); and that of
recollection (*reminiscentia* and *anamnesis*). In broader and more common
contexts, *memoria* refers to both storage and reminiscence. Indeed, when
described as an aspect of rhetoric, it refers to training and discipline in a
whole craft of memory, *ars memorativa*, comprising techniques for storing
a memorial inventory that are designed to facilitate more productive
recollection. Though the two activities are closely related, the one being
dependent upon the other, for clarity's sake it is best to follow ancient
example and discuss *memoria*, at least initially, separately from *reminiscentia*. Thus, this chapter is concerned first with the nature of memory-
storage, of what is stored and how, and then with the question of what
recollection is and how it was thought to proceed.

A caveat to this method of proceeding is in order. The monastic
traditions of the early medieval centuries in the West are not primarily
concerned with those definitional problems that later occupied the scholastic philosophers, but are directed towards the practice of meditational
prayer. G. R. Evans has noted that "[t]he notion of memory poses a variety
of problems which seem to have held few attractions" for pre-scholastic
scholars.[1] This is not because they neglected their memories, but rather
because *memoria* was thought of as the praxis of liturgical and devotional
prayer, as I demonstrated in *The Craft of Thought*. Thus, while there are
virtually no medieval treatises *de memoria* much before the twelfth century,
there are a number of writings on prayer, meditation, and the study of
Scripture, which employ some basic features of practical memory-work
that we find also in antiquity, without evidencing much (if any) interest in
memory and recollection as philosophical concepts. Yet the psychological
descriptions of memory and recollection, most fully articulated by Aristotle
and his heirs, account for certain basic themes in medieval practice and for

some of the terms used in rhetoric to discuss *memoria*, such as the notion of places, the importance of images, and the somatic–aesthetic emphasis given to the workings of memorial storage and recollective procedure. So, without wishing to label these general practices as Aristotelian in any ideological sense (they appear in un-Aristotelian and pre-Aristotelian works too), I will discuss the Aristotelian analysis of *memoria* at some length in this chapter, despite the fact that it was not known directly in the medieval West until the twelfth century, because it most adequately explains how and why practical mnemotechnique was supposed to work, and glosses some of its basic terminology.

THE MEMORY-IMAGE

Systematic philosophical and medical discussions of what we would now call the neuropsychology of memory are solidly based, both in late anti-quity and in the later Middle Ages, on the familiar descriptions by Aristotle, found chiefly in *De anima* and the short treatises on recollection, sleep, and dreaming known collectively as the *Parva naturalia*. During the Middle Ages, the Arabic and Hebrew commentaries on Aristotle, chiefly of Avicenna and Averroës, were used extensively as well. What is said about memory in the fourth-century AD medical compendia based on Galen reflects these same traditions, and was the basis for medical knowledge of the workings of memory. Memory is treated in these related traditions as the final process in sensory perception, which begins with the stimulation of the five senses and becomes the material of knowledge through the activities of a series of internal functions, known to the Middle Ages as the inward sense(s).

The development of conceptions of inward senses has been ably traced by several scholars, notably H. A. Wolfson in a 1935 essay in the *Harvard Theological Review*.[2] One difficulty shared by many of these accounts, however, is that in so carefully delineating the subtle variations among the accounts in Aristotle and his commentators, they inevitably leave the impression that the distinctions among the various aspects of the interior sense were more precise and absolute than in fact they are in the texts. Avicenna, in some ways the most careful of the Arab commentators, varies in his own use of several terms, for example whether he refers to "interior senses" or "interior sense."

Wolfson's essay does an admirable job of showing the complexity and variability of medieval descriptions of the interior senses, but even he does not quite convey the dimension of the problem. His table of correspondences among Arabic, Hebrew, and Latin texts of the various terms for the internal senses demonstrates his apt observation of the "remarkable care and comparative uniformity with which the technical Arabic terms are rendered into Latin."[3] But the confusing inconsistencies that do indeed exist are found not primarily in translation or the specific enumeration and definition of the parts of the internal senses, but in the varying perception of the describer concerning the function of his definitions – as physician, as a philosopher, as theologian, as rhetorician, as curer of souls. In addition to the philosophical and medical traditions, there is a largely independent doctrine of interior senses within Christian spiritual traditions, deriving from Origen and other early Church teachers like Augustine, who addressed their concerns to the Biblical problem of how directly human beings can experience God in vision and prayer: when Moses is said to see God, what exactly is happening?[4] These were not concerns for Aristotle.

The explanation given by the ancient and medieval academic writers for how the mind knows and what kinds of knowledge it is capable of must be understood in the context within which the various works on the soul were written. Even philosophical works are products of their time, and it is important to acknowledge their cultural matrix. Students of history have long recognized that philosophical answers are specific to time and place, but one needs also to keep in mind that philosophers have not, in fact, asked eternal questions.[5] The questions themselves proceed from assumptions embedded deeply within a culture's habits of mind, those presuppositions about human and cosmic nature that are absorbed in earliest education and often survive to color in some degree all subsequent experience, even of the rarest individuals.

One fundamental assumption that lay behind the psychological questions framed by Aristotle's medieval heirs was that human beings have two distinct kinds of knowledge – of "singulars" or particular material things, and of abstract principles or concepts. Discussions of the internal senses address the problem of how people know their own experience(s) in terms of how we can come to understand abstract concepts when the input to our brains is in the form of individual sensory impressions. A second assumption within which psychological explorations were framed was that the whole sensing process, from initial reception by a sense-organ to awareness of, response to, and memory of it, is somatic or bodily in nature.[6] Finally, Aristotelians, in particular, assumed that everything created, even knowledge, has an immediate, proximate material cause. Aristotle says that acts of recollection occur "because one change is of a nature to happen after another," either of necessity or by habit.[7] Such a statement makes sense only when read in the context of his belief that things are caused by and cause other things, one after another, contiguously or proximately.

The medical interest in the improvement and maintenance of memory is a continuing theme in ancient and medieval writings on the subject. One of the more influential late medieval "arts of memory" was written by Matheolus, a physician of Perugia. That memory and recollection could best be understood as a physical process involving physical organs is both fundamental to the whole idea of memory *training*, and quite foreign to much post-Cartesian epistemology: it will be helpful, therefore, to begin with the anatomy of memory. All the different interior faculties, wits, or senses described in ancient philosophical and medical literature after Galen (that is, after 212 AD) are operations of one organ, the brain. Aristotle, however, and the medical tradition in which he wrote, supposed that two organs were involved in the production of memories: the heart, which received all externally derived impressions, and the brain, to which this information was relayed and where it was stored.[8] The controversy over whether the brain or heart was primary was resolved medically in the Alexandrine schools. Herophilus of Chalcedon and Erasistratus of Ceos described (perhaps after human dissection) two parallel systems in the body, one of blood vessels that centered in the heart, and the other of spinal marrow and nerves that centered in the brain. To the brain was attributed sensitivity, motion, and neurological functioning, and to the heart warmth and "vital spirit." This model of human physiology prevailed for nearly 2,000 years.[9]

But, even though the physiology of consciousness was known to occur entirely in the brain, the metaphoric use of *heart* for memory persisted. Memory as a function of the heart was encoded in the common Latin verb *recordari*, meaning "to recollect." Varro, the second-century BC grammarian, says that the etymology of the verb is from *revocare* "to call back" and *cor* "heart."[10] The Latin verb evolved into the Italian *ricordarsi*, and clearly influenced the early use in English of "heart" for "memory." Chaucer often uses the phrase "by heart" as we still use it, and while he was perhaps echoing the medieval French phrase "par coeur," there are also much earlier uses of the metaphor in English. *The Middle English Dictionary* records an early twelfth-century example of *herte* to mean "memory"; there is an Old English use of *heorte* to mean "the place where thoughts occur," *cogitationes*.[11] Since the common Old English verb meaning "to remember" was made from the noun *mynde*, "mind," it seems probable that the metaphorical extension to memory of the English word *heorte* was made on the direct analogy of the Latin metaphor in *recordari* and its derivatives. Certainly, the existence of *recordari* in Latin is the justification for Jerome's assertion that, in the appropriate Biblical contexts, *cor* is a common metaphor for memory.[12]

Neither Aristotle nor Augustine nor Thomas Aquinas had a conception of mind or mental activity like ours.[13] *Soul* is not the same thing as *mind*, as most moderns who are not philosophers are inclined to think. In an essay on the development of the "mind–body problem," Wallace Matson calls attention to Aristotle's comment in *De anima*, "If the eye were a living creature, its soul would be its vision [or its ability to see]."[14] Aristotle's fundamental understanding of soul, which was preserved to a degree by his medieval descendants, was that it is not a "thing" (ghostly or not) but "a kind of organization and functioning that certain pieces of matter have." Prior to Aristotle, even the soul was thought to be a thing, "an interior double, which both pushes and orders the body around."[15] *Soul* is the whole complex of organization and function of a human being; *mind* is invoked to explain that aspect of its function relating to its ability to understand and to acquire wisdom.

Brain physiology and the formation of memories

For Aristotle, emotions and even judgments are in some sense physiological processes, though they are more than just that. Memory-images, produced in the emotional (sensitive) part of the soul are "physiological affections [meaning both "a change" and "a disposition to change in a certain way"], in some sense of 'is' analogous to that in which a house is bricks. But it is not 'simply' this."[16] These images impress the material of the receiving organ – that is a chief implication of the seal-in-wax archetype. Aristotle goes on to explain that young and old have poor memories because in each group the body is in flux and therefore does not retain images well (*De memoria* 450a 32). Later he remarks that people whose humors are out of balance are sometimes better at recollecting than remembering, or the reverse. Those who are melancholic are too fluid to retain images well and so recollect uncontrollably: "The reason for recollecting not being under their control is that just as it is no longer in people's power to stop something when they throw it, so also he who is recollecting and hunting moves a bodily thing in which the affection resides" (453a 14). Dry people on the contrary form images more slowly but are better at retaining them, while dwarfs and people "whose upper parts are especially large" have poor memories because they have more weight resting on their perceptual organs (453a 31), and the images fail to persist.[17]

This conception of the essentially somatic nature of the memory's images continued through the Middle Ages. Medical recipes and dietary advice devoted to memory's maintenance and improvement are common. Many of these go back to ancient or Arabic sources, and all reflect the basic Galenic anatomical description that placed memory in the posterior portion of the brain. They follow ancient physiological theory in believing that the health of all organisms is best maintained through dietary manipulation of the balance of humors. One of the most famous physicians of the late Middle Ages was Arnaldus de Villanova, Chaucer's "Arnold of Newe-Town," a Catalan who died in 1311. He translated many medical works from Arabic to Latin, and wrote several tractates of his own. His name is attached to one of the most widely printed medical compendia of the late Middle Ages, *Philosophi et medici summi*, though not all it contains is his.[18] Among the contents is a collection of medical aphorisms, *Doctrina aphorismorum*, which contains some dietary prescriptions and recipes for aiding the memory, and a separate, brief treatise, "De bonitate memoriae."[19] Many of the same prescriptions occur also in the fifteenth-century memory treatise which I have mentioned earlier, the *De augenda memoriae* by the physician, Matheolus of Perugia.

Since the brain is moist and cool, it needs to be protected against overheating of all sorts. Drunkenness is especially bad, but so are all sorts of immoderate or superfluous activities, including the sexual.[20] Too much *meditatio*, however, can also be bad; Arnaldus prescribes "temperate joy and honest delight" as beneficial for maintaining memory (and, as we shall see, the idea that the memory should not be crammed at one sitting, but fed temperately only until it is satisfied, not satiated, is a commonplace in teaching).[21] A diet which includes fatty meats, strong wine, vinegar and all sour things, legumes such as beans, and especially garlic, onions, and leeks is very bad for memory. (It is a wonder that Chaucer's Summoner has any mind left at all.) These are all very hot foods of the third or even fourth degree.[22]

Generally, whatever is good for the health of the body also aids the memory, so various purges can be efficacious.[23] Matheolus advises a seven-day regimen of drinking sugared water for several days instead of wine (since sugar was thought to have medicinal value perhaps it would seem to safeguard the water). Certain herbs, especially ginger and coriander, when chewed or taken in powdered form, are particularly good. Arnaldus and Matheolus also suggest bathing the head in a concoction which contains laurel leaf, camomile, and a honey-derivative, and Arnaldus also recommends frequently bathing the feet in a similar potion.[24] Physical prescriptions, however, are secondary to the need for memory training and practice. Matheolus's medical advice comes briefly at the end of several paragraphs devoted to the training advice of Thomas Aquinas, Hugh of St. Victor, and Cicero; Arnaldus says that the chief way to strengthen and confirm memory is through "concentration [*solicitudo*] and frequent recollection of what we have seen or heard."[25]

In his discussion of memory as a function of the sensitive soul, Thomas Aquinas follows the outline of his chief sources, Avicenna and Averroës, and his master, Albertus Magnus. He enumerates the interior senses in the *Summa* during his discussion of human psychology, especially in Ia, Q. 78, article 4. Four powers are described: common sense; the fantastic (imagination: "as it were a storehouse of forms received through the senses"); the estimative; and the memorative. That power called estimative in animals is called the cogitative in humans, or the *ratio particularis*. In his "De potentia animae," cap. 4,[26] Thomas defines the powers more particularly, enumerating five this time: the *sensus communis*; *phantasia* (retentive imagination); *imaginativa* (the composing imagination); *aestimativa seu cogitativa* (called the latter in human beings, and also *ratio particularis* or "collativa intentionum individualium," the opinions, beliefs, prejudices, of a particular individual human); and *memorativa*. But the composing imagination (*imaginativa*) is elsewhere combined with *imaginatio* (or *phantasia*) and called simply *phantasia seu imaginatio*.

In addition to the memory of sensorily perceived objects, Thomas Aquinas distinguishes a type of memory which he calls "intellectual." This distinction arose in part to resolve the problem of how one could remember conceptions, since one's memory stored only phantasms of particular sense objects or composite images derived from particular sense objects. The type of memory which recalls abstractions, things created in thought rather than sensorily perceived, is a part of the intellect; Thomas defines it in article 6 of Q. 79 (*ST* I), as "a power to keep thoughts in mind," rather than only individual things, and it is peculiar to human beings. Animals have memories too, but only of discrete experiences – they cannot generalize or predict on the basis of what they remember. But concepts "are not retained in the sense part of the soul, but rather in the body–soul unity, since sense memory is an organic act" (ad. I). Human memory is thus both material, as it retains the impress of "likenesses," and yet more than that, for people can remember opinions and judgments, and predict things, based upon their memories.

The concept of "intellectual memory" is attributed by Thomas Aquinas to Augustine, although in *De memoria*, Aristotle distinguishes the two kinds of memory (449b 30ff.), as he also does in *De anima* in his effort to qualify Plato's doctrine of recollection. Aristotle says that both concepts and "singulars" are known through images – sensory objects by the likenesses we get through our senses, and concepts by images which we associate with them. "Memory, even the memory of objects of thought, is not without an image. So memory will belong to thought in virtue of an incidental association, but in its own right to the primary perceptive part."[27] When we think of the concept "triangle," Aristotle says, we think of a triangle, even though we understand our image to be a conceptual model, "as in drawing a diagram."[28] No human being is capable of thinking entirely abstractly without some sort of signifying image. Thomas Aquinas, though differing from Aristotle in how and where images for thought were retained, also believed that no human thinking could take place without some sort of image.

The two major faculties of the sensory soul which Aristotle describes in *De anima* are the common sense (*sensus communis*) and the imagination. *Sensus communis* is the receptor of all sense impressions. (Avicenna defined it as "the center of all the senses both from which the senses are diverted in branches and to which they return, and it is itself truly that which experiences.")[29] It unites and compares impressions from all five external senses, but it is also the source of awareness. It both receives the sensation of hearing a sound and realizes that hearing is taking place.[30]

While all animals have sensation, not all have imagination – yet imagination is not thought either. It is the process in all animals capable of learning (like dogs, horses, birds, and perhaps bees and spiders) whereby *phantasmata* are formed and move the creature to action. Human imagination, however, involves some quasi-rational activity, for humans are not just moved by imagination's products, but judge and form opinions about them. Human imagination is what Aristotle calls "deliberative" (*bouleutikē* or *logistikē*): "Imagination in the form of sense exists, as we have said [in *De anima* III, ii], in other animals, but deliberative imagination only in those which can reason" (*De anima*, III, xi, 434a 5ff.). Pure sensation is always true, enjoying something of the status which contemporary philosophers accord to what some of them call "raw feels"; but imagination can be false.[31] It is therefore a more rationalizing activity than the elementary sensory receptiveness of the common sense.

Aristotle's definitions of the stages in the sensory/consciousness process can be classified in two ways: (1) whether or not actively conscious behavior is involved; and (2) as types of interior activity. According to the first kind of classification, *sensus communis* and imagination (in humans) are differentiated from one another; so too are "believing" and "thinking," and memory and recollection. In this classification, the "faculties" or interior senses are six in number, pairs of receptor (passive) and conscious (active) operations. But described as types of interior activity, Aristotle distinguishes only three: the activity of forming the mental images (*phantastikon*); the activity of reacting to or forming opinions about these images (*dianouti-kon*); and the activity of recalling those images and reactions (*mnēmoneu-tikon*). The threefold classification of mental activity was authoritatively fixed by "Galen"'s immensely influential medical compendium in the anterior, medial, and posterior parts of the brain, as described by ancient anatomists. Medieval encyclopedists, like Bartholomaeus Anglicus, often paired "passive" and "active" states of these three functions, ascribing them to these distinct areas in the brain, which were described as cavities or chambers in the brain's soft matter, filled with "animal spirits"– from *anima*, the soul as energy – that power the various processes of thinking.[32]

Aristotle's great medieval Arabic and Hebrew commentators elaborated, and, to some extent, continued to localize, the somatic psychology of their Greek sources, to a degree that no student of medieval psychology can afford to ignore. Their description attempts to fill in (usually by compli-cating) that of Aristotle, both detailing more precisely the physical nature of the sensory process, including memory, and reifying the non-corporeal aspects of thinking, especially about abstract knowledge-bodies like con-cepts. Though they do not introduce an actual "mind–body problem," Avicenna and especially Averroës do seem to emphasize a mind–body split by their insistence that human intellect, as part of an independent "agent intellect," can directly consider abstractions. This characteristic of their psychology is usually related to the attempt, in late Alexandrine philoso-phy, to reconcile Plato (as Neoplatonism) to Aristotle.

Avicenna's long commentary/compendium of *De anima* and the *Parva naturalia* is the *Liber de anima*, composed in the early eleventh century and translated into Latin in the twelfth. In the fourth part, Avicenna details the powers of the soul that are involved in translating sense impressions (which he also thought to be in some way corporeal) into thought. First, there is the *sensus communis*, having the Aristotelian functions of receiving and combining external impressions and of basic awareness (knowing that one is sensing). Next, he defines *imaginatio*, solely a retentive faculty: "that [power] detains the sensible form which is called *formalis* and *imaginatio* and it does not categorize [*lit.* separate] it in any way."[33] Scholastic writers sometimes called this function *vis formalis*, as indeed Avicenna himself does here. It is often paired with *sensus communis* and located in the paired front "ventricles" or chambers of the brain.

There is also, however, a "deliberative" kind of imagination (as Aristotle suggested), one which has a composing function, joining images together: "the construction out of images of things existent, new composite images of things non-existent, or the breaking up of images of things existent into images of things non-existent."[34] As Wolfson suggests, this is basically Aristotle's "deliberative imagination" (*phantasia logistikē* or *bouleutikē*), by which "we have the power of constructing a single image out of a number of images."[35] This power of composing an image in both humans and animals is joined to a power of judgment, whereby we form an opinion of the image we have composed. This was called in Latin *estimativa*, a translation of the Arabic word *wahm*, introduced into the classification by the Arabic Aristotelians.[36] Latin scholastic writers re-defined *estimativa* as something like "instinct" in animals, the reaction whereby a lamb, seeing a wolf for the first time, knows to fear it, or seeing its mother knows to follow her. They called the human power *cogitativa*, defined as a conscious, though pre-rational, activity.[37]

Avicenna's scheme also distinguishes between the form and *intentio* of a sense-image, every such image being composed of both. Each aspect, form and *intentio*, of the sense-image has its own apprehending faculty and a store-house into which it goes. *Intentio* means opinion about or reaction to something. It also means something less definite, related to the concept in rhetorical and literary theory of "point of view." Since our knowledge comes to us through our senses, every image impressed in our memories has been filtered and mediated through our senses – it is not merely "objective." Our senses produce affects in us, changes such as emotions, and those effects include memories themselves.

Thus to say that all memory-images are made up of both likeness and intention is to say that the way we have perceived something is an inevitable necessary part of every image we have. Our recollections are never just neutral (or "factual" as we prefer now to say). Our memories store likenesses of things as they were *when they appeared to and affected us.*[38] This analysis – we should note – requires that all memory-images have some experiential and affective quality, which each phantasm acquires in the process of being made in the brain. Form and *intentio*, the completed phantasm, then is stored together as a single memory-phantasm in the *virtus custoditiva* or *virtus memorialis*, becoming the experiential basis of knowledge. Here again Avicenna is following Aristotle, who says in I, i, of *Metaphysics* that "experience is formed of many memories."[39]

3. Cambridge, University Library MS. Gg 1.1, fo. 490v. From an anthology of eclectic
materials, made *c.* 1330 in England (West Midlands); the greatly various texts were written
by one scribe, in Anglo-Norman and in Latin, with illuminations by a single artist. This
diagram of the brain is discussed in Chapter 2.

A late medieval diagram shows these processes well (figure 3). It is in a mainly French-language manuscript, Cambridge University Library MS. Gg 1.1, written in England in the fourteenth century. This book was evidently made for an aristocratic household, which still conducted its culture primarily in French, though there are Latin and even a (very) few English works in it as well. Amongst some Latin prayers and many French histories and romances is written a summary of Aristotelian doctrine about the brain, which also incorporates this picture diagram of its processes, as then commonly understood. The manuscript picture diagrams human cognitive process as described in the late medieval tradition of Aquinas, deriving from Aristotle via Avicenna: indeed the textual summary states that it shows thinking as "tractat Thomas in prima parte summe," as Thomas analyzes it in the first part of his *Summa theologiae* (the part that contains Aquinas's teaching on human psychology, though the terms used accord in many ways with Avicenna's analysis more than with Aquinas).

In this diagram, the various activities involved in thought are drawn as *cellae* or compartments, linked by "channels" (*nervi* in Latin), which the artist has drawn leading from the eyes (as similar *nervi* do from all the sense organs) and between the various activities in the brain. It is important to understand that this drawing is a diagrammatic representation, not an anatomical drawing. It was drawn in order to make clear the relationships of activities involved in the process of thinking, but the first three activities shown in this diagram as if sequential were actually thought to occur simultaneously.

The diagram shows how sensations are channeled from the various sense organs (in this drawing just the eyes are shown with channels, but similar *nervi* communicated to all the sense organs) to the *sensus communis*, which is also identified as *fantasia*, pairing "passive" and "active" aspects as Avicenna had done. These are fed to the *imaginatio* or *vis formalis*, which puts mental images together – simultaneously, *estimativa* acts on these contents of *imaginatio*, as a phantasm is constructed of likeness (*formalis*) and belief (*estimativa*). The process produces something wholly mental, a conceptual form that human intelligence can know and work with. The materials for thinking are thus shown as mental creations, *phantasmata*, a word taken by scholastic commentators from Aristotle's treatise, but which occurs as well in Quintilian's rhetoric, translated in Latin as *imagines*. It is important to notice that the resulting mental image was considered to be composed of input from all the senses. In the context of thinking, the word *imago* in medieval Latin was not limited solely to the visual sense, though it is also true that the visual was regarded as the primary instrument of cognition for most people. And finally, the images are themselves emphatically fabricated. *Fantasia*, *estimativa*, and *vis formalis* are all agents which put separate bits and responses together into a whole sensory experience – they are not just recording devices.

These *imagines* are made present to the mind as the materials of understanding through the activity called *cogitatio*, "cogitation, thinking," and from them ideas and thoughts are constructed. In this diagram *cogitatio* receives the phantasms put together by the image-making power (*vis formalis*) and they are made into concepts by *vis imaginativa*, the activity of imagining and conceptualizing (pairing abilities to receive and to act in the fashion characteristic of this diagram, and of Avicenna's analysis). Our conceptions in the forms of phantasms, mental images, are finally retained and recollected by memory, *vis memorativa*, the final stage of this constructive process. Notice that memory, like thought and imagination, is also *vis*, an agent, a power, not just a receptacle.

The path between memory and thinking must be two-way, because memories have to be recalled as well as stored. So a sort of valve was posited, which would allow images to pass into memory, and also to be recalled for cogitation. This was called the *vermis*, the little worm-like body drawn in the diagram between *cogitatio* and *memoria*. Moreover, it had been observed that people often lower their heads in order to think and raise them when trying to recollect something. This was taken as evidence for the action of the *vermis*, opening as needed for recollection, and closing for concentrated thinking once one had received from memory the materials one needed. Without such a valve, it was thought, memories could crowd unbidden into the mind, overwhelming and distracting rational thought. The *vermis* is a gatekeeper, of a sort.

It is striking how entirely imagination is implicated in cognition and in memory by this medieval analysis. This aspect is the most astonishing, most alien, from the stand-point of our own cognitive psychology. The vestiges of our sensations are collected up at the start of the process in the *sensus communis*, but from the instant they are received in bits and pieces from their various sources, fictive powers, *fantasia*, *vis formalis*, and *vis imaginativa*, go to work. This faculty may or may not make an image that is accurate or faithful as a representation of something else: the important thing for the procedures of recollection is that such images are constructed. They are fashioned by "gathering up" matters (*componendi*, composing them) into a common location.

Thomas Aquinas: a seal impressed in wax

Thomas Aquinas shared the somatic psychology of his sources concerning the nature of human perception and the process whereby the soul knows; if anything, he insisted more completely than the Arabic commentators on the "embodiment" of all kinds of human knowledge.[40] All thinking utilizes the brain's phantasms: "Avicenna erred in saying that once the mind had acquired knowledge it no longer needed the senses. For we know by experience that in order to reflect on knowledge already gained we have to make use of phantasms, and that any injury to the physical apparatus underlying these will tend to prevent our using the knowledge we already have."[41] Thus all stages and varieties of knowledge for human beings, from the most concrete to the most abstract, are shaped in some way within a physical matrix. The phantasms are produced by *imaginatio*, the image-making power, which, like memory, is an "affection" (to use Aristotle's term) or "motion" (to use that of Averroës) of the soul, motions which are physiological although not only or simply that, in the way that a house is bricks but not just bricks.[42]

In his lectures on *De anima*, Thomas describes the process of sensory perception as involving either "material" or "spiritual" change. He gives his definition in the context of his discussion of the operations of the five external senses. He says, as do his sources, that taste and touch perceive by direct contact with their objects, whereas the other three senses perceive through "media." But of those three, "the sense of sight has a special dignity; it is more spiritual and more subtle than any other sense."[43] The senses of touch and taste are composed of all four elements, as the body itself is, but the other three of air and water.[44] (Keep in mind throughout this discussion that the brain, while composed like all the body of four elements, is especially moist.) The act of perception for all the other four senses involves some kind of "material" change or addition; the organ receives material qualities directly from the object emitting them. So, in touch and taste "the organ itself grows hot or cold by contact with a hot or cold object," in smell, there is "a sort of vaporous exhalation," in hearing "movement in space" of reverberation.[45] But sight causes a wholly "spiritual" change, the likeness is received in the eye "*as a form causing knowledge, and not merely as a form in matter.*"[46]

The likeness received by the eye is formed by light, the nature of which is crucially relevant to the way in which a visual "appearance" affects the eye. Thomas Aquinas says that light is neither wholly physical nor wholly spiritual, for "it is impossible that any [wholly] spiritual or intelligible nature should [fall within the apprehension of] the senses; whose power, being essentially embodied, cannot acquire knowledge of any but bodily things."[47] But light is not physical either, for it does not behave like a body having mass.[48] The likeness of an object, progressing to the eye through air, is formed by light and received "immaterially" in the following way:

> the recipient receives the form into a mode of existence other than that which the form has in the agent; when, that is, the recipient's material disposition to receive form does not resemble the material disposition in the agent. In these cases, the form is taken into the recipient "without matter," the recipient being assimilated to the agent in respect of form and not in respect of matter . . . Aristotle finds an apt example of this in the imprint of a seal on wax. The disposition of the wax to the image is not the same as that of the iron or gold to the image; hence wax, he says, takes a sign, i. e. a shape or image, of what is gold or bronze, but not precisely *as* gold or bronze. For the wax takes a likeness of the gold seal in respect of the image, but not in respect of the seal's intrinsic disposition to be a gold seal. Likewise the sense . . . is not affected by a coloured stone precisely as a stone, or sweet honey precisely as honey.[49]

Once again, he says, the distinction between a spiritual change as here described and a material change is that in the latter case the recipient (a sense organ) "acquires a material disposition like that which was in the agent"; that is, it receives heat or cold or smell particles or reverberating air – some matter – emitted from what it is perceiving.[50]

The crucial features of Thomas's understanding of "spiritual" and "immaterial" in this context lie in his appeal to the ancient image of the seal in wax. For the wax does form a physical likeness of the original seal. What he evidently means by "spiritual" is that the wax material does not take on the gold or bronze of the original, *but not that nothing physiological at all happens to it*. As Myles Burnyeat has argued, for Aquinas Aristotle's notion of "spiritual" change is the act of perceiving itself, which certainly affects us even though the sense organ itself does not change (unlike touch, for example, when the skin becomes cold in sensing cold). The seal's image is not just ghostly like that of a photographic slide projected on a screen, but is a sort of imprint that effects a real change in the perceiver. The phantasms are in some respect physiological; they are materially caused (in Aristotle's terms) by the nature of the brain. What Thomas says here he understood in terms of Aristotle's four "causes" (or aspects) of all created things: "material," "formal," "efficient," and "purposeful." What the eye takes from the object via air and light is its "formal" aspect but not its "material" one, and this aspect causes the eye to change in the sensation we call "sight." The change in the eye occurs in the same manner in which phantasms are recorded in memory, like a seal in wax.

A further context for understanding the quasi-physical nature of the phantasms is found in Thomas's comments on *De anima*, III.iii. Referring to Aristotle's statement (in William of Moerbeke's translation) that "these images dwell within and resemble sense experiences," he says, "images ... 'dwell within' in the absence of sensible objects, as traces of actual sensations; therefore, just as sensations arouse appetitive impulses [emotions] whilst the sensed objects are present, so do images when these are absent."[51] The phantasms themselves are "movements started by actual sensations,"[52] and memory is, in definitions deriving from Aristotle, a "delayed motion that continues to exist in the soul."[53] Thus in some physical sense – just how is difficult to understand because the writers seem themselves unsure on this point – recollection involves a re-presentation of images imprinted in the matter of the brain's posterior ventricle,[54] which are then "scanned" or "seen" as objects by the intellect in some way analogous to that in which the eye perceived them in the first place. "The phantasms in the imagination are to the intellect as colours to sight; as colours provide sight with its object, so do the phantasms serve the intellect"; knowing differs from sight in that "understanding is an act proper to the soul alone, needing the body ... only to provide its object [the phantasms]; whereas seeing and various other functions involve the compound of soul and body together."[55]

Thomas's description of how knowledge based on experience-derived concepts comes about is also instructive in understanding how he regards the corporeal/spiritual nature of phantasms. We come to know a concept like "curvature" by means of a hypothesis, an "as though" proposition:

When ... the mind understands actually anything precisely as curved, it abstracts from flesh; not that it judges the curved thing to be *not* flesh, but it understands "curved" without regard to flesh ... And it is thus that we understand all mathematical objects, – as though they were separated from sensible matter, whilst in reality they are not so.[56]

We understand universals by considering "certain aspects ... of sense-objects ... in separation or distinctly, without judging them to exist separately."[57]

Here Thomas rejects a Neoplatonic view that universals themselves are imprinted in the soul, and that in sense-objects we recognize or recollect these prior implantations; he also, clearly, rejects the Avicennan–Averroist view that direct knowledge of separately existing universals is possible. Indeed, he again shows himself to be a better Aristotelian than many of the commentators he was following. As Sorabji comments, Aristotle's belief that biological growth and conscious activity are both equally powers of the soul could lead to the sort of materialism which concludes that conscious activity is therefore simply another biological process. But instead, he (and Thomas Aquinas with him) "prefers to deny that biological growth is 'simply' a physical process – which is not however to say that it is a mental one [in the modern sense]. Growth is also a development towards an end. And desire, perhaps, is an efficient cause of action towards an end."[58]

Similarly, for Thomas, objects of thought (e.g. triangle, curvature, whiteness) are re-presented in the individual, psycho-somatic phantasms produced by sense-objects, but they are not merely such traces in the brain. They are abstracted by a process of comparison and contrast, "related to a unity in so far as they are judged by one intellect."[59] But even in describing so purely mental an activity as abstraction seems to us to be, a physical analogy persists. Thomas, as we have seen, regards the production of phantasms as a process of physical changes ("motion"); thus, in sight, "the colour-affected air itself modifies the pupil of the eye in a particular way, i.e. it imprints on it a likeness of some colour, and … the pupil, so modified, acts upon the common sense."[60]

We have followed the progress of the likeness, the seal impressed upon the stuff of *imaginatio* and memory, until it is presented to the intellect as an object of thought, not of sense only. And we have seen that Thomas regards abstracted ideas as being *as if* distinct, not as actually existing separately from the phantasms in the memory. But in his discussion of this process in *Summa theologiae*, Thomas explains that because the phantasms are products and forms in sense organs, and are of individual objects, their mode of existence is different from that of the intellect – how then can they cause knowledge? They must somehow be impressed upon the receiving intellect as color-affected air modifies the pupil of the eye, an organ itself composed of air and water and thus able to be a medium between the light-generated, air-borne likeness and the moist brain. The intellectual impression is mediated and formed "by the power of the active intellect, which by turning towards the phantasm produces in the passive intellect a certain likeness which represents, as to its specific conditions only, the thing reflected in the phantasm. It is thus that the intelligible species is said to be abstracted from the phantasm; not that the identical form which previously was in the phantasm is subsequently in the passive intellect, as a body is transferred from one place to another."[61]

Granted these serial processes are increasingly spiritual and immaterial, it is still crucial to notice that for Thomas Aquinas the activity of thinking and the activity of having a sense perception are fundamentally analogous, not fundamentally different. Images, representative likenesses, are fundamental to knowing (one must have knowledge of something) even if they have to be produced in something which by definition has no matter to be formed. That this is so is a symptom of how basic the simile of the seal in wax was to Thomas's understanding of knowledge, perception, and memory. For St. Thomas, the soul is neither a ghost in a machine nor the machine itself. It is "embodied," as the form which "causes matter to be."[62]

The implications of this belief were well realized by Thomas Aquinas's great pupil, Dante, when, at the end of his *Paradiso*, memory and speech both fail him. Angels, says Dante, have no need of memory for they have continuous understanding,[63] but human beings must know by remembering physically formed phantasms. Of direct knowledge of God, such as that indicated at the end of the *Paradiso*, the memory "can form no adequate image," in Gardner's phrase (we recall the scholastic aphorism, *veritas est adaequatio rei et verbi*), and so it fails the intellect, bringing back nothing but an inadequate shadow or impression of the vanished vision.[64] The bodily matrix of memory is also clear in Thomas Aquinas's belief that sensory memory does not survive death, for it has "no activity apart from the corporal organ."[65] The memory that is immortal is what he calls "intellectual memory," since the intellect does survive death. But this is not true memory. Intellectual memory is "the notion of memory" (a conception of having had a memory when one was still alive in one's body); after death, the soul can still regard past events which are preserved in its intellect, and it can recall these (for recollection is an intellectual activity). But it can form no new memories when it no longer has a body.[66] Because memory requires a body, the souls in Dante's *Inferno* are forever stuck in their recollected pasts, unable to form new memories in hell, yet cut off also from the continuous vision that nourishes the blessed souls and angels.

Dream-images and memory-images

Other kinds of images were thought to arise from the imagination. It will be useful to consider these briefly, as a way of distinguishing them from memory-images. Imagination produces a dream-image in a different manner, though from the same materials. Aristotle says that the mental images which come in dreams arise spontaneously, not in response to a controlled process like recollection; in fact this is their chief difference from the memory-images that are the subject of my study here. Dream-images are created by the *vis imaginativa*, as are all phantasms.[67] They are in the same class as after images, hallucinations, and other irrational images, the product of aroused, imbalanced emotions (as perception is distorted by anger or lust) or of raw sense-data unformed by judgment (as when we see the land moving as we ride through it). Such images are themselves just sense-data, *aisthēmata*, rather than being the imprint of a sense impression after some time has elapsed, Aristotle's basic definition of a memory-phantasm. To put the matter in modern psychological terms, Aristotle does not consider that a memory is a memory until it has been securely stored in a retrievable manner in the "long-term memory." In sleep, the controlling *sensus communis*, the seat of awareness, is not functioning. So the external senses, if stimulated, produce unprocessed raw data; there are also residual movements, effects, left over from material received during the day.[68] All of this uncontrolled material can stimulate the imagination, but with the *sensus communis* and all other judgmental activity in the inner sense suspended, the resulting mental images pose a special interpretive problem, for they must be judged after the fact, as it were, as to their truth or falsity, whether they are of divine origin and predictive of the future, or whether they are simply the body's way of adjusting the balance of humors, or the product of random, raw *aisthēmata*.

While Aristotle acknowledges that some dreams can be true, such things do not seem to interest him very much, and he says little about them. But Averroës and Avicenna are both greatly interested in prophetic dreams, which they regard as the province of those with especially well-formed imaginations. Avicenna discusses the prophetic imagination, "that is, what is genuinely prophetic in the image-making power."[69] Dreams of the future result from a direct action of angelic intelligences upon the mind in sleep, acting upon the imagination. He also recognizes inspirations "which suddenly fall into the soul [*quae subito in animam cadunt*]," unrelated to previous knowledge or experience. Such inspiration is of various kinds, "sometimes it is from the intellect, sometimes by means of divination, and sometimes it is from poetry, and this happens according to aptitude and habit and custom."[70] These inspirations, Avicenna says, arise from causes

which assist the soul for the most part unknown and for the most part [they] are like sudden apparitions, which do not remain in a manner so that they can be sought out in recollection, unless the mind hastens to aid them with an already-held memory.[71]

Avicenna underlines here the relationship among the images formed in heightened states such as trances and epilepsy, in dreams, and those required in memory. The images produced during dreams and trances will disappear unless they are associated with images that are already in memory storage, already familiar and accessible to recollection. Thus even direct inspiration requires the immediate assistance of human memory, though in a way more mysterious than that of ordinary dreaming or consciously controlled recollection.

Meticulous mental imaging – mental painting, really – is a feature of trained recollection, even when one may be "recollecting" an experience recorded in someone else's words. In his *Epitome* of Aristotle's *Parva naturalia*, written about 1170, Averroës writes of individuals with peculiarly gifted powers of concentration, who can form accurate images of things just from their description by others: "In this manner, it is possible for a person to form the image of an elephant without his ever having actually seen one." Such a feat can only be achieved by all three faculties (imagination, cogitation, and memory) acting together, and is possible only for humans because it is an intellectual operation. Such concentration is "exceedingly difficult" and "will only occur in the case of those who exercise their minds in solitude." Averroës is speaking of *consciously controlled* procedures here, and it is note-worthy that he believes that the power of imagining predictively and originally can be achieved by conscious meditation as well as by sudden inspirations. But ordinarily it is in sleep or trance, or in particular cases like epilepsy, that the faculties will all unite and the dreamer "will behold the wonders of the world."[72]

Before turning the discussion directly to the processes of recollection, let me summarize for the sake of emphasis the chief features of a memory-image. Most importantly, it is "affective" in nature – that is, it is sensorily derived and emotionally charged. It is not simply an abstraction or a mental ghost, despite its critical usefulness to all rational processes. Nor does the language of computation adequately describe what a memory was thought to be – it is not a mere algorithm or schema of the sort that accounts for what a machine does, though, as we will see, many mnemonic techniques function, at least in part, like algorithms. But they are never just that. Successful memory schemes all acknowledge the importance of tagging material emotionally as well as schematically, making each memory as much as possible into a personal occasion by imprinting emotional associations like desire and fear, pleasure or discomfort, or the particular appearance of the source from which one is memorizing, whether oral (a teacher) or written (a manuscript page). Successful recollection requires that one recognize that every kind of mental representation, including those in memory, is in its composition sensory and emotional. Recollection *may employ* schemes, but it *is like* reading a book, that is, an event involving judgment and response (*intentio*) in addition to intellect.[73]

One other feature distinguishes a memory-image from every other sort. Aristotle says that "Memory is of the past," and "all memory involves time."[74] Because time is bound into their nature – memories are presently existing images of things that are past – memories differ from other sensorily pro-duced images, as recognition (of something present) differs from recollection (a matter which I discussed in Chapter 1). Their temporal nature also means that memory's re-presentation is less importantly mimetic, or objectively reiterative of the original perception, than it is temporal, because it makes the past perception present. Aristotle says that we judge time-lapses and the relative duration of time by an imaging process similar to that by which we judge magnitude (449b 30ff., and 452ab), by constructing a sort of scale model in the mind. Aristotle spends a good deal of his brief treatise on this particular problem, suggesting a solution which Sorabji describes in pp. 18–21. What is important to later thinkers about this discussion is Aristotle's insist-ence that memorial *phantasmata* are both representations of things (in the senses discussed in Chapter 1) and "re-presentations" of experience no longer present. Time is a dimension of all images in the memory.

Thus, recollection was understood to be a re-enactment of experience, which involves cogitation and judgment, imagination, and emotion. Averroës and Aristotle both insist on this: "the one who recollects will experience the same pleasure or pain in this situation which he would experience were the thing existing in actuality."[75] Memory's success is heavily dependent on the recollector's skill in being able to form memory-images that are "rich" in associations, as "iconic" (to use another term from neuropsychology) as possible. All mnemonic advice stresses the benefits to be gained from forming memories as scenes that include personal associations. Hugh of St. Victor, for instance, stresses the need to impress the circumstances during which something was memorized as part of the associational web needed to recall it: the sort of day it is, how one feels, the gestures and appearance of one's teacher, the appearance of the manuscript page, and so on.

RECOLLECTION

In his *Libri rerum memorandarum* (1345), Petrarch gives the following account of the recollective abilities of one of his friends:

It was enough for him to have seen or heard something once, he never forgot; nor did he recollect only the subject [*res*], but the words and time and place where he had first learned it. Often we spent entire days or long nights in talking: there was no one I would rather listen to; for after the passage of many years the same things being spoken of, if I were to say much more or less or say something different, at once he would gently admonish me to correct this or that word; and when I wondered and inquired just how he could have known this, he recalled not only the time in which he would have heard it from me, but in the shade of which holm oak, by what riverbank, along what sea shore, on the top of what hill (for I had walked long distances with him along the coasts), I recognizing each particular.[76]

Striking in this account is the friend's mnemonic use of unrelated, experiential detail to mark what we think of as objective information. Some contemporary psychologists are inclined to think that the memory used in reproducing information accurately (called "rote" or "semantic" memory) is unrelated to what is called "event" or "episodic" memory, our ability to recall events in vivid detail from our own past, because personal memories are subject to re-creation and inaccuracy, whereas the usefulness of rote memories (such as remembering that $6 \times 7 = 42$) depends exactly on their unchangingness. But in Petrarch's account, recollection of personal experiences is used to ensure greater accuracy of memory, an accuracy which he recognizes when he acknowledges that his friend, recollecting the event as a whole, was able to correct Petrarch's own memory of the information – quotations and learning – they had exchanged. Personalizing bits of information helps to distinguish one bit from another, and thus is an aspect of the mental addressing system itself. Each memorized bit, in this technique, is regarded in the first instance not as information to be reproduced but as a personal event, with full phenomenological status. Accuracy comes about through the act of recreating in memory the complete occasion of which the accurate quotation is a part.

The whole matter of memory error seems to be quite differently conceived by the ancients from the one that fuels modern anxieties about "making mistakes." For us, making a mistake of memory is a failure in accuracy, a failure exactly to iterate the original material. In antiquity and the Middle Ages, problems involving memory-phantasms are described as heuristic (recollective) rather than as reproductive problems, and are due to a failure to imprint the phantasm properly in the first instance, thus causing confusion and recollective loss. One must be careful to form one's *imagines* securely and distinctly in the first place, and by repetition and practice ensure that they are in long-term memory. One must make them sufficiently distinct from one another, and use a set order with a clearly established beginning, like "one" or "A." One should not tire the memory by trying to memorize too much at a time, or too quickly, for this produces an over-loading problem. Forgetting is a technical error, due to such things as insufficient imprinting or mis-addressing, and errors of recollection are thus perceptual in nature, if the mind's "eye" cannot see clearly or looks in the wrong place. But if one's images are clearly made, and if one's routes to them through the mass of individual phantasms stored in memory are properly marked, and fortified through practice, one will safely and securely find one's place. As Quintilian says, "however large the number [of items] we must remember, all are linked one to another like dancers hand in hand, *and there can be no mistake* since they join what precedes to what follows, no trouble being required except the preliminary labor of memorizing" (my italics).[77] A common image for items associatively grouped in memory is that of *catena* or chain; perhaps the very notion of *texta* itself, which literally means "something woven," derives from the same mental phenomenon. And the language that describes the formation of associations as "hooking" material to other things leads to a metaphor of recollecting as fishing: as one pulls up one's line, all the fish on one's hooks come with it (as painted in the border shown in figure 28).

The idea also informs the common metaphorical extension in Latin of the word *silva*, "forest," to mean a mass of unrelated and disordered material. Within his memorial forest, a trained student, like a knowledge-able huntsman, can readily find the places (*loci*) where the rabbits and deer lie. Quintilian observes that:

just as all things do not grow in every country, and you would not find a particular bird or animal if you did not know its birthplace or its haunts, while even kinds of fish differ . . . so every Argument is not found everywhere, and we have therefore to be selective in our search.[78]

The spatial nature of this mental search is clearer in the Latin: "ita non omne argumentum undique venit ideoque non passim quaerendum est." As the huntsman finds game and the fisherman fish, so the student finds his stored material – by knowing its habits and habitats. Accuracy is a feature of the memory-image which is determined at the imprinting stage. Quintilian counsels having someone read aloud from a text so that one can check the accuracy of one's image of it during the process of setting it in the memory, and to check oneself periodically by re-reading. Evidently forgetting was a familiar phenomenon, indeed a necessary aspect of creating memories, but the solution for ensuring a measure of accuracy for one's semantic memories lay in frequent practice and testing oneself (XI. ii. 34). The greater challenge was to secure a rich recollection of material through one's inventory schemes.

Recollection as investigation

The first part of Aristotle's *De memoria* defines the nature of the memorial image and how such images are stamped upon the soul, like a signet ring in wax. The second part of the treatise deals with the process of recollection. For Aristotle, recollection is the active, intellectual process, distinct from the passive, receiving nature of memory. Sorabji (p. 35) suggests that Aristotle thought of it as distinct from memory in part because the Greek verb for "to recollect" is passive, "to be reminded of," and so the recollector must become the conscious agent, who associates ideas with one another, "one thing putting you in mind of something else." (In this psychology, spontaneous recollection, though recognized, is not valued; it is too risky and irrational.)

When we recollect "starting in thought from a present incident, we follow the trail in order, beginning from something similar, or contrary, or closely connected."[79] The important thing is to have a starting-point (*arché*), and to have the things to be remembered set in an order that can readily be searched: "whatever has some order, as things in mathematics do, is easily remembered."[80] This is what remembering from places (*apo topon*) also affords, for "people go quickly from one thing to another, e.g. from milk to white, from white to air, and from this to fluid, from which one remembers autumn, the season one is seeking." The "places" Aristotle appears to be talking about in this passage are instances of individual visual or verbal associations. But another system of "places" discussed at greater length in *De memoria* is more consciously systematic.

Sometimes it is best, Aristotle says, in recollecting a series of things, to begin at a medial position because then one can remember either of the two things to each side of it. Evidently, as Sorabji comments, Aristotle is describing a mnemonic technique "done through some system of images."[81] The system Sorabji reconstructs is quite specific and elegant, in the mathematical sense of that word. Images are "placed" in threes, each triad containing (perhaps as its middle term) a numerical symbol (a similar technique is recommended in *Rhetorica ad Herennium*). The images are scanned when we need to recollect, but associating them in triads marked by an individuating device such as a number allows one to scan more quickly, by being able to skip over several sets until one arrives at a suitable starting-place; it also allows one to "visit the images that are next door on either side" ("neighboring," Sorabji's translation of *suneggus*), instead of going through a whole series one after another each time. Undoubtedly such a procedure would be useful in remembering a composition of one's own (which is the task most ancient writers on rhetoric address, as do their modern commentators) but it is equally useful as a technique for recalling the work of others, a summarized treatise, for example, or a set of "common places" (*koinoi topoi*) which one had read and stored in one's memory library and which one wished to refer to in composing one's own work. Aristotle highly recommended the systematic cultivation of memory to his students in dialectic. According to Diogenes Laertius, he wrote a book on mnemonics, and he refers several times (notably in *De anima*, 427b) to a system of memory training, such as the familiar memorizing of places (*topoi*). In the *Topics*, he says he wants students to memorize arguments, definitions, and the *topoi* of argument as defined in *Topics* II–VII; furthermore the *topoi* should be memorized by number so they can be quickly scanned during debate.[82]

It is the spatial, somatic nature of memory-images that allows for secure recollective associations to be formed, according to a variety of consciously applied techniques, training, and diligent practice. Recollection is like reasoning: Thomas Aquinas says that human being not only have memory as animals do, as a spontaneous remembrance of things past, but they also have it in a particularly human way, as reminiscence, "a quasi-syllogistic search [*quasi syllogistice inquirendo*] among memories of things past in their individuality."[83] But because it is also a physiological process, recollection is subject to training and habituation in the manner of all physical activity. The most powerful associational connections are formed by habit, *de consuetudine*, rather than by logic, *de necessitate*. Logical reconstruction is universal to all human beings in all situations: six times seven is always forty-two, and seven times seven is seven more, or forty-nine. But, while "white" may remind me of "milk," it may remind you of "snow" and someone else of "lilies," and thus lead all three of us in different, unrelated associative chains, none of which is inherently (*de necessitate*) truer or better than another. Such chains are individually habitual, unlike six times seven. All ancient mnemonic advice takes this fact into account by counselling that any learned technique must be adapted to individual preferences and quirks. One cannot use a "canned" system, nor will every system work equally well for everyone.[84] The ability to recollect is natural to everyone, but the procedure itself is formed by *habitus*, training, and practice.

Aristotle demonstrates the associational nature of memory by observing that one sometimes can recollect something in one way and sometimes not. Sometimes, if we want to remember C, we can get to it via B, but sometimes B doesn't work, and we need to remember D in order to set up the "chain" that gets us to C. "The reason why one sometimes remembers and sometimes not, starting from the same position, is that it is possible to move to more than one point from the same starting point" (452a 24), for example from "white" to "milk" or "lilies." A "chain of succession" is set up in recollection, "for the impulses follow each other by custom, one after another" (451b 22). "By custom" (Sorabji's "by habit") translates the Greek "gar ethei," literally "by repetition."[85]

Thomas Aquinas and the other scholastics elaborated Aristotle's observations on the associational, "habitual," nature of recollection. Commenting on Augustine's discussion of the trinitarian nature of the human soul (memory, intellect, and will), Thomas Aquinas says that Augustine did not think of them as distinct powers but "by memory he understands the soul's habit of retention; by intelligence, the act of intellect; and by will, the act of the will." Memory is a proclivity or disposition (*habitus*) of the soul rather than a power or activity itself. "As Augustine proves, we may be said to understand, will, and to love certain things, both when we actually consider them, and when we do not think of them. When they are not under our actual consideration, they are objects of our memory only, which, in his opinion, is nothing else than a habitual retention of knowledge and love."[86]

The habit is a mediator between a power and its object, for "every power which may be variously directed to act, needs a habit whereby it is well disposed to its act."[87] All virtues and vices are habits, good or bad (see II–I, Q. 55). Defining memory as *habitus* makes it the key linking term between knowledge and action, conceiving of good and doing it. Memory is an essential treasure house for both the intellect and virtuous action.

Memory and the habits of virtue

In Aquinas's theology the influence of Cicero is apparent in his discussion of the four cardinal virtues,[88] whose names and attributes themselves are taken from "Tullius's First and Second Rhetoric" (i.e. *De inventione* and *Ad Herennium*) though reference is also always made to *Wisdom* 8:7: "for [wisdom] teacheth temperance, and prudence, and justice, and fortitude, which are such things as men can have nothing more profitable in life."[89] Prudence, the first of them, is also called by Cicero *sapientia*, a word he used to translate the Greek *sophia* of his sources.[90] Prudence, says the *Ad Herennium*, "is intelligence capable, by a certain judicious method, of distinguishing good and bad; likewise the knowledge of an art [*scientia cuiusdam artificie*] is called Wisdom; and again, a well-furnished memory and experience in diverse matters [*rerum multarum memoria et usus conplurium negotiorum*] is termed Wisdom."[91] Cicero himself defines prudence as:

the knowledge of what is good, what is bad and what is neither good nor bad. Its parts are memory, intelligence, and foresight. Memory is the faculty by which the mind recalls what has happened. Intelligence is the faculty by which it ascertains what is. Foresight is the faculty by which it is seen that something is going to occur before it occurs.[92]

As he adapts these texts in his own thought, Thomas Aquinas addresses the three basic meanings of prudence given in *Ad Herennium*. Classical rhetoric had defined as one aspect of prudence knowing the procedures and intricacies of an art, or what we now might call craft "know-how." In his general discussion of the nature of virtue, Thomas considers the question of whether art (artifice) can be considered as relevant to speculative knowledge or only to mechanical knowledge. He responds that even purely intellectual activities require art; for the construction of a sound syllogism, or of an appropriate style, or the work of measuring or numbering all involve something of artfulness, of craft. Art is here defined as knowing how to make something well.[93] All craft is acquired through habit (repetition), but it is an intellectual or "speculative" habit, not a moral one:

Since, therefore, habits of the speculative intellect do not perfect the appetitive part, nor prompt it in any way, but affect only the intellective part directly, they may indeed be called virtues inasmuch as they make us capable of a good activity ... yet they are not called virtues ... as though they ensured the right use of a power or habit. Because he possesses a habit of a theoretic science, a man is not set thereby to make good use of it ... That he makes use of it comes from a movement of his will. Consequently a virtue which perfects the will, as charity or justice [or prudence], ensures the right use of these speculative habits [such as any art]."[94]

Next, Thomas Aquinas distinguishes "know-how" from the ethical nature of prudence, thus departing from, or rather refining, as we shall see, this part of the classical description in order to emphasize and isolate clearly the essentially ethical character of prudence. As art is knowing how to make things well, prudence is knowing how to do well: "prudence stands in the same relation to ... human acts, which lie in the effective application of powers and habits, as art does to external productions."[95] While the definition of prudence is closely associated with that of art, in itself prudence is a moral virtue, channeling the will and appetites, not perfecting intellectual activities, although like all virtues it is under the control of reason. Prudence is

a virtue of the utmost necessity for human life. To live well means acting well. In order to perform an act well, it is not merely what a man does that matters, but also how he does it, namely, that he acts from right choice and not merely from impulse or passion ... Man is directed indeed to his due end by a virtue which perfects the soul in the appetitive part, the object of which is a good and an end. For a man to be rightly adapted to what fits his due end, however, he needs a habit in his reason; because counsel and choice, which are about things ordained to an end, are acts of reason. Consequently, an intellectual virtue is needed in his reason to complement it and make it well adjusted to these things. This virtue is prudence. And this, in consequence, is necessary for a good life ... Art is necessary, not that the artist may lead a good life, but so that he may produce a good and lasting work of art. Prudence is necessary, not merely that a man may become good, but so that he may lead a good life.[96]

Prudence involves both reason and will, an "intellectual virtue" which also directs and "perfects" the emotional, desiring will. It requires knowledge but it acts to shape up our ethical life so that we may live well, and not merely be good, in the way that a carving or a building can simply "be good."

Prudence as *sapientia*, "wisdom," comprises the suitable use of all knowledge, practical and speculative – including, let it be noted here, the making of poems. It thus includes dialectic, rhetoric, and physics, or knowledge arrived at by arguing from probable premises, knowledge arrived at by persuading on the basis of conjectured truth, and knowledge arrived at through demonstration.[97] This classification of all human knowledge as a part of prudence is also found in later medieval writers, such as Brunetto Latini, who in his *Trésor* states that prudence ("sapience") contains all sense and all teaching, and it also knows all times ("tens"). Echoing *De inventione*, although he says his immediate source is Seneca, Brunetto gives the definition of prudence we have already noted: "c'est le tens alé par memoire, de quoi Seneque dist, ki ne pense noient des choses alées a sa vie perdue; et du tens present par cognoissance; et du tens a venir por porveance."[98] Prudence comprehends not only all human knowledge but also temporality. The definition of it given in *De inventione* makes this clear: its parts are temporally related, memory being of what is past; intelligence of what is; foresight of what is to come.

The temporal nature of prudence is stressed by Thomas Aquinas when he comes to defining its exact nature; his first topic under the parts of prudence is whether memory is one of them. He concludes that it is, for:

Tullius [*De invent.* ii.53] places memory among the parts of prudence ... Prudence regards contingent matters of action, as stated above [II–II, Q. 47, art. 5]. Now in such like matters a man can be directed ... by those [things] which occur in the majority of cases ... But we need experience to discover what is true in the majority of cases: wherefore the Philosopher says [*Nic. Ethics* ii.1] that "intellectual virtue is engendered and fostered by experience and time." Now experience is the result of many memories as stated in *Metaphysics* i.1, and therefore prudence requires the memory of many things. Hence memory is a part of prudence.[99]

By memory, Thomas clearly means here not just the natural power of the sensitive soul described by Aristotle but trained memory, the memory which is a treasury of many memories.

Thomas's meaning is made apparent when one contrasts his quotation of these words from the *Metaphysics* with that of his teacher, Albertus Magnus. Albertus, citing the same *Metaphysics* passage in *De bono*, Q. II, a.I, writes that the power of experience is perfected by "multae enim memoriae eiusdem rei" – many memories of the same thing – which is actually what Aristotle himself wrote.[100] When Thomas Aquinas, however, cites the same passage, he writes that experience results "ex pluribus memoriis," from several different memories. The memorial experience that founds prudence is not iterative but concatenative, "plural" in the sense of the motto of the United States, those many memories contained in the varied quantity of his sources. E. K. Rand has written eloquently of their role in Thomas's compositional style:

St. Thomas has learned from many men of wisdom, but on the present occasion they are summoned to court [to discuss the nature of temperance], summoned from their chambers in his mind. I am not going to name them all, but they are hovering outside the courtroom in crowds, ancient Greeks and ancient Romans, members of all the philosophical schools, some of their poets, as we have seen, and Christian poets like Ambrose, doctors of the Roman church and of the Greek, Popes all down the line, saints and heretics – at least the mighty Origen – writers of the early Middle Ages from England, France and Spain, writers of the Renaissance of the twelfth century, writers of his own day, the Hebrew Rabbi Moses, or Maimonides, the Arabs with Averroës at their head, mystics, monastics, and metaphysicians, writers of lawbooks and decretals, Church councils and liturgy, yes, Holy Scripture, Old Testament and New and the glosses thereon.

The material from secular Roman authors alone quoted in the *Summa theologica* is remarkable: it includes Cicero, Juvenal, Ovid, Terence, Seneca, Boethius, Macrobius, Caesar, Livy, Sallust, Valerius Maximus, Varro, Vegetius, and Virgil.[101] It is an immensely rich set of memories, but it can be paralleled in any number of other medieval works. The point to realize is that Thomas's experience was consciously made up from them all, a mighty chorus of voices able to be summoned at will from the tablets of his memory. The very usefulness of memory as a treasury of knowledge and experience lies in its ability to be nurtured and trained. Memory is a "habit of retention," as Thomas says in *ST* Ia, Q. 79, art. 7. Thus, "the aptitude for prudence is from our nature, while its perfection is from practice or grace. And so Cicero observes that memory not only is developed by nature alone, but owes much to art and diligence."[102]

The nature of the memorial phantasm as *passio* or *affectio animi* is important to understand, for this idea is basic to the notion of trained memory as the *habitus* that perfects, indeed makes possible, the virtue of prudence or moral judgment, and to the corollary idea that memory is the faculty that presents (or re-presents) experience, the basis upon which moral judgments must be made. As the subsequent history of the words *passio* and *affectio* shows, the making and re-presentation of a *phantasm* is also closely bound up with the physiology of emotion.

Since each phantasm is a combination not only of the neutral form of the perception but of our response to it (*intentio*) concerning whether it is helpful or hurtful, the phantasm by its very nature evokes emotion. This is how the phantasm and the memory which stores it help to cause or bring into being moral excellence and ethical judgment. Every emotion involves a change or movement, whose source is the soul, but which occurs within the body's physiological matrix: such "affects" are "movement[s] of the soul through the body," as Theodore Tracy happily translates *De anima*, 403a 24.[103] Thus the phantasm is "conceived as a controlling factor in the whole mechanism of emotion and action, with which moral excellence is concerned."

The word which Aristotle uses to classify the memorial phantasm is *pathos*, translated by William of Moerbeke as *passio*:[104] the *pathos* is what a sense perception causes in the soul as a kind of image, the having of which we call a memory.[105] Since it is a physical change or "affect," a phantasm is also an "affection" or *passio*. Memory itself is neither perception nor conception, but a "condition," *habitus* (Greek *hexis*) or "affection" (*pathos*) touched off by these, after some time has passed, and a phantasm has been formed.[106] Memory is *hexis* or *pathos* in that "it is a *state* or *affection* . . . that follows on perceiving, apprehending, experiencing, or learning" – all of which require the production of phantasms.[107] This basic connection between the process of sensation which ends in memory, and that of human emotional life is fundamental for understanding the crucial role memory was thought to have in the shaping of moral judgment and excellence of character.

In his *Nicomachean Ethics*, Aristotle says that ethical excellence, character (*ēthos*), results from habituation (*ēthos* as, literally, one's haunts and accustomed places).[108] The organism's *hexis* or *habitus* is a matter of custom, particular emotional responses and acts performed in the past and remembered, which then predispose it to the same response in the future.[109] Both vices and virtues are habitual dispositions, formed in this way. What develops, as Tracy describes it, is a "moral organism" akin to and embodied in the physical organism.[110] Experience is made from many repeated memories, which in turn are permanent vestiges of sense perceptions: "Thus [a] sense-perception (*aisthēseōs*) gives rise to [a] memory (*mnēmē*), as we hold; and repeated memories of the same thing give rise to experience (*empeiria*); because the memories, though numerically many, constitute a single experience. And experience, that is the universal when established as a whole in the soul – the One that corresponds to the Many ... – provides the starting-point of arts (*technēs*) and sciences (*epistēmēs*); art in the world of process (*génesis*) and science in the world of facts (*to on*)."[111] Experience – memories generalized and judged – gives rise to all knowledge, art, science, and ethical judgment, for ethical judgment, since it is based upon habit and training and applies derived principles to particular situations, is an art, and part of the "practical intellect," that is, directed to the world of process and change rather than of essence and unchanging Being ("to on").

Quintilian defines *hexis* as that "assured facility" (*firma facilitas*) in any art which supplements, bends, and transcends its rules, and constitutes what we call mastery.[112] As the psychologist George Miller observed, learning can be regarded as the acquisition of "richer" and better mnemonics. Donald Norman describes a fine instance of this in posing the old problem of Cannibals and Missionaries, who all want to get from one side of a river to the other but have only a boat that carries two, and neither cannibals nor missionaries want to be left alone with one another. Their early efforts to solve this problem take his students many moves and much time, but gradually the problem is reduced to a few seconds and a half-dozen moves as the rules of this art, derived from many memories of the same thing, are worked out.[113]

Hexis is physiological, as the memory is trained to respond with certain movements, just as a dancer's muscles are, but is also reasoned, for it is facilitated and consental rather than automatic response. Thomas Aquinas makes this distinction between "automatic" and "considered" response the crux that differentiates the *prudentia* of humans from that of animals, for though animals have a certain kind of prudence, theirs is entirely by natural instigation ("ex eo quod instincter naturae moventur"), whereas the human virtue is "ex ratione," from considered judgment. And because this is so, human prudence requires both memory of the past and the ability to recollect it in a considered manner, for prudence (meaning something like "the ability to make wise judgments") can project into the future only because it also knows the present and remembers the past.[114]

The *hexis* or orientation of the moral organism which disposes it to act righteously is prudence. And this learned disposition or virtue in turn is the product of "repeated individual emotional responses [what I have called reactions, the *intentio* part of each phantasm], leading to action in a variety of situations."[115] Hence, the ability of the memory to re-collect and re-present past perceptions is the foundation of all moral training and excellence of judgment. Moreover, the representation produces an emotional response; since it is an *affectio* it is experience as genuine as what initially produced it. Averroës writes of memory-images, "Since that which is to be recalled is similar to the thing comprehended by [a person] in actuality, the one who recollects will experience the same pleasure or pain in this situation, which he would experience were the thing existing in actuality. It is as if he brought the thing to be recalled into effect . . . Accordingly pain can occur in connection with a thing to be recalled or pleasure too, in the same way as it would occur, were the thing existing in actuality."[116]

Trained memory (*memoria*) is "one of the conditions required for prudence," an integral or enabling part of the virtue.[117] Thomas Aquinas quotes Tullius, but he could also have quoted his own mentor, Albertus Magnus. Albertus's discussion is in some ways clearer and fuller than Thomas's, with respect to just how memory can be regarded as a habit and why it is an attribute of prudence; and so we might begin our discussion of how memory was trained in the late Middle Ages with Quaestio II, "De partibus prudentiae," articles 1 and 2, of Albertus's treatise *De bono* (translated in Appendix B).

The first article of this question is "Quid sit memoria." Albertus quotes Cicero to the effect that the parts of prudence are memory, intellect, and foresight, corresponding to the three tenses. First, he considers in what way memory can be a part of prudence, since he earlier had defined memory as simply a function of the soul, not a trainable characteristic (a feature required of something that is a *habitus* and thus a virtue). Prudence is knowing how to do what is good or bad, a knowledge which in turn depends upon past experience, because we can only judge of the future by what is past. Memory can be considered in two ways, as the storage capability of the brain, or as its recollective process. As the store of what is past, memory is the nurse and engenderer of prudence and so a part thereof. As the process of recollection, memory is a habit; recollection is a natural function which can be strengthened through training and practice. This makes it truly necessary in order for prudence to exist. Albertus concludes this article by defining memory as "habitus animae rationalis," a trained facility of the rational soul.

He next considers more precisely in what way memory displays the characteristics of *habitus*, and this leads him directly to a lengthy discussion of "artificial memory," specifically the Ciceronian technique of places and images, *loci* and *imagines*, and of "memory for things" and "memory for words," taken from the "Second Rhetoric" of Tullius, the *Ad Herennium*, III.[118] Albertus starts with Tullius' consideration of the distinction (echoed in virtually every ancient treatise on the subject) between natural and artificial memory, that is, whether memory is a native talent merely confirmed by practice or whether it can actually be improved. He concludes, as the ancients had, that while artificial memory schemes cannot make a naturally poor memory good, they can improve and perfect the potential of a naturally sound, normal memory:

> Therefore we say with Tullius that the kind of memoria which relates to human life and justice is two-fold, that is, natural and trained or "artificial." That is natural which by virtue of its talent for finding-out things remembers easily something it knew or did at an earlier time. The "artificial," however, is one which is made from an orderly arrangement of images and places, and, as in everything else art and virtue are a perfection of natural talent, so also in this. What is natural is completed by training.[119]

By adopting Tullius' definition of memory as a habit and the condition for prudence, which is in turn the repository of all liberal knowledge and ethics, Albertus Magnus and Thomas Aquinas both make the conscious cultivation of memory and the practice of the memorial arts a moral obligation as well as a scholarly necessity. The training of memory fits Thomas's definition of a moral virtue perfectly, such virtues being called "from *mos* in the sense of a natural or quasi-natural inclination to do some particular action. The other meaning of *mos*, i.e. 'custom,' is akin to this: because custom becomes a second nature, and produces an inclination similar to a natural one."[120]

The moral aspect of memory training is crucial to understand as we examine the role of memory throughout the medieval period. Memory could be aided by an assortment of tools, ranging from conscious mnemonic systems to written notes on wax tablets or even paper, but these were no substitute for conscious training. For the trained memory was not considered to be merely practical "know-how," a useful gimmick that one might indulge in or not (rather like buying better software). It was co-extensive with wisdom and knowledge, but it was more – as a condition of prudence, possessing a well-trained memory was morally virtuous in itself. The medieval regard for memory always has this moral force to it, analogous to the high moral power which the Romantics were later to accord to the imagination, genetrix of what is best in human nature. As I have noted, the memory feats of saints are frequently stressed in hagiography, even of saints who were not scholars (like Francis of Assisi). This was done not to show off their intellectual prowess, but to stress their moral perfection.

In this heavily Aristotelian chapter, I have, inevitably, concentrated on scholastic traditions in the theology of prudence and character. But scholars writing before the full revival of Aristotle also saw the connection between memory and the molding of moral character, in terms explicitly of the seal-in-wax trope. Hugh of St. Victor addresses the moral education of novices in this manner:

For, [when a seal is stamped] a figure that is raised up in the seal appears depressed in the impression in the wax, and that which appears cut out in the seal is raised up in the wax. What else is shown by this, than that we who desire to be shaped up through the examples of goodness as if by a seal that is very well sculpted, discover in them certain lofty traces of deeds like projections and certain humble ones like depressions.[121]

The *dicta et facta memorabilia*, exemplary deeds and words of others impressed into our memories like a seal into wax, shape our moral life in shaping our memories. One can recognize in this trope how thoroughly embedded in the neuropsychology of memory ethical action was considered to be, and how in stamping the material of the brain with both a "likeness" of sensory experience and a personal response to it, a memory phantasm also shaped the soul and judgment.

THE ARCHITECTURAL MNEMONIC

A device of memory art based specifically on houses – which I will call hereafter the "architectural" or "Herennian" mnemonic, terms more accurate than Frances Yates's "Ciceronian mnemonic" and less misleading than the Renaissance's overly global "the art of memory" – is described most fully in *Rhetorica ad Herennium*, which is dated to *c.* 86–82 BC, just after Cicero's *De inventione*, and possibly composed by someone who had the same teacher as Cicero.[122] The basic principles are now familiar to most scholars, thanks to the efforts of Frances Yates and Paolo Rossi, but a brief description is perhaps in order here by way of introduction. There are three chief ancient sources: Cicero's *De oratore* (in which it is summarily described in Book II, 350–360), the *Rhetorica ad Herennium* Book III (the most detailed account), and Book XI of Quintilian's *Institutio oratoria*.

According to the account in *Ad Herennium* III, the backgrounds are like wax tablets (*cerae*) or papyrus, and the arrangement of the images on them is like writing; subsequent delivery is like reading aloud. The backgrounds must be arranged in a series, a certain order, so that one cannot become confused in the order. One can thus proceed forwards from start to finish, or backwards, or start in the middle (one might recall here the artificial memory system described in Aristotle's *De memoria et reminiscentia*, which also allows one to scan, sort, and move about mentally in a similar way).

The formation of the backgrounds in the mind should be done with special care and precision, "so that they may cling lastingly in our memory, for the images, like letters, are effaced when we make use of them, but the backgrounds, like wax tablets, should abide" (III, 18, 31). One should practice daily seeing one's backgrounds and placing images on them. It is also useful, in order to keep track of where one is, to place a mark on every fifth or tenth one – a golden hand, or the face of a friend named Decimus. In memorizing backgrounds, one should avoid crowded places, because too many people milling about confuse and soften their outlines. Background *loci* should be well lighted but not glaring; they must not be too much alike but differ enough in form to be clearly distinguishable one from the next; they should be of moderate size and extent, "for when excessively large they render the images vague, and when too small often seem incapable of receiving an arrangement of images" (III, 19, 32). (Notice that grouped images are placed in a scene within a single *locus*, serving like a stage; the analogy between memory art and theatre is ancient and persistent.)[123] If we are not pleased with the real backgrounds available to us, we may create some in our imagination and "obtain a most serviceable distribution of appropriate backgrounds" (III, 19, 32).

These backgrounds should be viewed from about thirty feet away, "for, like the external eye, so the inner eye of thought is less powerful when you have moved the object of sight too near or too far away" (III, 19, 32). Both the "auctor ad Herennium" and Cicero use the word *intervallum* in articulating this rule, meaning "the distance between two points." I understand this word differently in the context of mnemotechnical advice from the way it is translated by Harry Caplan, the Loeb editor. He refers it to the distance between the background places themselves. Now, while one is advised to make these distinctive from one another in order to avoid overlapping and confusion, the *Ad Herennium*'s author explains the need for the rule quoted above in terms of the viewer's ability to see an object clearly. This concern also accords with an aspect of mnemonic advice from the Middle Ages.[124] So I understand *intervallum* to refer to the distance of the viewer from the background, optimally (according to Tullius) thirty feet; it is thus a principle of perspective, the viewer's stance in relation to the background.

The images to be placed in these backgrounds are then described in detail. The principles governing their creation are consistent with ancient observations that recollection is achieved through association, and that images, especially visual ones, are more easily and permanently retained than abstract ideas. So we associate the materials of memory through a system of consciously selected visual–verbal puns or pictures, whatever will serve to fix the association of image with idea. One can use such a system to remember things (*memoria rerum*) or to remember "words" (*memoria verborum*). Remembering "things" means remembering subject matters, the main words in quotations, the chief theses of an argument, the gist of a story, or the like. Remembering "words" means exact word-for-word memorization, and should be reserved for an extract from the poets (III, 19, 34) – the *Ad Herennium* recommends the practice for children, and for adults only as an exercise to sharpen memory for matters (III, 24). In each kind of memorizing, punning images are used to make orderly association, but he admits that word-for-word memorization in this fashion is cumbersome and burdens the mind; exact memorizing is better served by repeating a passage two or three times to set it in the memory by rote before one begins to attach images to it (III, 21, 34).

Much the same advice is found in Cicero's *De oratore* but more briefly because the subject "is well known and familiar" (II, 87, 358).[125] Visual images are the keenest of all and best retained by the memory; auditory or other perceptions are retained when attached to visual ones (II, 87, 357). Images are retained more easily than abstract thoughts, but they "require an abode," for "the embodied cannot be known without a place" ("corpus intelligi sine loco non potest").[126] One needs a large number of *loci*, distinctly visible, and at moderate distances (*modicis intervallis*), and images that are "lively, sharp, and conspicuous, with the potential to present themselves quickly and to strike the mind." Practice will form the necessary habits for mastery of these skills, and Cicero mentions several methods of forming suitable images, involving homophony, puns, rebuses, and the like. All this mental image-forming, he says, should be practiced "according to the systematic approach of a consummate painter, who keeps the different localities distinct from each other by employing a variety of shapes [*modo formarum varietate locos distinguentis*]" (II, 87, 358), a phrase which Rackham, the Loeb translator, observes "denotes what we call 'perspective.'"[127] One should remark here Cicero's important, though commonplace, comparison between the forming of images and painting; one should also remark that he acknowledges the importance of the viewer's perspective.

Quintilian has sometimes been regarded as skeptical of the whole idea of artificial memory, but, as Frances Yates observed, this reputation is not founded.[128] He extolls memory highly – "all learning depends on memory" ("omnis disciplina memoria constat": *Inst. orat.*, XI, ii, 1) – and believes, like all the authors of antiquity, that a natural memory can and should be cultivated by practiced techniques. It is memory which "makes available to us the reserve of examples, laws, rulings, sayings, and facts which the orator must possess in abundance and have always at his finger-tips"; it is the treasury of eloquence, "thesaurus hic eloquentiae"(XI, ii, 1).

Quintilian's skepticism is directed towards the image-making schemes to accomplish "memory for words," such as that described in *Ad Herennium*. How, he says, can such a cumbersome method enable one to grasp a long series of connected words, such as the five books of the second process against Verres (Cicero's *Verrine Orations*)? One cannot even represent every sort of word by an image (for instance, conjunctions). Quintilian admits that one might devise a method of shorthand symbols (*notae*) as Metrodorus is said to have devised, but he himself counsels learning a long work by dividing it into short sections, which one then memorizes one at a time, so that by frequent and continuous practice one learns the words in each brief section, and then unites the fragments in order (XI, ii, 28). He suggests embedding cues (*notae*) to stimulate the memory, especially in passages hard to recall – these cues could take the form of associated images or some other method (perhaps numerical or other *notae*). He also suggests learning a passage by heart from the same wax tablet upon which it was originally written down, thus effecting a transfer from the external tablet to the tablet of memory, and counsels reading passages aloud once or twice over so the mind is "kept on the alert by the voice" (XI, ii, 32–34). For memory work, the voice should not rise above a murmur, however. It also helps if another reads aloud to us so that we can test what we have memorized, identify hard passages, and mark them. By such means, he says, he has trained his own natural memory, which is not at all exceptional. And he ends with his famously skeptical assessment of reported feats of prodigious memory, such as those of Theodectes, supposed to be able to remember any number of verses after a single hearing: "We ought to believe [such a thing], however, simply because believing it gives us hope" (XI, ii, 51).

It is noteworthy that Quintilian's reservations are directed more at schemes which promise accurate "memory for words" than at "memory for things." This attitude is compatible with the basically ethical value given to memory training. Memory for words, like any merely iterative reproduction of items in a series, can deteriorate rather quickly into mere trickery, and is associated by Quintilian with sophistical rhetoric (a prejudice which extends at least into the thirteenth century, as we will see in Chapter 4). Even the *Ad Herennium* commends memory for words primarily as good exercise for memory for things. *Memoria ad res* compels the recollector to actively shape up material for an occasion, whether as composer or viewer or reader, and thus is ethically more valuable, consistent with the moral emphasis given to rhetoric by Cicero, Quintilian himself, Augustine, and the traditions of monastic prayer. Especially in composition, memory for things is preferred to rote iteration, even when the speaker has accurate command of the original words. This is, of course, exactly the reverse of modern prejudice.

Quintilian's reservations concerning elaborate schemes of *loci* and *imagines* have reinforced our own modern puzzlement in the face of such an apparently cumbersome and odd procedure. Even Frances Yates, who studied these schemes so thoughtfully, confessed herself puzzled by their seemingly cluttered nature, especially that for *memoria verborum*. What purpose could they serve, except demonstrating "vanity and ostentation in a man who, where memory was concerned, took more pride in his art rather than in his natural powers," as Quintilian says of Metrodorus (XI, ii, 22). Quintilian's criticism of the Greeks (and one should note that all the people whose extravagant claims he criticizes are non-Romans, though similar claims, as we know from Pliny, were current concerning the prodigious memories of Julius Caesar) is likely to have been in part a Ciceronian pose, that of the practical, sparely educated Roman. This is the persona adopted in *De oratore* by both Crassus and Antonius, the heroes of the dialogue, both men highly learned in Greek but affecting to despise "Greeklings." "Crassus," Cicero says, "did not so much wish to be thought to have learned nothing, as to have the reputation of looking down upon learning, ... while Antonius held that his speeches would be the more acceptable to a nation like ours, if it were thought that he had never engaged in study at all" (*De orat.*, II, 5). Quintilian, we recall, was modeling himself upon Cicero's example, against excesses of artifice and style that he detected in Seneca and Tacitus. Though this literary context may help to explain Quintilian's skeptical pose regarding the Greeks, it does not help to ease our modern skepticism concerning how the system of backgrounds and images could work for many people, as it evidently did, being "well known and familiar" to Cicero's audience.

A remarkable demonstration of how it might work has come recently
in psychological literature. The distinguished Soviet neuropsychologist,
A. R. Luria, published a lengthy case-study (*The Mind of a Mnemonist*) of a
Russian journalist of prodigious memory, who became a professional
"mnemonist" or performing memory-artist. Luria studied him over a
thirty-year period, from the 1920s through the 1950s, testing him frequently
and asking him in detail about the systems he had worked out for retention
and recall. The system used by Shereshevski, the subject (whom Luria refers
to as "S." in his study), was almost exactly that of the ancient architectural
mnemonic, based upon "places" and "images," although he was entirely
self-taught in memory arts. Luria himself seems unaware of the ancient
system; at least he does not mention it. Moreover, Luria refers to an
account of a Japanese mnemonist, who had also worked out a system of
"placing" images very similar to that of S.[129] The study of S. gives valuable
insight into the praxis of the ancient system.

Luria observes first that everything S. recalled was in the form of words
(including numbers, nonsense syllables, and seen or described objects) and
that he responded to hearing words by at once converting them into vivid
and remarkably stable visual images. He did this on a word-by-word basis,
so that to recall a long series of words he needed to find a way of
distributing his mental images in an orderly row or sequence. He seems
most often to have used a street which he visualized in precise detail in his
memory, often a street in the town he grew up in but also streets in
Moscow, where he then lived – Gorky Street served him often. As Luria
describes the process: "Frequently he would take a mental walk along that
street . . . beginning at Mayakovsky Square, and slowly make his way down,
'distributing' his images at houses, gates, and store windows. At times,
without realizing how it had happened, he would suddenly find himself
back in his home town . . . where he would wind up his trip in the house he
had lived in as a child" (p. 32). This technique enabled S. to reproduce at
will a series from start to finish, or in reverse order, or from any point. He
could also tell at once, given one word in a series, which word occurred on
either side of it, its "neighbors," so to speak (we recall Aristotle's similar
description of this recollective phenomenon in *De memoria*).

His recollection of these visual images was so stable that when asked to
recall passages or series he had memorized even years earlier he could do so
promptly and accurately. Luria and his associates concluded quickly that
S.'s memory was essentially limitless and gave up trying to measure its
capacity. The key to this capacity was the stability of his images and places.
As Luria concludes, "the astonishing clarity and tenacity of his images, the

fact that he could retain them for years and call them up when occasion demanded it, made it possible for him to recall an unlimited number of words and to retain these indefinitely."[130]

Nonetheless, S. did occasionally make errors. Luria determined, however, that these were not errors caused by loss but errors of *perception*. In revisiting his places, S. sometimes failed to notice or saw badly an image which he had placed in a poor location. As S. described these errors to Luria:

I put the image of the *pencil* near a fence ... the one down the street, you know. But what happened was that the image fused with that of the fence and I walked right on past without noticing it. The same thing happened with the word *egg*. I had put it against a white wall and it blended in with the background ... Sometimes I put a word in a dark place and have trouble seeing it as I go by. (36)

His solution to the problem was as follows:

What I do now is to make my images larger. Take the word *egg* I told you about before. It was so easy to lose sight of it; now I make it a larger image, and when I lean it up against the wall of a building, I see to it that the place is lit by having a street lamp nearby ... I don't put things in dark passageways any more ... Much better if there's some light around, it's easier to spot then. (41)

Crowds and noise confused him (37) because they interfered with his ability to perceive his images and places, and stray noise confused his concentration. S. described his problem: "You see, every sound troubles me ... it's transformed into a line and becomes confusing. Once I had the word *omnia*. It got entangled in noise and I recorded *omnium* ... and the more people talk, the harder it gets, until I reach a point where I can't make anything out" (39).

S. had trained his memory "for words" rather than "for things," in the ancient sense. His grasp of entire passages of a text, his ability to form coherent images associated with the meaning of a long passage, was far from good. If a story were read to him, especially at a rapid pace (S. required a pause of 3–4 seconds between items in order to form and place his images), he would complain that, since each word called up an image for him, they began to collide with one another in a hopeless muddle (65). He was best at recalling items in a series, or brief connected passages which he could remember as though they were parts of a scene. His capacity for recalling thousands of such series, however, was virtually limitless in space and, over time; indeed, S.'s chief problem, especially after he became a professional performer, was how to forget, a problem which presented itself to him as how to erase images he had formed. He tried mentally burning an image sequence he no longer needed, and he tried writing it down (unwittingly putting to the test Thammuz's fears about the danger of substituting writing for memory). Thammuz needn't have worried. Neither technique had the least effect on S.'s memory. Finally S. realized that he could simply will a specific series of images not to appear, and they would not come up (66–71). This clear indication of his conscious control was a great relief to him.

One test Luria set for S. was to remember the first four lines of the *Inferno*. S. knew no Italian, and so made images of Dante's words from Russian homophones. This was the method he described using to memorize the first line, "Nel mezzo del cammin di nostra vita":

Nel – I was paying my membership dues when there, in the corridor, I caught sight of the ballerina, Nel'skaya.
mezzo – I myself am a violinist; what I do is to set up an image of a man who is playing the violin [Russ.: *vmeste*], together with Nel'skaya.
del – There's a pack of Deli Cigarettes near them.
cammin – I set up an image of a fireplace [Russ.: *kamin*] near them.
di – Then I see a hand pointing to a door [Russ.: *dver*].
nostra – I see a nose [Russ.: *nos*]; a man has tripped and, in falling gotten his nose pinched in the doorway [*tra*].
vita – He lifts his leg over the threshold, for a child is lying there, that is, a sign of life – vitalism. (45–46)

His system for the other three lines was similar, though he devised a different scene of related images for each line. Sixteen years later, without warning, Luria asked him to repeat these lines for him and he did so, flawlessly and effortlessly.

Shereshevski's technique for recalling after so long an interval is also discussed by Luria. It made no difference to S. whether a series were presented orally or in writing. He had practiced his imagining technique to the point where he could find images quickly even for words he had never heard before; for common words, he tended to use the same images over again. Once remembered, he had no difficulty in recalling, whether the interval had been a day, a month, or many years. But he needed first to place himself mentally back in the situation in which he had first committed the series to memory. As Luria describes it:

S. would sit with his eyes closed, pause, then comment: "Yes, yes . . . This was a series you gave me once when we were in your apartment . . . You were sitting at the table and I in the rocking chair . . . You were wearing a gray suit and you looked at me like this . . . Now, then, I can see you saying . . ." And with that he would reel off the series precisely as I had given it to him at the earlier session. If one takes into account that S. had by then become a well-known mnemonist, who had to remember hundreds and thousands of series, the feat seems even more remarkable. (12)

One final characteristic of S.'s method is worth remarking. Luria stresses that the highly intricate technique he had developed was at its basis entirely natural to him, essentially a matter of spontaneous recollection by his memory aided by consciously applied method. The "techniques he used were merely superimposed on an existing structure and did not 'simulate' it with devices other than those which were natural to it" (63). The author of *Ad Herennium*, introducing his strikingly similar mnemonic, comments that "the natural memory, if a person is endowed with an exceptional one, is often like this artificial memory [*similis sit huic artificiosae*], and this artificial memory [*haec artificiosa*], in its turn, retains and develops the natural advantages by a method of discipline" (III. 16.29). The use of the demonstrative pronoun in the Latin text seems to me significant. *This* method, the author is saying, builds upon the memory's natural disposi-tions. So too S.'s memory system – to say nothing of that of the Japanese mnemonist who used a similar one – was natural, developed by practice but entirely self-generated and self-taught.

There are a number of ways in which Luria's study of S. can provide useful insight into the basic neuropsychology of the descriptions we have of the architectural and other mnemonic schemes. First, Luria was especially impressed by S.'s synaesthesia, or apparently simultaneous and unsorted sensory perceptions, especially of ear, eye, and nose (though all five senses were involved). He "saw" sounds as visual shapes, and his memory-images often produced sensations of vibration or smell for him, as well as sight. This natural tendency was greatly increased by his mnemonics, for everything coming in to his mind was turned into an image. The essentially visual nature of these images was psychologically crucial. Sounds were only con-fusing to S. unless they were translated into particular clear visual images. It was the images which provided the stability over time to S.'s recollective power. Medieval memory advice stresses synaesthesia in making a memory-image. Memory-images must speak, they must not be silent.[131] They sing, they play music, they lament, they groan in pain. They also often give off odor, whether sweet or rotten. And they can also have taste or tactile qualities. I will have more to say about this later, but it is worth commenting on here, since synaesthesia was considered to be so vital to S.'s success.

In the second place, S.'s process of recollection was a process of percep-tion; he mentally walked through his memory places and looked at what was there. This accounts for the essentially perceptual nature of ancient advice on the preparation of *loci*, that they be properly lighted, moderate in size and extension, different enough from one another in shape that they can't be confused, not crowded, that the images in them be of moderate size and neither too large nor too small, and that they be made clearly distinct from their background.

Third, S.'s problem with overloading, experienced when words were read to him too rapidly, or when he tried to grasp a lengthy passage as a whole, suggests why all the ancient Roman writers, from the *Ad Herennium* author through Quintilian, had their doubts about the ordinary utility of "memory for words" when tied to images like these. Fourth, and as a counterbalance to the previous point, S.'s ability to recall thousands of short series of words, even though he had trouble grasping long connected passages, sheds light on the ancient advice to memorize lengthy passages piecemeal, in short sections which can later be united. As Hugh of St. Victor writes, the memory rejoices in shortness ("memoria brevitate gaudet"); the experience of S. should caution us, however, against assuming that in saying this Hugh meant that only brief extracts of longer works could be retained in the memory. Any long work can be considered as a number of short series joined together – indeed, this is exactly Quintilian's advice. And as separate series, a virtually limitless number can be retained in a good, trained memory.

Fifth, and in some ways the most important for our purposes, S. was completely uneducated in mnemonics. The system of backgrounds and images he devised was self-taught, refined by trial and error. He never seems to have discovered the principle of "memory for things" that every ancient writer on the subject is at pains to emphasize as the key to the successful composition and delivery of an oration. This, surely, was because his prodigious feats of memory were treated as freakish, and he himself as a vaudeville act, his art perceived to be a mere curiosity without social usefulness and ethical value. Moreover, he was rewarded only for his iterative accuracy – creative composition was not his aim. The situation in the ancient and medieval worlds, needless to say, was far different. By providing such tantalizing parallels, S. can teach us how the memory system described in these treatises is true to human psychology, but there is much about the actual use of memory in education and composition during the Middle Ages that S.'s experience cannot tell us.

CHAPTER 3

Elementary memory design

THE NUMERICAL GRID

The architectural mnemonic was not the only, or even the most popular, system known in the Middle Ages for training the memory. In her 1936 study of the subject, Helga Hajdu mentions various alternative systems, including an elaborate digital method of computation and communication that also served mnemonic purposes, discussed in the treatise *De loquela digitorum* ascribed to Bede; various mnemonic verses that serve both scholars and laity, such as the university students' mnemonic for remembering the various types of syllogism ("Barbara Celarunt Darii," etc.) and the execrable rhyming hexameters used by lawyers as a mental index to the various collections of laws; and various counting devices, like the rosary and the abacus, which involve manipulating physical objects in a rigid order as an aide-mémoire in calculation.[1] There are rhyming catalogues of medieval libraries which were intended to be memorized by the monks,[2] and there are Alexandre de Villedieu's 4,000 rhymed hexameters setting forth the rules of Latin grammar, the *Doctrinale*. One of the earliest and longest-lived poems in English is the mnemonic for the months of the year: "Thirty days hath September, April, June and November."

Interesting as these particular items are, however, they are too limited in purpose or too bound to a particular situation, such as the monastery or the law court, to be of much interest in considering how memories were trained by a wide variety of people to make a securely searchable inventory of a variety of texts and other material (what Albertus Magnus lumps together as *negotia*, a word usually understood as "business," but in the context of memory-training it translates better as "matters," "content," or even "stuff"). Other systems of memory training clearly surpassed that described in the *Ad Herennium*, in both their longevity and their broad applicability to all spheres of learning. And, unlike the Herennian mnemonic, they were widely disseminated in the Middle Ages (not just the humanist circles in papal Avignon and in Tuscany), and find their way into practical writings on the subject of memory well before the fourteenth century.[3] In this chapter, I will be concerned with two simple schemes used in memory training. They employ the most common of locational heuristics, the order of numbers, and that of the alphabet. In order to demonstrate their ubiquity, I must appeal to the reader's patient willingness to pick the way through the eclectic evidence that I have gathered up in this chapter.

Learning by heart: Hugh of St. Victor on memorizing the Psalms

How to use a number scheme is described by Hugh of St. Victor in a text virtually overlooked by modern scholars, the Preface to his *Chronicle*, also called "De tribus maximis circumstantiis gestorum," translated in Appendix A. Hugh's description is one of the fullest, and clearest, of any mnemonic system. The method utilizes psychological principles similar to the method using images in background places, but in this case the system of *loci* is numerical, and the images are short pieces of text written into the numbered backgrounds, as though within the cells of a grid. The images of written text are impressed also as they appear in the particular codex from which they were first memorized, including their location on the page (recto, verso, top, middle, bottom), the shapes and colors of the letters themselves, and the appearance of each page including marginalia and illuminations, to make a clear visual experience. Finally, Hugh advises that the physical conditions under which one had memorized the original material should also become part of one's total recollection of it – in modern psychological terms, to make of it an "episodic" not just a "semantic" memory.

This Preface was composed about 1130, and is addressed to novices (*pueri*) studying Scripture in the cathedral school of St. Victor. It precedes a *Chronicle* of Biblical history, set out as columns – seventy folio pages in the fullest versions – of names, dates, and places, which the students were to memorize as an elementary part of their education in *sacra pagina*, or the study of the Bible. The Preface was unpublished until 1943, when it was edited by William M. Green (there appear to have been no previous printings at all).[4] The manuscripts suggest that the preface, while having some local success, never achieved the wide dissemination of *Didascalicon*, the work which earned Hugh a reputation for being an important proponent of *ars memorativa* in the later Middle Ages and Renaissance.[5] There are several manuscripts of the Preface alone; Green comments that, while portions of the *Chronicle* tables were "often omitted with much resultant confusion and variety in the manuscripts, the text of the prologue . . . is usually well preserved."[6] There are 34 surviving manuscripts of the Preface (compared to 125 of *Didascalicon*), nearly all written in the twelfth and thirteenth centuries, though there are 2 from the fourteenth, and 1 from the fifteenth century. Of those whose provenance is known, most are claustral.[7] The largest number of manuscripts is French, as we would expect, including several from St. Victor. So, the evidence suggests that this particular treatise was not regarded as major or original enough to deserve wide dissemination, despite its author's eminence, and that it sank into oblivion by the early fourteenth century, because it had been superseded by or incorporated into other pedagogical tools. Its very ordinariness, however, makes it important to my study.

Hugh's method displays the principles basic to classical mnemonics, as we find them described by Aristotle, Tullius, Cicero, and so many others. One must have a scheme of places in a rigid, easily retained order, with a definite beginning. Into this order one places the components of what one wishes to memorize and recall. As a moneychanger (*nummularius*) separates and classifies his coins by type in his money-bag (*sacculum, marsupium*), so the content of wisdom's store-house (*thesaurus, archa*), which is the memory, must be classified according to a definite scheme. Without retention in the memory, says Hugh, there is no learning, no wisdom. "Indeed, the whole usefulness of education consists only in the memory of it."[8]

The example Hugh gives is how to memorize the Psalms. There are 150 in all, and to learn them one constructs a series of mental compartments, numbered consecutively from 1 to 150 – in other words, a rigid system of cells that has a definite starting-point. To each number is attached the first few words (the *incipit*) of each psalm, so that as one visualizes the number one, one simultaneously visualizes "Beatus vir qui non abiit"; upon seeing the number twenty-two one also sees the text "Dominus regit me"; and so forth. In Hugh's scheme the images are the written words as they actually appear in a manuscript and the *locus* is simply a numbered box, but the incidental difference of this scheme from the architectural one is less important than its fundamental psychological similarity; they both employ a system of consciously adopted, rigidly ordered backgrounds as a grid which is then filled with the images constituted by the text.

Hugh also counsels that this same method of numerical ordering can be used to learn the text of an individual psalm. Under number twenty-two, for example, one might visualize a subsidiary set of consecutive numbers.

To these one attaches the rest of the text, in short pieces (verses) – however many one needs to complete the task. The crucial task for recollection is the construction of the orderly grid through which one can bring to mind specific pieces of text. This enables one "when asked, without hesitation [to] answer, either in forward order, or by skipping one or several, or in reverse order and recited backwards" whatever is in the memorized text as a whole. And it also enables one to construct mentally a concordance of the text, thus disputing quickly and surely, making citations to authorial texts by number alone.[9]

This scheme will work for any book of the Bible (or for any text at all, for that matter). A long text must always be broken up into short segments, numbered, then memorized a few pieces at a time. We have some clue as to just how short "short" was from the length of verses in the medieval format of the Psalms, and from the number of words enclosed in *cola* and *commata* divisions. Obviously, optimal length varies slightly from one individual memory to the next, but the medieval texts of the Psalms generally contain more verse divisions than do modern texts. Psalm 23 (Vulgate 22), for instance, is six verses long in the printed King James Bible, but has nine divisions in the Latin Paris text of the thirteenth century. The longest of these is the first, containing thirteen words; by contrast the King James contains thirty words in verse four and twenty-two in verse five. The fewer number of words per division in the medieval format accords with the real limits of human working memory, that is, how much one can safely take in during a single *conspectus*, or mental glance (to use the terminology of the memorial *artes*).[10]

Hugh's mnemonic advice is addressed to students, but not to children just learning to read. This is evident when we ask ourselves at what point in a monastic education such a work would become useful. The *linea* or number grid he describes imagines the psalms in their textual order, from 1 onward to 150. The heavy emphasis which is placed upon the *incipit* or first phrase of each psalm is also noteworthy. Though, he says, one may make subsidiary cells in the grid for each verse of a psalm, its initial words receive Hugh's most careful attention, as the cues and starting-off points for recollection of the whole. Yet, as described, this exercise seems at odds with what we know of the monks' usual recitation practices, and thus needs some further exploration.

At St. Victor, as in all monasteries at this time, novices first learned the Psalms by heart in the liturgical offices, as they had for centuries, chanting the words to melodies, perhaps accompanied as well with processional movements and postures. Entire texts became rote-retained through this exercise. The liturgical order of psalms is not, however, that of their textual order. Rather, the liturgical order groups all the Psalms in weekly cycles, assigning them to particular offices in a variety of ways that is quite independent of textual order. So if a novice already had all the Psalm texts by rote from chanting the liturgical offices, what could be the point of learning them again in a different, textual order by means of the grid device Hugh describes? Evidently it was not to learn the Psalms by rote – that had already been achieved. Those *pueri* whom Hugh addressed already had their rote memory of these texts.

The goal must be further study, to be able to find a specific text without the need to repeat the whole liturgical sequence. And that is what Hugh counsels: "dispose it in such a manner that when your reason asks for it, you are easily able to find it." *When your reason asks for it* refers to the rational, investigative procedures of recollection. The device Hugh describes is good not for habitual, rote retention (melody, gesture, and physical location are superior for that purpose), but for quick recollection and retrieval, for creative study and for invention in situations such as preaching, teaching, and debate. Hugh's advice is for more advanced students, not for beginners. Indeed, the lists of historical markers in the *Chronicle* which this advice prefaces are not matters for beginning readers, but for serious students of the Bible.

The numerical grid provides random, multiple access points to material *already* in memory, enabling someone to work with and make something new from their rote memory store. The mnemonic cue, which is the *incipit* of the verse, crucially provides the starting point for recollection of each rote-retained textual chunk. And if a text has been retained with care and frequently practiced (conditions provided for by the divine office), each cue will reliably call forth the whole.[11] The essential task is to impress rote memories as a complete experience, made as particular as possible. To that end:

we [should] also pay attention carefully to those circumstances of our matters which can occur accidentally and externally, so that, for example, together with the appearance and quality or location of the places in which we heard one thing or the other, we recall the face and habits of the people from whom we learned this and that, and, if there are any, the things that accompany the performance of a certain activity. All these things indeed are rudimentary in nature, but of a sort beneficial for youths.[12]

Advice to pay particular attention to manuscript layout, where and how a text is presented on a page, is commonplace, and I will discuss other examples of it shortly. Hugh counsels as well to set our memories within

the seasons and times, and the performative expessions and gestures that
occured when one first learned the verses. Such experiential cues are
perhaps best explained with reference to liturgical performances, for
which time and season are crucially important. Thus Hugh addresses
situations of memorizing both from written books and also from physical
performance. The two modes reinforce one another, both providing additional experiential cues to the rote-retained segments, which help to recover
them richly within one's investigative grid.

Hugh's advice to divide the text duplicates that of Quintilian, as it also
articulates the experience of Shereshevsky, who had difficulty remembering
long passages of connected words, but none at all in retaining an apparently
limitless number of short segments. Any long text can be treated as though
it were composed of a number of short ones:

> For the memory always rejoices [says Hugh] in both brevity of length and fewness in
> number, and therefore it is necessary, when the sequence of your reading tends
> toward length, that it first be divided into a few units, so that what the memory
> could not comprehend as a single expanse it can comprehend at least in a number.[13]

This is advice which Hugh repeated in *Didascalicon*. In this treatise
Hugh extolls even more the dependency of all wisdom (*sapientia*) and the
liberal arts upon memory, training which is now sadly decayed because
students do not learn proper habits:

> We read that men studied these seven [arts] with such zeal that they had them
> completely in memory, so that whatever writings they subsequently took in hand
> or whatever questions they posed for solution or proof, they did not thumb the
> pages of books to hunt for rules and reasons which the liberal arts might afford for
> the resolution of a difficult matter, but at once had the particulars ready by heart.
> Hence, it is a fact that in that time there were so many learned men that they alone
> wrote more than we are able to read.[14]

Hugh's Preface shows this same contempt for the cumbersome, inefficient,
and happenstance method of turning the pages of a book to look for a text
that one needs. Do you think, he asks the students, that people wanting to
cite a particular Psalm turn over the pages of a manuscript hunting for it?
"The labor in such a task would be too great."[15] It is also striking that Hugh
makes an exact correlation here between the amount stored in one's
memory and the amount of written composition one produces.

But Hugh's most practical advice in *Didascalicon*, a work which teaches
the arts of reading as its title indicates, is to gather (*colligere*) while reading,
"reducing to a brief and compendious outline things which have been
written or discussed at some length."[16] Again the principle of dividing a
long text (*prolixius*) is to be observed, because, Hugh says, the memory is

lazy and rejoices in brevity.[17] Therefore, we ought to gather something brief and secure from everything we learn, which we can store away in the little chest of our memory.[18]

One should not assume that Hugh meant that one should retain only a compact summary of what one has read; what he means is that one should break prolixity, a long text, into a number of short, securely retained segments which can be gathered in the memory. This method of study certainly leads to florilegia, as it leads also to Bartlett's *Familiar Quotations* and *The Oxford Dictionary of Quotations*. The phrase "brevem ... et compendiosam summam," "a brief and compendious summary," might seem self-contradictory, except that Hugh is clearly giving the same advice he spells out more fully in his *Chronicle* Preface, memorizing a compendious summation of brief segments of the text one is trying to master – the scholar's method of note-taking, in other words, except written in the memory instead of on note-cards. It is worth recalling by those who might dismiss such advice as mere florilegiality, born of distaste for the comprehensive knowledge of a text, that note-taking and serious scholarship are not exclusive activities. How compendious the summation of a text might be would depend on the industry and talent of each individual reader, and the importance to him of a particular text.

This principle of grouping or "gathering" respects the limits of working memory. It is called "chunking" in neuropsychology now.[19] While the storage capacity of memory is virtually limitless, the amount of information that can be focused upon and comprehended at one time is definitely limited, to a number of units somewhere between five and nine; some psychologists express it as a law of "Seven plus-or-minus two."[20] So one of the fundamental principles for increasing mnemonic (recollective) efficiency is to organize single bits of information into informationally richer units by a process of substitution that compresses large amounts of material into single markers. In this way, while one is still limited by one's capacity to focus on no more than six or seven units at a time, each unit can be made much richer. As the psychologist George Miller has written (without being aware that he was echoing one of Hugh of St. Victor's favorite images), if my purse holds only six coins I can carry six pennies or six dimes; similarly, it is as easy to memorize a list containing a lot of information coded into "rich" units as it is to memorize one containing "poor" units, for the limiting factor is the number, not the nature of each item. Miller describes grouping in this way:

The material is first organized into parts which, once they cohere, can be replaced by other symbols – abbreviations, initial letters, schematic images, names, or what have you – and eventually the whole scope of the argument is translated into a few symbols which can be grasped all at one time.[21]

This is exactly what Hugh counsels doing when he substitutes number-coordinates for the verses of a Psalm – the active, working memory first focuses on the number, and then that numerical address leads to the text placed within it, itself composed of a few words at a time, grouped into phrases. In recollection, one first focuses on the informationally richest sign, say "Psalm 23." That stands in for a set of six sub-units or verses (in the King James Version), and one might focus on one number amongst those, perhaps the number two. That sign in turn both stands for and cues the words "He maketh me to lie down in green pastures; he leadeth me beside the still waters," themselves grouped into five syntactic sub-units or phrases. A fairly common method of citing texts in commentaries and other learned material, especially Psalm texts (the most widely known by heart), was by the initial letters of each word, so that, for example, "Beatus uir qui non abiit" (Ps. 1:1) could be written "b. u. q. n. a." This is another substitution process of the sort Miller adduces, a means of making psychologically richer units. It saved work for the scribe, but it also served as a memory note of effective brevity, for readers who were expected to know the words referred to such signs.

Because of the substitution process that creates rich units, one can skip material, rearrange it, collate it, or whatever, simply by manipulating a few digits mentally – recalling the second verse of every Psalm, perhaps, or reciting a couple of Psalms by alternating verses from one with the other, maybe one in ascending order and the other in the reverse. Any number of impressive parlor-tricks (ancient and medieval pedagogy would have called them exercises) can be played, for one is actually just counting a few digits at a time. One can also use the ability conferred by this process for serious ends, such as marshaling texts on a particular topic, as Hugh suggests in his Preface, by *proferentes numerum*, "fetching forth ... its number,"[22] that is, memorizing only the numerical coordinates to a text under the topical key-word. These coordinates then trigger recollection of each separate text. It would indeed be possible to conduct a substantive discussion of doctrine by numerical citations alone among scholars who knew their Bible in this fashion.

Division and composition

There is a trope in late medieval university prose called a *divisio* or a *discretio*: we might call it a summary outline or even a set of study notes. Such a "division" comprises the main topics of a particular subject under study, and one finds them in the margins of academic manuscripts such as the Decretals and the Sentences, works designed for commentary and disputation. A fine example is in the fifteenth-century Bolognese manuscript of the Decretals (a canon law text) reproduced in figure 4. This *divisio* concerns papal powers, and the subdivisions of the topic spew forth from the beak of a memorable imperial eagle, each written on a wavy line emanating like speech from the eagle's mouth. The whole image provides a unique, succinct, and effective cue for these subject matters, indicating how they are related in content and what their underlying theme is, for these powers all relate to the crucial fourteenth-century tension between the papacy and the lay monarchs who both sponsored it and fought each other through its offices and influence.

Two late Roman grammarians, Consultus Fortunatianus and Julius Victor, define the process and goal of division clearly, and since each was quite influential throughout the history of medieval pedagogy, it is worth pausing over what they have to say.[23] Both are disciples of Quintilian and Cicero (the Cicero of *De oratore* and *De inventione*, not the "Auctor ad Herennium").

Julius Victor, more or less a contemporary of Augustine's, alludes briefly and disparagingly to the art of memorizing by *loci* and *imagines*. For him, memory as a subject in rhetoric is chiefly important for composition: "Memory is the firm grasp of things and words for the purpose of invention."[24] The goal is plainly stated: memory is not retention for its own sake but rather the raw material of further creation. Julius Victor cites Cicero's *De oratore*, I, 18 (a passage that became famous in the later Middle Ages), to the effect that memory is a treasure-house (*thesaurus*) of everything an orator needs, safe custodian of the *verba* and *res* required in thought and invention. But Quintilian is his major source. Paraphrasing *Institutio*, II. vii. 2–3 and XI. ii. 37, he advises learning by heart both your own and others' written compositions, but recommends particularly, as Quintilian does, that one learn the best compositions of the orators, historians, and other worthies by heart, for then one will carry within oneself models for imitation and sources for substance and style.

For both written and purely memorial activities, *divisio* and *compositio* are most useful. He who correctly puts together the basic structure of an oration can never err (*errare*).[25] This will hold true not only when one arranges the questions to be addressed, but in expounding them as well – if the first and second and so on are bound together correctly, then one will securely remember the whole following content. In its root meaning, Latin *errare* does not invoke the need for accurate representations of external objects, but rather the dangers of chaotic, unplanned mental movement. It

4. University of Oxford, Bodleian Library MS. Lat.th.b.4, fo. 21v. An eagle marks a legal topic (*distinctio*) summarizing the principles of papal power, in a copy of the Decretals, signed by the scribe in Bologna, July 1241.

invokes the concept of staying on a path and not straying aimlessly. Having clearly marked routes – a map or "disposition" – is basic to a task conceived in such terms. Similar advice concerning the advantages of properly dividing a theme for the sermon is a feature of late medieval *artes praedicandi*, as we shall see. *Divisio* means dividing a text into short segments for memorizing, and *compositio*, putting the segments together in an order, arranging them properly from one to two to three, and so on.[26] The advice is a cliché of classical rhetoric, from the pen of a very ordinary professor of the subject, but it is a most valuable cliché.

One needs, as Aristotle said, a starting-place, a beginning clearly marked "One." By dividing and composing, a person is constructing a series of numbered sequences for each text one memorizes, whether it be one's own work or a set piece from one of the great stylists of the past. Quintilian's otherwise cryptic advice (*Inst. orat.*, X. vii. 7) to orators always to have before them the *modus* and *finis* of their speech, "and for this division is absolutely necessary," makes some sense when one understands *divisio* in its mnemonic context. The order of numbers cues both the *modus* or "way" and the *finis* or "goal" for a speech; it allows for digression and all sorts of extempore speaking, while keeping one from losing one's way, or forgetting how much one has left to cover or one's chief points.

The mnemonic requirement for a firm starting-point also gives a practical context for the critical importance given in medieval commentary to the title of a work, an emphasis that often seems to us bizarre. *Titulus* is derived from "titan," says Remigius of Auxerre, because it is the illuminating "sun" of the entire text. The *titulus* was one of the basic analytic categories or *circumstantiae* that every student had to know about a work. Mnemonically speaking, the starting-point of a text is its title; everything else in both the text itself and its accompanying commentary will be linked in an order from this point.[27] The Benedictine Rule required that each brother be given a codex at the start of each Lent, which he was to read "in order from the beginning."[28] Reading in order is a mnemonic requirement, as well as an injunction to read the whole book and not just the bits we like (a habit less likely in Benedict's time than it is now, when we are far more accustomed – and able – to skim our regularly printed books). As he makes the book his own in his memory, each monk must give particular care to its starting-points for those are the key to its order, and thus to his ability to recall it. "Begin at the beginning" was made a moral duty in the Rule in part because of its fundamental mnemonic importance, for *memoria*, as mindful attentiveness, was the necessary attitude of meditation.[29]

Fortunatianus, also of the fourth century, wrote an art of rhetoric in three books in the form of a dialogue.[30] For what he says about memory, Fortunatianus relies almost entirely on Quintilian's advice in *Institutes*, XI, 2. Memory is a mixture of natural ability and artifice, or training; nature is served by art and art aided by nature. Simonides, Charmadas, and Metrodorus Scepsis taught the art of memory; what Simonides learned from his experience at the banquet was that memory is best aided by orderly marked-out places (*sedes*) in the soul; when we have such places, we can bring things together, whether we compose in writing or mentally (*ad scripta vel cogitata*).

Fortunatianus then says that the best procedure for memorizing is first to divide a long piece into sections. Next we memorize by constant and intense concentration (*continua et crebra meditatio*), and then we join one piece to the next in numerical order, until we have learned the whole. "What assists memory the most? Division and composition; for order serves memory powerfully."[31] Those passages we find hard to memorize should be additionally marked with *notae*. We should repeat often what we have learned, and write passages down on wax tablets. To exercise our memories, we should begin by memorizing poems, then orations, and then harder material such as legal writings. Reciting in a low voice or murmur is also a very useful technique (*voce modica et magis murmure*). We also retain better and recall more clearly what we have learned at night, when distractions are few. (Much of this advice is also in Martianus Capella, who copied many passages from Fortunatianus; its antecedents are in Quintilian.)

One of the commonest and oldest distinctions made in memory advice is between memory for things and memory for words; we find it already in *Dialexeis*. The meaning of "memory for words" is clear, even to us, for it denotes the exact repetition of a word that we identify with memorization. What exactly constitutes "memory for things" is somewhat less self-evident. The distinction drawn in *Ad Herennium* is probably the clearest of the ancient accounts. There, memory for things means organizing memorial cues by means of a composite scene of mental images associated with various key-words and subjects (illness, poison, heir, will, witnesses). Memory for words also involved constructing images, but seriatim, following the exact syllables of the original words, and is to be used to set words in foreign languages or proper names (the sort of exercise "S" performed to recollect Italian words he did not understand).

Fortunatianus considers when one ought to select one method over the other. Should we always learn word-for-word (*ad verbum*)? Only if time permits; but if it doesn't we should retain only the main matters (*res*), and suit our own words to them later, according to the occasion.[32] It is a very bad practice to have to excuse ourselves and refresh our memories by a prompt, or by reference to a book. If your memory is poor or time is short, do not tie yourself down by trying to speak word-for-word from memory, for if you should forget even one word in a series it will lead to an awkward pause or to silence. So it is best to remember *res* rather than *verba*, for one can suit words to the *res* as occasion demands (*de tempore*) and not run the risk of needing prompting or forgetting altogether.

Word-for-word rote memorizing of a number of outstanding literary and Scriptural texts was also always considered to be the essential base of education. Fortunatianus and Julius Victor both were addressing students who learned a set of canonical poetic texts, works in meter by Virgil, Ovid, and Horace. Quintilian advises acquiring such a memorial foundation in earliest education, and we have John of Salisbury's admiring account of how his master, Bernard of Chartres, set daily memorizing exercises of this kind for his pupils.[33] But many writers gave paraphrases of texts, even when manuscripts containing the complete text were available to them. The reason is not far to seek. They are quoting from memory *sententialiter*, according to the matter or *res*, rather than word-for-word. The amount of material learned by each method probably varied according to an individual's talent and time, as Fortunatianus here acknowledges. One finds even the poetry of the *Aeneid* sometimes quoted approximately. Pierre Riché cites two Merovingian examples: *Aeneid*, I. 90, "Et crebris micat ignibus aether," becomes "Crebris micantibus ignibus ex aethere," and *Aeneid*, II. 794, "Par levibus ventis volucrique simillima somno," is rendered as "Par levibus ventis similisque somno volucri."[34] In each instance of adaptation the chief words are remembered but the syntax is completely altered in the first, moderately changed in the second. Fundamentalists will object that the author's sense has also been altered, and they will be correct. But by late classical and medieval standards, the *res* in both instances is preserved, even though the *verba* are changed.

The important thing to realize is that such alteration can result from a choice made consciously by the memorizer and writer – it does not automatically reflect poor training or a faulty manuscript. On its face, alteration like this is completely neutral. Modern scholars tend to assume that accuracy of reproduction is a function of continual access to written texts, and thus that the extent of an author's reliance upon his memory can be gauged in inverse proportion to the fidelity of his quotations. I think this is a naive assumption. It is clear from what Fortunatianus says that he urged his students always to memorize the canonical texts in the first instance. Only if one is pressed for time should one fall back on memorizing the *res* (it is also clear that *res* could mean anything from a summary aphorism to all the main words of a text). From advice in various early monastic rules, it is clear that students then were obliged to memorize important texts accurately and in full.[35] Monastic reading, of course, meant *meditatio*, as Dom Leclercq has so well described it: "The *meditatio* consists in applying oneself with attention to this exercise in total memorization; it is therefore, inseparable from the *lectio*. It is what inscribes, so to speak, the sacred text in the body and in the soul."[36]

The Rule of Ferreolus observed, "anyone who wishes to be worthy of the name of monk is forbidden to be ignorant of letters; he must also hold all of the Psalms in his memory"[37] – *psalmos totos*, "in their entirety" – a task that commonly took two to three years, though gifted individuals could manage it in six months. The mnemonic practice which informs this command also informs the admonition of the sixth-century (?) *Regula magistri* that monks on a journey who had not yet mastered the Psalms should provide themselves with tablets on which the text was written, so that when they stopped they could sharpen their memory with the help of their companion.[38] This requirement is also derived from ancient mnemonic practice: recall Quintilian's comment that it is of great value when one is practicing in order to fix one's memory, to have someone else read aloud the material, so that one can check the accuracy of one's recollection against the reading.

The book which Christians, both clergy and educated laity, were sure to know by heart was the Psalms. It has been observed that Augustine wrote not only in Latin but "in Psalms," so imbued is his language with their phrasing and vocabulary; the same could be said of any number of Christian writers. Nor was it only the Psalms which were so intimately known; Pierre Courcelle has shown the extent to which Gregory the Great and other writers might be said to write "in Augustine."[39] Such intimacy can be achieved only by long and thorough familiarity with a text as a whole, not just a few aphorisms. As Riché observes, "to know how to read was to know one's Psalter"; even Merovingian lay aristocrats, especially the women, knew at least a few Psalms *verbaliter*, word-for-word.[40]

Accuracy of recollection was a helpful skill to nurture in an age of few manuscripts, many of uncertain quality. The *Regula magistri* counsels that the scriptures be retained in memory partly so that if a codex has lacunae or lacks the commentary (*textum lectionis*), the missing parts could be supplied or expanded from memory.[41] There is no point in debating whether or not their faith in the accuracy of memory was misplaced, for some individuals have highly accurate recollection and others do not. The point to understand is rather that one's memory was *expected* to be not only copious but accurate (the reverse, one might observe, of expectations now). Nor is this characteristic only of the period from the sixth through ninth centuries, when the availability of books was at a minimum. Writing his *Dialogus* while in exile in Munich and away from the libraries that nurtured him earlier, William of Ockham apologizes not for the inaccuracy of his memory but for the fact that circumstances prevent him from having access to all the latest documents in the ongoing controversy, and so his treatise is incomplete – it was imperfect in that sense. Thomas Aquinas, living in a century far richer in books than the sixth, still stored his reading from various libraries in his memory, to be pulled forth as a seamless golden chain, *Catena aurea*. The ability perfectly to replicate the contents of one's memory again and again, forwards, backwards, and in all sorts of combinations, remained a revered skill at least until the end of the Renaissance.

"Memoria rerum"

The "inaccuracy" we find so frequently in medieval citation can often be the result of a deliberate choice on the authors' part, either at the stage of initial memorizing or (and I think more frequently) at that of composing. Medieval scholars' respect for accuracy in copying texts has been repeatedly demonstrated (despite complaints about particular errors), and it is justly observed that without the labors in scriptoria throughout the Middle Ages virtually no ancient literature would be known to us today. Yet the same people who honored the exact copying of even non-Christian texts quote these same works erratically, at times precisely, at times so paraphrased and adapted as to alter them almost beyond recognition. The one sort of activity is verbatim memorization, the other *memoria rerum*, memory of subjects. Both can employ mnemonic techniques, such as those just described. In the traditional ancient and medieval education in liberal arts, word-for-word rote memorizing is associated particularly with grammar, the fundamental work in language upon which both dialectic and rhetoric built. Training in *memoria rerum* was associated with the tasks of rhetoric, specifically invention and delivery.[42]

The fourteenth-century English Dominican Thomas Waleys, a careful scholar of decidedly non-florid style (Beryl Smalley remarks that, unlike Robert Holcot, Waleys "seldom made a mistake" in the attribution of a source),[43] advises against rote memorizing of one's own composition in his *De modo componendi sermones* (c. 1342), for:

Words fall out of a facile memory, and from such a trivial action, the memory of what one is saying is thrown in confusion, because the words (rather than concepts) do not present themselves. Often, from forgetting a single syllable, one botches the whole thing. Thus, the preacher can be confounded because he has bound himself to words rather than to their substance.[44]

Waleys also disapproves of relying on an overly polished style, composing the whole sermon in rhythm, or too many divisions of the text, for these devices also engender mistakes of recollection and the consequent confusion of the preacher. So too does citing too many authorities. Forgetfulness and its attendant embarrassment is the fault of the preacher who strives to excel in mere ingenuity ("qui in curiositate conatur excellere").

To ward off such preacher's perils ("periculum praedicatori"), one should memorize not word for word, but according to the *sententia* of one's authorities ("sententiam auctoritatum plene et distincte retineat"). By this advice, Thomas Waleys means that one should remember the most important words, but not worry about the lesser ones:

And if there are words in these authorities [i.e. the texts] which are singularly weighty in merit, one should especially strive in memory to retain and speak about them, taking fewer pains with the others. And this for sure, that there are many authoritative texts of the saints which, because of their length and obscurity, it is better and more useful to elucidate according to their sense alone than to recite word for word. And given that they can be recited word for word [by the preacher], where the authorities are obscure at all, their meaning can be set forth in other plain words, for, when they are not understood by the listeners they lack all profit.[45]

Waleys makes several interesting distinctions in this section, beginning with a basic one between *sententialiter*, "by the sense-units," and *verbaliter*, "word for word" – a variation on the ancient distinction between memory for matter and memory for words. Synonyms for these two abverbs are *summatim* and *verbatim*. Waleys's advice is directed towards the delivery of an already composed sermon; the preacher should retain his *sentence* or subject matters, and deliver his sermon with the aid of his *memoria* ("memoriter retinere et dicere"). This procedure is preferred to exact recitation for reasons of security as well as elegance.

Sententialiter may also have a technical meaning in the context of mnemonics, one that links the mnemonic value of the colon divisions marked off in a written text with the advice to remember "by the *sententiae*." A *sententia* was not merely an impressionistic division, but, according to a well-known definition by Isidore of Seville, coincides with a colon; it is a coherent though not complete semantic unit, and a number of such *cola / sententiae* make up the completed, distinct thought that is a *periodus*.[46] So remembering material *sententialiter* would mean to remember it in chunks the equivalent of colon-divisions, by its constituent ideas or *sententiae*, rather than by word-for-word reiteration. Two verbs, *retinere* and *dicere*, are used by Waleys with the adverb *sententialiter*; by contrast, the verb *recitare* is used twice with *verbaliter*. *Recitare* is the verb also used for the elementary school-room exercises in which children train their memories first by rote, word-for-word.

Essentially what Thomas Waleys says here is also Cicero's advice in *De oratore* and elsewhere, that one prepare a speech for delivery by remembering it according to its topics and major parts, rather than word for word. For Thomas Waleys, the fault of an overly ingenious preaching style is that one may literally lose one's way in it, for one must learn an ornate composition word for word, and that method risks losing everything in the memory loss of a syllable.

But, Thomas Waleys is quite clear, one does not choose absolutely between *summatim retinere* and *verbatim recitare*. Waleys says that the preacher knows his memorized texts *verbatim*, and then adapts them to the occasion and to the circumstances of his auditors – "dato quod verbaliter recitentur," "given that [the texts] can be recited word for word [by the preacher]." Whether or not we believe that all preachers conformed to this behavior, it is significant that Waleys expects it as a norm. Fortunatianus gave similar advice: we should learn texts verbatim whenever we can, but, so long as we are careful to convey the substance of our original, we may accommodate it in our own words to the occasion. Those accustomed to medieval texts are familiar with the results.

Some years ago Theodore Silverstein recognized that Adelard of Bath had certainly had direct knowledge of Cicero's *De natura deorum*.[47] His demonstration depended on recognizing that Adelard had reproduced the *res* of a passage in Cicero, though he had not quoted it *verbaliter*. The Latin of the two texts, Silverstein wrote, is similar "in the way the ideas . . . march together step by step, but their language is not quite the same." Nonetheless, Silverstein boldly rejected the notion that an (unknown) written intermediary had to have intervened between Adelard and Cicero to account for these differences. He writes, "such a text . . . has thus far not appeared in evidence and will, one may guess, be difficult to find." Once the phenomenon of *memoria summatim* is recognized by modern scholars, textual genealogies can allow greater flexibility and perhaps less speculation than they have in the past..

Even Scripture is altered to accord with the particular occasion a writer is addressing. An example occurs in a section of Hugh of St. Victor's *De archa*

Noe, a meditation on monastic virtues composed about 1140.[48] Hugh's theme is that the tree of wisdom is firmly rooted in faith, and he is chastizing those sinners who flaunt their lack of faith, not fearing the Lord. He quotes Psalm 72:2–3, but slightly alters the text to make it emphasize his immediate occasion: "Mei autem pene moti sunt pedes, pene effusi sunt gressus mei; quia zelaui *in peccatoribus* pacem peccatorum uidens."[49] The Vulgate reads "quia zelaui *super iniquos*." Frequently Hugh will add an *inquit* or an *autem* to a text to improve the transition between his words and those of a quotation (scholars still do this, of course), or he will change an inflection to fit the syntax of his own sentence. He also often incorporates fragments of text into his own words, making them virtually into items of his own vocabulary, the sense of quotation being almost lost. So Proverbs 8:31, where Wisdom speaks of herself "ludens in orbe terrarum; et deliciae meae esse cum filius hominum,"[50] is quoted as follows: "Hec est sapientia, quae aedificavit sibi domum, quia *ludens in* orbem *terrarum* delicias suas dicit *esse cum filiis hominum*." Such adaptive freedom is enabled by complete familiarity with the text, the shared memory of it on the part of both audience and author, and hence a delight both in recognizing the familiar words and in the skill with which they have been adapted to a new context. It is also evident that superficial changes in wording like these were not regarded as affecting the text's substance, even in the case of Scripture. They fall within medieval norms of correct quotation and use.

Memorizing *sententialiter* greatly increases the efficiency of recollection. George Miller has observed that a hypothetical sentence can be thought of as 100 letters or 25 words or 3 phrases or 1 proposition. If one considers a sentence as 1 proposition, one will obviously be able to grasp it more effectively and securely than if one regards it as 100 letters. It is, says Miller, "those larger, subjective units, loosely called ideas, that we must count to determine the psychological length of any text."[51] This is what ancient and medieval writers called *memoria rerum*.

Hugh of St. Victor, in *Didascalicon*, describes his own practice as a student, in terms of his favorite image of the trained memory as an orderly money-bag:

How many times each day would I exact from myself the daily debt of my bits of sophomoric wisdom [*sophismata*],[52] which thanks to the principle of shortness I had symbolized in one or two maxims in abbreviated form, so that indeed I held in my memory both the payouts [*solutiones*] and the numerical order of virtually all the propositions, questions, and objections which I had learned.[53]

In this context, *solutio* refers to the information "paid out" from memory's store, as the skillful money-changer pays out coin. This store is in the form of pieces of wisdom, *sophismata* or *dicta*, the bits into which texts are divided. And they are marked for recollection (*signare*) by having been reduced, according to the rule of *brevitas*, to one or two sayings "in abbreviated form" (*in pagina*) and numbered in order.

Hugh uses the word *pagina* in a specialized manner here that is recognized only in dictionaries which cover late Roman and medieval Latin: Du Cange and the *Thesaurus linguae latinae. Pagina*, like *(s)cedula* (discussed in the next part of this chapter), refers both to a type of physical surface and, by extension, to the sort of thing written on such a surface. Latin *pagina* is derived from the verb *pango*, "to fasten," and refers to the rectangular boards covered with wax that, fastened together, made up a set of tablets.[54] The constraints of the surface required writing in columns. Obviously, *pagina* refers to such physically shaped surfaces, as when Cicero, for example, writes of "filling a page" (*complere pagina*).[55]

But what one wrote on a *pagina* was what we call notes, that is, ephemeral memoranda, abstracts, computations, the rough drafts of compositions that were to be fully composed later, either in oral delivery or written onto papyrus or parchment in fair hand. The meaning of *pagina* was extended in later Latin to include this other meaning – a memorandum, something that is in a form abbreviated for further study and application.[56] Du Cange cites a letter of Ambrose, in which he says to his correspondent that he is sending him a little present, this short letter, because his friend wanted him to *paginare*, "examine in brief and informal form," some things concerning the interpretation of the Old Testament.[57] Similarly, Paulinus of Nola wrote that the laws of God were written on stone *in pagina*, meaning they were set down *breviter*, without all the commentary.[58] In medieval Latin, one finds the word *paginator*, the person who ornamented the pages with pictures and drawings. This task is associated with the work of the *rubricator* or *miniator* (the word from which Modern English "miniature" derives), the person who worked with red pigments to mark the text with short-form summaries, digests, and pointings of its contents, *in pagina*. It is worth noting that *rubricare* and its vernacular derivative *rubric* had dual meanings also.[59]

After one has divided a text, clearly marked its constituent pieces, and placed the segments onto one's numerical grid, the next principle, according to Hugh's Preface, is to memorize each bit in such a way that one sees it clearly and distinctively. One should always read a text from the same codex, so that the features of the page on which the particular segment of text appears become part of one's mnemonic apparatus. "Indeed I consider nothing is so useful for stimulating the memory as this," Hugh writes.[60] The layout of the many folio leaves of names, places, and dates which comprise his *Chronicle* was evidently designed by Hugh himself. Each page is in four columns, with headings in red introducing groups of ten items or less (figure 5).

Formatting the page of memory

The lay-out Hugh adopted for his *Chronicle* was clearly influenced by that of the Canon Tables of Eusebius, added to virtually all early medieval Bibles.[61] Compiled in Greek around 331, they were later translated into Latin. The elements of their design, which show parallel passages in the four Gospels, are very old and scarcely vary over their history (a ninth-century example is reproduced in figure 6). Passages are cited by number (including numbers over 200 – instead of chapters and verses, Eusebius divided the Gospels into sections) without any written text.[62] There are ten tables in all, the first showing concordant passages in all four Gospels; the next three show concordances among three of the four; the next five those among any two; and the last one lists passages unique to each of the four. The tables are laid out in columns (one meaning of *in pagina*), the numbers listed one after another vertically, and architectural columns are drawn to separate the four main vertical spaces on the page, together with arches and other architectural elements representing a classical façade.

It has been suggested that, in this context, an arcade motif may derive from the ancient mnemonic advice to use buildings – including *intercolumnia*, the spaces between columns – as backgrounds for things to be remembered.[63] Certainly *intercolumnia* is one of the most enduring types of memory locus. Within each rectangular space made by the columns in the Eusebian Tables, the name of the gospel is written at the top, and then the chapter numbers of the synoptic passages are recorded. Horizontal lines, sometimes colored, are drawn between every four numbers (in the Greek text) or five (in the Latin); the effect is to divide the page into a series of small rectangular bins, none holding more than five items. Such a layout is clearly designed for mnemonic ease; as Hugh of St. Victor tells his students about his own similar design: "Now indeed you have enough to do to imprint in this fashion in your memory the matters which are written out below, according to the method and diagram for learning by heart demonstrated to you earlier."[64]

The presentation of the manuscript page in medieval Bibles provides one of the most interesting contexts for understanding Hugh's injunctions to his young pupils concerning the need to divide material for memorizing, the mnemonic value of textual lay-out, and the requirement always to use

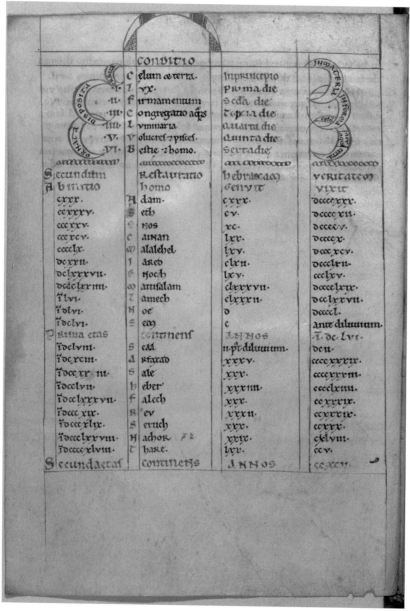

5. Paris, Bibliothèque nationale de France MS. lat. 15009, fo. 3v (French, twelfth century). Hugh of St. Victor's column format for his *Chronicle*. The headings and section markers are in red and blue ink, alternating. From the library of St. Victor, this is likely to be either the archetypal manuscript of this text, or very close to it.

6. New York, Pierpont Morgan Library MS. M. 860, fo. 8v (France, between 857 and 862). A page of Canon Tables from a Gospels made in the monastery of St. Martin in Tours.

the same codex. Typical of so-called "Paris format" is an English Bible of the late thirteenth century, now in the Huntington Library (EL 9 H4). Each book is divided into numbered chapters and subdivisions called *cola* and *commata*, using a scheme devised in Paris at the end of the twelfth century by the English scholar, Stephen Langton, later cardinal and archbishop of Canterbury.[65] Each chapter begins with a colored initial, alternately red and blue. The text of each chapter is presented in prose form, unbroken except for the punctuation of the *cola* and *commata*. Each chapter is numbered, in Roman numerals with alternately red and blue colored elements. These numbers also have distinctively drawn colored pen lines and circles in them – these, plus the colored initial, for which there are two or three different forms for the commonest letters, give each folio opening a unique appearance. The running heads at the top of each opening are also distinctively colored and drawn with differentiated pen ornamentation. Since this Bible is a small one, the differences in the design of the running heads from one opening to the next are quite noticeable.

The Psalms, together with collections of maxims like Cato's *Distichs*, were the elementary reading text throughout the Middle Ages, from late antiquity onward.[66] And Hugh of St. Victor evidently regarded their mastery as a beginning task, among the *puerilia*. But in the majority of medieval Bibles, the Psalms, unlike the divisions in all the other books, are unnumbered. Moreover, whereas in Carolingian Bibles the Psalms are written in verses, Bibles of the thirteenth century and later characteristically wrote them out as units of prose. The reason for this change undoubtedly is that the Bible at this time began to be issued as a single bound volume, often quite small, even pocket-sized, whereas in the earlier Middle Ages it was usually issued in separate volumes of full folio size.[67]

However, in these later Bibles the verse divisions are indicated by colored initials, alternately red and blue. Each psalm begins with a large colored initial, sometimes fully decorated, other times just drawn large, red or blue alternately. It is interesting that the Huntington Library's manuscript of Richard Rolle's fourteenth-century English Psalter (HM 148) preserves this format for the Latin text of the Psalms written above Rolle's translation of it and of Peter Lombard's commentary. Each Psalm's verse division has its initial letter colored alternately red or blue, the first initial of each Psalm is a large blue letter with distinctive red pen decoration surrounding it, and the color scheme is repeated, like a color-code, for the English translation, and the commentary which follows. These markers alternate between red and blue. An effort is made in the writing of the book to distinguish each memory-sized chunk as a unique visual image. Since in fixing one's images for storage (which required time, and at least two or three separate passes over the written text), one made sure to use the same codex – as all memory advice stressed – the mnemonic usefulness of such decorative elements is apparent.

Even what we hear must be attached to a visual image. To help recall something we have heard rather than seen, we should attach to their words the appearance, facial expression, and gestures of the person speaking as well as the appearance of the room. The speaker should therefore create strong visual images, through expression and gesture, which will fix the impression of his words. All the rhetorical handbooks contain detailed advice on declamatory gesture and expression; this underscores the insistence of Aristotle, Avicenna, and the other philosophers, on the primacy and security for memory of the visual over all other sensory modes, auditory, tactile, and the rest. Hugh as well insists that acoustically received material must be translated to visual terms and so fixed in memory. We recall that for the memory-artist, S., it made no difference whether material to be retained was presented to him orally or in writing – his visualization technique was the same.

Though the psychological principles are identical, such image schemes are far more sophisticated, complex, and learned. The commonness of the number-grid is indicated by its use to format the Bible, and by its traces in other scholarly contexts, such as the style used to cite the Decretals and other non-Scriptural texts.

Orality, literacy, memory, and citation of texts

The numerical grid imposed on Scripture by its division into numbered chapters and verses was first printed in the Geneva Bible of 1560. But Scripture had been divided into brief segments before Jerome, and indeed dividing by chapter goes back to the scholars of the Masoretic text. (We should remember that ancient texts were commonly copied without any divisions except for the fixed number of syllables that constituted a line of writing – students learning to read were taught how to divide up the text on their own. This was the practice for writing texts through about the third century AD.) Jerome divided in the classical fashion of *cola* and *commata*; so did Cassiodorus, who used not only these divisions of the text but chapter divisions and headings as well.[68] The late medieval Bible is divided into numbered chapters, using the scheme of Stephen Langton, together with the Cassiodorian division of the book of Psalms into *cola* and *commata*, which Alcuin had made standard. The essential utility of such division for memorizing the Biblical text was obvious to Langton, who glosses as follows Jerome's warning, made in his prologue to the Vulgate text of Joshua, that both reader and copyist should diligently preserve the divisions of the text: "by divisions, that is by chapters . . . which truly are most valuable for discovering what you want and holding it in your memory."[69] Dividing was not a casual task: Langton took thirty years to work out his chapter divisional scheme, perfecting it through classroom testing.[70]

Langton's chapter divisions superseded various earlier divisional schemes. This whole matter of the relationship between how scholars laid out a text in their memories, cited it when they made reference to it, and how scribes composed it on a manuscript page is well illuminated by a study of these habits prior to about 1200 AD. The problem is important because some anthropologists and historians of technology seem to assume that there is a direct and simple correlation between the form something takes in writing and the way a person is able to think of it, in the same way that a washing-machine's design determines how clothes washed in it will be washed. The fashion for defining writing as a technological innovation of the same sort as television and the automobile, or the heavy plow and moveable type, seems to me fraught with difficulties. Why I think so will be apparent from the following study of citational habits, page lay-out customs, and the use of the mental numerical grid for remembering Scripture during the early Christian and Carolingian periods.

It is apparent from remarks of St. Augustine, who used the pre-Vulgate, Old Latin text of the Bible, that the Psalms at least were taught to him and his audience in an order that was numerically designated. In his commentaries on the Psalms, which began as sermons, he prefaces his comments on Psalm 118 (119), with an observation about his compositional habits. He apologizes for delaying so long, though he has expounded all the others, partly in sermons, partly by dictating additional material, but Psalm 118 is long and extremely difficult.[71] He refers to this Psalm by number ("psalmum centesimum octauum decimum"). Of another Psalm, 125, he says, "Now you remember, *according to the order taught to us*, this Psalm is one hundred twenty-five, which is among those Psalms whose title is 'A song of degrees'" (my emphasis).[72] From the manner of address, it would appear that this commentary began as a sermon, as many did, and Augustine clearly assumes that everyone in his audience will know which is Psalm 125, "according to the order taught to us." Similarly, in commenting on Psalms 100, 104, and 105, he refers to them by number, though his usual habit is simply to begin by referring to "this Psalm" (*iste Psalmus*) without further identification. He does not find mystical significance in these numbers;

indeed, his attitude towards their numbering seems quite purely practical. Yet, commenting on Psalm 150, Augustine engages in a memorable *tour de force* of associations, expounding several possible numerical divisions of the Psalms; clearly their numbers were known also to Augustine's lay audiences. Such compositional dilation upon the *secretum* of numbers, is a trope, and it remained so in medieval preaching. No doubt the preachers believed that a numerological *mysterium* was divinely concealed in the texts (interpreters usually believe that what they find is "in" the text). Yet it is also true that the technique is a most effective inventory tool, open to use by mortal authors – witness Dante's *Commedia* and, in the English tradition, the work of the *Pearl* poet. It is worth remarking that *any* heuristic instrument, such as a number, can be treated as a reified sign. A mathematician once explained to me the difference between numerology and number-theory this way: the one (numerology) wants to explain everything, the other explains nothing but itself.

Referring to Psalms by number is not, however, Augustine's style of citation when marking a quotation. It was the universal custom in early medieval scholarly composition not to use numbers at all when citing sources. Passages from Scripture especially are often quoted without any attribution; the audience was expected to recognize the source from memory. New Testament texts may be introduced by a phrase such as "the Lord said" or "So the Apostle says," without naming the particular gospel or epistle being quoted; prophetic books of the Old Testament are cited by name ("Isaiah says") sometimes, but the historical books often are quite unattributed. And the Psalms, perhaps the most frequently quoted of all, are almost always completely unattributed; even the phrase *ut ait in psalmis*, "as it says in the Psalms," is unusual. Augustine was being quite untypical of himself when, in the *Enarrationes*, he cites a text as being "in Regnorum secundo libro," "in II Kings."[73] Occasionally he will introduce a quotation from a Psalm by *in alio psalmo*, "in another Psalm," but usually he simply quotes a verse in complete confidence that his audience will know it.

Jerome often refers to the Psalms by number, even in order to introduce a quotation from one. He also uses the less exact (from our point of view) citational style of Augustine, but, for example, he introduces a quotation from Psalm 44 by writing, "Legimus in quadragesimo quarto psalmo," "We read in Psalm 44,"[74] and one from Psalm 9 by "de quo in nono psalmo ... dicitur," "concerning which [the devil] it says in the ninth Psalm."[75] Books of the Bible, including the Pauline epistles and historical books of the Old Testament are often cited by name, unlike Augustine's practice. Jerome does this not only in his commentaries, but also in his letters. For instance, in his letter (no. 53) to Paulinus of Nola on the study of Scripture, he introduces a quotation of Psalm 118 by its number.[76] Jerome also numbered and referred by number to the book-divisions of his own works; thus in the introduction to Book 8 (*octavus liber*) of his *Commentary on Isaiah*, he refers to "books six and seven above."[77] Such variations in citational style continue through the early Middle Ages; Bede, for example, in his treatise on the figures and tropes of Scripture refers to the Psalms by number. But Carolingian manuscripts are the first written books to indicate occasionally in the margin the name of the book from which a quotation is cited, although such information was frequently not copied by later scribes.[78]

It would seem from early references to Psalms by number, so at odds with the citational conventions then prevalent, that one should not presume that the form of a citational style limits the abilities of scholars and their audiences to conceive of and designate texts in other ways. It is obvious from the works of these fourth-century Christians that the Psalms not only had a fixed order, but that they were taught and memorized by their number in that order. The earliest monastic rules, including Benedict's, discuss the order of the Psalms for divine office by referring to their numbers (see chapters 9 and 18 of the Benedictine Rule). Indeed, the method described by Quintilian of dividing a long text into short sections, memorized seriatim or *per ordine*, lends itself to just such a method of memorial storage, and suggests that the numerical grid principle is very ancient indeed. Quintilian's advice itself implies numbering the segments produced by *divisio* of a long text, so that one can join the second piece to the first, and so on (*Inst. orat.*, XI. ii. 37).

There is also clear evidence that the verse divisions of each Psalm were numerically designated as early as the time of Augustine. The word *versus* is used by Augustine to refer to the divisions within the Old Latin text (though it was Cassiodorus who established the divisional scheme used in the medieval text of the Psalms)[79] and these verses have numbers. So, in his commentary on Psalm 6 (referred to as "sextus psalmus" in his comments on Psalm 11's titulus),[80] he speaks of the first verse and second verse of the Psalm. These verses are somewhat different from those similarly designated in the Vulgate text. Though the divisions themselves differ, clearly the principle of dividing by verses was known. These divisions were imposed on the text only in memory. They are not marked in the early Christian codices we possess – indeed even word divisions are not indicated.[81] It thus appears that versions of the numerical grid system described by Hugh of St. Victor for memorizing and mentally concording the

Scriptural text were taught commonly at least by the fourth century, and probably were applied to texts well before then.

Alcuin regards the numerical order of the Psalms as so ancient and fixed that he indulges in some exegesis regarding the symbolism of a particular Psalm's place in that order. In his commentary on Psalm 118, he says that he has reckoned the patterns worthy of comment ("eruendas rationes") for all the numbers in the Psalms, "that is, why are all the penitential Psalms consecrated in a number containing sevens? and why is Psalm 118 divided into twenty-two sections, of which each one has eight verses? or what is the reason for there being fifteen Psalms designated in their titles 'a song of degrees'?"[82] Invoking the text from Wisdom (11:21) that God created the universe (including Scripture) by number, order, and measure, he proceeds to analyze the significance of the numbers in the format of Psalm 118. For our purposes, however, what is significant is the simple but profound fact that Alcuin thought of the text as formatted in terms of a numerical grid, twenty-two sections of eight verses each, and that he also thought that the Psalm, which itself had a number in the order of the whole book (118), incorporated subsets of numbered divisions in sections and verses. This is the mnemonic format which Hugh of St. Victor taught in 1130, and is in the tradition of numerically designated divisions which we find in the fourth century.

But the first Bibles to write out the complete format of chapter and verse are mid-sixteenth-century, and virtually no medieval scribes wrote in the numbers of the *verses* in any Scriptural book; chapter numbers were copied in routinely only beginning in the thirteenth century.[83]

There is, in other words, a lag of well over a millennium between the time the numerical grid was certainly in common use for dividing Scripture, and its first complete appearance on a physical page. It is clear in this instance that people had laid out the Bible on a grid in their memories for over 1,000 years before they bothered to express that grid in writing, and for at least 400 years before they thought it important even to suggest it in their scholarly citational habits.

In his treatise on sermon composition, Thomas of Waleys makes a comment that is illuminating of this whole matter. Advising preachers how to cite the Bible and patristic authorities during their sermons, Thomas suggests that although some cite the Psalms by number, others omit such numerical citation, referring instead generally to "the Psalter," since the Psalms are so commonly known:

Next, whenever a particular Psalm is cited, it is also referred to as the fortieth or thirtieth, or in another similar manner. Others however omit such citation, and only say: "This is found in the Psalter," *and the reason is that the Psalms are generally well known.*[84] (my emphasis)

This comment by Thomas would seem to explain why, even in late medieval written Bibles, the Psalms are commonly unnumbered while in all the rest of the books the chapter numbers are included. The Psalms are unnumbered because they are so well known, having been memorized as a first book – people have their own schemes for recalling them (some recite them with their numbers, some do not), and a cue is enough to bring forth the whole text in recollection. In written texts such as moral treatises and treatises on preaching, well-known texts such as the Psalms and Epistles are commonly referenced by the first few words of a phrase only, for example, "Beatus vir &c." Or in some treatises, one finds a verse referenced solely by the first letters of the words, on the model, adduced earlier, of "b. u. q. n. a." for Psalm 1:1. These references could only be useful to readers who had memorized verbatim the texts being cited.[85]

Thomas of Waleys says, though, that thematic sentences taken from every other part of the Bible must be cited by chapter and book. This comment indicates how widely used some sort of numerical grid was as a mental filing system. The style for citing the *Decretum*, used in glosses and other contexts throughout the Middle Ages, was according to the number of the large division (*distinctio*, *quaestio*, or *causa*) followed by the introductory word or phrase of the particular canon referenced, "xxxij c. multorum" or "xxiv c. cum itaque." If two or more canons in a given *quaestio* or *distinctio* began with the same words, they might be distinguished as, for example, "c. Si quis i, Si quis ii," etc. Similar forms were used for citation of the various volumes of decretal collections compiled after Gratian's catalogue.[86] Obviously a canon lawyer was expected to have pretty well memorized the entire set of Decretals in order to be able to use these references without a great deal of wasteful "turning the pages." William of Ockham, in his *Dialogus*, speaks of his relief at having stocked his memory with so much material, including all the Decretals, when he found himself exiled in Munich; Peter of Ravenna, a fifteenth-century Italian lawyer, claimed (as we will see) that adopting his version of an alphabetical mnemonic enabled him to learn all the decretal collections.

Yet there were clearly risks in citing too many numbers while one spoke. Thomas of Waleys advises that supplementary authorities, Biblical and patristic, should not be fully cited by book and chapter number, but by book alone. If one insists on citing every chapter number it often happens, when bringing together several authorities, that a chapter number falls out of the preacher's memory, and one then could bring forth another section than the one intended. Wherefore, he says, he praises the practice of former times when preachers did not cite chapter numbers in their delivery, but only when they wrote their sermons down. He concludes, "I think their method was better because it was safer [*tutior*] than the modern method by which chapter numbers and books are cited together."[87] Before dismissing this as the advice of an irredeemable pedant terrified of being caught out by a colleague, let us consider it in terms of the practical difficulties attendant on the numerical grid as a method for recalling text.

The grid serves essentially as a coding and filing system for the orderly and ready recollection of material. In using a mnemonic, however, one does not normally call out its coordinates, whether one's grid be the architectural places or this numerical one. The grid is essentially arbitrary, in the sense that it is not part of the material placed within it, any more than a file is part of what it contains. However, wrong coordinates will send one to the wrong part of the file, and thus to the wrong text, causing a devastating loss of place. Thomas advises articulating only the name of the work cited, a safer thing to do since it isn't a part of the grid. It is not the file itself, only the name of the file. Indeed it is striking that he advises avoiding articulation of the code whenever possible, even of the Psalms, if one can get away with it. Only in the more secure situation of a corrected, written version should the numerical grid be articulated, when any miscitation can be worked out. And his advice is given for *safety's* sake.[88]

Not every preacher followed Thomas's advice in this matter; he himself suggests that it is a bit old-fashioned, and of course the sermons we have preserved are all in written form, with all citations given. But it is a significant point that medieval citations are given *before* the text more frequently than after it. The anterior position serves to cue the mental grid. Our mode of citing after a quotation, in parentheses or a footnote, is designed solely to send a reader to a printed source that he or she must find elsewhere. Our citations are referrals, not access cues to a mental grid of texts.

Indexing systems devised in the monasteries and, later, the universities seem all to have served the dual function of being both tools for finding texts initially and also for noting them in the memory, as mnemonic hooks. Not only numbers could serve such a purpose: the Dominican system, devised for the Bible concordance, of citing by book, chapter number, and letter (A–G) to indicate the position of a text within the chapter was widely disseminated. The Rouses describe a bookmark of the thirteenth century, which explains the key to the pagination scheme of the volume in which it is found, a Cistercian manuscript in which pages are marked with a combination of letters and dots.[89] One side of the bookmarker says: "Ut memoriter teneatur alphabetum taliter ordinatur: a .a :a a:," etc. Evidently this reference scheme was designed in part to provide a memory grid for the readers. On the reverse of this bookmark, the strip of parchment is divided into seven equal sections, marked A through G, the location scheme also used by the Dominicans within chapter divisions. One held this side against the edge of the page to provide the finely tuned location for the text. A number of other such bookmarks are known.[90]

As Richard and Mary Rouse say of all these various coding and filing schemes, "they emerge with striking suddenness in the West, to the point that one may say that, probably before 1220, certainly before 1190, no such tools existed; and that, after the 1280s, the dissemination and new creation of such aids to study were commonplace."[91] Of the sudden proliferation of written tools there is no doubt; as there is also no doubt that the same order (the Dominicans) chiefly responsible for creating them is also chiefly responsible for the dissemination of mnemonic devices based on places, including the Herennian one. It is also true that during the thirteenth century schemes for memory training were disseminated into the general culture in France and especially in Italy, via vernacular translations and adaptations of the architectural and other memory-training techniques. We therefore should not assume that these multitudinous study aids replace memory as a fundamental tool; instead, they often were thought of as memory systems first and manuscript aids second. This suggests that reading and memorizing were taught as they were in antiquity, as one single activity, and, further, that the monastic understanding of what one does in reading, so well described by Dom Leclercq, not only persisted but became part of general culture in the thirteenth, fourteenth, and later centuries, for reasons that had as much to do with the moral value of *memoria* in meditation and prayer as with its utility. But this is a subject for later chapters.

Furthermore, the proliferation of written guides to these various heuristic schemes in the twelfth and thirteenth centuries does not mean that there were no indexing mnemonics in use earlier. Hugh's Preface describes an indexing scheme in great detail, long before 1190, and, for reasons I have indicated, it seems most likely he was describing a well-known, persistent technique. Indeed it is likely that all these schemes – numbering of chapters, alphabetizing (the memory scheme which Aristotle described in *De memoria* was an alphabetical one), page indexing by number and/or letters – are medieval adaptations of schemes known since antiquity as memorial schemes. With the Rouses and other scholars, I suppose that a chief reason for the proliferation of written indexing schemes was that more people had need of organized textual material and that there were more texts to be consulted after the twelfth-century infusions from Spain and Sicily. Once the scholarly community was enlarged beyond the monastery, the need for written transmission was greater, and priests and friars who need to preach have need of preachers' tools. But this did not occur at the expense of memory; indeed the written schemes themselves are to be used as memory grids, *ut memoriter teneantur*.

One other intriguing practice which indicates the tenacity and pervasiveness of the methods described by Hugh of St. Victor is that of quotation itself, and the related practice of what Hugh calls "gathering," *colligendum*. The medieval verb *quotare* first makes its appearance, according to the *Revised Medieval Latin Word List*, early in the thirteenth century (which does not mean it was unknown earlier). Derived from the adjective *quot*, "how many," it meant "to number" a book, dividing a longer text into numbered subdivisions, such as chapters. Robert of Basevorn discusses quoting in chapter 31 of his *Forma praedicandi*, written in 1322. After the prayer, the theme is restated and quoted, "quotandum quantum ad librum et capitulum." For authorities other than the theme, it is not necessary to give the section number "secundum modum modernum" (apparently, like Thomas of Waleys, Robert did not like the new custom of citing every authority by chapter number), though one may number books in a series (like I and II Kings), or one may also give a chapter number in a book which explains another book (Gregory's *Moralia in Job*, for instance, which comments direcly on Job). The correct form is, "Gregorius primo, vel secundo, Moralium super illud Job." But masters and professors of theology may "quote" (numerically divide) anything:

It is permitted, indeed it is their prerogative, for masters and professors of sacred theology to quote everything in a carefully worked-out manner [*exquisite*], since in regard to this matter much deference is given them by others, because of the testimony of their excellent teaching and display of humility regarding their responsibilities, and because of the dignity and honor of their rank.[92]

So the practice of quoting, marking, and numbering a text for citation seems to have been the special prerogative of the most learned members of the university, who alone are able to quote *exquisite*.

The quotation of patristic texts is a feature of thirteenth-century scholarship, and made possible the compendia of authorities designed for sermon composition, such as *distinctiones* collections, textual *concordantiae*, and other *libri rerum memorandarum*. Often in these collections, each quote is cited by book and chapter number (and in some by the further refinement of A–G division), the two basic coordinates of the grid that serve not only to help find the quotes in a complete text of their parent work but to place them in a memory file, so that, considering Avaricia, for example, would bring forth a number of texts, each labelled in a mental file called "Avaricia." Indeed, for most preaching friars, working far from large libraries, the citations could only have served as memory coordinates.[93]

It is likely that the passion of many late medieval preachers for numbering sermon divisions – what has been called the scholastic or university method of the thirteenth century – is related to the nature of this numerical grid. Thomas Waleys says that numerical division of the theme in the modern style is not just a gimmick, but most useful for both the preacher and his auditors:

Indeed if only one division of the theme be made, still that division will be beneficial as to those subjects, as much for the preacher as for the hearer. For the moderns began not just because of a vogue, as others believe, to divide the theme, which the ancients did not customarily do. Especially it is useful for the preacher, because division of the theme into separate parts affords an opportunity for dilation in the later development of his sermon. For the hearer truly it is most useful, because when the preacher divides the theme and afterwards develops the parts of the division in order and clearly, both the matter of the sermon and the form and manner of the preaching is more easily understood and retained; that will not be the case if the preacher proceeds unclearly or without order and by a confused structure.[94]

Of special interest in this advice is the assumption on Thomas Waleys's part that both preacher and auditor relied on the numerical system for retaining discourse, for the key both to successful dilation and to retention is orderly division by number. This manual was written within a university setting, in which preacher and hearers alike were scholars, but the same method was used in preaching to the laity.[95] The fourteenth-century Dominican preacher, Giordano of Pisa, whose sermons were taken down by dictation while he spoke, used the method of division constantly. Since he preached commonly two or three times a day, Friar Giordano often only got through the first few divisions of his sermons, though he always announced all his themes in order in his introduction. When exhausted, he would promise to continue where he left off at a later time – and he did, invariably picking up exactly where he left off. These sermons were taken down as they were preached; they were not later corrected.[96]

Robert of Basevorn's quoting schemes

Several excellent examples of how thematic division works mnemonically can be found in Robert of Basevorn's treatise on preaching. For a sermon on the Passion, Robert suggests the following "division" of the text: "Jesus iterum clamans voce magna emisit spiritum," Mt. 27:50 (I will quote the Latin text here because the word-play, essential to its mnemonic effectiveness, cannot be reproduced in an English translation):

Hic notantur: Passionis utilitas, *Jesus*; patientis potestas, *clamans*; humanitatis veritas, *voce magna*; patiendi libertas, *emisit*; separationis acerbitas, *spiritum.*[97]

This is the basic division into five, a portion of the theme plus a rhyming catchphrase which in some way (not always clear to me, I confess) abstracts the major idea to be developed from each of the five divisions.

Then comes the subdivision, also in five parts:

Subdivitur tunc sic: Quinque sunt vocales, scilicet *A E I O U*, quae omnem vocem faciunt. Sic quinque vulnera Christi omnem sonum, sive doloris sive gaudii faciunt. Vide *in manibus A* et *E*: [Jer. 31:3] "Attraxi te miserans" etc. [Is. 49:16] "Ecce in manibus meis descripsi te"; *I in latere*: talem enim figuram imprimit vulnus lanceae, hoc est "ostium arcae" quod "in latere," etc. in Gen. [6:16] et in Joan. [20:27]: "Infer digitum tuum huc et mitte in latus meum, et noli esse incredulus," etc.; *O* et *U in pedibus*: [Ps. 8:6] "Omnia subjecit Deus sub pedibus ejus." Ideo ut consequaris dicas facto: [Job 23:11] "Uestigia ejus secutus est pes meus."[98]

No one will have any difficulty in recognizing this counsel to be at once typically medieval and, from a modern standpoint, bizarre to the point of intellectual decadence. Yet the scheme proposed is eminently sensible as a mnemonic both for composing and for delivering a sermon, as well as providing auditors with a clear structure within which they can grasp and retain the major points of the sermon.

This example, like many others, combines a variety of mnemonic structures, which in this case are also reflected in its compositional structures.[99] The theme is the Passion, and the preacher elects to divide by fives, a number with evident associations to his subject because there were five wounds in the crucifixion. A mnemonic rhyme composed of summary catchphrases organizes the main division in five. Then, in the subdivision, one remembers the five wounds, imposing upon the structure of those five another five, the five vowels, or *voces*, perhaps used because of the word's punning association with *voce magna*, the third division of the text which deals with the theme *humanitatis veritas*. (Punning of all sorts is fundamental in mnemotechnic; one encounters visualized homophony throughout the history of written mnemonic advice, as a principle both for forming images and for association of ideas.) To each of the five vowels is attached a text beginning with it. Five vowels, five wounds; the basic composition is complete, combining a scheme of *loci* and *imagines* that incorporates a numerical grid, on which are "placed" brief texts and other sorts of visual images. As hermeneutic, an interpretation of their meaning, attaching these particular texts to the five vowels is grotesque non-sense, but as an elementary device for retaining and recollecting them – as heuristic – it is both simple and effective. One can return to the theme of one's composition after a detailed exposition of any of its pieces and readily find one's place.

Robert of Basevorn's other examples follow the same principles. For a division into six of the theme, "Ego vox clamantis in deserto, parate viam Domini," he suggests using the six basic syllables of the chant, a pun on "vox clamantis." To these six notes – ut, re, mi, fa, sol, la – are attached the texts for the subdivision, as follows:

1) UT filii lucis ambulate; 2) REvertere, revertere, sulamitis, revertere, revertere ut intueamur te; 3) MIsere animae tuae placens Deo; 4) FAcite dignos fructus poenitentiae; 5) SOLve vincula colli tui, captiva filia Syon; 6) LAvamini, mundi estote.[100]

This is a most revealing application of the technique called solmization, for it shows that Robert of Basevorn understood that the device was primarily a mnemonic, and could thus be utilized in non-musical contexts. It also suggests how much more broadly the function of a mnemonic was understood then than it is now, when we restrict it to reiterative tasks.

The principle of attaching a syllable to a particular musical value or "degree" was known in antiquity, and indeed is found in virtually every culture.[101] It is most notably discussed in the Middle Ages in a letter of Guido d'Arezzo to the monk, Michael. There is evidence that solmization was used in medieval Europe before Guido, but the Benedictines were certainly happy to give him credit for having "invented" it, and the system he describes became the dominant one, indeed the foundation of what Westerners still use. Guido's syllables are taken from a hymn to John the Baptist, "Ut queant laxis"; these syllables then became the names of the six parts of a hexachord, at that time the unit organizing musical tones. As Guido wrote to Michael:

You will then have an altogether easy and thoroughly tested method of finding an unknown melody . . . After I began teaching this procedure to boys, some of them were able before the third day to sing an unknown melody [to them] with ease, which by other methods would not have been possible in many weeks.[102]

His system is designedly mnemonic, "if you wish to commit any note or neume to memory,"[103] whether you knew the melody before or not, "quem scias vel nescias." For the system of places forms a kind of alphabet. Indeed,

Guido's analysis of the purpose and function of musical notation seems to derive from Isidore of Seville's definition of the purpose of letters, that is, to hold things in memory, including what we do not already know. Just as the alphabet enables us to hear again and retain in memory the voices/words of those who are not actually present and whom we have never heard or seen in the flesh, so musical notation is, in this way, like an alphabet (and so says John of Salisbury, in a passage I will examine in the next part of this chapter).

Here, as well as in any other medieval text, we can understand that craft rules (*artes*) were thought to be, as Aristotle says, built up from repeated, remembered experiences, the principle being to recognize and organize likeness. This could then be applied, even to things never seen before and encountered for the first time. This is not mnemonic in the restricted sense that moderns tend to understand it, but in the larger sense of how all learning takes place. Learning is regarded as a process of discovering more effective, efficient, inclusive mnemonics – for memory, as Hugh of St. Victor says, is the basis of learning. To learn the alphabet (and numbers were designated by the alphabet, too, we should keep in mind) was to be possessed of a set of infinitely rich mnemonics – not only a skill that would enable one to read signs on a piece of vellum, but a key opening the door to the whole cultural complex of institutionalized practices signified in the word *memoria*. This is an analysis of learning that differs from our own in its emphasis upon memory and memorial cues, and it is very far from restricted to rote tasks. It places rote in the service of creative thought.

Whatever the number of one's sermon division, Robert of Basevorn recommends attaching a set of symbols or markers that incorporate that number and can be used as a mnemonic for the subdivisions. For example, besides the two already described, Robert suggests the seven mercies of God, the eight Beatitudes, the nine orders of angels, the Ten Commandments, the twelve hours of the day. But eleven, he says, is almost never used, and never a number greater than twelve, for one will lose track. This observation is borne out in a catalogue of such numbered groups of items that was made anonymously and attached, as Book IV, to Hugh of Fouilloy's *De avibus*. Though many threes and sevens, fours, sixes, tens, and nines are listed, there are only two elevens – and nothing greater than twelve.[104] It is also useful, Basevorn says, to break up a larger number; for example, subdividing an initial division of nine into three sets of three, since there are so many threes that finding them presents no problem. Mary and Richard Rouse comment, concerning a sermon of Alan of Lille on the Trinity, that it is "an extravaganza of triplicity" – so too they well characterize the sermons of Innocent III as amounting to "a sequence of lists" of threes or fives or fours or sevens.[105] The subject matters so grouped are the *singulars* of which Hugh of St. Victor speaks, sorted and stored like coins of similar size in the properly numbered compartments of the memorial store-house.

THE ALPHABET AND KEY-WORD SYSTEM

The number grid which Hugh of St. Victor describes was but one of several memorial heuristics taught in the Middle Ages. Memory training, we learn from Quintilian, was an elementary component of learning to read and to write. The numerical coding seems best designed to remember and to collate (that is, move discrete pieces of texts about in various combinations) longer works, like the Psalms, although it clearly can be used for a variety of other purposes as well. But in addition to such a task, a memory library needs to have cross-referencing systems, and these also seem to have been taught among the educational basics.

Quintilian speaks both of memorizing a text in (numerical) order, and of marking the passages one especially wants or needs to remember with mental *notae*. *Notae* are discussed twice in relation to memory training. First, describing the system of *loci* and *imagines*, Quintilian suggests imprinting in orderly progression a spacious house with many rooms, and then marking the items to be remembered by a *nota*, either an associative sign (an anchor to remind one of navigation, for instance) or a key-word, for even people who lose the thread of what they are saying can put their memory back on track with a single cue. These *notae* are then placed in the orderly series of rooms. He prefers, however, a simpler system, yet one still using *notae*. After one divides a text into short sections, and has repeated these to oneself two or three times and perhaps written them down as well, one then marks passages one especially needs to recollect with *notae* which one has invented for oneself.[106] Martianus Capella some 400 years later also advises using *notae* to mark passages, and the word is found commonly in memory advice, and ubiquitously written out in the margins of manuscripts against passages that either the scribe or a later reader thought to be especially important for remembering.

Notes and places

It is unclear from Quintilian and other writers whether these *notae* or *notulae* are to be inscribed on the physical page or only in memory, as

Hugh of St. Victor counsels; clearly some were made physically, for marginal marks do occur in manuscripts, copied by scribes to help users of the books. But since every reader is advised to make *notae*, most mnemonic signs must have been devised mentally, especially when books were used by many different readers over several generations. In manuscript margins from the twelfth century on, one finds commonly the word, *nota*, addressed to the reader. It is the imperative singular of the verb *notare*, "make a note," and it points out an important or difficult passage that the reader might wish particularly to mark with a *nota* of some sort of his own to help remember it.

Mental marking is mnemonically advantageous because each individual makes up his own system of *notulae*, his own filing system, and, as we know from *Ad Herennium*, one's own *notae* and *imagines* are to be preferred to memorizing a pre-existent system, because such exercise stimulates the memory more fully and fixes it more securely. Hugh of St. Victor describes a completely mental system; Robert Holcot, in a text we will examine again later, says that as he reads he imagines a memory-image projected onto the particular text that he wishes to remember, and he gives detailed instructions in his commentaries for making these. Yet the written manuscript containing them is a plain one, rubricated but without any drawing or decoration. Only in the margin, opposite each verbal picture, is written the single word *pictura*. Perhaps we might understand the word in this context not as a noun, but, on the analogy of *nota*, as a command to the reader that he is to make a picture from the written description, evidently in his mind.[107]

At the end of the English Middle Ages, Stephen Hawes writes of the orator tucking into his memory "sundry ymages," not only for the "mater . . . lyke to the tale" but also in a "recapytulacyon" ("re-chaptering" or "cross-heading") of each image by its "moralyzacyon," a general ethical topic or "commonplace" heading. Much material – how much would have to vary individually – seems to have been assumed to be filed away not as a complete text (or not only as a complete text) but as sets of extracts "noted" in the memory. The verb *tractare*, meaning to "draw out" or "extract," is frequently used of a process of reading as well as of a genre of composition. To "tract" a text while reading it means to pull out of it the various matters that one wishes to squirrel away in one's memorial inventory. Then, when composing a tract (the gerund form, *tractandum*, is used to indicate this activity), one begins by collecting on a particular subject all the material, together with appropriate commentary, that one had previously drawn out of one's reading and filed away under a letter or a key-word or some other *nota*.

A late but important description of memory-work by the fifteenth-century Italian jurist, Peter of Ravenna, who wrote one of the works on the art of memory most popular in the Renaissance, states that a well-trained memory is most like a book containing both text and glosses. "For I daily read all my lectures of Canon Law without a book; but if I should have a book before my eyes, I deliver the textual concordances [*textum*] and glosses from memory so that I should not seem to omit the least sylla-ble."[108] Thus, at the end of the fifteenth century, when printed books had become almost common, a law professor might still lecture regularly without a book, and could supply his lecturing apparatus more accurately and completely, he says, from his memory than by depending on a book.

Peter's memory-places were arranged alphabetically: "on the nineteen letters of the alphabet I have placed twenty thousand extracts of both sorts of law." I will come back to this passage shortly to discuss exactly how he says he did this, but for now I want to stress his use of the alphabet as his ordering device. He uses, he says, the regular alphabet, but also "human figures in place of the letters and thus living, vivid images."[109] For the sake of vivid images, unusual ones of the sort memory can easily fix on, he can make use of a sort of human alphabet to indicate the various letters. He even suggests using the forms of enticing women for such a purpose: "illae enim multum memoriam meam excitant," "these greatly stimulate my memory," though, he adds, this is not a technique for those who loathe women or who cannot control themselves.

Evidence that alphabets were commonly used as a mnemonic ordering device is scattered but persistent in both ancient and early medieval books. Aristotle describes (in *De memoria*) the use of letters of the Greek alphabet as an ordinary method for ordering memorized material. But if one is using an alphabet to file lots of different topics, one might well need more than one set of such places to accommodate one's material, lest one's memory be overwhelmed by trying to crowd too much into one place (a persistent warning in memory texts). To avoid this, one needs more than one set of alphabets, containing different forms though having still a rigid, easily recoverable, order. That is what Peter of Ravenna was doing with his human alphabets.

It is a curiosity of medieval books that tables of Greek, Hebrew, Coptic, runic, and even wholly imaginary alphabets are found side by side in a number of monastic manuscripts. It is also an insufficiently explained curiosity that books containing the Bestiary, moralized descriptions of animals both real and imagined, are found commonly in monastery libraries. Scholars have wondered what function such apparently puerile, unscholarly material might serve to justify its preservation. I will return to this question in Chapters 4 and 7, to make my case more fully, but my hypothesis is that they functioned not only to delight and intrigue medieval students but to provide them with mnemonically valuable heuristics, orderly foundations or sets of mnemonic *loci*, which can continue to have value throughout one's education (a lifetime project). In this context, such a list of letters does not serve primarily to form words (and indeed in the case of imaginary alphabets, no words are to be formed) but to supply sources of *notae*. They have more in common with notarial abbreviations and punctuation than they do with the phonemic graphemes of an intelligible language.

Learning an alphabet is a part of grammar. This is also the point at which one lays down one's fundamental mnemonic apparatus. Mnemonic writers like Thomas Bradwardine and John of Garland assume their students have certain sets of images already in their memories – in addition to alphabets and numbers, these include the Zodiac and the "characteristics of animals," *voces animantium*, a collection of attributes that derives from the various versions of the Bestiary, a work that itself goes back to Alexandrine Greece. Ordered lists of this sort, I propose, were deliberately memorized in order to serve as potential mnemonic heuristics, the seats (*sedes*) into which one could place the variety of diverse material one would acquire in one's education and reading.

Morgan Library MS. M 832, a manuscript written and painted in the last half of the twelfth century at the monastery of Göttweig in Austria, contains in its first folio the letters of five alphabets – Hebrew, Greek, Latin, Scythian, and Runic, taken from Hrabanus Maurus "De inventione linguarum." The rest of the manuscript is a Bestiary.[110] In light of the mnemonic role of alphabets and of the *voces animantium*, finding the two sorts of material together in a single manuscript makes some practical pedagogical sense, for such a manuscript would have served the monks by providing them with material to help them form sets of memory-places (indeed, it is hard otherwise to give a practical reason for twelfth-century Austrian monks to learn such alphabets as Scythian or Runic).

There is evidence of scholars using both imaginary and real alphabetical sets later in their careers. Robert Grosseteste's scheme of referencing symbols is derived eclectically from various alphabets, and many of his *notae* are imaginary. The Bolognese rhetoric master, Boncompagno da Signa, lists in his *Rhetorica novissima* (1235) a variety of signs and symbols that are useful as artificial aids to natural memory, including *deposita alphabeta*, and describes as well how he has used an imaginary alphabet as a memory code. By this means, he claims, "within thirty days I have memorized the names of five hundred students. And I also affirm, which will seem more remarkable, that in the sight of all I have named every one by his own name, not omitting his surname and where he was from: wherefore, together and singly, they were overcome with admiration."[111]

Boncompagno's feat may appear pallid in comparison with some of the feats of memory described by other scholars, but my concern is not with his talent but with his method – using an imaginary alphabet. Bernhard Bischoff describes some manuscripts from the ninth and eleventh centuries in which the names of the months and of numbers in Greek, Hebrew, and Coptic are given in parallel columns. Such lists, he says, "worked like magnets" in attracting names from other languages as well, but "I think . . . these lists and enumerations in general cannot be regarded as the result of, or as an attempt at genuine language study. They might rather be regarded as a symptom of a naive curiosity which manifests itself also in the collecting – it is a kind of collecting – of foreign and strange alphabets which can be observed in manuscripts from the eighth century on and continued to post-medieval times," collections which included, indiscriminately, both real and invented alphabets.[112] Such a long life would suggest that readers found utility in these lists (after all, *curiositas* or the useless collecting of knowledge was regarded as sinful); they provided collections of *notae* that might be useful in schemes for memory coding, and supplemented, as a reader might wish, those with which he was already familiar.

Writing and memory

It was Isidore of Seville, that chief conduit of ancient pedagogy to the medieval West, who defined the function of written letters in terms of their memorial utility. Alphabets are a kind of *notae*, and these written letters were invented "in order to remember things. For lest they fly into oblivion, they are bound in letters. For so great is the variety of things that all cannot be learned by hearing, nor contained only in memory."[113] Writing is a servant to memory, a book its extension, and, like the memory itself, written letters call up the words of those that are no longer present. Two things are worth emphasizing in Isidore's definition. First, the primacy of memory over writing, which one encounters as well in a text like Plato's *Phaedrus*, is still present here in Isidore. Secondly, writing and memorizing are regarded by Isidore still as essentially the same process: writing is an activity of remembering, as remembering is writing on the tables of the mind. And all textual *notae*, such as marks of punctuation, or editorial signs and the shorthand symbols and abbreviations known properly as *notaria*, are of the same class as letters. Isidore defines a *nota* as "figura propria in litterae modum posita," "a distinctive shape used in the manner of written letters." Isidore's understanding of a note, or for that matter of a letter, is not the same as our own, and this philological fact must be considered carefully. In modern linguistic theory, graphemes ("letters") represent one or more phonemes, the units of meaningful sound that convey sense in any language; thus philosophical issues of adequacy and truth of representation can meaningfully apply to them. But a mnemonic cue does not represent anything necessarily. Its effectiveness resides entirely in its satisfactory performance as a mental marker, a reminder. Once it has successfully cued the matter it marks, its function is completed. For mnemonic cues, as indeed for tools generally, their "adequacy" is in respect of a task rather than an idea or theory. A screwdriver is adequate to its task when it drives a screw successfully. This is a fundamental definitional distinction, that must always be taken into account in medieval discussions of the nature of *litterae*, especially those contexts, chiefly pre-scholastic, in which the writer claims that written letters are "like" the *notae* of recollective investigation.

By defining the essential utility of written letters as memorial in nature – writing is to keep us from forgetting – Isidore gives a remarkably succinct statement of a principle tenet of pre-modern pedagogy. A student in ancient schools (and these earliest accomplishments were the work of the nursery, according to Quintilian) first learned his letters, beginning with their names even before their forms, though Quintilian prefers, he says, that children learn the two together, endorsing especially the use of ivory alphabet-blocks for children to play with. In a custom deriving from Greek education, Latin letters were learned from A to X and then backwards from X to A, and then in pairs, such as AX, BV, CT, DS, and so on. Finally, breaking the order entirely, they were taught in all various combinations.[114]

Quintilian rightly stresses that such a method teaches children to learn letters individually, not just in rote order.[115] But the exercise also induces a facility for *calculating* with the alphabet, that is moving it around quickly and surely in all sorts of both common and odd combinations. Such facility is very useful for the kind of mnemonic shuffling necessary for composition, and would create an alphabetical heuristic as flexible as a numerical one. As Quintilian says, "the elements of reading and writing are entirely a matter of *memoria*";[116] he meant not only developing memorized content but, of equal importance, the capability for secure, rapid, and capacious system-building which characterizes trained *memoria*. "Memory . . . is very necessary to the orator; there is nothing like practice for nourishing and strengthening it, and, since the age-group of which we are now speaking cannot as yet produce anything on its own, it is almost the only faculty which the teacher's attention can help develop."[117]

After individual letters, instruction proceeded to syllables (ba-, be-, bo-, bi-, bu-, etc.) and then to words; all this time, writing was also taught, the student doing exercises on his wax tablet to complement the mental exercises performed on the tablet of his memory. Reciting was part of the reading–writing process from the very beginning. Quintilian recommends that students learn reading, recitation, and writing from material that contains sound moral advice,[118] the sayings (*dicta*) of famous men and lines from the poets. As Marrou says, "A la lecture et à l'écriture est intimement associée la récitation: l'enfant apprend par coeur les petits textes sur lesquels il s'est exercé, à la fois pour se former et meubler sa mémoire."[119] "To form one's character and furnish one's memory" – they were the same goal in educational practice and philosophy from antiquity throughout the Middle Ages (and indeed well into the twentieth century).

Reading required careful preparation, including learning the proper use of punctuation. Marrou mentions traces of such student-originated preparation still observable on papyri (which were written without any sort of punctuation, even word divisions), where strokes have been made, by students not the scribe, to separate the words and lines, and to cut words up into syllables for scansion.[120] *Cola, commata,* and *periodi* served a dual purpose; they marked the sense- and pause-divisions, and they also cut the text into the brief segments that could be memorized as a single unit. Quintilian says that a period should never be too long to be recited or read in a single breath. It also must not be "too long to be retained in the memory" as a single, intelligible unit.[121] A period contains at least two *cola*, Quintilian says, units that are not self-standing but are yet "rhythmically complete," *sensus numeris conclusus.*[122] The use of rhythm to define units of prose is also mnemonically valuable, of course, for rhythm serves the synaesthetic requirements of rich mnemonics. A basic memorial unit is the colon, a short segment of text that is coherent (it is, says Isidore, a *sententia* – "sentence," in Middle English), and is marked by a medial point in many manuscripts.[123]

Notae also included short-hand marks and abbreviations. Systems of such marks, numbering many hundreds, were taught as the *notataria* to ancient and medieval notaries and lawyers; students were taught the complex system of Latin abbreviations that we encounter in medieval manuscripts. Thomas Bradwardine concludes his treatise on artificial memory (completed soon after 1333) by saying that "one who has learned the notary art will attain the highest perfection" in the craft of memory.

John of Salisbury's *Metalogicon*, written some fifty years after Hugh of
St. Victor's *Chronicle* Preface, is particularly interesting for the light it
sheds on what was thought to be the link between memory and *notaria*.
Like Hugh, John of Salisbury characterizes memory as "the mind's treasure-
chest, a sure and reliable place of safe-deposit for perceptions."[124] Memory is
a natural gift, but, like all natural abilities, must be cultivated and trained
(here John echoes both *Ad Herennium* and *De oratore*).

John of Salisbury especially laments the decline of training in *notaria*.
He is discussing punctuation, and evidently thinking of what Isidore called
the *notae sententiarum*, the editorial marks devised in antiquity for textual
scholarship. These little notes, which "indicate the mode of what is written
and show [what] is clear or obscure, certain or doubtful, and so on" were
powerful tools, "highly effective for both comprehension *and retention* [my
italics]." They are to reading and memory what notes are to the chant.

> That such great import has existed in such tiny notations should not seem strange,
> for [musically knowledgeable] singers likewise indicate by a few graphic symbols
> numerous variations in the acuteness and gravity of tones. For which reason such
> characters are appropriately known as "the keys of music." If, however, the little
> notations we spoke of above gave access to such [a powerful key to knowledge],
> I am surprised that our forefathers, who were so learned, were not aware of this, or
> that the keys to so much knowledge were lost.[125]

Two things are being spoken of at once here. First of all, he speaks about
the particular system of editorial *notae* (obelisk, apostrophe, etc.) described
by Isidore of Seville, which John claims is no longer taught, and the secret
of which has been lost. John of Salisbury also recognizes the general
importance of all kinds of *notae* for memory training, for he assumes that
these strange marks, like all the other *notae*, are memory aids, necessary for
both retention and comprehension. And though the knowledge of some
systems of ancient *notae* and memory coding are now obscure, still grammar, including memory, must be studied at least from the books we do
have. For "if all the books of the grammarians are not available, it is still
very helpful, for the interpretation of what we read, to have fixed in our
memory even this fragmentary survey" (the *Metalogicon* itself).[126]

That the *ars notaria* was associated specifically with memory training is
also suggested by a twelfth-century gloss on the *Ad Herennium*, the so-
called "Alanus" gloss, which may be the work of Alan of Lille, although no-
one can say certainly.[127] Commenting on the passage in Book III, in which
Tullius cautions against those Greek works which offer lists of pre-formed
imagines verborum, because they are both inadequate in scope and less
effective for memory than images one makes oneself, the glossator writes

that the author "did not have the notarial art in mind."[128] He clearly knows, as did John of Salisbury, that *notae* are important for memory, and recognizes in his comment that the accumulation of *notae* that one learned in the advanced studies of this art helped to perfect the training of memory.

Indices and chains

Memorial *notae* were commonly used for concording schemes. Of these, the prototype is an alphabetical heuristic, which has left many traces in the organization of written texts. The existing account of it, which describes its use with a degree of detail comparable to what Hugh's Preface tells us about the number grid, is very late (fifteenth-century). Still, what it describes is borne out by the actual design of medieval concordances, *distinctio* collections, and other preachers' tools. And we also have Aristotle's succinct account of an alphabetical memorial system in *De memoria*, Quintilian's reference to key-words to aid recollection, and certain other evidence which we will look at soon. This alphabetical system produces what is essentially a *catena*, in which a key-word or phrase acts as the hook for several bits of stored material, the indexing words themselves being stored alphabetically. The monastic practice so well described by Dom Leclercq, "whereby the verbal echoes [of Scripture] so excite the memory that a mere allusion will spontaneously evoke whole quotations,"[129] is a version of this type of memorial organization.

The description occurs in the testamentary letter by Peter of Ravenna which I cited earlier in this discussion; it prefaces the memory rules which form the body of his book, *Fenix*.[130] As is the custom of such advertisements, the language is self-congratulatory and inflated, but the method itself is credible, and borne out by other evidence. Peter says he has "placed" 20,000 legal extracts, 1,000 texts from Ovid, 200 from Cicero, 300 sayings of the philosophers, the greater part of Valerius Maximus, 7,000 texts from Scripture, and other chunks of his learning on 19 letters of the Roman alphabet. If he searches the letter A, for example, he is able to produce immediately texts and examples from learned sources on a variety of subjects, "de alimentis, de alienatione, de absentia, de arbitris, de appellationibus, et de similibus quae jure nostro habentur incipientibus in dicta littera A," "about provisions, about foreign property, about absence, about judges, about appeals, and about similar matters in our law which begin with the letter A."[131] Or, if a sacred context is wanted, out come texts on Antichrist, on worship (*adulatio*), and other subjects. Or on natural history, texts from Ovid, Valerius, and Cicero can be produced on

A-beginning animals. And when he gets all the way through, he can immediately go back and begin his lists over again. Even allowing for boasting, this is impressive and Peter clearly intended it to be so to his contemporaries.

But as interesting as the quantity of information held is the way it is organized. A letter of the alphabet acts as the primary key or *locus* or file. Then texts are placed in the file by a secondary key, a word beginning with the primary letter. In Peter's scheme, the key-words are themselves arranged also by general topic: natural history, sacred subjects, vices and virtues, etc. And the confirmation of his orderly arrangement lies in his ability to replicate his lists. In other words, the memory in this scheme is organized like a subject index of texts.

Peter of Ravenna says that though he stored his materials alphabetically, he pulled in from his memory both glosses and concordances according to their position with respect to the text. A much earlier instance from which, I think, we can infer that an alphabetically sorted set of glosses is intended to be used in this same way, keyed to words as they occur in their textual order, is Jerome's index and gloss of the Hebrew names in the Bible. This, together with Eusebius's canonical tables, was one of the most familiar of scholars' tools. It was incorporated into a larger alphabetical glossary of the whole Bible from at least the thirteenth century (as part of the "Paris" format). But Jerome's original construction of the index applies the principles of the memorial heuristics I have described.[132] In its written form, Jerome's index is first catalogued by a particular book of the Bible, beginning with Genesis and proceeding in canonical order. The Hebrew words occurring within each book are then grouped alphabetically. But they are not fully alphabetized, that is, not beyond the initial letter. Instead they are given in the order in which they occur in the actual text. So the first word glossed in Genesis, under A, is "Aethiopiae" (1:13), followed by "Assyriorum" (1:14), "Adam" (1:19), "Abel" (4:2), "Ada" (4:19), and so on. The first word under G is "Geon," the name of one of the rivers flowing from Eden in 1:13, followed by "Gomer," a son of Japheth mentioned in 10:2, "Gergesaeus" at 10:16, and the place-names "Gerara," "Gaza," and "Gomorrha," given in the order in which they occur in 10:19.

In a preface, Jerome describes how he came to make this index, and what his intention was. He says he was urged by two of his conventual brothers, who considered him to be notably proficient in Hebrew, to bring together and expand glosses and explanations of Hebrew names in the Old Testament that had been made by Origen and Philo; "and, excited by the usefulness of this suggestion, I reviewed each book according to the order of the Scriptures, renewing the old edifice with new attentiveness."[133] Each book at a time, following the order of the written text, is exactly what the extant index shows. But notice that Jerome considers this scheme to be especially *useful*, particularly user-friendly in contrast to the work of his predecessors. Other sorts of glossaries are known from early periods. For example, the Old Latin glosses of the Gospels, which were copied into the late seventh-century Book of Durrow, represent traditions independent of Jerome but even older. But these glosses in the Book of Durrow are alphabetized out to the second or third letter, not geared to their occurrence in the text as Jerome's are.[134]

The order followed in Jerome's compilation responds to principles of mental concording, and the mnemonic principles which he assumed that its users would also have. Absolute alphabetical ordering is a scheme best adapted to the needs of readers working from a written codex physically open in front of them, the way readers now work. In such a circumstance, it is much easier to find words listed in completely alphabetical order, the way a modern dictionary is, than to find them in a partially or initially alphabetized list.[135] But for someone who is speaking (or preparing to speak) from a text either written in a very large pandect volume of the sort kept at the altar, or mentally held in discretely numbered and memorized *divisiones*, Jerome's system is actually much quicker and easier than a modern list would be, for one discovers the glosses in the order of their occurrences in the text. To find any of the glosses one needed for further exposition, one can simply follow the order of the text itself, as Peter of Ravenna centuries later described himself doing when he lectured from his law books.

That this method, useful only to someone working primarily from memory, continued in use is indicated as well by a small continuous gloss on the whole Bible, including Jerome's prefaces, that is written out, after the fully alphabetized dictionary of Hebrew words, at the very end of a French Bible of *c.* 1325 (Huntington Library MS. HM 1073). It is sometimes supposed that full alphabetization constituted progress so apparent that it inevitably replaced such methods as Jerome's (and is a sure indication of literacy driving out memory), yet in this manuscript of the late Middle Ages both sorts of organization appear, the one for a large amount of encyclopedic material, the other for a much shorter, more selective amount, keyed to long-familiar texts. The individual glosses are very brief (about one colon apiece) and each is marked by a red or blue paraph, colored alternately, and they follow exactly the order of the text from Genesis on. It would be a simple task to slip these glosses into one's memorial places, and bring them out at the proper locations (*loci*) in the text, as Peter of Ravenna did.

All of these schemes bespeak the assumption that a good memory is a library of texts, and a thoroughly catalogued and indexed one at that. And in this intimate relation between memory and page, the memory performs the greater part of indexing and organization. The structure of the various schemes is geared to the requirements of the memory. One might well wonder why Jerome bothered to classify the Hebrew names alphabetically at all; why not just give them in the order in which they appear in each book? If Jerome had composed with the understanding that his index would always be physically open before his readers, as they recited their way all the way through Genesis each time they used his list, he might have done such a thing. But since he expected his list to be used to compose a mental gloss that would be available to someone speaking on a memorized text, he knew practically that such a scheme would not work, for it would overwhelm the active memory. "Memory rejoices in brevity": one consequence of this is that individual items must be grouped and clustered into classifications and sub-classifications in order to provide recollection with the means of finding them surely and quickly. This fundamental psychological principle underlies all indexing systems. As Quintilian says concerning *partitio*, the orderly arrangement of all our propositions, "it follows nature as its guide" and is the greatest of aids to memory.[136]

Another interesting example of a subject concordance is the famous indexed *Tabula*, compiled by the English Franciscans Robert Grosseteste and Adam Marsh, around 1235–1243.[137] The marginal notes Grosseteste habitually made in the books he owned are a striking feature of his work; his library, left to the Franciscan convent at Oxford, was valued for these annotations as well as for the books themselves. As R. W. Hunt has written, "More books containing autograph notes by him have perhaps survived than of any other medieval writer of comparable eminence."[138] Most of these marginalia are subject-headings or corrections to the manuscript. Often they simply identify the source of a quotation in the text. But there are also extensive cross-references; for instance, in a copy of Boethius's *De consolatione philosophiae* Grosseteste added "a dozen references ... to various works of Augustine,"[139] citing, as was the custom, by title and book number, no more. He also added punctuation divisions to this particular Boethius, which had been copied without them.

A typical page of one of his books, known to be annotated in his hand, is reproduced (from Bodleian Library, MS. Bodley 198) as the frontispiece to D. A. Callus's *Robert Grosseteste, Scholar and Bishop*. The writing is a highly abbreviated cursive akin to the *littera inintelligibilis* used by Thomas Aquinas for his dictation draft of a portion of the *Summa contra Gentiles*. Such notation, in similarly abbreviated writing, is sometimes found in other scholars' manuscripts. But Grosseteste's books are also filled with marks (*notae*), each of which is keyed to a particular topic, that serve as a subject index to the book's contents. The key to these *notae* was found by Professor Harrison Thomson, bound with a Bible now in the Municipal Library of Lyons (Lyons MS. 414). Fifteen folios preceding the Bible contain a topical concordance of texts from Scripture and the Fathers, each topic being marked by a sign or *nota*. The first four pages of this concordance give an index of the signs; there are just over 400 of these, and Thomson comments that it would be "no inconsiderable task" just to remember them (though no harder than remembering the thousand-plus signs taught to Roman notaries). "All the letters of the Roman and Greek alphabets, mathematical figures, conjoined conventional signs, modifications of zodiacal signs, and additional dots and strokes and curves are pressed into service. There seems to be no recognizable system behind the choice of a sign for a given subject."[140] This last observation suggests strongly the nature of these *notae* as purely heuristic, deriving from a privately devised scheme for finding discrete bits of information, of exactly the sort commonly advised for memory design.

The concordance of texts itself follows this directory in the Lyons manuscript. Nine major classifications were used, called *distinctiones*, but the copyist has written only "ad dist. vi et parum plus," ". . . and a little more."[141] The main headings are divided into sub-topics, and the *notae* are keyed to these. Professor Hunt has transcribed a typical entry: "[℈] Quomodo philosophia accipienda sit a nobis," "How philosophy may be understood by us."[142] There follow the citations, first those to the Bible, and then, in a separate paragraph, those to the works of the Fathers and more recent theological writings. Citations to pagan authors are given off to the right, in a separate column. Thomson and Hunt both conclude that the purpose of the compilation was to serve as a subject index to Grosseteste's books. Hunt observes that the system continued to be used among the Franciscans in the second half of the thirteenth century, for other books so marked have been found.[143]

But how, for whom, and why was the compilation written out? The possible answers to these questions remain somewhat mysterious. Thomson suggests that Grosseteste used the signs so that as he rapidly thumbed his books he could find appropriate passages on a given subject, without the bother of re-reading. "For an ecclesiastic as busy as Grosseteste was, the gain was considerable, but it entailed an initial reading and indexing that must have demanded extremely close attention."[144] To this observation of Thomson's, we should join the remark of the Franciscan regent-master at Oxford in 1316–1317, William of Alnwick, who, in a disputation, challenged his opponent's reference to one of Grosseteste's marginal notes made in his copy of Aristotle's *Physics*. Alnwick says that Grosseteste wrote in the margins of his books "when some noteworthy thought occurred to him . . . so that it should not escape his memory, just as he also wrote many 'cedulae' which are not all [authoritative]. What he wrote disconnectedly in the margin of his copy of the *Physics* is of no greater authority than the other cedulae he wrote, which are all kept in the library of the Friars Minor at Oxford, as I have seen with my own eyes."[145]

It seems to me most likely that Grosseteste's indexing system was devised by him originally for his own use as a tool both for his own books, and crucially, for his memory. The *notae* are both formed and used according to the familiar pedagogical principles, placed against passages of a text that one particularly wishes to remember, or that are especially important or difficult to recall. Grosseteste is unusual only in having drawn his *notae* so systematically with pen and ink, instead of mentally projecting them as he memorized his passages. Perhaps the fact that these were his own books rather than belonging to a whole community freed him to do this.

But we should be as grateful to Grosseteste's penwork as we are to Hugh of St. Victor's elementary Preface, for it gives us an instance of just how the sort of memorial subject concordance which a medieval student was expected to devise for himself was put together. Given the compositional habits of the time, it is unlikely that Grosseteste expected to thumb constantly through his manuscripts to find material for his voluminous work. We may usefully remember Hugh of St. Victor's admonition: "Too great would be the labor in such a task." Thomson rightly observes that the initial effort to read and index the books was clearly immense; indeed that is so, but it is exactly the sort of concentrated, thoughtful *meditatio* required in medieval study to memorize, ruminate, and make one's reading one's own. At the end of it, Grosseteste had a mental concordance of considerable scope and power; his ability to cross-reference and "quote" (in the medieval sense) his Boethius, to compile his *tabula*, and indeed to compose all those tracts and commentaries and letters, scientific and pastoral works, in addition to his duties both at Oxford (a place with very few books in his day)[146] and as bishop of Lincoln, attests to a memory supremely and securely designed, a remarkable, though by no means rare, realization of the ideal and goal of a medieval education.

Other evidence of the memorial function of the Grosseteste–Marsh tabulation, besides what is obvious from its method of creating *loci* by classification and sub-headings, lies in the fact that each entry follows a design that is almost, but significantly not quite, identical. First come the Biblical citations, in canonical order; then, in a separate group, the Fathers, beginning with the Latin Fathers (in the order Ambrose, Jerome, Augustine, Gregory), the Greek, and finally any recent theologians. Off to the side on the right are the references to pagan writers – Latin, then Greek, then Arabic.

But the individual works of authors such as Augustine (whom Grosseteste cites far more often and variously than anyone else) are not always given in the same order. If the index were being made *de novo*, solely from a physical book, one would expect the compiler to index all the citations to it at the same time, each citation under its appropriate heading in Grosseteste's scheme. This should have the effect of causing citations from a particular work to appear always in the same order relative to other works by that author. But this is not the case. Similarly, were the work being compiled from individual slips marked with a citation (an unlikely possibility), one would expect a constant order among the works cited, especially since all the numbers of the book- or chapter-divisions are given in order (as "Augustinus: ep. 9. 11. 15. 20. 38. 50. 57; De civ. dei li. 10, 11, 12, 13," etc.).[147] Why carefully order the one, but not the other, if one were organizing separate slips of parchment? That the design extends as far as authors, and then skips, as it were, to chapter numbers (the order in which a particular work is recalled), suggests that the citations are given in the order in which Grosseteste had stored them in memory, and not only from a physically manipulated source.[148]

So why was the subject concordance written down (though incompletely)? Presumably to be of use to other scholars, as indeed it proved for a long time to be. Grosseteste's *tabula* amounts to a florilegium without the texts themselves being written out. A note in the manuscript tells us that Adam Marsh extended his master's signs and classifications; indeed, space is left under some entries in the Lyons manuscript, presumably for additional entries. This concern for expansion suggests that Grosseteste's system became public, presumably when his library came to the Oxford Franciscans. The index guides a student with access to this particular library to making his own index by memorizing those passages to which the *notae* lead him.

Another interesting use of alphabetical organization is the second part of Book II of Albertus Magnus's treatise, *Mineralia*.[149] Here the chapter headings state the nature of the organizing principle: "De lapidis pretiosis incipientibus ab A," "Concerning precious stones beginning with A," and so on through Z. This would seem to reflect the way Albertus had organized his material mentally. Especially interesting is the fact that the names are not in absolute alphabetical order under each letter; so under B there are Balagius, Borax, Beryllus; under C, Carbunculus, Chalcedonis, Calcaphanos, Ceraurum, Celidonius, Celontes, Cegolites. Peter of Ravenna's lists also are not absolutely alphabetical; this suggests someone arranging material mentally rather than alphabetizing written-out words with the aid of slips, simply because it is easier mentally to organize material using a few letters at a time than to alphabetize fully a number of long words. The latter is better done when one can manipulate written words physically, as anyone who has had to prepare an index will recognize. His method suggests strongly that Albertus is using a mental alphabetical heuristic, which he has simply transposed to a written document, writing on the page as he had written in memory before.

One alphabetizing principle that seems very odd and useless to us is employed in the index to a late thirteenth-century manuscript of *Sentences* commentary by the Dominican friar Richard Fishacre, who died in 1248 (Oxford, New College MS. 112).[150] The indexing words are arranged not according to initial letter but by their vowel combinations; in other words, by syllables rather than by letters. An explanation of the system is given (fo. 322):

this preceding index is arranged according to the order of the vowels in the alphabet, and according to the manner of their combinations [with consonants]; if you wish therefore promptly to find those things which are contained in the preceding book, take the subject concerning which the passage is made (principally) or should be made, and regard the vowel of its syllable, or of each of its syllables if it should be a two-syllable word; and having recourse to the index you should find the vowel or vowels written in the margin and ordered as previously said. And opposite the word you will find written the folio number, the page number, and even the line number in which you will be able to find what you seek; knowing this also, that "a" designates the first column [of the book opening], "b" the second, "c" the third, and "d" the fourth.

Accordingly, the index begins with monosyllables in "a" ("pax," "laus," "pars"); then bisyllables having "a" in each syllable ("adam"); then "a" plus "e"; "a" plus "i"; "a" plus "o"; "a" plus "u"; and so on through all five vowels singly and in combination. Only the first two syllables of multisyllabic words are considered for indexing purposes. This produces a list in which *locutio* and *pondus* both precede *locus*, *pax* precedes *amor*, and *terra* precedes *spera*, for the initial consonants are not considered in the scheme.

Fishacre's indexer belonged to a culture that still learned to read Latin by recognizing syllables. They were the basic units from which words were thought to be built. Word-recognition and retention was basically a matter of syllable-recognition. Thomas Bradwardine's advice for word-memory is to make an image for each of the five vowels, and then for each possible combination of one consonant plus vowel. Remembering a whole word consists of stringing together the various images one has pre-formed for its syllables. The Fishacre index is based upon a similar understanding of how words are recalled, simplified to a string of no more than two. Why the compiler virtually disregarded the order of the consonants accompanying the vowels is mysterious. Evidently, in his mental arrangements, all the possible "a" syllables were grouped together, as Albertus Magnus grouped things by their initial letter. A scheme that groups by syllables is not inherently less useful as a mental heuristic than one which groups by initial letter. There were nineteen letters in the Roman alphabet, twenty-one if one includes "x" and "z," but these were rarely used as initial consonants. But the Fishacre index allowed forty-five groups altogether, so that there are actually many fewer items within each cell of this grid than there are in initial-letter schemes. It should be noted, however, that no other surviving index uses this heuristic.

A mental library of *dictiones* and a library of physical books used the same heuristics. Having already discussed at length the enduring image of the trained memory as a library, I will conclude this chapter with a brief reflection on their parallel cataloguing systems. The cupboard-like press in which medieval books were kept could be called an *armarium*, "cupboard," or a *columna*, "column," the word used in a library catalogue from 1400.[151] The books in these medieval *arcae* or *armaria* were labeled according to schemes of letters and numbers, sometimes used separately, sometimes in tandem. The sources we have for this information are library catalogues and sometimes the books themselves, mostly from the twelfth century and later. Typically, each book-press was assigned a letter, and each shelf (*gradus*) in it a number, starting from the bottom shelf to allow for expansion.[152] Sometimes another, subsidiary, number was assigned to each volume to indicate its place on its *gradus*. Often also the lettered bookcase carried a legend indicating the subject of the contents therein. Alphabetizing as a heuristic scheme for libraries dates at least to the

Alexandrine Library.[153] The lay-out of the library and the design of the scholars' memories imitate one another. Some of the best evidence for the similarity medieval scholars perceived between what is read and written in memory and in books is the way in which heuristic schemes taught for organizing one's memorial *arcae* were also used, when collections became large enough to need them, to organize the manuscript codices in their wooden *arcae*.

CHAPTER 4

The arts of memory

The mnemonic techniques that I have described so far are basic, their elementary nature attested by their ubiquity. *Divisio* and *compositio* are processes required by the physiology of memory itself, at least as the pre-modern world understood it. But it is important to keep in mind that in considering medieval *memoria* we are dealing with more than just a set of techniques or a descriptive psychology, yet also a more specifically realized value than ghostly ideas (like "the Gothic") which modern students have attached to some philosophy or other, or to a metahistorical *mentalité*. From antiquity, *memoria* was fully institutionalized in education, and like all vital practices it was adapted continuously to circumstances of history. *Memoria* unites written with oral transmission, eye with ear, and helps to account for the highly mixed oral–literate nature of medieval cultures, which many historians of the subject have remarked. Yet it is also clear that the later Middle Ages, from the eleventh century onward, was a far more bookish culture than the earlier medieval centuries had been. *Memoria* was adapted to that change, without – as a set of practices – losing its central place in medieval ethical life. In this chapter I will focus on this change by considering the revival in the thirteenth century of the Herennian architectural mnemonic which I described in Chapter 2.

The medieval history of the particular mnemonic practice expounded in *Rhetorica ad Herennium* and espoused also by Cicero in *De oratore* is briefly summarized. Even by the time of Quintilian (first century AD), the method of projecting images into architectural places and making theatrical scenes of them, though still known, was considered cumbersome and gimmicky. Mnemonic practices continued to be cultivated – Quintilian enumerates a number of them in Book XI of *Institutio oratoria* – but the elaborate image-games and exercises to strengthen *memoria verborum* are not repeated there. Instead, Quintilian stresses mnemonics for the disposition of one's subject matters when speaking *ex tempore*, and using rebuses and puns to recall unfamiliar words or especially important items. This practical attitude persists in the rhetorical teaching on memory of the fourth and fifth centuries. Indeed there is little evidence of anyone, ancient or medieval, systematically teaching the *Rhetorica ad Herennium* before the end of the eleventh century. However, in considering the medieval understanding of rhetorical craft, including *memoria*, a historian must clearly distinguish between those methods described and used in actual practice, and what is described in and disseminated solely through the two ancient rhetoric textbooks known in the Middle Ages as the "vetus rhetorica" (Cicero's early work *De inventione*) and the "rhetorica nova" (the *Rhetorica ad Herennium*). The medieval titles refer not to the actual order of composition of these works (for in fact their compositional order is the reverse, though they were made close in time to one another) but to the order in which they were incorporated into the medieval curriculum of rhetoric, for the *Rhetorica ad Herennium* was not much taught at Bologna, Oxford, or Paris before the thirteenth century. Its first widely used commentary, and thus the first evidence of its entering a broadly influential curriculum, is the Parisian "Alanus" commentary of the late twelfth century. Bolognese masters of the first part of the thirteenth century, such as Boncompagno da Signa, report it as little taught, though Boncompagno had clearly read it, for he parodies its medieval title in his own work of 1235, *Rhetorica novissima*. Herennian *memoria* plays no direct role in the development of medieval memory craft before the thirteenth century, and when it was revived in university teaching after 1250, it was within the context of an extraordinarily rich, diverse understanding of *memoria*, which had developed in monastic traditions of ruminative meditation and the composition of prayer. Monastic *memoria* is more like what is now called "mindfulness" than what many psychologists deem to be memory, a discipline of attentive recollection and concentrated reading of texts in the Bible (*lectio divina*), which took place during the daily office and in private meditation, and formed the core of monastic life. But it should not simply be translated as "mindfulness" because the activity of *lectio divina* assumed a searchable inventory of remembered materials far richer than any student might be expected to acquire today. These practices are analyzed historically and aesthetically in my study of *The Craft of Thought*, and additionally demonstrated in the twelfth-century works brought together in *The Medieval Craft of Memory*. When the Herennian architectural mnemonic described by Frances Yates and others was revived in the late medieval universities, it was within these well-established monastic practices. One cannot separate it out from them without seriously distorting late medieval and early modern method and understanding.[1] Whether they acknowledged their debt or not (and, being "modern," most did not), the Renaissance writers on the art of memory wrote still from within a profoundly medieval context.[2]

In the late thirteenth century the architectural method enjoyed a revival, having been commended as the best method by both Albertus Magnus and Thomas Aquinas.[3] The revival of Tullius' art of memory occurred in the context of the classicizing fervor of the early humanists, among whom, for the purposes of this history, we must include the friars chiefly responsible for the Aristotelian renaissance that brought back into scholarly circulation his *De anima* and its appendices, the *Parva naturalia* including *De memoria et reminiscentia*. Aristotle gave a philosophical explanation for and authoritative vindication of using arbitrary associations as a basic mnemonic tool. Both Thomas's and Albertus's commentaries on *De memoria* use the memory advice of the *Ad Herennium* as their prime example of the application of Aristotle's general precepts concerning the associative nature of recollective searching. In addition to the Aristotelians, the self-described Ciceronians of early humanist Italy played an important role in the revival of the Herennian mnemonic; indeed, some evidence points to the circle around Brunetto Latini as one agency of this revival. And it is the identification of the Herennian mnemonic scheme with humanism that led to its dominance in the memory texts of the Renaissance, many of which emanate from a milieu that is Italian and also Dominican. To that story, however, I will return after examining more particularly medieval schemes.[4]

JOHN OF GARLAND (C. 1230) AND THE BESTIARY

The sources of the specific medievalness of the arts of memory I will discuss now are not attributable to handbooks and manuals, such as some (unknown) non-Ciceronian body of rhetorical precepts. They are related instead to manuscript painting conventions, the Bestiary, and various conventions of pictorial diagrams. In the early Middle Ages, *memoria* is discussed not in the context of how best to teach rhetoric, but rather in writings on meditation and prayer, in which a diagram-like picture (*pictura*) is created mentally, which serves as the site for a meditational *collatio*, the gathering into one place of the various strands of a meditated composition. A particularly illuminating and complex example utilizing the principles of medieval memorial picturing is Hugh of St. Victor's treatise "On constructing Noah's ark," which I will discuss at length in Chapter 7.[5]

That text is not, however, an art of memory produced within the universities, the subject of the present chapter. In particular I will examine three academic texts which defined "arts of memory," written by John of Garland, Albertus Magnus, and Thomas Bradwardine. They all incorporate a medieval understanding of the precepts of *memoria* that has wrought a thorough sea-change upon the Herennian mnemonic. I have chosen to discuss them out of chronological order because neither Bradwardine nor John of Garland show any close affinity to the *Ad Herennium*, but Albertus does – therefore, John of Garland and Bradwardine are good examples of medieval mnemotechnical principles, not derived directly from the classical text of Tullius. Albertus wrote about one generation after John of Garland did, and Bradwardine some ninety years after Albertus.

It is often the confused student who can teach us the most about unstated general assumptions. One revealing account of memory training from the early thirteenth century is the garbled adaptation of the *Ad Herennium* on memory, found in John of Garland's *Parisiana poetria*. John acquired his education in Paris, and taught there as well, except for a brief sojourn at Toulouse. He wrote in the 1230s, by which time the Aristotelian winds of the university were starting to blow upon the *Ad Herennium* but had not yet shaped it into respectability. In his treatise, John recommends as most necessary for poets organizing their material in invention (composition) the "ars memorandi secundum Tullium," "the art of remembering according to Tullius." But it is evident from what he says that John of Garland had little of a historian's concern for what the first-century BCE Tullius was about. His confusion is instructive, however, for it is that of a man educated in a different memory keying system, trying to relate the strange terms of *Ad Herennium* to those with which he is familiar.

What he was familiar with was the system of keying mnemonically on *locus, tempus, et numerus*, as we found those terms used by Hugh of St. Victor – page design, memory occasion, and an ordering system that places items to be remembered in a grid design.[6] To this basic knowledge, acquired as part of his own early grammatical training, John of Garland tries to add the learned rules of the Herennian mnemonic. The discussion occurs in Book II, devoted to what John calls selection of readings – literally, their binding-together (*alligare lecta*), John's psychologically suggestive term for invention. Having discussed what sorts of material to select and the various tropes and figures (mostly drawn from Geoffrey of Vinsauf's *Documentum*), all in terms of a vaguely defined notion of stylistic levels, John proceeds to the art of remembering. The discussion is brief and wholly geared to comprehending what John thinks is being said in

Ad Herennium. After his discussion of *memoria*, John of Garland proceeds immediately to give examples of well-composed letters, the subject matter of *ars dictaminis*, the "art of the dictamen" (whose intimate basis in the arts of *memoria* I will discuss in Chapter 6). *Ars dictaminis*, and the related *ars notataria* or *notaria*, the "art of notation" or short-hand, in which the system of Latin abbreviations was taught to students of law and theology, are both closely associated with discussions of *memoria*, as these begin to reappear in handbooks of rhetoric in the later Middle Ages.[7] John of Garland's placement of his discussion in the *Parisiana poetria* underscores one of his basic assumptions, namely that selecting and gathering material one has read is the heart of successful composition, and that this can occur only because one has a trained memory.

John of Garland says that the art of remembering is essential for selecting ("electio") and organizing material. So, as Tullius says, we should place ("disponere") in our minds an open space ("area"), in a place neither too bright nor too gloomy, because these qualities are harmful to retaining and selection. The area should be thought of as divided into three principal parts and columns ("per tres partes principales et columpnas"). In the first column, subdivided in three, we place "courtiers, city dwellers, and peasants," together with their particular concerns, duties, and the things pertaining to them. If one's teacher (of rhetoric, in this instance) should say something in class having to do with these three levels of audience, we place it in the appropriate section of the first column. In the second column we mentally mark off ("intelligi distingui") our source texts, "exempla et dicta et facta [deeds] autentica,"[8] including the source of each, which we have read in a book or hear in class. To aid in recalling a particular text, we should also mentally note the circumstances under which we first heard it, "the place in which, the teacher from whom, his dress, his gestures," or the page upon which we read it, whether it was light or dark (referring to the hair- or skin-side of the parchment), "the position on the page and the color of the letters." This advice is noticeably similar to that given 100 years earlier in Hugh of St. Victor's *Chronicle* Preface (see Appendix C).

Finally, in the third column we should imagine written out the sounds of all sorts of languages and the characteristics of animals ("omnia genera linguarum sonorum et vocem diuersorum animancium") and etymologies, interpretations, and summary definitions ("ethimologias, interpretationes, differentias").[9] These should be in alphabetical order ("secundum ordinem alphabeti"). So when the teacher makes an etymological explanation or we hear a word in a language we do not know, we put it in this column, together with something that marks it. Word and sign together we gather ("collocemus") in the third column. Whenever we hear an unfamiliar word, we relate it by sound to one we know and so, associating one with the other, store the unfamiliar safely in our memory. The eagle and summary *distinctio* shown in figure 4 would seem to derive from such memory advice as this, though John wrote in Paris and the eagle summary–picture was drawn in Bologna a decade later, suggesting that John's mnemonics were not unique.[10]

While it is clear that John did not fully understand the *Ad Herennium*, he did understand the system he learned himself. And so the *Ad Herennium*'s rule of using *intercolumnia* for backgrounds is understood as the columnar design of a manuscript page, rather like the design Hugh devised for his pupils to help them memorize those seventy folio pages of the most important data for their study of Scripture. There are more examples of medieval "misreadings" in this text. The *Ad Herennium* advises using architectural locations with few people in them, meaning "open" in that sense, but John freely adapts this rule to his students' circumstances. The open *area* is like a vacant page to be written upon in columnar format, with subdivisions upon it for the various categories of subject. And on this vacant page we write in three columns the material we learn: first, what is relevant to decorum and style; second, all the authoritative texts we read or hear, which we write down as though they actually were on a page, marked and colored, each with its source and each also with whatever associative details of *locus* or *tempus* (in Hugh of St. Victor's sense) help us to recall them. The making of John's second column itself requires all the mnemonic utilities that Hugh of St. Victor counsels by way of dividing, marking, and gathering authorities.

The third column is of particular interest. It is ordered alphabetically in the memory, as *distinctio* collections and concordances were on the page. To help us remember hard words and words in languages we do not know (such as Hebrew and Greek) and the etymologies, interpretations, and *distinctiones* requiring such material, we should associate words we do not know with those we do. Although there is irreduceable imprecision in John of Garland's language here, I think informed guesswork will help us through some of the murk. The two chief memory aids (*notulae* of a sort) which John mentions are "omnia genera linguarum sonorum et vocem diuersorum animancium," or "all kinds of sounds of languages and the *voces animatium* of diverse animals."[11] Using the "sounds of languages," coincidental homophonies between sounds in a known tongue and the sound of unknown words, is a simple and effective mnemonic (by *omnia genera* John means to include vernaculars as well as Latin). Robert of

Basevorn's advice to use the syllables of the chant or the five vowels to recall texts in a sermon division is a slight variation of what John counsels here. And we recall that Luria's subject, Shereshevski, recalled the words of Dante's unknown Italian by associating their sound with words familiar to him in Russian.

The *voces animantium* is a list of the habits and physical features thought to characterize the animals and birds; it was disseminated both as a simple listing (the form it takes in such sources as Isidore) and, in an expanded semi-narrative form, as the Bestiary, versions of which were a standard element in Western education from at least Alexandrine Greece.[12] Scholars have not entertained the possibility of a mnemonic function for the Bestiary, but what John of Garland says concerning the usefulness of *voces animantium* to help mark material is very suggestive, especially taken in conjunction with other evidence. As we will shortly see, Thomas Bradwardine also uses mental pictures drawn from the Bestiary and from the traditional depictions of the Zodiac signs for mnemotechnical purposes.

The Bestiary was thought of as a beginner's book, an entertaining way of retaining moral precepts. This does not exclude it from being of use to learned readers too, but its primary audience was student novices and the monks who taught them. Despite its pictorial and pleasurable content, it was found commonly in monastery libraries, even those of the Cistercian reform. This fact is particularly significant, for the Cistercians frowned on idle image-making, and are responsible for an unadorned style both of architecture and of manuscript painting. In such an apparently hostile environment, only some over-riding perception of its utility could account for the Bestiary's continuing presence and dissemination among these monks.[13]

A book from the English Cistercian library of St. Mary's, Holmecultram, makes a particularly interesting study from the standpoint of mnemonic technique. It is an early copy of an Anglo-Norman version of the Bestiary, composed about 1130 by Philippe de Thaon for Adeliza of Louvain, Henry I's second queen. The manuscript is in the British Library now, MS. Cotton Nero A. v, and the first eighty-two folios of it are the original, twelfth-century book from Holmecultram. The Bestiary is preceeded by a mnemonic rhyming poem on the dating of Easter, and by several doggerel stanzas, also in Anglo-Norman, describing the traditional images of the Zodiac and the Calendar. The fact that this book is in Anglo-Norman indicates that it was for students who were beginning their studies and not for the adult scholars, who would have known Latin (it is the only Anglo-Norman book in Holmecultram's library).

Philippe de Thaon's Bestiary is presented as a memory-book. In each of its pictures of the animals, the verses admonish the reader to remember particular pieces of the description as well as the whole: "Aiez en remembrance . ceo est signefiance," "Hold in memory . this is important." The Bestiary is described by its author as a "gramaire," or elementary book, derived from "Physiologus" (supposed to have been the original author of the Bestiary) and Isidore of Seville, whose *Etymologiae* contained a listing of the *voces animantium*. Thus the contents of this book were understood to be among the essentials of a medieval education, for, together with the grid-layout described by Hugh of St. Victor, the Bestiary and Calendar/Zodiac images were also elementary mnemotechnical tools, the students acquiring a repertory of images along with their store of basic texts and chants.[14]

But how were they used? Here John of Garland supplies an important clue. The Bestiary descriptions are laid away so that one can use them later to mark material for recollection. They do not themselves supply an orderly memory grid, nor (probably) were the Zodiac signs used for a grid. Instead, one uses the rigid order of numbers and/or alphabet to lay out one's basic grid, but then one might use such vivid images to further mark the material for immediate, secure recollection. What the Bestiary taught most usefully in the long term of a medieval education was not natural history or moralized animal fables but mental imaging, the systematic forming of "pictures" that would stick in the memory and could be used, like rebuses, homophonies, *imagines rerum*, and other sorts of *notae*, to mark information *within* the grid.

It is important that the Holmecultram Bestiary is not illustrated. Its pictures are entirely verbal, they are not drawn on the page. This forced the students to make the pictures carefully in their minds, to paint mentally, thus learning one of the most critical of inventive techniques. (As we will see in Chapter 7, decoration of one's mental book remained basic in mnemotechnique, even after pictorially graphic images became a much commoner feature of medieval books, including Bestiaries.)

John of Garland counsels that the *voces animantium* are to be laid alphabetically on one's memory-page. We may recall, from Chapter 3, how Peter of Ravenna says that he had alphabetized lists of all sorts of material stored in his memory places, which he used to mark the thousands of textual segments he had collected. Visual alphabets, in which the letters are given the shapes of animals, birds, or tools, are very common, as Frances Yates observed, in fifteenth-century treatises on memory, but derive "almost certainly . . . of an old tradition."[15] Often, the name of the animal or bird also begins with the letter it is made to represent.

Some elaborate drawings are found in Host von Romberch's *Congestorium*,[16] the product of a late fifteenth-century German Dominican, whose "congestion" of lore (and it certainly is that) concerning memorial heuristics seems to conserve the traditions of his order. Romberch's schemes incorporate what is in the *Ad Herennium*, but add to it an enormous amount of advice on how to fashion complex grid systems based both on alphabetical and on numerical orders. Several of the alphabetical ones involve animal images; in one case, the letters are associated with animals whose names begin with those letters, so that for A one might think of an eagle (*aquila*), for B an owl (*bubo*), for N a bat (*noctycorax*), etc. Peter of Ravenna, we recall, could pull forth a string of beasts beginning with A or B or whatever letter of the alphabet. In another case, Romberch suggests using animals or various implements whose figures are bent into the shapes of the various letters. The printed text (1533) offers several pages of these, a number of which look very like the twisted shapes of birds and other beasts used to decorate initials in manuscripts from the early Middle Ages on. Romberch evidently sought to preserve the mnemonic efficacy of such manuscript decoration, attested to by Hugh of St. Victor. But instead of seeing these drawn on a page, one used them mnemonically to mark a text or *distinctio* (which is basically an ethical commonplace, a set of texts remembered *ad verbum* or *ad res*, which together define a moral topic).[17]

A remarkably fierce animal suddenly looms into a Biblical *interpretatio* by the Dominican scholar, Hugh of St. Cher (d. 1263), which may help to shed light on how the *voces animantium* could be used for organizing material in the memory. It occurs in his comment on the phrase *in medio umbrae mortis*, Ps. 22:4.[18] "Et nota," he says in a phrase which, I have already suggested, is both an invitation to remember (in reading) and a trigger for recollection (in composing), "quod inter omnes peccatores, detractores proprie dicuntur umbrae mortis," "among all sinners detractors are most fittingly called of the shadow of death." For death indeed spares no-one but carries off everyone equally; likewise detractors detract from everything. Wherefore, a detractor is signified by a bear (*ursus*). A bear has a great big voracious mouth, just like a backbiter or detractor. And it has three rows of teeth, which Hugh of St. Cher proceeds to moralize in terms of a backbiter's nasty characteristics.

Where did the bear come from? Judson Allen, who carefully studied this matter, says that Hugh's comment is found in no other Psalter gloss; it is his own. Hugh of St. Cher cites the most famous bear in Scripture, the one with all the teeth in Daniel's dream (Dan. 7:5). This text supplies the details of the image: "tres ordines erant in ore ejus, et in dentibus ejus," "there were three rows in the mouth thereof, and in the teeth thereof" (Douay translation; the King James Version differs markedly from the Vulgate).

The bear has a wide, devouring mouth, as does death, as do backbiters –such connections are clear in the Daniel text, for the bear is commanded to "Arise, devour much flesh." And the connection of death with biting is clear and traditional, made by means of the homophony of Latin *mors*, "death," and *morsus*, "bite." Furthermore, though Latin *dectractor* has no homophonic or etymological connection to *mors* or *morsus*, the late Latin participle *mordentem*, from *mordere* "to bite" and, by a metaphorical extension, "to make a caustic comment," clearly connects to "detractors" in meaning, and to "death," "biting," and "teeth" in sound. The Old French word, *mordant*, "bitter speaking," would have been familiar to Hugh, for he was French; he may well also have known the word *backbiter* from English students at Paris. Such a mnemonically useful tissue of homophonies accords with John of Garland's advice regarding the use of the sounds of all kinds of languages to help fix etymologies and interpretations in the memory. But none of these words requires a bear.

I suspect that the reason why a bear entered Hugh of St. Cher's compositional memory is because the word *ursus*, like *umbra*, starts with a U. *Ursus*, together with its *voces* – the most vivid of which is its big mouth, according to Isidore, who derives *ursus* from *os*, "mouth" – and texts relevant to it, such as this obvious one from Daniel, would be stored in Hugh's memory under "U," helping to mark etymologies, distinctions, and interpretations of words and texts which also start with "U." And so, when composing his *distinctio* on *umbra*, his U-animal comes to mind, and it has characteristics (*voces*) which, happily, can this time be pressed into service of the point he wishes to make. In other words, what first led Hugh to a bear was not some hermeneutical or iconographic correlation, but the simple fact that *ursus* and *umbra* have the same initial letter. The word *ursus* was thought to originate in *os*, *oris*, hence "teeth," and a link to the happy homophony of *mors* and *morsus*. So the bear's appearance in the written text is a vestige of Hugh's mental organizational scheme. That it also serves his interpretation is, of course, why that connection is preserved in the final composition.

John of Garland's memory advice confirms certain features as standard in medieval mnemotechnique. In particular, treating the memory as though it were an area divided linearly into columns within a grid seems distinctly medieval. Hugh of St. Victor describes the elements differently, but he too says to treat memory as a *linea*, a line of cells in a numerically addressed grid. The earliest source of such a lay-out is unclear, but linearly formatted diagram pages, such as Eusebius's Canon Tables, were widely known and used from earliest times.[19] The development of tabular lay-outs and the advice to use them mnemonically went hand in hand, since there is a clear, persistent theme in all medieval mnemonic advice: to take advantage of the presentation of the physical page as a fixative for memory.

THOMAS BRADWARDINE, *ON ACQUIRING A TRAINED MEMORY* (C. 1335)

John of Garland's presentation of *memoria* in his *Parisiana poetria* is too informal to be a complete art of memory. A proper art requires general principles and a system which one can apply to a variety of circumstances, and these are not features of John of Garland's mnemonic advice. But a medieval treatise on memory that does meet the criteria for being an art, yet owes as little to Ciceronian sources as does the advice of John of Garland, is the *ars memorativa* attributed to Thomas Bradwardine, mathematician and theologian at Merton College from 1325 to 1335. Subsequently, he was chancellor of St. Paul's and prebend of Lincoln, then a chaplain to Edward III, and finally he died of the plague in August, 1349, a month after his consecration as archbishop of Canterbury. Bradwardine is best known for his participation on the orthodox side in the debate regarding the roles of predestination, grace, and free will, through his theological tract, *De causa Dei*, "the case for God." His other work is mathematical in nature – a tractatus on proportions, one on the problem of squaring a circle, a speculative arithmetic, and a speculative geometry. And then there is the tract we are concerned with here, *De memoria artificiali adquirenda*.

This treatise belongs to Bradwardine's Merton years.[20] It is of considerable interest that it was not composed by a professional teacher of rhetoric, like John of Garland, nor for elementary-level students, but by a theologian and professor of natural philosophy lecturing for university students. The work exists in three manuscripts: British Library MS. Sloane 3744, British Library MS. Harley 4166, and Fitzwilliam Museum (Cambridge) MS. McClean 169. All are English in origin, of the late fourteenth century and the first part of the fifteenth, the work itself being datable to 1333–1335. The McClean version is part of a book, the work of a single scribe, containing other scientific material, astrological, herbal, alchemical, and mathematical in nature. The Sloane manuscript version in contrast is a digest of Bradwardine's advice; it was written in a single pamphlet, together with a treatise on heraldry. It is also incomplete, missing the discussion of memory for syllables and memory for words, and containing a different, abbreviated conclusion. The McClean manuscript contains a version that is nearly three times the length of that in Sloane 3744. The text in Harley 4166 contains about two-thirds of the material in McClean, with which its readings agree closely. Harley 4166 is a book made up of a number of isolated fragments bound together; because of this it is no longer possible to tell how the original manuscript was copied, and it appears to have been unbound for a long time.[21]

Bradwardine's treatise is interesting on two grounds. First, it codifies mnemonic advice of the sort that exists piecemeal in a few sentences in other medieval documents, and secondly, though some of its precepts resemble ones in the classical architectural mnemonic, Bradwardine obviously draws on a different tradition. His *ars memorativa* has been treated by some modern scholars as though it were in the *Ad Herennium* tradition, but it is not.[22] It articulates a completely medieval art of images in places, which owes very little directly to the *Ad Herennium* and is not associated by Bradwardine with any ancient authority. The incidental similarities between Bradwardine's rules and those of "Tullius" are explained by two factors, one being certain enduring requirements of human recollection (such as having a rigid, easily reconstructable order to the backgrounds; making visually remarkable and emotionally laden associations through images; and the rule of Seven Plus-or-Minus Two), and the other being a few continuous pedagogical traditions. For, as in the case of the advice given by Hugh of St. Victor, there is no reason to believe that Bradwardine created a wholly new art of memory. At most, he was drawing together in a single handbook advice that had been practically, if not so systematically, available for centuries. And, as we will see, these same conventions are to be found not in a textual tradition but in manuscript painting traditions from the early Middle Ages. This suggests to me that the mnemonic role of book decoration was consciously assumed from the beginnings of the book in the West; we have seen other evidence of this close link in the specialized vocabulary of memory techniques as well.

It is in a few generalities rather than specifics that Bradwardine's system resembles that described in the *Ad Herennium*, written 1,500 years earlier. Bradwardine distinguishes many of the basic terms of memorial art: memory for subject matters and memory for words, natural and artificial memory, the archetypal metaphor of memory as a surface onto which letters are written, and the very idea of places and images. But both the manner and specifics of his presentation are quite different from what is in *Ad Herennium*. He begins by describing six general properties of places or locations (*loci*): the size, shape, and characteristic features of a single location, and the number, order, and distance away that characterize a set of such background locations.

A *locus* should be of a size neither greater nor smaller than what the eye can take in at a single glance – a small garden or a cloister are ideal in their extent. In shape it should be rectangular, like a page or a tablet. This is a striking and significant difference between Bradwardine's rules for the *loci* and those of the Herennian mnemonic. It clearly is related to both John of Garland's and Hugh of St. Victor's use of the word *locus* to refer to the presentation on the page of the textual matter to be remembered. The *locus* should be a lighted, completely open space, with no distracting detail of its own. It must be neither too dark nor too glaringly illuminated. One should not imagine a crowded location, such as a church or marketplace. One should use real places, which can be visited and re-inspected frequently, in preference to wholly imaginary ones, which are trickier and would require greater mastery to keep clearly and unchangingly in mind.

The places in their ordered sets should contrast with one another in color as well as content. Bradwardine describes making a first set of five locations on the theme of a field: the first might be a waste field, the second a green garden, the third the same field at harvest, the fourth the field after harvest when only the stubble remains, and the fifth the field blackened by burnt stubble. (It is of some interest, I think, that Bradwardine uses the common motif of the seasonal changes as a set of memorative locations.) One multiplies one's available locations in such sets of five, Bradwardine counsels, working upward from ground-level to the upper storeys, as though of a building. After the set of fields, he describes a set of flat raised locations: a large couch, an armoire, a table, a tomb, an altar. Then come roofs (wood shingles, thatch, slate, tile, and lead) and terraces (floored with earth, greenstone, tiles, straw, or carpeting). By multiplying sets of five in this manner, one never has to think of more than five closely related locations at any one time, but one can also extend the multiplying process as much as one chooses, though Bradwardine suggests that no more than ten related sets be constructed at one time, lest the fabrication become too unwieldy.

For one must be able to keep track exactly of each location in relation to the others in its own and related sets. So the places must have contiguity (or "neighborliness," to use Aristotle's word) and direction – as the order of numbers and alphabets have both of these basic features. Without such a rigid schematic order, one cannot find places easily, nor can one move about or gather them together. I have stressed before the shuffling requirement which a memory system must address – Bradwardine's method of multiplying sets in fives does this. These locations are the mental bins of one's inventory, each of similar size, shape, and illumination, and each of a monochromatic color but the colors contrasting with those of the other locations in its set (the carpeted flooring of the fifth member of Bradwardine's fourth set suggests that a simple pattern within the monochrome was tolerable). One relates these to one another basically in the manner in which people construct a grid or matrix, as sets of empty boxes, built one on top of the other, and addressed individually by means of a pair of coordinates that places them within the matrix.

One final feature of the locations concerns what Bradwardine calls *distancia* and *distancia intercepta*. By this term he seems to mean what we call perspective, both with respect to the position of the observer and with respect to the distance depicted *in* the location itself, foreground and background. The observation point is frontal, and far enough away from the scene that everything in it can be seen clearly, fully, and at once. There is no suggestion here, as there is in the *Ad Herennium*, that the mental eye's perspective will change as one imagines a walk through it – in the Bradwardinian account, the eye is positioned optimally, so that one takes in the whole location at one glance. Additionally, within the location, whatever detail (a hill, perhaps, or a tree or a couch) is needed to set the image is depicted, but no *distant* background is shown, for this might distract from the clarity of the mnemonically important image. Thus, a mnemonic scene in its background may have some shallow suggestions of setting, but no deep perspective. Bradwardine says that the "distance" in the location should be void – a single color or a simple design. Both of these perspectival conditions are common in early medieval painting. Indeed the picture-page of the sixth-century Gospels of St. Augustine (figure 29) provides an excellent illustration of such a locational arrangement, frontal perspective, and emptiness of distance. One finds such features still in late medieval painted scenes.

Into the cell-like arrangement of locations in tiers, one places the *imagines*. Bradwardine gives several general rules for the construction of memorial images for content (*res*) and images for words. This organizational feature of his treatise is another significant difference from the *Ad Herennium*, for it clarifies the fact that as images, those employed for various mnemonic functions do not differ significantly in their characteristics. Memorative images should be of moderate size, but that is their only moderate feature. Because the memory retains distinctly only what is extraordinary, wonderful, and intensely charged with emotion, the images should be of extremes – of ugliness or beauty, ridicule or nobility, of laughter or weeping, of worthiness or salaciousness. Bloody figures, or monstrosities, or figures brilliantly but abnormally colored should be used, and they should be engaged in activity of a sort that is extremely vigorous.

These figures are to be grouped against the plain background in an active scene, their relative positions acting as cues to the order of the material with which they are associated. So, the image for the first matter to be recalled is placed towards the front of the location, its torso occupying the center. Then the second image is placed on its right hand, and it is helpful if the central image has limbs or some means of attaching the other images to itself physically. The third and fourth images (if they are needed) are attached serially to the right of the second. A fifth image is attached to the left side of the central image, with the following ones joined serially to it. To read this composite, one begins in the center, then looks right as far as one can, and then returns to the center and looks left. The figures are joined to one another in an active, even violent, manner. The first image is to strike or hold the second with its right hand, the third to ride around the second, and so on, so that these vigorous activities "will be, as it were, a fastening together of their order in the series." One can have three or five or seven images in a single group but not many more, because one tends to lose track over seven. And within each image the order of precedence is rigid: central front, then right, then left, and foreground over background figures. It is clear from Bradwardine's description of these groupings that the locations have some depth to them; the figures do not occupy just a flat plane, but are impressed memorially in the manner of a carved relief.

Bradwardine's chief example for grouping images in locations is the twelve signs of the Zodiac. It is an odd group for him to pick in a sense, because these signs are examples neither of memory for content nor of memory for words; it is tempting to find a reason in the persistent use of memorial systems based on the signs of the Calendar.[23] If this were the case, the twelve signs themselves would be intended only as markers for yet other material. Bradwardine does not in fact use them here for anything other than as examples to illustrate the basic principles he has already given for the characteristics and arrangements of images in a location. He could, most likely, expect all his students to be familiar with them already, not as concepts (they are hardly that) but as images of the purely fictive, associational kind that is basic for memorative discovery.

He groups the twelve images in two mental locations. Aries, the ram, is figured in the center of the first location, with the second sign, Taurus, to its right. In front of Taurus is Gemini, the Twins, born either from a woman or from the Bull (in order to avoid having an extraneous image). One of the twins plays with a Crab. To the left of Aries is Leo, who attacks Virgo. Virgo holds Libra in her right hand, while with her left she tries to balance Scorpio in the scales. These eight images, whose order and linkage in the scene cues their actual order, in the manner which Bradwardine earlier defined, are all in the first location. The remaining four form a scene in a second location: Sagittarius is placed in the center, shooting arrows at Capricorn, who holds Aquarius in his right foot and Pisces in his left, while pouring forth water for the fish from the water-vessel. The images are brilliantly colored, especially with red, white, and gold, and every color is described as the superlative of its type in hue and intensity.

But what is most surprising, to our more priggish sensibilities and expectations, is the emphasis on violence and sexuality which runs through all the interaction of the figures in each scene. A super-white ram is kicked by a super-red bull with super-swollen testicles (so one will be sure one isn't looking at a cow or a heifer), which the ram in turn kicks so hard that blood flows copiously. To its left, the ram is also kicking a rampant lion in the head, causing another wound. The lion is attacking a beautiful maiden, whose whole left arm is dreadfully swollen from the wound inflicted by a scorpion, which she is trying to balance in her scales. The twins are ripped from the womb of a woman whose parturitional wound extends to her breast. Or they are being born grotesquely from the bull. The twins are most beautiful, but one is being pinched dreadfully by a horrible crab, and is weeping while trying to free his hand, while his twin caresses the monster "in a childish way." The images of the second location are less violent but no less grotesque, as a rampant goat, shot with arrows by a bowman (and so bleeding profusely), carries a water-jug in one front foot and fish in the other, for which it pours out water from the jug. And the whole account concludes, matter-of-factly, with Bradwardine's comment that, having constructed such scenes, one can recite their contents in whatever order one wants, forward or backward.

Not all of Bradwardine's images are violent, though all are vigorously extreme, in conformity with a basic principle for memory-images – namely, that what is unusual is more memorable than what is routine. One remembers abstract concepts by a concrete image: sweetness by an image of someone happily eating sugar or honey, bitterness by an image of someone foully vomiting. Wholly abstract ideas like God, angels, or the Trinity can be attached to an image "as painters make it" or, later in the treatise, "as it is usually painted in churches." This is more direct evidence that every sort of image, whatever its source or placement, was considered to have some memorial utility. But we will consider this matter further in a later chapter.

Images are used for memorizing *verbaliter* or *sententialiter*. In accord with elementary pedagogical practices, Bradwardine's method for remembering words verbatim is to analyze them as chains of syllables, marking each syllable with an image. He discusses memory for words as both *memoria sillabarum* ("memory-by-syllables") and *memoria oracionis* (by which Bradwardine does not mean "oration" but the quotation from the Bible which forms the basis for a sermon); the one is basically an extension of the other. First one analyzes the whole number of possible syllables, for each of which one finds an image of something whose name begins with that same syllable. These syllable-hooks can come either from Latin or from vernaculars, including dialects.

As an example, Bradwardine takes the sentence (alluding to the English victory over the Scots in the second battle of Berwick in July, 1333): "Benedictus Dominus qui per rege Anglie Berewicum fortissimum et totam Scotiam subjugavit," "Blessed be God who through the English king subjugated mightiest Berwick and all of Scotland." To remember the first phrase of this sentence, he says, one might make a scene composed of a Benedictine monk ("Benedictus") in the center, with a Dominican friar to his right ("Dominus"); the monk holds out his left hand to a cow ("qui," a bilingual pun), as though he was dancing with her, for the cow is imagined upright on her hind feet, displaying very large, red teats. In turn, the cow holds a partridge ("perdix," for *per*) in her left front foot. The scene in the second location comprises a king ("rex"), holding an eel in one hand ("anglia") and a mighty bear ("Bere-wic") in the other. For the last phrase of the sentence, one might construct a scene of someone named Thomas ("totam"), who is with one hand subduing a Scot ("Scotiam"), and with the other holds a marvellous yoke ("sub-*juga*-vit"). These scenes are startling and very funny, in the grotesquely humorous manner of fourteenth-century English paintings in the margins of the religious books with which Bradwardine was likely familiar.[24]

Many of the puns in Bradwardine's examples are bilingual, depending on homophonies from Latin, English, and English dialect words. For instance, the Latin syllable *qui* sounded to him like the northern dialect pronunciation of English "cow," which was [ki]. Actually northern [ki], spelled 'cy' or 'ci,' is the plural form, but Bradwardine was, after all, a southerner. What is also apparent is that he pronounced Latin like a Frenchman, so that *qui* comes out as [ki] instead of [kwi]. This is a fine instance of using the sounds of every sort of language as a memory aid, the advice we found in John of Garland.

The syllable images obey rules of calculation rather than any sort of naturalism, by which I mean that their function in a particular context takes precedence over their realistic nature. For example, to remember the syllable "ab-," one might picture an *abbatus*, "abbot." For the reverse syllable, "ba-," one can either remember a separate object, whose name starts with "ba-" (Bradwardine suggests *balistarius*, "crossbowman") or one can simply reverse the position of the abbot, so he appears upside-down. For a three-letter syllable, such as "bal-," one adds to the "ba-" image some feature which stands for the added letter. For example, "L" is readily associated, for an Englishman, with a bent elbow, which both forms an "L" and sounds like English "elbow." The position of the elbow-image in relation to the abbot image establishes whether the syllable is "bla-" or "bal-" or "lab-." When the "l" comes first, it is shown at the abbot's head; "lab-" is an abbot with an elbow held over his head. If the "l" is medial, the elbow is held in the middle of the image; "bla-" might be an upside-down abbot holding his elbow at his waist (or a rightside-up crossbowman doing the same). If the "l" is last, as in the syllable "bal-," it figures at the bottom of the image. "Bal-" is figured, humorously, as an upside-down abbot chewing on an elbow. It is interesting that a style of marginal drollery in use in England at about this time (seen, for example, in the Rutland Psalter) features several images of dismembered limbs, some being chewed on by grotesque creatures. I will explore some of the general connections between manuscript marginalia and memory-images in Chapter 7; there are a number of specific parallels between the changing styles of the two that argue for their link, and this is one of them.[25]

Such image-making is governed by positional concerns, a kind of additive calculation in which the position of the elbow (in Bradwardine's example) relative to the rest of the image functions algorithmically, as does the position of a number in the columns of tens in the algorism itself. The same locational calculative principles are at work in Bradwardine's advice to use images for numbers, such as a unicorn for one, or a lamb with seven horns for seven, or dismembered hands with only nine digits for nine, or – interestingly from the standpoint of mathematical history – either a zero or full hands for ten. These images one uses to calculate by the algorism, the method of calculation based upon tens which we commonly use today, but which was then relatively new to Europe. This calculational bent is appropriate to Bradwardine's personality, but it is quite different from what the *Ad Herennium* has to say about making images for words. And it is fascinating to contemplate a mathematician like Bradwardine calculating mentally through the use of such lively pictures; after all, the much simpler system of Arabic numbers was then commonly in use. The algorism was part of this new system; Bradwardine nonetheless counsels the use of these vigorous calculational pictures. Apparently he thought that their vigor made them more useful for mental work than the more abstract notational system. The sources of these number-pictures are interesting too: the unicorn is from the Bestiary, most of the other images are from the Bible and/or the common iconography of church painting and sculptures, and the images involving fingers most likely derive from their common use in daily calculation.

Bradwardine's images can be the stuff of Grand Guignol, but they are also funny. The image of an abbot, already subject to imaginative indignities by being reversed each time one wants to remember "ba" instead of "ab," is made fully ridiculous when we encounter a saintly Benedictine dancing to his left with a white cow holding a partridge and standing on her hind legs, while with his right hand he either mangles or pulls the hair of St. Dominic ("Benedictus Dominus qui per"). Or the imperial king holding a struggling eel in his right hand and a bear by its tail with his left ("rege Anglie Berewicum"). The puns move easily between Latin (*anguilla*, eel and *Anglie*) and English (*bear* and *Bere[wic]*). It is like a mental game of charades, or childrens' rebus games, utilizing several languages and every source of image. But for Bradwardine and his contemporaries, such games have serious scholarly utility because their culture was still profoundly engaged with thoughtful memory work. No opprobrium of childishness or frivolity or obscenity or inappropriateness attaches to such image-making. The disgusting and the silly, the noble and the violent, the grotesque and the beautiful, the scatalogical and sexual are presented, one after another, and usually as part of the same scene, just as memory dictates.

The one thing that cannot be tolerated is dullness or quietude or any failure to rivet the attention. These are shocking images, that make us recoil or laugh out loud, but their shock value is useful for the specific mental tasks involved in memory work. And while the very notion of *useful* sex, violence, and laughter would be, for our own prurient and priggish age, an ultimate jadedness, titillation (and it is that) for Bradwardine is a necessary component of the art of memory, serving pious functions like meditation and preaching. We could consider the use of such images as a kind of extreme instance of the Augustinian dictum that the things of this world are to be enjoyed as they prove useful to the good, rather than as ends in themselves. But one can certainly also understand, in this context, the motive for St. Bernard's admonition to the Benedictines of Cluny that monks should have no need of grotesque figures to help them meditate, and the continuing caution throughout the period against the sin of *curiositas*, "distraction," especially in meditation.

Bradwardine's approval of lively images in memory-work can be paralleled in other medieval texts. One of the most striking features of Albertus Magnus's analysis of memory is his enthusiastic commendation of the usefulness of vivid metaphor to secure recollection. Albertus treats the nature of recollection and the Herennian mnemonic specifically in his treatise *De bono*, Question II, article 2 (translated in Appendix B). This work was written during the 1240s, while he was in Paris. Albertus's precepts (which we might think of as prefatory explanations of an art of memory) were thus composed 115 years later than Hugh of St. Victor's elementary advice, 20 years later than John of Garland's unsystematic account of *memoria*, and predate by 88 years Bradwardine's fully fledged art of memory. He is a pivotal figure in the acceptance of the *Ad Herennium*'s art of memory, which came, after him, to dominate medieval university and then humanist teaching. Albertus is the earliest medieval philosopher to argue systematically for the Herennian art as the best of all the arts of memory. He is also about the earliest to speak of an *art* of memory (*ars memorativa*) rather than just to use the general term *memoria* for an eclectic collection of empirical advice. Finally, Albertus sets his art of memory in the context of moral philosophy rather than in a discussion of rhetoric; this too represents a change from earlier pedagogical treatises.

Albertus's discussion is set up in the usual scholastic manner, queries and responses both being drawn in part from the discussion in the *Ad Herennium* itself. Albertus is concerned specifically to recommend this art: "ars memorandi optima est, quam tradit Tullius," "the best method for recollecting is that which Tullius taught." His justification is made on moral grounds as well as practical ones. Tullius' memorial art especially is valuable for the ethical life and judgment as well as for an orator ("ad ethicum et rhetorem"), since moral judgments are expressed in particular acts and it is therefore necessary that their basis (i. e. prudence) be incorporated in the soul in corporal images (Q. II, a.2, *solutio*). They cannot be retained in images, however, except by the memory. "Unde dicimus, quod inter omnia quae spectant ad prudentiam, summe neces-saria est memoria," "Wherefore we say that, among all the matters which pertain to prudence, the most necessary is *memoria*."

It is important to recognize that Albertus is defending not memory training, which he takes for granted, but this particular system. Certain of his questions address either insufficient definition in Tullius (e.g. objection 10) or apparent contradictions between what is found in *Ad Herennium* and in Aristotle (e.g. objections 3 and 7) or in Aristotelian psychology, as already commented upon by Albertus in his own treatise on the soul (e.g. objections 2 and 13). He also addresses those hostile to the whole scheme as being altogether too curious and elaborate. Such hostility did in fact exist among previous generations of Parisian masters, as we will see.

Albertus is much interested in the ancient system's use of vivid visual images against precisely visualized backgrounds set in order; it is this feature that makes Tullius' system the best. He is obviously working with Tullius' text, trying to adapt it to thirteenth-century circumstances and the memory training with which he is familiar; the results are instructive. He considers, for example, what the phrase "aut natura aut manu" means (*Ad Her.* III.16.29), since Tullius doesn't clearly define it, and suggests (probably correctly) that it refers to kinds of *loci*, the cloister-garth (*pratum*) being an example of a natural place, a house or an intercolumnar space of an artificial one ("made by hand," *manu*; see resp. 10).

Judging by his comments on the five principal characteristics given for desirable background images, Albertus clearly understands that they are designed for ease in perception as one walks through one's places in memory, seeing images on backgrounds. "Confusion," he writes, "is engendered either in respect to the background-place or the matters located in it or to that which by its action makes visible the background and what is in it."[26] If one crowds too much into one location, one will confound one's images: "it heaps up a great many images, and so these images break up in the soul and do not remain, just as a great number of waves break up in water."[27] This effect, however, is not what the *Ad Herennium* gives as the reason to avoid crowds; the concern there was with the initial making of backgrounds, and to avoid imprinting crowded places because of their adverse effect on the clarity of the backgrounds.

One can also be confused if one's places are too much alike, too close together or far apart, or improperly lit. Images must be seen clearly, for "something glaring confounds sight" whereas obscurity impedes it; in either case the images are not properly imprinted and therefore cannot be seen with the inner eye. Following these general guidelines, each person can form his own places from diverse sources. A comparison of the sources enumerated by Albertus with those in the *Ad Herennium* again indicates that Albertus had adapted his source. Tullius mentions these specific examples: *aedis* (a house), *intercolumnium* (the space between columns, a colonnade), *angulus* (a recess), *fornix* (an arch), all clearly Roman architectural items. Albertus's examples are equally clearly medieval: *templum* (a church), *intercolumnium*, *pratum* (cloister-garth), *hospitalis* (hospice or hospital). The only shared word is *intercolumnium*, though Albertus surely had a different sort of columned space in mind (perhaps a cloister or a columned church interior) than did the author of *Ad Herennium*. In fact, *intercolumnium* is the only specific kind of location in the architectural mnemonic that has an unbroken history – perhaps this is due to the continuing use of columns to mark off memory groups in the various tabular formats, such as the Canon Tables. These columnar formats feature images of architectural columns, often joined by arches, to frame the textual material.

Albertus's account of the *Ad Herennium*'s advice concerning image-making shows his fascination with the procedural details of this system. He gives first a complete account of the technique for creating images-for-things. He uses the examples given in the *Ad Herennium*, but it is clear that not all of its details are familiar to him:

we place in our memory "a sick man in bed, who is a figure of the deceased, and we place the defendant standing by the bed, holding in his right hand a cup, in his left hand tablets, and a physician standing upright holding the testicles of a ram," so that certainly in the cup should be the memory-cue of the poison which he drank, and in the tablets should be the memory-cue of the will which he signed, and in the physician may be figured the accusor and by the testicles the witnesses and accessories, and by the ram the defense against matter being adjudicated.[28]

Albertus's attempts to comprehend this scene show his editorial efforts to understand the Latin of a culture far outside his experience. Most notable is his change of the original "medico testiculos arietinos tenentem" to "medicum astantem tenentem testiculos arietinos." In the original text, the defendant and the sick man are the only two human figures in this scene, the defendant holding cup, tablets, and on his fourth finger (*medicum*, used in the ablative singular, is an abbreviated noun-form of the phrase *digitus medicinalis*) the ram's testicles (in ancient Rome money bags could be made from the skin of ram's testicles).[29] Albertus adds a third figure to this scene, a physician (*medicus*, used in the accusative singular) who is standing also by the bed, and he holds the ram's testicles. And why a ram? Since they are noted for their territorial defensiveness, the ram can signify the proceeding against the defendant. What is clear from this ingenious adaptation is Albertus's effort to visualize a *similitudo rerum*. His particular misunderstanding here proves precisely his understanding of the general method.

But a more taxing passage awaited him, the description of the technique of *similitudines verborum* for memory of words, using as its example the line, apparently cited from a popular Roman play, "Iam domum itionem reges Atridae parant," "Now for their journey home the kings, sons of Atreus, prepare." Every commentator on the *Ad Herennium* has floundered about here. A major portion of the difficulty is attributable to the fact that the images which the *Ad Herennium* suggests one use to remember these Latin words are visual puns which depend entirely on contemporary allusions – a reference to two celebrated Roman families, in one instance, and to two well-known contemporary actors in the other. To remember the first half-line one thinks of Domitius "raising hands to heaven while he is whipped with thongs by the Marcii Reges" ("iam domum itionem reges"), both Domitius and Rex being names of distinguished Roman families. Caplan, the Loeb translator, comments that the scene "is doubtless our author's own creation," and it is difficult to understand why it involves whipping, except as an instance of the general principle of forming images related to one another through violent activity. The second half-line is recalled by a scene of the two famous actors, Aesop and Cimber, making ready for their roles as Agamemnon and Menelaus in a play about the trials of Iphigenia ("Atridae parant").

Albertus's attempt to deal with this passage was complicated by an incorrect manuscript reading, one he apparently selected over the more correct one, for both versions were known to him. For *domum itionem*, "journey home," his version read *domi ultionem*, "revenge at home." So in Albertus's account (see Appendix B) somebody named Domitius is being whipped (in revenge for something) by martial (that is, "warlike") kings. Then, having made a certain sense of the scene in the first memory location, he makes a hash of the one in the second. The original text advises that to remember the phrase "Atridae parant," one should imagine two well-known actors, Aesop and Cimber, preparing for their roles as Menelaus and Agamemnon ("the sons of Atreus") in a play about Iphigenia. Here again Albertus was not helped by his chosen manuscript (one of the so-called "E recension"), which left out the explanation in the original text (see *Ad Her.* III.21.34) that the two named figures were actors preparing for their roles in a play.[30] Besides leaving this information out, Albertus's version had also added the adjective *vagantem*, "wandering," as an adjective modifying the name, Iphigenia. So what Albertus found in his manuscript was a reference to two people named Aesop and Cimber who either prepared Iphigenia for wandering, or incited her to wander. Albertus tried to make a mnemonic association by linking the notion of "preparing"

with that of "wandering," for, as he observes, one who prepares (*parat se*)
for something wanders about.

Those who have also struggled with obscurities in ancient texts cannot
help admiring Albertus for plunging into this crux instead of silently
reporting it, though in this case discretion might have served him better.
The nature of his effort indicates again his grasp of the essential features of
the method and purpose of image-making, if not of this particular example
of it. He raises these two specific instances of image-making from *Ad
Herennium* as the basis for others' objection to the whole method (objection 10), on the grounds that it is is metaphorical and obscure, and therefore a hindrance rather than a help to memory. Better to remember the
things themselves (the actual words of a text) than to adopt this cumbersome, confusing method.

Albertus defends the method with vigor precisely because it is metaphorical, grounds that must be of interest to students of medieval fictional
literature. He quotes almost in full the advice of *Ad Herennium* on the
making of striking and unusual images, and replies at length to possible
objections (objs. and resps. 16–21). The images one composes must be
striking and vivid, rare and unusual, "quae quasi mirabiles sunt, imagines
nobis constituamus" (obj. 20). What is unusual and marvelous strikes us
and is retained in the memory more than what is ordinary ("mirabile plus
movet quam consuetum"); moreover, what is marvellous, by its forceful
impression on us, causes us to remark it, and that engenders both inquiry
and reminiscence. For this purpose, fabulous metaphorical images, composed from marvels ("compositae ex miris") are best: "metaphorica plus
movent animam et ideo plus conferunt memoriae." For as Aristotle says (in
Metaphysics, I.1, where he also says that experience is made of many
memories), this was why the earliest philosophers wrote their ideas down
in poetry, because fables composed of marvels were more moving to the
memory and to inquiry ("fabula, cum sit composita ex miris, plus movet").
All inquiry begins in wonder ("ex admirari"), he continues, quoting the
Metaphysics again (I.2), for the start of philosophical thought is in wondering about causes, about befores and afters and whys. Though he does not
explicitly invoke it, Albertus clearly makes an etymological connection
between *miris* and *admirari*, and thus a relationship of some compatibility
between *fabula* and *philosophari* – the link between them being through the
requirements of inventive memory.

Some of his work shows Albertus's use of a technique of composing vivid
visual images, which incorporate the principle of being marvellous and
active. Familiarity from memory training with the technique of vigorous

image-making, even in the context of theological debate (where it becomes a useful tool for keeping any sort of discourse in mind), provided a scholarly audience with a habit of encountering such imagery even in the context of commentary and treatise, without finding it inappropriate. And Albertus's stress upon the mnemonic *usefulness* of what is marvellous and unusual gives a crucial ethical justification for using even fantastical or salacious or violent images. Albertus makes it clear that the criterion for creating mnemonic images is not decorum but utility. Because the memory is physiologically constituted in such a way that it better retains what is unusual and emotionally charged rather than what is expected or routine, material must be marked with those sorts of images. Students of literature have always remarked the penchant for strikingly peculiar allegory in many of the pre-modern arts. But it may well be that some of what we suppose to be allegory, and thus to have a specifically iconographic meaning (if only we knew what it was), is simply a mnemonic heuristic.[31]

Albertus's *Postilla in Isaiam* (commentary on Isaiah), of which a reliable modern edition exists, affords several interesting examples of Albertine imagination. First, as is also true of Aquinas's work, quotations from pagan authors, including the poets, are much in evidence. In this commentary, he quotes from Cicero twenty-three times, most frequently from *De inventione*; he also quotes "Homer," Horace (five times), Ovid (seven times), Martial, Vitruvius, and Virgil, among several others. Moralized stories of the pagan gods, including Jupiter, Priapus, Venus, and the jackal-god Anubis, also find their way into his commentary. Frequently these tales are used to point the Augustinian moral that the pagan gods were no better than devils, corrupt; indeed one of Albertus's richest sources is *The City of God*. Another is evidently from some sort of early version of *Ovide moralisée*, so popular later in the century and into the following one. Commenting on the phrase "in auribus meis" (Is. 5:9), Albertus says:

Wherefore in the fables of the poets in Ovid [*Met.* II, v, 47ff.] great Jupiter, who represents the god of gods, when he needed to strike down Phaeton, who was burning up the sky and earth and all therein, took up his javelin beside his ear, that he might clearly teach that it is judicious first carefully to listen and weigh the merits of the persons and their causes, and then to smite the killers.[32]

But not all of Albertus's vivid visual images are so self-evidently literary in character. For example, commenting on Is. 35:6, "Then shall the lame man leap as an hart," Albertus moralizes the verse with an unusual image rather like the "curious, emblem-like 'pictures'" found by Beryl Smalley in Holcot's *Moralitas*.[33] "The soul," Albertus says, "has two feet, that is intellect and emotions. When they are equal, and emotion is made equal in truth to the intellect, then a man walks well. If however one or the other is bent, the intellect through error or emotion through desire, a man is lame."[34]

Two other examples are also curious. In commentary on Is. 47:2, Albertus writes of the phrase *revela crura*, "make bare the thigh," that it is a custom of prostitutes to reveal their legs in order to incite desire. "Wherefore Venus was painted with her skirt raised to reveal her leg that she might provoke lust."[35] Smalley discovered this passage, and comments on it that its source is not in any pictorial tradition for "the mythographers all represent Venus as naked . . . Curious and of an observant turn of mind, [Albertus] may have seen or read some study of her wearing a dress. Maybe he simply invented her as a personification of harlotry."

Then there is the ram which runs amok in the middle of Albertus's commentary on Aristotle's *De memoria*, composed between 1254 and 1257, when Albertus had left his teaching career in Paris for an administrative one in Cologne. Invoking the *Ad Herennium* on the making of memory-images as a practical instance of Aristotle's understanding of how memory works by association, he comments on the phrase "testiculos arietinos" (*Ad Her.* III.20.34). Frances Yates translates the passage as follows:

> For example, if we wish to record what is brought against us in a law-suit, we should imagine some ram, with huge horns and testicles, coming towards us in the darkness. The horns will bring to memory our adversaries and testicles the dispositions of the witnesses.[36]

Yates wonders wittily whence such a vigorous beast could appear: "How has it managed to break loose from the lawsuit image to career dangerously around on its own in the dark?" She suggests perhaps the connection had something to do with the Zodiac, or perhaps was just the result of too many lonely nights of study. But the explanation is more prosaic. The testicles are in the ancient source, of course, but the charging ram bearing them was added in the earliest known commentary/gloss on it, *Etsi cum Tullius*, which is most probably the work of William of Champeaux, the teacher of Abelard and founder of the school of St. Victor in Paris; thus it dates from the early twelfth century.[37] This aggressive ram with large testicles – both a pun on *testes*, "witnesses," and a sign for the adversarial nature of the legal proceeding – features as well in the other twelfth-century commentaries, and had become the standard academic gloss on this passage by the time Albertus wrote.[38]

Before proceeding to discuss the circumstances within which the Herennian mnemonic was revived, let me summarize the features which seem to be distinctively medieval in the memory advice we have examined in John of Garland, Thomas Bradwardine, and Albertus Magnus. With respect to the memory *locus*, these are: (1) a plain-colored or simply patterned background, with just enough suggestion of depth to be able to position the images in relation to one another in a scene; (2) the observer positioned frontally in respect to this scene, at a distance from which the whole composition can be taken in completely at a glance; (3) a clear and consistent arrangement of the images, which enables them to be read off in sequence – this sequence can be from the center to either side, or, in a circular arrangement, clockwise or counterclockwise (we will see examples of these in Chapter 7). With respect to the *imagines*, they are: (1) their grouping in a scene in which the order among them is expressed through physical action; (2) the use of vivid, unusual, and extreme images; (3) the use of images from a variety of sources, including the Bestiary, the Calendar, and all other sorts of painted or sculpted forms, such as those found commonly in churches and in books.

The placement of the memory locations is diagrammatic, frequently within a grid. One of the most popular of late medieval ethical manuals was an allegorical treatment of the game of chess, composed by the Dominican friar, Jacopo da Cessola, around 1300. It was one of the works printed by William Caxton. In an excellent essay on this work, Raymond DiLorenzo commented that it uses mnemonic technique to integrate the ethical material which the friar has composed as a set of *memorabilia*, "things-to-be-remembered." The mnemotechnique used is the chessboard, a grid, into which *imagines* (the chess pieces, described with vivid and unusual detail) are fitted. Jacopo prefaces the work, which is basically a florilegium, by saying that chess was invented by a philosopher who sought to correct a tyrannical king. As they played the game, the philosopher instructed the king in the virtues and vices that attached to each piece. Thus the game itself became for the king a mnemonic of kingly virtue and responsibility, a Rule for Princes presented in a form that embeds its own mnemonic – the form of a grid filled with images, familiar to medieval audiences as a basic format for the page of memory.[39]

The earliest medieval *artes memorativae* belong to the thirteenth century – or, more precisely, the earliest written medieval *artes* belong to this period. In Alcuin's dialogue with Charlemagne on rhetoric (ninth century), the king asks his teacher, Alcuin, if there are any specific precepts for *memoria* (trained memory), which is the noblest aspect of rhetoric ("nobilissima . . . rhetoricae parte"). There are none, replies Alcuin, except disciplined exercise in memorizing ("ediscendi exercitationem"), practice in writing, and the discipline of cogitation or mental composition. One should also avoid drunkenness (which is harmful to any discipline of soul or body). *Memoria* is a store-house, custodian of invention and cogitation, of "things" and "words," and without it "even the most eminent of the speaker's other talents will come to nothing." Charlemagne's question about precepts is another way of asking whether *memoria* is an art or not. Alcuin takes for granted that *memoria* is a study, involving discipline, training, and practice. But he apparently saw no need (at least for Charlemagne) for a complex set of related precepts in addition to the elementary principles of memory training. He thought of memory as a consciously constructed inventory, a library, a store-house of material in the form of both "words" and "things." But his advice to the emperor does not go farther, to suggest a systematic art of memory.[40]

This bias, if that is what it is, in favor of teaching rhetoric students a few mnemonic principles instead of a systematized art of memory can also be found in Quintilian and in the late Roman rhetoricians of the fourth and later centuries. In *De oratore*, Cicero speaks of an architectural mnemonic art as so well-known that it needs no elaborate description.[41] But, 150 years or so later, Quintilian, while not rejecting totally the notion of making an art of memory, plays down its utility and that of other such *artes*. Evidently a fashion favoring practice and discipline in the elements of memory training over more elaborate, curious (and Greek) *artes* had begun to dominate Roman pedagogy; this bias is consistent with Quintilian's judgments against using pre-fabricated mnemonic *imagines* and all other quick prescriptions for memory training. Of course, the *Ad Herennium* also counseled against substituting others' schemes for one's own; this is a traditional pedagogical caution, the basis of Plato's warning in *Phaedrus* against substituting textbooks and recipes for teachers and disciplined practice. But Quintilian's bias towards philosophical rhetoric and against the sophistical excesses he saw in his contemporaries like Seneca is reflected again here in his remarks about the usefulness of *artes memorativae*. Instead, he stresses the elementary aspects of memory training, reserving the various arts for it to those of advanced ability – and to teachers of dubious reputation (or so he implies).

The emphasis in the rhetoric schools on the elements rather than on an advanced *techne* of *memoria* is found still in the fourth century. Julius Victor wrote that "for impressing memory some teach observations of a great many places and images, which do not seem effective to me."[42] Since he took a great deal from Quintilian, it is not surprising to find this opinion, and it also indicates that during the centuries after Quintilian wrote, his judgment continued to predominate, despite the fact that Cicero himself spoke favorably in *De oratore* of using memory arts based on images in places. Julius Victor in turn greatly influenced Isidore of Seville and Alcuin. Yet, as we have seen, Julius Victor does give instructions in the basic mnemonic preparations: division, memory "for subjects" and "for words," using memorial *notae*, meditation, and composition. So it seems that in later antiquity and the earlier Middle Ages a memorial *ars* such as that taught in the *Ad Herennium* was regarded in standard pedagogy as marginally helpful at best, and that the focus of memory training was on its elements, instilled through practice and discipline, but without emphasizing a universal body of principles. To use the traditional categories, *memoria* was taught as a *studium*, a collection of empirically proven guidelines, but it was not a systematic *ars*, as it apparently had been regarded in the time of Cicero and would be again by the end of the thirteenth century. The distinction I am making is between what we would call a craft, learned by apprenticeship, and a scientific discipline that can be taught from a textbook.

Although arguments from silence are not worth much without positive, corroborating evidence, it is interesting that Augustine makes no mention of an art of memory, though trained as a teacher of rhetoric and though he is one of the great philosophers of memory. Frances Yates attempted to make a case for his having been a practitioner of the Herennian art, on the basis of his descriptions of memory's power in Book x of *Confessions*, of which the following is typical:

See, in the measureless plains and vaults and caves of my memory, immeasurably full of countless kinds of things which are there either through their images (as with material things), or by being themselves present (as is the knowledge acquired through a liberal education), or by registering themselves and making their mark in some indefinable way (as with emotional states which the memory retains even when the mind is not actually experiencing them, although whatever is in the memory must be in the mind too) – in this wide land I am ... free to run and fly to and fro, to penetrate as deeply as I can, to collide with no boundary anywhere. So great is the faculty of memory, so great the power of life.[43]

The metaphors Augustine uses here are archetypal: one did not need to practice the Herennian art to believe that memory was locational in nature, like a vast cave with many inner caverns in which all experience was inventoried, and that it had immense power which training could enhance. Indeed, though copied as one of Cicero's works, the *Rhetorica ad Herennium* was not much commented on or quoted until late in the eleventh century. The earliest ancient references are in scattered sources from Jerome (in works from 395 and 402) through Priscian (early sixth century). None of these are to the memory section, it should be noted. Its influence is not extensive until after the mid twelfth century, and even later.[44]

When it was first revived, its memory advice was received with skepticism. John of Salisbury (who knew Quintilian's *Institutes* better than most of his contemporaries) alludes to arts of memory: "Seneca most readily promised to teach the art for furnishing memories, of which I certainly wish I were a master; but as far as I know, he did not actually teach it. Tullius seems to have applied himself to this in [*Rhetorica ad Herennium*] but the latter is not of much help to me."[45] And Geoffrey of Vinsauf, writing at the turn of the thirteenth century, dismisses the *Ad Herennium*'s art completely: "Tullius relies on unusual images as a technique for training the memory, but he is teaching himself; and let the subtle teacher, as it were in solitude, address his subtlety to himself alone."[46]

Instead, Geoffrey counsels the traditional elements of memory training: division, placing the pieces in a rigid locational order (one, two, three, etc.), marking material with mental *notae* for secure recollection from the storage-bin (*cella*) of memory, respecting the limits of short-term memory (*brevitas*), and not stuffing too much in at one time, for the store-room of memory responds well only while it is having fun, and so must be treated well ("Cellula quae meminit est cellula deliciarum"). The problem with a method like that described in the *Ad Herennium* is that it is gimmicky and ready-made, whereas no single group of markers (*notae*) will work equally well for everyone. Everyone should make little markers of his own choosing and devising, for those are "safer," *tutior*, for recollection. One should note the concern Geoffrey expresses for the *safety* of a recollective scheme – Thomas of Waleys has the same concern.[47]

One other early medieval writer on memory should be considered here, because he is credited by Frances Yates as being the one who "handed on the art [of memory] to the Middle Ages."[48] This is Martianus Capella, a fifth-century teacher whose allegorical encyclopedia on the seven liberal arts, *The Marriage of Philology and Mercury*, became influential after the turn of the first millennium. Martianus treats *memoria* in the traditional way, as a part of rhetoric. But he is rarely mentioned as a proponent of an art of memory and never, to my knowledge, linked with the precepts of Tullius. What Martianus describes under *memoria* are some of the elementary rules of ancient mnemotechnique, but nothing that constitutes an art of memory, let alone repeats what is peculiar to the architectural art of the *Ad Herennium*. Indeed, the advice on memory training that is advocated by

Cassiodorus (d. 590), whose *Fundamentals of Divine and Secular Letters* became perhaps the most important academic text for the early Middle Ages, is not that of Martianus Capella but of Consultus Fortunatianus (a late fourth-century rhetoric master), from whom Martianus Capella copied a great deal. As we saw in Chapter 3, Fortunatianus's advice belongs to the elementary pedagogy of how to memorize a text, which one can find as well in Quintilian. Like Martianus Capella, Fortunatianus represents the mnemotechnical pedagogy which Augustine, Marius Victorinus, and other teachers in late antiquity valued.

Martianus Capella says that while memory is a natural talent, it may be assisted by training. The craft of memory has only a few rules and requires much practice; but by it words and things can be grasped quickly and surely. Memory-for-things is easier and less time-consuming than memory-for-words, though the latter may be employed to recall hard words or particular words one has trouble remembering. Simonides invented the art from his experience when a banqueting hall collapsed, and he was able to identify the victims because he had attached their names to the places where they were seated. Order is thus the key to the precepts of memory training. The order is memorized as a set of distinctive mental locations into which one puts images of things to be recalled – for example, if one wants to remember a wedding, one would place the image of a girl in a saffron wedding veil; if a murderer, a sword or other weapon. "For just as what is written is contained in wax and letters, so what is committed to memory is written into areas as if on wax and in page-form [*in cera paginaque signatur*]."[49] But since much labor is required for remembering, we should write down what we wish readily to retain. If the material is long, divide it into shorter sections for ease of memorizing. It is useful to mark with *notae* things we want particularly to recall. When memorizing, one should not read aloud but meditate upon the material in a low murmur. It is best to exercise the memory at night, when silence aids concentration.[50]

The ultimate sources for all of this lore are *De oratore* and Quintilian's *Institutes*, not the *Ad Herennium*. Martianus himself provides the particular examples. A particular order – *this* order – is memorized ("is [ordo] ... meditandus est") as a set of distinctive, well-known (and well-lighted) locations ("in locis illustribus"). Into these locations the likenesses of objects ("species rerum") and images of subject matters ("sententiarumque imagines") are gathered ("collocandae sunt"). Rather than a procedure like that for forming places advised in the architectural mnemonic, what Martianus counsels is a prototype of advice like that of Hugh of St. Victor (and others, as we shall see) – to make a diagram, *linea*, in one's mind that acts as a schematic ordering device for material that is then put into it. This is the commonest type of medieval description for what one does in forming memory places, and it is not the same kind of procedure as that described in the *Ad Herennium*. Bradwardine's sets of places in fives, one on top of another as in a matrix, is more like constructing a diagram than it is like walking through a house one knows familiarly. The schematic quality is distinctively medieval.

From the time of Quintilian then, *memoria* seems to have been commonly taught as an elementary practice, consisting of a few basic rules and some common-sense advice, eclectic, empirical, pragmatic, but not a unitary discipline with a full methodology. This study concentrated on the essentials and was suspicious of what seemed to be shortcuts. Are there any precepts? Charlemagne asks Alcuin. None, is the reply, only discipline, training, and exercise. In this exercise, the importance of *notae*, or *signa* as they are also called, was universally acknowledged, including *imagines* of every kind, any of which could be used for mnemonic associations. What makes an image a mnemonic is not its nature but how it is used. Any image *used* as a mnemonic, by virtue of that use, is classified as a mnemonic image. These can – and did – include all kinds. It is important to note that none of these early medieval writers expresses any hostility towards using mental images for memory work – their motives are not iconoclastic or doctrinal, even when iconoclastic controversies were current.[51] And they are not prescriptive concerning what kinds of images to use. Their principle seems rather to have been to use "whatever works."

Boncompagno da Signa, writing in 1235, discusses no systematic art of recollection, no principles for constructing mnemonic *notae*. Instead he lists virtually everything made as a potential memory aid, for somebody in some circumstances. Every sort of sign, starting with language itself, helps us to remember something. Indeed, for Boncompagno, any interpretative activity is essentially a matter of recalling something to memory. So, the cock that crowed when Peter betrayed Jesus was a memorial sign (*memoriale signum*) by which Peter recalled Jesus' prophetic words. All books, all pictures, images, sculptures, all cruciforms, all insignia of rank and station, banners, alphabets, methods of calculation, notches cut in sticks to record loans and repayments (tallies), the stories told to children which record the events of history, even the jargon of thieves – everything has a memorative function by which God reminds us of Himself and we remember the world we experience. Boncompagno's version of Neoplatonism, which is evident, is less interesting in this context than his notably eclectic list of mnemonic images. He has a philosophy of memory (of a sort) but he has no *ars memorativa*, no principles on which to explain how these diverse kinds of *signa* work.[52]

Another specialized term, in addition to *nota* and *signum*, that defines a function of images used memoratively, is the phrase *imagines rerum*. All these terms belong to the common pedagogy of memory and are not specific to a version of an *ars memorativa*. They are distinguished by function, *nota* being reserved for any sort of mental marker one uses to file and cue stored material. *Imagines rerum* traditionally seem restricted to the function of public speaking, declamation, and hence composition. Though no admirer of memory arts, Quintilian does favor making *imagines rerum* for one's subject matters when preparing a speech. Eloquence, he writes, depends upon an orator's emotional state. The mind of the speaker must be emotionally as well as intellecually engaged.

Quintilian uses the term again when he discusses in greater detail how emotions are stirred in the orator. To do so one is much helped by vivid images, "which the Greeks call *fantasiai* . . . whereby images of things absent are again presented in our minds" (*Inst. orat.*, VI, 2, 29). These *imagines* can generate the very emotions in the orator which he seeks to awaken in his audience, and cause him to re-experience what happened:

shall I not see the assassin burst suddenly from his hiding-place, the victim tremble, cry for help, beg for mercy, or turn to run? Shall I not see the fatal blow delivered and the stricken body fall? Will not the blood, the deathly pallor, the groan of agony, the death-rattle, be indelibly impressed upon my mind?[53]

But *imagines rerum* are also critical for retaining the order and flow of a speech – a mnemonic function. Unless one can speak with order, copiousness, and style, one is not speaking but only ranting. To produce such ordered pattern:

those vivid conceptions (*rerum imagines*) of which I spoke, and which, as I remarked, are called *fantasiai*, together with everything that we intend to say, the persons and questions involved, and the hopes and fears to which they give rise, must be kept clearly before our eyes and admitted to our emotions.[54]

It is the *imagines* that can be fixed by the mind's eye and that arouse again both one's intent and and one's procedure (*intentio*) concerning one's subject matters, so these are the key to holding any discourse in our memories. One is not trying to store away entire written texts through their agency (even if one were so unskilled an orator as to have written one's complete speech down in advance), for words alone are easily lost and cannot be reconstituted, if one were to stumble or need to depart suddenly from one's prepared theme. Martianus Capella advises the use of vivid *imagines rerum* in the service of what Bradwardine much later called *memoria orationis*, to help remember the chief subjects of one's speech (the veiled bride, the sword).

Bradwardine also advocates using *imagines rerum*, vivid images which cue the main points one will develop extemporaneously in one's talk. These *imagines rerum* in their memory places act as focal images for the speaker's meditation. The places order the major stages of the speech; the *imagines rerum* in each location (supplemented, perhaps, by particular words remembered through *imagines verborum*) trigger the memory through their associational power to recall various parts of one's mental library. *Imagines rerum* can act as compositional sites and cues that can "gather in" (*re-colligere*) much related material laid down elsewhere in memory, because they invite the orator's mental eyes to stay and contemplate. This function is also emphasized in medieval advice about the work of memory. It accounts for the particularly medieval use of the verb *remember* to describe what one was doing when one meditated in vivid picture-form on hell and heaven, two places one could never have visited oneself and thus could not actually remember, in our sense. Yet meditation, as we will see in the next two chapters, was thought to be a particular activity of memory. The use of *imagines rerum* as sites for memorial composition (*compositio*) was analyzed as a kind of remembering. Medieval diagrams as images of subject matters require one to stay and ponder, to fill in missing connections, to add to the material which they present. They are the instruments and machines of thought.[55]

TEACHING AN ART OF MEMORY IN UNIVERSITIES

Memory became a "speculative" art, given serious attention in universities, about the year 1250, while continuing as always to be an elementary skill to be mastered by all who claimed to read. This distinction is important to keep in mind when considering the history of any "art of memory." Of the three writers whose mnemotechnique I discussed earlier in this chapter, only John of Garland was a teacher of rhetoric. Albertus Magnus was a professor of theology and logic; so was Thomas Bradwardine. Yet it was John of Garland who produced an old-fashioned pragmatic of mnemonic advice, despite using some of the terms of the *Ad Herennium*. These he would have learned from masters who used the "Alanus" gloss, which attempts only to explain the ancient treatise's hard words and to paraphrase some of its sentences. Ten or fifteen years after John of Garland, in the same university setting though in a different faculty, Albertus Magnus wrote his sympathetic and philosophically systematic commentary on the *Ad Herennium*'s precepts for an art of memory based upon images in places, giving it a seriousness which it did not lose again until well after the Renaissance. It seems, thus, that university rhetoric teachers had little role in the academic development of medieval arts of memory.

Commenting on the intellectual situation of *memoria* at the end of the twelfth century, G. R. Evans remarked that "[t]he elements of a formal art of memory and of a formal study of the faculty of memory, based on older authorities, are all present in the twelfth century schools ... What was missing was a stimulus – perhaps in the form of an individual scholar with a special interest in the topic – to bring the elements together."[56] We may safely conclude that this individual scholar was Albertus Magnus. Though we know very little about his early life, it seems probable that he studied at Padua during the first decade of its foundation as a *scholium* around 1222. Padua was founded by scholars from Bologna – indeed the influence of Boncompagno da Signa on its rhetoric curriculum was strong from the start. But Padua was also noted as an early center for the study of Aristotle's *libri naturales*, including the brief essays of the *Parva naturalia*, and if Albertus was there, it was the natural history books that he studied, rather than rhetoric.[57]

Three commentaries on the Herennian memory art were made before that of Albertus Magnus (though it should always be noted that Albertus's comments on the *Ad Herennium* advice are made in the context of a treatise on ethics and a commentary on Aristotle). The earliest is that in a gloss known as *Etsi cum Tullius*, likely the work of William of Champeaux, made in Paris early in the twelfth century. It was followed a decade or so later by a commentary of Thierry of Chartres. Towards the end of the century, perhaps in the 1180s, a third commentary was made, the work of a "magister Alanus," who may or may not have been the famous teacher and Latin poet, Alan of Lille. This became the standard text for the thirteenth century and later. All of these commentaries were Parisian in provenance, and reflect the teaching of rhetorical *memoria* in Paris. The first commentary specifically on the *Ad Herennium* made after the twelfth century is an early fourteenth-century Italian one, possibly from Bologna, called, from its introductory words, *Plena et perfecta*.[58]

The only one of the twelfth-century commentaries to be published in a modern edition is that of Thierry of Chartres, composed in the 1130s, a full century and more before Albertus Magnus's commentary on Aristotle's *De memoria*. Thierry was a teacher at Chartres, and later chancellor, in the first half of the twelfth century, a contemporary of Hugh of St. Victor and of

John of Salisbury's teacher, Bernard of Chartres. His interest in rhetoric is primarily in its organization of topics; he is best known for his studies in the Old Logic of Aristotle and in Plato. His commentary on the *Rhetorica ad Herennium* is preserved only in a single manuscript of the twelfth century. It has been edited by K. M. Fredborg, probably its first publication since then.

What Thierry has to say about Tullius' mnemonic techniques "hardly goes beyond mere paraphrase," as Fredborg notes, and only one of his remarks about the memory section (an explanation of the characters Domitius and the *Martii Reges* which figure in the example given by Tullius for *memoria verborum*) is picked up by any of the writers who immediately followed him and used his comments in their own work.[59] Like his contemporaries, then, Thierry seems to have been little interested in the Herennian mnemonic, or in contributing to its revival as a practical tool for oratory, nor does he appear to have understood significantly better than they did what it was all about. He comments on it because it is part of Tullius' text, paraphrasing almost exactly what it already says, glossing words, explicating grammar, explaining the mythological allusions.

Nonetheless, Thierry's commentary is not without interest, because of the intelligence of his comments and his generally positive stance towards his subject. He exhibits none of the outright scorn for the Herennian memory scheme that we find in John of Salisbury and Geoffrey of Vinsauf, though they both wrote a good deal later in the twelfth century than he did. He expands the skepticism, apparent in the *Ad Herennium* itself, concerning the utility of memory for words – this sort of thing, he says, is useful as an exercise only, and to remember verses from the poets.[60] He then rehearses in paraphrase the example in the *Ad Herennium* of how to remember the verse "Iam domi ultionem [*sic*] reges Atridae parant." And he adds an example of his own: if you should want to remember the first two lines of Book II of the *Aeneid* ("Conticuere omnes intentique ora tenebant / cum pater Aeneas lecto sic orsus ab alto est [*sic*]"), you might imagine someone sitting on a couch ("sedentem in lecto") and reciting something, while surrounded by many intent listeners ("multos intentos ad audiendum").[61] This is a perfectly sensible image – rather more sensible than those given as examples in the *Ad Herennium* – but it does not, in fact, exemplify the advice of Tullius to construct visual homophonies that will cue a line for you word-by-word. It is much more like an image *ad res* than an image *ad verbum* in the manner of the *Ad Herennium*.

Yet the vocabulary of the ancient mnemonic advice does not seem wholly foreign to Thierry. He gives a sympathetic and comprehensive explanation of *imagines rerum* and their value to orators, of the reasons why memory craft can benefit natural talent, and of the need for practice and disciplined exercise in making sets of numbered locations. He is clear about what the locations are and how the images are fitted into them, why the locations remain stable while one changes the images to suit the needs of each particular orational cause. He understands the reason for having a fixed order among the locations, so that one can go backwards as well as forwards, or in whatever way one wishes. He knows that *intervalla* refer to *locorum distancias,* the distance in the mind's eye from which one views the locations, for one's view of the content will be confounded if one's view-point is situated too close or too far away.[62] He understands that grotesque, unusual, wonderful images excite the memory, and need to be used instead of ordinary or routine ones. And he approves the advice in Tullius against relying entirely on ready-made images instead of finding one's own. It is only in regard to *memoria verborum* that he seems dubious, and in this he is in the company of Quintilian and the anti-Sophist Roman tradition.

Yet Thierry's commentary seems to have had virtually no influence on either his contemporaries or later writers – certainly Albertus Magnus was not influenced by Thierry's clear explanation of that wretchedly difficult crux concerning Aesopus, Cimber, Iphigenia, and the sons of Atreus. Had he known Thierry, Albertus might not have given such a muddled gloss of this passage. Albertus and the other later memory writers got their understanding of memory locations, images for things, and images for words in other ways, most likely from the commentary of "magister Alanus," who was muddled in just the places that Albertus was. The fact that Thierry is so clear about most of the *Ad Herennium*'s memory terms and descriptions of technique is of greater significance than the few moments of hesitation he displays, for it supports the conclusion that many of the basic concepts of memory advice from late antiquity remained current in the twelfth century – current enough for an exceptionally intelligent commentator, like Thierry of Chartres, to explain the gist of the *Ad Herennium* on memory with understanding, if without enthusiasm.

MEMORY AND DIALECTIC IN THE VERBAL ARTS

The reassessment of memorial art was given a crucial intellectual impetus by the translation into Latin of Aristotle's *De anima* and its related treatises, including the one on memory and recollection. This material was first translated by James of Venice (the Old Translation), and had begun to circulate widely by about 1200.[63] Albertus commented on it during the 1240s, his years at Paris. As we have seen, he connects Aristotle's comments on the associative nature of memory and the principles by which it operates with the example of the advice and images adduced in *Ad Herennium*. He is the first Western scholar to have done so. His pupil, Thomas Aquinas, does the same, both in his own *De memoria* commentary and in the *Summa* (1272). By mid-century the art of making memorial images in backgrounds, and more importantly, the idea that *memoria* could be treated as an art, with principles and structure, even though its specific application varied so much with individual experience, had been accepted as philosophically and logically reputable. As a result of this circumstance of its revival, the art of memory is often dissociated from the study of rhetoric in the later Middle Ages, and treated instead as a part of logic, or ethics – as in Albertus Magnus's treatise "on the Good" – or natural philosophy. Separate memorial *artes* and essays on strengthening memory were typically composed and circulated as independent treatises, often in anthologies of works on natural philosophy, a description that fits well both of the manuscripts in which copies of Bradwardine's treatise are found, and the essays of Matheolus of Perugia, Peter of Ravenna, and the most popular art of memory of the late fifteenth century (printed throughout Europe), that of a Spanish physician, Jacobus Publicius.

The linking of memory arts to dialectic and the discovery of arguments goes back to Aristotle's *Topica* at least. As I pointed out earlier (in Chapter 3), Aristotle specifically mentions there that the topics or seats of argument are stored in the mind using a method like that of the arts of memory. This particular text of Aristotle was not lost in the Middle Ages: it became a part of the medieval curriculum known as the old logic. Cicero wrote an extended adaptation of Aristotle's work in his own *Topica*, a work known as well in the Middle Ages. But it was through Boethius's sixth-century treatise *De differentiis topicis* that the topics of argument, seen as analogous to the places of recollection, gained full currency in the earlier Middle Ages, for this work was an elementary text on reasoning and logic.[64] The idea that recollection, *memoria*, is itself a reasoning procedure, which makes use of orderly series of mental topics (places) for the procedure of investigation, is fundamental from antiquity onward both in dialectic and in rhetoric. In each of these linguistic arts, the compositional task requires invention (discovery and recovery) of arguments, matters, and materials, which in turn derive their power and persuasion from the mental library one put away during the study of grammar. The initimate connections among the three arts of the trivium, habituated throughout a medieval scholar's entire reading life, should never be forgotten or set aside in our own desire to analyze them separately.

All three of the twelfth-century commentaries on *Ad Herennium* address the issue of how to classify memory art within the standard curriculum, and all three regard it as both rational and persuasive, part of both dialectic and rhetoric. The "Alanus" commentary, which dominated teaching of the text known as Cicero's New Rhetoric (the *Rhetorica ad Herennium*) through the thirteenth century, paraphrases its initial definition of *memoria* as a "treasury," by calling it *camera argumentorum* as well, invoking again the "topics"-of-argument model familiar in dialectic. Albertus Magnus and Thomas Aquinas both discuss recollection (and the need to store memory in such a way as to enable effective recollection) as a procedure of rational investigation. They do so in the context of commenting on Aristotle's *De memoria*, but they did not need to learn this from him, for it was a pedagogical commonplace. The commentary called *Plena et perfecta* puts the matter succinctly. To the question whether arts of memory are to be considered part of dialectic or rhetoric, the master replies that they belong properly to both, for "memory is taught as a part of dialectic just as it is of rhetoric."[65]

It was Aristotle who made these rules comprehensible through his analysis of the imagistic and associative working of recollection. A manuscript of the first decade of the fifteenth century (Ambrosiana MS. R.50. supra) appends a poem of forty hexameters setting forth rules for the art of memory to the Latin translation of Aristotle's *Nicomachean Ethics*. Though it does not go so far as to attribute these verses to Aristotle himself, it is clear that the connection – even a sort of authorship – between Aristotle and the arts of memory had become by then something of a commonplace. The renewed Aristotelian connection was not the first comprehend recollective procedures as forms of reasoned investigation – they had always been regarded as that. Its twelfth century commentaries recognized just such a rational system in the *Ad Herennium*'s advice on rhetorical *memoria*. Nor was it new to discuss memory within the context of ethical philosophy, as Albertus Magnus and Thomas Aquinas both did (Thomas discusses it with the virtue of prudence in the *Summa theologiae*, and Albertus in his treatise *De bono*). In so doing, these two friars were following well-established Ciceronian practice, for Cicero discussed the virtue of prudence, and defined memory as part of it, in his first rhetorical work, *De inventione*, the rhetoric text best known throughout the entire Middle Ages. The parts of prudence, Cicero wrote, are "memory, intelligence, and foresight," *memoria, intelligentia, providentia (De invent.* II. 53).

But it was new to treat *memoria* as a separate study within psychology considered as a natural science, as both scholars did in their commentaries on Aristotle's *De memoria*, and as Averroës had done in his *Epitome* of Aristotle's psychological works. Aristotle's *De anima* and its companion treatises are associated with neither rhetoric nor dialectic nor ethics. The lasting, distinctive contribution made by the two Dominicans, building on one another's work and on their Arabic forebears, was to rationalize the arts of memory as a distinct subject in natural science, not solely within dialectic and rhetoric (including that aspect of rhetoric, articulated by Cicero, that dealt with civic virtues such as prudence and sound judgment). Classifying the arts of memory within a scientific subject (psychology) that was separable from the language arts of argumentation and invention "put ... artificial memory on an altogether new footing," as Frances Yates rightly observed.[66] It was this new Aristotle-based classification that made possible the extravagant scientific claims made for mnemonic art in the Renaissance, as a speculative subject on its own. In the early eighteenth century, Diderot re-classified the arts of memory as part of dialectic (the invention of arguments), as Pierre Ramus had earlier done in the seventeenth century. Though they do not say so, their scheme was not unprecedented, but rather a return to the situation of mnemonic practices in the twelfth- and early thirteenth-century medieval curriculum, as instruments of verbal invention.

Yet the academic recovery of Aristotle's major psychological texts is not sufficient to explain the immediate popularity of *ars memorativa* in circles that included theology students and professors, students of law, friars, and (especially in Italy) bureaucratic clerks, merchants, physicians, and notaries. A translation of the memory section of *Ad Herennium* appeared in Italian not later than 1266, only a few years after Albertus Magnus's discussion of it in *De bono*, and before Thomas Aquinas commended it in the second part of his *Summa*. And a French version was made by Jean d'Antioche at the end of the thirteenth century, as part of a translation of the *Ad Herennium*.[67] The explanation for this popularity lies in cultural and educational factors that greatly increased people's need and opportunities for speaking publicly, to a variety of audiences both clerical and lay. These came into prominence during the latter twelfth century, and were fully developed during the thirteenth and fourteenth centuries.

Unlike the situation in the earlier Middle Ages, when public oratory was the responsibility primarily of abbots and bishops, addressing one another or monks in their cloisters or a few aristocrats, the culture of the medieval university called for public disputations, sermons, and other forms of oral address on the part of all students as well as professors. Lawyers had always needed to retain quantities of detailed material and to be able to speak disputationally; the study of law expanded greatly after the twelfth century. The Fourth Lateran Council of 1215 encouraged greater participation by the laity in the life of the church, the chief vehicle for which was to be vernacular sermons. The lay culture of courtiers and merchants also incorporated the need to speak well publicly during the thirteenth and fourteenth centuries.[68]

We can trace these social developments in the rapid proliferation from the thirteenth century on of memorial *artes* – some based mainly upon Tullius, some (like Bradwardine's) clearly not. They are written in Latin and in the vernaculars, especially Italian and French. Often they are the work of Dominican friars, though other orders and even laymen (especially in the fourteenth century) were also active transmitters. Whatever their content and provenance, however, they are all called *artes memorativae* after the twelfth century, though the term is rarely used before then during the Middle Ages when *memoria* is discussed.

It is a phenomenon of the very greatest importance to this study of what I have called "memorial culture," that the Dominican order, which was responsible for developing many of the most useful tools for the study of written texts during the thirteenth century, was simultaneously the most active single proponent and popularizer of memory as an art, and especially of the principles of Tullius. The Dominicans developed the written concordance to the Bible, devised indexing schemes for texts that were to continue in use for centuries (they are responsible, for example, for the referential scheme of dividing a column of text into areas marked A through G), and compiled many collections of *distinctiones, quaestiones,* and other scholars' and preachers' aids. Of course the Franciscans and other fraternal orders compiled similar reference tools, and practiced techniques of traditional *memoria* that eventually also came to be called *artes.* But Albertus Magnus and Thomas Aquinas are the two earliest theologians to commend particularly the art of memory which Tullius taught as being the best of all. These two great saints exercised their influence for several centuries in ensuring Dominican sponsorship of the Herennian architectural mnemonic.[69]

Preaching friars and theology students were not the only groups in the thirteenth century who took up *ars memorativa* with enthusiasm. The mid-thirteenth-century Italian translation of Tullius, the earliest vernacular one, was probably made by a Florentine jurist, Bono Giamboni,[70] who also translated Brunetto Latini's *Trésor* into Italian from French. It is closely associated in the written record with a collection of rhetorical precepts, chiefly from the *Ad Herennium*, made by a Dominican, Guidotto da Bologna. Brunetto Latini himself was a great Ciceronian; his *Trésor* is a compendious florilegium of things to be remembered from classical writers on a variety of ethical and rhetorical subjects. Though it does not include Tullius' memory art, there is some basis for thinking that such compilations were thought of specifically as memory books, and their compilers revered at this time in Italy as major exponents of *ars memorativa*. Bono Giamboni's translation soon was attached, as a final appendix, to an early Italian ethical florilegium, *Ammaestramenti degli antichi*, compiled around 1300 by the Dominican friar, Bartolomeo, of the convent of San Concordio in Pisa.

The author of the *Ammaestramenti* supplement (Bono, lightly edited by Bartolomeo) makes clear why he considers an art of memory to be necessary for all educated men, including laity:

if a man has the wisdom to know well how to understand things, and also has wisdom and justice, which is the firm desire to want to arrange things well, and to want to do it rightfully, he must know how to speak ... for without speech his goodness would be like a buried treasure ... We have already seen the first thing a speaker must know, how he is to learn to speak good, ornamented, and ordered speech, as I have shown you. Now I wish to show you the second thing a speaker must know in order to speak perfectly, which is how his speech may be held in memory, for no one will speak well if when he speaks he does not have it clearly in mind.[71]

The art of memory is specifically an aid for speakers, not for learners, for composers, not for readers. This distinguishes it most clearly from the elementary rules of memory training. But, like all memory training, it was considered to be an ethical as well as a practical imperative.

CHAPTER 5

Memory and the ethics of reading

There is no questioning the fact that written material came increasingly into use from the eleventh century on; the reason that more manucripts survive from the later Middle Ages is because more were made. The making of scholarly compendia is a response to this increase, and the larger educated, book-needing public that created it. There is an increase not only in bulk, but in the complexity of indexing and classifying schemes that one does not see before the late eleventh century, and it is evident that, though they derive from mnemonic principles in use for centuries, they seem much too technical to have served directly as a mnemonic – for them to be useful as memory devices, a user would need some prior training and familiarity with basic mnemonic principles.

But these facts do not seem to have altered significantly the value placed on memory training in medieval education, nor to have changed the deliberate cultivation of *memoria*. Medieval culture remained profoundly memorial in nature, despite the increased use and availability of books for reasons other than simple technological convenience. The primary factor in its conservation lies in the identification of memory with creative thinking, learning (invention and recollection), and the ability to make judgments (prudence or wisdom). Writing, as we have seen, was always thought to be a memory aid, not a substitute for it. Children learned to write as a part of reading/memorizing, inscribing their memories in the act of inscribing their tablets. Writing itself was judged to be an ethical activity in monastic culture. A twelfth-century sermon says, in part: "Let us consider then how we may become scribes of the Lord. The parchment on which we write for Him is a pure conscience, whereon all our good works are noted by the pen of memory." The orator then proceeds to moralize the various implements of writing: pumice, knife, pen, ruler, chalk, ink, and so on.[1]

COMPOSITION AS GATHERING (OCKHAM, RICHARD DE
BURY, AND PETRARCH)

In 1330, the Franciscan friar William of Ockham, virtually interdicted from
the intellectual community of Western Europe by Pope John XXII for his
teachings challenging papal power, found himself living at the Franciscan
convent in Munich. There he spent the rest of his life. Having been a
member of university communities at Oxford, Paris, and in Italy, where he
had access to the best libraries in Europe, his isolation at Munich was
distressing to him, not least because there he had virtually no books, nor
means of obtaining them, for the Pope had warned that nothing was to be
sent to him. Ockham makes this quite clear at several points in his
Dialogus, the long dialogue on the limits of papal power between a master
and his pupil, which contains a few pieces (chiefly Part II) written earlier,
and much new material.[2] The work was in circulation by 1343; it appears to
have been unfinished, because, while Ockham names the matters he
intended to include in Part III, the manuscripts all break off in that part,
each at different places and none complete.

Ockham's situation as a scholar is a dramatically extreme case that
demonstrates quite clearly the necessary role that memorial training and
transmission continued to play in both education and scholarly dialogue
throughout the Middle Ages, even as the number of books increased.[3]

In the first part of *Dialogus*, Magister or Master, Ockham's persona, tells
his pupil that, in order to conduct his arguments properly, he needs various
books and materials he cannot get, a theme sounded frequently throughout
the work, "but you know I do not have any of [various writings he has just
spoken of] and those [men] absolutely refuse to communicate to me [the
materials I spoke of] concerning governance."[4] He complains again in the
prologue to the third part of not having the books he wants: "I can in no
way introduce [my subject] beyond the preface since I am unable to come
by precisely the books I consider necessary." To which the pupil responds
that he is sure this fear will not restrain his master. And it did not.[5]

The Master counsels his disciple whenever he can to extract and memorize material from a wide variety of sources; indeed, if the Master had not
done so when he had the opportunity, he would now have no hope of
access to even the most fundamental texts, the Bible and the collections of
canon law. The pupil asks how one gets knowledge of subjects like imperial
rights and papal powers? "Complete knowledge about them – which you
recall is to be drawn out of books of sacred theology, and of both kinds of
law, that is canon and civil, of moral philosophy, and from the histories of

the Romans, and especially of the emperors, and of the greatest pontiffs, and of other peoples – should be most patiently extracted and solidly built up. By which means alone I have hope of obtaining the Bible and the books of church law." And he again apologizes if, under the circumstances, he seems to make an imperfect or awkward book. His pupil responds by saying that even though in these days circumstances prevent the making of a perfectly complete work, "it is still useful not to remain wholly silent, because we may provoke those with a good supply of books into perfecting and completing the work."[6]

Professor Miethke has observed that polemical writing, a genre that requires the utmost currency for its effectiveness, was often composed, even in the fourteenth century, on the basis of a scholar's memory of the work to which he was responding, or even on hearsay accounts of texts, rather than on written copies. Written copies of new work, treatises, disputations, and the like, were difficult to obtain, even if one lived close to their origin in both place and time. There are very few fourteenth-century manuscripts of *Dialogus*, yet it is clear that Ockham's ideas had tremendous currency and occasioned bitter controversy throughout Europe, even in his own lifetime. In 1343, Duke Albert of Austria is said to have supported the position of the emperor, Ludvig of Bavaria, against the papacy, because he was persuaded by the emperor's report of the ideas in a "dialogus" produced by Master William of Ockham. Obviously papal interdict did not in fact prevent even Ockham's current work from circulating out of Munich, and, given the conditions, the chief method of such circulation, Miethke thinks, would have been oral, well in advance of written copies.[7]

It is important to recognize that Ockham's memorial training occurred as a part of his ordinary education, and that he expects his students to fill their memories as a part of their ordinary education. (The Magister in *Dialogus* has no reason to suppose his student will be exiled as he was, yet he urges him to fill his memory just the same.) Ockham did not educate himself with the idea that he might go to Munich, nor was he, as a student, the captive of provincial schools having, in consequence, infrequent access to libraries. His whole scholarly life until 1330 was spent in the greatest of European universities, his circle the most bookish of the time. And still it is clear that he read to memorize, that in composing he was able at will to draw extensive resources from his memorial library. He does indeed ask those with access to a supply of books to perfect his work, but what Ockham meant by "perfect" is not "to correct" in our sense (as a modern scholar, forced into similar circumstances, might beg indulgence for inexact citations, pleading a faulty memory). Ockham means to complete or fill in and add more; he apologizes for only skimming the surface of his analyses and expositions of the subject ("de prefatis ... nullatenus intromittam"), for if he had the latest material he would be able to fill out the contents he had earlier stored in his memory. This incomplete and prefatory work composed largely from memory fills 551 folio pages with material that is certainly not of an elementary nature.

Evidently Ockham's memory did not contain dim recollections of a few commonplaces learned in grammar school, and evidently too he did not pause frequently during composition to find references in his books, for he had none. Nor could he consult extensive indices in the library of the Munich Franciscans, or thumb through his own books for marginal *notae* marking passages pertinent to imperial power in order to do his research. And the thought of Ockham and his companions escaping down the Rhône from Avignon to Italy with a trunkful of parchment slips (to say nothing of persuading his papal jailors, who were suspicious precisely about his opinions, to let him keep such a heap of slips during four years of imprisonment) is simply silly. Yet exactly these activities – frequent consultation of indices, thumbing books to pick up previously marked passages, writing citations onto parchment slips, even "scissors-and-paste" composition – have all been presumed by many medievalists to have been the methods by which scholarship was conducted during this period. We are even solemnly told that Hugh of St. Victor was the last teacher to recommend a good memory as a scholarly necessity.[8]

It has been known for a long time that the publication of information during the medieval period often occurred by means of sermons and such oral forms. So Bernard of Clairvaux's preaching of the Crusades was disseminated quickly through Western Europe both by direct preaching on his part and by others preaching what he had said.[9] This was also an early Church custom; Cyril of Alexandria composed many sermons which he sent to all the bishops of Greece, who, in turn, memorized them and preached them to their own congregations.[10] All sorts of material was disseminated in this way; a famous example is the invention of eyeglasses, first disclosed in a sermon preached in February of 1306 by the Dominican friar Giordano (who belonged, incidentally, to the same convent at Pisa as did Bartolomeo da San Concordio).[11]

Observations by modern scholars that many full commentaries, such as that on Cicero's *Ad Herennium*, sprang up virtually fully formed in the late eleventh and early twelfth centuries (as did so many other written scholarly tools) are best explained by their compilers having been able to draw upon a stock of glosses and comments, developed and disseminated orally over a long time from one generation of masters to the next in monastery classrooms, and from one monastery to another via travelling scholars. John Ward aptly describes this as a "gloss potpourri . . . the accumulating mass of rhetorical wisdom [which] came to form a kind of anonymous pool, from which pitchers were drawn almost at random." The schoolroom, as he says, was a very conservative place, in which particular glosses might have a life of a millennium or more. It was also one of the most important locations for the preservation and dissemination of eclectic oral lore, for in it students learned to lay down pieces of text and commentary together in memory, via the sorts of heuristics I discussed earlier. Indeed, the piece-by-piece nature of memory storage may help to account for the line-by-line nature which most of the earliest commentaries took.[12] In an important sense, every ordinary gloss was essentially a florilegium of Important Things To Remember, at least in the judgment of its compilator, arranged in an order for easy storage and recollection.

The astonishing precision with which the Rouses have been able to date the emergence of complex glossating apparatus within a couple of decades in the twelfth century suggests strongly that the written versions express an existing oral tradition.[13] They were written down then rather than at an earlier time because a large, new public of university scholars needed to be accommodated. University activity heavily depended on oral forms, from the lecture itself, to the oral (and orational) nature of examinations, *disputationes*, and *sermones*. In lecture, students studied from books open before them, but it is significant, I think, that the manuscript illuminations typically show them without pens.[14] They would have mentally marked the important passages, as Hugh counsels, by memorizing them from the same codex each time (a problem solved when students owned their own copies of major texts), noting the shapes of the letters, the position of the text on the page, and then filing segments of it appropriately away, with the teacher's comments "attached" to the textual image. By contrast, a modern student in class or the library without a pen is a lost soul.

But in the minds of modern scholars oral transmission raises the question of accuracy; we tend to dismiss memory as a reliable disseminator and instead look solely to writing (manuscript copies or letters) as the agent for all varieties of accurate transmission. Yet, as I have observed before and will again here, medieval scholars simply did not share our distrust of memory's accuracy. Remembering Ockham's desire for "perfection" (and his comment can be multiplied endlessly in scholarly works throughout the Middle Ages), what was valued was completeness, copiousness, rather than objective accuracy, as we understand and value it now. In this as in much else, medieval assumptions about the occasionalness (temporality) and the plenitude or "copiousness" of literature are at odds with modern textual fundamentalism.

Richard de Bury's love for books was not that of a mere bibliophile, but a scholar's love (as Petrarch recognized).[15] Yet it is not at all clear in *Philobiblon* that every volume he saved from dust and dirt was saved physically. Some – how many we cannot know – he collected in memory and later had his secretaries write out from dictation. He tells us this directly, but it is also clear from the way he talks about books, what they are, and of what use, that trained memory and the book are closely linked – even for him, in the mid fourteenth century, the avid collector of one of Europe's greatest private libraries.

Bury closes his first chapter with a catalogue of metaphors for books, many of which we have already encountered as metaphors primarily for memory: *thesaurus, scrinium, favus* ("honey-comb"), and a couple that suggest he had encountered Hugh of St. Victor in some form (or at least shared some of his commonplaces): *arca Noe, lignum vitae,* and *scala Jacob.*[16] Most of these reappear elsewhere in his treatise as motifs for both books and the memorial activities of scholarship. For in Bury's prose, as in that of so many other writers, the two are practically interchangeable. Having a good memory is virtually as good as having the book itself, and better than having an untrustworthy written copy of it. Such play, it seems to me, can be found in a passage such as the following, when Bury describes his collecting habits in Paris, "the paradise of the world."[17] There, he says, are to be found delightful libraries above little rooms redolent of sweet aromas, "super cellas aromatum redolentes" (p. 70, line 2), which include the cloisters ("prata") of the Academy, the by-ways ("diverticula") of Athens, the walks of the Peripatetics, the promontories of Parnassus, and the porches ("porticus") of the Stoics. And then follows a catalogue of classical and Christian authors, after which Bury says that "having unbound the strings of our treasuries and our *sacculi*, we distributed coinage with a joyful heart, and we recovered by this ransom priceless books from mud and grit."[18] I do not wish to argue that Richard de Bury bought no books, for it is evident both from *Philobiblon* and contemporary accounts that he bought and transported for his personal library a great many, though whether there were really five cartloads, as the Durham chronicler has it, may be wondered at.[19] But I do wish to point out that the language in this passage plays heavily with common metaphors for memory training as well as with the literal action of buying books. *Thesaurus, sacculus,* and the actions of redeeming the words of authors with a payment and of dispensing coins from one's *sacculus*, joyous heart (memory) and all, are all metaphors we commonly encounter in works about memory, and it seems to me that Bury may well be engaging in a playful scholarly conceit here, meaning perhaps that where poorer scholars depended upon the *sacculi* of their memories to redeem books, he had tangible coin to pay. Or perhaps he means (for I don't think he was mean-spirited) that he depended on both the *thesaurus* of his purse and that of his memory to ransom wisdom from dirt and neglect; he uses the plural forms of both *thesaurus* and *sacculus*, after all.

Twice Bury comments directly on how he depended on the industry of others to collect books, especially the most recent of works. In chapter 4, the neglected books are made to complain of how shabbily they have been treated, but comment favorably on virtuous clerks who use them properly, that is, memorize them:

First of all it behooves you to eat the book with Ezekiel, that the belly of your memory may be sweetened within ... Thus our nature secretly working in our familiars, the listeners hasten up gladly as the magnet draws the willing iron. What an infinite power of books lies down in Paris or Athens, and yet sounds at the same time in Britain and Rome! In truth while they lie quietly they are moved, while holding their own places they are borne everywhere in the minds of their listeners.[20]

Later Bury describes his network of clerical searchers, who reported to him orally every new discourse and argument, no matter how half-baked and unfinished, from every part of Christendom, exactly the correspondents denied by edict to Ockham. They are like keen hunters after rabbits, like men setting nets and hooks for every little fish ("pisciculus"):

From the body of Sacred Law to the notebook of yesterday's bits of sophomoric discourse, nothing could escape these searchers. If a devout sermon sounded in the fountain of the Christian faith, the holy court of Rome, or if a new question was aired with novel arguments, if the solidity of Paris ... or English perspicuity ... had set forth anything concerning the advancement of knowledge or the explanation of faith, this immediately was poured into our ears still fresh, unerased by any word-scatterer and uncorrupted by any idiot, but from the purest pressing of the wine-press it passed directly into the vats of our memory for clarifying.[21]

These two passages demonstrate clearly that oral transmission from one memory to another was still an important and respected aspect of the dissemination of learning in academic and administrative circles during Bury's time. Books can stay physically on their shelves in Paris and yet move to the centers of England and Rome, if they have been transmitted by one who imitates the prophet Ezekiel and first consumes (memorizes) their contents. Everything from authoritative canons to the latest controversy is reported directly to him orally, memory to memory – not having to go through the unreliable medium of scribal copying. It is worth pausing over this last statement, for it is so foreign to modern assumptions that one may slide over it. The ignorant, word-scattering, cloudy-headed idiots who would erase ("denigratum") or otherwise spoil the texts in transmitting them are the professional copyists and secretaries into whose charge the copying of books for university scholars had now passed. Bury is saying that he regards the memorial transmission of a trained cleric as more reliable than the written copy produced by one of these scribes.

MEMORY, DIGESTION, AND RUMINATION IN MONASTIC READING

When one's first relationship with a text is not to encounter another mind (or subdue it, as one suspects sometimes) or to understand it on its own terms, but to use it as a source of communally experienced wisdom for one's own life, gained by memorizing from it however much and in whatever fashion one is able or willing to do; when one's head is constantly filled with a chorus of voices available promptly and on any subject, how does such a relationship to the works of other writers differently define the meanings of such literary concepts as "reader," "text," "author?" In the next part of this chapter I would like to examine in some detail just what a medieval scholar meant when he said that he had read a book. I am not focusing here on the activity called *lectio*, "study," though that is the word actually derived from *legere*,[22] but rather the activity which, in each individual reader, must succeed *lectio* in order to make it profitable, that is, *meditatio*.

Hugh of St. Victor well defines the difference between *lectio* and *meditatio* in his *Didascalicon*. *Lectio*, "reading" or "study," trains one's natural *ingenium* by the order and method ("ordo et modus") of exposition and analysis, including the disciplines of grammar and dialectic. Meditation begins in study ("principium sumit a lectione") but "is bound by none of study's rules or precepts. For it delights to range along open ground, where it fixes its free gaze upon the contemplation of truth, drawing together now these, now those ideas, or now penetrating into profundities, leaving nothing doubtful, nothing obscure. The start of learning, thus, lies in *lectio*, but its consummation lies in meditation."[23]

In Hugh of St. Victor's *De archa Noe*, the ark of studies which one builds board by board in one's memory, the entire process of learning centers in meditation. The Ark of Wisdom/Prudence ("arca sapientiae") has three storeys, which represent three stages of moral judgment: correct, useful, and habitual (*rectus, utilis, necessarius*). I am in the first storey of the ark when I begin to love to meditate on (that is, memorize) Scripture, and my thoughts freely (*libenter*) and often consider thereby the virtues of the saints, the works of God, and all things pertaining to moral life or to the exercise of the mind. I can then say that my knowledge is correct, but it is not yet useful, for of what use is knowledge hidden away and inactive? But if I not only know but act in a way that is good and useful, so that the virtues I have learned to admire in others I make my own ("meas faciam") by disciplining myself to conform at least outwardly to right living, then I can say that the understanding of my heart is useful, and I will then ascend to the second storey. When the virtue I display in works is mine internally as well, when my goodness is completely habitual (that is, a state of being) and necessary to me, then I ascend to the third storey, where knowledge and virtue become essential parts of me (become "familiar" or "domesticated," to use another common metaphor).[24] What Hugh describes here is a process of completely internalizing what one has read (and one must remember that *habitus* is used like Greek *hexis* in all these discussions), and the agency by which this is accomplished is *meditatio*, the process of memory-training, storage, and retrieval.

Petrarch supplies one of the most revealing analyses of reading in the late Middle Ages. Like Ockham, Petrarch was clearly no backward provincial, clinging to outmoded ways of study. Yet Petrarch's name is linked with those of Cicero and Thomas Aquinas in many Renaissance memory texts as one of the chief proponents of an artificial memory system, a reputation that seems to be based not on his having written a book of memorial technique but on his copious florilegial collection of commonplaces, *Rerum memorandarum libri*.[25]

Petrarch was greatly devoted to the writing of St. Augustine. He carried a pocket-sized copy of the *Confessions* everywhere with him, and used it on at least one occasion for *sortes Augustinianae* exactly on the model of Augustine's own *sortes Biblicae* in the garden, recounted in *Confessions* VIII.[26] The very custom of using books for *sortes* is an interesting example of regarding books as personal sources whose function is to provide memorial cues to oneself, divine influences being able to prophesy through the images of letters on the page just as they can during sleep through the images written in the memory.

Petrarch composed three dialogues with Augustine which he called his *Secretum*, not designed for publication until after his death.[27] In these he confesses his doubts and sins to the saint through the mouth of his persona, Francesco. Francesco bewails the frailty of his body, the disgust he feels for Milan, "the most melancholy and disorderly of towns" which assails his soul daily with its clamor and dirt. Augustine reminds him of many literary works addressing this problem, including one of his own; do these not help him? Well, yes, says Francesco,

at the time of reading, much help; but no sooner is the book from my hands than all my feeling for it vanishes.

AUG: This way of reading is become common now; there is such a mob of lettered men ... But if you would imprint in their own places secure notes [*suis locis certas notas impresseris*] you would then gather the fruit of your reading.

FRAN: What notes?

AUG: Whenever you read a book and meet with any wholesome maxims by which you feel your soul stirred or enthralled, do not trust merely to the powers of your native abilities [*viribus ingenii fidere*], but make a point of learning them by heart and making them quite familiar by meditating on them ... so that whenever or where some urgent case of illness arises, you have the remedy as though written in your mind ... When you come to any passages that seem to you useful, impress secure marks against them, which may serve as hooks in your memory [*uncis memoria*], lest otherwise they might fly away.[28]

The margins of Petrarch's books are full of such marks.[29] This passage makes quite clear that Petrarch used them, at least in part as did Grosseteste, to construct his mental concordance of texts, each hooked into its own place in his memory by a key. There they provide the matter for prudence, the experience upon which Francesco can draw in need, a remedy for distress written in the mind ("velut in animo conscripta"). The process whereby what he takes from his texts is imprinted ("impressere") is meditation.

And it is clear from what he says that such memorizing is done according to a learned and practiced technique. One does not rely upon *ingenium*, "aptitude," one hides the fruits of reading in the recesses of memory ("in memorie penetralibus")[30] and through practice makes one's reading familiar to oneself, domesticates it (to use Albertus Magnus's word), makes it one's own. Perhaps no advice is as common in medieval writing on the subject, and yet so foreign, when one thinks about it, to the habits of modern scholarship as this notion of making one's own what one reads in someone else's work. "Efficere tibi illas familiares", Augustine's admonition to Francesco, does not mean "familiar" in quite the modern sense. *Familiaris* is rather a synonym of *domesticus*, that is, to make something familiar by making it a part of your own experience. This adaptation process allows for a tampering with the original text that a modern scholar would (and does) find quite intolerable, for it violates most of our notions concerning accuracy, objective scholarship, and the integrity of the text. Modern scholars learn all they can about a text, making sure they know the meaning of every word in it. So did medieval scholars; that was what *lectio* was for. But a modern scholar is concerned primarily with getting the text objectively right, treating it as an ultimate and sole authority. We are taught to legitimate our reading (by which we mean our interpretation or understanding) solely by the text; we see ourselves as its servants, and although both the possibility and the utility of such absolute objectivity have been called into question many times over the last century, this attitude remains a potent assumption in scholarly debate, even for those most wedded to reader-response theories.

But the medieval scholar's relationship to his texts is quite different from modern objectivity. Reading is to be digested, to be ruminated, like a cow chewing her cud, or like a bee making honey from the nectar of flowers. Reading is memorized with the aid of *murmur*, mouthing the words subvocally as one turns the text over in one's memory; both Quintilian and Martianus Capella stress how murmur accompanies meditation. It is this movement of the mouth that established rumination as a basic metaphor for memorial activities.[31] The process familiarizes a text to a medieval scholar, in a way like that by which human beings may be said to familiarize their food. It is both physiological and psychological, and it changes both the food and its consumer. Gregory the Great writes, "We ought to transform what we read within our very selves, so that when our mind is stirred by what it hears, our life may concur by practicing what has been heard."[32] Hugh of St. Victor writes of walking through the forest (*silva*) of Scripture, "whose ideas [*sententias*] like so many sweetest fruits, we pick as we read and chew [*ruminamus*] as we consider them."[33]

The various stages of the reading process are succinctly described at the end of Hugh of St. Victor's *Chronicle* Preface (Appendix A). All exegesis emphasized that understanding was grounded in a thorough knowledge of the *littera*, and for this one had to know grammar, rhetoric, history, and all the other disciplines that give information, the work of *lectio*. But one takes all of that and builds upon it during meditation; this phase of reading is ethical in its nature, or "tropological" (turning the text onto and into one's self) as Hugh defines it. I think one might best begin to understand the concept of levels in exegesis as stages (*gradus*, "stairs") of a continuous action, and the four-fold way (or three-fold, as the case may be) as a useful mnemonic for readers, reminding them of how to complete the entire reading process. *Littera* and *allegoria* (grammar and typological history) are the work of *lectio* and are essentially informative about a text; tropology and anagogy are the activities of digestive meditation and constitute the ethical activity of making one's reading one's own.

The ruminant image is basic to understanding what was involved in *memoria* as well as *meditatio*, the two being understood as the agent and its activity. Though monastic theology developed the idea of meditation in terms of prayer and psalmody, its basis in the functions of memory continued to be emphasized. *Ruminatio* is an image of regurgitation, quite literally intended; the memory is a stomach, the stored texts are the sweet-smelling cud originally drawn from the gardens of books (or lecture), they are chewed on the palate. Gregory the Great says that in Scripture "uenter mens dicitur," thereby adding *uenter* to *cor* as a synonym for memory in Scripture.[34] Six centuries later, Hugh of St. Victor, discussing *memoria* in *Didascalicon*, says that it is imperative to replicate frequently the matter one has memorized and placed in the little chest, *arcula*, of one's memory, and "to recall it from the stomach of memory to the palate."[35]

Composition is also spoken of as *ruminatio*. In one of his sermons, Augustine says that he has been caught unexpectedly by a mistake in the day's reading – the lector read the wrong text. "Since I hadn't prepared a sermon for your graces on this subject, I acknowledge that it is a command from the Lord [through the lector's error] that I should deal with it. What I intended today, you see, was to leave you all chewing the cud [*vos in ruminatione permittere*] ... So may the Lord our God himself grant me sufficient capacity and you some useful listening."[36] Nothing in the sermon text we now have distinguishes this sermon from Augustine's premeditated ones. Even assuming editorial revision, convention evidently required that an orator's improvisations be as artfully composed as any other work. To speak ex tempore requires a well-provided, well-practiced, and accessible inventory, as Augustine compellingly demonstrates in this sermon.

Another example, the most famous of all, is in Bede's account of the English poet, Caedmon, who changed what he learned by hearing in *lectio*, or sermons, into sweetest poetry by recollecting it within himself ("rememorandum rerum") and ruminating like a clean animal ("quasi mundum animal ruminendo").[37] Caedmon's rumination occurs at night, the optimal time for such activity; the fact that he was a cowherd may be coincidental to the story, but Bede emphasizes it so much that one suspects he thought the detail significant in the context. Philip West has suggested that his profession suits his ruminative activities; perhaps the ancient link between poets and ruminative animals, found in many cultures, has some connection with the rumination of composition.

Metaphors which use digestive activities are so powerful and tenacious that digestion should be considered another basic functional model for the complementary activities of reading and composition, collection and recollection. Unlike the heart, no medical tradition seems to have placed any of the sensory-processing functions in the stomach, but "the stomach of memory" as a metaphoric model had a long run. Milton, his biographers agree, mentally composed a store of verses each day, which he then dictated to a secretary. John Aubrey comments that while Milton had a good natural memory, "I believe that his excellent method of thinking and disposing did much to help his memory," a clear reference to the kind of training, disciplined practice, and deliberate design ("disposing") that had always been features of classical memory-training. And Milton's anonymous biographer, speaking also of his mental composition, remarks that if the poet's secretary were late, "he would complain, saying he wanted to be milked."[38]

Likening the products of mental rumination to those of digestion led to some excellent comedy; one thinks at once of Rabelais and of Chaucer's *Summoner's Tale*. But the metaphor was also realized seriously. There is a remarkably graphic statement of it in the *Regula monachorum* ascribed to Jerome, though composed probably in the twelfth century. The writer speaks of the various stomach rumblings, belchings, and fartings that accompany the nightly gathering of the monks in prayer. But, he continues, as a famous pastor has said, just as smoke drives out bees, so belching caused by indigestion drives away the inspiration of the Holy Spirit. Belching and farting, however, are caused by the preparation and digestion of food. "Wherefore, as a belch bursts forth from the stomach according to the quality of the food, and the index of a fart is according to the sweetness or stench of its odor, so the cogitations of the inner man bring forth words, and *from the abundance of the heart the mouth speaks* (Lk. 6:45). The just man, eating, fills his soul. And when he is replete with sacred doctrine, from the good treasury of his memory he brings forth those things which are good."[39] No comment is needed on this text, so very odd and even irreligious to us, except to observe that I can think of few more cogent statements of the curious consequences deriving from ancient and medieval notions of the soul's embodiment than this serious, pious linking of the sweetness of prayer and of the stomach. The notion of the Spirit (*flatus*) as a breath or wind is Biblical; modern scholars, accustomed to thinking of this trope as a mere figure of speech, would never make the connection with a fart (also *flatus*) that this medieval writer did. It stems from exactly the psychosomatic assumptions that directed medical writers to prescribe foot-soaking, head-washing, and chewing coriander to improve memory, sweetness of the mouth and stomach being evidently as necessary to the healthy production of memory as a stress-free body (with relaxed feet and a non-itching scalp) is to productive concentration. Modern scholars who think they have observed subversion, class rivalries, or even a ribald "medieval unconscious" at odds with its piety in the vomiting, shitting, farting, and belching that characterize the hybrids in some late thirteenth- and fourteenth-century English manuscripts containing texts such as Psalters and Decretals – texts which require much memory work – would do well to ponder the pervasive, Biblically based, monastic trope of prayer as spiritual flatulence. It was often intended to provoke laughter and humility, but its use in books of meditation is not unconscious, nor should we assume it to be impious.[40]

The monastic custom of reading during meals is described in some texts as an explicit literalizing of the metaphor of consuming a book as one consumes food. A late *Regula* for women adapted from the writings of St. Jerome makes the connection clear: there should be reading during meals "so that while the body is fattened [*saginatur*] with food, the mind should be filled [*saturetur*] with reading."[41] Benedict's Rule says that "while the brothers are eating they should not lack in reading";[42] the somewhat later *Regula magistri* gives the reason why in words much like those of the later rule I just quoted.[43] Every brother who has learned his letters should take his turn reading during meals, "so that there should never be a lack of restoration for the body nor of divine food, for as Scripture says, man does not live by bread alone but in every word of the Lord, so that in two ways the Brothers may be repaired, when they chew with their mouths and are filled up through their ears."[44] The Rule for women continues by characterizing how each sister should follow the reading. With absorbed, intent mind ("mens sobria intenta sit"), she should actively, emotionally enter into the reading. She sighs anxiously when, in prophecy or historical narrative, the word of God shows enmity to the wicked. She is filled with great joy when the favor of the Lord is shown to the good. "Words do not resound, but sighs; not laughter and derision but tears."[45] This last comment is a reformation of one of Jerome's dicta, that "the preacher should arouse wailing rather than applause,"[46] itself an idea that accords with the advice given by Quintilian and others that an orator must above all arouse the emotions of his audience. This Rule admonishes against laughter because, like applause, derision is associated by the writer with detachment and disengagement from the material, tears with the opposite. The state of being "engaged with" and "totally absorbed in" the text (as I would translate the adjectives *sobria* and *intenta*) is necessary for its proper digestion.

Commentary on the two moments in Scripture (Ezekiel 3:3 and Revelation 10: 9–11) in which a prophet is given a book to eat that is sweet as honey in the mouth underlines the need to consume one's reading.[47] "Therefore we devour and digest the book, when we read the words of God," says Hugh of Fouilloy in the twelfth century. "Many indeed read, but from their reading they remain ignorant ... others devour and digest the holy books but are not ignorant because their memory does not let go of the rules for life whose meaning it can grasp."[48] And Jerome, commenting on the Ezekiel text, says "when by assiduous meditation we shall have stored the book of the Lord in the treasury of our memory, we fill our belly in a spiritual sense, and our bowels are filled, that we may have with the Apostle the bowels of mercy (Coloss. 3:12), and that belly is filled concerning which Jeremias said: 'My bowels, my bowels! I am pained at my very heart' (Jer. 4:19)."[49]

Biblical study provides a model for other literary study. In the same part of the second dialogue in *Secretum* we looked at earlier, Augustine says that one needs a store of precepts from one's reading, in order to guard against sudden emotion and passion – anger, for instance. Yes, replies Francesco, he has found much good on this matter not only in philosophers but in poets as well. And he proceeds to give an interpretive reading of *Aeneid*, 1, 52–57, the description of Aeolus in the cave of the winds:

As I carefully study every word, I have heard with my ears the fury, the rage, the roar of the winds; I have heard the trembling of the mountain and the din. Notice how well it all applies to the tempest of anger ... I have heard the king, sitting on his high place, his sceptre grasped in his hand, subduing, binding in chains, and imprisoning those rebel blasts.[50]

And he demonstrates his interpretation by appealing to the last line of Virgil's description, "mollitque animos et temperat iras" (1. 57); this, says Petrarch, shows that this passage can refer to the mind when it is vexed by anger.

Augustine praises the meaning which Francesco has found hidden in the poet's words, which are so copious and familiar in his memory. For, "whether Virgil himself meant this while he wrote, or whether, entirely remote from any such consideration, he wished only to describe a maritime storm in these verses and nothing else,"[51] the lesson which Francesco has derived concerning anger is truthful and well-said. Extraordinary as this opinion is to a scholar brought up on notions of the inviolate authority of the text, we should not assume on the other hand that Petrarch's words, in the mouth of his revered mentor, indicate only an extreme subjectivity. *Virgil's* words remain significant themselves as the subject of the disciplines associated with *lectio*, and a source of wisdom and experience (via memory) for anyone who cares to read and remember them. The focus for Petrarch at this point is rather on what the individual reader makes of those words, and that focus is not scientific but ethical.

Virgil's words, having been devoured (or one might say harvested), digested, and familiarized by Francesco through *meditatio*, have now become *his* words as they cue the representational processes of his recollection. It is as though at this point the student of the text, having digested it by re-experiencing it in memory, has become not its interpreter, but its new author, or re-author. Petrarch has re-spoken Virgil; re-written Virgil, we would say with strong disapproval. But the re-writing which is acknowledged in what both Augustine and Francesco say, is seen as a good, not for Virgil's text, which is irrelevant at this point except as it has occasioned Petrarch's remembrance, but for Francesco's moral life.[52]

Hugh of St. Victor's Preface to the *Chronicle* (Appendix A) gives usefully succinct definitions of the three "levels" of Biblical exegesis which indicate quite clearly which belong to the activity of *lectio* and which to *meditatio*. *Littera* is the subject of grammatical and rhetorical study; *historia* is the foreshadowing relationship of one event in the Bible to another, and is what is often also called *allegoria*. After these disciplines comes *tropologia* (which is more like what we think of as "allegorical"); it is what the text means to us when we turn its words, like a mirror, upon ourselves, how we understand it when we have domesticated it and made it our own, and that is the special activity of memorative *meditatio*, the culmination of *lectio* but bound by none of its rules, a free play of the recollecting mind. "Holy Scripture," wrote Gregory the Great, quoting Augustine, "presents a kind of mirror to the eyes of the mind, that our inner face may be seen in it. There truly we learn our own ugliness, there our own beauty. There we know how much we have gained, there how far we lie from our goal."[53] As we do this, the text's initial sweetness may well turn to indigestion and pain, as it did for St. John, but such dolor is to be welcomed. For, as Hugh of Fouilloy comments on Apocalypse 10:11, "He certainly suffers pain in his stomach who feels affliction of mind. For this can be understood because, while the word of God may begin by being sweet in the mouth of our heart, before long the mind [*animus*] grows bitter in doubt against itself." And he quotes Gregory, "We devour the book when with eager desire we clothe ourselves with the words of life."[54]

The psychology of the memory phantasm provides the rationale for the ethical value of the reading method which Petrarch describes. A properly made phantasm is both a likeness (*simulacrum*) and one's gut-level response to it (*intentio*), and it is an emotional process that causes change in the body. The insistently physical matrix of the whole memorative process accounts for Petrarch's slow, detailed refashioning of Virgil's description. The active agency of the reader, *discutiens*, "breaking up" or "shattering" (one could even translate "deconstructing") each single word as he recreates the scene in his memory, is emphasized: "Ego autem audivi ... audivi ... audivi." He re-hears, re-sees, re-feels, experiences and re- experiences. In this way, Virgil's words are embodied in Petrarch's recollection as an experience of tumult and calm that is more physiological (emotional, passionate) than mental, in our sense. Desire underlies the whole experience, changing from turmoil through anger to repose.[55] The recreated reading becomes useful precisely because in the heat of passion Petrarch's emotions replay that process of change, for he can remember what right action *feels* like. That is not a logical decision process, but one of desire and will guided through the process of change by remembered habit, "firma facilitas" or *hexis*.

I have noted before that the medieval understanding of the complete process of reading does not observe in the same way the basic distinction we make between "what I read in a book" and "my experience." This discussion by Petrarch, I think, makes clear why, for "what I read in a book" *is* "my experience," and I make it mine by incorporating it (and we should understand the word "incorporate" quite literally) in my memory. One remembers the boast of Chaucer's eagle in *The House of Fame* that he can so palpably represent "skiles" (arguments) to his students that they can "shake hem by the biles" (*HF*, II, 869–70), the avian manner of making them one's dear friends.

In this way, reading a book extends the process whereby one memory engages another in a continuing dialogue that approaches Plato's ideal (expressed in *Phaedrus*) of two living minds engaged in learning. Medieval reading is conceived to be not a "hermeneutical circle" (which implies mere solepsism) but more like a "hermeneutical dialogue" between two memories, that in the text being made very much present as it is familiarized to that of the reader. Isidore of Seville, we remember, in words echoed notably by John of Salisbury, says that written letters recall through the windows of our eyes the voices of those who are not present to us (and one thinks too of that evocative medieval phrase, *voces paginarum*, "the voices of the pages").[56] So long as the reader, in meditation (which is best performed in a *murmur* or low voice), reads attentively, that other member of the dialogue is in no danger of being lost, the other voice will sound through the written letters. Perhaps it is not inappropriate to recall again, having just spoken of Petrarch, the Greek verb, *anagignôskô*, "to read," but literally "to know again" or "remember."

TWO WAYS OF READING

A great deal has been written on the subject of audible reading in antiquity, and its apparent replacement by silent reading at some later time. Reading aloud is assumed to have been the more common method, and those who believe that there is sharp contrast between orality and literacy have made much of a change from one form to the other, seeing it as a shift of sensibility from the "earmindedness" of orality to the "eyemindedness" of literacy. Judicious scholars of this school have always known that silent reading to oneself was also practiced in antiquity, but have insisted that it was regarded as strange and uncommon.[57] It seems to me, however, that silent reading, *legere tacite* or *legere sibi*, as Benedict and others call it,[58] and reading aloud, *clare legere* in *voce magna* or *viva voce*, were two distinct methods of reading taught for different purposes in ancient schools and both practiced by ancient readers, and that they correspond roughly to those stages in the study process called *meditatio* and *lectio*. They clearly acquire additional meanings, perhaps even a whole theology, in medieval monastic culture;[59] and university library statutes suggest that reading silently (*legere tacite*) may have become more noiseless in a university reading room than the phenomenon of the same name may have been in a monastic cell.[60] But I think these developments themselves were founded in and continued to be based upon these distinctive but complementary, elementary pedagogical procedures, the *viva vox* of lecture and the *vox tenuis*, as it is called sometimes, of memory and meditation.[61]

The *locus classicus* for any discussion of ancient reading habits is, in fact, from late antiquity: Augustine's description in the *Confessions*, VI, iii, of Ambrose reading:[62]

Now I regarded Ambrose himself as a fortunate man as far as worldly standing went, since he enjoyed the respect of powerful people . . . I had not begun to guess, still less experience in my own case, what hope he bore within him, or what a stuggle he waged against the temptations to which his eminent position exposed him, or the encouragement he received in times of difficulty, or what exquisite delights he savored in his secret mouth, the mouth of his heart [memory], as he chewed [over Your bread] [*occultum os eius quod erat in corde eius, quam sapida gaudia de pane tuo ruminaret*] . . . There were questions I wanted to put to him, but I was unable to do so as fully as I wished, because the crowds of people who came to him on business impeded me, allowing me little opportunity either to talk or to listen to him. He was habitually available to serve them in their needs, and in the very scant time that he was not with them he would be refreshing [*lit.* remaking] either his body with necessary food or his mind with reading [*aut corpus reficiebat necessariis sustentaculis aut lectione animum*]. When he read, his eyes would travel across the pages and his mind would explore the sense, but his voice and tongue were silent [*lit.* stilled] [*sed cum legebat, oculi ducebantur per paginas et cor intellectum rimabatur, vox autem et lingua quiescebant*]. We would sometimes be present, for he did not forbid anyone access, nor was it customary for anyone to be announced; and on these occasions we watched him reading silently in that way [and never the other] [*sic eum legentem vidimus tacite et aliter numquam*],[63] and so we too would sit for a long time in silence [*sedentesque in diuturno silentio*], for who would have the heart to interrupt a man so engrossed [*tam intento*]? Then we would steal away, guessing that in the brief time he had seized for the refreshment of his mind [*reparandae menti suae*], he was resting from the din of other people's affairs [*feriatum a strepitu causarum alienarum*], and reluctant to be called away to other business. We thought too that he might be apprehensive that if he read aloud, and any closely attentive listener [*ne auditore suspenso et intento*] were doubtful on any point, or the author he was reading used any obscure expressions, he would have to stop and explain various difficult problems that might arise, and after spending time on this be unable to read as much of the book as he wished. Another and perhaps more cogent reason for his habit of reading silently was his need to conserve his voice, which was very prone to hoarseness. But whatever his reason, that man undoubtedly had a good one.

I have quoted this description at length because I think it is often misread. It presents an excellent contrast between the two kinds of reading, *lectio* and *meditatio*. Ambrose withdraws over a book into silence, *meditatio*, even though others are present. Augustine contrasts it specifically here with the activity of *lectio*, delivered in a loud voice to a listener who freely asks questions. In meditational reading, Ambrose, the reader, is *intentus*; in the other kind, the listener is *suspensus* and *intentus*.

In a scholarly tradition going back to Norden (1922), Balogh (1927), and Hendrickson (1929), Augustine's response is characterized as one of "surprise and wonder" at Ambrose's "strange" habit.[64] I do not find these traits in what Augustine says, however. Instead this seems to me a sympathetic portrait of a very busy man's efforts to make time for the kind of scholarly study that refreshes him, written (we should remember) by a man who by then was himself a very busy bishop, subject to exactly the interruptions and demands he shows us in Ambrose. What surprises Augustine is that

Ambrose never seemed to read in *the other* way, though others were present ("et aliter nunquam"). This situation helps to explain the slight defensiveness of Augustine's last remark about Ambrose's weak voice, responding to what might be seen as his rudeness or failure in duty. Saving the voice is a reason given for using *vox tenuis*, in addition to its usefulness for memorizing, in the rhetoric of Fortunatianus, who was more or less Augustine's contemporary.

The basic contrast in Augustine's portrait of Ambrose is carried in the two words *strepitus* and *tacitus*.[65] Meditative reading is Ambrose's means of acquiring *silentium* amid the *strepitus* of his daily activities, even in the common room where his petitioners gathered. To repair his mind ("reparandae menti suae" – we notice again the underlying motif of building), Ambrose refrains from *lectio* and engages instead in *meditatio*.

Strepitus, especially for Augustine, means "loud noise, confusion, rumbling," and other sorts of disordered, unconcentrated, busy noise, the interruption that daily congress creates. At the end of Book IX of the *Confessions*, Augustine laments the contrast between the meditative conversation between Monica and himself, as they talk alone (*soli*) and gradually ascend to mystical contemplation ("venimus in mentes nostras et transcendimus eas, ut attingeremus regionem ubertatis indeficientis, unde pascis Israel in aeternum veritate pabulo"),[66] and descend back to the chattering noise of the mouth where words are born and die ("ad *strepitum* oris nostri, ubi verbum et incipitur et finitur"; my emphasis). The contrast here is exactly that made in his description of Ambrose, and casts some additional light on it. For Augustine never says that his conversation with Monica ceases; all the verbs continue to be in the first person plural, indicating shared activities. Being *soli* and *taciti* does not mean being "solitary" or "private" in a modern sense, nor does it mean "quiet" in our sense; it has rather to do with the difference between their concentrated, attentive, meditational conversation and *strepitus*, between rumination and chit-chat. Indeed, *while they are speaking* ("dum loquimur"), they touch a little ("modice") that eternal life, "toto jictu cordis," "with an all-out thrust of our hearts." The heart-thrust here should, I think, be understood as a figure for a particular effort of recollection, as Augustine plays on the root of Latin *recordari* (*cor, cordis*).[67]

Whether or not the vocal chords are used is a secondary difference between the two methods of reading. This distinction is well defined by Isidore of Seville in some brief memory advice that he gives in his *Sententiae*. After advising that one divide a long text in order to memorize it according to the memorial principle of *brevitas*, he says that memory is also much better aided by silent reading than by reading aloud: "Silent reading is more acceptable to the senses [meaning here the interior senses engaged in making memories] than full-voice; the intellect is better trained [*lit.* constructed] when the voice in reading is quieted, and in silence the tongue is moved. For by voiced reading the body is tired and the voice's sharpness is dulled."[68] Ambrose's silent reading is not a function of whether his lips move or not, but of his single-minded concentration, the solitude and silence he creates for himself, even in a busy room.

Augustine begins his description of Ambrose with the metaphor of rumination; Ambrose's hidden mouth of his recollecting heart ruminates the texts of Scripture. Such reading was nourishment for his mind, as food was for his body (yet another instance of the digestion–rumination metaphor associated with *meditatio*). When he read for this purpose, his eyes were led over the page as his recollecting mind cracked open its meaning ("cor intellectum rimabatur"). The verb *rimor* is related to the noun *rima*, meaning "crack, fissure," and was used originally in an agricultural context to mean "turn up" or "tear open" the ground. *Rimor* is used by Virgil of a vulture feasting on entrails, and by Juvenal of an augur pouring over the heart of a sacrificed chicken.[69] All of this indicates that meditative reading, *legere tacite*, was a slow, thorough process in keeping with its memorative function, one in which each word was examined thoroughly ("broken into pieces") as one stored a piece of text away together with its heuristic associations. *Rimor* is an intensely energetic, suspenseful, concentrated, and meticulous activity, which gives a vigor to meditation that the placid image of cud-chewing may not.

This concentration is described as *tacitus, intentus*, a state in which, in this scene, both Ambrose and his companions are in long-lasting silence ("diuturno silentio"). *Silentium* is also a word found in late-antique rhetorical texts, those of the tradition Augustine was educated in, in connection with the *meditatio* necessary for *memoria*. Thus, Martianus Capella advising on the techniques of memory describes how to produce the state of concentration necessary for firm recollection: texts to be learned are not "read in a loud voice, but are more usefully meditated in a murmur; and it is clear that the memory is stimulated more readily at night than during the day, when also the silence everywhere helps, nor is concentration interrupted by sensory stimuli from outside."[70] *Silentium* is the accompaniment and also the result of being *intentus*, of *meditatio*, and *memoria* (which is why memory is easier at night) but it is evidently not incompatible with the vocal *murmur* which, together with writing on one's *tabulae*, helps greatly in memorizing.[71]

Intensity is also part of the attitude the student needs listening to his master's *lectio*; Augustine describes how such a listener would respond, if only Ambrose were reading "magna voce." Since listening students had to memorize the commentary as they heard it, clearly the *intentus* necessary to remember had to be part of their mental attitude as well. In both *lectio* and *meditatio*, *intentus* refers to the absorbed, suspenseful attitude, "hanging on each word," which the memory needs for success. This is mental silence, lack of noise (*strepitus*), mental solitude; modern students certainly recognize the state, but we associate it with "individual creativity" rarely achieved, rather than with an ordinary requirement for reading, or indeed most kinds of writing. Antiquity and the Middle Ages associated it with memory and recollection, and when they speak of silence and solitude in such a context, this state of attentive concentration is what they usually mean. They also thought that it could be taught, and encouraged practice and techniques for achieving it.[72]

This understanding of silence is still evident towards the end of the Middle Ages in the work of a scholastic rather than monastic writer, Thomas Aquinas. When, in the *Summa theologica*, he digests for his readers Tullius' memory rules, Thomas alters one of them in a significant way. The *Ad Herennium* states that "solitude" conserves the sharp outlines of memory-images ("solitudo conservat integras simulacrorum figuras"); Thomas changes the reading to "solicitude" ("sollicitudo conservat integras simulacrorum figuras").[73] He does so, I think, because he understood the essential importance of a memory's being an *affectus* or *pathos*, that is, he knew the sensory-emotional nature of the state we call concentration (and think of as entirely mental). *Sollicitudo* is best translated in English as "worry," as a dog is said to worry a bone; it is conceptually like Augustine's use of *rimor* and Petrarch's of *discutere*. After nearly a millennium of monastic development of the twin ideas of "solitude" and "silence," the quality of intense, aroused attention implied in *meditatio* even in ancient pedagogy, and its fundamental necessity in the disciplines of memory, was completely apparent to Thomas Aquinas. For him, *solitudo*, in the context of memory training, is synonymous with *sollicitudo*, that attitude of mind which vexes or worries the emotions and the sensations, in order to engage in the activity of making, storing, recalling memory-images, to the exclusion of outside *strepitus* and bustle even when it is going on immediately around one. Thomas's success at producing this state in himself is attested to by the many stories of his peers. And without that degree of emotional concentration, memory fails.

Thomas Aquinas's biographers associated his deep concentration with his prodigious memory; Francis of Assisi's biographers do as well. Thomas of Celano writes: "whenever he read in the Sacred Books, and something was once tossed into his mind, he indelibly wrote it in his heart. He had a memory for [whole] books because having heard something once he took it in not idly, but with continued devout attention his emotion-memory [*affectus*] chewed on it. This he said was the fruitful method for teaching and reading, not to have wandered about through a thousand learned discussions [*tractatus*]."[74] *Affectus* in this description is the agent by means of which rumination and memorization take place; in other words, remembering is an activity in which the emotions must be engaged in order for it to occur at all.

FLOWERS OF READING I: HELOISE

"The method of reading consists in dividing," says Hugh of St. Victor, "modus legendi in dividendo constat."[75] Reading fundamentally proceeds by *divisio*. This meant that every text one learned was stored and recalled basically as a series of short sequences, whether one knew it from start to finish, as many ancients knew Virgil and Homer, and many Christians knew several books at least of the Bible; or whether one learned a number of set passages from it, as I learned Shakespeare's plays; or whether one learned only its aphorisms and maxims. The ordering of these texts, their *compositio* or *collatio*, was a function of the mnemonic heuristics one imposed on them (I am speaking purely in terms of how a student learned, not of how texts were copied by scribes). It is this fundamental feature of the memorial design and its method that made it possible for a single segment of information to be cross-filed, so that one could, for example, find Psalm 1, verse 2, in the mental file containing the words of Psalm 1 in complete textual order and in that dealing with the subject of *lex Domini*. One could thus think of it in several different settings, leading to the process of "composition" in the modern English sense. It is no wonder that early writers considered building metaphors to be so apt both for reading and for composing, for each memorized chunk is like a plank or brick one places into a memory design.

From at least Alexandrine times, a favored form of elementary textbook was the florilegium, or compilation of extracts and maxims derived from the great writers of the past. It was as popular with Christians as it had been with pagans. I have alluded to this literary form many times during my study, but I now want to look at the genre in greater detail. Its essence is well defined by the title of Petrarch's contribution to it, *Libri rerum memorandarum*. A florilegium is basically the contents of someone's memory, set forth as a kind of study-guide for the formation of others' memories. The contents are what Hugh of St. Victor called *sophismata*, others more commonly called *dicta* or *dictiones*, and they are presented either *verbatim (ad verba)* or *summatim (ad res)*.

The most familiar variety brings together ethical topics, vices and virtues and socially useful habits, such as those for study or for civic behavior. Such compilations are common in antiquity; Cicero says, attributing Aristotle, that Protagoras was the first to gather together and write down the "rerum illustrium disputationes" or commonplaces (*communes loci*).[76] Aristotle's word for the "special topics," as distinct from the general categories such as antithesis or similarity, is *eidē*, and they were so called because they belong to the practical, particularized realm of political and ethical life. In Roman rhetoric, the commonplaces were moral in nature; Quintilian must warn his readers that he is using the word in an unusual sense when he applies *communis locus* to the "places of argument" (*Inst. orat.*, v. x. 20–21). Most often, they were arranged by moral categories, "in adulterium, aleatorem, petulantem," or categories of evidence, "de testibus, de tabulis, de argumentis."[77]

A good example of a scholar's florilegium is the Carolingian encyclopedia of Hrabanus Maurus, *De universo*. In the preface to it which he addresses to his former colleague, now bishop, Haimon, Hrabanus describes his motive for undertaking the work. He recalls that they were students together, reading a multitude of books not only of divine learning but also of natural history and liberal arts. Since then, divine providence has released Hrabanus from external cares, but called Haimon to pastoral duties as bishop, where he must contend not only with the pagans to the east, but with a fractious populace. Wherefore, says Hrabanus, "I considered that I might confect in writing something pleasing and useful for Your Holiness: in which you might have briefly annotated in selections for your recollection [*ob commemorationem*] things which previously you had read in many large codices completely in the stylish discourse of orators . . . . While I was treating all these things carefully, it came into my mind that, according to the custom of the ancients who put together many things concerning natural history and etymologies of names and words, I might myself compose for you a little work in which you would have written down [something] concerning not only natural history and the literal meanings of words, but also the spiritual sense of those same things, so that you could find, continuously placed together, both the literal and spiritual meaning of each single thing."[78] And that is exactly what *De universo* is, a web of *interpretationes* of the various matters relevant to Scripture, arranged by key-words that are themselves organized not alphabetically but "logically" (starting with God and the angels). Much of it, including the organizational key-words, is taken directly from Isidore's *Etymologiae*. But collated continuously (*continuatim*) with Isidore, as Hrabanus promises, are interpretations or *sensus*, both *litterales* and *mystici* of the various Scriptural items. These are most likely Hrabanus's own lecture notes here collated for Haimon; much of their content was also used in the elementary Scriptural gloss compiled for beginning students in the early twelfth century called the *Glossa ordinaria*.[79]

The purpose of Hrabanus's compilation is not to substitute for the study of original texts, but to provide cues for recollecting material read earlier. This is a convention of the genre, florilegia being understood to be volumes only of extracts, the notes which students took on their reading. And these notes are memorative in both origin and purpose. Hrabanus describes himself as a student carefully extracting ("mihi sollicite tractandi") from his studies, and the sources from which he gathers are much like those William of Ockham drew from 500 years later, and recommends that his students draw from in turn – books of sacred learning, moral philosophy, and histories (but, as one would expect, Ockham's memory gardens included a great deal of canon law as well). Perhaps more concretely than any other genre, the florilegium is the essential book of memory.

But why bother to compose them? Especially if one is expected to be familiar as well with the full works from which these flowers are plucked? The reason has everything to do with the difference between reading as lecture and reading as meditation, meditation being an activity of dividing and composing. We must remember that a trained and well-provided memory was regarded throughout this long period not as a primitive learning technique but as the essential foundation of prudence, *sapientia*, ethical judgment. The choice to memorize or not isn't like deciding to trade in one's old typewriter for a word processor. Composition was considered to be a memorial activity too; a preacher making a sermon must draw upon his memorial store-house. It is, after all, for the purpose of composing that Ockham advises his student to stock his memory, so that he may recall what he needs.

As a compositional and devotional aid, a florilegium is a promptbook for *memoria*; that is clearly how Hrabanus Maurus understood it. Such compilations provide the materials (and in some cases also suggest a format) for the *memoria* of those who must lecture publicly and extemporaneously, as Bishop Haimon needed to do in his sermons. Isidore of Seville succinctly articulates this requirement by remarking aphoristically that "*Lectio* requires the aid of memory."[80] The various types of florilegial books have been intensively studied recently, and it is clear that those of the scholastic centuries (the thirteenth and fourteenth centuries primarily) differ in format and in type of content from earlier ones, and from the late medieval and Renaissance compilations of the humanists. Monastic compilations are primarily meditational in nature, designed for an audience of varying sophistication, whereas the scholastic florilegia, like the *Manipulus florum* or *Handful of Flowers* studied by the Rouses, are often highly technical, even jargonish textbooks for clerics composing sermons. These arose to fill a particular market demand to which I have already alluded: the greatly increased population of university scholars and preachers. Many of these scholastic florilegia are organized so technically that they would be hard to memorize as such, but their usefulness assumes an already well-trained memory. They are thus still memorial promptbooks, made *ob commemorationem*, but a derivative sub-genre for specialists. Indeed, as Christina von Nolcken has shown, the specialization of preachers' florilegia into collections of Scriptural *distinctiones* (or scholastic definitions) and sermon *exempla* was reorganized in the fourteenth century in a more compendious form of various sorts of material from an array of sources. Their entry-headings were moral topics.[81] The resulting composition was one that a late twelfth-century cleric approvingly characterized as "adorned with flowers of words and sentences and supported by a copious array of authorities. *It ran backwards and forwards on its path from its starting-point back to the same starting-point*" (my emphasis). The memorial principle of such organization is evident, and as von Nolcken comments, these features remain impressively constant.[82]

　　In a careful study of pre-scholastic florilegia, Birger Munk Olsen notes that monastic collections follow a number of different principles of order, sometimes even in different sections of the same compilation.[83] These range from clear ordering schemes by moral topic, some even alphabetically arranged by topic or *incipit*, to those in which extracts are arranged by author, to ones showing no discernible order at all, including those "mini-florilèges" which are nothing but short pieces copied onto margins or the blank pages of manuscripts. Extracts themselves range in length from single lines to lengthy passages. The audience intended is sometimes beginning students; several address *pueri* in their prefaces, but (as we saw with Hrabanus) adult scholars are mainly addressed. This fact again confirms their nature as meditational prompts or sources for a memory already basically trained, rather than as a primary-school text. The compiler of *Florilegium Duacense* says that, because there are so many books and human memory is so yielding ("madida memoria"), "from a multitude of books I have plucked a few [matters] among a great many, which seemed to me most useful and necessary"; these one can read and meditate and learn by heart, for they are kept "non scriniis aut armariis, sed archa pectoris," "not in treasuries nor in bookcases but in the chest of memory."[84] By these extracts, the needy soul is cured, the healthy preserved, the weary recreated, the hungry fed, the simple soul may be instructed, the scholarly one aroused, the impoverished one gain something worth noting down.

It is interesting that rigidly structured compilations exist side by side with those that seem totally nonstructured, for it confirms again that the form itself of a work like this cannot be trusted as an indication of whether or not its contents were to be memorized, nor in what manner. An unorganized compilation could hardly be used unless it were to cue an already-formed *memoria*, readers slipping the material into their own heuristic schemes, as they had been taught to do. But collections that come with their own organization were also designed to stock or cue the memories of their users, as is apparent from such a late, vernacular, Dominican product as Bartolomeo's *Ammaestramenti*. Moreover, it is not clear always that the compilers themselves distinguished their audiences carefully; the author of *Florilegium Duacense* clearly thought his readers would include both adults and beginners.

Florilegia have retained their immense popularity until the present. The justification for their use goes back to ancient pedagogy, and is well described by Quintilian. Once a child learning to read progressed from syllables to whole words, his writing exercises (which kept pace with his reading) consisted of writing out words, especially hard words, on the ancient principle that one should always concentrate on what is difficult, for then the mastery of what is easier is also accomplished. He was also set to copy lines, which he memorized for reciting during this task, repeating them in a murmur while he wrote.[85] Because memory was so intimately and constantly involved, Quintilian urges that "the lines set for copying should not be meaningless sentences, but convey some moral lesson. The memory of such things stays with us till we are old, and the impression thus made on the unformed mind will be good for the character also. The child may also be allowed to learn, as a game, the sayings of famous men and especially selected passages from the poets (which children particularly like to know). Memory is very necessary to the orator."[86] Such an exercise, in other words, is not useful *except* as these bits of reading are memorized, or as they recall to mind matter previously stored away. In providing the maxims for discourse, they provided the materials of character too.

Texts such as Cato's *Distichs* provided such elementary material, as did the Psalms.[87] Quintilian's advice is echoed by Julius Victor, and we see the same practice centuries later in the teaching of Bernard of Chartres, described by John of Salisbury:

> Bernard used also to admonish his students that stories and poems should be read thoroughly, and not as though the reader were put to flight like a spurred horse. Wherefore he always insistently demanded from each one, as a daily debt, something committed to memory.[88]

Cassiodorus provides one of the best medieval statements of the virtue of acquiring such material, the *topica* as he calls them, stored in memory. "Clearly [*memoria* is] a remarkable sort of work – that in one place could be gathered together whatever the mobility and variety of the human mind was able to learn by inquiring about the sensible world through various postulates – it contains the free and willful mind; for wherever it turns itself, whatever thoughts it enters into, of necessity the human mind falls into some one of those common places earlier mentioned."[89] The commonplaces are understood here to be habits of thought, habits of character as well, the *hexis* or *firma facilitas*, complete mastery of subject and self, that Quintilian understood *hexis* to mean. One cannot think at all, at least about the world of process and matter ("in sensibus ... per diversas causas"), except in commonplaces, which are, as it were, concentrated "rich" schemata of the memory, to be used for making judgments and forming opinions and ideas.

This is really no more astonishing than saying that one cannot think without opinions, or without categories. But it is true that the nature of those opinions for medieval students was more consciously literary in origin than is the nature of most of our received opinions, which we like to think are factual instead (some people I know even claim to have factual opinions). And this memorized chorus of voices, this everpresent florilegium built up plank by plank continuously through one's lifetime, formed not only one's opinions but one's moral character as well. Character indeed results from one's experience, but that includes the experiences of others, often epitomized in ethical commonplaces, and made one's own by constant recollection.

Abelard relates the following famous and instructive anecdote about Heloise:

> I admit that it was shame and confusion in my remorse and misery rather than any devout wish for conversion which brought me to seek shelter in a monastery

cloister. Heloise had already agreed to take the veil in obedience to my wishes and entered a convent. So we both put on the religious habit, I in the abbey of St. Denis and she in the convent of Argenteuil which I spoke of before. *There were many people*, I remember, who in pity for her youth tried to dissuade her from submitting to the yoke of monastic rule as a penance too hard to bear, but all in vain; she broke out as best she could through her tears and sobs into Cornelia's famous lament:

> O noble husband,
> Too great for me to wed, was it my fate
> To bend that lofty head? What prompted me
> To marry you and bring about your fall?
> Now claim your due, and see me gladly pay . . .

So saying she hurried to the altar, quickly took up the veil blessed by the bishop and *publicly* bound herself to the religious life.[90] (My emphasis)

Heloise quotes from Lucan's poem, *Pharsalia*, the verses with which Pompey's wife, Cornelia, greets her husband after his shameful defeat in battle, offering to kill herself in sacrifice to placate the gods. In his study of the episode, R. W. Southern states the parallel: as Cornelia offers herself to death to save her husband at the moment of his greatest shame, so Heloise sacrifices her life that Abelard might overcome his shame, for "[l]ong before Abelard had seen himself as the modern Jerome, Heloise had seen herself as the modern Cornelia."[91] It was a natural thing for her to do, because these lines from Lucan were in her memory, they helped to make up her experience. Since Heloise read in the medieval way Hugh of St. Victor describes, she did not see herself as Cornelia in the sense of assuming or acting a role. Rather, Cornelia's experience, given voice by Lucan, had been made hers as well – so much her own that she can use it, even, perhaps, with irony, in such an extreme personal situation.

Literary fragments of florilegial length, *dicta et facta memorabilia*, are a frequent (though to our eyes peculiar and somewhat embarrassing) accompaniment to medieval moral decisions. Augustine, at the very moment of his greatest personal anguish, thinks immediately of the hermit Anthony, as he hears the mysterious command *Tolle, lege*, and picks up the Book to read whatever his eye chances on.[92] One sometimes gets the impression that a medieval person, like Chaucer's Dorigen, could do nothing (especially in duress) without rehearsing a whole series of exemplary stories, the material of their experience built up board by board in memory, and, as Gregory says, transformed into their very selves, so that even in moments of stress the counsel of experience will constrain a turbulent and willful mind. If the task is properly done, as Cassiodorus says, the mind of habitual necessity (a meaning of *hexis*) will have a "place" for anything it may encounter, whatever the circumstances.

A modern woman would be very uncomfortable to think that she was facing the world with a self constructed out of bits and pieces of great authors of the past, yet I think in large part that is exactly what a medieval self or *character* was. Saying this does not, I think, exclude a conception of individuality, for every person had domesticated and familiarized these *communes loci*, these pieces of the public memory. It does underscore the profound degree to which memory was considered to be the prerequisite for character itself. The link is suggested in the fact that Greek *charaktêr* means literally "the mark engraved or stamped" on a coin or seal; by transference, the word came to mean "distinctive mark" and hence the "distinctive quality" of a person or thing, and ultimately also "type" (of person) or "style."[93] The word's literal meaning continued to be recognized, however; in *Orator*, Cicero translates it with the Latin word *forma*, which had a similar range of meanings.[94] One basic conception of a memory phantasm, as we have seen, employs exactly the same model, that of "seal" or "stamp," in wax most commonly, but also on a coin (as in Hugh of St. Victor's *Didascalicon*). The Greek concept of *hexis*, crucial to an understanding of moral behavior, is a predisposition that "stamps" or "forms" the embodied soul towards behaving in certain ways rather than others. Perhaps here as clearly as anywhere else in ancient and medieval culture, the fundamental symbiosis of memorized reading and ethics can be grasped, for each is a matter of stamping the body–soul, of *charaktêr*.

Heloise's moment of moral decision is articulated as a rhetorical action. This is the most telling feature of the entire incident. It gives us a clear way of understanding just how ethics and rhetoric were thought to coincide, and as there has been a great deal of misunderstanding about this, especially in the modern school of Exegetical criticism, I want to analyze her action carefully.

Exegetical critics believe that literature is ethical in nature, but they think of the ethical use of texts in entirely normative and definitional terms. All medieval literature, they believe, was thought to promote charity, and the only value of the specifics of a text, its "literal level," is as an instance of a universal and normative moral principle. But the direction of this analysis runs exactly counter to that of any rhetorical situation. Rhetorically conceived, ethics is the application of a *res* or generalized content (most often expressed in a textual maxim) to a specific, present occasion *which is public in nature*, because it requires an audience. Rhetoric composes commonplaces by a process of adaptation. Normative or transcendental analysis, in contrast, discovers a universal, timeless principle amid the detritus of the event, and its moral truth is unconditioned by audience, occasion, speaker, or text. But rhetoric does not normalize an occasion, it occasionalizes a norm.[95]

What is so striking, and so strikingly medieval, in Heloise's action is her articulation of her own present dilemma and decision by means of her memory of a text in the public domain (as we would say). She re-presents Cornelia in her own present situation; the text from Lucan provides a temporal and spatial meeting-ground, a common place, between a public memory and her personal situation, and gives her a way of talking about herself in the present. Heloise is "making a commonplace" even as she speaks to her grieving friends and relatives, and in the process she is re-presenting Cornelia. Or rather, she implies, both Cornelia's action and now her own are part of a definitional copiousness, which can be usefully held together within a common memory locus – that is why the presence of an audience is so crucial. And copiousness, as I argued in Chapter 1, is not a process of analytical definition so much as it is compiling a memory place that is most like a florilegial entry, an indefinitely expandable grouping of *dicta et facta* on some common theme or subject. And, as I also have said, these themes ("Justice," "Wifely Chastity," "Disgraced Husbands") do not function as a-priori definitive norms, but as labels, the mnemonically necessitated listing of the memorial chest. And, of course, sayings and stories can be listed in more than one place, for, like ethics itself, they are copiously – rhetorically – defined.

The presence of an audience would appear to be crucial to the making of the ethical action. This simply reminds us that a rhetorical conception of ethics requires that its social and public nature be stressed. But it is remarkable that instances of moral judgment in medieval literature seem so often to require both a literary text and an audience to complete them, whether the audience is in the work itself or is created by a direct address to readers (Petrarch speaks to Augustine about Virgil, Dorigen utters a formal complaint "as ye [that is, we readers] shal after heere").

The function of this audience, however, is not to supply a norm. It is to supply a memory. Heloise's friends and relations try to dissuade her "in pity for her youth"; sobbing so that she can scarcely speak, Heloise breaks out "as best she could" with Cornelia's lament and takes the veil. The scene is deliberately made memorable – perhaps even contrived to give the appearance of spontaneity, in the best traditions of Ciceronian rhetoric – and speaker and audience together collaborate in this. Memorableness, enabled for this occasion by the quality some writers have called "performance" (and to which we might apply the rhetorical term, "delivery") would, in fact, seem to be the necessary source of the ethical nature and efficacy of Heloise's act.[96] And the mediator of the action is a piece of a literary text. Why? Because it is that which is common to both the subject and the audience, a piece of their common memorial florilegium. If the audience did not recognize Heloise's quotation, the scene would lose its ethical effectiveness. Instead of talking about ethical rules in medieval culture, it would be truer to speak of ethical memories, contained in texts as *dicta et facta memorabilia*; they are not ethical algorithms or universal definitions, but are "copious," like literature. And they require not to be applied (like a theorem) but to be read, interpreted.

This brings us back to the third element in the complete, ethically valorized action – Heloise herself. For it is her memory that is the first mover, as it were, of the whole incident. Clearly, she is not, in our sense, expressing herself. Self-expression is a meaningless term in a medieval context – on that point I agree with the Exegetes, for there was no concept of an autonomous, though largely inarticulate, individual self, to be defined and given a voice against social norms. Heloise is not expressing herself, but neither is she simply expressing Lucan. She is expressing her "character," which is a function of *memoria*.

So instead of the word "self" or even "individual," we might better speak of a "subject-who-remembers," and in remembering also feels and thinks and judges. In other words, we should think of the apprehending and commenting individual subject ("self") also in rhetorical terms. Her subjectivity is located in Heloise's memory, including her whole florilegium of texts, one of which she invents (in the ancient sense) for this occasion, thereby investing it, the occasion, and her own action with common ethical value, and giving her audience something to think about.[97]

It seems to me that the basic notion of a memory-place as a commonplace into which one gathers a variety of material is essential to understanding how the process of ethical valorizing occurs. In considering what is the ethical nature of reading, one could do much worse than to start with Gregory the Great's comment, that what we see in a text is not rules for what we *ought* to be, but images of what we *are*, "our own beauty, our own ugliness." It is this which enables us to make these texts our own. We read rhetorically, memory makes our reading into our own ethical equipment ("stamps our character"), and we express that character in situations that are also rhetorical in nature, in the expressive gestures and performances which we construct from our remembered experience, and which, in turn, are intended to impress and give value to others' memories of a particular occasion.

Thus, the entire ethical situation in Abelard's account is socially and rhetorically conceived: it requires a recollecting subject, a remembered text, and a remembering audience. These, of course, are also the three ingredients found in virtually all medieval narrative literature. What makes a poem like Chaucer's *The Book of the Duchess* ethical is its construction: a recollecting subject (the dreamer, the Man in Black), remembered *dicta et facta* (the dream itself, fair White, the Ovidian tale of Ceyx and Alcyone), and the remembering audience (the dreamer who listens to the Man in Black, and we readers).[98] That the poem also talks generally about death, love, or honor does not in itself make it an ethical poem. Rather, the ethical content is made by both the common and specific topics of death, love, and honor, recollected and spoken by somebody to somebody else in this poem, which thereby lodges as an experienced event in the memories of its audience, memories that are made up equally of *imagines* (likenesses) and *intentiones* (feelings). Ethics is inseparable from the copiousness of the text itself and its effect upon the *memoria* of its audience and witnesses. It is interesting to reflect that the psychoanalytical situation is in some respects parallel to the one I have just described, for the same three ingredients are present: recollecting subject, remembered *dicta et facta* in all their copiousness, and a remembering audience. But psychoanalysis is neither public nor social in its occasion, and it is therefore not truly rhetorical, despite these structural similarities. Nonetheless, psychoanalysis often presents itself as a modern version of *memoria* (and sometimes as a modern version of ethics too), though in fact by privileging the concepts of privacy and subjectivity it is greatly different from medieval *memoria*. Jacques Lacan sounds very much like Cassiodorus when he writes that: "[Psychoanalytic] recollection is not Platonic reminiscence – it is not the *return* of a form, an imprint, an eidos of beauty and good ... coming to us from the beyond. It is something *that comes to us from the structural necessities, something humble*" (my emphases).[99] But of course the "structural necessities" that Cassiodorus meant when he spoke of the containers of trained memory that give shape to the uneducated mind (I would have used the adjective "private," but it is too anachronistic) were neither generic attributes of Man, nor infusions from some vague cultural mentality, but were the publicly held commonplaces laid down according to a manner and method that everyone knew and approved.

FLOWERS OF READING II: FRANCESCA

Italian and French humanism of the thirteenth and fourteenth centuries is studded with vernacular florilegia, including Brunetto Latini's *Trésor*, written in French for the circle at Avignon (*c.* 1266) but soon translated into Italian. A modern editor of *Trésor* writes disparagingly of it as a compilation of compilations, which "contains no element of imagination, no artistic pretension."[100] Yet Dante has memorialized it as Brunetto's chief work, the fame of which will live forever. And Petrarch did not disdain to produce an ethical florilegium (in Latin, to be sure, but for a lay audience), derived mainly from Valerius Maximus' very similar compilation (known by its medieval title, *Dicta et facta memorabilia*), though Valerius Maximus was also much admired and studied at this time.

It is certainly true to observe that ethically directed florilegial compilations are distinctive (though not original) products of the early Renaissance, from *Trésor* (1266) to such an Erasmian product as *Adagia* (1508). As Thomas M. Greene has observed in a fine essay on the *Adagia*, "the impulse, whatever it was, that produced this [florilegial] text and its thousands of companions, has to be regarded with some curiosity."[101] Clearly it was an impulse distinct from, though not in conflict with, the equally typical humanistic one to restore the original purity and wholeness of ancient texts. These two activities are fundamentally adaptations of the two kinds of reading, *lectio* and *meditatio*, which had been developed in medieval schools. The desire to establish true texts evolved from the scholarship of grammar and rhetorical study, a careful restoration and analysis of textual *litterae*. This sort of study – together with commentary and the questions it invokes and responds to – were traditionally the tasks of *lectio*, a master reading a text aloud to his students, responding to questions, elucidating hard passages, and, above all, establishing the text. In monastic tradition, *lectio* encompasses all the disciplines of the sacred page; Hugh of St. Victor makes this clear in the program he sets forth in *Didascalicon*. But *lectio* is the preface to, and must be completed by, *meditatio*, if study is to be a truly moral, useful activity. This link between studious reading and meditative composition based upon the flowers culled from reading goes back to the Rome of St. Jerome and is very much a heritage of ancient rhetoric. Jerome wrote to Pope Damasus that "to read without also writing is to sleep."[102] The humanist impulse to compile florilegia directs the literary enterprise specifically to forming, from humanist sources, the ethical character of the laity, while at the same time confirming one's own memory and providing an occasion for meditative composition. Making florilegia is an unbroken tradition of medieval pedagogy; these humanist examples in the genre broaden it to include exactly the audience to whom the humanist memory-texts are also directed: lawyers, physicians, merchants, aristocrats, and clerical bureaucrats of all sorts, the components of the extensive secular society coming into existence in southern, and then later northern, Europe.

And in this enterprise, the florilegial books of ethical instruction compiled by the regular clergy also played their part.[103] Even in fourteenth-century England at least one such compendium was made for personal meditation and not primarily as a preachers' manual. At the very end of the century, John of Mirfeld, an Augustinian canon of St. Bartholomew's, Smithfield, made his *Florarium Bartholomei*, which he prefaces by saying that it provides a "storehouse" of material "which every Christian soul needs for its virtuous behaviour and its salvation … Understand, however, that [these texts] are not to be read amidst tumults, but in quiet; not speedily, but one subject at a time, with intent and thoughtful meditation."[104]

Bono Giamboni's role as *translateur* of both *Trésor* and Tullius on memory is revealing, for it connects both *Trésor* and the *Ammaestramenti* with memory training, for which the Herennian precepts offered a human-istically approved method, more authentically classical (perhaps this is what was thought) than methods associated with university training, such as those taught by Thomas Bradwardine. Bartolomeo, the Italian Dominican, begins his florilegium with the passage from Cassiodorus (cited *sententialiter* and in the vernacular) which I quoted earlier in this chapter: "Siccome dice Cassiodoro: Lo senno umano se egli non è ajutato e restaurato per le cose trovate d'altrui, tosto puote mancare del suo pro-prio", "As Cassiodorus says: human judgment if it is not adjusted and restored by things found in [the works of] others, promptly will fall short of its true nature."[105] There are few clearer statements of this eminently florilegial formulation concerning the nature of human character, and the role which public memory, enshrined in books, must play in the development of individual ethical behavior.

Human beings are born imperfect, needing to be completed. To be sure this Augustinian doctrine is thought of in terms of vice and virtue, but it is very easy, especially if one thinks in modern popular-Freudian terms, to fall into an essentially Manichaean understanding of the process as a kind of war between the superego and the unconscious. It is truer to the assump-tions driving the compilers of florilegia to think of character in terms of completion or filling-out or building (the root concept in Latin *instruo*, "instruct"). Public memory is a needed ethical resource, for its contents complete the edifice of each individual's memory.

Therefore, says Bartolomeo, it behooves a wise man not to rest content with his own ideas, but by diligent study to search out those of others. Of course, not all of their wisdom can be contained in a little book, and so, he says, he has taken pains to gather or pluck (like flowers) [*raccogliere*] their wisdom, as he best can. Bartolomeo then describes the basic order he has followed in his compilation; clearly, however, Bono's translation of the Herennian precepts was soon also considered to be an appropriate addition to it. Memory technique was attached to such florilegia not as an after-thought but as an integral part. It provided the method whereby the flowers of study could be made not only *recti*, but *utiles* and *necessarii* too. Bono's translation was well adapted for such collections, as is apparent from his prefatory remarks, which address the ethical nature of learned discourse, regarding mnemotechnique as an essential means to that greater end.

I would like to close this chapter by examining for a moment the reading-seduction of Paolo and Francesca in Canto v of Dante's *Inferno*. This scene brings together in a particularly compressed and fruitful manner several of the aspects of reading that I have discussed, and I would like to meditate on it in terms of three of its key words: memory, desire, and reading. Francesca begins with memory, re-presenting her past, "the time of your sweet sighing," in response to Dante's request. "There is no greater pain than to recall the happy time in misery [*ricordarsi del tempo felice / nella miseria*]." Her recollection is of reading, itself a memorative, recol-lective activity:

We read one day for pastime [*diletto*, "delight"] of Lancelot ... Many times that reading drew our eyes together and changed the colour in our faces, but one point alone it was that mastered us; when we read that the longed-for smile [of Guinevere] was kissed by so great a lover, he who never shall be parted from me, all trembling, kissed my mouth. A Galeotto was the book and he that wrote it; that day we read in it no farther.[106]

Modern readers, concentrating on the failings of the lovers' judgment, tend to see in this story only an example of passion overmastering reason, and to blame Francesca for her self-serving words that put the onus for her actions on the book and its author. Or, if they are keener moralists, they blame the lovers for wasting their time on such trash in the first place when they should have been reading sterner stuff. Or the story is read as a caution against leaving a young man and woman alone together at all. In any case, the consensus seems to run, Paolo and Francesca are to be blamed for improperly reading the book by allowing it to arouse their emotions.

This interpretation accords well with modern notions (usually attrib-uted to "Augustine") that medieval people thought texts to be authoritative maps for their actions, readers being totally passive in the face of what they read.[107] But as I hope my study has helped demonstrate, this scholarly fiction is manifestly untrue. Medieval reading was highly active, what I have called a "hermeneutical dialogue" between the mind of the reader and the absent voices which the written letters called forth, at times literally in the murmur of ruminative meditation. In this scene, it is not an idle detail that Paolo and Francesca read together, and thus aloud. If such activity does not occur, reading has not truly taken place for the memory has not been engaged. Thus, reading is first a sensory activity ("diletto," delight); when the senses and emotions are engaged, when imagination forms its images and cogitation responds affectively to them, memory and recollection can occur. And *only* when memory is active does reading become an ethical and properly intellectual activity. What therefore activates Paolo and Francesca's desire? The activity of reading itself, just as Francesca says.

Recall for a moment Hugh of St. Victor's description of the three-stage process of reading–meditation. First, one focuses on the example, next one acts in imitation of it, and then one internalizes the imitation so that one's own vital power (*virtus*) is permanently changed. The moment such a change occurs is the moment of desire, and, with it, of will. It is also the moment during which the full process of meditative study is completed; when, in Gregory the Great's words, what we read is transformed into our very selves, a mirror of our own beauty or ugliness, for we have, like Ezekiel, eaten the book. The end of Francesca's remembering to Dante, and the end of the lovers' desire, is also the end of their reading ("that day we read no farther").

This understanding of what medieval reading was supposed to be complicates the pathos of this tale as no mere moralism can. No wonder that Dante swoons "like a stone," emotionless and thus memoryless, from the effort of his remembering (both at the time, listening to Francesca, and later writing it down) of her remembering of their remembering of the story memorialized in the book. *Ricordare* and *leggiare* and *amare* are simultaneous activities, necessarily accompanying each other. Paolo and Francesca are reading properly here, recreating the exemplary scene, rewriting it in their own memories. But having eaten the book with Ezekiel and St. John, they find in the experience a fitting echo of the *Apocalypse* account, as its sweetness turns bitter. Their fault is not in having read the *Lancelot* in the first place, nor is it simply in allowing their reading to create desire; it is in reading "no farther," imperfectly in the medieval sense of "incompletely."

In the ongoing hermeneutical dialogue that the process of reading was understood to be, the question of when and how to divide looms rather large. This is another aspect to the irony and pathos of Francesca's last words, to their reading "no farther." Comments like this are fairly common in medieval literature. One instructive parallel occurs in *Piers Plowman*, when Lady Meed boasts to Conscience that she has read the Bible and lives by the text "Omnia autem probate," "try out all things" (1 Thes. 5:21). To which Conscience replies that she should have read the rest of the sentence, "quod bonum est tenete," "hold fast to that which is good."[108] Similarly here, Paolo and Francesca are not wrong to utilize Lancelot and Guinevere as instructive examples, nor to re-write their story in their own memories, but they didn't finish the sentence. This presents their fault as one of poor *divisio* and incomplete reading, rather than of wrong interpretation according to some transcendental norm. One clause alone is the problem – "solo un punto."

In the *Inferno*, the pair read the scene from the French prose *Lancelot* to the moment when Guinevere kisses her lover. Also present with the two main characters in *Lancelot* is Galehot (Galeotto), Lancelot's faithful companion, who has arranged the meeting and actually suggested the kiss. To one side, out of earshot, are Guinevere's lady-companions, including the Lady of Malehaut, and Galehot's seneschal. The kiss is described in a paratactic sentence, made up of several clauses or *cola* marked in the manuscripts with a point, *punto* in Italian. Each *punto* marks out a memory-sized piece, in the traditional manner of textual punctuation.

The sentence begins thus: "Et la roine voit li cheualiers nen ose plus faire. si le prent par le menton & le baise deuant galahot asses longement." That is presumably where Paolo and Francesca stopped reading. Had they read the next clause of the sentence after the point, they would have read that Lancelot and Guinevere's illicit love-making was instantly discovered: "si que la dame de malohaut seit quele le baise."[109] Now the Lady of Malehaut is in love with Lancelot herself, has just imprisoned him and tried to seduce him (unsuccessfully), and she is Big Trouble. Guinevere, immediately after the kiss, swears Lancelot and Galehot to secrecy (of course), but it is by then too late – for the Lady of Malehaut has already seen and comprehended, and cannot be trusted. Indeed (to learn from this example) every illicit love affair has its "Lady of Malehaut," and it is only a matter of time (often not long) before she shows up; thus their fear of her watchful and dangerous eyes, to those who have read far enough in their book to be concerned about her, should be enough to check passion. But Paolo and Francesca failed to get to the crucial "point."

I am not suggesting that the lovers' only fault was one of punctuation – yet they did not punctuate wisely. "Solo un punto" did them in, says Francesca, one little mark of punctuation. But *modus legendi in dividendo constat*. And since *divisio* produced the building-blocks of memory, and hence of education and character, punctuation was not an altogether trifling affair. It was crucial, as it still is, to the intelligibility of a text, but it was also crucial ethically, given the role that reading and memorizing played in the formation of moral judgments. We recall that Stephen Langton spent over thirty years "coting" the Bible, and that Robert of Basevorn reserves the practice of quotation (or "cotation") only to the most learned and skilled of doctors. Scholastic quotation is a form of punctuating, as all textual division is. In a letter describing his own habits of study, Ambrose writes of working long into the night to punctuate perfectly the ancient teaching of the Fathers, and to fix it firmly in his memory by continual, familiar practice and in slow increments – as an aid to which he writes down his studies with his own stylus. *Ad unguem distinguere* is the idiomatic phrase he uses, meaning to "mark off, divide up" or "punctuate" or "decorate," "to a hair" (literally "to a finger-nail") or "exactly." Since what he says of the nature and circumstances of his studies rules out the possibility that he was decorating the "senilem sermonem" that occupied him, he seems to have been doing what the scholastics called quoting his texts, and making them familiar and habitual to himself at the same time in leisurely stages ("lento quodam figere gradu"), using his own hand and stylus, in the best school fashion, to fix the impression in his memory. In that way he is sure not to just blow the words about ("deflare") to an attendant scribe taking dictation, but to hide them away ("abscondere"), in his memory-receptacle where all *lectio* should be hidden safely.[110] Thus Paolo and Francesca's failure to read further, even one *punto* more, is one that reverberates within the whole tradition of the methods of reading developed in the elementary schools of antiquity and the Middle Ages. The Lady of Malehaut in the person of Francesca's husband, Giovanni Malatesta, discovers them instantly and fatally, just as the book warned – if only they had not divided their reading at the point where they did. It is not the least of the many pathetic ironies in Dante's scene that lovers who failed to divide perfectly in life will never be parted in death.

CHAPTER 6

Memory and authority

THE INTENTION OF THE WORK

This chapter explores connections between memory work of the sort I have been discussing, and medieval assumptions about the nature of authority and authorship. Composition is the activity which links them, and most of this chapter discusses in detail the process itself of composing texts designed for oral or written delivery, as it was taught and practiced in schools. Composition is one of the two activities of meditation, and the complement to *divisio* in designing a memory for inventive recollection. As division is the mode of reading, as Hugh of St. Victor says, so composition – the placing together of pieces laid away by division and marking – is the mode of text-making, what we, imprecisely, call writing. The memorized chunks culled from works read and digested are ruminated into a composition – that is basically what an author does with authorities.

It is also important to recognize that there are two distinct stages involved in the making of an authority – the first is the individual process of authoring or composing, and the second is the matter of authorizing, which is a social and communal activity. In the context of memory, the first belongs to the domain of an individual's memory, the second to what we might conveniently think of as public memory. Texts are one important medium of this social memory-bank, the archival *scrinia* available to all, from which, by the methods already examined in this study, an individual could store, by the sense (*sententialiter*) or word for word (*verbatim*), the chests of his or her own memory.

The distinction between *res* and *verbum*, as we have come to understand it in the context of memorial practices, is at the heart of medieval views of how one should deal with the texts that, along with other publicly held things like buildings, paintings, songs, and melodies, make up the available *res*, materials. For *memoria rerum* involves an adaptation of the original language for mnemonic and compositional purposes rather than its complete iteration. Thomas of Waleys, we recall, distinguished between reciting and retaining and speaking; *recitare* is word-for-word repetition of a text *verbaliter*, whereas *retinere et dicere* is recollection *sententialiter* (according to the sense of its principal words) in order to facilitate composition. Reciting is what children do when first learning to read, but recollection is associated, as we have already seen, with the investigative activities of invention and new composition, the tasks of rhetoric and poetry.

We will consider in some detail what the *res* was taught to be in the compositional process; this will make its role somewhat clearer. The *res* or matter of a literary text was considered as something extra- or pre-linguistic, for which words are to be discovered from one's memorial store as one transforms it into present speaking. These words mediate the public appearance of the *res*, rather as clothes may be said to mediate the public appearance of a person (to use a favorite metaphor) – they suggest and conceal, they give clues and cues, they reveal but never completely. The notion that a text has both *res* and *verba* posits the idea or meaning that lies within speech as some sort of construct partly independent of and greater than the words from which it is constructed, and to which these words can serve as a route or guide. There is, as it were, *an intention of the text* which can, and indeed must, be translated from one mind to another and adapted to suit occasions and circumstances. This adaptation was not believed substantively to alter the enduring *res* (or *sentence*, as it was called in medieval English), which is in a continual process of being understood, its plenitude of meaning being perfected and completed. The adaptation process, which is the work of interpretive commentary and meditative reading is crucially what makes the public, the authorized text.[1]

In considering medieval views of textual authority, one needs always to keep in mind that *auctores* were, first of all, texts, not people. When the old woman in Chaucer's Wife of Bath's tale, in order to win an argument, vows that "auctors can I fynde, as I gesse," she means that she can find in her memory store specific quotations from textual sources, not that she can find people who write. The *intentio auctoris* or author's intention – a common category of the scholarly introduction to a text known as the *accessus ad auctores* – was defined by Albertus Magnus in a tautology that equates the author's intention with the words in the text: "the intention of the speaker as expressed in the letter is the literal sense."[2] Consequently, there *is* no extra-textual authorial intention – whatever *intentio* there is is contained in the words of the text. All meaning develops from them. Albertus's definition invokes the commonplace of Isidore of Seville, that the *litterae* of writing are representations both of a voice and of words spoken. But the words (*voces*) in turn are signs of things – *res*, the concept one keeps coming back to in all pre-modern discussions of rhetoric, language, and the role of *memoria*.

The word *auctor* was thought to be derived from the verbs *agere*, "to act," and *augere*, "to grow." A second word, *autor*, was related through etymology to Greek *autenthēs*, "authentic," but medieval dictionary-makers distinguished the two words, one spelled with a *c* and one without, quite carefully. *Auctoritas* derived from *auctor*, and was defined by Hugutio of Pisa in about 1200 as "sententia digne imitatione," "a saying worthy of imitation." Thus, both authority and author were conceived of entirely in textual terms, for an author is simply one whose writings are full of authorities. And an author acquires authority only by virtue of having his works retained *sententialiter* in the memories of subsequent generations.[3]

Author-texts are retained and imitated *ad res* because it is there, not in their actual words, that their authority lies; this is the assumption in Hugutio's definition. It is related directly, I think, to the memorial distinction between iteration and imitation, *recitare* and *retinere*, *memoria verborum* and *memoria rerum*. Both the word *auctor* and the later synonym, *originalis*, are related closely to the traditional metaphor of literature as a great river flowing over time from a *fons* or source. So, when Jerome wrote of the Bible as *originales libri*, he meant something like "originating texts," progenitors of a whole family of textual descendents, especially commentaries and other adaptations, which are the indication, or authorization, of a work's institutional standing in the public, communal memory.[4]

Let us look again at Petrarch's comment, through the mouth of Augustine, concerning the meaning he finds in the Cave of the Winds passage in the *Aeneid*, for Petrarch a major *auctor*:

I cannot but applaud that meaning which I understand you find hidden in the poet's story, familiar as it is to you; for, whether Virgil had this in mind when writing, or whether without any such idea he only meant to depict a storm at sea and nothing else, what you have said about the rush of anger and the authority of reason seems to me expressed with equal wit and truth.[5]

Petrarch has responded to this text's *res*, amplifying it through first familiarizing it in his memory (by *divisio*) and then writing it anew in words that do not reproduce the actual language of the *Aeneid*, but rather adapt its sense to Petrarch's own situation (*compositio*). Were we to think of this exegetically, we could say that Petrarch gives these lines a tropological interpretation. But the point is that his interpretation is not attributed to any intention of the man, Virgil, but rather to something understood to reside in the text itself. Authorial intention in itself is given no more weight than that of any subsequent reader who uses the work in his own meditative composition; the important intention is within the work itself, as its *res*, a cluster of meanings which are only partially revealed in its original statement. Petrarch supports his reading by appealing to some of the words in this passage that suggest anger and turmoil, but he does not suggest that these meanings were ever Virgil's intent – they may or may not have been, it is unimportant. What keeps such a view of interpretation from being mere readerly solipsism is precisely the notion of *res* – the text has sense within it which is independent of the reader, and which must be amplified, dilated, and broken-out from its words, as they are processed in one's memory and re-presented in recollection. Amplifying is an emotional, image-making activity as we have seen, and it is just this quality that makes it ethically profitable. More importantly than growth in knowledge, reading produces growth in character, through provisioning – in *memoria* – the virtue of prudence.

CONSIDER THE BEES

Composition starts in memorized reading. The commonest way for a medieval author to depict himself is as a reader of an old book or a listener to an old story, which he is recalling by retelling. In monastic meditation, the old book was something in the Bible; later in the Middle Ages, old books were also secular and vernacular. It is well to consider the commonplace of the reader/author as a bee. This trope came most familiarly to the Middle Ages in the form given to it by Seneca, whose letters were a standard item in the medieval curriculum of rhetoric, or *ars dictaminis* as it came to be more commonly called during the twelfth century.[6] Seneca wrote: "We ought to imitate bees, as they say, which fly about and gather [from] flowers suitable for making honey, and then arrange and sort into their cells whatever nectars they have collected."[7] Composition begins in reading, culled, gathered, and laid away distinctively in separate places, "for such things are better retained if they are kept separate"; then, using our own talent and faculties, we blend their variety into one savour which, even if it is still apparent whence it was taken, will yet be something different from its source ("ut etiam si apparuerit unde sumptum sit, aliud tamen esse quam unde sumptum est appareat").

I mentioned this variation of the store-house metaphor for memory in Chapter 1; like the rest of those metaphors, this one too should be understood not as a mere decoration but as a complex model of the process of composition and authorship. As a model it is a variant also on that of digestion, as indeed Seneca realized: "the food we have eaten, so long as it retains its original character and floats in our stomachs as a mass, is a burden; it passes into tissue and blood only when it has been changed from its original form. So it is with the food which nourishes our mind . . . We must digest it; otherwise it will only come into our acquired memory-store [*memoria*] and not pass on to become part of our own abilities [*ingenium*]." Merely to store memory by reading is an incomplete process without composition, for composing is the ruminative, digesting process, the means by which reading is domesticated to ourselves. Indeed the two tasks require one another – Jerome echoes this same principle when he says that there is no point to reading if one does not also compose and write.[8]

This familiar trope of the bee has been extensively analyzed as a model for classical, medieval, and Renaissance assumptions concerning the nature of literary imitation, the relationship of authors to their antecedents, and the changing way in which these assumptions have been understood.[9] I have no desire here to rehearse work which has been so ably and thoroughly done. But the scholars who have analyzed it most comprehensively have started from the preoccupations of Renaissance writers defining themselves against a medieval world which they sought to reject (while often unaware, inevitably, of the extent to which they were themselves still its products), and in the course of such analyses a particular medieval understanding of the trope has, I think, been rather slighted and misrepresented. To get at this particular medievalness, I must emphasize that, in this trope, composition, like reading, is assumed to depend on a memory properly stored with discrete, immediately recoverable *loci*. For Seneca, *memoria* is not an alternative to creativity (which is how I would understand his use of *ingenium* in this passage) but the route to it. He does not disparage *memoria*, but only its undigested, parrot-like use.

Memory is the matrix of all human temporal perception. This too is a medieval commonplace, nowhere so eloquently explored as in the final books of Augustine's *Confessions*. *Memoria* makes present that which is no longer so in actuality; indeed, as we have seen, this temporal understanding of memorial representation is more emphasized, at least in medieval analyses, than its mimetic one. Prudence, the ability to make judgments in a present context about both present and future matters, is founded upon *memoria*, and traditionally was represented with three eyes, looking to past, present, and future. But memory remains, by its nature, of the past – a thing cannot be in memory until it is past. This insistence is basic in medieval

Aristotelian (and Augustinian) psychology, as I emphasized in Chapter 2. Therefore, to say that memory is the matrix within which humans perceive present and future is also to say that both present and future, in human time, are mediated by the past. But the past, in this analysis, is not something itself, but rather a memory, a representing of what no longer exists as itself but only in its memorial traces.

It seems to me that this is quite different from insisting, as Renaissance and modern scholars have done, that the past is mediated by the present. The change in emphasis, in the direction of mediation, if you will, is critical. It seems to be typical of modern (Renaissance) consciousness to give the past, like other scientific subjects, objective status apart from present human memories. As a result, perhaps, a Renaissance scholar worried that the past had been distorted through the mediation of the present, and sought to recover or resuscitate the dead past itself. In his book on Renaissance literary imitation, Thomas M. Greene has emphasized how the language of necrology and revival is woven into those scholars' anti-quarian and philological projects.[10] By contrast, Augustine journeyed through his memory not to find his past but to find God, his present and future. And it is clear that Augustine assumed that the way to God lay only through the re-presenting of his past in memory; he has no interest in his past except as it provides him with a way and ground for understanding his present.[11]

Few features of medieval scholarship are so distinctive as an utter indifference to the pastness of the past, to its uniqueness and its integrity on its own terms, as we now would say. Ordinarily, medieval scholars show no apparent interest in archaeology or historical philology, and the representation of classical or Biblical figures in medieval dress is continually amusing to modern audiences of their art and literature. Yet it is evident as well that medieval scholars realized that language and societies had changed significantly over time; Chaucer and Dante commented famously on the phenomenon, but the acknowledgment is found often much earlier as well. Indeed, the division of modern from ancient was first formulated at the beginning of the Middle Ages.[12] It simply doesn't seem to have been thought to be of paramount importance.

This omnitemporality in medieval thought, as Erich Auerbach called it, is usually attributed to a prevailing belief in the eternity of God and consequent emphasis upon divine continuity in human history. The dogmatic cause is surely important, but no more so, I think, than the particular character of the medieval institution of *memoria* by means of which texts of past authors are constantly related in and through present minds (the dual meaning of the

English verb *relate* is important here, for it captures both the positioning and re-speaking of these texts). The sole relic of the ancients with which medieval scholars vigorously concerned themselves was written texts; this choice itself is interesting, for there were other artifacts of antiquity still readily visible. But only the letters which compose texts can speak (for letters are signs of voices/ words no longer present); only they can be related to the present and future, and thus become the material of prudence.

The most comprehensive model of the medieval view of what constituted *memoria* is the medieval book itself, especially those fully marked up codices, punctuated and ornamented to the last, precise hair (*distincti ad unguem*, to adopt what Ambrose said of his textual labors). As codicologists speak of paper or parchment or stone as a support for writing, so the book itself is the chief external support of *memoria* throughout the Middle Ages. In its lay-out and ordering, it serves the requirements of readers who expected to engage it in their own memories. It also often records the memorial gatherings of a whole community of readers over time, presenting in its multiple margins the graphic display of a *catena* or chain of comments upon the source-text. The distinctive format of the glossed book, used especially for law compendia and certain Biblical texts, but later also for secular authors, is the most satisfying model of authorship and textual authority which the Middle Ages produced (see figures 10 and 11), as many scholars have recognized.[13] Let me emphasize once more, that a book does not mimic a memory; its relationship to *memoria* is not that of a mirror or copy, any more than letters on parchment mime their contents. Their relationship is functional; the book supports *memoria* because it serves its requirements, some of which are biological, but many of which, in the memorial cultures of the Middle Ages, were institutional and thus conventional, social, and ethical.

COMPOSING A WORK: INVENTION

But before examining the finished product, the book itself that both results from and furnishes *memoria*, it will be helpful in the rest of this chapter to consider in detail how the act of making a text was thought to proceed, in order to stress its origins in the activities of memory. I think it will become clear during my discussion that the terms "oral" and "written" are inadequate categories for describing what actually went on in traditional composition. I would propose the term "memorative composition" instead, and stress its close affinity to the metaphors of digestion and rumination, examined in the previous chapter.

It is clear, both from descriptions of pedagogy and from the practices of individual writers, that much of the process of literary composition was expected to occur mentally, in mature authors, according to a well-defined method that had postures, settings, equipment, and products all its own. The drafts that resulted were designated by different names, which do vary a bit according to the particular writer, but each of which denotes a fairly well defined stage of composition. These are, first, *invention*, taught as a wholly mental process of searching one's inventory. It involves recollection primarily, and occurs with postures and in settings that are also signals of *meditatio*; indeed, it is best to think of invention as a meditational activity, and indeed Quintilian so designates it. This meditation involves both the discovery and *disposition* of the subject matters, and it results in a product called the *res*, a term familiar also from the pedagogy of memory training. More complete than what modern students think of as their outline, the *res* should, according to Quintilian, be formed fully enough to require no more than finishing touches of ornamentation and rhythm. In other words, the *res* is like the rougher drafts of a composition, with much room left still for shaping, rearranging, and adjustment.

The post-invention stage involves elaboration, of both form (disposition of parts) and style. Its products are called *dictamen*; it might, but need not, involve writing instruments. As will become clear, the *dictamen* is most like what we now call a formal draft; a number of versions, each unfinished, could be involved in its making. *Compositio* covers three closely related activities: *formalization*, or taking one's *res* and giving it final form as a composed piece; *correcting*, by both adding and emending, but also by comparing and adjusting the revisions to make sure the words fit one's *res* in intention and adequacy as much as possible (changing one's *res* drastically at this stage would indicate a lack of proper invention); *polishing*, artfully adjusting one's expression to make it stylistically striking, persuasive, and memorable in all its details (the medieval *ars dictaminis* addresses this specifically). For the stage of *compositio*, a set of waxed tablets or other informal (easily correctable) writing support could be used, on which one might write down all or parts of one's *res* to make stylistic tinkering easier. But, depending on one's maturity and experience, this process could, like invention, be completely mental.

When the *dictamen* was shaped satisfactorily, the composition was fully written out on a permanent surface like parchment in a scribal hand; this final product was the *exemplar* submitted to the public. (Often a scribe's fair-copy was submitted once again for a final corrective collation by the author or author's agent before the exemplar was made available for further copying.) The word "writing" properly refers to this last inscribing process, which the author might do himself, but usually did not. Saint Anselm's biographer, Eadmer, clarifies this when he describes how he wrote his biography of Anselm:

> when I had first taken the work in hand, and had already transcribed onto parchment a great part of what I had drafted in wax [*quae in cera dictaveram pergamenae magna ex parte tradissem*], Father Anselm himself one day called me to him privately and asked what it was I was drafting and copying [*quid dictitarem, quid scriptitarem*].[14]

Eadmer was reluctant to comply with his abbot's request, knowing Anselm's humility, but showed his work in the hope that Anselm would correct it. In fact, Anselm did so, deleting some things, approving others, and reordering some material. But, as Eadmer feared, Anselm's reticence showed itself a few days later when he called Eadmer in and told him to destroy all "the quires in which I had put together the work." Eadmer obeyed the letter of Anselm's order and destroyed the quires after first copying their contents into others.

In this admission of guilt, Eadmer makes clear the distinction between the composing and copying stages. Of the first, he uses the verb *dictare*, of the second *scribere*. *Dictare* is done *in cerae*, "on wax"; *scribere* is the action whereby the *dictamen* is *traditum*, "transcribed," to parchment. Since Eadmer did his own copying the distinction is an interesting one, for it indicates that Eadmer thought of the two activities as different, even when the same person performed them. *Dictare*, for Eadmer, evidently simply means to compose, without any suggestions of oralness (one can dictate with one's stylus on wax); *scribere* is what a scribe does, even when the scribe is also the author. One needs to be careful not to over-generalize Eadmer's consistent distinction, for there are instances when the verb *dictare* means dictate to a secretary, as Thomas Aquinas did, sometimes from a written *dictamen* (in *littera inintelligibilis*) and often directly from memory.[15] And *scribere* is used in contexts when the author is still composing. But the fact that these two verbs sometimes overlap in meaning does not indicate that the two processes, of composing and of transcribing in secretarial hand, were undifferentiated. The author produces a *res* or *dictamen*; that which is a *liber scriptus* is in a formal hand on parchment, and the product of a scribe.

The distinction is long-lived. Chaucer makes it, in English, when he begs his scrivener, Adam, that he should "after my makyng . . . wryte more trewe."[16] Once the work was written out, it was corrected by the author (Chaucer complains of the amount of rubbing and scraping of parchment he must do after Adam's work), as Anselm corrected Eadmer's written composition, and equally, as Bernard of Clairvaux and Augustine corrected the reports (*reportationes*) of their oral sermons. It is important to realize that the written version of a text was considered to be a scribal or secretarial product and not an authorial one *no matter who the scribe was*. All written texts are presumed to need emendation and correction; *emendare* is also a stage of the composition, formation, and "authorizing" of a text, which follows the fair-copy product. This is very different from the status which a printed text has now, for a medieval text was not presumed to be *perfectus*, "finished," even though it had been *scriptus*, "written." The first task which both ancient and medieval elementary students performed in school when they had written copies of texts before them was *collatio*, in which the *grammaticus* read aloud from his text while the pupils emended theirs; thus the introduction a child had in school to a written text was as something that needed to be checked and corrected.[17]

COLLECTING AND RECOLLECTING

Having sketched these stages out, I now want to examine in more detail how they are related to the procedures of trained recollection.In Book X of his *Institutio*, Quintilian describes an unskilled student in the throes of starting a composition (the stage of invention), as lying on his back with eyes turned up to the ceiling, trying to fire up his composing power by murmuring to himself, in the hope that he will find things in his memorial inventory to bring together into a composition. (Quintilian doesn't approve of such desperation, preferring that one compose more calmly, but that is not germane to my present concern.)[18] If a modern teacher were to describe such a scene of typical desperation, she would not do it in these terms. Instead, someone would be described with pen in hand, seated at a desk amid heaps of crumpled paper. And while the person might have a desperate or vacant look, while he might get up to pace the floor or stare out of a window, he would be silent, returning constantly but silently to his pen and sheets of paper (or her computer screen). And when composition finally began, that too would be silent (even though, in fact, many people still subvocalize while actually composing). What Quintilian describes, however, is a student murmuring during recollective meditation in order to compose. And this he regards as the typical initiating activity of composition – what one does in order to get "the idea" for a work.

The mental activity which Quintilian's desperate author is attempting to stimulate is *cogitatio*. This is one of the functions of the inner sense, and, as we saw in Chapter 2, while it gets defined with somewhat different emphases in the various accounts of human psychology, it is the ability to compose. The process is shown in the late medieval brain diagram in CUL MS. Gg. 1.1 (reproduced as figure 3 and discussed at greater length in Chapter 2), which explicitly invokes Thomas Aquinas as its authority. To review, *vis cogitativa* in medieval psychology works with the imaginary things conjured by *vis aestimativa* and the *vis formalis* or *fantasia*. According to Avicenna, who defines it most stringently, it is the compositive human imagination, or the activity of taking the individual phantasms produced by imagination (*vis formalis*) and putting them together with other images, mainly those previously stored in memory. In the diagram shown in figure 3, *vis cogitativa* is also called *vis imaginativa*, and a striking feature of the diagram is how imagination and its materials are implicated at every stage in the process of making thoughts. *Vis imaginativa* corresponds to what Aristotle calls the deliberative imagination, a combination of *phantasia* with *dianoia*, or the power of constructing with conscious judgment a single image out of a number of images.[19] Some medieval psychologists distinguished the simple act of putting images together from the act of judging the result, and use *vis imaginativa* for the former, reserving *vis cogitativa* for the judging faculty.[20] But throughout its long history, *cogitatio* is basically the activity of putting images together in a consciously recollected, deliberative way. Though it is often translated into modern English as "thought," one should never forget that the *vis cogitativa* is an activity of *animus*, the sensory-emotional soul; it therefore is never as abstractly intellectual as the modern word implies. Its judging power is based in emotion, the sort of thing that causes a lamb, seeing a wolf, to run in fear. For Aristotle, the cogitative activity (*dianoētikē psychē*) is "the faculty which judges what is to be pursued and what is to be avoided," what is good and what is evil, not after intellectual consideration but as an initial responsive judgment; cogitation, he says, also comprises the functions of combination and separation.[21] So the act of invention, carried out by cogitation, was thought to be one of combining, or "laying together," in one place or compositive image or design, divided bits previously filed and cross-filed in other discrete *loci* of memory. The result was a mental product called the *res*, the model of one's composition. It is this that an orator or preacher would lay up in *imagines rerum* when preparing to speak, and its close kinship is apparent to the technique of memorizing texts according to their *res*, which one would then shape to suit a particular occasion.[22]

For composition in the Middle Ages is not particularly an act of writing. It is rumination, cogitation, dictation, a listening and a dialogue, a gathering (*collectio*) of voices from their several places in memory. The fifteenth-century Italian physician, Matheolus of Perugia, wrote that *meditatio* is derived from *mentis dictatio*.[23] The ancient writers frequently speak of the importance of listening to what one is composing. In *Heroides*, Ovid's Leander writes that "having spoken in such words to myself in a low murmur, the rest my right hand talked through with the parchment."[24] Thus, the *vox tenuis* which accompanied meditative reading seems to have accompanied composition as well; we might recall the story of Thomas Aquinas's conversations with Saints Peter and Paul that so disturbed his *socius*. I have used the phrase "hermeneutical dialogue" to describe the relationship between a reader and his reading in *meditatio*; it applies also to composition, for indeed that hermeneutical dialogue constitutes the process of composing, as reading and other experience is gathered together and domesticated in memory.

But what exactly was this process of *collectio* thought to be, as it relates to our own acts of composing? One of the boldest and most complete accounts comes from Augustine, as one might expect. During his meditation on *memoria* in Book X of the *Confessions*, Augustine speaks of how the sense impressions are "impressed" in the mind as images stored up in the wondrous cells of memory.[25] Then he proceeds to discuss *cogitatio* and *collectio*, as the power and particular activity involved in making ideas, creating thoughts. *Cogitando* [thinking] is "nothing else but by meditating to gather together those same things which the memory did before contain more scatteringly and confusedly." Augustine's use of *colligere*, deriving from the verb which means both "to collect" and "to read," carries in this context a specific meaning of gathering together the memories of what one has read and stored in separate places earlier, as well as a general meaning of collecting up earlier experiences of all sorts.

We discover ("invenimus") such things as concepts and ideas when by the activity of thinking we collect ("cogitando quasi colligere"), and by the act of turning our *animus* we attend to ("animadvertendo curare"), those things which our memory was holding here and there, unarranged in any particular design ("passim et indisposite"). These we gather together in our memory, so those matters which formerly lay scattered from each other and unnoticed ("ubi sparsa prius et neglecta latitabant") now readily occur to us as part of our familiar mental equipment ("iam familiari intentioni facile occurrant"). The process Augustine describes is generally recognizable from other writers too, for this is what was later called *vis cogitativa*. *Cogitatio* finds matters held in various memory-places and collects them into one place, ready at hand ("ad manum posita") for our intellect's further attentions and uses.[26]

How many matters of this kind our memory holds, Augustine continues, placed ready at hand . . . things which we say we have learned ("didicisse") and know ("nosse"). If we stop recollecting them ("recolere") then once again they break apart and slip away ("dilabantur") into the remoter recesses of our memory ("in remotiora penetralia"), whence we must draw them together again ("cogenda rursus") in order to know them again. Knowing, *cogitandum*, derives its name from this action of continually gathering dispersed images and matters together ("ex quadam dispersione colligenda"). For *cogo*, "draw together," and *cogito*, "cogitate," are derivative one from the other, as are *ago*, "do," and *agito*, "do continually," and *facio*, "make," and *facito*, "make frequently."[27]

So learning is itself a process of composition, collation, and recollection. But the result of bringing together the variously stored bits in memory is new knowledge. It is one's own composition and opinion, *familiaris intentio*. This is the point at which collation becomes authorship. Augustine understood this quite well in his own composing experience, for he speaks of the process of *cogitatio/collectio* as an expansive one; paradoxically perhaps, the act of bringing memory-images together into a single, compositive design is the path to enlarged understanding. "I know . . . but I do not understand," he says in one of his sermons, drawing a characteristic distinction, "yet cogitation makes us expand, expansion stretches us out, and stretching makes us more capacious."[28] For Augustine, the pieces brought together in *cogitatio* make a sum greater than its parts. Knowledge extends understanding not by adding on more and more pieces, but because as we compose our design dilates to greater capacity and spaciousness. New knowledge, what has not been thought, results from this process, for dilation leads ultimately even through the deepest caves of memory to God. Augustine characteristically speaks of this as a transit through memory. How shall I reach God? he asks. "I shall pass through [*transibo*] even this power of mine which is called memory; I shall pass through it to reach Thee, sweet Light." God is indeed beyond memory, but the only way there is through and by means of it. Augustine gives the process a metaphysical twist, but his description of how invention occurs as an activity of *memoria* belongs clearly to the ordinary pedagogy of rhetoric.[29]

In practice, invention was an intensely emotional state, more so than we now associate with thinking. We have very few specific medieval accounts of people doing what we call composing. Among the best are those of Thomas Aquinas, and Eadmer's description of Anselm, written around 1100.[30] The work in question was the *Proslogion*; Eadmer reports what Anselm told him of the great difficulty he experienced composing it:

partly because thinking about it [*haec cogitatio*] took away his desire for food, drink and sleep, and partly – and this was more grievous to him – because it disturbed the attention [*gravabat intentionem ejus*] which he ought to have paid to matins and to Divine service at other times. When he was aware of this, and still could not entirely lay hold on what he sought, he supposed that this line of thought [*hujusmodi cogitationem*] was a temptation of the devil and he tried to banish it from his mind [*repellere a sua intentione*]. But the more vehemently he tried to do this, the more this thought pursued him [*tanto illum ipsa cogitatio magis ac magis infestabat*]. Then suddenly one night during matins the grace of God illuminated his heart, the whole matter [*res*] became clear to his mind, and a great joy and exultation filled his inmost being. Thinking therefore that others also would be glad to know what he had found, immediately [*ilico*] and ungrudgingly [*livore carens*] he wrote it on writing-tablets [*rem . . . scripsit in tabulis*] and gave it to one of the brethren of the monastery for safe-keeping.[31]

There are a number of interesting features to this description. Eadmer describes the activity of composition as one of profound concentration, a meditative withdrawal that takes one from food, sleep, and even the most sacred routines of the day. This activity is described in the repeated terms *intentio*, "concentration," and *cogitatio*, "mulling over." This *cogitatio* is spoken of initially as an enemy; Anselm wants to repell it ("repellere"), but it more and more aggressively and hostilely took over ("infestabat") his *intentio*, even when he turned it to the liturgical office (which is to be performed also with *intentio*). So obsessed is he that he fears the devil is tempting him. Then, of a sudden, *cogitatio* is completed (Eadmer attributes the grace of God) and only at that moment is a product, called the *res*, committed to a writing surface – but to one that is traditionally associated with unfinished work and with the formation and functions of memory. By no means has it yet been "authorized," that is, become an *auctor* or source-text for other minds and memories to use.

I have already stressed that *cogitatio* involves recollection since it uses memory-images; however, it is a pre-intellectual process even though it involves making judgments, for these are emotionally and intuitively based at this point rather than logically so. Like meditative reading, invention is not, to use the categories of medieval psychology, a process of the intellec-tual soul, but primarily of the sensory-emotional one, dependent upon the images stored in memory and the effectiveness of the heuristic structures in which they have been laid down there.

This antiquated language conceals from us an important characteristic of memorial cultures, one I have stressed before but that is worth pointing to again. Alexander Murray has reminded us that what constitutes rational behavior is, to some considerable extent, a matter of culture. His *Reason and Society in the Middle Ages* traces how reasonableness as a category of thought was influenced in the later Middle Ages by a tension between monastic culture, whose roots were in the disciplines of meditational prayer (among other things), and intellectual culture, which developed in the urban ambience of the universities. These tendencies existed equally in the same institutions and even the same individuals. They were not often perceived as tensions in conflict, but their eventual incompatibility is reflected in our sharp division now between reason and emotion, to the point of assuming them to be incompatible altogether.[32] In the teaching and practice of composition, however, the monastic cultivation of meditational prayer, itself evolving from practices in the ancient schools, remained dominant. This stressed that feeling and sense, the bases of memory, are key components of creativity, as we can readily see from the fact that medieval *cogitatio* translates, as I emphasized in Chapter 2, not as our phrase "reasoning out" in logic, but as "mulling over" and getting the sense of an idea.

Quintilian assures his students that *cogitatio* can be greatly helped by an orderly consideration of the case, but that order is not necessarily what we would call logical or intellectual. It is a heuristic structure which we follow by habit rather than deriving it anew from each separate occurence; that is, we follow a set form or procedure we have memorized. (For example, we might apply an invention procedure like the adverbial questions which my school-teachers taught me: who, what, where, when, how, why? Or, were we medieval clerics needing a sermon on a text, we might use the heuristic of the four levels of interpretation.) Reason alone cannot help that frantically murmuring student, for he has not yet gathered up his memory-images to the point where reason can process them. All that can help is a recollected heuristic, a trained memory which proceeds by habit and emotion, pre-rationally.

The highly emotional state described by Quintilian is very like that of Anselm as he desperately sought what he couldn't quite find ("nec adhuc quod quaerebat ad plenum capere valens"). We recall also what Thomas Aquinas's biographers said of his habit of intense prayer: "At night ... he would rise, after a short sleep, and pray, lying prostrate on the ground; it was in those nights of prayer that he learned what he would write or dictate in the day-time. Such was the normal tenor of his life – a minimum of time allowed to sleeping and eating, and all the rest given to prayer or reading or thinking or writing or dictating."[33] Such physical accompaniments of *cogitatio* are apparent in all the accounts of composition, prostration being its common posture; Quintilian's student lies down on his back,

Thomas Aquinas face-downwards. It is a position designed to shut out external stimuli, especially visual ones, which would serve to confuse or distract one's recollective eye as it looks through its inventory of places, for both *strepitus* and *turba* are great mnemonic enemies.

The emotions (*affectus*) are the starting-point, as they must be in order to engage *memoria* and *cogitatio*. Reginald, Thomas Aquinas's *socius*, said of him that "in his soul, intellect and desire [*intellectus et affectus*] somehow contained each other . . . his desire [*affectus*] through prayer, gained access to divine realities, which then the intellect, deeply apprehending, drew into a light which kindled to greater intensity the flame of love."[34] Desire begins the ascent to understanding by firing memory, and through its stored-up treasures the intellect is able to contemplate; the higher its understanding, the more desire flames in love as it both gets and gives more light. It is a sentiment worthy of Dante himself. So Anselm, searching his memory places for the pieces he can't quite find to complete the design which his meditation is constructing, fears the devil, fears the intense emotion that has invaded his body as well as his thoughts, keeping him from food and sleep as well as from liturgical prayer. So Thomas falls prostrate in tearful prayer. But the products of this non-logical, obsessive, emotional activity are closely reasoned monuments of scholastic logic, the *Proslogion* and the *Summa theologica*.

It is significant that the times when both Anselm and Thomas Aquinas are described as being particularly distraught are when they are stuck, searching for connections they can't quite get hold of. "Once at Paris," writes Gui of Thomas Aquinas, "when writing on Paul's epistles, he came upon a passage which quite baffled him until, dismissing his secretaries, he fell to the ground and prayed with tears; then what he desired was given him and it all became clear."[35] Thomas wept in order to solve an intellectual difficulty; Anselm behaved like a monk in love until his rational problem came clear. A modern scholar similarly blocked would go to the library or thumb through notes. By such transports of fear and desire, Thomas and Anselm expected to stimulate their memorial libraries. Gui reports that Thomas never set himself to compose without tearful prayer, and "[w]hen perplexed by a difficulty he would kneel and pray and then, on returning to his writing or dictation, he was accustomed to find that his thought had become so clear that it seemed to show him inwardly as in a book the words he needed." It is clear also from Gui's account that Thomas deliberately and habitually cultivated the posture of prostrate prayer in order to produce a solution to a specific compositional problem.[36]

THE *DICTAMEN*

After invention comes the process of shaping the *res* into the version called *dictamen*. The mental activity required is still what the philosophers called *vis cogitativa*, but rhetoricians appear to use *cogitatio* for the revision stage of composition. (This is a bit confusing because Eadmer speaks of Anselm's invention stage as *cogitatio*, perhaps because he was not a teacher of rhetoric.) One is still composing, but working on a much more complete form of the text than at the start of *inventio*. There seem to be a number of terms used for this stage – Fortunatianus and Julius Victor both call this *compositio*; Quintilian reserves the word *cogitatio* for it; Augustine calls it *collectio*; for Hugh of St. Victor, as we shall see, it was a kind of *collatio*. In any event, the root concept is still a recollective one, bringing matters together, collecting from different places, into a designed text (*res*) which now exists in a common place in one's memory. A related distinction is made by the scholastic terms for these two stages, invention and composition, called respectively *forma tractatus* and *forma tractandi*. The *forma tractatus* corresponds to the *res* of a text, the content arrived at during invention, or the drawing of material – both out and together (the root meaning of *traho*) – into a fully coherent textual argument. The *forma tractatus* can then be shaped up and refined stylistically in a *forma tractandi*. The continuous, polishing nature of this latter activity is indicated in the fact that a present participle is used for it (*tractandi*), whereas the *res* is finished (*tractatus*) when invention is complete. A tract (*tractatus*) is philosophical or moral argumentation without stylistic embellishments or figures; the basic expression of reasons, ideas, logical connections, and all structural elements such as divisions belong to the *forma tractatus* and the various figures of style to *forma tractandi*. Such definitions follow naturally from the pedagogy and practice of composition I have described. The distinction is correlative to that between *memoria rerum* and *memoria verborum*, and also to the emphasis given to the former in the pedagogy of *memoria*.[37]

Fortunatianus says that *memoria* has two essential objects: that material be securely retained, and that it be directly (*cito*) retrievable. This is essential not only for composing that makes use of writing but "immo et cogitatio," "especially cogitation."[38] Later, speaking of Simonides' artificial memory system, he remarks that for "scripta vel cogitatio," "writing or cogitation," we should place together orderly heuristic cues and memorial *similitudines*. Julius Victor makes a similar distinction between composing during which we write ("scribimus") and that we do in cogitation ("cogitamus"), both of

which depend on the same processes of *divisio* and *compositio* that characterize a trained and designed memory.[39]

Both these writers are distinguishing between methods of composition,
one which involves writing on a physical surface and one which is entirely
mental, involving no written draft at all. One should take careful note that
neither writer suggests that the two styles of composing require different
mental preparation or procedures, or that one involves memory and the
other not. Indeed, as presented, the difference is no more significant than
our individual preferences for revising in longhand or at a machine. We see
similar idiosyncrasy of choice in the compositional aids of writers throughout the Middle Ages. The same writer may choose sometimes to work with
a wax tablet and other times not. Thomas Aquinas, we recall, wrote out
portions of his *res* for the *Summa contra Gentiles* in *littera inintelligibilis*.
These pages show the signs of revision and tinkering that characterize
the shaping up of a *dictamen*. But for the composition of *Summa theologiae*
(a longer and more complex work) he worked most often without writing
anything down at all, calling a secretary in when he was finished to take
down his dictation in fair hand. Quintilian, advising that prose rhythm is
an effect to be worked on carefully, relates approvingly that Plato tried out
the first four words of the *Republic* in a variety of orders on his wax tablets
in order "to make the rhythm as perfect as possible," because this small
elegance could be better worked on with the help of a tablet. Quintilian
himself, however, does not encourage dependence on such physical aids. It
is important to keep in mind that Quintilian was addressing the requirements of orally delivered compositions, the need to be able to revise and
change, digress and add, freely and confidently during delivery itself. So the
various techniques he discusses are derived in response to such a situation.
But these same techniques were applied to compositions designed to be
read, and the drafting stages in the production of a final exemplar are
virtually the same; the production of a *res* and then a *dictamen* follows the
same successive steps, whether the *dictamen* was then read to a scribe or
delivered publicly.[40]

When was the stylus to be used? Here again individual habits obviously
varied, but Quintilian describes in detail the received pedagogy that lies
behind the distinctions made by later teachers and practioners. The elementary preparation for eloquence is writing, he says in Book X (on
composition); a beginner must write out maxims and sayings on wax
tablets "as carefully and as much as possible." Writing is crucial because
it forces us to concentrate, and its slowness makes us attentive and
careful, for "as deep digging makes the soil more fertile ... so progress

which is not sought by superficial means yields the fruits of study more generously and retains them more faithfully [*fidelius continet*]."[41] In other words, one writes as an aid to storing memory: "This [writing] is where the roots [of oratory] lie, this is where the foundations are, this is where the wealth is stored in the emergency reserves of our treasury."[42] The *aerarium* was the public treasury ("sanctiore aerario conditae"). Quintilian's metaphor elegantly captures how the contents of a particular orator's memory, no matter how hidden away, are nonetheless public both in sources and in use for common social good.

A beginner must also learn how to cultivate the circumstances needed in all meditational activity. Young students should seek out solitude, silence, and seclusion, and learn to pursue their task with utmost concentration and involvement.[43] Gestures accompanying strong emotion will likewise serve to stimulate the mind (*animus*), and so important is this gestural stimulus that one should not follow the example of those foolish authors who start dictating right away to scribes, lest the presence of another inhibit us (recall how Gui says Thomas Aquinas sent his secretaries away before he prostrated himself in tears).[44] The author should learn not to compose in "the heat and impulse of the moment," dashing off a speedy draft as some do, who call such a thing their *silva*, literally meaning "forest" but used metaphorically here for unshaped materials. One should exercise care from the outset "to shape the work ... in such a way that it needs only to be chiselled [*caelandum*] into shape." Here Quintilian advises that the *res* of one's composition be carefully planned out in one's mind before it is committed in any way to formal written form.[45] Finally, even as beginning students, we should "acquire the habit of making concentration [*intentio*] overcome all hindrances. If you concentrate wholeheartedly on the work in hand, nothing that strikes your eye or your ear will get through to your mind [*animum*]."[46] Therefore, wherever we are, in a crowd, on a journey, at a party, we must practice fashioning a secret inner sanctuary (*secretum*) for our cogitations.

Quintilian stresses one matter in regard to the lay-out of the waxed tablets. Waxed tablets best serve excision and correction (though people with poor eyes may have to use parchment in order to see the letters better – parchment slows down the writing process, however, and so may hinder thought). Excision and correction were, of course, vital in revision but so was addition and what we might think of as digression. Dilation, *dilatio*, allowing space for matter that might occur to you while you revise, is just as necessary as excision. As a beginner writing one's *res* onto tablets, one should, says Quintilian, be sure to allow such space physically, in the form of blank leaves, and also be sure not to cover all the space of the tablet page, but leave generous margins.[47] The practice seems self-evident, and I don't wish to belabor it, but it underscores how the original text, the *res*, was conceived of as a mental location into which new material was collected from other places, amplified and adapted, as one refined one's *dictamen* for delivery to an audience. For Quintilian does not recommend that one continuously recopy one's revised text to make a clean copy seamlessly incorporating such additions. A set of written tablets would show visually just what was original and what was added (erasures are not so apparent on wax as on paper because the end of the stylus smooths the wax out). This is the visual image of his prepared oration which a young student would set in his memory places before the exercise of delivery, not as a clean or fixed document but rather as the memorandum of a work, a palimpsest of the series of his compositional drafts. It is a procedure that invites ongoing digression and commentary.

Having learned to revise with stylus and tablets, a student advances to the technique of *cogitatio* proper, the ability to revise mentally (Quintilian is using the word *cogitatio* to refer to a technique, not simply to the natural psychological process). "Proxima stilo cogitatio est," he writes, "our next topic is mental preparation [*cogitatio*], which itself derives its strength from writing, and is a sort of halfway house between the labour of writing and the chanciness of speaking impromptu [*extemporali*]." It is more frequently used by mature orators than either of the other two extremes of method, solely writing and then memorizing verbatim, or solely speaking extempore.[48] Eventually, through practice, we will develop our skill to the point where we can rely as surely on what we have prepared by cogitation alone as what we have written out word for word and memorized. *Cogitatio*, however, requires an especially careful conception of the order of the composition, so that we may take advantage of things occurring to us at the moment (those which we would add in the margin if we were using a tablet). Such a composition "must be so conducted as to allow us to depart from it or return to it with ease ... the most important thing is to bring with us ... a ready prepared and reliable store of speech; all the same it is deeply stupid to reject any gift the moment [*temporis munera*] brings."[49]

"The greatest fruit of our studies, the richest harvest of our long labours is the power of improvisation [*ex tempore dicendi facultas*]," especially for an advocate who cannot always count on having time to prepare himself, and must instead rely on the agility and readiness which he has acquired by practice and training. *Ex tempore dicendi* is emphatically not unprepared. Ancient and medieval extempore speaking is the highest expression of artistic mastery and learning. Quintilian discusses at length the procedures by which one can master what we now would call improvisation: commenting on the ancient idea of what we might call talent or artlessness (being *atechnē*, without art), he says that such a gift "will only be useful if it is based on the art of which we have spoken, so that an intrinsically irrational activity comes to be grounded on reason." Artlessness is especially the product of art, impromptu speaking the product of preparation. One must first of all know the way of one's speech ("Nota sit primum dicendi via"), the order and route through which the points of an argument proceed, from first to second to third and so on. *Divisio* is absolutely essential to establish the "modum et finem," "definite bounds and limits," of a composition "which cannot exist without a Division" of the material. The mind must be so trained that it can pay attention to the invention, arrangement, and style both of what we are saying at the moment and what we will say next, for an extemporaneous speech must especially exhibit "an orderly, formal, and fluent manner." To achieve this, a speaker must not only have his immediate subject in mind but be able mentally to look ahead and "have in sight everything on the road and around it, and see not only the end, but all the way up to the end."[50]

To ensure such facility, Quintilian counsels that, together with all the relevant questions, persons, and arguments, we must keep before our mental eyes *rerum imagines* or *phantasiai*. The phrase is used technically here, to refer to those vivid images of subject matters, those which we have associated with the *res* of our composition. Their function is not only to keep track of the composition's form (as it is in *Ad Herennium*) but to awaken the emotions of the orator.[51] "Maxima enim pars eloquentiae constat animo; hunc adfici, hunc concipere imagines rerum … necesse est," "eloquence is mainly a psychological matter: it is the mind which must be emotionally stirred and must conceive images."[52] Rhetoric mainly involves functions of the sensory soul, forming, combining, reacting to, storing, and recollecting the *imagines rerum* which are critical to eloquence. Elsewhere, Quintilian more particularly describes the value of the *phantasiai* to the orator, for thereby "the images of absent things are presented to the mind [*repraesentantur animo*] in such a way that we seem actually to see them with our eyes."[53] By this the orator is moved and thus is enabled to move others. The purpose of such images is not description but persuasion.

The mature orator will use all three methods of composition which he has learned. He will write out and memorize some of his speech (perhaps the beginning) and may use his tablets as he is composing to perfect particular phrases, he will above all carefully plan out and prepare the bulk of his oration by meditation and cogitation, and be able to adapt to sudden turns of a case, or to sudden inspiration, by speaking extempore when he wants to. Cicero himself kept notebooks ("libellos") of his memoranda; Quintilian says he will allow the use of such jottings, which may even be held in the hand and occasionally glanced at while speaking. But he urges that we not write down anything that we cannot investigate as well in memory ("quod non simus memoria persecuturi"), lest we be enslaved by our prefabricated composition and unable to take advantage of the momentary chances and opportunities a particular occasion may present.[54]

Throughout the Middle Ages, preaching included much *ex tempore dicendi*, as one might expect. The Dominican friar Giordano da Pisa (1260– 1310, he who first publicized eyeglasses) can be quite frank about his freedom. "I thought of preaching to you not about this, but about something else; but when it pleased Him that I should be so fluent in this, thank God this has really been a good sermon. But anyway I want to tell you a little about what I had planned to say."[55] On another occasion, "I am so full, and I have so much in me, and I am so rich that I do not know what to say to you: I have said nothing of what I prepared, not a thing."[56] The friar's sermons were taken down by reporters, whose comments are preserved;[57] this *reportatio* represented the first written version of the work, which Friar Giordano seems not to have subsequently corrected.

The written *reportatio* was customarily submitted to the author for emendation before being published. Deferrari quotes from Gregory Nazianzus's farewell sermon: "Farewell, ye lovers of my discourses, in your eagerness and concourse, ye pencils [*graphides*] seen and unseen, and those balustrades, pressed upon by those who thrust themselves forward to hear the word."[58] These human pencils continued to be a fact of life in both the lay and learned circles throughout the Middle Ages; it is, I think, worth noting that Gregory refers to them as simple machines. He is, of course, being witty but his wit tells us something quite profound about the way in which the reporter's role was regarded. The scribe as such is not a thinking being, a reader or scholar, certainly not an *auctor* himself, but a mere pencil, performing the humble and subservient task of writing.

Christian sermons were thus composed and published in the manner of all ancient orations, worked out mentally in the ways that Quintilian describes, written down at the time of delivery by reporters and then often corrected by the author before being made available for further dissemination in an exemplar. The Greek church historian, Socrates, says of Atticus, bishop of Constantinople: "Formerly, while a presbyter, he had been accustomed after composing his sermons, to commit them to memory, and then to recite them in church; but by diligent application, he acquired confidence and made his instruction extemporaneous and eloquent. His discourses, however, were not such as to be received with much applause by his auditors, or to deserve to be committed to writing."[59] Atticus demonstrates exactly the sequence of training and proficiency which Quintilian describes, even though his results were disappointing to his congregation. And we must also notice that a sharp distinction is made between Atticus's writing and memorizing his composition verbatim for oral delivery (regarded as a mark of ineptitude), and the exemplar written by a scribe which marks a text deemed worthy to be preserved.

St. Augustine composed mentally with much happier results than poor Atticus. In a 1922 article, R. J. Deferrari gathered much of the extensive evidence in Augustine's sermons which indicates the cogitative and extempore nature of their composition, among which this remark may stand as typical. In an Easter sermon on the text "et Verbum erat apud Deum" (Jn 1:1), Augustine speaks of how the "inner word" (God's *res*, as it were, which by grace informs human speech) is translated into ordinary discourse. The speaker has planned his sermon in his mind as an inner word which he will varyingly express to fit the occasion. "For I who speak with you," he says of his own habitual practice, "before I came before you, I mentally composed [*cogitavi*] in advance what I would say to you. When I was composing what I would say to you, already a word was in my mind. Nor would I be speaking to you, unless I had previously thought about it in my mind."[60] This mixture of prior *cogitatio* and purely *ex tempore dicendi* is a common feature not only of Augustine's sermons but of those of his contemporaries, Roman and Greek, and clearly continued throughout the Middle Ages. Not only does Augustine's *De doctrina christiana* assume that preachers will compose in this way; so, as we have seen, do the later medieval *artes praedicandi* of Robert of Basevorn and Thomas Waleys. The reason for numerically dividing sermons is to allow the preacher to take off on an extempore digression without losing his place in his premeditated design (he would have no need for such an aid if he were reading from a written text) – or to speak in terms of memory-design, to allow him to compose (gather together) material from other memorial *loci* into the *locus* where the eye of the mind is following its text. Friar Giordano's admittedly extemporaneous sermons employ numerical *divisiones* just like pre-planned ones, pulled in from the numbered bins of his memorial treasury.[61]

Yet we must be careful not to regard the informal style of the popular sermon as caused by its predisposition to extempore composition.

Quintilian, speaking for the central tradition of classical rhetoric, does not associate particular compositional methods with any of the three kinds of style distinguished in that tradition, nor with any particular genre of discourse. There are, however, two fatal errors in delivery which an orator can make (and these cautions are repeated by every writer on the subject through the Middle Ages). The first is to lose one's way in one's oration, hesitate, or be reduced to needing a prompt. The second is to appear in any way to be reciting word for word a prefabricated text. Quintilian counsels various ways of avoiding this, such as seeming to grope for a word, pausing, perhaps wondering aloud how to answer an opponent's charge, and other devices which give the effect of spontaneity. But genuine spontaneity is equally bad if one cannot achieve the same level of crafted eloquence one attains by careful *cogitatio*; that is why *ex tempore dicendi* is reserved only to masters whose memories are fully stored and effectively designed.[62]

This ability to appear unrehearsed despite elaborate preparation is what the Romans considered the crowning achievement of rhetorical *memoria*, regarded in the context of performance. In all the rhetorical textbooks, *memoria* precedes *pronuntiatio* or delivery and the discussion concerns how to achieve facility and the mastery of memorial design necessary for this end. The assumption that writing is handmaid and servant to memory is once again demonstrated in this ancient prejudice against any composition appearing to have been written down in advance of delivery. Cicero says of the great orator Marcus Antonius that "his was the best memory, with no suggestion of prior meditation [*erat memoria summa, nulla meditationis suspicio*]; he always seemed unprepared to begin speaking, but he was so well prepared that after he had spoken it was the judges that rather appeared to have been insufficiently prepared for defending their position."[63] I know of no more succinct demonstration of how greatly we misunderstand when we reduce ancient and medieval *memoria* to our word "memorization."

TWO MEDIEVAL AUTHORS AT WORK

I would now like to consider two case studies of medieval authorship, which indicate in practice the distinctions I have drawn so far. The first is Hugh of St. Victor's *De archa Noe*, a wide-ranging commentary on Genesis 6–7; the second continues Eadmer's account of Anselm composing his *Proslogion*. In his preface to *De archa Noe*, Hugh describes how the work began as an exchange "in conventu fratrum," "in a gathering of the brothers," while he sat once with them responding to their questions. His *sermones* on that occasion so pleased them that he decided to write down what he had said: "However, because I knew certain things to have been especially pleasing to the brothers, I specially wanted to commit them to the care of my pen in a *collatio*, not so much because I thought them worthy to be written but because I recognized that material new to that occasion [literally "unheard before then"] would be yet more pleasing in this way [i.e. written down]."[64] In other words, *De archa Noe* began as an oral exchange between Hugh and a gathering of his fellow canons of St. Victor, the sort of *lectio* that Augustine hoped he might have (but didn't) with Ambrose. Such a discussion session, during which the master responds to questions, and comments on a base text by extending its meaning with reference to other texts, is called *collatio* by Isidore of Seville: the word also referred to the monks' daily meal.[65]

Hugh's oral *collatio* on that occasion becomes then the basis for the composition which he commits to writing. This written version is what he actually calls his *collatio*. Again, the link of reading, composition, and food is apparent; *De archa Noe* itself was certainly read at monastic *collationes* of various sorts, the mental meal to accompany the physical one. Evidently, in its many uses, *collatio* retained the idea of gathering together, of texts with one another, of masters and students, and of monks over their reading in chapter and at meals. It is also an informal stage of composition, between purely oral exchange and something that has achieved the finish which makes it worthy of the scribe's ministrations. In short, it has the status of a *dictamen*, something Hugh felt free to alter even as he wrote it out.

At the end of Book II of this work, Hugh introduces a verbal device in the form of a tree, the *arbor sapientiae*, which is an avatar of the first *lignum uitae* and grows in holy hearts as in an invisible Paradise, embodying allegorically both the Tree of Knowledge in Eden and the Tree of Life in Revelation. The figure is introduced with a set of characteristic epithets, a series of fifteen rhyming phrases of three words each (one is actually six words made up of two apposite phrases).[66] Having given the list, Hugh announces to his audience that he and they should rest for a little while because his sermon has gone on to the point of tedium.

He takes the matter up again in Book III. He will expand, he says, each item in the series announced at the end of Book II: "[h]ic ipsius incrementi gradus, quos ibi breuiter et summatim perstrinximus, latius per singula prosequendo explanamus."[67] The phrase *breuiter et summatim* reflects also Hugh's advice on memory in *Didascalicon* (III. 11); this third book of *De archa Noe* may be considered an application of what Hugh says there. Each summary phrase is expanded as a chapter in Book III, in the same

order announced at the end of Book II. So the first phrase of the passage in
II. xvi, describing the tree "per timorem seminatur" ("planted by fear") is the
first subject developed in Book III: "First there it is said of wisdom that it is
planted by fear" (alluding to Prov. 1:7, "the fear of the Lord is the beginning
of wisdom"). The second phrase, "per gratiam rigatur" ("watered by grace"),
is the subject of the next chapter, and so on, in unviolated order. The order
of the phrases themselves follows that of the growth of the tree and its
fruit: planting, watering, the seed sometimes being sterile, sometimes root-
ing, germinating, opening, growing, strengthening, greening, leafing and
branching, flowering, fruiting, ripening, being harvested, and finally eaten.

This compositional structure is mnemonic. The orderly stages (*gradus*)
in the growth of a tree provide Hugh's heuristic as he composes. To each
step, Hugh has attached a Biblical quotation about wisdom, usually a verse
or two defining the word *sapientia* as a virtue or quality (*timor Domini*,
gratia, *dolor*, *fides*, etc.). So the basic mnemonic order is the stages of tree-
growth to which the thematic texts on wisdom are linked. Each growth-
stage with its primary text is the subject of one chapter, and is stated in a
rubric at the start. Within this essential structure, a number of excursive
topics are developed from a phrase or word of the rubric; these may bring
in other linked texts. Basically the structure is that of a concordance, or
catena, in which the parts are associated by key-words, each of which pulls
other texts and sayings with it, "compounding with interest," as Hugh's
Chronicle Preface promises. With a composition planned on such complex
chains of materials, it is easy to understand why the metaphor of fishing
came to be commonly associated with memory work.

We know that Book III is extempore because Hugh tells us so at its end.
He apologizes that the whole thing has been a digression from his real
subject, which was the building of the *arca sapientiae*. He says that it
ballooned (or blossomed) from his discussion in the second Book, and
that he had not planned it:

> But now, while we have been following out the by-ways of our exposition, we have
> digressed a long way from what we had proposed. Wherefore for this also we beg
> your indulgence, because, as I truly confess, most often in this treatise we have
> invented many more things while writing than we have written down having
> already worked them out. So likewise in this matter I blush to confess my fool-
> ishness. Now, however, we will continue by returning to our plan, concerning the
> making of the ark of wisdom.[68]

Despite his assurance to us in the Prologue that the version he is setting
before us is, though informal, a *written* composition, Hugh includes this
lengthy extemporaneous digression, for which he apologizes with red face

as being far from his initial proposal. Are we to conclude from this that Hugh was as prone to spontaneous digressions when he was writing as we would expect a speaker to be? And that the heuristic structures of his memory-library are as apt to show (or be disguised) in a written composition as in a spoken one? It is evident that we must.

A great deal has been made of what is called the oral style of medieval sermons, and its supposed differences from written style or authorial style. Oral style, in this theory, is characterized by repetition, verbal formulas, digressions, especially of a colloquial or informal kind, and parataxis above all. Written style, by contrast, is hypotactic and periodic in the Latin manner, marked by subordination and sub-divisions; it contains longer and more unusual words, is nonrepetitive, and self-consciously artful. This distinction has been raised in this century to the status of a truism in literary analysis, but, unlike many truisms, this one isn't true. It rests upon a genuine tautology, which causatively associates the stylistic features of a particular text whose compositional conditions are known with its method of composition; these features are then used to demonstrate that the text was composed in a particular way.[69]

What can we deduce from style alone about the methods by which a work was composed? Nothing at all. Medieval writers extended the classical canons of stylistic decorum by applying them not just to content and genre but to types of audience. Thus a sermon preached to the people would require a popular style in order to be understood, while one preached to a learned audience would require a more evidently formal, grand style. But medieval writers did not associate the levels of style with compositional methods. Hugh clearly had no real objection, despite his blushes, to leaving his meditation on *arbor sapientiae* as Book III of his written text; indeed, if he did not confess it himself, there is no way from its style that one could tell he was composing extempore, so little does the third book differ in terms of sentence structures, vocabulary, complexity and artfulness of expression, from the others. The composition of *De archa Noe*, according to what Hugh tells us, involved at certain points all three of the compositional methods described by Quintilian: it began as a premeditated *collatio* with an orderly *praepositum* (proposal), it was written with a stylus, and it was also at times *ex tempore dicendi*. Moreover, it is typical that medieval composition involved all of these methods.[70]

Eadmer's account of Anselm tells us some interesting things about the status or authorization of the various products of the compositional stages. The written product of Anselm's lengthy and arduous cogitation (which we have already examined) is called by Eadmer a *res*. This Anselm wrote onto tablets as soon as he had finished his completed design. Eadmer tells us that Anselm gave these wax tablets to the brothers for safe-keeping. After a few days, he asked for them again but they could not be found. So, "Anselm wrote another draft on the same subject [*aliud de eadem materia dictamen*] on other tablets, and handed them to the same monk for more careful keeping."[71] But these tablets were found thrown on the floor, their wax broken and scattered. The monks collected the pieces and brought them to Anselm, who was able to piece the wax together and with difficulty (*vix*) recover the writing. "Fearing now that by some carelessness it might be altogether lost, he ordered it, in the name of the Lord, to be copied onto parchment [*pergamenae jubat tradi*]."[72]

Eadmer calls what was on the first set of tablets *res* and the second *dictamen*. Anselm's *res*, when lost, is easily recovered by him from memory; he asks for the tablets after some time has elapsed, finds they are missing, but is untroubled by their loss. But the second set, the *dictamen*, he pieces together with difficulty, and decides to have copied onto parchment at once to prevent their loss. This suggests that the *dictamen* was a much revised, expanded, and polished version of the *res*, which cannot be as readily reconstructed. It would also seem that Anselm, in the eleventh century, was more inclined to use a stylus and wax tablets for composition than was Thomas Aquinas in the thirteenth. I mention this as a caution against interpreting the differences in their techniques as influenced by something more than individual choice.

Eadmer tells these stories of Anselm's difficulties in composing *Proslogion* not to talk about his compositional methods – for to him there was nothing noteworthy in them – but as moral tales, to indicate that Anselm's work was not taken seriously at first by his fellows, when it was in its pre-exemplary state. The long time that *Proslogion* spent on wax tablets before it went onto parchment is meant to convey this under-valuing, as also is the astonishing carelessness of the monks entrusted with it. (Only the devil – if he were responsible for the breakage – seems to have understood its significance.) But on parchment the text will become safe – it is worth noticing that the motive for making the exemplar is safety.

This initiates another stage in the full composition of *Proslogion*. Parchment support makes the text not only safe but public. This decision by Anselm was made, Eadmer says, "livore carens", ungrudgingly, invoking a venerable commonplace that attributes the publication of a work to the author's generosity, humble spirit, and freedom from envy. It is interesting that the sin resisted is envy. We moderns with our firmly held assumptions about intellectual ownership and the consequent possibility of intellectual theft, might be inclined to attribute non-publication to avarice, miserliness. Attributing envy, however, suggests that the motive was thought to be pure malice, an act against society itself. So an author who does not share his work and launch it, as it were, into the stream of literature, is thought to be guilty of a sin against community. The last step of authorship is to overcome such envious feelings and submit one's work to the communal process of authorization through public comment and readerly response.[73]

The end of Eadmer's story of the finishing of *Proslogion* comes with Gaunilo's criticism of its arguments, and Anselm's further response, both of which he incorporated into the text itself:

> This work came into the hands of someone who found fault with one of the arguments in it, judging it to be unsound. In an attempt to refute it he wrote a treatise against it and attached this to the end of Anselm's work. A friend sent this to Anselm who read it with pleasure, expressed his thanks to his critic and wrote his reply to the criticism. He had this reply attached to the treatise which had been sent to him, and returned it to the friend from whom it had come, desiring him and others who might deign to have his little book to write out at the end of it the criticism of his argument and his own reply to the criticism.[74]

Anselm's humility is exemplary, but, unlike Eadmer, that is not what I find interesting in this account. In the first place, we note that an unknown reader, Gaunilo, composed a criticism of Anselm's text which he simply wrote out as though it were a continuation of it. Moreover, he is not the one to send it to Anselm; a friend of Anselm's does this, sending a copy of the text with Gaunilo's addition which has come into his possession. This behavior would get a modern reader a stiff fine, if not jail, but Eadmer finds it unremarkable, not reproving Gaunilo's manner of publication in the least. And indeed scholars familiar with medieval readers' habits of simply adding material as they choose to texts by someone else will not be surprised either. It is a mark that one's work has been truly read, and made his own, by someone else, and this in turn is another way of indicating that it is gaining authority – in the word's basic meaning of "growth" – as it generates further texts.

In this history of the *Proslogion*, we can observe the initial stages of its socialization, as it were, as it enters a public memory-bank and becomes literature. In order for the authority of the original work to come fully into being, it is necessary that there be a Gaunilo, as it also requires Anselm's reply to him – and the many comments, pro and con, that it has generated since. For a text demonstrates its authority not by closing down debate but by accumulating it – that is what we learn from Eadmer's tale about what constituted the originality of a text for a medieval public. Notice that Anselm, welcoming Gaunilo's response (there is less of humility in this than joy at being finally taken seriously in a way his own careless brothers had not done), adds his own comments to Gaunilo's, and instructs that both sets of comments be incorporated as the end of the text in all subsequent copying. His behavior suggests that once his work was made public (in an exemplar) Anselm saw himself as a co-equal reader along with other readers like Gaunilo, adding to the readerly flow that keeps the work alive and original in its proper sense. A modern author, responding to critics, will relegate them to the footnotes or to selective quotation; and we expect this because, to us, his authority attaches to him personally, *he* is author. But the way Anselm treats it, authority is a property of the *work*, proven by its ability to generate other work. Once the original exists, he places himself with Gaunilo as equally its reader, and what he thinks of the merits of Gaunilo's comments is given the status simply of more commentary, further dialogue.

This same observation concerning Anselm's attitude towards his written work is made by Brian Stock in his fine analysis of Anselm's description of the way he came to compose the *Monologion*, which began and was carried out in a way like that of Hugh of St. Victor's *De archa Noe*.[75] Stock emphasizes two matters: first, that Anselm regards his written version as the result of a process that is reductive and not complete; secondly, that the text both results from and remains the focal point of a dialogue Anselm has in his own mind (in *cogitatio*), with his clerical brethren (*Monologion* began as colloquia which his brethren requested him to write down), and finally with "a putative reading public."[76] In the case of Gaunilo's response to *Proslogion*, that public was putative no longer, and it is both significant and as typical as anything can be of the Middle Ages that Anselm immediately invited it, in writing, into his text. If his first written exemplum is "reductive" (in Stock's terms), it is so only as it offers the essentials for subsequent dialogue – indeed, it requires dialogue in order to achieve its proper textual function. Anselm says that *Monologion* began "in familiar conversation" ("sermones colloquendo") with his brother monks, thus, like Hugh, emphasizing the communal talk that started and will sustain his work. This is not just a monkish peculiarity, though the ideal of such a dialogue-text would be well realized in such a setting. The principle behind it is fundamental in the rhetorical tradition of text-making. As a composition, the written exemplum is expansive; it offers a "common place" which collects subsequent comments, glosses, references, as readers apply, adapt, restate, meditate upon it. Truly it is commentary and imitation which make a text an *auctor* – not the activities of its writer but of its readers. This has little to do, I think, with literacy, but everything to do with the institutional nature of literature in a memorial culture.

The author's *dictamen*, whether scribally transcribed or not, was thus a sort of memorandum of his composition at a particular stage, which he might reconstruct or revise almost continually, as he worked to perfect his *res*. In this sense, the modern notion of a finished work is quite foreign to medieval authorship. Authors would issue versions of a work which they still intended to perfect to scribes for copying onto parchment, perhaps in an effort to secure them, as Anselm wanted to do. Chaucer's *Troilus and Criseyde* circulated in at least one shorter version than the one we now possess, as its editor, R. K. Root, demonstrated long ago. A note by the scribe of the St. John's College, Cambridge, manuscript, before several blank lines on one folio page, indicates that "her faileth thyng þt is nat yt made," "here is lacking something that is not yet composed."[77] And the two versions, F and G, of the Prologue to *The Legend of Good Women* clearly represent different publications of the poem. The visions and revisions of *Piers Plowman* were once thought to be so unusual as to constitute *prima facie* evidence that multiple authors were responsible, but in fact the phenomenon is not uncommon in kind, though perhaps Langland was unusual in the degree of his revisions.[78] Petrarch habitually continued to revise autograph copies of his works after he had sent a version off for transcription and circulation; this is true of both his poetry and prose works.[79] And the revising process was not limited to the first author. Readers, in the course of familiarizing a text, became its authors too. No modern reader would think of adapting and adding to the work of someone else in the way that medieval readers freely did, sometimes indicating the difference by writing their own work in margins, but often not. The results concern every editor of a medieval text.

Perhaps because of the familiarity of their language, readers seem especially to have recorded in vernacular texts the ways in which they had made them their own, by adding passages, incorporating comments, respecting the *res* but not necessarily the *verba* in the manner in which *memoria* expands the words during meditation. The more amateur a production (one can really only use such a word after the thirteenth century), the more apt one is to find this, since these were made for use by families or small coteries. Among English works, the manuscripts of *Piers Plowman* are particularly notorious. Unlike the professional scribe, whose job was to copy not to read, an amateur writing for him- or herself was writing as a reader, whose task was to make one's own what one finds in texts. Rather than condemning them for this, we should understand that such wholesale commentary is a form of compliment, a readerly contribution to the text's continuation, and a judgment that it is worthy to be a public source for *memoria*.[80]

GLOSSING: MAKING A TEXT AN AUTHOR

I have spoken of the medieval book as a support for the various activities of *memoria* – no format shows better its compositional, meditational character and *catena* structure than the lay-out of the glossed books, which developed during the course of the twelfth century in France, particularly in Paris. They have been the subject of a penetrating study by Christopher de Hamel, who has demonstrated how they came into being soon after the compilation of the line-by-line Biblical commentary known as the *glossa ordinaria*.[81] This standard commentary was "simply a practical aid for students beginning on their study of the Bible," as G. R. Evans calls it, "distilling out the essence of the work of previous centuries" to present "a manageable and reliable" introduction in a brief, summary, and *ad res* form that was keyed specifically to the Bible text itself and did not try to address large questions or explore difficult matters.[82]

The glossed book's lay-out, difficult to set up and copy, was reserved for works that were among the most fully institutionalized (authorized in the sense I have been developing in this chapter) – the Decretals and compendious books of canon law, the Bible, especially the Psalms and the Pauline Epistles, and (by the late fourteenth century) the works of certain classical authors. The lay-out presents graphically the process of this authorization, for the compiled comments are written all around the author-text, keyed into it, *catena* fashion, via red underlinings, heuristic symbols, and other punctuation (in one early lay-out the Biblical words being commented on were written out in red and the commentary in ordinary dark ink).[83] They are also among the most fully decorated of books – and they are those which must be fully memorized. *Catena* is a mnemonic lay-out, elementary in memory training, in which the source text itself serves as the ordered set of backgrounds into which material is keyed. The complete format was developed for the commentary compiled by Peter Lombard for the Psalms and the Epistles, a revision of the older compilation by Anselm of Laon. It is possible that Peter Lombard himself devised the format, leaving it to professional scribes to carry out; this would not be unusual for a master to do, though the format is extremely complex in execution – one thinks of

7. Cambridge, Trinity College MS. B.5.4, fos. 146v–147r. The figure of "Augustinus" corrects one of the glosses. From Herbert of Bosham's Psalter, with the gloss of Peter Lombard. Bosham was secretary and advisor to Thomas Becket, who commissioned this project, carried out in northern France between 1164 and 1177.

Hugh of St. Victor's design for his *Chronicle*, and of Peter of Poitiers's diagrammatic *Genealogia*, both also twelfth-century French products.[84] The source-text is written in the center of the page on alternate lines in the large, careful hand known as *textualis formata*, and the commentary, hooked into it via key-words and phrases, is written in a smaller hand around it. One immediately sees the textual relationship of source to commentary; one is also provided with a mnemonically useful image to help to place the commentary safely in one's memory, *catena*-style. Recall how Hugh of St. Victor advises his students to pay close attention to the shapes of the letters and the colors on the page in order to fix a memorial image of the text – the glossed format seems deliberately designed to present memorable variations of letters (the different hands) and colors, for each page is unique. These different hands became conventionally used for these different kinds of text; the large hand developed into fully formed Gothic script; the smaller, squatter hand was used for commentary, even in books that did not reproduce a source-text. Clearly, they were used to form a visual cue to the sort of text with which one was dealing.[85]

One of the best-written of the glossed books of Psalms was made for Herbert of Bosham, chaplain, confidant, and biographer of Thomas Becket, probably in the late 1160s.[86] It was made in two large books, so extensive was the project; it presents the texts of both of Jerome's translations of the Psalms, the Gallican (based on the Greek translation of the Septuagint) and the Hebrew (based directly on the Hebrew text), with the commentary of Peter Lombard, which consists largely of excerpts from the major patristic commentators. The first volume (see figure 7) is now in the library of Trinity College, Cambridge (MS. B. 5. 4) and the second in Oxford (Bodleian Library, MS. Auct. E inf. 6).[87] One of their more original features is the use of painted figures to help fix the page as a mnemonically functional visual image. These figures usually inhabit the outermost margins of the page. The gloss itself is carefully annotated, with the sources of the commentary identified (Jerome, Augustine, Cassiodorus) and a system of patterned dots is established as a unique additional signature for each of the main sources (such indexing patterns seem to be quite common in glossed lay-outs; one thinks of the use of similar systematic *notae* for concording purposes which we see in Grosseteste's books, for example). The painted figures are a part of this apparatus: so, a bearded man labelled Augustinus (or Cassiodorus or Hieronimus) points a javelin at the commentary text. He holds a banderole on which is written a warning such as "Ego non probo" or "Hic michi caveat" or, as in figure 7, "Non ego"; it is significant that these figures mark where Peter Lombard misidentified or miscopied extracts, or where there is other disagreement. In addition to these figures, several of the Psalms have emblematic pictures painted next to their opening words; unlike the citational figures, these can occur in the inner margin where the gloss itself is written, as well as in the outermost one, suggesting that they too were considered essential in the gloss, and acted as markers for these particular Psalms. Unfortunately, both manuscripts were badly mutilated by someone who cut many such figures out of their pages, so that whatever system there may have been is now lost; it is apparent, however, that certain of these figures were deliberately repeated. A figure of "Ethica" holding a dove and a serpent, for instance, appears at the beginning of Psalms 4 and 11; the figure of a soul in flames, with the legend "Homo in igne, Deus in homine" is repeated at the beginning of Psalms 2, 8, and 81.

This textual format, serving the memorial lay-out of *catena*, is thus an applied mnemonic containing numerous visual helps to memory in its features, and also laying out graphically the relationship of the *auctor* and all its progeny, including their disagreements. The way in which the commentary is woven together around the *auctor* illustrates how the authority is understood as source-word rather than as final-word, the way we tend to understand it now. The pages shown in figure 7 were intended for study and meditation – they were not to be used by beginning readers directly but by their teachers. Moreover, Herbert of Bosham's books are not a single work but a whole library of materials, an encyclopedia of related knowledge gathered into its pages. Though drawn on a flat, two-dimensional page, each place occupied by a chunk of Psalm-text with its commentaries and glosses, it is conceived like a cube and used like a box or little room. The structure as a whole is thus composed of cells, like those in a beehive. Hugh of St Victor anticipated such a structure in his discussion of how to memorize the psalms (Appendix A), when he describes how one should conceive the basic *linea*, or diagram plan, as a set of compartments or boxes for associated materials, like the money-boxes used to store coins for rapid recovery. In a properly designed memory, just as on these pages, the verses of the source will be like a line with many hooks on it, and as one pulls in one part of it, all the fish will come along. To pull in one text is to pull all the commentary, as well as other texts concording with it. Source, glosses, citations, punctuation, and decoration are all married up together in a single memorial image which constitutes the text; one cannot meaningfully talk for long about one of these strands in isolation from the others, for that is not how they were perceived. They all serve *memoria* practically (they help to form the heuristics of order, unique address, division, and composition needed for safe storage and retrieval) and they also image its institutional nature. A work of literature was not taught in isolation, as an artifact produced by some person long dead whose particular intention we must now recover, but as an ever-rolling stream accumulating and adapting over time as it is collated with its multitude of readers. *Collatio* means all these things: bringing together of texts, conversations about texts, and feeding upon texts as one feeds at a community meal.

The glossed format remained very popular, especially for university use. A copy of the Gregorian Decretals with two distinct levels of identified commentary in it (law commentary was usually signed with the initials of the master responsible for it) plus additional comments in other hands shows in a wonderfully visual manner how the source-text has been wound about with generations of commentary. In this manuscript (Bodleian Library, MS. Lat. th. b 4, originally completed in July of 1241 at Bologna), the originating text is written in a large formal hand in two columns down the center of the page, with the commentary about it on all four sides (see figure 10).[88] Margins have been left between the two parts of the book and between the two columns of text; these contain ink decorations and comic drawings, such as a fox chasing a rooster (fo. 37) and a cat with a mouse (fo. 84v), or, as shown in figure 8, dogs and men hunting a savage boar. But these margins have themselves been written over with other commentary (though the drawings are usually left alone); in addition there are interlinear glosses in the main text. So the page presents a text that consists of a great many margins, those margins traditionally left for the memorial activities of readers over time. And these responses form an integral part of the public presentation of the text; indeed, in this manuscript, the originating text seems almost overwhelmed by its margins, as is perhaps suitable for a legal book. In earlier glossed books, scribes ruled an extra margin for current readers when the complex of written text and gloss threatened to crowd out the blank space of the page. Blank space is needed both to ensure a clean, crisp image of the text (for *turba*, "crowding," is a great enemy of memory) and to allow one to make one's own *notulae*.[89]

There are manuscripts in which the commentary has been written out in the margins, while blank space has been left for the main text, unfinished by the scribes. One such is Newberry Library MS. 31.1, intended for a text of Fulgentius on the pagan gods, with commentary by Pierre Bersuire (this text was the standard beginning of Bersuire's *Ovide moralisée*).[90] It is an odd way for a manuscript to be left, for usually the source-text was written first with the commentary fitted in. This manuscript was used despite what to us would be an insurmountable handicap, presumably by those who had

8. University of Oxford, Bodleian Library, MS. Lat.th.b.4, fo. 23v. Fully glossed page
from a Decretals written in Bologna, 1241. Notice how various readers have expanded
the number of margins with their own glosses. In the center margin are drawings of men
and dogs hunting a boar.

the source so well memorized that they attached the commentary to it mentally. In this regard, it is significant, I think, that this empty page space has been respected by readers, whose own notes are written in the expected place, outside the margins of the commentary, as though the unwritten space was also required in some way for the making of a proper memory-image keyed to the mentally supplied text – perhaps as a surface onto which textual cues could be projected in memory. In doing this they were following what had been standard before the invention of the glossed lay-out, when line by line commentary on the Bible text was written out continuously, without all the keys supplied in a glossed book, and a reader had to supply the appropriate Bible text from the grid in his memory.

So important is the acquiring of commentary to establish an *auctor*, that at least one medieval vernacular writer supplied an exemplar of his work in the form of a glossed book. There is a manuscript of Boccaccio's romance epic, *Teseida*, written entirely by Boccaccio himself, which is now in the Biblioteca Medicea Laurenziana in Florence (MS. Acquisti e Doni 325). It is on parchment, of course, written out with rubrics, initials, and even a few decorations, and space has been left for additional miniatures. It is obviously an exemplar, not a *dictamen*, so that its format was intended by Boccaccio to be copied by others. But it is a glossed book. The stanzas of the source-text are written in the large display hand reserved for *auctores*, and commentary, written in the appropriate script, surrounds it in the margins. These annotations, comments, and corrections are also Boccaccio's. As Giorgio Pasquali said of this manuscript, "[Boccaccio] began and continued in fits and starts to add notes at one or another point in his poem (at times brief interlinear interpretations, at times erudite excursus), without having completely compiled a running commentary," though he seems headed in that direction. In *Teseida*, Boccaccio is both the originator of his text, and its reader; his own commentary invites commentary from others. And, of course, *Teseida* itself is a re-presenting of the classical legend, with Statius quite clearly remembered – so Boccaccio as composer is also, simultaneously, a reader.[91] Evidently, Boccaccio considered the heart of the process of making literature to be not the production of a beautifully written-out final text, but the unending collocation which the author-text conducted with its readers in the margins, the background for memory. By giving his new work all the trappings of a glossed book, Boccaccio was claiming for it the immediate institutional status of an *auctor*.

In conclusion, I would like to look at the matter of plagiarism, as pre-modern centuries defined it. It is sometimes said that there was no plagiarism before there was a law of copyright; this is not true. But plagiarism was differently defined, as a matter essentially of poor *memoria*. Composition cannot occur without authors, used in the way we have seen in these last two chapters. One's audience will, of course, recognize them and their translation to the occasion of one's own design, for they are in the public memory. The *memoria* of the composer and the *memoria* of the audience are thus bound in a dialogue of textual allusions and transformations, and not to engage in it is the mark of a dolt.

Thus Quintilian scorns orators who simply repeat the words of others, or who boilerplate their own speeches, as much as he scorns those who appear to be rehearsing a word-for-word memorized speech. How shamed they should feel, he says, "by the detection of their wretched stock-in-trade, so familiar to the audience's memory, and worn to shreds, as it were, by doing numerous different services for poor men who want to put on a show."[92] *Ad res* memorizing supposes that the reader will recreate the original's *sententiae* in words that are at least partly his own; this freedom respects the fruitful *auctoritas* of one's source as ignorant parroting cannot. John of Salisbury, describing Bernard of Chartres's custom of making his students recite daily from the works which were to serve as their models, suggests a distinction between true and false imitation that is close to Quintilian's, and instructive:

if, to embellish his work, someone had sewed on a patch of cloth filched from an external source, Bernard, on discovering this, would rebuke him for his plagiary, but would generally refrain from punishing him ... if an unsuitable theme had invited this, he would, with modest indulgence, bid the boy to rise in [true] imitation [*ad exprimendam auctorum imaginem ... conscendere*].[93]

In a letter to Boccaccio in 1359, Petrarch writes of how he had thoroughly familiarized Virgil, Horace, Livy, Cicero, and some others:

I ate in the morning what I would digest in the evening; I swallowed as a boy what I would ruminate upon as an older man. I have thoroughly absorbed these writings [*michi tam familiariter ingessere*], implanting them not only in my memory but in my marrow ... But sometimes I may forget the author, since through long usage and continual possession I may adopt them and for some time regard them as my own; and besieged by the mass of such writings [*turba talium obsessus*],[94] forget whose they are and whether they are mine or others'. This then is what I meant about more familiar things deceiving us more than others; if at times out of habit they return to the memory, it often happens that to the preoccupied mind, deeply intent on something else, they seem not only to be yours but to your surprise, new and original ... I grant that I like to embellish my life with sayings and admonitions from others, but not my writings [*Vitam michi alienis dictis ac monitus ornare, fateor, est animus, non stilum*] unless I acknowledge the author or make some significant change in arriving at my own concept from many and varied sources in imitation of the bees . . . I much prefer that my style [*stilus*] be my own, uncultivated and rude, but made to fit, as a garment, to the measure of my mind, rather than to someone else's . . . each [writer] must develop and keep his own [style] lest . . . by dressing grotesquely in others' clothes . . . we may be ridiculed like the crow.[95]

This eloquent characterization of his own practices is less a Petrarchan manifesto of a new Renaissance spirit of individuality and freedom from dead authority than a restatement of the very medieval description of reading and composing we encountered, also eloquently, in Hugh of St. Victor on the Ark of Wisdom. The life is adorned with others' maxims so that by the process of domestication their character stamps the character of the man and becomes that of his style (and here we must remember that *stylus* means both pen and style in our sense of the word), cut, like good clothing, to one's own measure of ability, "ad mensuram ingenii mei." How the words of others become the measure of one's own mind is described earlier in this book, the digestion and rumination by which they are made mine, "michi tam familiariter ingessere". Familiarizing makes the wholesale appropriation of one's sources "honorable," for, like a bee, one has transformed the many nectars of the reading-flowers in one's memorial store-house into a single honey, "e multis et variis unum faciat." If they haven't been so processed, then the imitation is dishonorable.

We, of course, would still regard the results as plagiarism, so long as the idea was recognizable. Perhaps that is because we think of plagiarism as theft and authors as owners with enduring rights to their work. But for Petrarch, as for Bernard and Quintilian, plagiarism occurs when one unwittingly or from laziness quotes *verbatim* because one's memory-design has been overwhelmed by the over-crowded bits of one's improperly stored reading. That is a failure of memory, due to one's own neglect and sloth (including the kind of sloth that overworks the body); it is not perceived as a matter of theft. The plagiarist is detected by the superior memories of the audience he is trying unsuccessfully to impress. Plagiarism is to be avoided because it makes oneself appear ridiculous and shameful in public, like a clown in ill-fitting clothing, whose garments are not familiar to him. It is a failure of invention because it is a failure of memory, that educated *memoria* of the trained author, who knows how to speak without appearing to have memorized at all.

CHAPTER 7

Memory and the book

"PAINTURE" AND "PAROLE"

The importance of visual images as memorial hooks and cues is a basic theme in all memory-training advice and practice from the very earliest Western text we possess, the *Dialexeis*. In that pre-Socratic fragment, one is advised to fashion rebuses, or visual riddles based on homophonies, to recall the sound of particular words (*memoria verborum*) such as personal names, and also heraldic images, such as Ares for anger, to remember themes (*memoria rerum*). In a study of the architectural mnemonic, Herwig Blum sought to link this technique to the plentiful use of decoration, such as mosaic, frieze, and painting, in ancient buildings, both domestic (as at Pompeii) and monumental.[1] We have always known that certain classes of allegorical images, such as those in Renaissance emblem books, were to be used for meditational reminiscence, for their authors tell us so.[2]

The function of *picturae* in medieval cultures has been, I think, rather misunderstood. In 600 Pope Gregory the Great wrote a letter to the hapless bishop, Serenus of Marseilles, who had become concerned that some of his flock might be engaged in superstitious worship of the holy images in his church. To prevent this, he destroyed all the pictures, thereby scandalizing his entire congregation, which deserted him on the spot. This story has been understood as an early indication that medieval images were a strict form of iconography, pictorial writing. The art historian Emile Mâle analyzed the function of Gothic images as the literature of the laity, *laicorum litteratura*.[3] The Gothic cathedral, Mâle argued, was essentially a Bible in stone and glass, its images designed to substitute for the written word in communicating the stories of the Bible to a lay congregation which could not read and therefore, Mâle assumed, had no other access to their content. The notion that the medieval laity as a group could not read at all has now been largely discredited by the accumulation of contrary evidence, from even the earliest medieval centuries. Explanations such as Mâle's also played down the fact that books and churches restricted to learned groups and clerical use were also profusely pictured. But Mâle was not wrong to say that the cathedral was a non-verbal textual form, only in his understanding of what that statement meant to a culture that did not share the bias ingrained in our notion of representational realism.

For that is a non-medieval bias. Representation, as we have seen, was understood not in an objective or reproductive sense as often as in a temporal one; signs make something present to the mind by acting on memory. Just as letters, *litterae*, make present the voices (*voces*) and ideas (*res*) of those who are not in fact present, as Isidore said, so pictures serve as present signs of or cues to those same *voces* and *res*. Gilbert Crispin, the abbot of Westminster from 1085 to 1117, says this of *pictura*: "Just as letters are the forms and markers of spoken words, pictures exist as the likenesses [*similitudines*] and markers of written matters."[4] As used here by Gilbert, *similitudo* does not mean "likeness" in the sense in which a painting of a dog is "like" a dog, for he is discussing the visions of Ezekiel and Isaiah, in particular the four-faced creatures of the divine chariot, whose faces Ezekiel saw in his vision "in the likeness" of a man, a lion, an eagle, and a bull (Ez. 1:10). These creatures do not represent God, they are signs of the presence of God. The Latin verb *repraesentare*, "represent," is derived from the word meaning "present in time," *praesens*. Abbot Gilbert's is not a mimetic definition but a temporal one, in keeping with the traditions of both ancient and medieval philosophy and pedagogical practice; the letters and other images are signs (*notae*), not primarily by virtue of imitation but by virtue of recalling something again to memory, making one mindful as the prophet is made mindful. This understanding requires that pictures themselves function recollectively, as letters do.[5] It is equally true to say that letters can function as pictures of a sort, a theme explored in this chapter.

With reference to this very medieval notion of what a picture is for, we may look at what Gregory wrote to Bishop Serenus:

It is one thing to worship a picture, it is another by means of pictures to learn thoroughly [*addiscere*] the story that should be venerated. For what writing makes present to those reading, the same picturing makes present [*praestat*] to the uneducated, to those perceiving visually, because in it the ignorant see what they ought to follow, in it they read who do not know letters. Wherefore, and especially for the common people, picturing is the equivalent of [*pro*] reading.[6]

Several aspects of this characterization require comment. First, Gregory says that the picture is for learning a story, *historia*. It is not, in our sense, a picture of some thing but rather the means for knowing, memorizing, and recollecting the same matters or stories that written letters also record. Like Abbot Gilbert (who would likely have received the idea from him), Gregory insists that *picturae* are essentially textual in the way that they function. What writing makes present, pictures also present, namely "quod sequi debeant," what they should do. Looking at pictures is an act analogous to reading. And reading, as we have seen, is a complex activity involving both an oral phase, that of *lectio*, and a silent one, of *meditatio*, committing the substance of the text to memory in mental images that enable one to mull it over and make it one's own. That is the nature of learning it, "addiscere". So, as reading letters "praestat," makes present, a story – and the Latin is emphatically temporal in its meaning – so too does seeing a picture. "[P]ro lectione pictura est" – picturing does what reading does and so can stand in for it (the force of *pro* in this formulation) *because it is also an inventive, rhetorical activity*. By Gilbert's time, the use of images was justified theologically solely by their recollective value. Images are themselves words of a sort, not because they represent words in our sense of "represent," but because, like words, they recall content to mind.

Both textual activities, picturing and reading, have as their goal not simply the learning of a story, but learning it to familiarize and domesticate it, in that fully internalized, even physiological way that medieval reading required. But in order to profit from *pictura*, one must understand it rhetorically, as directly referential not to an object but to a narrative (*historia*) and thus to human mental processes involved in understanding (intellect) and persuasion (will). The *phantasm* or *imago* which the mind must shape out of the various data of the senses in order to know at all mediates to our intellects what our eyes take in. Phantasms, which are the materials by means of which people think, are mental "impressons" of our sensory experiences, used in constructing concepts that involve other mental materials as well, such as previous memories. A phantasm is not a direct transfer of whole experiences. This is a crucial point to comprehend about the psychology of images, especially in the medieval West. A physical image, such as a painting or a statue, cannot directly represent anything to a human mind because we humans can only understand what our senses have variously taken in by means of a phantasm constructed "spiritually" (Augustine's word – we now would probably say mentally or cognitively) by our imagination for use in our thinking. This psychology is found in Quintilian as well as Aristotle, Augustine, and Aquinas. The diagram of the version of it shown in figure 3 underscores the way in which human imagination is involved throughout the process of thinking. Augustine wrote that human memory is never of the actual past because it is the recollection of phantasms.[7] Bishop Serenus was scandalized by his flock, before he scandalized them, because they failed to recognize exactly this distinction. They took the images to be directly representational of things themselves, and, having thus objectified them, they reified and mystified them.

Picturae and *litterae* remain intimately linked in the later Middle Ages. A good example is the work of Richard de Fournival, who was a canon of Amiens cathedral in 1240, and its chancellor in 1246; later he became a canon of Rouen, and chaplain to Cardinal Robert de Sommercote. He died not later than 1260. He is remembered for a work that exists in many manuscripts of the thirteenth to fifteenth centuries, *Li Bestiaire d'amours*; so popular was it in its day that it acquired a critical answer from an unnamed woman, *Li Response du Bestiaire*.[8] Richard had designed his text as a picturebook, the writing and seventy-plus drawings of animals forming a unit. He explains his plan in a preface. All people by nature desire knowledge, he says, and because they live so short a time, they must rely upon the knowledge gained by others as well as their own experiences. To gain such knowledge, God has given the human soul the ability of memory.[9] Memory has two gates of access, sight and hearing, and a road particular to each of these portals. These roads are called *painture* and *parole*.[10]

Painture serves the eye and *parole* the ear. Both are equal means of access to the "house of memory," which holds all human knowledge of the past, and each has cognitively the same effect. But the *painture* of a text is not confined only to the pictures painted on a page, as Richard de Fournival makes clear. Its *painture* also includes the mental images which it raises in its readers'/listeners' minds: "When one sees painted a story, whether of Troy or something else, one sees those noble deeds which were done in the past exactly as though they were still present. And it is the same thing with hearing a text, for when one hears a story read aloud, listening to the events one sees them in the present."[11] It is significant that Richard uses the verb *veir* of what happens in memory both from something received from sight and from hearing. Because it is translated into predominantly visual images by the mind, even *lectio*, *lire*, "reading-aloud," creates *painture*. Thus, seeing is not confined to silent reading, any more than speaking is to reading aloud.

Because memory has these two gates, Richard says, he has designed his book to be especially memorable by enhancing both its *painture* and *parole*. In saying this he does not mean simply that he has put together a book with illustrations, although he has done this as well. "And I will show you how this text has both *painture* and *parole*," he continues: "For it is clear that it has *parole*, because all writing is made in order to signify *parole* and in order that one should read it: and when one reads it aloud, writing returns to the nature of *parole* [speech]. On the other hand, it is clear that it also has *painture* because the letter does not exist unless one paints it [that is, unless one gives it a visible form]."[12] Richard claims for his book rhetorical *energeia/enargeia*, or "bringing-before-the-eyes," that much-prized quality of vividness which takes hold of a reader's imagination and, especially in narrative, enables one to experience the events as though they were happening before one's very eyes and ears.[13]

"For I send you in this writing [*cis escrit*]," continues Richard, "both *painture* and *parole*, so that when I am not present this writing by its *painture* and by its *parole* will make me present to your memory."[14] Richard refers to his picture book, underscoring that it has both *painture* and *parole*, and that together both will make him present to its readers in their memories. This is a remarkable restatement of the idea, found in Isidore, that letters are signs of sounds (*voces*) which in turn signify things. A written word has both visual shape (its *painture*) and calls to mind sound (its *parole*); which one of these two senses affords the gate to memory thus depends not on whether a text was composed orally or in writing, but on how it is presented to its audience on a given occasion, whether by being read aloud or silently to oneself. The distinction Richard makes here is related to the long-standing, and at this time universal, one between *legere clare* and *legere tacite*, which require different tasks from a reader. In either case, the sensory gateway is always dual (though the proportions of seeing and hearing differ according to the two types of reading), for all words are both shape and sound by their very nature, and all sensory impressions are processed so as to act upon memory in the same way, making what is no longer physically before one present to the mind's eye. [O]*n les veïst*, "one sees them," says Richard of the events in the story of Troy, whether through looking at their pictures, reading and listening about them in words, or – best of all – both at once.

Thus the visual presentation of a text was considered, at least by the learned, to be a part of its meaning, not limited to the illustration of its themes or subjects but necessary to its proper reading, its ability-to-be significant and memorable. Malcolm Parkes has spoken of punctuation and other aspects of lay-out as the "visual grammar" of language, as necessary to comprehension as the pauses and accents of spoken language.[15] This is another way of saying, in essence, that language has both *painture* and *parole* in its nature, precisely what Richard is talking about.

The idea is articulated often. When, at the beginning of *La vita nuova*, Dante addresses his readers to explain the genesis of his work, he says that "in the book of my memory" he found "a rubric which says: *Incipit vita nova*. Under which rubric I find written the words which it is my intention to copy into this little book; and if not all, at least their substance."[16] Somewhat later (2: 10), he refers to words "scritte ne la mia memoria sotto maggiori paragrafi," "written in my memory under large paraphs." Charles Singleton has written cogently on Dante's use of this conceit to govern the progress and nature of his work, and the extent to which the image of himself as the scribe and glossator of a previously extant text is exploited.[17] In composing, Dante sees the work in visual form, written in his memory as pages with text, rubrics, and paraphs. Notice also that he treats his own work as though it were an *auctor*, which he will treat *sententialiter* as he wishes to adapt it, unconstrained by verbatim quotation.

In a similar fashion, the English poet, John Lydgate, begins a poem on "The Fifteen Joys and Sorrows of Mary" by describing how he came to write it. First, he saw a Pity "sett out in picture," that is, the painted scene we now call the Pietà. As he inspects this *meditacioun* closely (and the picture itself is termed the meditation), it resolves itself into "Rubrisshes departyd [separate rubrics] blak and Reed / Of ech chapitle a paraf in the heed / Remembryd first Fifteene of her gladynessys / And next in ordre were set hyr hevy-nessys."[18] Like Dante, Lydgate thinks of his poem as laid out in his memory like a written page, with an illumination, text, rubrics, and paraphs, a page of the book of his memory that seems in lay-out very like that of a fifteenth-century Book of Hours, which is the sort of memory book that a fifteenth-century poet's readers would know best. *Memoria* is stored and inventoried in such divisions, inscribed as visual images; this was the elementary pedagogy which Dante and Lydgate shared, and which long predates them both.

I have already mentioned a passage from Chaucer's *The House of Fame*, in which all the voices, the *parole*, of human beings are described as rising from earth to Fame's house, where they assume the shape of those who spoke them. It is an exceptionally exact realization in poetry of the traditional medieval understanding of what words are. These human *paroles* do more than just represent (in form and time) the *voces* of those who spoke them, they also come clothed in language's graphic form, its manuscript *painture*:

> Whan any speche ycomen ys
> Up to the paleys, anon-ryght
> Hyt wexeth lyk the same wight
> Which that the word in erthe spak,
> Be hyt clothed red or blak,
> And hath so very hys lyknesse
> That spok the word that thou wilt gesse
> That it the same body be,
> Man or woman, he or she.   (*House of Fame*, 1074–1082)

9. University of Oxford, Bodleian Library, MS. Bodley 717, fo. 287v (?Norman, late 11th century). The inscription above the drawing of the scribe reads "Imago pictoris et illuminatoris huius operis. Hugo pictor," "The image of the painter and illuminator of this work. Hugh the painter."

The figures are clothed in red or black, according to the ink in which the letters forming these words were written. Chaucer has peopled his House of Fame with literature that has both *painture* and *parole*. He also gives us a precise image of how *litterae*, written in black and red, are signs of *voces* (both voices and words) and *voces* re-present in our memories those no longer immediately present to us.[19]

The scribe who wrote out the letters was often identified as the painter or picturer of the manuscript. For example, a late eleventh-century manuscript, perhaps from Normandy (figure 9), pictures a monk named Hugo, with his scribal pen and knife, identifying the portrait as "imago pictoris et illuminatoris huius operis." Very similar is a portrait of a monk named Isidore in a manuscript of 1170 written for the cathedral at Padua, which calls him the painter of the manuscript, yet shows him in the act of writing. And the nun Guda wrote in her colophon, "peccatrix mulier scripsit quae pinxit hunc librum."[20] Indeed, the earliest medieval evidence suggests that at that time, too, the scribe was most often also the book's decorator, and that often when an author wrote out his own text he also punctuated and decorated it in a scheme that he intended copyists to preserve. The Latin verb, *distinguere*, means "divide up," "mark," "punctuate," and "decorate," all activities pertaining to the fundamental task of *divisio*. Thus, Jerome admonishes later copyists to preserve his punctuation of the Bible. There is evidence that Eusebius himself designed the Canon Tables named for him; the decoration of the fourth-century *Virgilius Augusteus* (MS. Vat. lat. 3256) was done by the scribes. The earliest illustrations in books occur at the beginning of sections of the text in order to mark its divisions, thus serving as what Carl Nordenfalk called "a kind of pictorial rubrics."[21] The Augusteus manuscript of Virgil has colored initials, the earliest surviving examples of this feature, at the beginning of the first line occurring on each page, but such large initials were soon used to mark the beginning of each major division of a text. The monks at St. Albans in the twelfth century described the finishing of a text by decorator and rubricator as a task of exacting division, "ad unguem," which they were proud to have done "irreprehensibiliter."[22] Though the forms of decoration and rubrication they put in their book were very different from those in fourth-century use, their phrase recalls that of St. Ambrose laboring over his books *distinguendam ad unguem*. Nordenfalk observes that book decoration was born of "the necessity of providing a dividing and supporting framework for tabular texts," such as lists of numbers, or names of persons and places, or "words divided into syllables by punctuation."[23] Such phenomena need the "visual grammar" that lines and columns provide because they have no grammar of their own. But whereas the earliest kind of decoration one finds in papyri is of this sort, I do not think that decoration was generated solely to organize lists. It is rather a subspecies of punctuation itself, and thus basic to reading and retention, for, to quote again Hugh of St. Victor's succinct aphorism: "Modus legendi dividendo constat." Manuscript decoration is part of the *painture* of language, one of the gates to memory, and the form it takes often has to do with what is useful not only to understand a text but to retain and recall it too.

Imagines rerum *in psalters for study*

One of the continuing themes in medieval manuscript illumination is the making of what some art historians have called word-pictures, or images linked to (or even substituting for) words through a visual pun. The technique is clearly related to the practice of making mnemonic *imagines*, and examples of it can be found which pre-date by many centuries the thirteenth-century acceptance of the *Ad Herennium*. One of the best-known examples is the Utrecht Psalter, of which a number of medieval copies were made. In it, *picturae* and *litterae* together make up the *littera-tura*, the text, and both address the ocular gateway to memory. The words, however, can also be sounded aloud, and so can also address its aural gateway, and as signs of *voces* the images do as well.[24] It is well to keep mind when considering medieval habits of study, that "silence" was neither necessarily nor often totally "quiet," without any sound.[25]

Though the manuscript was made in the vicinity of Reims in the ninth century, the style of its drawings reflects older models, Byzantine and even late classical. This suggests that these images belong to a long tradition of *imagines rerum* associated with the Psalm texts; if the images were thought to be especially useful – for example, for the memory work of meditative study – that would help to account for their longevity and continued copying, which is otherwise something of a mystery. Certainly the excellence of the Utrecht's system of Psalm images was recognized at the monastery of Christ Church, Canterbury, for it was used as a model in the making of other psalters. It was, for example, copied in the Canterbury scriptorium in a manuscript that still exists (British Library MS. Harley 603) but uses a different text of the Psalms than that in the Utrecht Psalter itself, the Roman text, based on the Old Latin versions, rather than Jerome's Gallican version, which used the Greek Septuagint.

If the images were used only as verbatim cues to specific syllables (as *imagines verborum*, in the language of memory art), these verbal differences between the Psalter versions would indeed pose a difficulty, but since they evidently were not, they have considerable value as *imagines rerum* for signaling the chief topics and key ideas of each Psalm in order. The method of *memoria rerum* and its fundamental role in meditational exercise accounts for the image schemes' value to generations of monks, for the English copies of the Utrecht Psalter are in fact adapted flexibly to the varied interests and circumstances over time of those making and using them. They are obviously study manuscripts. Two of them set out all three medieval versions of the psalms side by side, plus commentaries and glosses – and one, the Eadwine Psalter, also contains translations of Psalms into early English and Anglo-Norman. Tellingly, the designers of these later copies did not merely iterate the original images but changed them, added to them, and even made up new ones on their model.[26]

The Utrecht Psalter demonstrates very well some essentials of the technique known as *memoria rerum*. Like the others, this psalter is a study book, made not for novices just learning their Psalms *but for readers who already have the Psalms by heart*, and who therefore can recognize and profit from the subject- and topic-cues which the images provide. The images of each Psalm are drawn in a grouped scene at the beginning of each Psalm text; as a norm, they are read from left to right as one reads written text, though certain dominant images, such as those of Christ, can be placed centrally. Many engage in activities which underscore their relationships.

One example will suffice as an illustration of the technique used for each of the Psalms.[27] Psalm 148, *Laudate Dominum*, calls upon the various parts of creation to praise the Lord. It is fairly long, and needn't be quoted in full, but a summary of its constituent verses is useful for understanding the picture-scene which accompanies it in the Psalter (figure 10). The following are invited to praise the Lord: angels, hosts, sun and moon, stars, heavens of heavens and waters above the heavens (1–6); dragons and deeps, fire and hail, snow and vapors, stormy wind (7–8); mountains and hills, fruitful trees and cedars, beasts and cattle, creeping things and flying fowl (9–10); kings and all people, princes and judges, young men and maidens, old men and children (11–13), for God exalts "the horn of his people," Israel (14). The picture shows, at its upper center, a large figure of Christ ("Dominus") the Creator, in a mandorla – He is flanked by "angels." At each end of this upper space, or "heaven," are two gigantic figures drawn from the waist up, one holding up the "sun" and the other the "moon." Below the Christ are "mountains" and "hills." A "fire" is burning on them, and they are covered with "fruitful trees, and all cedars." On the ground, and in the tree branches, are "beasts, and all cattle, creeping things, and flying fowl." Beside the mountains and hills are two people, each with an open book (verse 6: "he hath made a decree which shall not pass"). They are at the head of four groups of people, "kings," "princes and judges" (dressed as soldiers), "young men and maidens," and "old men and children." At the bottom of the picture is shown "all deeps" and "dragons."

As is the case with Psalm 148, the picture of each Psalm in this Psalter provides a set of cueing images for its principal words and themes. These images cue verses which one can then complete by note recitation. It is incorrect to think of the images as substituting for the words, or as an aid for beginners who do not already know the texts by another means. The pictures are only a jumble if, on seeing them, one does not recognize the topics which the images elicit, or – equally important – the order in which the verses occur. As is the case with Hugh of St. Victor's *Chronicle* Preface (Appendix A), this mnemonic system is based on a prior-retained

10. Utrecht, University Library MS. 32, fo. 82v ("The Utrecht Psalter," France, near Reims, ninth century). Picture-summary for the text of Psalm 148.

foundation of verbatim memorization, acquired and fortified during the daily round of monastic offices by those using the Utrecht Psalter as it was by the novices of St. Victor studying history. The images provide a full *memoria rerum* of the Psalms.

Thus to term these images "word-pictures" is misleading, for the characterization mis-states their main function, which is to cue and trigger recollection of textual material that the reader already knows. They are agent images in the proper sense, for they are devices and tools. The method of *imagines rerum* is designed for those studying and composing colloquies, meditations, and sermons on the basis of those studies. They have an important practical function. The *imagines rerum* of a psalter such as the Utrecht lay out the essential subjects of each Psalm in a clear order, quickly apparent to one who recognizes the cues provided. In their groups the images are *clarus* (well lit), *rarus* (not crowded), and *solemnis* (disposed in coherent order). Evidently, internalizing such a system of images will draw in the habitually retained texts and topics to which each image is attached, providing a completely portable mental instrument, readily available on any number and variety of occasions, as needed – exactly the situation envisioned by Hugh of St. Victor in his advice to impose a *linea* or structure upon the rote-retained texts of Psalms (Appendix A). The psalters of the "Utrecht family" demonstrate very well how artificial memory schemes build upon a foundation of prior learning, not as substitutes or alternatives but as *notae* and *imagines rerum*, markers and cues to the mental library retained by heart which formed the foundation of ancient and medieval education.

Another example, painted in a style quite different from the Utrecht Psalter though also using *imagines rerum*, is the Cuerden Psalter now in the Morgan Library (MS. M 756), made in England, probably Oxford, around 1270. The use of word-pictures is unusual in thirteenth-century English art, more typical at this time of French art. There is a donor picture in the book, which would indicate the involvement of a lay patron, but Dominicans are also pictured frequently in its pages, suggesting that this order had a role as well in its making.[28]

Each Psalm in this book has an initial which contains a rebus-like picture of key words within the Psalm. Psalm 38 starts "Dixi custodiam vias meas ut non delinquitur in lingua mea. Posui ori meo custodiam cum consisteret peccator adversum me," "I said I will take heed to my ways, that I sin not with my tongue: I will place a guard on my mouth when the sinner comes before me." The initial of this Psalm in the Cuerden Psalter ("D") shows a nimbused Christ seated at the center of the picture (figure 11). David with

11. New York, Pierpont Morgan Library MS. M. 756, fo. 60r ("The Cuerden Psalter," England, Oxford, *c.* 1270). Initial of Psalm 38 (39).

his harp is shown to His left, and Christ covers David's foot with His own. The Christ figure looks to His right, where the same David figure is shown kneeling, and pointing to his extended tongue: his foot also is covered by Christ's. The position of these three figures suggests the mnemonic principles which Bradwardine's treatise expounds, though they were drawn some seventy years earlier. Christ is in the middle, and to His left (our right) is David, who is the subject of the first word in the text, *Dixi*. Christ steps on David's foot, thereby joining the figures in an action of hitting, touching, striking, or something similar. The left side of the scene provides an image of chief words in the second and third phrases of the first verse, *non delinquitur in lingua mea* and *posui ori meo custodiam*. To remember the correct order of the words, one first looks to the right and then to the left of the central figure, their orderly joining being indicated by the actions of the central image, covering a foot in one case and looking in the other.

Another good example of the sort of *imagines rerum* that occur in the Cuerden Psalter is the initial to Psalm 72, *Quam bonus* (figure 12), which shows a crippled man moving about on his knees, while balanced by two low stools which he holds in his hands, while a second stooped figure with a staff goes behind him. This image refers to verse 2 of this Psalm, "mei autem pene moti sunt pedes, pene effusi sunt gressus mei," "but as for me, my feet were almost gone; my steps had well nigh slipped."

The initial of Psalm 52 (figure 13), which begins "Dixit insipiens," shows, on the left, a figure of the fool with a club, eating a round loaf of bread. This figure is often found in psalters, to mark the initial of Psalms 13 and 52, which are virtually identical texts. (The round loaf refers to verse 4 [modern numbering], in which the "workers of iniquity" are said to "eat up my people as they eat bread.") But other figures appear in the initial as well as the fool. These refer to verses 2 and 3; at the bottom of the round space inside the D are two male figures lying on the ground together in what appears to be a homosexual embrace: they are those who "are corrupt and are made abhominable in their inquities" (verse 2). To the right and top of the space, a nimbed Christ looks down and points to two other male figures, one of whom is tonsured: these refer to verse 3, "God looked down from heaven on the children of men to see if there were any that did understand, or did seek God." Reading this scene counter-clockwise from the top produces the correct order of the verses: "Dixit insipiens," "Corrupti sunt," and "Deus de celo prospexit."

One sees this impulse to provide textual pictures in late medieval vernacular manuscripts produced by lay scribes, so it is not confined, at least by the end of this period, to Latin productions. These vernacular productions are often done in a style that is idiosyncratic and bears little relationship, either in iconography or in execution, to the books produced by professional workshops. This makes their use of pictures all the more interesting as an indication of what readers thought they needed in order to profit from a book.

12. New York, Pierpont Morgan Library MS. M. 756, fo. 105v ("The Cuerden Psalter," England, Oxford, *c.* 1270). Initial of Psalm 72 (73).

Among such manuscripts, a copy of *Piers Plowman* in the Bodleian Library (MS. Douce 104, written in 1427) contains drawings on almost every page, which relate to the poem in several different ways. Some are *imagines rerum* related to the content in a manner that we recognize easily,

13. New York, Pierpont Morgan Library MS. M. 756, fo. 79r ("The Cuerden Psalter,"
England, Oxford, *c.* 1270). Initial of Psalm 52 (53).

such as the drawings of the Seven Deadly Sins. So, opposite the text's brief
description of the courtesan, *Pernel prout hert*, is drawn a woman-dandy
who wears a gorgeous robe and a belt with golden balls on it (fo. 24). The
text describing Gluttony is written over a drawing of a figure with a cup
and a swollen belly (fo. 29) – here the relationship of word and picture is
made concrete. Others of the pictures are associated with the marginal
tituli; for example, opposite text discussing the duties of knights is a knight
with the words "nota de kny3thod" written across it (fo. 35v).

Still other images follow the precepts for *imagines rerum* by cueing either
chief words or concepts of the text with which they are associated. For
example, opposite a discussion of Charity appears the figure of a young
man in hose and doublet holding a round mirror – this evokes (but does
not explain) the line "Ac I seygh hym neuere sothly but as my-self in a
miroure" (fo. 74). A speech by Free-Will (Liberum Arbitrium) on how
Holy Church is a love-knot of loyalty and faithful belief is accompanied by
a drawing of a man hanged on a gibbet, an allusion not to the theme of the
speech but to one line in it, "And þeues loueþ and beleuþ hateþ and at þe
last be hongyt" (manuscript reading) (fo. 79; see figure 14). Finally, a
number of images are not obviously related to particular texts but recur
at intervals in the margins, probably according to the reader's own system;
chief among these is a figure suggesting meditation, shown either as a

14. University of Oxford, Bodleian Library, MS. Douce 104, fo. 79r (*Piers Plowman C.* XVII. 118–148). Text in Hiberno-English dialect, manuscript made in Ireland in 1427, likely by a single scribe–illustrator, with annotations made soon afterward by another scribe writing the same hand. The drawing of a man on a gibbet cues the text, "And þeues loueþ and beleuþ hateþ and at þe last be hongyt" (line 138). Over the figure's legs seems to be written (the ink is badly rubbed) "Nota de mandatu," "Make a note concerning the commandment," in reference to the underlined verses in Latin, lines 140a–c.

seated man holding his head on his hands (fos. 54, 63) or as a male head shown gazing pensively at the text (fo. 65).[29] Made in Ireland in 1427, fifty years or so after Langland's poem, Douce 104 is a unique production, written in Hiberno-English dialect by an Irish scribe and decorated either by the same person or by a painter he worked with closely. Kerby-Fulton and Despres argue that it is the work of a single scribe-illustrator – perhaps a clerkly maker not unlike Langland himself – who made this book for his own use and that of his friends.[30] Many *Piers Plowman* manuscripts seem made for personal use by admirers of the work. Though it is not without skill and training either in its writing or in its decoration, Douce 104 shows few signs of derivation from the court culture of the age. But neither does *Piers Plowman*. The text is basically that which modern editors recognize as C, but it contains a number of odd and idiosyncratic readings, suggesting that it may have been at least partly a production for meditation in the manner of *memoria rerum*.

MENTAL PICTURES

Painture, as Richard de Fournival's comments make clear, is a function of words themselves, not only of what we think of as painting. Through ekphrasis and related figures, one could paint with words alone, making imaginary pictures that never seem to have been realized in what we would consider to be a pictorial way. Such verbal *picturae* are addressed directly to the memory of the reader, for it is in one's own *vis imaginativa* and *memoria* that they are given picture form. The author is a painter, not only in that the letters he composes with have shapes themselves, but in that his words paint pictures in the minds of his readers.

By the same token, the graphic forms in a book talk, they have *parole*, sometimes literally represented in the form of a voice-scroll, the cartoon-like banner that emerges from a figure's mouth. All the carefully painted letters made by a scribe signal *voces*, words conceived of as sounding. In the useful counsel which he appended to his florilegial *Ammaestramenti degli antichi*, discussed at the end of Chapter 4, Fra Bartolomeo advised sounding texts aloud while one read them, for ears and eyes help each other to confirm memory. There is not the sharp division of seeing from hearing, the visual from the verbal, that we have become so accustomed to making that we are often unaware of how unusual it is. The carefully fabricated aural-visual synaesthesia (often including the other senses too) common in medieval arts articulates and supports, among other things, a psychological need to make mnemonically rich images; one recalls how crucial a role synaesthesia played in the successes of Luria's subject, the memory-artist, S.

Examples of verbal pictures which are described as paintings even though no drawing accompanies them are frequent in medieval literatures, both Latin and vernacular. Some interesting examples from the fourteenth century were described by Beryl Smalley in her book on the English classicizing friars, especially Robert Holcot, the Dominican who was closely associated with Richard de Bury.[31] Smalley discusses the verbal pictures of two friars in particular, Holcot and John Ridevall, a Franciscan who lived somewhat before Holcot. Ridevall's pictures are found in his *Lectura* and Holcot's in his *Commentary on the Minor Prophets*, both works addressed to clerics, who would have used the material in composing their own sermons. Smalley includes an index of seventy such pictures, culled from these works and others, and also prints a partial transcription of the ones in the Bodleian Library manuscript of Holcot's commentary (MS. Bodley 722).[32] Smalley was concerned particularly with the sources of these images; it is clear from her discussion that some of their attributes are conventional, found even in classical literature, and some were apparently invented. My concern here is with the form in which they are presented.

Ridevall calls his images *poeticae picturae*, which are "painted according to the poets [*pingitur a poetis*]."[33] But they are not extracted from earlier authors, for they cannot be found in the sources he cites. They are, however, pictorial in their details, not abstract or simply narrative. And Ridevall insists that these pictures are images that he and his sources painted. If we take what Richard de Fournival has to say about the way words paint pictures and apply it here, it will help us to understand Ridevall's meaning. His classical authors did indeed paint these images in a sense, but as ekphrases and other figures with stylistic vividness addressing imagination. They arise from earlier texts but through the medium of his own image-making, as a means for remembering. Smalley comments of the pictures that "[t]heir many . . . traits could hardly be illustrated," and concludes that they were never intended to be other than textual in form, "aural aids" to be used in preaching to keep his audiences attentive and concentrated.[34] She is quite right in observing this. And a textual picture is as good as a painted one in addressing memory work, for it can be painted by imagination without the constraints of paint and parchment. Holcot's are also emblematic pictures. They function as compositional aids, the use which their intended clerical audience would most readily have for them. Indeed, they are *imagines rerum*, which relate the parts of a theme like Faith or Sloth through a set of images, each of which is associated with one of its aspects (or divisions, in scholastic language).

A good example is Holcot's picture of Charity:

This is said according to Augustine's seventh sermon on John [vii, c. 4]: no one can say what sort of face love has, what shape, what stature, what sort of hands or feet she has. Nonetheless she has feet, for they lead to the church. Whence from this image, it is possible to describe charity or love as a queen placed [*collocata*] on a throne, of elevated stature, of a well-made shape, married to Phebus, strengthened by children, nourished with honey, with a four-sided face and gold-appearing clothing, having hands stretched out dripping with liquid, ears open and straight, eyes flaming and devoted in wifely fashion, and goat-like feet.[35]

In other of Holcot's pictures, the attributes are also numbered, and the images are partially developed as a sermon might be, with texts, *exempla*, further definitions, and explanations. As Smalley notes, each attribute of the image is moralized by Holcot with a "string of quotations"; indeed, as she also observes, the *distinctio* is a "precursor of the 'picture.' Holcot's Child [one of these images] could be rewritten as a *distinctio*."[36] Holcot's pictures are scholastic definitions brought vividly before the eyes; given both color and motion they are *imagines agentes* in the sense developed by the *Ad Herennium*, a text regularly taught in the fourteenth century, when Holcot composed his commentary.[37]

The manuscript calls each of these definitions "pictures," indicating them in the margin with the words *depinctio* or *descriptio*, but the pages are completely without graphic decoration beyond the essentials of punctuation. These pictures are evidently entirely addressed to mental imagining, an aspect of the memory-directed *painture* which any text has. Holcot says as much himself. Of the picture of Idolatry, which is associated by him with the text of Hosea 9:1, he writes that he places the painting of Idolatry "over" the letters "Noli letari," which begin the verse.[38] He says the same thing about his other pictures – each is placed above ("super") a particular text with which it is associated. These mental pictures organize the glosses to these verses and, as in a glossed book, are to be visualized above or upon the text, "super illam litteram," exactly in the way written glosses are made upon their authoring text. And the image has been mentally projected onto the letters of the page, as a way of remembering and organizing not simply a text but a whole apparatus of glosses from which one could develop a sermon.

Hugh of St. Victor: the construction of Noah's Ark

One of the most characteristic features of twelfth-century pedagogy (which we know chiefly through Biblical commentary, sermons, and meditational works) is the use of pictures, both verbal and graphic, that are presented as diagrams serving to consolidate, summarize, and fix the main subjects to be attended to. In *The Craft of Thought* I discussed in much greater detail how this feature emerges in the twelfth century, rooted firmly in the meditational practices developed in monastic life of the previous centuries. In the rest of this section, I would like to examine two of these in particular, which are roughly contemporary, and both of the mid twelfth century: Hugh of St. Victor's *Little Book on the Construction of the Ark* (*Libellus de formatione Arche*) and Hugh de Fouilloy's *On the Dove and the Hawk* (*De columba et accipitre*), a part of his Bestiary-style treatise *On Birds* (*De avibus*). Only one of these (Fouilloy's) was drawn, presumably to an exemplar made by the author.[39] The other (Hugh of St. Victor's) was never drawn, and, despite the elaborately visualized and visualizable pictures Hugh paints in his words, no scribe of its fifty-three surviving manuscripts seems to have attempted even a crude approximation of it. Evidently a medieval reader did not need to have pictures drawn on a parchment page in order to understand that a book or text had *picturae*.[40]

Hugh of St. Victor's text is called in various manuscripts "De pictura archae" or "de visibilia pictura archae" or "depinctio archae," as well as by what has become its modern title, *Libellus de formatione arche*. It is also frequently presented as the fifth book of Hugh's other commentary on this same subject, *De archa Noe*.[41] Beryl Smalley called it a diagram, and she was clearly correct.[42] *De formatione arche* is a cosmography – a combination of *mappa mundi* and *genealogia*, together with mnemonics for the vices and virtues (including the monastic virtues), the books of the Bible, a calendar, and other assorted categories of information – all put together as an elaborate set of schematics imposed upon the Genesis description of Noah's Ark. Hugh had likened the building of the Ark to the building of a medieval education, all tucked away in its various compartments with the pathways between them clearly marked – this treatise is a kind of demonstration of this governing figure, the archetypal memorial *arca*. Hugh himself calls it a "machina universitatis" (col. 702A), containing both a *mappa mundi* and a *linea generationis*, a world map and a historical genealogy. And it organizes for mental storage the chief themes of Hugh's commentary "moralized," here presented both *summe* ("in summary") and *breviter*.

The Ark is presented in two projections, one as a flat plane seen from above (called the "planus," "plan"), the other an elevation ("altitudo") or cross-sectional view, and Hugh moves between these two as his purpose changes. Moreover, the details of the model are often incoherent, impossible to graph completely because they shift and change. A successful ekphrasis invites one to draw it, but it can only fully be so with the mind's eye, which is invited by the words to augment, to color, to fill in, and straighten out their gaps and silences as part of the experience of hearing or seeing them. And, indeed, Hugh's picture only works as a mental encyclopedia, whose lineaments can merge and separate and shuffle about in the way that mental images do, but ones fixed on a page cannot.[43]

On a flat, rectangular surface – like the page of a book or a tablet, the page of memory – Hugh says that he draws and paints ("depingere," "pingo") a diagram.

First, in order to show in a figure the religious significances of the Ark of Noah, I find the center of the plane [which is also the plan] on which I want to draw the Ark, and there I fix a point. Around this point I make a small square, which is like the cubit from which the Ark was constructed. And around this square I make [*circumscribo*] another, a little bit bigger than the first, in such a way that the space between the two squares looks like a band around the cubit. Next, I draw [*pingo*] a cross in the innermost square in such a way that the four limbs of the cross meet each of its sides, and I go over [*circumduco*] the cross with gold. Then, I colour in [*colore uestio*] the spaces between the four angles of the cross and those of the square: the two above with red, the two lower ones with blue; in such a way that the one half of the cubit resembles fire, with its bright red colour, and the other half resembles a cloud with its blue. Next, in the band around the cubit, above the cross I make [*scribo*] an alpha [A], which is the beginning. Opposite that, under the cross, I make an omega [Ω], which is the end. Next to the right limb of the cross I make a chi [X], which is the first letter in Christ's name. The chi [X] signifies the decalogue of the law, which was given first to that ancient nation, as being elect and rightly placed at the right hand. Next to the left limb of the cross, I make [*pono*] a C [resembling the lunate form of sigma, ϲ], which is the final letter in Christ's name. C, in that it stands for 100, signifies the perfection of grace, which was first given to the gentile nations; the gentile nations, before they received the faith, were at first not in favour, and so they belonged on the left hand. Then in the space within the band I paint two bands of colour: a band of green inside, and a band of purple outside. In the middle of the golden cross, I paint [*pingo*] a yearling lamb, standing.[44]

Aspects of this diagram are fashioned in accordance with familiar mnemonic advice of the most elementary sort. An empty, rectangular space is marked off into distinct compartments, each in turn painted with coded information recorded in both writing and pictorial images. These images function as cues, *imagines rerum*, for remembering highly complex material; both the images themselves and their relationship to one another are mnemonically important. Once he has described its basic construction, Hugh then makes a lengthy moralization of the features he has placed in his mental diagram. The nature of this moralization is crucial to understand; Hugh himself explains it at the end of this treatise:

I have said these things about the drawing of our Ark [*de arche nostre*], so that if it please anyone to gaze inwardly [*intueri*] upon the elegance of the Lord's house and His miracles (which are without number), he might at the same time rouse his emotion [*affectus*] with this examplar. (*De formatione arche*, XI. 119–122)

Notice first that Hugh is clearly describing his own composition, "our Ark." Since much of the content is similar, but in an abbreviated form, to the concerns of Books I, II, and IV of *De archa Noe*, this diagram would appear to be at least a version of the mental plan or *imago rerum* from which he spoke his *collatio*.

Hugh had spent quite a lot of time in *De archa Noe* on the details of lodging within the Ark, and he refers to this previous discussion. Concerning the raven released after the flood he remarks (*De formatione arche*, VIII. 12): "I discussed all these things more fully in my book about the Ark [*in eo libro quem de archa dictaui*]." From remarks of this sort, it seems clear that Hugh regarded his picture of the Ark (*pictura arche*) as related to this other treatise, the *De archa Noe*, to whose themes and concerns this diagrammatic treatise refers. Hugh's *pictura arche* is thus not a picture of the Ark in the sense of being an illustration, even in allegory, of that object in Genesis; it is rather a picture-summary of Hugh's colloquies, and aids the related rhetorical processes of memory and invention. (It should always be remembered that medieval summaries can occur either before or after the text they accompany.) The diagram of the Ark does not include the material in Book III of *De archa Noe*; of course we remember that Book III, which I examined in my previous chapter, is a digression from his original plan. This diagram is personal to Hugh, yet is presented to others as an example which may provoke someone else's imagination and memory, their *affectus*.

Thus the diagram and its values are not seen by Hugh as prescriptive, nor are they exactly what we think of as iconographical, if by iconography we understand the images to represent fixed, generally accepted meanings. Rather, it employs just that kind of associational heuristic which the scholastic writers distinguished from universal logic, and defined as particular to reminiscence. Basic to the pedagogy of memory is the caution that each individual must make up his own set of associations – what works for one will not automatically work for all. Because of this, the values which the images are given by one author can only be exemplary, not universally normative (as mathematical images are). In his moralization of the images in his diagram (and by "moralization" Hugh meant the process of giving something personal valuation or signification, "making it mine"), Hugh explains what his own associations with them are, but these are not consistent.[45]

So, for example, the purple color of the border of the central cubit may represent the blood of Christ's passion, and the green the rewards of grace which it made possible. Or, the purple may signify Christ's blood and the green the water by which, in Noah's day, the world was judged. Or purple might be the damnation of the wicked and green the liberation of the good. The moralizing procedure gathers an increasingly dense store of associations around the focal image, as the composer looks mentally at his images, down different chains of thought and in different contexts. It is important to notice how these associational chains vary – they may even be contradictory, as they are in the example I have just given. That is because the technique addresses the task of reminiscence. Hugh's memory diagram of the Ark is an investigative device for meditation and composition.

Having completed his picture of the central cubit (its importance to the Ark based on Genesis 6:16), Hugh turns to the plan of the whole structure that extends out from it. A quadrangular figure is drawn again around the midpoint, but this one corresponds in the ratio of its sides to the dimensions of the Ark itself, being six times as long as it is wide (Hugh admits, however, that this is an awkward ratio, and so for convenience's sake four to one is more easily managed). Across this area four lines are extended, two laterally and two vertically, forming a cross in the middle. The distance between each pair of lines corresponds to the dimensions of the central square, so that they cross exactly under the cubit. The rectangle of the Ark itself is oriented east and west in its long dimension, east being directed to the top (*sursum*) of the mental page and west to its bottom (*deorsum*). The north side is also called the right (*dextera*) and the south the left (*sinistra*), though this nomenclature is not consistent.[46]

Within the perimeter of the large rectangle, two others are drawn about the central cubit, one inside the other in such a way that their angles are formed at points equidistant along the diagonals of the outermost rectangle. Thus there are four quadratures in the planar projection: the central square or cubit, and the three rectangles, each four to six times as long as it is wide. The three rectangles are the three main decks or chambers (*mansiones*) of the three-storey Ark. And drawn across the whole plan are the two sets of double lines described earlier, which meet under the middle cubit.

Hugh then turns to a description of the elevation. In this projection, the double lines which are drawn latitudinally across the Ark and under the central cubit are seen to represent the halves of a central column that runs up the middle of the Ark, through the center of each of its storeys. Atop it, the central cubit sits like a crown or capital, imbricating the central beams, and forms a lantern window, the only source of light for the structure beneath. From the central imbrex, the beams extend downwards to the exterior walls of the Ark, forming the roof. At the bottom of the column is the Ark's entrance. The whole structure looks like a cut-off pyramid, exactly as Hugh describes the Ark in *De archa Noe*, "ad similitudinem curtae pyramidis."[47] The description of these three basic models – of the central cubit and of the Ark's plan and elevation – comprises chapter 1 of the *pictura* of the Ark.

On an actual page, plan and cross-section would have to be shown as separate drawings. But Hugh describes raising the central column and pulling up the three decks into a three-dimensional figure, and then, as he fills in the various pieces of the picture he is able to move back and forth between the planar projection and the elevated one. This is done mentally, in imagination. Hugh says:

> If you wonder what I mean when I say we should make a column, think of it this way: raise up the cubit that lies in the middle of this band so that it drags the band itself up with it, as though the band were folded over the center. And thus, both halves of the band hang downward toward the floor of the Ark, forming planes themselves, and they are joined to the floor of the Ark at the edges, so that it looks like an upright column.[48]

Book two describes this central column, "now that the column is standing in the middle of the Ark" (I. 108). It signifies the Tree of Life and the Book of Life together, the Book being its northern hemisphere and the Tree its southern; its north also represents Christ's human nature and its south half His divinity. These associations summarize Hugh's lengthy moralization of the column of the Ark in Book two, sections 6–8 of *De archa Noe*. On the plan, however, the column is shown splayed out, as it were, so that the arms of the cross which are directed towards the north and the south represent these two faces of the column. They are differentiated by color also, the north being green, the south sapphire. Floor beams extend across each of the three rectangles to meet the roof beams which extend diagonally from under the central cubit to the largest perimeter; these form the three decks.

Next, Hugh focuses on the longitudinal band (*zona*), which extends from one end to the other under the cubit. This band represents the "longitude" of the Church, that is, its life extended in time. The upper half of the figure, from the top of the Ark to the central cubit represents history from Adam to the Incarnation, the lower half, time since the Incarnation. In the upper half are written the names of the generations from Adam to Christ; in the lower the succession of apostles and popes.

Within this diagram, Hugh singles out the twelve patriarchs and the apostles for a particular mnemonic. Midway down the upper half, the name "Judah" is written – centrally, because he was the first-born. About it and to the right are written the names of the next three patriarchs; to the left, the remaining eight, from Dan to Benjamin. Superimposed on these names are busts of the twelve, what Hugh describes as "images from the chest up" of the sort which the Greeks called *eikones*, and which sometimes are seen carved in stone tablets.[49] Thus the twelve appear in order in their places, name and image together, "like the senate of the City of God."

Just below the central cubit is written "Peter," and to left and right about him, also in a semicircle, the names of the rest of the apostles, six to the right and five to the left. We recall that in Bradwardine's memory-art the order of items in a series depended on groupings to the right and left of a central figure. To each apostle's name are also attached the images that mark him – *cum suis iconibus*. When completed, the rank of apostles together with the rank of patriarchs "like the twenty-four elders sitting around the throne in the Apocalypse" (II. 91), that is, the central cubit pictured with the Cross and Lamb. Following this figuring of the apostles is written the succession of popes, through Honorius (d. 1130), and the remaining space is for those who will live after us, through the end of time.

But the historical diagram has more refinements. It is also divided into three unequal parts, one extending from Adam to the patriarchs, the second from the patriarchs to the Incarnation, and the last through the bottom half of the whole figure. These correspond to the times of the natural law, the written law, and grace. Hugh marks these by painting three border stripes down the long sides of the Ark. But the stripes are not of equal width, for the outermost is broader than the two others, and the middle one is narrowest of all. They are painted in three colors: green, yellow, and violet, whose relative position in the lines corresponds to the division of time being represented. Green is outermost (the broadest line) during the time of natural law, yellow during the written law, violet during the time of grace. Violet is in the middle (the narrowest) at the time of natural law, yellow in the time of grace, and green in the time of written law. The innermost stripe is yellow during the time of natural law, violet in that of written law, green in that of grace. The three colors represent, says Hugh, the three kinds of moral action possible to human beings – motivated by natural goodness, motivated by God's revealed law, and motivated by grace. All three sorts have been present on earth in every period of history, but the proportions have varied, in the manner recalled by the distribution of the colors in the border stripes.

The elevation of the Ark also shows the ship's ladders, by which one mounts from one storey to the next. These, says Hugh, are placed about the center column at the intermediate points of the compass, called by Hugh the east- and west- "frigor" and "calor," (north-east, north-west, south-east, and south-west). These associate the storeys with ascents from vice to virtue and to holiness. So, from "the cold of the east" (the north-east) which Hugh labels pride, one ascends first to fear, then to sorrow, then love. From the "cold of the west," which is ignorance, one ascends to knowledge, meditation, and finally contemplation. From "the heat of the east," which is fervid zeal of spirit, one ascends to temperance, to prudence, and finally to fortitude. There are 12 ladders in all, 4 about the column, on each of the 3 decks. Each ladder has 10 steps, for a total of 120, and on the steps, alternating by gender, are 60 men and 60 women, who represent the 60 warriors of Israel who surround the bed of Solomon (Cant. 3:7), and the 60 queens (Cant. 6:8) who mount up to his embrace.

But the ladders contain far more detail than this. Those 3 on the northeast are inscribed with the 30 books of the Bible, in order, 10 on each as though each step of the ladder were a book.[50] And each book is divided on the outside (as it were, on its spine – books were still usually stored flat in their cupboards at this time) into three *gradus* (steps), corresponding to the three modes of Biblical interpretation: literal narrative, allegory, and tropology or moralizing. Each of the ladders also has an inscription, appropriate to its role in the three stages of virtuous ascents which Hugh analyzed previously. For the north-east, the ascent from pride, the three stages were fear, sorrow, and love. So the first ladder has inscribed on it: "Here ascend those who fear hell, with Isaiah calling and saying, 'Their worm will not die, and their fire will not be put out.' (Is. 66:24)." This is the last verse in Isaiah. At the top of the first ladder is the book of Lamentations, tenth in Hugh's Bible. On the second ladder is written, "Here ascend those who mourn the exile of the present life, because of the vessels of the Lord's house that were taken away captive into Babylon." At the top of this ladder is the book called Paralipomenon or Chronicles; the last event it tells of is the beginning of the Captivity. The third ladder in the series is labelled, "Here ascend those who sigh for their native land, who await the return of their spouse, saying 'Come, Lord Jesus Christ.' (Apoc. 20:21)." This is the last verse of the Apocalypse, and the last in the Bible.

In the next three chapters of Hugh's treatise, the ladders are pressed into the service of a greatly elaborated moralization of the vices and virtues. The details of this are a bit hard to describe, so a translation of part of it may provide a useful sampling of this section. Hugh gathers in material by using the four directions, the boxing of the compass, which he introduced earlier:

the four evangelists are also drawn in the four corners of the Ark. In the cold of the east is the lion, to frighten those who are swollen [with pride]. In the the cold of the west is the eagle, to give light to the blind. In the warmth of the west is the bull, to slay the flesh. And in the warmth of the east is the man, to call man back to his origin. [Hugh previously says that the south-east, the direction of zeal, is where man was created – these compass points are part of a geographical-historical-moral *mappa mundi*.] Through the Book of Life, which faces the north, ascend those from the cold of the east and from the cold of the west, and therefore a hand with an open book stretches downward from the top of the lower ladder on the inside, coming from the Book of Life, chastising on the one side and teaching on the other. On one side, the reproof is written: "Woe, woe, woe" (Apoc. 8:13), and on the other, the teaching of Judah: "In the beginning God created the heaven and the earth" (Gen. 1:1) . . . On the Tree of Life ascend those coming from the warmth of the east and the warmth of the west. Therefore two branches extend downwards from the top of the ladder, one on each, one with leaves, the other with fruit; both come from the Tree of Life, nourishing some and offering shade to others. The virtues, moreover, are depicted opposite each ladder on the part to the inside in the following way. Fear ascends first from the cold of the east opposite the Book, naked, since it has thrown down the clothes of pride because of the fire and worms that are drawn under the foot of the ladder. On the second ladder, Grief is depicted [*depingitur*] and next to it, the carrying away into Babylon beginning with Joachim and then coming down crosswise to the foot of the second ladder and finally exiting from the Ark for Babylon, which is located at this point on the map of the world. Next to the third ladder, Love is drawn [*pingitur*] as one of the virgins with a burning lamp and a container of oil, awaiting the arrival of her betrothed. Each of the virtues reaches upward with one hand, in the position of someone climbing. (*De formatione arche*, IV. iv. 224 - v. II)

Other *imagines* of the virtues inhabit the other ladders. The ladder of desire (*concupiscentia*) starts in the bottom of the Ark's hold, on the south-west quadrant of the column, with a figure of a bare-breasted girl otherwise covered by branches from the Tree of Life; opposite her a devil-seducer blows fire from his nostrils and mouth. Higher up on this same ladder a naked man is beaten with switches, in order to express, in the manner of an *imago rei*, the virtue of patience. The figures on the ladders to the north-west, the direction of knowledge, begin with a person coming out of a cave, his face veiled, who falls down at the foot of the ladder, striking a rock and shattering the vessel he is carrying – this is the image for Ignorance, "which destroys the wholeness of the soul with its various errors." On the second ladder sits Meditation, gathering up the pieces of the broken soul. And on the third ladder, Contemplation, depicted as a *faber* (smith), joins the fragments and liquifies them as though in a furnace with a pipe that runs into the central cubit as though in a mint for coins, reforming the fractured soul through the fire of divine love in the likeness of God. On the fourth set of ladders, those on the south-east, Temperance is painted like a house-holder seated at his family table; Prudence like a journeying pilgrim who flees the world; and finally Fortitude, dressed in a cloud, like one who has rejected the world and is raised on high.

Hugh allows his Ark-diagram to complicate almost endlessly, as it devel-ops in his recollective meditation. There are many room-ettes (*mansiunculae*) within the Ark itself, which the Bible refers to but does not describe. But Hugh thinks that some were built like nests into the outer wall of the Ark, for the amphibious animals who can live neither entirely in water nor entirely on dry land. The rooms within the Ark itself, of which there are a great many (though again, the Bible says nothing about them), represent places men-tioned in the route of the Exodus, from Rameses in Egypt to Jericho on the bank of Jordan. This map is fitted onto the various temporal and moral categories which Hugh has already associated with the directions and areas of the main figure, so that each location on the map is treated as though it were a mental box filled with links to variously related materials, analogous to the manner in which the design of Herbert of Bosham's psalter packs individual Psalm verses with their extensive commentary.

Surrounding the whole Ark are ellipses, which diagram Hugh's cosmol-ogy. The innermost of these represents the zone of air, and is divided into quadrants that correspond to the four parts of the world, which is the rectangular Ark itself (these four are the areas formed when the cross is laid out onto the largest rectangle). In each quadrant of this ellipse a figure is painted to recall one of the four seasons, and the twelve winds are disposed on it as well at the appropriate compass points. Another zone is projected outside this one and divided into twelve parts; in it are represented the twelve months together with the twelve signs of the Zodiac. Surrounding the calendar ellipse is the figure of Divine Majesty, His shoulders and head rising above the top of the whole figure and His feet extending below it, thereby seeming to contain all things in His embrace, in the conventional manner one sees in many such figures at this time. About Him are two seraphs with extended wings, between whom and the figure of Majesty are painted the nine orders of angels, forming a semicircle about the Throne. Included also is a chain of six circles extended from the top of the genealogy to the Throne; in each of these is written a rubric which summarizes in order the work of a day of creation.[51]

Hugh de Fouilloy: The Dove and the Hawk

No paintings of Hugh of St. Victor's Ark exist; this is one of the stronger evidences that it was never intended to be realized graphically, for a distinctive trait of both pedagogy and spiritual exercise in the twelfth century is painted diagrams and drawings both in books and on parchment rolls, like posters, developed for teaching and meditational use in conjunction with treatises. Many illustrated treatises remain in which the drawings and structuring devices have been copied faithfully and extensively along with the texts accompanying them. Some, such as Richard of St. Victor's plans and drawings of the visionary Temple-complex in Ezekiel, are very complex: manuscripts of this work, composed at St. Victor not long after Hugh of St. Victor's treatises on Noah's Ark, faithfully and completely copy the set, evidently because they were recognized to be essential to the commentary. Yet Hugh of St. Victor's Ark remains, as it began, a richly imagined ekphrasis.

One example of a treatise that always had painted pictures is by Hugh de Fouilloy (also called Hugo de Folieto), known usually now as *Liber aviarium* or *De avibus* ("On Birds"), the first nineteen chapters of which are actually a separate composition concerning the dove and the hawk (indicated quite clearly in the manuscripts by the phrase "Explicit de columba et accipitre," though the edition in the Patrologia Latina does not show this). Hugh de Fouilloy entered the priory of St-Laurent-au-Bois in the village of Fouilloy (Folieto) near Corbie in 1120, became its prior in 1152, and died about twenty years later.[52] This priory was absorbed in 1223 by the large Benedictine foundation at Corbie; as a result, Hugh de Fouilloy was forgotten and his work – which remained popular – was attributed to his contemporary, Hugh of St. Victor, until the eighteenth century. In addition to his book of birds, he wrote several other short treatises which focus on picture diagrams, including "The Wheels of True and False Religious" and "Concerning Shepherds and Their Sheep." Carlo de Clercq, the modern historian who has worked most extensively on Hugh de Fouilloy and his picture treatises, has concluded that while he did not probably execute any of the existing manuscript drawings himself, Hugh did supply the design for them and intended them to be an integral part of his texts. Indeed, in his two wheel treatises, the wheel diagrams are identified as "capitulum 1," the explication forming the succeeding chapters of the works. In other words, the picture is not an illustration of the text or even a diagram accompanying it, but as much a part of it as the words themselves. Modern editors who do not pay attention to this are violating what Hugh composed, for they are in essence arbitrarily deleting chapters from his work.[53]

Hugh's treatise on the dove and hawk and other birds was soon attached to another treatise, on animals, and so became part of one of the chief versions of the Bestiary. An independent section of anonymous authorship was also added, which lists the *voces animantium* in alphabetical order (and chapter II of Hugh's own treatise on the dove and hawk also lists the dove's *voces* in summary form). Hugh's drawings for his own treatise were often partially and poorly copied by later scribes and illuminators, but several manuscripts preserve the whole cycle.[54] For our purposes here, the most interesting of these pictures are the first two, each containing a good bit of text in addition to drawing. Both are summary *picturae* of, respectively, the first prologue and the first eleven chapters of the treatise.

The first summary picture is a simple *imago rerum* of the first preface, which Hugh addresses to a fellow monk, Hugo Rainerus, who is known only from this text. He describes how this Hugo has begged him to write what follows concerning the dove and the hawk, and how, while he, Hugh de Fouilloy, has come to the contemplative life from a clerk's vocation, his fellow monk came from the military life – thus in his own life, Hugo Rainerus has combined the features of the hawk and the dove, which flies far away into solitude. Both the hawk and the dove share the same perch, and so "I am from the clergy and you from the military. We come to conversion that we might sit in the life of the Rule as though on a perch."[55]

The *imago* which Hugh devised for this text (figure 15) shows a cleric and a knight in two locations within a frame of dual arches separated by a column through which runs a single pole or perch. Over the knight is perched a hawk, over the clerk a dove. On the archway is written "Ecce in eadem pertica sedent accipiter et columba," "Behold on the same perch sit the hawk and the dove." On the perch is written "Hoc pertica est regularis vita," "this perch is the life of the Rule." Above the knight is written "miles," above the clerk "et clericus," and on the column which separates the two is written "activa" (next to the knight) "et contemplativa vita," next to the clerk. On the external wall of the knight's location is written "paries bonorum operum," "the wall of good deeds," and on the other external wall, "paries sanctorum cogitationum," "the wall of holy thoughts."[56] The motto about good deeds on the knight's wall refers to a sentence in which Hugo characterizes his fellow as one who was "accustomed to seizing domestic fowl, [but] now with the hand of good deeds may bring to conversion the wild ones, that is, [seculars]."[57] So the first of Hugh de Fouilloy's *imagines* presents in straightforward fashion the *res* or *sententia* of this first prologue. The images are set in

15. University of Oxford, Bodleian Library, MS. Lyell 71, fo. 3v (Italian, *c.* 1310). Hugh of
Fouilloy's picture of his Preface to *Concerning the Dove and the Hawk*.

two locations, architecturally characterized, and they speak the chief points
of the text which they represent. They are *paintures* with *paroles* in the
manner which Richard de Fournival describes, for the *parole* of the painting
is taken from the accompanying text, and the painting derives directly from
the *painture* in the text's metaphoric, picturing language.

The next picture of the treatise (figure 16) is more complex, as the text it
summarizes is longer, but the composition follows these same principles.
The treatise on the dove is an exegesis of Psalm 67:14: "Si dormiatis
intermedios cleros [*terminos* in the Hebrew version], pennae columbae
deargentatae, et posteriora dorsi ejus in pallore auri," "If you sleep among
the midst of lots, you shall be as the wings of a dove covered with silver, and
the hinder parts of her back with the paleness of gold." This dove, which
occurs in a Psalm recalling the Exodus, is collated with two other doves – the
one which Noah sent out from the Ark, and the dove of the Holy Spirit. The
peculiar word *cleros* in this verse in the Septuagint Psalms is understood by

16. University of Oxford, Bodleian Library, MS. Lyell 71, fo. 4r. Hugh of Fouilloy's
picture of the chief themes of *Concerning the Dove and the Hawk*.

Hugh to be a Greek word meaning, in de Clercq's phrase, "attitudes . . .
selon les circonstances de la vie."[58] *Cleros* is translated into Latin by Hugh as
sors, sortis, usually translated in modern Latin dictionaries as "fate," but better
translated in this context as "outlook on life," or "mentality."

Several features of this picture show some affinity with Hugh of St. Victor's Ark picture. First, there is a large central image of the dove, which relates all the various *res* of this treatise as the Lamb draws together those in Hugh of St. Victor's work. Though this diagram is circular rather than rectangular, it is a circle imposed upon a rectangle that is enclosed in a colored frame – the basic shape of the tablet of memory. The organization of this diagram, with the dove at its center and the topics of the work radiating out from it, is an accurate guide to the method of the work itself, in which a number of Biblical texts using the word *columba* radiate out from the central concept. The chief themes of the treatise are written in summary phrases or *tituli* in locations within this framed rectangular space. It would be too tedious for this chapter to show exactly the correlation of these phrases with the full text; briefly, those written immediately about the wheel-like circle surrounding the dove are taken from chapters 2–4, which have to do with defining relationships among the alloted ends (*sortes*) of the Old and New Testaments, and the contemplative life. The two rectangular locations just outside the wheel and the four smaller circles in the corners summarize the color symbolism of the dove, which Hugh discusses in chapters 5–10 (chapter 11, as I said earlier, is a summary listing of the traditional attributions of the dove). Around three sides of the margin just inside the outer frame is written the fourteenth verse of Psalm 67; across the bottom of this margin is a title for the picture: "Exprimit hanc mundam sine felle columbam," "it portrays this pure dove without bitter taint." The words in this picture are all written in red, at least in the Lyell manuscript, confirming their status as mnemonic rubrics for the text which the diagram accompanies.

Hugh de Fouilloy says that his treatise is directed to an audience of "illiterati." But the context in which he uses this word affords one of the better chances we have to understand its meaning for a learned, monastic writer like Hugh de Fouilloy. Obviously, as de Clercq has astutely remarked, given the amount of written Latin in Hugh's pictures, most of it employing abbreviated forms, they cannot have been intended for illiterates in our present understanding of that word. Nor can his audience have been laity who knew no Latin, or who could only mouth the syllables and sound the words, without being able to comprehend them. Hugh says that he summarized these matters in order to satisfy the wish of Hugo Rainerus "to paint the dove whose 'wings are silvered and whose back is pale gold,' and to build [novice minds] through a picture [*per picturam simplicium mentes aedificare*] . . . so that what the mind [*animus*] of [the less learned] could scarcely comprehend with the mind's eye, it might at least discern with the physical eye, and what their hearing can scarcely perceive their sight might do so."[59] In a second preface, Hugh de Fouilloy restates this point: "What writing signals to the teachers, a picture does to those less educated ... I therefore labor more that I may please the unlearned than that I might speak to the learned and, so to speak, pour juices into a vessel already full."[60] Hugh de Fouilloy restates the old idea that picturing and writing are the same thing intellectually but in different media. To this, he adds the observation, also very traditional, that the memory (that is, the whole process which takes place in the *animus*) more readily retains something seen than something only heard – an observation which seems to me clearly derived from the experience of an education which was mostly presented in an aural form. It is worth emphasizing his concern for those beginning students who have not yet learned how to do this, how to see mentally the *painture* in the textual *parole* which they receive. This concern, in turn, reflects a fundamental belief that all input to the mind had to be imagined (see figure 3).

But the term *illiteratus* involves yet one more, related, assumption, basic to the medieval epistemology of signs.[61] It is a common medieval humility trope that we are all, in varying stages, *illiteratus* in respect to the perfect knowing of God. It derives immediately, in its choice of words, from the belief that *litterae* are a category of signs; this being so, like all signs, they are necessary to mediate truth to the limited and incomplete minds of human beings. Hugh de Fouilloy defends himself for making a treatise on such a mundane subject as the dove by noting that he is not being silly or merely entertaining, for both David and Job left divinely truthful lessons for us through metaphor when they wrote of birds. Isidore noted, in a basic definition, that "figures are extremely useful in gathering. For subjects [*res*] which by themselves are least comprehensible, are easily grasped by a comparison of things [*comparatio rerum*]." This comment occurs in his chapter "De conlatione" (to which I have referred before) in which he discusses various aids to memory, including reading a text frequently, breaking a long piece into short bits, and reading *sub silentio*, in a murmur.[62]

The comparative terms in which Hugh de Fouilloy defines his audience (*simplicior* as against *doctior*) makes it clear that his audience is the beginning students of the monastery, postulants for whom the treatise with its pictures will serve both as a way of organizing for mnemonic effectiveness some basic exegetical material on the dove and the hawk, and also as an exemplary model of how to make *imagines* for remembering other exegetical collations. The picture reduces the words to their *res*, the outline of topics and principal words, which, in speaking, one would amplify and elaborate. The verb Hugh uses for his pictures, in addition to *pingere*, "paint," is *decrescere*, "reduce in size," that is reducing prolixity to memorable *brevitas*, according to the principle of storing mnemonically rich units. Hugh de Fouilloy's remarks point to an elementary pedagogy of making such compositional images as a technique for remembering.

'DISTINGUISHING' THE BOOK

Marginal notes

I would like now to suggest a few additional ways in which the requirements of mnemonic technique may have specifically influenced the decoration of medieval books. Book decoration was thought to provide sources of mnemonically valuable images, and examples to encourage the making of other such images. But influence sometimes also went the other way, as we have seen in the case of pictures, where mnemonic principles such as making *imagines rerum* directly influence the making of a graphic image. The symbiotic relationship between memorial effectiveness and the lay-out of books throughout the Middle Ages is apparent at the level of principle and general rules; the more difficult problem is know to what extent the selection of images and decorative elements reflected particular mnemonic techniques and themes.

I have grouped my observations into three general categories: marginalia, classroom diagrams, and compositional *imagines rerum*, though it should be kept in mind that the three kinds do not always neatly sort out from one another. Perhaps it could be said that marginal images serve the function of textual heuristics and mnemonic storage – the need for *divisio* – while the diagrams invite further "gathering" and meditational recollection. Yet, having said this, one must instantly qualify the statement by noting that *inventio* and the mnemonic task it serves, *compositio*, are tasks equally of finding and gathering material into one place from a number of previously stored places. Indeed, these twin tasks are no better distinguished from one another than memory is from recollection. Still, one must start somewhere (a fundamental mnemonic principle); and having said that, I have acknowledged that my definitional structures (like a great many others) are more useful as inventive devices than as stating fact.

In his general advice on memory training (*Inst. orat.*, XI. ii. 27–49), Quintilian emphasizes three basic mnemonic principles: first, the utility of *imagines*, often of the rebus variety, for both memory-for-words and memory-for-things; second, the necessity of proper *divisio* and *compositio* both for memorizing and for composing, for one "who has got his Division right will never be able to make mistakes in the order of his ideas" (*Inst. orat.*, XI. ii. 37); and third, always to copy and memorize from the same wax tablets when one first commits something to memory, because the appearance of the writing, its visual image including any *notae* that may accompany it, is especially key to success.

A book made some fifty years after Hugh of St. Victor wrote indicates, as clearly as any medieval book I know of, a conscious effort by its makers to use images solely because they are mnemonically valuable. It is a copy of Augustine's *Enchiridion*, which was made and decorated in England at the end of the twelfth century for the Cistercian abbey of St. Mary's in Holmecultram, Cumbria. It is now Huntington Library MS. HM 19915.[63] There are several other texts in this book, but it is the *Enchiridion*, an elementary primer of Christian faith, that I want to consider here.

In most respects, HM 19915 is an ordinary medieval book of its period. It has summarizing *tituli* in the margins, which seem to be written in the same hand as the main text. Each chapter is numbered, and has a descriptive heading. Two- and three-line initial letters are colored alternately in red, green, and light blue, the colors used in other Holmecultram books of this same period.[64] Most of these initials have some simple filigree penwork either in or surrounding them, of a sort compatible with the generally sober style which art historians have associated with the Cistercians. The text is divided into *cola* and *commata*, and is rubricated appropriately. And highly stylized forms of the word *nota*, written in black ink, each distinct, appear in several of the margins opposite important text; these seem to be contemporary with the text itself, and indeed it is most likely that the same scribe, most likely a monk of the house in whose library the manuscript was housed, wrote, punctuated, and decorated it.

The unusual feature of this manuscript is that its marginal notations and *tituli* are each enclosed in an elaborately drawn image, each one unique, each colored in washes of several hues (figures 17–19). Several of the enclosing forms are geometrical (a square, a lozenge), some are architectural (steps surmounted by a column and tablature), some are banners on which the *titulus* is written, and some – the most surprising of all – are animals.[65] There is one showing two dogs' heads ringing each end of a banner, on which is written the *titulus* which summarizes that part of the text (figure 17); one is a dragon breathing forth a pall of smoke on which is written a command to the reader to mark (*signa*) a particularly apt bit of text (figure 18); another shows a dog chasing a hare, their tails forming a

17. San Marino, California, Huntington Library MS. HM 19915, fo. 5r (English, *c.* 1200). Detail of dogs' heads and a banner marking a *titulus*, "Quid sit proprie spes," "What is properly hope," keyed to Augustine's *Enchiridion*. From the library of the Cistercian monastery of St. Mary's Holmecultram, Cumbria.

18. San Marino, California, Huntington Library MS. HM 19915, fo. 46r. Detail of a dragon marking the *Enchiridion*, with the annotation, "Signa utilissimam sententiam breuemque," "Mark this most useful and brief aphorism."

19. San Marino, California, Huntington Library MS. HM 19915, fo. 36v. Drawing of a dog and a rabbit marking a notation that reads: "Signa humanam benevolentiam," "Mark human goodness," also for Augustine's *Enchiridion*. It seems apparent from the grammar that *Signa*, like the common *Nota*, is an imperative directed to the reader.

ring in which is written the notation, "Signa humanam benevolentiam," "Mark[:] human benevolence" (figure 19).

The function of *tituli* as mnemonic helps, a part of the rubrification of a written text, is well understood. They are found from antiquity, and they present the longer content of a text, the *prolixitas*, in a brief summary (*breviter*), a "résumé des chapitres," as Samuel Berger calls it in his history of the Vulgate Bible.[66] Written in the margin, *tituli* became part of the apparatus of the Bible at an early period; they could be either summaries, as we understand that word, or a quotation of the first few words in a textual division. In other words, they present the text according to the principles of *memoria rerum*, in which the *sentence* (to use the Middle English word) and principal words are used to cue the memory.

Enclosing the *tituli* in images, as in HM 19915, was evidently done to enhance their mnemonic function, by adding to something which was already understood to be mnemonic in function (the *titulus*), an attribute (the lively image) known particularly to impress memory. There is no other plausible reason for adding such images, because they are not related iconographically to the text they accompany, nor do they serve mechanical needs of a scribe or binder, as catchwords do. I have examined all of the manuscripts still extant from Holmecultram (there are eleven); others have marginal titles, sometimes enclosed in geometric or architectural forms, but none have the elaborate designs of HM 19915. Furthermore, these designs occur in only one of the works copied in this manuscript, Augustine's *Enchiridion*. As a primer of faith, the *Enchiridion* was a text that beginning students needed to learn. These vividly decorated *tituli* and notes would help them. The cultivation of images as recollective devices in such a basic book is an important link in the evidence which establishes that one of the earliest tasks taught in learning to read was learning to mark text with mnemonically useful mental images.

Marginal notations, glosses, and images are an integral part of the *painture* of literature, addressing the ocular gateway to memory and meditation. Indeed, the margins are where individual memories are most active, most invited to make their marks, whether physically (as in the ubiquitous "NOTA" command or a pointing finger, sometimes drawn with a string around it, or crudely sketched human and animal heads, or, especially in later manuscripts, implements such as shovels) or only in their imagination.[67] But the images in medieval books function in other mnemonically significant ways. These include rebus-like images which pun visually on certain words or themes of a text, all sorts of diagrams, and pictures that are of the type which Lydgate suggestively called *meditaciouns*, focal images like the "pity" (*pietà*) which he saw in his mental book, and which can stimulate a recollective composition of texts.

As we have seen, the observations that memory is easily overwhelmed by too solid or lengthy a diet, that it requires pleasing, that it retains best what is unusual and surprising, that memorizing is best served when one fixes what one is learning within a fully synaesthetic context, are standard features of mnemonic advice in the twelfth and thirteenth centuries. It is significant that the style of painting drolleries in manuscript margins comes into widespread use in the mid thirteenth century, along with the fashion for the thematic sermon (the sort of composition served by Bradwardine's *memoria orationis*), at the same time that the mnemotechnique described in the *Ad Herennium* was revived, under the twin sponsorship of the first humanists and the Dominicans.[68] The grotesque creatures, the comic images of monkeys and other animals mimicking human behavior, images that are violent, ugly, salacious or titillating, noble, sorrowful, or fearful possess the qualities recommended for memory images by the *Ad Herennium*. This may represent an instance where a particular mnemotechnique did influence a new style in book decoration, though one should remember that the general principle of making extraordinary images to influence memory was known all along.

In addition to discrete marginal images, some manuscripts employed *bas-de-page* (bottom margin) pictorial narratives. These, commonly, refer either to saints' lives or to well-known comic cycles like the Renart stories or Aesop's fables, or to fabliaux such as "the squire who laid eggs."[69] A fourteenth-century manuscript of the Decretals, written in Italy but illuminated in England, provides a virtual feast of such narratives, most carrying over several pages. It belonged to the priory of St. Bartholomew's, Smithfield (where John of Mirfeld was a canon), and it is now in the British Library MS. Royal 10. E. IV. The Decretals are a digest of canon law, and required memorizing in order to be fully useful. It was one of the essential books that William of Ockham insisted his pupil store away. The bottom margins of the Smithfield Decretals are filled with stories told entirely through pictures, like a running cartoon. These are not illustrations of the text; many have no apparent relationship to the material in the text which they accompany. There are saints' lives, with their usual complement of grotesque incident; a salacious story of a friar who seduces a miller's wife and murders her husband (fos. 113v–117); and a number of animal fables, some involving characters from the Renart cycle, and some seemingly made up. Two involve a group of killer-rabbits, who track down a human hunter and truss him up, and then capture a hunting dog, try him in a rabbit-court, and hang him (figures 20–24).[70]

20. London, British Library MS. Royal 10. E. iv, fo. 62r. Written in Italy, painted in England some forty years later). The start of a sequence of *bas-de-page* narrative pictures: a hunting dog is wounded by a rabbit-archer.

21. London, British Library MS. Royal 10. E. iv, fo. 62v. Two rabbits tie up the dog.

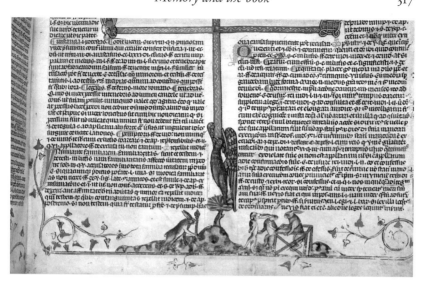

22. London, British Library MS. Royal 10. E. IV, fo. 63r. The dog is tried before a rabbit-judge.

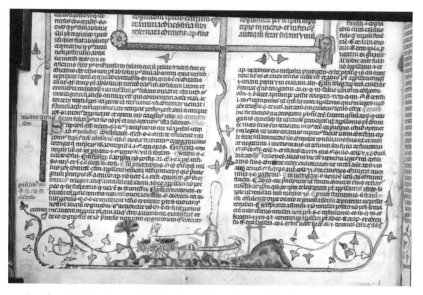

23. London, British Library MS. Royal 10. E. IV, fo. 63v. The dog, bound and gagged, is taken in a cart to the gallows.

24. London, British Library MS. Royal 10. E. IV, fo. 64r. The dog is hanged. A rabbit
thumbs its nose at the corpse, while brandishing a victory banner.

But there is yet another sort of marginal image, both more ancient and
more persistent than the drolleries and grotesques. Certain classes of
images appear over and over in the margins from the earliest decorated
books through hand-painted printed books. These include jewels, coins,
birds, fruit, flowers (sometimes shown with insects sucking their nectar),
and scenes of hunting and fishing, by both animals and humans. Examples
of several of these, from a Book of Hours made around 1440 in Utrecht for
Catherine of Cleves, the Duchess of Guelders (The Morgan Library MSS.
M.917 and M.945), are shown in figures 25–28 and figure 1.[71] As metaphorical tropes, these same classes of image figure persistently in the
pedagogy of invention and memory, those two processes for which books
are the sources and cues. Of course there were major shifts in painting style
and in the market for books as they became more numerous and widely
available. But, as we have seen, the assumption that writing is the servant of
memory persisted over a long time. Trained memory is a store-house, a
treasure-chest, a vessel, into which the jewels, coins, fruits, and flowers of
texts are placed. The reader gathers nectar from these flowers to furnish the
cells of memory, like a bee (figure 26). Coins and other treasure are perhaps
the most common of memory tropes; they also have a complementary
association (as do gold, pearls, and rubies) with the Biblical treasures of the

25. New York, Pierpont Morgan Library MS. M 917, p. 240 ("The Hours of Catherine of Cleves"; Utrecht, *c.* 1440). Coins used as a border, as in the common trope of memory as coins to be laid away in one's memory treasury.

26. New York, Pierpont Morgan Library MS. M. 945, fo. 20r ("The Hours of Catherine of Cleves"; Utrecht, *c.* 1440). Bees in a hive and gathering nectar from flowers in the border, as in the common trope of memory as the gathered flowers of reading (*florilegium*) to be culled by readers as bees gather nectar in their hives.

ſte ſanctus pro lege dei ſui
certauit uſqʒ ad mortem et
a uerbis impiox non timuit.
fundatus enim erat ſupra fir
mam petram. V. Corona au
rea ſuper caput eius: expreſſa
ſigno ſanctitatis glorie ho9s.
Oremus: Conuerti Alia an.

27. New York, Pierpont Morgan Library MS. M. 917, p. 247 ("The Hours of Catherine of Cleves"; Utrecht, *c.* 1440). Caged birds, used as a border, as in the common trope of memory as birds caged or penned in coops.

28. New York, Pierpont Morgan Library MS. M. 917, p. 266 ("The Hours of Catherine of
Cleves"; Utrecht, *c.* 1440). Fish used as a border. Notice that they form a chain,
one fish fastening itself to the next, and that the chain is drawn by fishhooks, like the
'hook' that draws a *catena* or chain of texts.

Kingdom of Heaven (figure 25). Some Books of Hours have pilgrims' badges as a marginal decoration; a book such as this was traditionally thought of as a *scrinium*, a shrine, the pilgrim's object.[72]

Birds, a common and long-lasting element in book decoration from the early programs for the Canon Tables to the elements of Insular interlace to the margins of psalters and Books of Hours, have also a very long association with thoughts and memories, as we saw in Chapter 1. Birds, like memories, need to be hunted down (by a fowler or hawker, a common variation on the general motif) or stored up in a cage or coop, as in figure 27. They are also part of the Christian motifs of the Tree of Life and Book of Life, so clearly linked to one another exegetically, as in Hugh of St. Victor's *De formatione arche.* Jesus likened the kingdom of Heaven to a mustard seed that grows into a tree so large that all the birds of the air might live in its branches: "et fit arbor, ita ut volucris caeli veniant, et habitent in ramis ejus" (Mt. 13:32). This exemplary tree is also, by the mnemonic technique of collation, the Tree of Life thus linked to the Book of Life, as Hugh says. Another ubiquitous trope employed in marginal images is wrestling, with hands, feet, arms, and sometimes hair-pulling, alluding to the common idea (Biblical as well as classical) of meditation as exercise (*meletē*), and of ascetics as spiritual athletes.[73]

Such images are not iconographical, nor do they illustrate or explain the content of a particular text. They serve the basic function of all page decoration, to make each page distinct and memorable, but their content is not only specific to the particular page on which they are drawn. One should consider them as images which serve to remind readers of the fundamental purposes of these books – Bibles, psalters, decretal collections, prayer books – books that are made for study and meditation, to be mulled over. They contain matter to be laid down and called again from their memorial store-houses, shrines, fiscal pouches, chests, vases, coops, pens, cells, and bins. A very early example makes my point. The Codex Alexandrinus, a fifth-century Greek Bible, has drawings of an empty vase into which a *titulus*, written in increasingly shorter lines, seems to fall as though in a stream. This simple image serves as a reminder that the words of God pour forth in a stream from the book into the vessel of memory, and that one's task is to be sure they are laid away there properly.[74]

Metaphors of fishing, hunting, and tracking down prey are also traditional for recollection. Aristotle speaks in *De memoria* of how people recollect from some starting-point: they "hunt successively" (451b19). The verb he uses is *thēr-áma*, "to hunt or fish for something." The same image is incorporated into the very definition of recollection by Albertus Magnus: "reminiscenti[a] nihil aliud est nisi investigati[o] obliti per memoriam," "recollection is nothing but the tracking-down of something hidden away in memory."[75] The metaphor is also used, elaborately, by Quintilian, who, defining the places of argument laid down in memory, likens a skillful orator to a huntsman or fisherman who knows exactly the habits and haunts of his game (*Inst. orat.*, V. x. 20–22). The metaphor in the word *error*, both error and wandering, is an aspect of this same idea, for one who wanders through the *silva* (meaning both forest and disordered material) of his untrained and inattentive memory is one who has either lost the footprints (*vestigia*) that should lead him through, or never laid them down properly in the first place.

Hunting and fishing go together in this trope of memory. The mnemonic *notae* which one uses to get around one's store-house are called both tracks (*vestigia*) and hooks (*unci*). Geoffrey of Vinsauf, discussing *memoria*, advises students to be diligent and practice the contents of their memorial store, laid away with markers of whatever sorts of *notae* suit them. Otherwise, they will be like a cat, which wants the fish but not the fishing.[76] Fish are fairly common in a number of manuscripts, sometimes drawn crudely by a reader opposite a portion of text, thus functioning like a "NOTA" admonition.[77]

Many manuscripts' margins contain images that seem to grow out of the words and into the margins, a kind of emphasizing bracket that becomes the shape of a hand or a head. Heads are very common, possibly because the head is the seat of memory. Heads also can be differentiated more easily than pointing hands (which can be provided with a string or a cuff, but not much else), for they can wear a variety of headdress, be male or female, frontal or in profile, and so on. A head, drawn with a text-balloon such as modern cartoonists use, as though it were mindful of the words of a *titulus*, occurs in a margin of the Winchester manuscript of Malory.[78] This image clearly indicates that this reader understood drawings of heads to be a part of a book's mnemonic apparatus.

Diagrams

A prominent feature of medieval book art is the use of diagrams. The Canon Tables, written *intercolumnia* – between arched columns that are decorated with birds and floral motifs – are one very early example, which we find in books from the earliest medieval centuries (figure 6). The typical lay-out of the Calendar, marked by images of the Zodiac and (later) the labors of the months, is another. In fact, one of the more intriguing aspects of Hugh of St. Victor's Ark-picture is its gathering of many common medieval diagrams into one place, and, if one adds the columnar format he employed for his *Chronicle*, it is clear that Hugh was accustomed, both in teaching (*lectio*) and in his own meditational composition, to using virtually every major genre of diagram common in the twelfth century – ladders, trees, circles, columns, maps, and genealogical charts – all enclosed within the rectangular shape of the memorial page. Even more interesting is Hugh's assumption that basic pedagogy consists in the ability to use such structures readily to perform tasks of mnemonic calculation (collating texts, for example). His own practice indicates that such recollective skill is, in large measure, what he is referring to in his aphorism, "the whole usefulness of education consists only in the memory of it" ("In sola enim memoria omnis utilitas doctrinae consistit").

In many ways, Hugh of St. Victor is a twelfth-century version of Quintilian, not an innovator of technique so much as an admirably clear, practical guide to the best pedagogy of his time. This pedagogy employed visual aids and diagrams to an extent that many modern historians have noted. For example, in his descriptive catalogue of English Romanesque illuminated manuscripts, C. M. Kauffmann writes that "the pictorial diagram . . . became one of the typical features of Romanesque art."[79] But most of these diagrams had been in common use for centuries before the twelfth, as mnemonic compositional aids – one thinks, for example, of the ladder with which Benedict organized the steps (*gradus*) of humility in the seventh chapter of his Rule.

Indeed, it is a much-remarked-on medieval characteristic to treat the space in a full-page drawing diagramatically, that is, with images placed in specific locations, often grouped about a large central figure, often in an architectural setting, often with related images enclosed in roundels or other geometric forms, usually with a border, and commonly with inscriptions, like *tituli* or rubrics, to be associated with the figure and to help associate the figures with one another. The justification for this practice is mnemonic necessity. The framework of the page provides a set of orderly *loci*; furthermore, this frame remains constant while the images in it change from page to page – that is the manner of a diagram, and it is also the manner of the page of memory, *imagines rerum* imposed upon a set of geometrically defined places in an orderly framework or grid.

Examples of this format span the whole period that we call the Middle Ages. The Gospels of St. Augustine (Cambridge, Corpus Christi College MS. 286), made in Italy or Gaul in the sixth century, was at Canterbury during the Middle Ages, and is thought to have been brought to England

29. Cambridge, Corpus Christi College MS. 286, fo. 125r ("The Gospels of St. Augustine"; Italy or Gaul, sixth century). A picture-page, showing a grid format and frontal perspective towards figures set against a plain background. Compare the instructions for forming memory locations in Thomas Bradwardine's *De memoria artificiali*.

from Rome by St. Augustine himself. A full-page picture (figure 29) groups figural scenes of the Passion week, many containing textual tags, into a grid of twelve cells, each set in a border. The whole rectangular construction is enclosed in another border painted around the vellum page. The outer border demarcates the *area* or flat surface of the page, just as the memory-page in Hugh of St. Victor's Ark *pictura* has a border enclosing it. The *loci* are small quadratures within this, three across in each of four tiers, clearly separated from one another by a red-colored border. Some of the individual *imagines* are given a rudimentary background; others are set in what has been called "hierarchical" space, wherein the figures are grouped in such a way that the main figure, the first in the order, appears in the center and larger than the subsidiary figures grouped to its right and left.

The background is simple, a single color, providing no more than the barest suggestion of a setting for the figures. And the perspective of the viewer is from the front and central, the qualities that define *distancia* in the mnemonic advice that has survived from later centuries. In fact, this page exemplifies so many of the rules for making mnemonic locations described by Bradwardine that one might, at first, wonder if he must have seen it; the manuscript was, after all, at Canterbury. Yet the details of Bradwardine's examples are not those of the drawings in the Gospels of St. Augustine. Their similarity in principle, however, suggests strongly that the same general rules that governed the making of the sixth-century Gospels' page were still a part of medieval mnemonic pedagogy in the fourteenth century.

The picture-page in this Gospels provides a complete set, in order, of *imagines rerum* for the Passion story, drawn not from a particular gospel but synthesizing all four accounts. The picture-page comes between the gospels of Mark and Luke; it is thought that similar pages, with images from the earlier life of Christ, were placed before Matthew and between Matthew and Mark, and that a page showing events from the Passion to the Ascension preceded John. Such a placement is usual in early medieval Gospels, which were large books designed for study within a monastery community.[80]

Picture-pages in medieval books had cycles of popularity. A much later example is a Flemish Psalter of the second half of the thirteenth century (The Morgan Library MS. M.183), which contains four such pages. M. R. James's catalogue description of this manuscript demonstrates clearly how the individual subjects of the images are inserted into a framework that is stable in all four of these pages – stable not only in shape and configuration, but in the type of content that occupies the different parts of the frame.[81] Again, the places within the frame are separated clearly from one another by borders; the *imagines rerum* refer to sixteen main events in the life of Christ and to various saints. This framework is quite elaborate, though its relationship to the common grid-format is evident.

Such *imagines rerum*, either painted only mentally or also on parchment, share many features with the teaching diagrams which the later Middle Ages produced in abundance. Diagrams were a common feature of medieval classrooms. One of the better-known, and most widely used, was in a tree form, composed by Peter of Poitiers towards the end of the twelfth century. It is the genealogy of Christ, called *Compendium historiae in genealogia Christi* or, simply, the *Genealogia*, and it is quite like the *linea genealogia* we encounter in Hugh of St. Victor's *De formatione arche*, composed a half-century earlier.

Beginning with Adam, the names of Christ's predecessors are listed in order, with a brief biographical sketch. The names and their relationships are indicated by lines and, usually, circles, with pictures of the chief events, such as the Temptation of Adam and Eve and the Flood – often also the diagram known as the Tree of Jesse is included. A version of the diagram seems to have had an independent existence by the early thirteenth century. An early thirteenth-century chronicler reports that Peter of Poitiers had "designed for the benefit of poor clerics trees painted on skins that displayed the history of the Old Testament."[82] Much copied, often incorporated into universal chronicles from the twelfth through the fifteenth centuries; the *Genealogia* was also translated into several vernaculars, including English, and had an exceptionally long run in the classroom.

Frequently, the *Genealogia* was written on a continuous roll of parchment rather than in a codex. Three examples in the Bodleian Library are of some interest. An English codex of the second quarter of the thirteenth century (MS. Laud Misc. 151), which contains both this text, in Latin, and Peter Comestor's *Historia scholastica*, belonged to Cardinal Morton (d. 1500) at one point in its history, and the first leaf pictures both his coat of arms and a rebus for his name, a drawing of a cask, or "tun," with the letters "mor" written on it. A roll (MS. Barlow 53), dating from the early fifteenth century, is an English translation of the *Genealogia*, with its preface. And finally, another roll, MS. Lat. th. b. 1, also English and from the first half of the thirteenth century, is especially interesting because its companion roll (MS. Lat. th. c. 2), which may have been attached to it at one point, contains diagrams of the Seven Deadly Sins, the Seven Gifts of the Spirit, and so on. The genealogy roll begins with a drawing and exposition of the Menorah or seven-branched candlestick, proceeding to enumerate a number of items in sevens and also in threes before it gets to Peter's diagram itself. Such a digest of preaching aids would be a useful tool for classroom lecture as well as for sermon making.[83]

Peter of Poitier's preface makes it clear that his format is a memory aid. Considering the length of holy writ, he says, he has digested the genealogical information and presented it in this form so that students may retain it in memory, as in a money-bag (*quasi in sacculo*). He uses the same image for memory used by Hugh of St. Victor in his *Chronicle* Preface, that of a *sacculus* or compartmentalized money-pouch, in which coins of various sizes can be carried, each in its place without loss or confusion. As I showed in my first chapter, this image is a common variant of the archetype of memory as *thesaurus* or *arca*. And Peter goes on to say that his scheme, though useful for all, is particularly so for those students who feel overwhelmed by the bulk of historical material; with the aid of his diagram, that daunting prolixity, having been made subject to the eyes, can be committed to memory and its usefulness realized.[84]

In his section on rhetorical memory, Geoffrey of Vinsauf (who was Peter's contemporary) emphasizes the mnemonic value of *formae*: "*loca, tempora, et formae* and other similar *notulae* are sure ways to lead me to [what I have stored away]."[85] He does not define what these *formae* are. The word can mean "shape" or "outward appearance." But it can also mean "geometric shape" or "outline" – the sort of thing that a diagram is,[86] and given the fondness of the twelfth-century classroom for diagrams, this was what Geoffrey probably meant. Diagrams formed of concentric circles, rose diagrams (which are not confined to windows), the primitive chart that forms the *Genealogia*, Hugh of St. Victor's columns of persons, places, and dates for his *Chronicle*, ladder diagrams, and the veritable forest of trees used to illustrate the relations of parts of a subject whether it be preaching or vices and virtues – all such *formae* are common features in manuscripts too, especially in the twelfth and thirteenth centuries.[87]

There is one more famous diagram worth considering here, described by John of Garland. I discussed in Chapter 3 John's instructions for composing a three-columned memory tablet that was to include all the *voces animantium* (chiefly animal names), words in various languages, and so on, in alphabetical order; some manuscripts of John's text include a partial schematic drawing of this, but it was clearly designed as a mental structure, infinitely expandable as such schemes are. John also mentions a diagram "quam pre manibus habimus," "which we have in our hands," the so-called Rota Virgili or Virgil's Wheel.[88] This circular diagram is also drawn in some manuscripts of the *Parisiana Poetria*, and it shows a series of concentric circles divided into three wedges, within which comparisons, likenesses, occupations, animals, plants, and implements are written that pertain to John's subject, the three different kinds of audience to be considered in determining stylistic decorum. Virgil's Wheel was clearly a mnemonic diagram that his students held; it is likely that it could be physically manipulated, as its concentric circles suggest.

This figure of the rhetorical Rota Virgili may provide the connection between the Latin word *rota*, "wheel," and the English phrase "by rote." *Rote* is "of obscure origin," according to *OED*, although it appears as though it should be derived either from Latin *rota* or from French *rote*, "way, route." As *OED* states, however, there has been "no evidence to confirm the suggestions."[89] My review of the evidence does not confirm a derivation either, but it may help to strengthen the suggestion in favor of the Latin over the French.

"By rote" appears in English in the fourteenth century meaning both "reciting (prayers, speeches, and the like) from memory" (an essentially neutral usage) and, in a pejorative way, "reciting unintelligently or by formula." For Chaucer, the word on its face is neutral, meaning "from memory exactly," a synonym of verbatim memory. The first clearly pejorative uses of the word (which are from the fifteenth and sixteenth centuries) modify "rote" with "mere" or "pure." "Rote" had also a generalized meaning of habit or custom, that which memory produces. The earliest *OED* citation, in a poem by William of Shoreham written probably in the 1330s, refers to a bad habit as a "wikked rote"; habitual knowledge is what the classroom *rotae* were designed to instill. John Gower speaks of the ancient pagans' "rote" (custom) in his *Confessio amantis* (VI, 1311), interestingly in the context of knowing magical arts and sorcery (things that scholars, whose memories were sure to be trained, would dabble in).

The clearest link between English "by rote" and the rhetorical tradition which included using the Rota Virgili diagram is in Chaucer's Pardoner's Tale, when the Pardoner describes his rhetorical tactics and how he adopts his speech to his audience:

> Lordynges, quod he, in chirches whan I preche,
> I peyne me to han an hauteyn speche
> And rynge it out as round as gooth a belle,
> For I kan al by rote that I telle.
> My theme is alwey oon, and evere was:
> *Radix malorum est cupiditas.*   (VI, 329–334)[90]

The Rota Virgili showed schematically how to adopt one's speech to particular kinds of audiences, something at which the Pardoner is especially adept. Notice how he distinguishes between his theme, which is always the same, and his ability to vary it to suit the particular occasion and congregation, *ex tempore dicendi*, a boast he repeats in lines 412–420 when he describes how he has insulted particular enemies in his sermons. I have hardly settled the etymological puzzle here, but the possibility of a link with memory devices like the Rota Virgili is suggestive. It is also easy to see how, if it referred to a mnemonic schoolroom diagram, "speaking by rote" could come to mean "speaking by mere formula."

Wheel-diagrams were not limited to the teaching of rhetoric. Wheels that move and are intended to be manipulated are common enough artifacts in manuscripts. For example, two moving wheels are found in Bodleian Library MS. Bodley 177, a collection of scientific pieces made up of four separate manuscripts written in the last part of the fourteenth century. On fo. 63v there is a simplified astrolabe, made of two freely moving concentric parchment disks, and on fo. 62r a wheel that reveals the letters of the Latin alphabet in various combinations. This latter is constructed from a vellum disk in which holes have been cut, its center pierced, and a thong tied through it to the back of the leaf on which it is placed, allowing it to move freely. Hugh de Fouilloy's wheels imply movement, most obviously those of his treatise on *True and False Religious*, which depict the rising and declining patterns of the lives of a good and a false monk.

One medieval figure who is important in the history of memory design and arts, but about whom I have had little to say because he has been thoroughly studied by Frances Yates and R. J. Hillgarth, is the late thirteenth-century Spaniard, Ramón Lull (1235–1316; the last version of his art was written 1305–1308).[91] Lull's art was designed to be both a key to universal concepts and a meditational memory art; his evangelical motivation, to preach persuasively in multilingual Spain, is significant in comprehending the importance he gave to inventing successful methods for *imagines rerum*. Indeed the missionary spirit remained the significant motivator as well for those friars and Jesuits who taught memory schemes as part of their evangelism in Mexico, China, and elsewhere.[92] Though Lull did have some influence in the late Middle Ages, he is more important in the context of early modern figures like Giordano Bruno and Camillo, with whom Yates is most occupied. Lull's is an extremely subtle, complex, and learned system, not at all for beginners. Nor is it, as Yates points out, at all like the system of *loci* and *imagines* described in *Ad Herennium*. Yet it did not come out of nowhere. Yates relates it to the Neoplatonism of Scotus Eriugena. But many of its characteristic uses of symbol and figure have much commoner origins.

Frances Yates attributes two apparent innovations to Lull. First, he "designates the concepts used in his art by a letter notation, which introduces

an almost algebraic or scientifically abstract note into Lullism." And
secondly, he uses diagrams extensively, such as concentric circles, rotating
triangles within a circle, ladders (steps), and trees, to "introduc[e] movement into memory."[93] But diagrams such as these, which all imply the sort
of movement and manipulation of which Yates speaks, were a common
feature of the medieval elementary classroom, precisely for the purpose
of memory training. So was the use of letter notation to organize concepts.[94] Hugh of St.Victor's *De archa Noe* is a universal diagram, designed
to organize a large amount of disparate information in a readily available, mnemonically effective, way. This fact suggests that such diagrammatic *machinae universitatis* were encouraged in medieval pedagogy well
before Lull.

For mnemonic purposes, diagrams, like other sorts of images in medieval books, have a combination of two functions: they serve as fixes for
memory storage, and as cues to start the recollective process. The one
function is pedagogical, in which the diagram serves as an informational
schematic; the other is meditational and compositional. The functions
were more elegantly formulated in the ancient and medieval advice to
students, that *memoria* consists in *divisio* and *compositio*. There are a
number of diagram-like pages in liturgical and devotional books throughout the Middle Ages, whose function is of this latter sort. In his classic
study of a much-copied sequence of such theological diagrams from the
late Middle Ages, the *Speculum theologiae*, Fritz Saxl commented: "A wealth
of wisdom is displayed, which slowly reveals itself to the patient reader who
does not mind the absence of a well-defined general lay-out ... Each
picture ... must be pondered again and again."[95] Such diagrams are like
the seventeeth-century emblems – indeed, they may well be their medieval
predecessors. They compose a place for a meditative recollection by picturing
various theological and devotional themes. Their obscurity and partialness
are deliberate; as deliberate as is the clarity of a pedagogical diagram such as
the *Genealogia*.

The most easily accessible now of these late medieval diagram-encyclopedias
is the De Lisle Psalter (British Library MS. Arundel 83-II), all published in a
volume edited by L. F. Sandler. Only the drawings now exist, but in the
original book they preceded a psalter made for an English layman, Robert
de Lisle. These drawings, made in the early fourteenth century, are copies
of a group of pictures devised towards the end of the thirteenth century by a
Franciscan friar working in Paris, John of Metz. The whole group was the
Speculum theologiae or, in England, *The Orchard of Consolation*, names
which suggest both the encyclopedic intention of their maker and their

contemplative purpose. (Recall Gregory the Great's admonition that, in our true reading, we see as in a mirror, *speculum*, our own vices and virtues.) The word "orchard" was used in the title of other medieval English vernacular works of devotion, such as *The Orchard of Syon*; it is a variant on the ancient "flowers of reading" (*florilegium*) trope, these being the fruits of meditational *memoria* presented as materials for yet further meditation. Three of the diagrams in the *Speculum theologiae* are known to have originated from texts, as pictures, *imagines*, of their *res*: a "Tree of Life," a "Tree of Vices and Virtues," and a "Cherub," the diagram-picture which is the content of a sermon-treatise attributed in the Patrologia Latina to Alan of Lille: *On the Six Wings* (of the Cherub [or Seraph]).[96]

These theological pictures, textually derived, are realizations on parchment of the kind of meditative imagining for compositional purposes that we encounter as well in Hugh of St. Victor's *De archa Noe*. They often have more in common with mnemonic rebuses than with the kind of schematic to which we now restrict the word "diagram." But they are rebuses of a very elaborate type. An ordinary rebus is an image-for-the-word, like the rebus of "Morton," which I described earlier in this section. These, however, are true *imagines rerum*, designed to call to mind the framework and contents of a composition, which each individual should ponder and elaborate further. They provide places for memorial gathering, *collatio*, in the manner which Hugh de Fouilloy provided for his treatise *On the Dove and the Hawk*.

The spectacular pages of some of the earliest books of the Middle Ages, the Insular gospel books designed for lectionary use and study, can be considered in this way. The carpet-pages of interlace that grace such Gospels as the Book of Durrow (late seventh century) or the Book of Kells (around about 800?; figure 30) are most like diagrams in the way in which they treat space. For example, Jacques Guilmain has demonstrated the simple, orderly geometry upon which the forms of ornament in these carpet pages rests. As he comments, the making of these pages "is an art that cannot be described simply as a catalogue of its component parts, for just as significant is the syntax of those parts . . . all details relate to the wholes as completed fabrics."[97] Moreover, they are not pages which one can easily digest; like the texts they introduce they must be looked at and looked at again, ruminated, absorbed and made one's own. The figures that peek through the interlace are not apparent until one looks long enough to begin putting together what seems at first fragmentary. It is a process such as the one Hugh of St. Victor describes as the journey from ignorance to contemplation; one first sees only an overwhelming jumble of fragmentary

30. Dublin, Trinity College MS.A.1 (formerly MS.58 "The Books of Kells"; Ireland or
North Britain (?Iona), about 800?), fo. 34r. The first page of the Gospel of Matthew (the
text is Mt. 1:18: "Christi hic generatio"), showing "Chi-rho-i" in large letters. Two
sedentary cats and several mice, two of which are nibbling a communion wafer, can
be made out at the right of the bottom of "Chi." To the right of them, at the base
of the stem of "rho," is a black otter eating a salmon.

detail, then as one meditates one begins to collect the pieces, and then in contemplation forges a meaningful pattern.

In a famous description, which some scholars think may be that of the Book of Kells itself, the twelfth-century historian, Gerald of Wales, recounts his encounter with such a book. It is remarkable not so much because of its apparently realistic depiction of the artistry of one of these Insular manuscripts as because of its articulation of a process of seeing, reading, and meditation that, Gerald says, fulfilled his ordinary expectations to an extraordinary degree:

> Look at [the forms in this book] superficially with an ordinary casual glance, and you would think it is an erasure, and not tracery. Fine craftsmanship is all about you, but you might not notice it. Look more keenly at it and you will penetrate to the very shrine of art. You will make out intricacies so delicate and subtle, so exact and compact, so full of knots and links, with colors so fresh and vivid, that you might say that all this was the work of an angel and not of a man. For my part, the oftener I see the book, and the more carefully I study it, the more I am lost in ever fresh amazement, and I see more and more wonders in the book.[98]

What Gerald describes is not an act of picturing or illustration, but an act of reading, in the monastic understanding of what reading is. It is basically a rhetorical practice, an act of *memoria* in which the figures grouped in the picture are designed both to recall and to stimulate further mental image-making in the reader. Pages that consist of a framework alone, without super-imposed images, are especially suggestive. An example is the carpet-pages of the Book of Durrow. Here empty rectangular panels are set in a framework of interlace, some panels having a plain-colored background, some a simple interlace design, like the empty places into which particular *imagines rerum* may be projected, and then erased and used again for other occasions and other texts – and by a variety of people, as is fitting for a book made to be pondered.[99]

The ornamentation of a medieval page does not consist of images to be memorized precisely. Instead, they are presented as examples and invitations to the further making of such images. Nothing could prevent a lazy user from employing such cues only to trigger rote memory. This was recognized as praying only with the lips, and excoriated as a form of sloth. But for a serious reader, one willing to become mindful of reading and ponder it, like Mary, in her heart, all memory advice is clear that one should not rely on ready-made images, one should learn to fashion one's own, for only this exercise will concentrate the mind enough to ensure a safe investigation of one's memory. A true memory-image is a mental creation, and it has the elaboration and flexibility, the ability to store and sort large amounts of information, that no pictured diagram can possibly approach.

There is a built-in indeterminacy of meaning, and even of relationship of parts, to medieval diagrams, for they follow the logic of recollection – which is associative and determined by individual habit – and not the universal logic of mathematics. Like the *tituli*, the rubrics, and the punctuation, the picture-diagrams are a part of the apparatus of a text – aiding its mnemonic *divisio*, surely, but deliberately inviting meditation, *compositio*, as well, the recollective process by means of which a particular reader engages a particular text (with all that includes) on a particular occasion.

The idea that manuscript decoration had a practical use is now broadly adopted by codicologists and art historians; as Christopher de Hamel has observed, "Decoration is a device to help a reader use a manuscript."[100] But, as I hope this chapter has shown, if we take a wholly utilitarian approach to decoration, especially if we identify it with some pre-conceived notion of literate as opposed to oral culture, we will misunderstand its full function as much as we did when we thought of it as only decoration, or as a help for those who couldn't read. Like reading, of which it is a part, decoration is practical in the medieval understanding of that word, having a basic role to play in every reader's moral life and character because of its role in the requirements of memory practices.

Every medieval diagram is an open-ended one; in the manner of examples, it is an invitation to elaborate and recompose, not a prescriptive schematic. Hugh of St. Victor did not think that he had produced a model of what the Ark was really like, whether at the literal, allegorical, or moral levels; this is apparent from the way in which he freely adds to the Genesis account of its lineaments and freely contradicts his own previous interpretations. Once again, we can see how his whole attitude towards a text differs from ours; it isn't, to him, a definitive statement of fact or experience but an occasion for rumination and meditation, for the engagement of *memoria*. Invitations to meditate further are found throughout his Ark *pictura*. After describing his elaborately painted ladders, for example, Hugh remarks, "There are many other things that could have been said about these [figures] that we must skip over here out of necessity."[101] But the reader may stay to meditate and contemplate and learn from the examples which Hugh has provided.

The rhetorical indeterminacy of a medieval diagram extends as well to all the elements that "distinguish" a medieval page. Iconography, in art as well as literary criticism, treats images as direct signs of some thing, as having an inherent meaning that will be universal for all readers. But, like the painted letters, all the other decorative elements are signs that act directly only upon memory. In the memory of a particular reader they will become meaningful as I make them mine. And memories, as we have seen, are differently stored, having different tracks and associative paths. The one thing that a manuscript image must produce in order to stimulate memory is an emotion. It must be aesthetic in the ancient sense of this word. It must create a strong response – of what sort is less important – in order to impress the user's memory and start off a recollective chain. That combination of image and response makes up the memory-image, and *only then*, when the fully formed image is in memory, can it become a matter of thought.

Let me take as a last example of this distinction the famous black otter eating a salmon that is tucked into the bottom border of the *rho* on the Chi-rho page at the beginning of Matthew in the Book of Kells (figure 30). It is very hard to find amid the myriad and apparently fragmentary forms on this page. But as I suggested earlier, the page is designed to make one meditate upon it, to look and look again, and remake its patterns oneself; the process of seeing this page models the process of meditative reading which the text it introduces will require. The letters on this page are virtually hidden away in the welter of its other forms; indeed, thinking of this aspect of its design, Françoise Henry calls it "a sort of rebus" (182). Yet it is not a true rebus, as are the visual puns suggested for remembering proper names by the author of *Dialexeis*. Nor is the Chi-rho page by any means a diagram-picture for the gospel of Matthew, even to the extent that *De formatione arche* is for *De archa Noe*. It helps instead to initiate the divisional and compositional process that is required to read Matthew, and it is this that makes it valuable to memory. In that process, the discovery of the successful otter, and – next to it – the two cats surrounded by mice they are too lazy to catch, surprises us with a shock of delight, whether or not we know the proverbs about lazy cats, or care to make a meditational link between industrious fishermen and cats who won't work for their food.[102] And, as Geoffrey of Vinsauf says, repeating a cliché of long standing, the memory-cell needs to be delighted as it works, lest too much heavy food give it indigestion. The emotion of surprise in itself makes the page effective in memory, whatever the meanings we may later give to its many forms.

Appendix A

HUGH OF ST. VICTOR: "THE THREE BEST MEMORY-AIDS FOR LEARNING HISTORY"[1]

My child, knowledge is a treasury and your heart is its strongbox. As you study all of knowledge, you store up for yourselves good treasures, immortal treasures, incorruptible treasures, which never decay nor lose the beauty of their brightness. In the treasure-house of wisdom are various sorts of wealth, and many filing-places in the store-house of your heart. In one place is put gold, in another silver, in another precious jewels. Their orderly arrangement is clarity of knowledge. Dispose and separate each single thing into its own place, this into its and that into its, so that you may know what has been placed here and what there. Confusion is the mother of ignorance and forgetfulness, but orderly arrangement illuminates the intelligence and secures memory.

You see how a money-changer who has unsorted coins divides his one pouch into several compartments, just as a cloister embraces many separate cells inside. Then, having sorted the coins and separated out each type of money in turn, he puts them all to be kept in their proper places, so that the distinctiveness of his compartments may keep the assortment of his materials from getting mixed up, just as it supports their separation.[2] Additionally, you observe in his display of money-changing, how his ready hand without faltering follows wherever the commanding nod of a customer has caused it to extend, and quickly, without delay, it brings into the open, separately and without confusion, everything that he either may have wanted to receive or promised to give out. And it would provide onlookers with a spectacle silly and absurd enough, if, while one and the same money-bag should pour forth so many varieties without muddle, this same bag, its mouth being opened, should not display on its inside an equivalent number of separate compartments. And so this particular separation into distinct places, which I have described, at one and the same time eliminates for the onlookers any mystery in the action, and, for those doing it, an obstacle to their ability to perform it.

Now as we just said by way of preface, a classifying-system for material makes it manifest to the mind. Truly such manifestation of matters both illuminates the soul when it perceives them, and confirms them in memory. Return, therefore, child, to your heart and consider how you should dispose and collect in it the precious treasures of wisdom, so that you may learn about its individual repositories, and when for safekeeping you place something in them, dispose it in such an order that when your reason asks for it, you are easily able to find it by means of your memory and understand it by means of your intellect, and bring it forth by means of your eloquence. I am going to propose to you a particular method for such classification.

Matters that are learned are classified in the memory in three ways; by number, location, and occasion. Thus all the things which you may have heard you will both readily capture in your intellect and retain for a long time in your memory, if you have learned to classify them according to these three categories. I will demonstrate one at a time the manner in which each should be used.

The first means of classifying is by number. Learn to construct in your mind a line [of numbers] numbered from one on, in however long a sequence you want, extended as it were before the eyes of your mind. When you hear any number at all called out, become accustomed to quickly turning your mind there [on your mental line] where its sum is enclosed, as though to that specific point at which in full this number is completed. For example, when you hear ten, think of the tenth place, or when twelve, think of the twelfth, so that you conceive of the whole according to its outer extent [along the line], and likewise for the other [numbers].[3] Make this conception and this way of imagining it practiced and habitual, so that you conceive of the limit and extent of all numbers visually, just as though [they were] placed in particular places. And listen to how this mental visualization may be useful for learning.

Suppose for example that I wish to learn the psalter word for word by heart. I proceed thus: first I consider how many Psalms there are. There are 150. I learn them all in order so that I know which is the first, which the second, which the third, and so on. I then place them all by order in my heart along my [mental] numerical line, and one at a time I designate them to the seats where they are disposed in the grid, while at the same time, accompanied by voicing or cogitation, I listen and observe closely until each becomes to me of a size equivalent to one glance of my memory:

"Blessed is the man," with respect to the first Psalm; "Why have the gentiles raged," with respect to the second; "Why, O Lord, are they multiplied," with respect to the third; this [much] is kept in the first, second, and third compartments. And then I imprint the result of my mental effort by the vigilant concentration of my heart so that, when asked, without hesitation I may answer, either in forward order, or by skipping one or several, or in reverse order and recited backwards according to my completely mastered scheme of places, what is the first, what the second, what indeed the twenty-seventh, the forty-eighth, or whatever Psalm it should be.[4] In this manner [disputants] demonstrate [that] the scriptures confirm their own arguments when, as they are about to use the authority of some one Psalm, they say this is written in the 63rd, this in the 75th, or whatever other Psalm, fetching forth for reference not its name but its number. For surely, you do not think that those who wish to cite some one of the Psalms have turned over the manuscript pages, so that starting their count from the beginning they could figure out what number in the series of Psalms each might have? The labor in such a task would be too great. Therefore they have in their heart a powerful mental device, and they have retained it in memory, for they have learned the number and the order of each single item in the series.

Having learned the Psalms [as a whole], I then devise the same sort of scheme for each separate Psalm, starting with the beginning words of the verses just as I did for the whole psalter starting with the first words of the psalms, and I can thereafter easily retain in my heart the whole series one verse at a time; first by dividing and marking off the book by [whole] Psalms and then each Psalm by verses, I have reduced a large amount of material to such conciseness and brevity. And this [method] in fact can readily be seen in the Psalms or in other books containing obvious divisions. When however the reading is in an unbroken series, it is necessary to do this artificially, so that, to be sure according to the convenience of the reader, [at those places] where it seems [to him] most suitable, first the whole piece is divided into a fixed number of sections, and these again into others, these into yet others, until the whole length of material is so parceled up that the mind can easily retain it in single units. For the memory always rejoices in both brevity of length and paucity of number, and therefore it is necessary, when the sequence of your reading tends towards length, that it first be divided into a few units, so that what the mind could not comprehend in a single expanse it can comprehend at least in a number, and again, when later the more moderate number of items is sub-divided into many, it may be aided in each case by the principle of paucity or brevity.

So you see the value to learning a numerical division-scheme; now see and consider of what value for the same thing is the classification-system according to location. Have you never noticed how a boy has greater difficulty impressing upon his memory what he has read if he often changes his copy [of a text] between readings? Why should this be unless it is because, when the image-receiving power of the heart is directed outward through the senses into so many shapes from diverse books, no specific image can remain within [the inner senses] by means of which a memory-image may be fixed? For when something is brought together to be fashioned into an image from all [the copies] indiscriminately, one super-imposed upon another, and always the earlier being wiped away by later ones, nothing personal or familiar remains which by use and practice can be clearly possessed. Therefore it is a great value for fixing a memory-image that when we read books, we strive to impress on our memory through the power of forming our mental images not only the number and order of verses or ideas, but at the same time the color, shape, position, and place-ment of the letters, where we have seen this or that written, in what part, in what location (at the top, the middle, or the bottom) we saw it positioned, in what color we observed the trace of the letter or the ornamented surface of the parchment. Indeed I consider nothing so useful for stimulating the memory as this; that we also pay attention carefully to those circumstances of things which can occur accidentally and externally, so that for example, together with the appearance and quality or location of the places in which we heard one thing or the other we recall also the face and habits of the people from whom we learned this and that, and, if there are any, the things that accompany the performance of a certain activity. All these things indeed are rudimentary in nature, but of a sort beneficial for boys.

After the classifications by number and place follows the classification by occasions, that is: what was done earlier and what later, how much earlier and how much later, by how many years, months, days this precedes that and that follows this other. This classification is relevant in a situation when, according to the varying nature of the occasions on which we learned something, at a later time we may be able to recall to our mind a memory of the content, as we remember that one occasion was at night and another by day, one in winter, another in summer, one in cloudy weather, another in sunshine. All these things truly we have composed as a kind of prelude [to our learning], providing the basics to children, lest we, disdaining these most basic elements of our studies, start little by little to ramble incoher-ently. Indeed the whole usefulness of education consists only in the memory of it, for just as having heard something does not profit one who cannot understand, likewise having understood is not valuable to one who either will not or cannot remember. Indeed it was profitable to have listened only insofar as it caused us to have understood, and to have understood insofar as it was retained. But these are as it were basics for knowledge, which, if they are firmly impressed in your memory, open up all the rest readily. We have written out this [list of names, dates, and places] for you in the following pages, disposed in the order in which we wish them to be implanted in your soul through memory, so that whatever afterwards we build upon it may be firm.

All exposition of divine Scripture is drawn forth according to three senses: literal, allegorical, and tropological, or moral. The literal is the narrative of history, expressed in the basic meaning of the letter. Allegory is when by means of this event in the story, which we find in the literal meaning, another action is signified, belonging to past or present or future time. Tropology is when in that action which we hear was done, we recognize what we should be doing. Whence it rightly receives the name "tropology," that is, converted speech or replicated discourse, for without a doubt we turn the word of a story about others to our own instruction when, having read of the deeds of others, we conform our living to their example.

But now we have in hand history, as it were the foundation of all knowledge, the first to be laid out together in memory. But because, as we said, the memory delights in brevity, yet the events of history are nearly infinite, it is necessary for us, from among all of that material, to gather together a kind of brief summary – as it were the foundation of a foundation, that is a first foundation – which the soul can most easily comprehend and the memory retain. There are three matters on which the knowledge of past actions especially depends, that is, the persons who performed the deeds, the places in which they were performed, and the time at which they occurred. Whoever holds these three by memory in his soul will find that he has built a good foundation for himself, onto which he can assemble afterwards anything by reading and lecture without difficulty and rapidly take it in and retain it for a long time. However, in so doing it is necessary to retain it in memory and by diligent retracing to have it customary and well known, so that his heart may be ready to put in place everything he has heard, and apply those classification-techniques which he will have learned now, to all things that he may hear afterwards by a suitable distribution according to their place, date, and person.

While [the circumstances of] time and number measure off length in the chest of memory, [the aspect of] place extends the area in width, so that the rest of the material may then be disposed in its locations. First, therefore, we will place in order our persons together with their dates, extending them from the beginning along the length of the time-line, [and] we will mark off our places, however many will adequately allow for the full extent of our summary, gathered up out of all the material. Now indeed endeavor to imprint in this fashion in your memory the matters which are written out below, according to the method and diagram for learning by heart demonstrated to you earlier, so that by experience you can know the truth of my words, when you perceive how valuable it is to devote study and labor not just to having heard the lectures on the scriptures or to discussion, but to memory-work.

The creation of nature was completed in six days and the renewal of man will be achieved in six stages. The world was made before time began, fashioned in six days, put in order in the first three days, and fitted out and decorated in the three following. On the first day was made light, on the second the firmament between the waters above and the waters below. On the third day the waters which were under the firmament were gathered together in one place, and dry land appeared, and produced green plants and those which make fruits. Behold the arrangement of the four elements. The heaven was stretched out above, next the air was made clear, next the waters were gathered together in one place, then the land was revealed. Its equipping and decoration followed.[5] On the fourth day lights – the sun, moon, and stars – were created for ornamenting the heaven. On the fifth day fish were created from the waters, and birds, birds for decoration of the air, fish for equipping the waters. On the sixth day were made the beasts of burden, wild beasts, and the rest of living creatures, for ornament of the dry lands.

At the very last, in fulfillment of all, humankind was created, Adam and Eve. When he was 130 years old, Adam engendered Seth. And Adam lived after he engendered Seth 800 years. Thus it is found in the Hebrew. However the authors of the Septuagint place 230 years before the birth of Seth, 700 after. And in all the period of Adam's life was 930 years. And likewise the others follow along in the columns of the diagram according to the true disposition of the Hebrew.

Appendix B

Next, the properties of prudence are investigated. And we follow the three categories of three philosophers, namely Tullius [Cicero], Macrobius, and Aristotle.

First Tullius says at the end of his First Rhetoric [*De inventione*]: "there are three parts to prudence: memory, intelligence, foresight." Macrobius, however, says in his *Commentary on the Dream of Scipio*: "the knowledge of prudence lies in intellect, circumspection, foresight, a willingness to learn, and caution." And Aristotle at the end of the first Book of his *Ethics* says that the intellectual virtues are prudence [*sapientia*], *phronēsis*,[2] and intelligence [*intelligentia*].

ARTICLE ONE: WHAT *MEMORIA* MIGHT BE[3]

Let us inquire first concerning the word *memoria*, which Tullius only mentions. And we will inquire in two ways, namely concerning what it might be in itself, and concerning the art of memory which Tullius teaches. First therefore let us examine what memory is. Tullius says that "memory is the faculty by which the mind recalls things that were in the past" [*De invent.* ii. 53, 160].

1. But it seems that according to this definition memory would not be a part of prudence. Memory, by means of which what has happened is recalled, is a function of the soul and not a characteristic capable of being developed by education and training [*habitus*], as is demonstrated in the questions *De anima* [Albertus Magnus, *De homine*, Q. 40, a. 1]; every part of prudence, however, is a matter of learning [*habitus*]; therefore memory is not a part of prudence.

2. Also, it was asserted above, that memory is a part of the sensory soul and not of the rational per se; prudence however is per se in the rational soul; therefore memory is not a part of prudence.

3. Moreover, to recollect things that have occurred is the action of a cognitive power; prudence, however, is a characteristic of ethical judgments [*moralium*]; therefore again memory is not a part of the virtue of prudence.

4. Likewise everything is directed and guided by something which is or can be; nothing of what has been, insofar as it has been, is or can be; therefore no direction is possible from past things, insofar as they are past. Whence this final conclusion follows, thus: all prudence is guided by present things, those things which are, or by future ones, those which can be; therefore no memory is a part of prudence.

5. Moreover, the recollection of something which happened comes about either by means of reason proceeding from a definite principle, or only by means of the forms of sense-objects. If it comes about in the first way, then to recall something past will be an act of reminiscence and not of memory, as appears from what was demonstrated earlier in my tract *De anima* [Albertus, *De homine*, Q. 41, a.1]. If however, it is by the second method, then the action of memory will not accord with the rational soul, and thus it will not be a part of prudence.

But on the contrary: Prudence is the knowledge of the good and evil of actions; this knowledge, moreover, is greatly aided by events that have already happened, because by means of the past it will know in what way it should manage itself in the future; therefore memory should be a part of prudence.

Likewise, in a certain decretal, Pope [Gregory IX] says: "From your past life we separate out what we should anticipate concerning the future." [Greg. IX, *Decret.* 2.23.6 i. f.] So memories of the past direct us regarding the future; therefore, memory is a part of prudence. Likewise the Philosopher says that "an intellectual power stands in need of experience and time." [*Eth. Nic.*, I, i, 1103a, 16–17] The Philosopher says elsewhere in the beginning of *Metaphysics*: "memory creates experience among men; many memories of the same thing make effective the power of a single experience" [*Meta.*, I.i, 980b, 20 – 981a, 1]. Therefore it seems that memory should be generative of prudence and a part of it.

SOLUTIO: We say that memory is a part of prudence, insofar as memory comes under the definition of reminiscence. When prudence distinguishes those things by which it is assisted from those by which it is impeded in its work, it is necessary for it to proceed by a process of inquiry, and thus necessary for it to progress from a pre-determined starting-point, and through intermediate probabilities to arrive at a working hypothesis;

and likewise since prudence proceeds from things that happened in the past, it uses memory, insofar as it is a function of reminiscence.

1. We reply therefore, that to recollect [*repetere*] things which are past comes about in two ways, that is from our natural predisposition, and this sort of recollection is only a psychological potential and imperfect in that it has no habitual method whence it might proceed. And there is recollection from trained habit, by which the past is recalled, whenever one wishes to recollect. And this can be a part of cognitive training [*in habitu cognitivo*], and then it is theoretical, or it can be part of moral training [*in habitu morali*], and then it is practical and is the virtue pertaining to prudence.

2. Replying to the next that *memoria*, insofar as it mixes itself up with reminiscence, belongs more to the rational soul than to the sensible soul, because reminiscence is as it were a kind of logical reasoning [*syllogismus*], as the Philosopher says, and so then *memoria* is a habit of the rational soul.

3. Replying to the next, that memory has two functions, that is, it is a condition for what we know rationally [*habitus cognitivorum*], and a condition for making ethical judgments [*habitus moralium*], and here it is discussed as a condition of making moral judgments, as I said.

4. Replying to the next, that the past so far as it is past brings nothing to our guidance in the present or the future. But memory takes in an event that is past as though it stayed ever-present in the soul as an idea and as an emotional effect on us, and so this event can be very effective for providing for the future. Moreover, I say "to stay in the soul as an idea," meaning an idea of good and evil, and "as an effect," meaning how much it affected positively or harmed those performing it.

5. Replying to the next, that *memoria* is understood by Tullius as the trained habit and not as the psychological faculty. However, "habit" does not fall under the heading of reminiscence so much as it does of memory, and so it is more readily discussed as memory than as reminiscence. Both memory and reminiscence indeed proceed from past events when they are past. But a past event when past creates no habitual effect except in memory, and so it is called *memoria* by Tullius. There are those, nonetheless, who say along with John Damascene and Gregory Nazianzus, that memory is the accumulation both of sensible objects and of intellectual ones, and so they say there are two faculties of memory, that is, one of the sensible soul and the other of the rational. But this is not said in the natural philosophy which Aristotle taught, or the other following him. What indeed appears to us concerning this matter can be expressly discovered in our treatise *De anima*.

ARTICLE TWO: CONCERNING THE ART OF MEMORY

Secondly, let us inquire concerning the art of memory which Tullius treats in his Second Rhetoric, at the end of Book III.

Let us determine what "artificial" memory might be. For Tullius divided the memory into natural and artificial, and he said our native memory was "something which is imbedded in our minds, born simultaneously with thought." And he says artificial memory is that "strengthened by a kind of inductive reasoning [*inductio quaedam*] and a system of rules."[4]

1. But it seems this is not so at all, because what he calls "natural memory" is either the activity of the soul, which is memory, or a particular habitualized action, by which this power is made fully effective. If it is the first sort of thing, then he speaks nonsense, because a power of the soul cannot be classified together with some one habitual characteristic and above all of the very same power. But the artificial memory is a habit and it cannot be a habit except of a power, which is memory. If it is the second sort of thing, then it would not seem to be of our nature, because habitualized training in remembering things is not inborn in us.

2. Moreover, what he says – that [*memoria* is] "what is imbedded in our minds, born simultaneously with thought" – seems to be opposite to what is good for our native memory. I showed indeed, in my treatise *De anima* [*De homine*, Q. 40, a. 3] that the best conditions for memory are cold and dry, whence we say the melancholics are the best at remembering. But the worst condition for thought lies in cold and dry, because thinking [*cogitatio*] is the repeated working-over [*coagitatio*] and running back and forth [*discursus*] of reason on the objects of memory [*memorabilia*], and for the operation of reason warmth and pliability or dampness work better. For what is warm moves vigorously and what is damp best responds to all movements. Therefore the best condition for natural memory is not generated together with thought.

3. Moreover, we should inquire concerning what this same person [Tullius] says about the artificial memory, that analogous argumentation [*inductio*] and a system of rules strengthen it, because these proceed from some reasoned principle by analogy or example or enthymeme or syllogism, when none of these is proper to memory but more to reminiscence, as Aristotle says in his book *De memoria et reminiscentia*.

4. Moreover, it should be asked what is the difference between an induction and a general rule. An inductive argument comes about when entirely from single cases a universal principle is inferred, and in

such a case a whole memory is generated as much of the natural as of the artificial. For the Philosopher says that out of many things, regarding which an example [*instantia*] is not already inventoried in the mind, *memoria* is created by the experience of the intellect. Thus the whole memory is made by the experience of generalizing from single cases [*ab inductione experimento*] among those things we have taken in [*acceptorum*]; thus this is not specific to the artificial memory.

5. Moreover, it appears from this that he should be wrong when he says *memoria* is made from a system of rules when induction suffices.

6. Likewise, a system of rules is a logic of universal principles; but a universal is generated by memory, as the Philosopher says; therefore what is generated by memory generates memory, which is impossible. Therefore Tullius says wrongly that *memoria* is created by a system of rules.

7. In connection with this latter point, we should inquire concerning the rules, which he teaches, that are attendant on this artificial memory. He says indeed that among them it is necessary above all to pay attention to those on which it is based: "the artificial memory consists of backgrounds and images." And he defines what he calls backgrounds thus: " By backgrounds [*loci*] I mean such scenes as are naturally or artificially set off on a diminished scale, complete, in a visually striking manner, so that we can grasp and embrace them easily by the natural memory – for example, a house, an intercolumnar space, a recess, an arch, or the like. An image is, as it were, a figure, mark, or portrait of a thing we wish to remember, such as the general class [*genus*] of horse, lion, eagle" and by this method it is sought. So when time is said to be more of the essence of memory than space, as something which falls within its very definition, why does not Tullius say that time is as necessary to pay attention to as place is?[5]

8. Likewise, a background represented "on a diminished scale" is a truncated and mutilated place; "completely" represented however is a background equivalent to the thing itself. Therefore it seems that "diminished in scale" and "complete" are contradictory with regard to the same object of memory, and thus by saying one thing about something the other will be false.

9. Moreover, to represent "in a strikingly visual manner" does not seem suitable for the background of all memory-objects, because not every sort of object-for-remembering is made in a visually marked place.

10. Moreover, what is a memory-place set off "naturally" and one "completely artificial?" These indeed ought to be defined but Tullius does not do so, either earlier or later.

11. Further, let us inquire concerning the rules which he makes to be observed about background-places and there are five in general. The first of them is that "it will be more advantageous to obtain places in a deserted than in a populous region, because the crowding and passing to and fro of people confuse and weaken the impress of images, while solitude keeps their outlines sharp." The second is that "places differing in form and nature must be secured, so that, thus distinguished, they may be clearly visible; for if a person has adopted many intercolumnar spaces, their resemblance to one another will so confuse him that he will no longer know what he set in each background." The third is that "the places ought to be of moderate size and medium extent, for when excessively large they render the images vague, and when too small often seem incapable of receiving an arrangement of images." The fourth is that "the places ought to be neither too bright nor too dim, so that the images may not grow obscure in shadows nor be dazzling from brilliant light." The fifth is that "the interval between the places should be of moderate extent, approximately thirty feet; for like an external glance [*aspectus*], so the inner glance of thought [*cogitatio*] works less well when you have moved too near or too far away."

12. So, let us inquire concerning these background-places. It seems indeed at first when he speaks concerning the faculty of reminiscence, that physical places are of no value for that which reminiscence deduces by a rational method. But physical backgrounds, at least ones of this sort, are in the image-making faculty.

13. Further, I held in my tract *De anima*, in the question "On *memoria*," that memory indeed retains for the soul not so much the images of sense objects but the impressions [*intentiones*] received from these images. Therefore it seems that images of physical places would not be especially valuable, but he ought to teach an art such that we may arrive at the concepts abstracted from them.

14. Likewise, to imagine is from *imaginatio*, which according to the Philosopher is the treasury of forms, and therefore is also called (*vis*) *formalis*. Thus it seems that these things are more of *imaginatio* than of *memoria*.

15. Further it seems that he has taught incompletely the rules for the backgrounds in which the images of things to be remembered are deposited, because many other things are useful as places for remembering besides those he defined: solitude, distinctness, intervals neither too great nor too small. Many people indeed remember sometimes by the opposite characteristics of places. Further, this same Tullius himself

adds a little further on: "if we are not content with our ready-made supply of backgrounds,we may create a region for ourselves and obtain a most serviceable distribution of appropriate backgrounds."

16. Additionally to this, let us inquire further concerning the images gathered in the places we spoke of. Tullius says indeed that in two ways we must hold likenesses for remembering, one way according to things, the other according to words. "Likenesses of things [*rerum*] are formed when we enlist images that present a general view or summation of the matter with which we are dealing; likenesses of words are established when the record of each single noun or word is kept by an image." Yet this technique which Tullius speaks of does not seem to be a useful skill but more of an impediment to remembering, for two reasons. Of which one is that there will be as many images according to his method as there are matters and words. Therefore their multitude would confound the memory. The second reason is because metaphors represent things less well than do the words themselves. If therefore we should refer the literal content in our material and words to images, as he teaches, we will be less quick to remember. For he thus teaches us to have recourse to images: "[if] the prosecutor has said that the defendent killed a man by poison, has charged that the motive for the crime was an inheritance, and declared that there are many witnesses and accessories to this act," we place in our memory "a sick man in bed, who is a figure of the deceased, and we place the defendant standing by the bed, holding in his right hand a cup, in his left hand tablets, and a physician standing upright holding the testicles of a ram," so that certainly in the cup should be the memory-cue of the poison which he drank, and in the tablets should be the memory-cue of the will which he signed, and in the physician may be figured the accusor and by the testicles the witnesses and accessories, and by the ram the defense against the matter being ajudicated. The same method is observed regarding images for words. But what is literal would affect someone more easily than what is non-literal, and so literal words will stimulate the memory more than metaphorical ones.

17. Moreover, Tullius himself says that "when we wish to represent by images the likenesses of words, we shall be undertaking a greater task and exercising our ingenuity the more; this we ought to effect in the following way." Suppose we wish to recollect these words: "Now their revenge at home [*domi ultionem*]" or "their home-coming [*domum itionem*]" (which is better) "the kings, sons of Atreus, prepare [*Iam domum itionem reges Atridae parent*]." In a background we must place Domitius, raising hands to heaven, while he is whipped with thongs by

the Marcian kings; this will be "now the kings their revenge at home". In the next place, Aesop and Cimber preparing wandering Iphigenia; this will be "Atridae making ready." That is, we should imagine someone who is beaten with sharp thongs by the Marcian kings, that is the sons of Mars, who aid Mars the god of war, for his own exile or for revenge, and because he who prepares himself for something wanders about, we represent wandering Iphigenia preparing Aesop and Cimber [*sic*].[6] These indeed are metaphorical words and obscure things not easy to remember.

18. Finally, let us inquire concerning those rules which Tullius gives for gathering images in such background-places. Indeed Tullius says that "the backgrounds are very much like wax tablets or papyrus, the images like the letters, the arrangement and disposition of the images like the script, and the delivery is like the reading." This does not seem possible. For letters are few in number compared to the number of word-elements, and, according to their diverse arrangements, they express whatever may be needed for speaking, as Democritus said happens in tragedies and comedies; but it would be necessary to have a great many images or they could not express the content in its literal kind.

19. If it is said definitely that a few images are enough, this indeed will be contrary to Tullius, because it appears from the above examples that it is necessary to have one's own likenesses of things.

20. Next after Tullius has taught what kinds of places we ought to employ, in a similar way he teaches what sorts of images we must seek out, that is, "we should set up the mental images of our likenesses to be as striking as possible, though not multiform or diffuse and changeable in nature, but we shall select images that are doing something; if we attribute to them exceptional beauty or singular ugliness; if we dress some of them with crowns or purple cloaks so that the likeness may be more distinct to us; or if we somehow disfigure them as by introducing one stained with blood or soiled with mud or smeared with red paint, so that their form is more striking, or by assigning comic effects to our images. For that too will ensure that we are able to remember more easily." From this it appears that it is not sufficient to have a limited number of images, so that according to their diverse arrangement each single one expresses a meaning to us, but we must have many, and these will not be less difficult to recall than the matters or universals themselves. Therefore the rules of Tullius are useless.

21. Moreover indeed, Tullius himself says regarding our images, in order that we may recollect by means of them, we require two kinds, that is in

disciplined study we constitute for ourselves images both spaced apart at intervals and strange, ones which are almost marvels. And he touches on the reason for each of these conditions, saying of the first thus: "But such an arrangement of images succeeds only if we use our notation to stimulate the natural memory, so that we first go over a given verse twice or three times and then represent the words by means of images." Likewise, in the same place: "art will supplement nature; for neither by itself will be strong enough, though we must note that theory and technique are much the more reliable." He also touches on the reason for the second condition, saying: "Now nature herself teaches us what we should do. When we see in everyday life things that are petty, ordinary, and common, we generally fail to remember them, because the mind is not being stirred by anything novel or marvellous. But if we see or hear something either incredibly decent or base in human beings, also unheard of, great, incredible, dangerous, that we are likely to remember for a long time."[7]

Likewise in the same place: "things which are immediate to our eye or ear we commonly forget; incidents of our childhood we often remember best, nor could this be so for any other reason than that ordinary things easily slip from the memory while the striking and novel stay longer in the mind." Again, in the same place: "Thus nature shows that she is not aroused by the common, ordinary event, but is moved by a new or striking occurence. Let art, then, imitate nature, find what she descries, and follow where she directs. For in invention nature is never last, education never first; rather the beginnings of things arise from natural talent, and the ends are reached by discipline."

From all these quotations it appears that for the artificial memory disciplined study is required in images and contents and words and much else besides, so that our images may be rare and conspicuous, and thus it seems that these may not be predetermined images which we employ for remembering all sorts of things, as we employ letters for signifying every sort of thing in writing. If because of this it is said that the images ought to be as numerous as the matters and words, Tullius says the contrary about what is good for memory, in the same book just before the end: "I know that most of the Greeks who have written on the memory have taken the course of listing images that correspond to a great many words, so that persons who wished to learn these images by heart would have them ready without expending effort on a search for them. I dis-approve of their method on several grounds." And he puts forth in general six reasons why what they say is wrong. Of which the first is thus stated by

Tullius: "first, among the immemorable [*sic* for *innumerabile*] multitude of words it is ridiculous to collect images [*mille* omitted]. How meager is the value these can have when out of the infinite store of words we shall need to remember different ones [second *aliud modo* omitted]?" The second reason is "why do we wish to rob anyone of his initiative, so that, to save him from making any search himself, we deliver to him everything searched out and ready?" The third is because "one person is more struck by one likeness, and another by another. Often in fact when we declare that some one form resembles another, we fail to receive universal assent, because things seem different to different persons; the same is true with respect to images, one that is well defined to us appears relatively inconspicuous to others; everybody, therefore, should in equipping himself with images suit his own convenience." The fourth reason is because "it is the instructor's duty to teach the proper method of search in each case, and, for the sake of greater clarity, to add in illustration some one or two examples of its kind, but not all, as for instance, when I discuss how to find an introduction, I give a method of search and do not write out a thousand kinds of Introductions. The same procedure I believe should be followed with respect to images." The fifth cause is because since memory is of two kinds, that is of things and of words, "lest we make memorizing too difficult, we should be content with memory for things," lest the number of words overwhelm what is memorized. The sixth and final reason is that we do not have training in memorizing-for-words unless it makes our *res* more readily memorable, indeed, "that by such training memory for things is confirmed in us, which alone principally is of practical use. In every discipline artistic theory is of little avail without unremitting exercise, but especially for memorizing theory is valueless unless made good by industry, devotion, toil, and care."

SOLUTIO: We say that art of memory is best which Tullius teaches, above all with respect to those things-for-remembering which pertain to how we live and to justice, and these memories chiefly relate to ethics and rhetoric because, since the action of human life consists in particular events, it is necessary that this art be within the soul through corporeal images; in these images however it will not remain except within the memory. Whence we say that among all those things which point towards ethical wisdom, the most necessary is trained memory, because from past events we are guided in the present and the future, and not from the converse. Indeed that necessity be in trained memory to the highest degree, Tullius proves by this argument, saying: "While an engrossing preoccupation may often distract us from our other pursuits, from memorizing nothing whatever can divert us. Indeed there is never a moment when we do not wish to commit something to memory, and we wish it most of all when our attention is held by business of special importance. So, since a ready memory is a useful thing, you see clearly with what great pains you must strive to acquire so useful a faculty, so that you will be able to judge having learned its utility." Therefore we say with Tullius that the kind of *memoria* which relates to human life and justice is two-fold, that is, natural and trained or "artificial." That is natural which by virtue of its talent for inventing things remembers easily something it knew or did at an earlier time. The "artificial" however is one which is made from an orderly arrangement of images and places, and, as in everything else art and virtue are a perfection of natural talent, so also in this. What is natural is completed by training. This however should be noted, that in all these matters I have been discussing, the word *memoria* is used instead of *reminiscencia*, for the reason determined above.

1. We reply to that which was questioned in the first place, by saying that Tullius defines "natural memory" as a power perfected by a natural habit and not an absolute power of the soul. Those people are called naturally good at remembering who have that ability either completely or mostly by nature, which others have by exercise of the art of memory, just as philosophers have said with regard to the divine intelligence, which knows all things by its very nature. And this kind of talented memory is with regard to its own disposition very well able to be compartmentalized and divided up exhaustively [*condividi*], in that it is itself a trainable power.

2. To the next I respond, because the word *memoria* is used in place of *reminiscencia*, likewise the condition beneficial for it accords more with what is beneficial for mental ingenuity than for the memorative power, in the way that reminiscence uses rational method and ingenuity in proceeding from one or many definite principles accepted in advance. And so this objection is not tenable.

3. I reply to the next, especially as it is most often the case that *memoria* is used in place of *reminiscencia* by Tullius, that since there is no recollection without memory, what is good for memory works also for recollection.

4. Replying to the next, that memory can be thought of in two ways, that is in respect to its objects or the psychological condition [*habitus*] left by these objects, and thus it is true that all memory is generated by inductive reasoning. But ready aptitude for memory-work is observed both in the action of memorizing and in retaining things-to-be-remembered, and

thus remembering is like a certain category of that art which is called the art of remembering, and thus it is generated not so much from inductive reasoning but by the many rules of organization for doing it. There are however these two in general for doing it, that is, an induction on the basis of one's memorial images, and a rule based on an organizational starting-point, from which the memory begins to proceed rationally in its action of remembering. As I said in the question "Concerning recollection" [*De homine*, Q. 41] recollection starts its procedure from a beginning determined by something acquired before or in respect to something forgotten. Whence it is necessary that within the soul there be something out of which it proceeds and something in terms of which it progresses. What it proceeds from is the starting-point, which Tullius calls rules. What it progresses in terms of are images, which are like letters within the soul, as Tullius says.

5. From this appears the solution to the next objection, which is that a rule is not useful in memory work.

6. I reply to the next, that a rule is generated out of the materials of memory on the basis of the things-worth-remembering from among those we acquired earlier, but it aids in the same activity, insofar as in the act of remembering it goes over the very same thing-worth-remembering, and thus nothing prevents memory from engendering something that previously was produced in itself.

As something closely connected to this, let us inquire concerning the rules which Tullius taught, in saying that these are the best, as he himself says, and one of them is accepted as a starting-principle, in terms of which first of all a matter [*res*] worthy-of-remembering moves along in the process of recollection, because, as Boethius says, every particular thing is created or has being in some place. But "place" [*locus*] is construed by Tullius here as that which the soul itself makes for storing-up images, and this also follows because, since reminiscence has no store-house except only the memory, and reminiscence is part of the rational soul, it is necessary that something which exists as part of reason be stored-up in corporeal images. Since however, something which exists as part of reason cannot, by means of its own nature, exist in corporeal images, it is necessary that it exist there in them through likeness and translation and metaphor, as, for example, for "joy" the most similar mental "place" [*locus*] is a cloister garth, and for "feebleness" an infirmary or hospice and for "justice" a courtroom, and so for the rest. And Tullius talks about "backgrounds" in such a way. The image however serves the memory as a likeness appropriate to a sentiment remembered through its separate parts, as afterwards will appear in the examples which Tullius gives.

7. In response to the problem concerning time, it appears of easy solution for, since all things remembered are past in time, time does not serve to classify things-worth-remembering and thus does not lead one more to one thing than to another. But a formal background mainly classifies through this feature, that not everything remembered is in one place, and it affects memory by this means, that it is formally composed [*solemnis*] and spare [*rarus*]. Indeed the mind more firmly latches onto things formally composed and sparely constructed, and likewise such things more strongly are imprinted in it and more strongly affect it.

8. Replying to the next, that a "small-scale" or "curtailed" space is so called by Tullius not literally nor certainly meaning smaller than the image of the things stored, but meaning more that the mind should not be spread excessively by traversing through imaginary spaciousness, like a field or a city; but the "place" is "small-scale" when the soul at once flies swiftly around its corners seizing the images hidden away in them. And through this appears the solution to the following objection because "small-scale" and "complete" are not contradictory, but being "small-scale" more ably restricts the straying of the mind, and "completeness" facilitates the whole matter being remembered.

9. I reply to the next by saying that because a conspicuous background more affects the soul, and although not every memorable thing is formed in a conspicuous place, nonetheless each thing-worth-remembering has to be put away in a likeness having a conspicuous background; so indeed this background-place is mentally grasped, as was said.

10. To that which was objected next, I say that Tullius by means of his examples does define the difference between natural backgrounds and those which are artificial. A cloister garden is a "natural" place, a house or intercolumnar space, on the other hand, is "artificial."

11. To the previous query concerning the rules for places which Tullius taught, I say that there are five, as he says, which especially create the best condition for remembering, and all are construed to prevent confusion in remembering. But confusion is engendered in respect either to the background-place or to the matters located in it or that which by its action makes visible the background and what is in it. And if confusion arises in respect to the matters in the location, then it will be the sort covered by the first rule, because a background, which one frequently makes use of while on one's mental tour [*obambulatio*], heaps up a great many images, and so these images break up in the

soul and do not remain, just as a great number of waves break up in water. If however confusion exists with regard to the background-place only, this is of three kinds, insofar as what affects its relative position. There is certainly the task of distinguishing one location from another, and on this principle the second rule is interpreted. Then, there is its comparableness and proximity to the matter to be remembered, and in this way the third precept is understood. There is next the extent [*spatium*] of the material, in terms of which the closeness or remoteness of one position from another is determined, and as far as this the fourth rule is interpreted.[8] If however the confusion results from the quality which on both sides makes us able to see what's going on, then it is a matter of obscurity or brightness, for something glaring certainly confounds sight and so it escapes from the mind and is not strongly imprinted; something obscure however does not sufficiently present things to view, and so again not much is imprinted by the one imagining. And thus it is clear through analysis in what ways these rules are interpreted.

12. To the next objection the solution appears through what was said earlier, because although reminiscence is situated within the rational soul, nonetheless it subjects itself to memory, and thus they bring together in the backgrounds the things-we-make-images-for [*imaginabilia*].

13. Replying to the next, the reactions [*intentiones*] which memory stores do not exist absolutely apart from the images of particulars, as is demonstrated in the same part of that treatise [*De homine*, Q. 40, a. 1]. And so these reactions are taken in at the same time along with the images, and therefore there is no need to have special rules for them.

14. Replying to the next, that imagination understood as the calculus of things-imaged, according to what the Philosopher says, by definition is slave to memory, because it is called "imagination" from its imitating an object, in that in shaping an object it causes us to have imitated that object, and that is, when by means of this imagining-action we arrive at what we earlier had taken in. The image-making-action however, which more properly is called *vis formalis*, contains the likeness according to what is received from the object into ourselves, and so more characteristically holds it insofar as it is a shape rather than a mental image. Because of this it is called *formalis* by the philosophers.[9]

15. I respond to the next problem, that Tullius did not teach imperfectly; it is necessary that he who learns about "place" should understand it under these different headings. But Tullius wished to say that various people will place for themselves different backgrounds, those indeed

which move them more. For some will place a church, from having turned their minds to churches, others an intercolumnar space, others a cloister garth, others a hospice, because they are affected by these; nonetheless it is necessary that anyone learn his background-place according to these five categories, because otherwise they will not engender memory but the confusion of mind which leads to forgetfulness.

16. Replying finally to the question concerning images for things and for words, that in truth these images convey much to the memory and are as much for the purpose of making the thing intelligible, as they are for producing copies.

    To that however which is tossed up in opposition, I reply that there are many literal matters but by transference a few are used to speak about many matters, and so although literal words make for more accuracy about the thing itself nevertheless the metaphors move the mind more and thus convey more to the memory.

17. Replying to the the next, that what is marvelous [*mirabile*] is more moving than what is ordinary, and so when images of this metaphorical sort are made up out of marvels [*ex miris*] they affect memory more than commonplace literal matters. So indeed early philosophers translated their ideas in poetry, as the Philosopher says [*Metaphysics*, 1.2, 982b, 15–20; cf. 1.3, 983b, 28–32, and Aristotle's quotation of Hesiod at 1.4, describing him as an early philosopher], because a fable, since it is composed out of marvels is more affecting. From this it appears that "from wondering [*ex admirari*] about befores and afters then and now is the beginning of philosophical thinking" [*Metaphysics*, 1.1, 982b, 11–12], because what is wonderful [*mirum*] by its vigorous motion causes questioning, and thence gives rise to investigation and recollection.

18. Replying to a further question concerning the rules for images of things and of words, that metaphors define many things in one, in that there are many likenesses within the one metaphor, and thus they are like letters, but it is true that the literal things themselves are many and confusing.

19. Replying to the next, that what Tullius means by "appropriate images" are ones which define by express and notable likenesses and not ones which are particular for each of one's memory-matters separately.

20. Replying to the next that in his examples Tullius touches on those which strongly move us and not those which are appropriate; those which strongly move us adhere in our mind for a longer time and more quickly occur to us.

21. Replying to the next that Tullius teaches that for study we require that
    every particular [*proprium*] bit of information adhere in our mind and
    indeed that each particular be attached to it by a metaphor, but even so
    such a way of studying will not sufficiently cause us to recollect, in that
    particulars of our education are excessively numerous and one effaces
    another. And therefore the art of remembering is executed by means of
    a few rules for backgrounds and images. Through this appears indeed
    the solution to the whole objection, and that which Tullius presents
    contrary to it clearly is to be conceded.

Appendix C

THOMAS BRADWARDINE: "ON ACQUIRING A TRAINED MEMORY"[1]

For a trained memory, two things are necessary, that is, stable locations and also images for the material. The locations are like tablets on which we write, the images like the letters written on them. Moreover, the locations are permanent and fixed, whereas the images are at one moment inked on like letters and at another erased. The background places must be made before the images, and so they should be treated first. With regard to these background places, six matters should be distinguished, that is, size, shape, nature, number, order, and intervening distance. Each place should be moderate in size, that is, as great as one's visual power can comprehend in a single look, such as a little garden or the space of a small room. Indeed memory is most powerfully affected by sensory impression, and especially by vision; therefore something appears to your memory just as it ordinarily appears to your vision.

The shape of a background should be like that of a rectangle. Concerning its nature, four things should be kept in mind: to wit, that the places should not be made so dark that they cannot be recovered easily or quickly from memory, nor made overly bright, for then they will interfere with the perception of the inscribed images. Secondly, your backgrounds should not be made in a crowded place, such as a church, the market, and so forth, because the images of the things crowding such places, which would occur in a crowd in your memory, may block other images of things that you intend to place there. So images should be put into regions deserted by men and empty. Thirdly, you need to know that it is very useful if your places are real rather than only imagined or made up, for real places one can frequently inspect, and thus through repetition mentally confirm and secure their appearance. But one can work with places of one's own imagining, if one chooses.

Fourthly, it is useful that contrasting backgrounds be formed (a principle that can also be demonstrated in connection with the number of the backgrounds). And so the first place might be like land unused and

361

empty; the second like a green garden; the third like land having hay strewn [over it] or produce as at harvest time; the fourth as having stubble after the harvest has been gathered; the fifth like black ground after the stubble has been completely burned. Then make for yourself another five places higher up, if you want, such as a large, high couch; then a cupboard; then a table; then a tomb; then an altar. Then if you want to climb higher through another five places, first place the roof of a house made of wood, second of thatch, third of stone, fourth of red tile, and fifth of lead. Then if perhaps you want another five, the floors of the upper-storey, the first as though of earth, the second as though paved in green stone, the third paved with tile, the fourth spread with grasses or straw, and the fifth furnished with carpets or cloths. These four sets of five suffice for the placement of all the things to be remembered – or perhaps ten of them or somewhat fewer, unless a man should want to work unheard of wonders.

It is particularly essential that your places have a continuous and straightforward order, so that your memory may find with dispatch all the inscribed images in their places easily, in forward order or backwards. As for the interval of the backgrounds, two things should be decided, that is, its size and its nature. Let it be a moderate amount, which differentiates the places suitably; its nature, however, should be vacant, an empty void.

On the part of the person remembering, to the extent that he fully surveys his locations, three things are usefully attended to, that is, a distinct and secure holding in memory of these places, which is achieved by frequently inspecting them, or at least thinking about them. Secondly, one should know at once, without having to calculate it, whatever number any of the places may have (in the whole order). Thirdly, when one must use one of the locations for a memory task, one should imagine oneself positioned at an optimal distance from it, and from there one should view that single place.

These precepts should suffice us in regard to the places; now let us go on to the images, about which there are four considerations: size, nature, order, and number. Their size should be moderate, as was said above regarding the backgrounds. But their nature should be wondrous and intense, because such things are impressed in memory more deeply and are better retained. However such things are for the most part not moderate but extreme, as something greatly beautiful or ugly, joyous or sad, worthy of respect or derision, a thing of great dignity or vileness, or maybe a person who has been injured with an enormous open wound flowing with a remarkable river of blood, or in some other way made ugly, having strange clothing and every bizarre embellishment, the color also very brilliant and intense, such as vivid, fiery red, and the whole color strongly altering its appearance. The whole image also should have some other quality such as movement, that thus it may be commended to memory more effectively than through tranquility or repose.

The ordering of images should be done in this way. First, for a subject matter that you want to remember, fashion for yourself an image of the size and nature just described, which you should place in the front of the first location. And if you can, make for the image you have fashioned a right hand and a left hand; and place the second image to the right of the first, so that with its right hand the image of the first matter holds, drags, or strikes the second image, or does something of this nature to it, or, oppositely, the second behaves in such a way to the first, so that their activity will be, as it were, a fastening together of their order in the series. And this method should be observed among all the images added in their turn in the same location. So, if you can, position the third as though riding around the second or doing something else around it, and to the third join the fourth, if you can; and on the left-hand side of the image attach the fifth, and to the fifth the sixth, if you can.

But if you do not want to gather so many images into one background, place the first image as I have indicated, the second to the right, and the third to the left, and then crossing over into the second background, in it and in any following ones you will place as many images as you like. But you should pay careful attention that the torso of an image comes before any of its other parts in the series of things to be remembered. And a hand or foot and its attachments that is closer to the front of the place comes before a more distant part and its attachments.

As to the number of images, you should note that in one place three images can be placed suitably, or five or seven, but not many more, lest a superfluous multitude of them should blur their distinctiveness. With respect to the images, moreover, two things are helpful for the person remembering. First he should not make up his images for himself too speedily, but taking sufficient time he should impress every part of it by concentrating profoundly and steadily. The second thing is that he should with equal diligence commit to his memory not just the image itself, but also its order in relation to what immediately precedes and follows it, so that as he may wish he may recollect everything easily, going forwards or backwards.

But one achieves recollection in two ways: in an easy way, that is only by the subject matter [i.e., *memoria rerum*]; in another difficult way, that is by the very words [i.e., *memoria verborum*]. You need to have this two-fold art of remembering. First, I will treat memory for the subject matter. Things to be remembered are of two sorts, some sensory and some abstract. Of the sensory things, some are visual and some not. Of those visible some are overly large, some overly small, and others are average. I will speak in the first place about those that are average.

Suppose that someone must memorize the twelve signs of the Zodiac, that is the Ram, the Bull, etc. So he might, if he wished to, make for himself in the front of the first location a very white ram standing up and rearing on his hind feet, with golden horns. And he might put a very red bull to the right of the ram, kicking the ram with his rear feet; standing erect, the ram with his right foot might kick the bull in his large and super-swollen testicles, causing a copious effusion of blood. And by means of the testicles one will recall that it is a bull, not a castrated ox or a cow.

In a similar manner, a woman may be placed before the bull as though laboring in birth, and in her uterus as if ripped open from her breast may be figured coming forth two most beautiful twins, playing with a horrible, intensely red crab, which holds captive the hand of one of the little ones and thus compels him to weeping and to such signs, the remaining child wondering yet nonetheless touching the crab in a childish way. Or the two twins might be placed there being born not of a woman but from the bull in a miraculous manner, so that the principle of economy of material may be observed. To the left of the ram a dreadful lion might be placed, who with open mouth and rearing on its legs attacks a virgin, beautifully adorned, tearing her garments. With its left foot the ram might inflict a wound to the lion's head. The virgin might hold in her right hand the scales, for which might be fashioned a balance-beam of silver with a cord of red silk, and weights of gold; on her left may be placed a scorpion horribly stinging her so that her whole arm is swollen; and also she could strive to balance the scorpion in the aforementioned scales.

Then in the front of the second location might be placed an archer with suitable equipment, holding an astounding bow fully extended, in which might be an even more astounding arrow, and he could strive to shoot arrows at a goat standing erect slightly farther back in the same location, remarkably hairy and shaggy, having a weird-looking horn and a golden, luxuriant beard. And he might hold in his right foot a most remarkable jug full of water, in his left foot unusual fishes, onto which he pours crystal-clear water from the water-vessel. And if it should be necessary to remember more things, one may place their images in the following locations in a similar manner. Having done so, the person remembering is able to recite these things in whatever order he may want, forwards or backwards.

If however you wish to recall things of extreme size, whether large or small, of the sort such as the world, an army, a city, a millet seed, an iota, or the smallest of worms, one makes average-sized images of them, perhaps of the sort that are depicted by manuscript decorators, or one can acquire the memory of such things through another thing that is opposite, similar, or in some other way analogous to them. If you want to recall sensory phenomena that are not visible, as for instance sweetness, place someone feeding himself with something sweet, like sugar, honey, milk, or happily tasting something else of this sort. But for bitterness, place someone feeding himself on something bitter and immediately vomiting it up in a disgusting manner. For foulness, place something smelling bad in the presence of someone else, who pinches his nostrils with one hand as though against the bad odor and with the other gestures contemptuously towards this thing. For things entirely abstract, such as are God, an angel, infinite space, and such matters, place an image as the painters make it, or you can secure its recollection by means of something that is contrary to it, similar, or analogous in another manner.

So much for memory-of-things, now memory-of-words demands its time; concerning which I propose this particular algorithm for remembering syllables presented to you, in order to commit a syllable artificially to memory. The person remembering should have for himself a ready-made image for any syllable always stored away by rote, which whenever he wants he is able freely to use, and he may do this in the following manner. He should consider and write down for himself the whole possible number of syllables, and should also consider the same number of easily visualizable things known to him, whose names in Latin or in his own language or in another language known readily to him may start with those syllables or coincide completely with them, which is even more useful. And because among diverse languages, and even among different speakers of the same language, frequently several different names for various things are used, and occur more readily to memory, it is not really possible to give specific advice that applies to all people. But each should take pains to adapt this advice for himself to his own way of remembering, and most prudently conserve his version without variation.

When, therefore, one wants to remember a certain syllable, one should place something whose name begins with that syllable, or may be totally coincident with it, in a particular location, as I demonstrated earlier, by means of which one may immediately recall the name of that thing whose first syllable it epitomizes, and one should work in a similar way with regard to any syllable. But whoever might wish to shorten this labor should do this using only the one language known to him whose instant recollection seems the most useful to him; though in any single language there are fewer syllables than all those which might be needed. But certainly, the principle behind this task of remembering syllables is extremely economical and very useful.

Every syllable is a vowel or is composed of a vowel and a consonant. For the five vowels make for yourself five images in this way: for 'A' make for yourself gold [*aurum*], a communion wafer [*azimus*], or Adam covering his naked genitals with leaves, or something else of this sort whose name begins with "A," or nouns of the same sort you might know in a language other than Latin that occurs to you more readily. For "E" place Eve, naked, hiding her prominent breasts with her long hair and her genitals with green leaves, or something else of the sort I indicated earlier. And for the remaining vowels you should make for yourself other images in a similar fashion.

For the shortest composite syllables, that is, ones constituted only from one vowel and a consonant, you should work in exactly the same way. So, for the "ab" syllable, imagine to yourself an abbot you know, dressed appropriately; for "ba" a crossbowman [*balisterius*] with a belt and the rest of the things that encumber him, and do the same thing for other syllables of this kind. If however you should wish to work more economically, let an upright abbot indicate "ab" to you, an upsidedown one "ba"; an upright crossbowman "ba," an upsidedown one "ab." And thus you can use only one image for pairs of syllables, according to its various positions.

For syllables of three letters, with two consonants at the extremes and a vowel in the middle, the technique is the same in every respect. So, for the syllable "bar" you might fashion Bartholomew, flayed; for "rab," Rahab the infamous harlot, or for this pair of syllables you might place only just the one or the other according to one or the other likeness (upsidedown or rightside-up), as I told you.

If however you wish to make the technique still easier, fashion for yourself images for all the consonants, or at least for those which occur often before or after syllables of two letters; of this sort are "r" and "l" and those like them – there are a few exceptions. For the "l" consonant, therefore, if you are English, you can imagine for yourself an elbow, which accords with that consonant both in name and shape. So, if you want to recall "bal," you might locate your image of the "ba" syllable, an upside-down abbot (or an upright crossbowman, if you'd rather use that) and he might hold the elbow by its middle sideways in his mouth (or in the other image it might be attached to the uppermost part of the crossbowman) in order to signify that the "ba" syllable must be followed by an "l." And the "lab" syllable may be signified by the same image in the contrary situation. But for remembering the syllable "bla," position a crossbowman holding his elbow in his hand at his waist, if you like, or under his belt, which should signify to you that "l" ought to be in the middle of the "ba" syllable, and in this way it will figure for you the syllable "bla." There are other syllables of more letters, and for them a skillful person can readily enough extend this technique. Let these examples, however, suffice for the technique of remembering syllables.

Now let us consider how to remember words, concerning which a technique of the same sort may be proposed for the remembering of a word that has been put to you to be artificially recalled. This technique follows from the previous one. All words have syllables in serial order, and so when a memory of the syllables has been secured, a memory of the words is also achieved. Another method however is shorter and handier, although more prone to cause error. This involves mixing memory for the things themselves with memory of their names. If you should need to recall a certain word which signifies to you a thing for which you can make an image, place for yourself the image of that thing itself instead of using the special memory technique for a word. And if an image of a thing known to you should present itself which would also serve for a word you propose to remember, if possible take the name of something which, in two or more of its syllables, sounds like that word. If however you cannot find one, at least find something whose name in its first syllable sounds like your word, which you can do according to the previous technique; and I should add further that, just as it is a fact that one can recollect a whole from its parts and the reverse, and sometimes the whole of a word from just its beginning, and one of two things that are alike by means of the other, or one of two contraries from the other, so also one can recall anything from something added onto it or in any way pertaining to it.

These matters having thus been disposed of, it remains to speak about how to remember sentences; the following algorithm may be proposed in order to recite any sentence presented to you. This one follows from the second one [concerning remembering words]. "Benedictus Dominus qui per regem Anglie Berwicum fortissimum et totam Scotiam subiugavit." ["Blessed be the Lord who by means of the English king subjugated most mighty Berwick and all Scotland."] For the first phrase, if you know someone named Benedict, or even Saint Benedict the Abbot, place him at the front of the first location; and if you have a lord you know, whom you just call "dominus," not using his actual name, place him injured in the face, pulled by the hair, mangled, or, in some way touched by the right hand of Benedict; or you might place there Saint Dominic or Emperor Domitian or someone known to you called by a similar name. For the third word and the fourth, which are monosyllables, proceed according to the technique for syllables; or for "qui" place a very white cow with very large very red teats, erect upon her hind legs, whose right front foot Benedict might hold with his left hand as though dancing with her. For indeed, a cow is called "qui" [*ky*] in northern English. In addition the cow, in a strange manner, holds in her left front foot a partridge [*perdix*], which will give the word "per" to your memory.

Then in the foreground of the second location you should bring together a king, resplendent in a crown and the other tokens of royal majesty, or if you should know well any king, or someone called or surnamed King, or one who in some game was a king, place him there, and let him hold in his right hand an eel [*anguilla*] wriggling about greatly, which will give you "England" [*Anglia*].[2] And in his left hand he might hold a bear by the tail or foot, which in English would signify the two first syllables of the word "Berwicum," and consequently the whole. From the other side of the bear might come mighty Samson or a lion, and strike that bear; and so this will figure to you "most mighty" [*fortissimum*]. Finally, the rest of this example could be fashioned in a third location in a similar manner, by placing there someone named Thomas, with his right hand subduing like a beast either a Scot or someone so named or surnamed, or someone whom you know to have campaigned vigorously in Scotland; and placing in his left hand an impressive yoke. This technique is for remembering material presented audibly, but certainly for remembering visual matter, such as recalling written things, one may make use of a similar method.

Now my pen must turn to remembering numbers. So, for "one" you might form a unicorn; for "two," Moses with his two horns, perhaps, or the two tablets; for "three," a tripod, or the Trinity as it is usually painted in churches; for "four," one of Ezekiel's creatures having four faces; for "five," Christ crucified with his five wounds; for "six," an angel with six wings; for "seven," the Lamb which has seven horns or eyes; for "eight" [*octo*], the emperor Octovian; for "nine," an angel clothed in a very white garment having nine very red transverse stripes, three above, three below, and three in the middle, which may signify to you the nine orders of angels, or this: a man with his thumb cut off, binding his wound with the other hand – for then indeed only nine digits will remain; for "ten," may be placed a zero or the Greek letter "chi"; and calculate the rest according to your skill in algorism. But one who has learned the notary art will attain the highest perfection of this craft.

Here ends the treatise of Master Thomas Bradwardine on acquiring a trained memory. Thanks be to God, says R[obert] Emylton.

Notes

PREFACE TO THE SECOND EDITION

1. *Conf.*, X. 8; translated by M. Boulding. Subsequent quotations are from this translation; any alterations are indicated by square brackets.
2. Ricoeur, *Memory, History, Forgetting*, 67.
3. Weinrich, *Lethe*, 10.
4. Bolzoni, *The Gallery of Memory*, 139–145.
5. See the description of this episode in Spence, *The Memory Palace of Matteo Ricci*.
6. On the dating of Hugh of St. Victor's works, see the entry by Roger Baron in the *Dictionnaire de Spiritualité*, s. v. *Hugues de Saint-Victor*. *Didascalicon* is one of Hugh's first works composed after he arrived in Paris in 1127; the *Chronicle* and its preface is somewhat later (around 1130, from internal evidence).

INTRODUCTION

1. Quoted from Miller, "Information and Memory," 44–45.
2. Infeld, *Quest: An Autobiography*, 263, 267, 272, 274–275.
3. "The Life of St. Thomas Aquinas" by Bernardo Gui, and Bartholomew of Capua, "Testimony at the First Canonization Inquiry." Translated by Foster, *Biographical Documents*, 50–51, 37; 107.
4. These sources are available in the *AASS*, March vol. 1, 655–747, in Prümmer, *Fontes vitae*, and in an English translation by Foster, *Biographical Documents*. See Foster's excellent bibliography, x–xii. The relationship between the various accounts is surveyed also by Mandonnet, "Pierre Calo et la légende de S. Thomas."
5. Dondaine, *Les Secrétaires*, esp. 10–25.
6. Dondaine, *Les Secrétaires*, 25.
7. See Foster, *Biographical Documents*, 44–45; Gui, c. 25; Tocco, c. 43.
8. Foster, *Biographical Documents*, 73, note 59.
9. Chenu, *Introduction à St. Thomas*, 245; see also Dondaine, *Les Secrétaires*, 20–22, and plate 37.
10. Foster, *Biographical Documents*, 38; Gui, c. 16; Tocco, c. 31.

11. Foster, *Biographical Documents*, 51; Gui, c. 32.
12. Chenu, *Introduction à St. Thomas*, 248–249.
13. The technique is described by Leclercq, *Love of Learning*, esp. 76–77.
14. Dondaine, *Les Secrétaires*, 19.
15. Foster, *Biographical Documents*, 38 (Gui, c. 16), 51 (Gui, c. 32), and 37 (Gui, c. 15).
16. Gui, c. 15.
17. Dondaine, *Les Secrétaires*, 51; Gui, c. 32; *Fontes vitae*, 89.
18. Dondaine, *Les Secrétaires*, 18. Walz, *San Tommaso d'Aquino*, 167–168, explains Evan the Breton's story as an oblique reference to a practice of leaving notes to a secretary to write up while the author slept; but this is not what the sources say took place. The typical postures of profound concentration and sleep were remarkably similar; see my discussion in Chapter 6.
19. "Epystolas de rebus maximis quaternas dictabat aliis, ipse manu propria quintam scribens." Petrarch, *Rerum memorandarum libri*, II. 2. There does not seem to be a contemporary source for this story, though Cicero flatters Caesar as one who "forgot nothing except his injuries"; "Pro Ligario," xii, 35. The story is told to illustrate Caesar's superior memory in the elder Pliny's *Natural History*, VII, xxv, 92. Petrarch quotes from both of these sources in his own recounting of the story. Cicero's account of the superior memory of his friend, the orator Hortensius, is in *Brutus* 87–88: in his encomium, Cicero emphasizes Hortensius's facility in speaking *sine scripto*, without written notes, an ability always much admired; see my discussion in Chapter 6.
20. *ST*, I, Q. 24, a. 1 resp.
21. Smalley, *Study of the Bible*, 148.
22. Legrand, *Archiloge sophie*, 24 (ed. Beltran, 145): "et pour tant est ce que on l'en estudie mieulx es livres enluminéz pour ce que la difference des couleurs donne souvenance de la difference des lignes, et consequanment de ycelle chose que on l'on veult impectorer. Et de fait les anciens quant ilz vouloient aucune chose recorder et impectorer, ilz mectoient en leurs livres diverses couleurs et diverses figures a celle fin que la diversité et la difference leur donnast meilleur souvenance." See Hajdu, *Das Mnemotechnische Schriftum des Mittelalters*, 114. The English translation is mine.
23. John Wyclif, "De veritate sacrae scripturae," cap. 6 (quoted by Smalley, "The Bible and Eternity," 84): "sed quinto modo sumitur scriptura sacra pro codicibus, vocibus aut aliis artificialibus, que sunt signa memorandi veritatem priorem, quomodo loquitur Augustinus."
24. Hildegard of Bingen (d. 1179) dictated her mystical visions in her own best Latin to a scribe, who took them down; then she had the written version corrected by a priest for any inelegancies. It is apparent from the descriptions of how she worked that she composed first probably in German, then translated that into Latin herself, dictated this version, and then had it finally corrected for solecisms. It is also apparent that she could understand Latin well enough to know whether the priest's corrections fairly represented her meaning. This represents a very different situation from that commonly assumed when moderns use the word "illiterate." See Derolez, "The Genesis

of Hildegard of Bingen's 'Liber divinorum operum.'" On the meaning of the term "illiterate," see also Clanchy, *From Memory to Written Record*, esp. 175–185.

25. The excellent studies by Clanchy, *From Memory to Written Record*, and Stock, *The Implications of Literacy*, are cases in point. Much of the early work on literacy was done in the context of the ancient world: a helpful account, which demonstrates that orality and literacy were complexly mixed even in ancient Greece, is Thomas, *Literacy and Orality in Ancient Greece*, and see also Harris, *Ancient Literacy*.

26. See Stock's fascinating dissection of the fundamentalist aspect of various eleventh-century heresies in his *Implications of Literacy*, 88–240. He does not identify this as fundamentalism, but rather associates it with literacy per se; the conjunction seems to me a bit of a red herring, however, because the determining distinction has to do with views of literature, which can exist among either oral or literate groups.

27. Smalley, "The Bible and Eternity," 89.

28. For example, see Kennedy, *Classical Rhetoric*, 98.

29. Greimas defines cultural values not as absolutes but as cultural and psychological modes, which allow adaptation and changes of behavior; see *On Meaning*, esp. chapter 8, "On the Modalization of Being."

30. These texts are now readily available along with a number of others discussed in this book, in Carruthers and Ziolkowski, eds., *The Medieval Craft of Memory*. My translations of Hugh of St. Victor's *Chronicle* preface, Albertus Magnus's discussion of trained memory in his *De bono*, and Thomas Bradwardine's treatise "On Acquiring an Artificial Memory" (appendices A, B, and C) appear in this edition in the version published in that anthology. I thank the Directors of the University of Pennsylvania Press for permission to use them.

CHAPTER 1

1. The phrase occurs in the beginning of *La vita nuova*, although the intimate connection of memory with writing is evident throughout his work (compare *Paradiso* 17, 91–92, where Cacciaguida tells Dante he shall carry things told to him about the future "scritto nella mente"). For a brief discussion of the memory-as-book metaphor, see Curtius, 326–332, but his whole previous discussion of "The Book of Nature" (chapter 16) is pertinent. E. G. Gardner has an excellent study of Dante on memory and imagination, in which he especially notes that for Dante memory was "mental writing"; "Imagination and Memory in the Psychology of Dante," esp. 280–282.

2. Havelock, *Literate Revolution*, 57. Eisenstein rightly emphasized the cultural effects of the "democratization" of the reading public made possible by numerous, cheap printed materials; *The Printing Press*, esp. vol. 1, 71–159, and *The Printing Revolution*, chapter 4. Good summary discussions of the state of literacy among various medieval laity at various times and in various places

are Parkes, "The Literacy of the Laity," D'Avray, *The Preaching of the Friars*, 29–43, and Clanchy, *Memory to Written Record*, 151–201. The ancient situation is discussed by Thomas, *Literacy and Orality in Ancient Greece*. For the situation in the later Roman period, comprising far more literate societies (by the narrow definition of "book-acquiring public") than any to be found again in Europe until the high Middle Ages, see also Harris, *Ancient Literacy*.

3. Cicero, *Partitiones oratoriae*, 26.

4. Max Black, *Models and Metaphors*, 219–243.

5. 450a 25; translated by Sorabji, *Aristotle on Memory*, 50. Unless otherwise noted, I have used Sorabji's translation of Aristotle's treatise throughout. Hett (LCL) translates: "for the movement produced [by a phantasm] implies some impression of sense movement, just as when men seal with signet rings." The Greek is "katháper hoi sphragizomenoi tois daktylióis" (text ed. Hett, LCL). *Daktyliós* (Liddell and Scott, s.v.) is a "signet-ring," a word used also by Plato in his version of this metaphor; Aristotle's verb is a synonym of the one Plato uses, meaning "to authenticate with a seal" (Liddell and Scott, s.v. σφραγ-ιζω).

6. Sorabji, *Aristotle on Memory*, 5, note 1; Plato uses the image in *Theaetetus*.

7. Sorabji, *Aristotle on Memory*, 5, note 2.

8. Richardson, *Mental Imagery and Human Memory*, contains a helpful review of current experimental work in this field, set within a solid philosophical framework. Two interesting books which attempt definitions of "representation" within the context of verbal and cognitive functions are Malcolm, *Memory and Mind*, and Fodor, *The Language of Thought*.

9. Chaytor makes much of this, *Script to Print*, 6–10. See also Eisenstein, "Clio and Chronos," and the essays in Küchler and Mellon, *Images of Memory*.

10. Albertus Magnus, *Postilla super Isaiam*, 11.6–9 (*Opera omnia*, vol. 19) on Is. 1:1, *quam vidit*: "Auditu enim satis certus non fuit, sed visu certificabatur, sicut dicit Horatius." The lines from Horace are *Ars poetica*, 180–181: "Segnius irritant animos demissa per aurem, / quam quae sunt oculis subiecta fidelibus."

11. Liddell and Scott, s.v. ΕΙΚΩΝ.

12. Jerome, *Commentarii in Hiezechielem* XII, on Ezek.40.4 (CCSL 75, 554, lines 177–182): "nihil enim prodest uidisse et audisse, nisi ea quae uideris et audieris, in memoriae reposueris thesauro; quando autem dicit, *Omnia quae ego ostendam tibi*, intentum facit auditorem, facit et cordis oculis praeparatum, ut memoriter teneat quae sibi ostendenda sunt, *Quia ut omnia ostendantur tibi, adductus es huc*."

13. Guido d'Arezzo, *Epistola de ignoto cantu* (Letter to Brother Michael): "Sicut in omni scriptura xx. et iiii. litteras, ita in omni cantu septem tantum habemus voces"; ed. Gerbert, *Scriptores*, vol. 2, 46. This letter can be dated from internal evidence to 1032.

14. A summary discussion of "mental imagery" as a concept in modern psychology is in Richardson, 4–24; he mentions "dual coding theory," in which pictures and verbal processes are considered to be alternative, independent methods of symbolic representation, and a "common coding theory," in which "a single system of abstract propositional representations" underlies

"all cognitive and mnemonic processes" (6). See also Malcolm's remarks on "The Picture Theory of Memory," 120–164.

15. Augustine, *De natura et origine animae*, IV.vii.9 (CSEL 60, 389, lines 7–19).

16. A version of the diagram is shown in the *New Grove Dictionary* s.v. *Solmization*. An account of it by Karol Berger in terms of mnemotechnical principles is in Carruthers and Ziolkowski, eds., *The Medieval Craft of Memory*. The early twelfth-century chronicler Sigebert of Gembloux wrote of Guido:

> Guido, Aretinus monachus, post omnes pene musicos in Ecclesia claruit, in hoc prioribus praeferendus quod ignotos cantus etiam pueri et puellae facilius discant vel doceantur per ejus regulam quam per vocem magistri, aut per visum [usum] alicujus instrumenti, dummodo sex litteris vel syllabis modulatim appositis ad sex voces, quas sola musica recipit, hisque vocibus per flexuras digitorum laevae manus distinctis per integrum diapason, se oculis et auribus ingerunt intentae et remissae elevationes vel depositiones earumdem vocum. *Liber de scriptoribus ecclesiasticis*, cap. 144. (PL 160, 579C)

Of interest in this account is not only the emphasis upon the eyes' importance to the success of Guido's two schemes, but also the specific mention of girls learning chant. Baddeley, *Psychology of Memory*, 235–254, describes some experiments on the nature of what he calls "auditory memory": these tend to focus on the ability to reproduce and recognize rather than to manipulate and adapt – a clear example of how different modern psychological understanding of "memory" is from medieval *memoria*.

17. Most current psychological experimentation points to the conclusion that the visual is indeed most important for the ability to recollect, whether "visual" includes "pictorial" or not. As Richardson puts it, "stimulus imageability is an excellent predictor of memory performance" (99). As a corollary to this, however, Richardson points out that mere "vividness" in a pictorial mental image is insignificant; what counts is its ability to create "relational organization" in the memory. Memory pictures need to be brought together in a coherent image or "scene" to be useful for accurate recollection; numbers, diagrams, and the alphabet are images with their own built-in organization, of course. For a cogent critique of problems that can arise from using words like "image" and "picture" to talk about what the brain actually contains, see Malcolm, *Memory and Mind*. Malcolm particularly warns against an "isomorphic" notion of "mental image," the idea that the shape of such an image is in some way like the form in which it is received; a version of this notion is assumed in assertions that the structure of thought is changed by the way in which text is presented to the memory; see esp. 143, 244–245.

18. See the first chapter of Baddeley, *Psychology of Memory*, discussing Ebinghaus in particular. A helpful gloss of the various terms used in contemporary neuropsychology for the processes of recollection is Dudai, *Memory from A to Z*.

19. Albertus Magnus, *Commentary on Aristotle's De memoria*, tract. 2, c.1: "[R]eminiscentia nihil aliud est nisi investigatio obliti per memoriam" (Recollection is nothing but the investigation by the memory of what has been forgotten); trans. Ziolkowski. In c. 3 of this same commentary, Albertus

distinguishes iteration from recollection. A succinct statement is the following: "Et ista est differentia in qua reminisci differt ab eo quod est iterato addiscere, cum reminiscentia possit moveri quodam praedictorum modorum in id principium quod est ante quaesitum jam in memoria, sive ex parte rei, sive ex parte consuetudinis. Iterato autem addiscens a talibus non movetur. Cum vero non investigat et movetur per aliquod principium, tunc non recordabitur vel reminiscetur" (This is how recollecting differs from rote learning, since recollection can be set in motion by any of the methods just mentioned, to discover that starting-point in the memory which is before what one now seeks, either through the nature of the subject matter itself or through his customary associations with it. A person learning by rote is not prompted by such things. When one neither investigates nor is cued by some prompting association, then one will not be recalling or recollecting) (my translation [which is certainly looser than my Classics colleagues would quite approve; it should be compared with Ziolkowski's more literal translation]). Albertus's whole commentary, as translated by Ziolkowski, is in Carruthers and Ziolkowski, eds., *The Medieval Craft of Memory*, and most of my quotations are from it. When medieval writers talk about *memoria*, in virtually every context other than when defining distinctions among the "inward wits," they mean *memoria* as trained reminiscence, as in the phrase *ars memoriae*. Simple iterative ability, or rote, is not a significant issue for them; see my further discussion of this matter in chapter 3 below.

20. For a fuller discussion of the derivation and changes in meaning of the English word *rote*, see Chapter 7 below, and *OED* s.v. *rote*. In the late fourteenth century, the word was beginning to acquire the pejorative meaning it now has, but as a secondary meaning.

21. Thomas Aquinas is clearer than is Albertus on this point. In his commentary on Aristotle's *De memoria*, Aquinas states that recollection, even when seeming to reconstruct logically, always proceeds from humanly originated associational habits rather than from anything necessitated by the nature of its object. See my further discussion in Chapter 2.

22. Plato, *Theaetetus*, 191D–E; cf. 194–195; translated by Cornford (*Collected Dialogues*, 897). Cf. the notes on this passage and on sects. 194–195 by McDowell, *Theaetetus*. See also the discussion of Cornford, *Plato's Theory of Knowledge*, 21–22 and 124, who particularly notes that non-sensory objects like thoughts are also said by Plato to be "stamped" upon (or "modelled in") the memory.

23. Liddell and Scott, s.v. εκμαγειον.

24. See the discussion and plate in Roberts and Skeat, *Birth of the Codex*, 111 and Plate I. The *tabulae* they show measure 9.1 × 5.7 cm, or about 3.5 × 2.3 inches. Needless to say, one could not get a great deal of fully formed writing onto one at one time.

25. The text is that of H. N. Fowler (LCL). Liddell and Scott, s.v. σημε-, also note the word was used to gloss Latin *clavis*, and with the adjective γραφε to mean "written characters."

26. Cicero, *De oratore*, II. 86–87. Quotations in this paragraph are all from this passage.
27. Fodor, 191; see also Gombrich, *Meditations on a Hobby-Horse*, 1–11, and Ellis, *Theory of Literature*, esp. 36–45. Richardson's discussion of the philosophical problem is in *Mental Imagery*, 25–42. An important discussion of the ancient meaning of "representation" is McKeon, "Literary Criticism and the Concept of Imitation," especially 155–157 in which McKeon distinguishes, vitally for the subject, between "copy" and "phantasm." More recent and complete is the discussion of imitation and representation by Trimpi, *Muses of One Mind*, especially Part Two.
28. Norman, *Learning and Memory*, 61.
29. Commenting on Aristotle's characterization of the memory "image" in itself, Nussbaum, *De motu animalium*, writes that his calling it both a *theōrēma* and a *phantasma* suggests that he thought its "pictorial" nature to be somewhat metaphorical, for a *theorema* "is most unlikely to be pictorial" (250). Thomas of Moerbeke translates the Greek text (450b 20) as follows: "Secundum quidem se ipsum, speculamen aut fantasma est, in quantum uero alterius, ut ymago et memorabile" (Aquinas, *Sentencia libri . . . De memoria*, cap. III. 112). Thomas Aquinas comments on this that an "image" can be something seen or thought of either in itself ("aliquid in se") or as an image of something else ("fantasma alterius"). Insofar as it is *of* some other thing ("alterius") which we have experienced in the past, it is considered as an image which leads-to (or discovers, heuristically) something other than itself and a starting-point for recollection ("sic consideratur ut ymago in aliud ducens et principium memorandi"; quoted from 115. 184–192). Aristotle himself seems to have believed, as did Plato, that the *eikones* had to be reasonably similar to the original, though the limits of this criterion are decidedly unclear when Plato can write, in the *Timaeus*, that time is an *eikōn* of eternity. Sorabji, 4, note 1, has a valuable discussion of the philosophical uses of the Greek word *eikōn*.
30. In this context, it may be helpful to consider Augustine's remark that, when we speak of things past or of anything not immediately in our presence, "we do not speak of the things themselves, but of images impressed from them on the mind and committed to memory." He claims here that our knowledge of anything, except when we recognize an object immediately before us, is not direct but is only of our memory of it. What we "know," therefore, is a mnemonic likeness (as signs are functional reminders), not the object itself. Remarks like this one should, I think, be considered in discussions of Augustine's much-vexed "Neoplatonism," because they do qualify what might appear from other parts of his work to be an unqualified belief in the Neoplatonic "realism" of memory and all signs. This comment is in *De magistro*; see Matthews, "Augustine on Speaking from Memory."
31. Among the basic ancient discussions are Aristotle, *Rhetoric*, and Cicero's *Orator*, a work better known to the later Middle Ages than any of Plato's several dialogues which comment on the matter. The changing ancient

perception of the relationship of rhetoric and philosophy forms a continuing theme in Trimpi's fine study, *Muses of One Mind*. Bruns, in a discussion of Descartes (*Inventions*, 63–64 esp.), observes that the modern era is characteristically epistemological, "wherein everything is thought to be determined or made intelligible by the workings of the [individual] mind"; ordinary speech is too error-prone and equivocal, too conditioned by the history of its usage to be of use to knowledge, and instead one seeks "a mathematical or systematized speech," which is pure precisely because history, time, and occasion have been purged from it. Such language would also be purged of memory, and recollection rendered useless in favor of a "purified" method.

32. For the development of this definition, see *TLL*, [s.v.] *adaequatio*.

33. Aristotle makes this clear especially in *Nicomachean Ethics*, 2. 6; the "mean" is not an arithmetically or statisically determined quantity but rather the principles of healthful diet or of virtue adapted to individual physiology and circumstances: "By the mean which is relative to ourselves I denote that which is neither too much nor too little, and this is not one and the same for everybody . . . an expert in any field avoids excess and deficiency, and seeks and chooses the mean – that is, not the objective mean but the mean relatively to ourselves" (trans. Wheelwright). The passage is cogently discussed by Trimpi, esp. 267–270. See also Tracy on the physiological foundations of ancient ethical ideas about the "mean" and "decorum." Unlike Trimpi, Tracy does not discuss their applicability to works of art and to the use of words.

34. See *TLL* and the *Dictionary of Medieval Latin from British Sources*, s.v. *adaequatio, adaequate*, and, for classical usage, Lewis and Short, s.v. *adaequo, adaeque, aequatio, aequalis*, and the form from which these concepts seem ultimately to derive, *aequus*, and the adverb *aeque*. The earliest surviving occurrence of *adaequatio* seems to be in Tertullian. The classical Latin adverb *adaeque*, "in like manner," glosses the Greek prepositional phrase "pros to ison," "towards the same." The development of the word in medieval philosophy towards an idea of greater and greater formal (logical) identity can perhaps be seen in the following citations given under *adaequatio* in *TLL*: (1) Grosseteste: "veritas propositionis est adaequatio sermonis et rei"; (2) Duns Scotus: "omnis propria racio intelligendi aliquid objectum per adaequationem representat illud objectum"; (3) Wyclif: "relatio adaequationis signi ad suum signatum, que relacio est 'ipsum esse verum,' cum sit adaequatio vel correspondencia ejus ad suum significatum." Wyclif uses the adverb to mean "fully" in this citation: "sic enim Deus uult, intelligit vel intendit rem esse, sic res est adaequate." One should note that relationship and thus "adjustment" is basic in all these uses, even when it is God who does the "adjusting" (God's "adjustment" results in perfection or completion of being, however). Even a perfectly adjusted "relationship" is not, it seems to me, the same thing as "objectivity" in knowledge, for the latter seeks to exclude from consideration anything but the-thing-in-itself, whereas the former always acknowledges the role of the knower in knowing the object.

35. The action of recollection is characterized as *interruptus* and *diversificatus*: Albertus Magnus, *Commentary on Aristotle's De memoria*, tract. II, cap. I (ed. Borgnet, vol. 9, 107–108).

36. This discussion owes a great deal to Markus, "Augustine on Signs," and Bruns, *Inventions*. See also Markus, "Signs, Communication, and Communities," which clarifies his earlier interpretation of what Augustine said in *De doctrina christiana*.

37. See especially Chenu, *Nature, Man, and Society*; Colish, *The Mirror of Language*; Markus, "Augustine on Signs"; Kenny, "Intellect and Imagination in Aquinas" and *Aquinas on Mind*.

38. Kenny, "Intellect and Imagination in Aquinas." See also Markus, esp. 76–82.

39. Augustine, *De trinitate*; see Markus, "Augustine on Signs." Augustine's use of "word" to refer both to the words humans use and to truth interiorized through grace, Christ the Word, has created a lot of confusion. Discussing the idea of the *verbum qui intus lucet*, Markus has noted that Augustine never did explain how this was related to human language. His analysis amounts, in fact, to "two theories of language," for the "inner word" is not a sign, as speech is, but is "essentially meaningful, and presents to the mind what it means ... [It is] the place of the mind's encounter with the object of its experience" ("res quam videndo intus dicimus," "the thing which by seeing inwardly we speak"); 78, quoting from *De trinitate* 14, 24. See also Markus, "Signs, Communication, and Communities." The inner *verbum* in Augustine seems to have more in common with the *res* spoken of in classical rhetoric and thus in rhetorical discussions of *memoria*; *decorum* and *adaequatio* are concepts which apply to it, as to all *res* when spoken in human discourse. This Augustinian "inner word" should probably be thought of as having a phantom capital letter: the *Verbum* of St. John's gospel; see Nash, *The Light of the Mind*.

40. Bruns, *Inventions*, is very good on this matter, esp. 17–43. It will be clear that Neoplatonism, especially in its most rationalist variety, differs markedly from this "practical" analysis. For a clear and most interesting account of how Neoplatonic rationalism exacerbated the "quarrel" between philosophy and rhetoric, see Trimpi, 200–240, and Bundy, *Imagination*, esp. 131–145.

41. Nussbaum, *De motu animalium*, esp. 241–255.

42. *Regula Benedicti*, Prol.

43. Aristotle, *De memoria*, 452b; see Sorabji's discussion, *Aristotle on Memory*, 18–21. The passage was commented on extensively in the scholastic Middle Ages. Augustine discusses also how the memory perceives time-lapses by a measuring mechanism located in memory-images (see especially his *De musica*, VI. 7–8; cf. *Conf.*, XI, 27). On the sharp differences between Aristotle and Augustine concerning the existence of time as a phenomenon also external to memory, see Janet Coleman, "Late Scholastic Memoria et Reminiscentia," esp. 23–30 and her *Ancient and Medieval Memories*.

44. Cicero, *De oratore*, II, 86. 354: "atque ut locis pro cera, simulacris pro litteris uteremur."

45. Translated and discussed by Yates, *Art of Memory*, 29–31; another English translation is that of Sprague. On the date of the work see Burnyeat, "Dissoi logoi," who underscores the lack of precise evidence for placing it. The text is in H. Diels and W. Kranz, *Fragmente der Vorsokratiker*, #90, vol. II, 416 (section 9 of *Dialexeis*). H. Blum discusses the possible mnemonic usefulness of Roman architectural design and ornamentation, 3–12.

46. John of Salisbury, *Metalogicon*, I, 13. 24–26: "Litterae autem id est figurae primo uocum indices sunt, deinde rerum quas animae per oculorum fenestras opponunt, et frequenter absentium dicta sine uoce loquuntur." This definition is an adaptation of Isidore of Seville, *Etym.* I, 3, 1, but Isidore says letters are themselves "indices rerum"; Clanchy suggests the change is due to John of Salisbury's care in the nominalist–realist controversy (202, note 1).

47. Cicero, *De oratore*, II, 87. 360: "tanquam litteris in cera sic se aiebat imaginibus in eis locis quos haberet quae meminisse vellet perscribere."

48. *Ad Her.* III, 17: "item qui mnemonica didicerunt possunt quod audierunt in locis conlocare et ex his memoriter pronuntiare. Nam loci cerae aut chartae simillimi sunt, imagines litteris, dispositio et conlocatio imaginum scripturae, pronuntiatio lectioni." See Caplan's note (208–209 in LCL edition), and his essay, "Memoria," which contains a good list of occurences of this metaphor in both classical and later writing. Renaissance use of the metaphor is discussed in Camden, "Memory: The Warder of the Brain." On the *Ad Her.* and other ancient systems, see Yates, *The Art of Memory*, and, more recently, Small, *Waxed Tablets of the Mind*.

49. Martianus Capella, *De nuptiis*, trans. Stahl and Johnson, vol. 2, 204. Ed. Dick, p. 269, lines 537–538 (V, 538): "sic quod memoriae mandatur, in locis tanquam in cera paginaque signatur." For an additional possible meaning of the phrase *in pagina*, see Chapter 3 below.

50. "Misericordia et veritas te non deserant; circumda eas gutteri tuo, et describe in tabulis cordis tui." Cf. Jeremiah 17:1: "The sin of Judah is written with a pen of iron, and with the point of a diamond; it is graven upon the table of their heart, and upon the horns of your altars."

51. On the close conceptual relationship of the "topics" of rhetoric, logic, and mnemonics in antiquity, see G. R. Evans, "Two Aspects of *Memoria*," and Sorabji, *Aristotle on Memory*, 26–34. The matter of memorial organization and design has received a great deal of attention from cognitive psychologists recently, particularly those involved in "cognitive science." Norman, *Learning and Memory*, is concerned with "the design of a memory," and notes that artificial memory systems (computers) are designed according to a "locus system," in which one first stores and then retrieves information by an addressing (heuristic) system. Bower ("A Selective Review," 1972), who has done some work on human retrieval schemes, notes that "pegword" systems are "powerful retrieval systems," the pegword acting as a "hook" for information. He has also noted success with various others of the schemes in use since antiquity – architectural locations, alphabetical orders, and hierarchical systems, in which a subset of categories is organized into a supercategory, and

those into still others; this is an efficient way to retrieve large numbers of items. On the success of such grouping or chunking systems, see also G. A. Miller, "Information and Memory." See also Feigenbaum, "Information Processing," and Reitman, "What Does It Take to Remember?" Versions of all these heuristics were also part of ancient and medieval memory design. What I find most interesting about the similarities between ancient and modern memory design is not that the ancients anticipated modern artificial memories (for they did not) but that human beings, faced with the problem of designing a memory (whether their own or a machine's), should repeat many of the same solutions.

52. Cicero, *Topica*, I, 5: "Therefore, since I had no books with me, I wrote up what I could remember on the voyage and sent it to you." This convention remained an authorial trope even in the late Middle Ages, suggesting its continued relevance to compositional technique; see the discussion of William of Ockham's *Dialogus* in Chapter 5 below. On the composition of Cicero's work, see Reinhardt's edition.

53. Cicero, *Topica*, I, 7–8: "Ut igitur earum rerum quae absconditae sunt demonstrato et notato loco facilis inventio est, sic, cum pervestigare argumentum aliquod volumus, locos nosse debemus; sic enim appellatae ab Aristotele sunt eae quasi sedes, e quibus argumenta promuntur. Itaque licet definire locum esse argumenti sedem, argumentum autem rationum quae rei dubiae faciat fidem." The *Topica*, along with a work by Boethius of similar title, was influential in the teaching of dialectic during most of the Middle Ages. See also *Inst. orat.*, V. x. 20–22. The best discussion of the ancient understanding of *topos* is still that of Cope, *An Introduction to Aristotle's Rhetoric*, 124–133.

54. Sorabji's discussion of the text is *Aristotle on Memory*, 31–34, and in his notes to this passage.

55. Aristotle, *De memoria*, 452a, 17; trans. Sorabji, *Aristotle on Memory*, 56.

56. Liddell and Scott, s.v. αναγιγνωσκω, and Lewis and Short, s.v. *lego, legere*.

57. Plato, *Phaedrus*, 275D; *Collected Dialogues*, 521.

58. Plato, *Phaedrus*, 276D; *Collected Dialogues*, 522.

59. Jacques Derrida has written at length on this passage from *Phaedrus*, from a viewpoint similar to the one I have taken here, though with his own particular objectives; see "Plato's Pharmacy."

60. Plato, *Phaedrus*, 274D–275A; *Collected Dialogues*, 520.

61. The suggestion that this story reflects a survival of oral traditional cultures was made by Notopoulos, "Mnemosyne in Oral Literature," and is often repeated in the writing of proponents of the "oral survivals" model for both ancient and medieval culture – see, e.g., Ong, *Orality and Literacy*, 59–61. But it is clear in the passage itself that Socrates is disparaging mere book-learning which pretends to substitute for learned truth. Socrates' own approval of writing books for the proper reasons is evident as well. See Curtius, 304, and Hackforth, *Plato's Phaedrus*, 162–164. Hackforth notes that Plato seems to have invented this story himself for this particular context, 157, note 2. Yates, *The Art of Memory*, 53, notes that this myth was used in the Renaissance to

justify extreme Neoplatonist schemes for an ultimately powerful "artificial memory"; on the admiration of the Greeks for Egyptian memories, see Havelock, 10. Egypt was "the mother of the arts" in one tradition passed along by Hugh of St. Victor; in another, the Hebrews are said to have taught the arts to the Egyptians; see Hugh of St. Victor, *Didascalicon*, III, 2. Martianus Capella says Thoth discovered all the arts; he was perhaps remembering the *Phaedrus*. See J. Taylor's note to his translation of *Didascalicon*, 210–211, note 3.

62. Clanchy, *From Memory to Written Record*, 7. But later Clanchy seems to contradict this position when he writes that "Literacy is unique among technologies in penetrating and structuring the intellect itself" (149). I agree with Clanchy's earlier statement, which seems also to accord with the findings of Scribner and Cole, *Psychology of Literacy*. This book reports a study of the introduction of script into a traditionally oral culture, and concludes that no general effects upon abilities to memorize or to think rational thoughts resulted. On the complex nature of literacies within oral cultures, see especially Finnegan, *Orality and Literacy*.

63. The variety of devices that have been used to model the working of memory and recollection is the subject of Draaisma, *Metaphors of Memory*. It makes a telling history, as each successive technological innovation is pressed into service in turn, from tablets to telephones to computers. What underlies all the changes which Draaisma presents is the tenacious belief that human recollection employs technique – it is not a whim of chance.

64. Ong, *Ramus*, 108.

65. This is one of the underlying themes of Clanchy, *From Memory to Written Record*. Rhetorical *memoria*, to which the *artes memorativae* most often refer, is concerned with invention (composition) – see Carruthers, *The Craft of Thought*. On the complex understanding of memory and history, especially in regard to questions of authenticity and "what really happened," see especially Janet Coleman, *Ancient and Medieval Memories*, and Geary, *Phantoms of Remembrance*.

66. Cassiodorus, *Institutiones*, II. 3. 17: "[M]irabile plane genus operis, – in unum potuisse colligi quicquid mobilitas ac varietas humanae mentis in sensibus exquirendis per diversas causas poterat invenire, – conclusit liberum ac voluntarium intellectum; nam quocumque se verterit, quascumque cogitationes intraverit, in aliquid eorum, quae praedicta sunt, necesse est ut humanum cadat ingenium." On the filing-cabinet metaphor, see (among many others) A. Clark, *Being There*, 67–69. I am indebted to John Sutton for introducing me to Clark's work on "connectionism"; what Cassiodorus describes in this text is in keeping with the extended-mind hypothesis of mental "scaffolding," exploited for the craft of thinking.

67. Jerome, *Epistula*, LX, 10: "Lectione quoque assidua et meditatione diuturna pectus suum bibliothecam fecerat Christi." The letter is Jerome's eulogy for the young priest, Nepotianus, written to his father, Heliodorus; Jerome honors Nepotianus' ability immediately to identify any and all citations, as

Jerome had witnessed at his own table. An ability we still honor in those who have mastered it, however unusual it may be, it is no magic trick but a refined, trained scholar's art.

68. Chaucer, *The Canterbury Tales*, I. 3115 and X. 26.

69. Liddell and Scott, s.v. θησαύρ-ισμα. In *Phaedrus* 276D, the phrase translated by Cornford as "collecting a store of refreshment for his own memory," which Plato uses when discussing what writing books is good for, is in Greek "heauto te hypomnēmata ["memoranda"] thēsaurizomenos" (ed. Fowler, LCL). It is noteworthy that for Plato his book is a store-house for his memory, its extension, not its substitute.

70. "Lay not up for yourselves treasures upon earth . . . But lay up for yourselves treasures in heaven."

71. "And when they had opened their treasures, they presented unto him gifts; gold, and frankincense, and myrrh."

72. Lewis and Short, s.v. Citations are to Columella, *De re rustica*, 8. 8. 1, 8. 8. 3, and 8. 9. 3; at 8. 14. 9 the pens for geese are also called *cellae*.

73. *Georgics* 4, 163–164 (Loeb translation). Virgil repeats this language in *Aeneid*, I, 432–433, where he likens the builders of Carthage to bees who "strain their cells to bursting with sweet nectar"; "cum liquentia mella / stipant et dulci distendant nectare cellas."

74. *De re rustica* 8. 9. 3; see also, for *loculamenta*, 8. 8. 3. Columella uses *loculamenta* for a bee-hive in II. 5. 2.

75. Martial, *Epigrams*, I, 117 (Loeb edition): "De primo dabit alterove nido / rasum pumice purpuraque cultum / denaris tibi quinque Martialem." Cf. *Epigrams* 7, 17: "Hos nido licet inseras vel imo / septem quos tibi misimus libellos" ("you may place the seven little books I send you even in your lowest pigeon-hole"). Seneca uses *loculamenta* in *De tranquillitate animi*, when, inveighing against those who collect books for show, he complains that such idlers have "bookcases built up as high as the ceiling" ("tecto tenus exstructa loculamenta"). These Latin words for Roman library fittings are discussed, together with citations, by J. W. Clark, *The Care of Books*, 32–36.

76. Virgil, *Georgics*, 4, 250. Medievalists and classicists spell the poet's name differently, classicists call him Vergil and medievalists Virgil (the usual medieval spelling). In order to avoid a possibly confusing double entry, I have adopted the medieval spelling throughout.

77. J. W. Clark, *The Care of Books*, 35.

78. *OED*, s.v. *pigeon-hole* (sb.), 7e.

79. Liddell and Scott, s.v. περιτερα-. Aristotle distinguishes between this bird and other species.

80. Plato, *Theaetetus*, trans. Cornford, 197d–199.

81. Philosophy speaks of the "pennas etiam tuae mentis quibus se in altum tollere possit adfiguram." On the development of the winged soul from this image in Boethius, see Pierre Courcelle, *La Consolation de Philosophie dans la tradition littéraire*, 197–199 and plates 119–124. As used by Boethius the image is Neoplatonic, as the soul, remembering, rises to its forgotten glory and perfection.

Courcelle stresses this connection, but the evidence does not, I think, support a conclusion that the notion is exclusively Neoplatonic.

82. J. E. Sandys, ed., *Aristotle's Constitution of Athens*, 186. J. W. Clark calls attention to this note (*The Care of Books*, 34, note 1) as suggesting that a pigeon-hole arrangement was used also by the Greeks for filing written material.

83. Cf. Hugh of St. Victor, *De archa Noe*, II. ii. 11 (CCCM 176, 35), who says the dove sent forth is mind/spirit: "Quod autem per auem anima significetur."

84. J. W. Clark, *The Care of Books*, 35; cf. the portrait of Ezra editing the Old Testament in the seventh-century *Codex Amiatinus*, discussed by W. Cahn, *Romanesque Bible Illuminations*, 33–34, and shown in plate 12. The deep wall-recesses that sometimes housed the wooden *armaria* of the later Middle Ages can be seen in a number of places. J. W. Clark, *The Care of Books*, has several pictures of them; see esp. Figures 20 and 25. Two good illustrations of self-standing wooden *armaria* are in Figures 27 and 28.

85. *Inst. orat.*, I, x. 7: "muta animalia mellis illum inimitabilem humanae rationi saporem vario florum ac sucorum genere perficiunt; nos mirabimur, si oratio, qua nihil praestantius homini dedit providentia, pluribus artibus egeat." Early Christian instances are discussed in relation to Biblical and other ancient antecedents by W. Telfer, "Bees in Clement of Alexandria"; see also the article by Jean Châtillon in the *Dictionnaire de Spiritualité*, s.v. *dulcedo, dulcedo Dei*.

86. The authorship of *Philobiblon* is discussed by E. C. Thomas, xliii–xlv.

87. Richard de Bury, *Philobiblon*, Prologue, 7.

88. This is Thomas's reading; earlier editors, however, read "per spirituales vias oculorum," a reading that makes better sense in terms of scholastic perception psychology; see my discussion of Thomas Aquinas's description of ocular perception in Chapter 2.

89. Richard de Bury, *Philobiblon*, I, 25 (ed. Thomas, 13, trans. 163, my alterations). It is interesting to notice the sexual metaphor that Bury uses to describe how reading acts upon the memorial store during meditation. Sexual metaphors for how reading acts upon the reader are common in clerical writing on the subject from the thirteenth century on, most familiarly in Jean de Meun. The trope is monastic in origin, centering on the *thalamus* or bedchamber of the *Song of Songs*; see *The Craft of Thought*, esp. 171–220.

90. Hrabanus Maurus, *De universo*, 22. 1 (PL III, c. 594C): "favus Scriptura est divina melle spiritualis sapientiae repleta."

91. Richard de Bury, *Philobiblon*, cap. 8, 136 (ed. Thomas, 76): "apes argumentosae fabricantes jugiter cellas mellis."

92. Hugh of St. Victor, *Didascalicon*, I, i.

93. [Gregory the Great], *Dialogues*, I. 4.10.122–125 (SC 260): "Super semetipsum sacros codices in pelliciis sacculis missos dextro laeuoque latere portabat, et quocunque peruenisset, scripturarum aperiebat fontem et rigabat prata mentium." The evidence for authorship of the *Dialogi* has been thoroughly reviewed by F. Clark, *The Pseudo-Gregorian Dialogues*, working in part from the comprehensive studies of the text by its Benedictine editor, de Vogüé.

Clark's work has shifted the balance of proof against the traditional attribution to the sixth-century pope, in favor of an author who was likely a monk working in the Roman curia in the later seventh century. The authorship is of no consequence to the point I am making here but it is nonetheless of general interest.

94. Lewis and Short, Du Cange, s.v. *scrinium*; see also the *Ox. Lat. Dict.* The *scrinium memoriae* may have been "of historical records"; cf. Lewis and Short, s.v. *memoria*. In a letter to a newly installed bishop, Gregory the Great gives instructions to make an inventory and put it in his church *scrinium*: "De quibus etiam secundum rerum inuentarii paginam desusceptum te facere uolumus, et in scrinium ecclesiae nostrae transmittere"; "concerning which, according to the memorandum of the inventory, we want you to make a receipt and transmit it to the archive of our church." Gregory had from the previous bishop such a receipt, which he sent "in scrinio nostro"; *Registrum epistularum*, III, 49.

95. Spenser, *The Faerie Queene*, II. ix. 56.

96. DuCange, s.v. *scrinium*.

97. Paulinus of Nola, *Epistula* 32. 16 (CSEL 29, 291. 10–11): "If a desire should take hold for meditating on the holy law / Stopping here one may pore over the sacred books."

98. Beeson, *Isidorstudien*, 162–163. The oldest manuscripts state that these and several other such verses which he composed were written on Isidore's book-presses ("scripta sunt in armaria sua"); J. W. Clark, *The Care of Books*, 47, note 2.

99. Beeson, *Isidorstudien*, 157; "Sunt hic plura sacra, sunt mundialia plura; / Ex his si qua placent carmina, tolle, lege. / Prata vides plena spinis et copia floris; / Si non vis spinas sumere, sume rosas." Note the allusion to the words of the voice to Augustine, "Tolle, lege." For a demonstration of Isidore's intimate familiarity with Augustine's *Confessions*, see Courcelle, *Les Confessions . . . dans la tradition littéraire*, esp. 235–253.

100. Alcuin, *Epistula* 22: "O quam dulcis vita fuit, dum sedebamus quieti inter sapientis scrinias, inter librorum copias, inter venerandos Patrum sensus" (PL 100, 175C). Here Alcuin calls the books themselves *scrinia*. Compare Richard de Bury, *Philobiblon*, ch. 7, 107, who calls the books that burned with the Alexandrine Library, *scrinia veritatis*.

101. F. Henry, *The Book of Kells*, 150.

102. See, for example, the exhibition catalogues, *Medieval Manuscripts and Jewelled Book-Covers*, of the John Rylands Library, Manchester, 1910 and 1938.

103. *MED* cites legislation that includes makers of *males* with other leatherworkers.

104. *OED*, s.v. *mail*, etymological note.

105. *Bevis of Hamptoun* 1297; *First Shepherds' Play* (*Prima Pastorum*), 224–225.

106. *Havelock*, 48; Chaucer, *The Canterbury Tales*, A. 694; *Piers Plowman*, B, V. 230; Layamon, *Brut*, 1769–1770. See also the Towneley "Magnus Herodes," where the king's soldiers boast they have "mych gold in oure malys," 453.

107. *MED*, s.v. *male* (a), cited from a fifteenth-century cookery-book.
108. On this portrait, painted on an oak panel and dated 1532, see Rowlands, *Holbein*, 82–83 and plate 74. The strongbox rests against the wall behind the merchant's arm.
109. *The Tale of Beryn*, lines 701–702.
110. On Chaucer's probable acquaintance with an architectural mnemonic (though not necessarily with the text of the *Ad Herennium*), see my "Italy, *Ars Memorativa*, and Fame's House" and "The Poet as Master Builder."
111. *Didascalicon*, I, 2; cf. John of Salisbury, *Metalogicon*, I, 11.
112. See Riché, *Education and Culture*, 461. Aldhelm, who died in 709, composed a sort of riddle on the subject of his books, which is called "De arca libraria"; the text is in Thompson, *Medieval Library*, 114–115.
113. Cited by Riché, *Education and Culture*, 461, note 99, from *Regulae magistri*, 17: "Simul etiam arcam cum diversis codicibus membranis et chartis monastherii."
114. John of Salisbury, *Metalogicon*, I, 11. 49–50: "Memoria uero, quasi mentis arca, firmaque et fidelis custodia perceptorum."
115. "Tollite librum istum, et possite eum in latere arcae foederis Domini Dei vestra."
116. This famous manuscript, which was brought to the Loire valley in the general exodus of books from Italy during the later seventh and eighth centuries, was first at Fleury and then, from the ninth century, in Tours, whence it was stolen in the mid nineteenth century, sold to Lord Ashburnham, and then recovered by the Bibliothèque nationale de France by the end of the century (its alternative name, the "Tours Pentateuch," acknowledges its long residence in that city). The book's making, provenance, and subsequent history is discussed most recently by D. Verkerk, *The Ashburnham Pentateuch*. The manuscript is also discussed by Cahn, *Romanesque Bible Illumination*, 26–29. Part of the evidence for placing the manuscript's making in Rome lies in the four legs on the closed chest: similar iconography occured in fifth-century mural paintings in the basilica of San Paolo fuor le mure in Rome (Verkerk, 165). Her arguments have not everywhere been accepted, and other scholars continue to believe, because of different affinities both textual and pictorial, that the manuscript is probably Spanish, perhaps with a North African connection. The date of late sixth to early seventh century has more general acceptance. Showing Noah's Ark as a boat became standard only later: see Unger, *The Art of Medieval Technology*, 39–40.
117. Smalley, *Study of the Bible*, 5, quotes Philo. A full analysis of architectural metaphors in Biblical exegesis is in de Lubac, *Exégèse médiévale*, 4. 41–60. Authority for this idea may be found in texts like Proverbs 24:3–4: "Through wisdom is an house builded; and by understanding it is established: And by knowledge shall the chambers be filled with all precious and pleasant riches." I discuss the architecture model, fundamental in monastic meditation practice, at length in *The Craft of Thought*.
118. Gregory the Great, *Moralia in Job*, epistula ad Leandrum 3. 109–114: "Nam primum quidem fundamenta historiae ponimus; deinde per significationem

typicam in arcem fidei fabricam mentis erigimus; ad extremum quoque per moralitatis gratiam, quasi superducto aedificium colore uestimus."

119. Du Cange, s.v. *mens*. Hugh says in *De archa Noe* that the *mens* holds time (Bk. II. i. 8–12). Dante's use of *mente* can sometimes be synonymous with *memoria* (for example *Inferno* 2, 7–9). Chaucer says of the dying Arcite: "For he was yet in memorie and alyve," in a context where we would use the word "conscious" (*Canterbury Tales*, I. 2698).

120. The various titles given to this work are listed in Goy, *Die Überlieferung der Werke Hugos von St. Viktor*, 212: these are only a few of the variants. In his edition for the CCSL, Sicard calls it simply *De archa Noe*, and the work formerly titled "De Arca Noe mystica" he has retitled *Libellus de formatione arche*. Sicard also commented extensively on the textual relationships of the two works, concluding that they indeed belong together; see also his *Diagrammes médiévaux*. The treatise *De archa Noe* was translated into English (from the edition in PL 176) by "a Religious of C.S.M.V.," *Hugh of St. Victor: Selected Spiritual Writings*. I will discuss *Libellus* in Chapter 7.

121. Jerome, *Commentarii in Hiezechielem*, esp. Books 12–14.

122. Hugh of St. Victor, *De archa Noe*, I. iii. 35–37 (CCCM 176, 10): "Huius uero spiritualis edificii exemplar tibi dabo archam Noe, quam foris uidebit oculus tuus, ut ad eius similitudinem intus fabricetur animus tuus."

123. Hugh of St. Victor, *De archa Noe*, I. iii. 236–238 (CCCM 176, 17): "quam cotidie sapientia edificat in cordibus nostris ex iugi legis Dei meditatione."

124. Jerome, *Commentarii in Hiezechielem* xii, on Ez. 40:4; CCSL 75 (554. 178).

125. Jerome, *Commentarii in Hiezechielem* i, on Ez. 3:5; CCSL 75 (32. 850–854): "Principia lectionis et simplicis historiae, esus uoluminis est; quando uero assidua meditatione in memoriae thesauro librum Domini condiderimus, impletur spiritaliter uenter noster et saturantur uiscera ut habeamus, cum apostolo Paulo, uiscera misericordiae."

126. Hugh of St. Victor, *De archa Noe*, II. i. 10–15 (CCCM 176, 33): "ita etiam in mente nostra preterita, presentia, et futura per cogitationem simul subsistunt. Si ergo per studium meditationis assidue cor nostrum inhabitare ceperimus, iam quodammodo temporales esse desistimus et quasi mortui mundo facti intus cum Deo uiuimus."

127. Hugh of St. Victor, *De archa Noe*, II. i. 42–43 (CCCM 176, 34): "Hec est archa, quam edificare debes."

128. Hugh of St. Victor, *De archa Noe*, IV. ix. 132–140 (CCCM 176, 115–116): "Hec archa similis est apothece omnium deliciarum uarietate referte. Nichil in ea quesieris quod non inuenias. Et cum unum inueneris, multa tibi patefacta uidebis. Ibi uniuersa opera restaurationis nostre a principio mundi usque ad finem plenissime continentur, et status uniuersalis Ecclesie figuratur. Ibi historia rerum gestarum texitur, ibi mysteria sacramentorum inueniuntur, ibi dispositi sunt gradus affectuum, cogitationum, meditationum, contemplationum, bonorum operum, uirtutum et premiorum."

129. Du Cange, s.v. *apotheca, apothecarii*. At least by the thirteenth century, the word seems sometimes to have meant specifically drugs and medicines

(s.v. *apothecaria*). In great houses in France, the "dessert chef" seems to have been called *apothecarius* (s.v. *apothecarii*, 4). It is worth recalling that sugars were relatively scarce and often considered to have healing properties.

CHAPTER 2

1. G. R. Evans, "Two Aspects of *Memoria*," 263. I discuss this matter at greater length in Chapter 4.
2. Wolfson's essay is both philosophical and philological in nature, tracing the usage of the Latin terms and how they translate Greek and Arabic (and Hebrew, where appropriate). Wolfson's essay should be read in conjunction with Bundy, *Theory of Imagination*, whose pioneering and deservedly influential study it corrects in some important aspects. A useful overview of Arabic-medieval medical doctrine is Harvey, *The Inward Wits*. Minnis briefly surveyed the function of *vis imaginativa* in "Langland's Ymaginatyf and Late Medieval Theories of the Imagination" – his essay begins to provide a corrective to overly stringent interpretations of medieval faculty psychology, though like many characterizations of what medieval people thought about imagination, it suffers from being too narrowly focused both in topic and in sources considered. See also the translated commentaries on Aristotle's *De memoria et reminiscentia* by Albertus Magnus and by Thomas Aquinas in Carruthers and Ziolkowski, eds., *The Medieval Craft of Memory*.
3. Wolfson, 115.
4. These doctrines are well reviewed in the *Dictionnaire de Spiritualité*, s.v. *sens intérieur*, and see also Rahner, "The Doctrine of the Spiritual Senses" and "The 'Spiritual Senses' according to Origen."
5. See Richard Rorty's comments in *Philosophy and the Mirror of Nature*, esp. 3–13.
6. See Matson, "Why Isn't the Mind–Body Problem Ancient?" 93.
7. Aristotle, *De memoria*, 451b 10ff. Though the actual role of the brain in sensory experience and memory was accepted generally, an additional role for the heart as the organ both of memory and of sensation remained. An excellent account of ancient teaching on the psychology of memory is in Coleman, *Ancient and Medieval Memories*. On the later medieval emphasis on the heart in literature, see especially Jager, *The Book of the Heart*. References to Aristotle's *De memoria et reminiscentia* are by Bekker number (I will use the short title *De memoria* from here on). Except where otherwise noted, I have used Sorabji's translation throughout.
8. Aristotle talks about the heart as the seat of perception in *Parts of Animals*, 666a 14ff., and *Generation of Animals*, 781a 20ff. What he says in *De memoria* about the processing of memory-images, however, might be interpreted as qualifying these other statements. On Aristotle's psychology, see the essays in A. O. Rorty, ed., *Aristotle's De anima*.
9. Wolfson, "The Internal Senses," esp. 69–74; see also Harvey, *Inward Wits*, 4–8. Early medicine and the contributions of the Alexandrine anatomists (third century BC) are discussed in standard histories; a place to begin is Vegetti,

"Hellenistic Medicine." On medieval medicine and medical practice more generally, see Siraisi, *Medieval and Early Renaissance Medicine*. Several early drawings of the brain, including the one from CUL MS. Gg 1.1 reproduced herein as figure 3, can be found in Clarke and Dewhurst, *Illustrated History of Brain Function*.

10. Varro, *De lingua latina*, VI, 46 (LCL, vol. 1, 214–215).

11. Bosworth-Toller, *An Anglo-Saxon Dictionary*, s.v. *heorte*.

12. See Chapter 1 above, note 124.

13. Rorty discusses how the "mind–body problem" was created in the Renaissance: *Philosophy and the Mirror of Nature*, esp. 39–69. See also the first chapters of Chalmers, *The Conscious Mind*. The classic exploration of the problem by Nagle, "What is it Like to be a Bat?," is an exceptionally succinct and well-crafted contribution that deserves more attention from literary historians and critics concerned with issues of subjectivity.

14. Aristotle, *De anima*, II, 1; cited by Matson, "Mind–Body Problem," 97.

15. Both quotations from Matson, "Mind–Body Problem," 96–97; the whole essay analyzes the intellectual matrix of ancient discussions of soul and body. An analysis strongly linking ancient psychology, sensation and memory, ethical behavior, and political life is that of Tracy, *Physiological Theory and the Doctrine of the Mean*, who concludes that for Aristotle, and also Plato, the essential model for understanding is physiological, based upon notions of health in the organism. Tracy's analysis has been corrected and nuanced by Martha Nussbaum, especially with respect to Aristotle's understanding of the so-called "practical syllogism" in ethical judgment; see her *De motu animalium*, 165–220, and *The Therapy of Desire*, 48–101. See also Cooper, *Reason and Emotion*, who particularly analyzes Aristotle's ethical and political ideas in terms of his views on judgment, persuasion, and "civic friendship."

16. Sorabji, *Aristotle on Memory*, 16. "Affection" and "emotion" are both words that must be understood physiologically – they affect and move the body. Nussbaum discusses the fact that for Aristotle emotion and judgment both can also be described in physiological terms, though they are not limited to such terms; Nussbaum, *De motu animalium*, 146–158.

17. Either the weight itself on perceptual organs or the excessive fluidity which Aristotle associated with dwarfism, or both, hinders the persistence of images and makes it difficult for the motion set up by a sensory impression in a human receiver to stop and be "fixed" as a memory-image; see Sorabji, *Aristotle on Memory*, 114.

18. Sarton, II-II, 893–900, gives Arnaldus's bibliography and the printed editions of his work; Arnaldus is discussed by Thorndike, *History of Magic and Experimental Science*, vol. 2, 841–861. More recently, see the edition by Garcia-Ballester, McVaugh *et al.* of Arnaldus's complete medical works, still in progress.

19. Arnaldus, *Opera omnia*, (Basle, 1585), in which see esp. *Aphorismorum*, cols. 243–244, and "De bonitate memorie," cols. 837–838; the latter appears to be a recension of the advice in *Aphorismorum*, together with some recipes for

memory enhancement "praised by the authorities," "laudata ab autoribus." The *Aphorismi de gradibus*, which appeared as vol. 2 (1975) of the complete edition of Arnaldus's medical works, is an important work on mixture, complexion, and "degrees," but has little to say about memory.

20. "Supervitet coitum superfluum et carnes facilis digestionis," "One especially should avoid unnecessary intercourse and easily digested meats"; Matheolus Perusinus, *De augenda memoriae* (Rome, [1494] iv.r.; I used the copy in the Newberry Library, Chicago). Advice against drunkenness is also given by Alcuin in his dialogue on rhetoric (ninth century); undoubtedly, some of these prescriptions were passed along orally, and some are based on continuing observation. It is well to remind ourselves that Avicenna's work is compendious; he is an originator in the pre-modern sense, not in our own.

21. That is, "gaudium temperatum et honesta delectio" (*Aphorismorum*, col. 244D); the likening of feeding memory to feeding the stomach is most fully expressed by Geoffrey of Vinsauf, but the memory–stomach metaphor is pervasive; it lies behind the standard monastic (and patristic) metaphor of *meditatio* as "rumination"; see Chapter 5, below.

22. *Guy de Chauliac*, 617, 620, and 627. Pepper is also of fourth-degree hotness, and so would presumably not be good for memory, although it is rarely mentioned as a specific prohibition.

23. Matheolus, *De augenda memoriae*, 4.v.: "Corpus teneatur mundum a super-fluitatibus vnde quottidie ventris beneficium et si non naturale fiat artificiale."

24. Arnaldus, *Aphorismorum*, col. 244E.

25. Arnaldus, *Aphorismorum*, col. 244: "Solicitudo et visorum seu auditorum frequens recordatio, memoriam corroborat et confirmat."

26. See Wolfson, "The Internal Senses," 120–122.

27. Aristotle, *De memoria*, 450a 10–15; Sorabji, *Aristotle on Memory*, 49; Wolfson, "The Internal Senses," 74–76.

28. Aristotle, *De memoria*, 449b 30. Nussbaum comments that it is not clear what sort of image Aristotle thought one utilized for concepts like "goodness" or "truth": *De motu animalium*, 266–267. Thomas Aquinas says that intellect itself retains "knowledge-forms" (it is *conservativa specierum*), concepts, and other things composed for thinking; see Kenny, *Aquinas on Mind*, 41–57, who explains what Aquinas meant by *species* and the relation of this concept to his distinctive psychology of an "agent intellect." Though this is a crucial difference in certain contexts (it is a major difference between Aristotle and Neoplatonism, and important as well in Christian descriptions of how an individual soul can be immortal), for the purpose of my discussion of memory in this chapter it would only be confusing to emphasize it.

29. That is, "centrum omnium sensuum et a qua derivantur rami et cui reddunt sensus, et ipsa est vere quae sentit"; Avicenna, *Liber de anima*, IV. 1; p. 5, lines 57–59.

30. Aristotle, *De anima*, III, ii, 425b 12ff. Aristotle, and indeed the whole classical—medieval tradition, did not distinguish between sound-as-heard and as vibration of air; for them, sound was sound and wasn't pertinent to the human

mind unless some abstracting process was involved. As Matson points out, this is one reason why they had no mind–body *problem*.

31. I realize that the concept of "raw feels" is a spin-off of the mind–body problem, and so on the historical grounds I argued earlier I shouldn't even introduce the language here; but I hope I will be forgiven. On "raw feels," see R. Rorty, *Philosophy and the Mirror of Nature*, esp. 24, 88–98. See also Nagle, "What is it Like to be a Bat?"

32. Harvey summarizes al-Razi's account (*c.* 900), 9–13, which in turn depended largely upon Galen. Four ventricles are described, a pair in front and two behind them, one following the other. *Imaginatio* is located in the front pair, *cogitatio* in the middle one, and *memoria* in the last one. The concept of vital spirits within the material body – one might think of these as the body's energy – is found throughout ancient and medieval psychology. They were carried and channeled by hollow vessels, the *nervi*, and were active also in the various ventricles of the brain, but exactly what they were composed of was a matter of dispute. The nature of the vital spirits was a critical concern for Descartes, but less fraught in earlier medical thought; see esp. Jacquart, "Medical Scholasticism," and Vegetti, "Between Knowledge and Practice." Sutton, *Philosophy and Memory Traces*, provides an account of Descartes's ideas about vital spirits that helps clarify his departures from previous thought.

33. Avicenna, *Liber de anima*, IV, i (ed. Van Riet, 6. 66–68): "Formam enim sensibilem retinet illa quae vocatur formalis et imaginatio, et non discernit illam ullo modo."

34. Wolfson, "The Internal Senses," 92.

35. Aristotle, *De anima*, III, xi, 434a 9–10.

36. Wolfson, "The Internal Senses," 86–95.

37. Wolfson, "The Internal Senses," 118–119.

38. Janet Coleman has some acute remarks on the importance of *intentio* and memory in "Late Scholastic Memoria." See the articles on *episodic* and *semantic* memory in Dudai, *Memory from A to Z*: these clarify importantly how modern analysis of memory has changed so radically from the ancient that it is difficult (though necessary) for historians even to use the same lexicon. See also Dudai and Carruthers, "The Janus Face of Mnemosyne."

39. This crucial, much-cited passage, is also found in Aristotle, *Posterior Analytics*, II, xix (100a).

40. As is apparent from Tracy, the notion of "embodiment" is elementary in Aristotle, and Aquinas rejects any modification of this idea in the area of how human beings know, specifically the implications in Avicenna and Averroës that direct knowledge of abstractions is possible. See Kenny, "Intellect and Imagination in Aquinas," and *Aquinas on Mind*, 89–99.

41. Thomas Aquinas, *In De anima commentarium*, Lectio 13 on Book III, par. 792. I quote the translation by Kenelm Foster; the Latin text is that of the Marietti edition (Turin, 1949).

42. Sorabji, *Aristotle on Memory*, 14–17; the image, from Aristotle's *De anima*, is commented on by Thomas Aquinas in par. 26 of Lectio 2 on Book I.
43. Thomas Aquinas, *In De anima*, Lectio 14 on Book II, par. 417.
44. Thomas Aquinas, *In De anima*, Lectio 1 on Book III, par. 570–574.
45. Thomas Aquinas, *In De anima*, Lectio 14 on Book II, par. 418.
46. Thomas Aquinas, *In De anima*, Lectio 14 on Book II, par. 417.
47. Thomas Aquinas, *In De anima*, Lectio 14 on Book II, par. 416.
48. Thomas Aquinas, *In De anima*, Lectio 14 on Book II, par. 406–414.
49. Thomas Aquinas, *In De anima*, Lectio 24 on Book II, par. 553–4.
50. Thomas Aquinas, *In De anima*, Lectio 24 on Book II, par. 552. The nature of Aristotelian "hylemorphism," that is, the idea I have been describing that perception occurs by causing physical changes in the organ that make it "like" what it perceives, is analyzed by Tracy, who sees it as a consequence of Aristotle's idea that the body is a balanced compound of the four elements, animated by a soul. These elements and their associated qualities (heat, cold, moisture, dryness) occur in paired opposites, which react when contact between them is established. "If the objective quality is strong enough, the qualitative change which it sets up in the medium evokes a corresponding change in the sense organ, i. e. the organ responds in the direction of that quality in proportion to its intensity. In so doing, the organ becomes *like* the objective quality" (Tracy, 207). But Burnyeat disagrees strongly with this interpretation, and argues that for Aristotle "spiritual" change does not in fact entail material change in the organ. See his analysis of Aquinas's commentary (arguing that Aquinas understood Aristotle well on this point), "Aquinas on 'Spiritual Change' in Perception." See also Nussbaum's discussion of hyle-morphism and Aristotle's concept of *pneuma*, 146–164. Thomas Aquinas, like Galen, located the *sensus communis* in the first ventricle of the brain. He also seems to make a sharper distinction than Aristotle does, between a sense like touch, which is directly affected by its object, and sight, whose "likeness" is "spiritual," in the way I am attempting to describe. For Thomas, sight is "like" its object as the imprint of a seal in wax is "like" the sealing-ring, an image which links the product of sight directly to the nature of the memorial phantasm. Clearly, the analogies between the external and inner "eyes" were far-reaching in Thomas's thought. See also Kenny, *Aquinas on Mind*, 88–117, on sensations, phantasms, and human knowledge of universals and particulars.
51. Thomas Aquinas, *In De anima*, Lectio 6 on Book III, par. 669.
52. Thomas Aquinas, *In De anima*, Lectio 13 on Book III, par. 792.
53. Quoted from Averroës, *Epitome of the Parva naturalia*, II, i; trans. Blumberg, 30.
54. For analysis of Aristotle's account, see Sorabji, *Aristotle on Memory*, 14–17, and Burnyeat, "Aquinas on 'Spiritual Change.'" An English translation of Aquinas's commentary on Aristotle's *De memoria* is in Carruthers and Ziolkowski, eds., *The Medieval Craft of Memory*, 153–188; see also the trans-lation of Albertus Magnus's commentary on the same text, *The Medieval Craft of Memory*, 118–152.

55. Thomas Aquinas, *In De anima*, Lectio 2 on Book I, pars. 19–20; see also *ST* Ia, Q.76, art. 1.
56. Thomas Aquinas, *In De anima*, Lectio 12 on Book III, par. 783.
57. Thomas Aquinas, *In De anima*, Lectio 12 on Book III, par. 782.
58. Sorabji, *Aristotle on Memory*, 17.
59. Thomas Aquinas, *In De anima*, Lectio 12 on Book III, par. 776.
60. Thomas Aquinas, *In De anima*, Lectio 12 on Book III, par. 773.
61. *ST* Ia, Q. 85, art. 1, obj. 4.
62. *ST* Ia, Q. 75, art. 5; also Q. 76 *passim*, but esp. arts. 1 and 3.
63. See *Paradiso*, 29, 76–81.
64. Gardner, "Imagination and Memory," esp. 280–282. The quotation is from 282. This passage has received some comment from Mazzotta, who sees the "failure" of Dante's memory as part of a conscious deconstructionist enterprise in the poem (*Dante: Poet of the Desert*, 260–267). Insofar as Dante's term "failure" is understood by modern interpreters to carry a negative *moral* connotation, it seems to me a wrong emphasis, and somewhat perverse, to label as a *moral* fault what is the intrinsic limitation of a biological mechanism (memory). See the comments of Freccero on "The Final Image" in his *Dante: the Poetics of Conversion*, 245–257.
65. *ST* Ia, Q. 77, art. 8.
66. *ST* Ia, Q. 79, art. 6, resp. obj. 2.
67. Sorabji discusses the difference very clearly, *Aristotle on Memory*, 11–12. Aristotle's discussions of the matter in both "On Divination in Dreams" and "On Dreams" are relevant.
68. Aristotle calls them "the movements of the senses when one is asleep"; *On Dreams*, 462a, 15–30. Averroës says that sleep is the "sinking of [the] common, perceptive faculty into the interior of the body"; *Epitome*, II, ii (trans. Blumberg, 33).
69. Avicenna, *Liber de anima*, IV, ii: "haec est propria prophetia virtutis imaginativae" (Avi. Lat., vol. 2, 19, line 61).
70. Avicenna, *Liber de anima*, IV, ii (Avi. Lat., vol. 2, 19–20, lines 68–70): "aliquando est ab intellectibus et aliquando est a divinationibus et aliquando est ex versibus, et fit hoc secundum aptitudinem et usum et mores."
71. Avicenna, *Liber de anima*, IV, ii (vol. 2, 20, lines 71–75): "quae adiuvant animam plerumque incognitae et plerumque sunt sicuti apparitiones subitae, quae non sunt residentes ita ut rememorari queant nisi eis succurrerit anima cum retentione appetita quia, quod potius agit anima, hoc est scilicet retinere imaginationem circa genus dissimile ab eo in quo erat."
72. Quotations in this paragraph are all from Averroës, *Epitome*, II, i, p. 28. These comments also occur in Albertus Magnus's commentary on Aristotle's *De memoria*, evidence of how widely spread this tradition was in teaching. Albertus follows his discussion of the image-forming ability's role in reminiscence by adducing the advice for making vivid memory-images found in the *Rhetorica ad Herennium*.
73. Sacks, *The Man Who Mistook His Wife for a Hat*, discusses the phenomenon now restrictively called "reminiscence"; he suggests that to restrict the term as

modern neuropsychology has may be an error of an overly mechanistic science, and comments that memories may be more like scripts or scores than algorithms; see 138–142, and the interesting case-study that is the title-essay of the book. Certainly both Aristotelean analysis and practical mnemonics recognized that recollection proceeds via a network of associations, the "richer" the better and the more secure.

74. *De memoria*, 449a 9ff.; Sorabji, *Aristotle on Memory*, 47–48.
75. Averroës, *Epitome*, II, i, p. 30. Aristotle stresses the emotional accompaniment of recollections in *De memoria*, 453a. This concept is close to what modern neuropsychologists recognize as episodic memory, which they sharply distinguish from semantic memory, a distinction not recognized in pre-modern psychology. Ancient and medieval students were taught to embed semantic details in episodic recollections as a mnemonic strengthener: see below.
76. Petrarch, *Rerum memorandarum libri*, II ("De memoria"), 13: "Vidisse semel vel audisse sat est, nunquam obliviscitur, nec res modo meminit, sed verba tempusque et locum ubi quid primum accepit. Sepe totos dies aut longas noctes colloquendo transegimus: audiendi namque cupidior nemo est; post annos vero suborta earundem rerum mentione, siquid forte plus minusve aut aliter dixissem, submissa voce confestim admonebat hoc me aut illud verbum immutare; mirantique et unde hoc nosset percunctanti non solum tempus quo id ex me audivisset, sed sub cuius ilicis umbraculo, ad cuius undam fluminis, in cuius maris litore, cuius montis in vertice – longinquas enim secum oras circuivi – me singula recognoscente memorabat."
77. *Inst. orat.*, XI. ii. 20: "Ita, quamlibet multa sint, quorum meminisse oporteat, fiunt singula conexa quodam choro, nec errant coniungentes prioribus consequentia solo ediscendi labore." This is a corrupted passage, though its general sense is clear: see Russell's note in his translation for the Loeb series, and the variant readings recorded in Winterbottom's Oxford Classical Texts edition. I have quoted Butler's old Loeb translation in this one instance; otherwise I have cited Russell's throughout.
78. *Inst. orat.*, V. x. 20–22.
79. Aristotle, *De memoria*, 451b 18ff.; in this one instance I have used the Loeb translation by W. S. Hett.
80. Aristotle, *De memoria*, 451b 29; see Sorabji's discussion of how recollecting (the mnemonic search) differs from remembering (the object of memory), *Aristotle on Memory*, 41–48.
81. Sorabji, *Aristotle on Memory*, 31.
82. Sorabji, *Aristotle on Memory*, 29–30. I discuss this important passage in the *Topics* at greater length in connection with the ancient method of using numbers as a recollective scheme; see Chapter 3.
83. *ST* Ia, Q. 78, a. 4, resp.
84. Quintilian comments that "we must, of course, invent" for ourselves the mnemonic images we use, unlike our background places, which may be real or fictive; *Inst. orat.*, XI. ii. 22.

85. Thomas Aquinas, commenting on this passage, defines the associative nature of recollection clearly: *In De memoria et reminiscentia commentarium* (hereafter cited as *In de memoria comm.*), Lectio VI, 379–383.
86. *ST* Ia, Q. 93, art. 7, ad 3. See also Q79, art. 7, ad 1.
87. *ST* II–I, Q. 50, art. 5, resp.
88. See especially Rand, *Cicero in the Courtroom*, 25–33, 103–112; in the matter of the cardinal virtues, Rand observes, Cicero was Thomas Aquinas's "constant companion and one of his respected authorities" (32).
89. Douay translation of Vulgate "sobrietatem enim et prudentia docet, et justitiam et virtutem, quibus utilis nihil est in vita hominibus."
90. Rand, *Courtroom*, 26–28; see also Loeb note on *De inventione*. The word *phronēsis*, sometimes also translated as *prudentia*, has a complex medieval history. Aristotle often links it with *doxa* or "judgment," but says that while animals also have *phronēsis*, only humans have *doxa*. Sorabji translates the word as "intelligence" (77–78), and the word clearly describes a sub-conceptual and sub-judgmental ability rather like what we mean when we say that our dog is "intelligent." But in the Middle Ages, *intelligentia* appears as one of the parts of prudence (along with memory and providence), following the definition of prudence given in *De inventione*, II, 160. This use of *intelligentia* is rendered as *phronēsis* by Albertus Magnus.
91. *Ad Her.* III, 2, 3.
92. Cicero, *De inventione*, II, 53, 160.
93. *ST* I–II, Q. 57, art. 3, ad 3.
94. *ST* I–II, Q. 57, art. 1, concl.
95. *ST* I–II, Q. 57, art. 4, resp.
96. *ST* I–II, Q. 57, art. 5, resp.
97. *ST* II–II, Q. 48, resp.
98. Brunetto Latini, *Livres dou trésor*, II, 59, lines 2–5 (ed. Carmody, 233–234). On prudence as containing all teaching, see II, 56–58; for example, "Mais ki bien consire la verité, il trovera que prudence est le fondement des unes et des autres; car sans sens et sans sapience ne poroit nus bien vivre, ne a Dieu ne au monde"; II, 56, lines 4–5 (230–231). The "Seneque" referred to is probably Martin of Braga (sixth century), Pseudo-Seneca, whose brief moral treatise, "Formula honestae vitae," was widely known during the Middle Ages: "Si prudens est animus tuus, tribus temporibus dispensetur. Praesentia ordina, futura praevide, praeterita recordare" (PL 72, 24C). I am indebted to Paul Gehl for this citation.
99. *ST* II–II, Q. 49, art. 1. Notice how Thomas Aquinas has brought together the texts on *ethos/ēthos* from the *Ethics* and *Metaphysics*.
100. See Tredennick's translation of the Greek text in the Loeb edition.
101. My quotation is from Rand, *Cicero in the Courtroom*, 61–62. A list of Thomas Aquinas's pagan sources is on 17–18 of this same book.
102. *ST* II–II, Q. 49, art. 1, obj. 2.
103. Tracy, *Physiological Theory and the Doctrine of the Mean*, 251. The influence of Aristotle's ethical theory, embedded as it is in emotional life as well as reason,

upon later antique and early Christian ethical philosophy is discussed by
Sorabji, *Emotion and Peace of Mind*. See particularly the discussion of
Seneca in this study, and in Nussbaum, *The Therapy of Desire*.

104. See the first sentence of Moerbeke's text, in Thomas Aquinas, *In De memoria comm.*

105. Aristotle, *De memoria*, 450a 25–30.

106. Aristotle, *De memoria*, 449b 24; for discussion see Sorabji, *Aristotle on Memory*, 1–2, for other uses of *hexis* and *pathos* in this sense in *De memoria*.

107. Sorabji, *Aristotle on Memory*, 1.

108. Aristotle, *Nicomachean Ethics*, 1103a 17ff.

109. Aristotle, *Nicomachean Ethics*, 1104a 27–30. In his commentary on this passage (*In decem libros ethicorum commentarium*, Bk. II, Lectio I, 247), Thomas Aquinas notes the pun in Greek *ethos*, and concludes, "Just so for us the word *moral* signifies something formed from habit, whenever it pertains to vice or virtue" (sicut etiam apud nos nomen moralis significat quandoque consuetudinem, quandoque autem id quod pertinet ad vitium vel virtutem). *Consuetudo* is defined as synonymous with *mos*, "custom." Furthermore, *virtus moralis* is described as "in parte appetitiva," and as such is based in something more like what we would call "physiological" than what we might call "rational" or even "mental."

110. Tracy, *Physiological Theory and the Doctrine of the Mean*, 229–231; the quotation is from 230. Tracy's analysis has been criticized as overly materialist by Hutchinson, "Doctrines of the Mean," 19, note 4, who notes that Galen made the same error in interpreting doctrines of Plato and Aristotle.

111. Aristotle, *Posterior Analytics*, II, 19; 100a 1–5.

112. Quintilian discusses *hexis* as *firma facilitas* in *Inst. orat.*, X, esp. parts i. 1 and i. 59, but all of X. i is pertinent to the matter of attaining mastery of oratory, as are his remarks on imitation in Book X. ii.

113. Norman, *Learning and Memory*, 74–80.

114. Thomas Aquinas, *In de memoria comm.*, Lectio I, 298.

115. Tracy, *Physiological Theory and the Doctrine of the Mean*, 229.

116. Averroës II, 1, p. 30; cf. also Aristotle, *De memoria*, 453a 15–30.

117. *ST* I–II, Q. 56, art. 5, obj. 3.

118. The *Rhetorica ad Herennium* and the *De inventione* were copied together during the Middle Ages; the *Ad Herennium* was not proven to be by someone other than Cicero until the sixteenth century, but there were suspicions earlier. On the dissemination of these texts and their traditions during the Middle Ages, see Cox and Ward, *The Rhetoric of Cicero*. Though classicists refer to the author of *Ad Herennium* as "auctor ad Herennium" or as "pseudo-Cicero," for the sake of brevity in my discussion I have adopted for him his early English name of Tullius. I use Tullius only for this author, however; Cicero gets credit for those things that are genuinely his. Calboli has made a case for identifying Cornificius as the anonymous author, but this has not won wide acceptance, and Tullius was the usual name assigned to the author by medieval scholars.

119. Albertus Magnus, *De bono*, II, art. 2: "Dicimus ergo cum Tullio, quod memoria pertinentium ad vitam et iustitiam duplex est, scilicet naturalis et artificialis. Naturalis est, quae ex bonitate ingenii deveniendo in prius scitum vel factum facile memoratur. Artificialis autem est, quae fit dispositione locorum et imaginum, et sicut in omnibus ars et virtus sunt naturae perfectionis, ita et hic. Naturalis enim perficitur per artificialem." Translated in Appendix B, below.

120. *ST* I–II, Q. 58, art. I.

121. Hugh of St. Victor, *De institutione novitiorum* (PL 176, 933B): "Figura namque quae in sigillo foris eminet, impressione cerae introrsum signata apparet, et quae in sigillo intrinsecus sculpta ostenditur, in cera exterius figurata demonstratur. Quod ergo aliud in isto nobis innuitur, nisi quia nos qui per exemplum bonorum, quasi per quoddam sigillum optime exsculptum reformari cupimus, quaedam in eis sublimia et quasi eminentia, quaedam vero abjecta et quasi depressa operum vestigia invenimus?" (translated by Bynum, *Jesus as Mother*, 97–98). According to his biographer, Anselm of Canterbury used this same trope for moral education, alluding as well to the ancient belief that the wax of memory is softer and better able to take impressions in youth than in age (Southern, *Eadmer's Life of Anselm*, 20–21).

122. Its composition is discussed by Caplan in the Loeb edition, vii–xxxiv, and see also the introduction by G. Calboli to his edition of the work (1993), and that of G. Achard to his.

123. A good, if somewhat controversial, treatment of this relationship is Enders, *Rhetoric and the Origins of Medieval Drama*; see as well her *The Medieval Theater of Cruelty*.

124. I have discussed this in some detail, with sources cited, in my chapter on "Memoria" in Cox and Ward, *The Rhetoric of Cicero*.

125. Cicero says he will not insult his audience by describing the scheme in detail: "ne *in re nota et pervulgata* multus et insolens sim" (my emphasis).

126. This idea was familiar to the early Middle Ages through Boethius, who articulates it in his translation of Porphyry's *Isagoge*. The relationship between mnemonic places or topics, and what came to be known as "topics" in logic is a vexed one, since there did seem, to many ancient philosophers, to be some sort of relation, and yet the mnemonic place has a physiological "location" that seems more ontologically real than the logical or even rhetorical topics do, both of which seem to be entities only of language rather than also of some sort of "space." Ancient and medieval philosophers worried the question of the ontological status of the logical topics without reaching any consensus; for a review of the problem at several stages in its life, see the final chapters of Stump, *Boethius's De differentiis topicis*. Though the problem is more one of philosophy than of practical pedagogy, uncertainty about it seems to be reflected in the way in which Aristotle's *Topica* and Cicero's work on the same subject are claimed by some writers on the topics of rhetoric and writers on mnemotechnique, as well as thought to be works of dialectic. I discuss this somewhat more in Chapter 3.

127. Translated by May and Wisse, *Cicero On the Ideal Orator*, 220–221. The translators comment that the passage is difficult, and their sense of it is often variant from Rackham's translation for the LCL. It seems unlikely that Cicero was thinking of "perspective," as Rackham has it: but distinguishing one's various places clearly from one another is a basic requirement of memory craft.

128. Quintilian's method is discussed in Yates, *Art of Memory*, chapter 2, to which I am much indebted, and also in Harry Caplan's essay "Memoria" in *Of Eloquence*.

129. Luria, *Mind of a Mnemonist*, 33, note. The connection between this case-study and the rules of the architectural mnemonic was first made by Sorabji, *Aristotle On Memory*, to which I am indebted. A number of mnemonists' techniques are discussed by Baddeley, *The Psychology of Memory*, 347–369.

130. Luria, *Mind of a Mnemonist*, 33–34.

131. For literary examples of using synaesthesic imagery for memory work, see Carruthers, "Chaucer, Italy, and Fame's House," and "The Poet as Master Builder."

CHAPTER 3

1. Most of these are described at least briefly by Hajdu, *Das mnemotechnische Schriftum*. A digital mnemonic from an early fourteenth-century Anglo-Norman manuscript is described in Hasenohr, "Méditation méthodique et mnémonique." The syllogism mnemonic is keyed, by the vowels of its various syllables, to the types of proposition that a syllogism can contain. A commonly used mnemonic verse for the ecclesiastical calendar, "Cisiojanus," is discussed by Kully. Several of these content-specific mnemonics are discussed in Eco, "An *Ars Oblivionalis*? Forget It!"

2. Thompson, *The Medieval Library*, 613. He describes an interesting verse-catalogue from St. Albans abbey of "all those [books] which are placed in the windows," 379.

3. The characteristics of these influential medieval schemes from late antiquity to the sixteenth century, with English translations of some key texts, are demonstrated in Carruthers and Ziolkowski, eds., *The Medieval Craft of Memory*. The university-based late medieval dissemination of the specific scheme described in the *Ad Herennium* is analyzed in Carruthers, "Rhetorical *memoria*," and see Chapter 4 below.

4. A portion of the *Chronicle* without the preface was published in the MGH. The prologue is discussed as a mnemonic text by Grover Zinn, "Hugh of St. Victor and the Art of Memory." A list of contents written on the end-paper of an early fourteenth-century manuscript of the text (B.n.F. lat. 14872) calls it an art of memory ("Tractatus, vel potius artificium memoriae"); this characterization of it was dismissed as "adventitious" by R. Baron (Zinn, 211, notes 2 and 3). For reasons that will become apparent in my next chapter, it is significant that the phrase "artificial memory" was used by a post-thirteenth-century reader to

describe this text, though it was not called that in the twelfth century, when it was first composed. (Goy, 40, ascribes this manuscript to the late thirteenth to early fourteenth century; it had been ascribed to the twelfth by Delisle.) That the number scheme was understood to constitute an "art of memory" by late medieval and Renaissance writers is apparent from the title of a manual for confessors by the Augustinian friar, Anselmo Faccio: *Memoria artificiale di casi di conscienza . . . disposto artificiosamente per via di numeri* (Messina, 1621).

5. Hugh's *Chronicle* does seem to have been known in England, though it remains unclear how long the Preface was studied. See Harrison, "The English Reception of Hugh of St. Victor's Chronicle."

6. Hugh of St. Victor, *De tribus maximis circumstantiis*, ed. Green, 486.

7. Goy, *Die Überlieferung der Werke Hugos von St. Viktor*, 36–43.

8. Hugh of St. Victor, *De tribus maximis circumstantiis*: "In sola enim memoria omnis utilitas doctrinae consistit"; ed. Green, 490, lines 39–40.

9. Hugh of St. Victor, *De tribus maximis circumstantiis*: "ut interrogatus sine dubitatione respondere possim, sive ordine prolatis, sive uno aut pluribus intermissis, sive converso ordine et retrograde nominatis ex notissa locorum dispositione, quis primus, quis secundus, quis etiam xxvii, xlviiii, sive quotuslibet sit psalmus. Hoc modo scripturas se affirmasse ostendunt qui, auctoritate psalmi alicuius usuri, hoc dixerunt in lxiii, hoc in lxxv, sive alio quolibet psalmo scriptum est"; ed. Green, 489, lines 36–41.

10. Brevity is one of Thomas Bradwardine's mnemonic principles – see Appendix C, and compare what both Hugh of St. Victor and Albertus Magnus have to say about brevity (appendices A and B). The fact that Latin is a syntactically more compressed language than English is also reflected in the greater number of words in the English translation, but is immaterial to the basic principle of mnemotechnical "chunking" and *brevitas* (one simply needs more divisions in English to accomplish the same task). Yet its greater compression may well have helped to make a better, more witty game out of mnemonic *brevitas*. On the important role of play in mnemotechnical art, see Chapter 4, below, and *The Craft of Thought*, esp. chapter 3.

11. Particular thanks to my colleagues Henrietta Leyser and Michael Clanchy, who realized the oddities and significance of this text in the context of monastic educational practice in ways I had overlooked.

12. Hugh of St. Victor, *De tribus maximis circumstantiis*: "Ego puto ad memoriam excitandam etiam illud non nichil prodesse, ut eas quoque quae extrinsecus accidere possunt circumstantias rerum non neglegenter attendamus, ut verbia gratia, cum faciem et qualitatem sive situm locorum reminiscimur ubi illud vel illud audivimus, vultus quoque et habitus personarum a quibus illa vel illa didiscimus, et si qua sunt talia quare gestionem cuiuslibet negotii comitantur. Ista quidem omnia puerilia sunt, talia tamen quae pueris prodesse possunt"; ed. Green, 490, lines 25–31.

13. Hugh of St. Victor, *De tribus maximis circumstantiis*: "Memoria enim semper gaudet et brevitate in spatio et paucitate in numero, et propterea necesse est ut, ubi series lectionis in longum tenditur, primum in pauca dividatur, ut quod

animus spatio comprehendere non potest saltem numero comprehendat"; ed. Green, 490, lines 6–9.

14. *Didascalicon*, III. iii, translated Taylor, 87. The standard edition of the Latin text is that of Buttimer; I cite it only when I think Taylor's translation needs to be modified.

15. Hugh of St. Victor, *De tribus maximis circumstantiis*: "An putas eos, quociens aliquem psalmorum numero designare volebant, paginas replicasse, ut ibi a principio compotum ordientes scire possent quotus esset quisque psalmorum? Nimis magnus fuisset labor iste in negotio tali"; ed. Green, 489, lines 42–44.

16. *Didascalicon*, III. xi, trans. Taylor, 93. "Colligere est ea de quibus prolixius vel scriptum vel disputatum est ad brevem quandam et compendiosam summam redigere"; ed. Buttimer, 60, lines 16–18.

17. *Didascalicon*, III. xi; "Memoria hominis hebes est et brevitate gaudet"; ed. Buttimer, 60, lines 24–25.

18. *Didascalicon*, III. xi; "Debemus ... omni doctrina breve aliquid et certum colligere, quod in arcula memoriae recondatur"; ed. Buttimer, 60, lines 26–27.

19. Dudai, *Memory From A to Z*, s.vv. *Capacity, Internal representation, Working memory*.

20. Miller, "Information and Memory." The limits of working memory have been known and studied for some time experimentally; some of the earliest experiments recorded in modern psychological literature are from the eighteenth century; see Miller, and also Norman, *Memory and Attention*, 98–124, and Dudai as in note 19 above.

21. Miller, "Information and Memory," 45. On the role of "gathering" in complex learning, see also Norman, *Learning and Memory*, esp. 80–116, and Bower, "Organizational Factors."

22. Hugh of St. Victor, *De tribus maximis circumstantiis*, ed. Green, 489, line 41.

23. Murphy, *Rhetoric in the Middle Ages*, 65–66, 80, 195–196.

24. Julius Victor, *Ars rhetorica*, cap. 23: "Memoria est firma animi rerum ac verborum ad inventionem perceptio"; ed. Halm, 440, line 11. This and subsequent quotations from Julius Victor are from Ziolkowski's translation in Carruthers and Ziolkowski, eds., *The Medieval Craft of Memory*. The twelfth-century gloss on Cicero's *De inventione* by Thierry of Chartres echoes this paraphrase: "[Memoria est] firma animo percipere, memoriter retinere que sunt apta ad inventione sive verba sive res, i.e. sententie" (Ward, *Artificiosa eloquentia*, vol. 2, 226–7, transcribed from Brussels ms. Bibl. Roy. 10057–10062).

25. Julius Victor, *Ars rhetorica*, cap. 23: "[N]am qui recte conpegerit orationem, numquam poterit errare" (ed. Halm, 440, lines 25–26). This is an interesting modification of Quintilian's original: "nam qui diviserit, numquam poterit in rerum ordine errare" (*Inst. orat.*, XI. ii. 36). Both "dividing" and "composing" are thought of as specific, definite tasks performed to ensure against error (failure of memory) by imposing a numerical order (one, two, three, etc.).

26. Julius Victor, *Ars rhetorica*, cap. 23: "In his autem, quae cogitamus, et in his, quae scribimus, retinendis proderit multum divisio et compositio ... Et si

prima et secunda deinceps cohaereant, nihil per oblivionem subtrahi poterit, ipso consequentium admonente contextu"; ed. Halm, 440, lines 24–25, 27–29. Cf. Quintilian, *Inst. orat.*, XI. ii. 36ff., and notice again the utter confidence that if one memorizes properly in order, one cannot err or forget.

27. The comment is made in Remigius's commentary on Donatus; see Minnis, *Theory of Authorship*, 19, 226 (notes 75, 77).

28. *Regula Benedicti*, cap. 48. 15–16: "In quibus diebus quadragesimae accipiant omnes singulos codices de biblioteca, quos per ordinem ex integro legant; qui codices in caput quadragesimae dandi sunt" ("In these Lenten days, they should each receive a separate codex from the library [*or* of the Bible] which they are to read straight through to the end. These books are to be given out at the beginning of Lent"). (Translated by Kardong, 383.) Alternative interpretations of this instruction understand *biblioteca* as "Bible" or "library," and *codices* either as "books" or as "the volumes" in which the Bible was bound in Benedict's time. But, as later monastic customaries make clear, medieval monks received other sorts of books as well. See Kardong's comments, 391–392, citing Mundò, "Bibliotheca, bible, et lecture."

29. The foundational connection of memory-work to meditative reading and visionary spirituality in monastic life is the subject of Carruthers, *The Craft of Thought*.

30. Halm's edition of Fortunatianus has been superseded by a critical edition, with extensive notes and introduction, by Lucia Calboli-Montefusco. Calboli-Montefusco provides a complete review of the evidence for Fortunatianus's career and works, including definitively correcting his given name to Consultus from the erroneous form (often found in older texts) Chirius Consultus. All subsequent references to Fortunatianus's *Artis rhetoricae libri III* are to this edition.

31. Fortunatianus, *Artis rhetoricae libri*, III, 13; "Quid vel maxime memoriam adiuvat? Divisio et conpositio: nam memoriam vehementer ordo servat." I quote from the English translation of Ziolkowski, in Carruthers and Ziolkowski, eds., *The Medieval Craft of Memory*, 295–297.

32. Fortunatianus, *Artis rhetoricae libri*, III, 13; "Semper ad verbum ediscendum est? si tempus permiserit: sin minus, res ipsas tenebimus solas, dehinc his verba de tempore accommodabimus."

33. John of Salisbury, *Metalogicon*, I, 24. 91–92: "he diligently and insistently demanded from each, as a daily debt, something committed to memory"; trans. McGarry, 69.

34. Riché, *Education and Culture*, 200, note 146. See also now Ziolkowski, "Mnemotechnics and the Reception of the *Aeneid*," for additional examples and a broader consideration of this topic.

35. A good review of the role of memorization in medieval pedagogy, which clearly sets forth the changing balance in late medieval university education from recitation and purely oral forms to reliance on books made available to students through the cheaper and faster copying methods of the university stationers' *pecia* system, is Riché, "Le rôle de la mémoire dans l'enseignement

médiéval"; he also notes the paradox that written arts of memory proliferate in step with the greater availability of books. On the role of recitation in early medieval Latin pedagogy, including evidence that passages from the ancient poets were sometimes chanted, see Ziolkowski, *Nota bene.*

36. Leclercq, *Love of Learning*, 90; see also 18–22, and cf. Riché, *Education and Culture*, 120–121.

37. "Omnis qui nomen vult monachi vindicare, litteras ei ignorare non liceat; quin etiam psalmos totos memoriter teneat"; *Rule of Ferreolus*, ix (PL 66, 963D); cited by Riché, *Education and Culture*, 115.

38. Riché, *Education and Culture*, 464; on the length of time needed to memorize, see note 117 on that page.

39. Courcelle, *Les Confessions*, Part II, chapters 1–3. On Gregory's indebtedness to Augustine, see esp. 225–231.

40. Riché, *Education and Culture*, 461–464.

41. "Hoc ideo constituimus ut frequentius aliqua meditentur et memoria teneant scribturas, Fratres, ut quando in quovis loco codix deest textum lectionis vel pagine si opus fuerit memoria recitetur": *La Règle du Maître*, cap. 49, ed. Vanderhoven and Masai, 241.

42. The kinds of memory-work associated with the seven different branches of the traditional liberal arts are discussed in Carruthers and Ziolkowski, eds., *The Medieval Craft of Memory*, 1–23.

43. Smalley, *English Friars*, 154.

44. Charland, *Artes praedicandi*, 335–6; "Verba enim de facili memoria excidunt, et ex levi actione sic turbatur dicentis memoria quod verba prius concepta non occurrunt. Immo, saepe cadens syllaba, cadit a toto. Tunc praedicator confunditur, quia se verbis plus quam sententiae alligavit." The brief quotations from Thomas of Waleys in my next few sentences are all from 336.

45. Charland, *Artes praedicandi*, 336; "Et si qua sunt verba in auctoritatibus illis quae sunt merito singulariter ponderanda, illa singulariter conetur memoriter retinere et dicere, de aliis minus curans. Et pro certo hoc habeat quod [multae] sunt auctoritates sanctorum quas propter sui prolixitatem vel obscuritatem melius est et utilius solum sententialiter dicere quam verbaliter recitare. Et dato quod verbaliter recitentur, ubi sunt auctoritates obscurae omnino, earum sententia est sub verbis claris aliis exponenda, ne, dum ab auditoribus non intelliguntur, careant omni fructu."

46. *Etym.*, I, xx.

47. Silverstein, "Adelard, Aristotle, and the *De natura deorum*"; quotations are from 82 and 84. Silverstein sets the two passages up in parallel columns, but they are too long to reproduce here, and I refer the reader to them for a textbook example of *memoria sententialiter.*

48. I use the name given to this treatise by Patrice Sicard in his edition for the Corpus christianorum (CCCM 176). In the PL, this work was called *De arca Noe morali.* Sicard has also accepted the view that the work which the PL edition called *De arca Noe mystice* is a summary picture of the major themes in *De archa Noe* (I agree with this view: see below, Chapter 7, and *The Craft of*

Thought, 243–250), and has renamed that work *Libellus de formatione arche* (also CCCM 176). Both these names have substantial support in the manuscripts. A discussion of the text with a complete English translation by J. Weiss is in Carruthers and Ziolkowski, eds., *The Medieval Craft of Memory*, 41–70.

49. "But as for me, my feet were almost gone; my steps had well nigh slipped. For I was envious at the foolish, when I saw the prosperity of the wicked." Cited at *De archa Noe*, III, iv (CCCM 176; 61. 66–68).

50. "Rejoicing in the habitable part of the earth; and my delights were with the sons of men." Cited at *De archa Noe*, III, vii (CCCM 176, 64. 28–30).

51. Miller, "Information and Memory," 46.

52. In Latin the word commonly means "a fallacy." But it does not mean that here; for instance, Richard de Bury in *Philobiblon* contrasts the permanence of sacred law to "yesterday's sophismata written in quaterni" (unbound pamphlets or memo-books). De Bury means that such things are without lasting value, rather than false in our sense. Once again, we have encountered a case where "false" means something more like "impermanent" or "incomplete" than completely "wrong." The use which Hugh of St. Victor makes of the word in the passage quoted links sophismata with the modern meaning of its derivative, *sophomoric*, meaning "the sort of wisdom possessed by students with lots more to learn."

53. *Didascalicon*, VI, 3: "Quoties sophismatum meorum, quae gratia brevitatis una vel duabus in pagina dictionibus signaveram, a memetipso cotidianum exegi debitum, ut etiam sententiarum, quaestionum et oppositionum omnium fere quas didiceram et solutiones memoriter tenerem et numerum"; ed. Buttimer, 114, lines 18–22. My translation differs significantly from Taylor's here, for I understand this passage in the context of Hugh's *Chronicle* Preface.

54. On ancient writing tablets, see Roberts and Skeat, *The Birth of the Codex*, 11–14.

55. Lewis and Short, s.v. *pagina*.

56. The entries in the *TLL* make this dual meaning clear; see s.v. *pagina*.

57. Ambrose to bishop Chromatius, written around 389, *Epist.*, VI. 28. 149–151 (Maurist number 50): "Hoc munusculum sanctae menti tuae transmisi; quia vis me aliquid de veterum Scriptorum interpretationibus paginare." Cf. *TLL* s.v. *paginare*.

58. Paulinus of Nola, *Carmen*, vi. 214–215 (CSEL 30): "uel quas ipse Deus leges interprete Moyse / condiderat, sacri quas seruat pagina saxi."

59. Du Cange, s.v. *paginator* and *rubrica*, *rubricare*.

60. Hugh of St. Victor, *De tribus maximis circumstantiis*: "Ego puto ad memoriam excitandam etiam illus non nichil prodesse;" ed. Green, 490, line 25. This point is discussed in much more detail in Chapter 7.

61. A thorough study of the Canon Tables is Nordenfalk, *Die Spätantiken Kanontafeln*, and see also Weitzmann, *Illustrations in Roll and Codex*. Hugh took much material for his own *Chronicle* from Eusebius's chronicle, also laid out in tabular form.

62. On the Eusebian and other early divisional schemes, see Robinson, *The Bible in its Ancient and English Versions*, 23, and also the *DTC*, s.v. Hugues de Saint Cher.

63. Blum, *Spätantiken Mnemotechnik*, 8: "Doch darf man sagen, dass der grösste Teil der römischen Malerei sich zur Einrichtung mnemonischer Stellen eignet"; see also Saenger, "Silent Reading," 375.

64. Hugh of St. Victor, *De tribus maximis circumstantiis*: "Nunc ergo satage ut ea quae subter describentur ita memoriae tuae imprimas, secundum modum et formam discendi superius tibi demonstratem"; ed. Green, 491, lines 29–31.

65. Leaving university life for Rome upon the election of his friend, Pope Innocent III, Langton was consecrated archbishop of Canterbury in 1207 against the wishes of the English king, John. After a period of exile at the abbey of Pontigny in France, Langton worked with William Marshal to produce Magna Carta (1215), which guaranteed liberties for the church as well as the barons. Langton fell out with Innocent III after the Fourth Lateran Council in 1215, supporting the young king, Henry III, against the papal legate, who was banished from England. Langton died in July 1228.

66. See esp. Riché, *Education and Culture*, 460ff. As lay devotions became an increasing concern in Europe after the thirteenth century, the Psalms were among the texts translated into the vernaculars, evidence of their ethical importance in meditational *memoria*. This period of vernacular translation needs to be distinguished carefully from the much earlier period, which produced translations of the Bible into Old English and other Germanic vernaculars, primarily for the use of clergy and a small audience at court; see Larès, "Les traductions bibliques: l'exemple de la Grande-Bretagne," in *Le Moyen Âge et la Bible*, 123–140.

67. On the character of the thirteenth-century pocket Bibles, developed as one of the tools for scholars "faced with the task of composing sermons" (280), see Light, "The New Thirteenth-Century Bible and the Challenge of Heresy." On the development of the various versions of the Bible during the whole Middle Ages, see Light, "Versions et révisions du texte biblique," in *Le Moyen Âge et la Bible*, 55–93.

68. *DTC*, s.v. Hugues de Saint Cher. *CHB*, vol. 2, 102–154, contains a good brief account of the development of chaptering in the medieval Bible; see also Berger, *Vulgate*, 316–327, especially with regard to early punctuation and stichometry of the texts. Jerome's use of *cola* and *commata* was much studied by medieval and Renaissance commentators; see especially Jerome's remarks in his preface to Joshua. On the ancient use of *scripta continua* much has been written; a useful account is in Marrou, *Education in Antiquity*. On the earliest medieval uses of word spacing see especially Saenger, *Space Between Words*, and Parkes, *Pause and Effect*.

69. Smalley, *Study of the Bible*, 222–224; she transcribes (224) MS. Cambridge, Peterhouse College 112, fo. 107, which I have translated here. Jerome's text is: "Monemusque lectorem ut ... distinctiones per membra divisas diligens scriptor conservet" (Jerome's prefaces are printed in R. Weber's text of the

Vulgate Bible). The Latin of Langton's gloss is: "*Per membra* id est per capitula...que valde necessaria sunt ad inveniendum quod volueris et ad tenendum memoriter."

70. Smalley, *Study of the Bible*, 224.

71. Augustine, *Enarrationes in Psalmis* on Ps. 118, preface: "partim sermocinando in populis, partim dictando exposui, donante Domino, sicut potui; psalmum vero centesimum octauum decimum, non tam propter eius notissimam longitudinem, quam propter eius profunditatem paucis cognoscibilem differebam" (CCSL 40, 1664. 3–7).

72. Augustine, *Enarrationes in Psalmis* on Ps. 125:1 (CCSL 40, 1844. 1–2): "Sicut iam meministis, ex ordine nobis tractantibus iste psalmus est centesimus uicesimus quintus, qui inter illos psalmos est, quorum est titulus, *Canticum graduum.*"

73. Augustine, *Enarrationes in Psalmis*, on Ps. 7:1 (CCSL 38, 35. 3–4).

74. Jerome, *Commentariorum in Esaiam*, VII, lines 32–33, on Is. 23:15–18 (CCSL 73, 314). Jerome refers to Ps. 44 similarly in Bk. II, lines 13–14, of this commentary, on Is. 5:1 (CCSL 73, 63). In the same location he says that "in sexagesimo septimo psalmo legimus" and then quotes what is now Ps. 67:16–17.

75. Jerome, *Commentariorum in Esaiam*, VI, lines 12–13, on Is. 14:16–17 (CCSL 73, 243). Commenting in Book VIII on Is. 26:10, he refers to Ps. 9 again as an authority on the devil– "de quo in nono psalmo scribitur" – and quotes verses 6–7 (see lines 30–33); CCSL 73, 334.

76. Jerome, Epistula LIII. 3. He refers to Ps. 72 by number in Epistula XXIII. 1, to Marcella, and obviously he expected her to know what he meant.

77. Jerome, *Commentariorum in Esaiam*, VIII, preface lines 1–2 (CCSL 73, 315): "Sextus et septimus superiores libri allegoriam quinti voluminis continent, quod olim historica explanatione dictaui." He refers to the books of his commentary, just completed.

78. Cf. Bede, *De schematibus et tropis*, 9. It is, of course, possible that these numbers, especially since they are written in notation (which is easier to insert) rather than as complete words (as Augustine's are), were added in copies made after Bede's death: Richard and Mary Rouse discuss briefly the citational style found in Carolingian manuscripts, which they describe as less than systematic, especially compared to the elaborate indices and marginal cross-referencing one finds in later medieval manuscripts (*Preachers, Florilegia, and Sermons*, 29).

79. *CHB*, vol. 2, 119, note 2.

80. Augustine, *Enarrationes in Psalmis* on Ps. 6:3 (CCSL 38, 29); he refers to *versus primus* and *versus secundus* of this Psalm in discussing the merits of a possible emendation (lines 12–13). The discussion of Psalm 11:1 is CCSL 38, 82. 1–2: "in sexto psalmo dictum est" ("it says in Psalm six").

81. Saenger, "Silent Reading," esp. 376–377, and now also *Space Between Words*. Some reservations about aspects of Saenger's thesis are spelled out in my review of it for *Early Medieval Europe* 10 (2001): 149–150.

82. Alcuin, *Expositio in Psalmis poenitentiae* (PL 100, 571C): "Sed primo omnium numerorum eruendas rationes ratum putavi, id est, cur etiam psalmi poenitentiae septenario numero consecrati essent? aut quare centesimus decimus octavus viginti duabus periodis divideretur, quorum singuli octo haberent versus? Aut quid rationis sit, quindecim esse psalmos, qui cantico graduum titulo praesignarentur?"

83. Huntington Library MS. HM 26052, an English manuscript of Augustine's *Enarrationes in Psalmis*, contains numbers in its margins which are apparently the verse numbers of each Psalm in order as Augustine discusses them. This is the only instance I have seen in which the verse numbers are written in. The text dates from the late twelfth century, and is rubricated; the Biblical texts are underlined in red. Opposite each of these, in the margin, the verse number is written, though this notation does not continue throughout the manuscript. The red underlining and verse numbering were evidently written in quite a bit later, probably in the fourteenth century. The verse divisions and numbers used are very like those found in printed versions of the Vulgate. A few other such instances undoubtedly also exist, but these rare exceptions do indeed demonstrate the rule.

84. "Tunc enim quandoque signatur ipse psalmus, et dicitur: *Psalmus xlus* vel *xxxus*, vel aliquo alio modo simili. Aliqui tunc omittunt signationem talem, et solum dicunt: *Istud habetur in Psalterio*, et ratio est quia psalmi sunt communiter satis noti"; Charland, *Artes praedicandi*, 346–347. One should note that the large, illuminated Psalters intended primarily for liturgical use usually contained the Psalm numbers, though not the verse numbers; this is true of such an early book as the Utrecht Psalter.

85. Examples of the form ending in "&c." are frequent in the fourteenth-century English poem *Piers Plowman*. Examples of the form giving only the first letters of words can be found in several manuscripts of the monastic text *De sex alis cherubin et seraphin*, e.g. Oxford, Bodleian Library, MS. Auct. D. 1.2, made *c.* 1200, probably at the convent of Llanthony, Gloucestershire. By no means are these isolated examples.

86. The citational conventions are explained in Diez, *Indices canonium, titulorum et capitulorum corpus juris canonici*, and the similar volume by the same authors covering civil law, *Indices ... corpus juris civilis*. I am grateful to Professor James A. Brundage for teaching some rudiments of legal citation to a Fellows' seminar at the Newberry Library.

87. Charland, *Artes praedicandi*, 347. "Ex signatione capituli accidit saepe inconveniens, nam saepe accidit, quando multae allegantur auctoritates, quod excidit a memoriis praedicatorum in quibus capitulis continentur auctoritates, et tunc allegant unum capitulum pro alio. Unde, ad vitandum istud inconveniens, recordor quod illo tempore aliquo pauci praedicantes actu signabant capitula; librum tamen signabant unde auctoritas fuit sumpta. Tamen, quando scribebant sermones, bene consueverunt signare libros et capitula. Credo quod modus iste fuit melior, quia tutior quam sit modus iste modernus quo capitula cum libris signantur."

88. It is quite common to find space left in the written version of a sermon or devotional text for the citation to be filled in; even so late a composition as Reginald Peacock's *Donet* shows this. On the relation between the stages of composition leading to the scribally produced text, see Chapter 6, below.
89. Rouse and Rouse, *Preachers, Florilegia, and Sermons*, 16. The Dominican concordance, a project overseen by Hugh of St. Cher, is described in *DTC*, s.v. Hugues de Saint Cher. See also Rouse and Rouse, "La concordance verbale des Ecritures."
90. Rouse and Rouse, *Preachers, Florilegia, and Sermons*, 16, note 30.
91. Rouse and Rouse, *Preachers, Florilegia, and Sermons*, 4. On the usefulness of *divisiones* for the composition of sermons, see also Minnis, *Theory of Authorship*, 155–157, who quotes the Dominican Master-General, Humbert of Rouen, to the effect that collections of these are "the arms of preachers" (156).
92. Charland, *Artes praedicandi*, 268–269: "Magistris autem et professoribus sacrae theologiae licet, immo eos decet, omnia exquisite quotare, quia quantum ad istud defertur eis ab aliis propter protestationem excellentiae magistralis et ostentionem humilitatis in deferentibus, et propter dignitatem gradus et honorem."
93. See Thomas Waleys's remarks about the mnemonic value of citation (Charland, *Artes praedicandi*, 347), quoted above. Christina von Nolcken, "Some Alphabetical Compendia," includes a typical example of a *distinctio* on a moral theme intended for use in preaching.
94. Charland, *Artes praedicandi*, 370; "Dato vero quod tantum una fiat divisio thematis, adhuc illa divisio erit bene ut illis, tam praedicatori quam etiam auditori. Non enim propter solam curiositatem, sicut aliqui credunt, invenerunt moderni quod thema dividant, quod non consueverunt antiqui. Immo, est utilis praedicatori, quia divisio thematis in diversa membra praebet occasionem dilatationis in prosecutione ulteriori sermonis. Auditori vero est multum utilis, quia, quando praedicator dividit thema et postmodum membra divisionis ordinate et distinctim prosequitur, faciliter capitur et tenetur tam materia sermonis quam etiam forma et modus praedicandi; quod non erit si praedicator indistincte ac sine ordine et forma confuse procedat."
95. Charland, *Artes praedicandi*, 110; on the overlap in form and method between "university" and "popular" sermons, see D'Avray, *Preaching of the Friars*, 123–125. Rivers, "Memory and Medieval Preaching," has studied in particular the use made of mnemonic precepts in the *ars predicandi* of the fourteenth-century Catalan Franciscan, Francesc Eiximenis; see also her translation of a generous section of Eiximenis's art in Carruthers and Ziolkowski, eds., *The Medieval Craft of Memory*.
96. See, for example, the sermons preached on February 23, 1305, in Sta. Maria Novella; Delcorno, ed., *Quaresimali Prediche*, numbers 3 and 4.
97. Charland, *Artes praedicandi*, 311: "Take note of these divisions: the utility of the Passion, "Jesus"; the power of His suffering, "crying out"; the truth of His humanity, "in a loud voice"; His freedom to suffer, "sent forth"; the pain of separation, "His spirit.""

98. Charland, *Artes praedicandi*, 311–312: "Then [the theme] is subdivided as follows: There are five vowels, AEIOU, which make up every word [with a pun on the double meaning of *vox*, "word, voice"]. Just so the five wounds of Christ make up every cry whether of joy or of sorrow. Behold "in His hands" the A and the E: "with loving-kindness I have drawn thee" [beginning with A in Latin] and Isaiah, "Behold, I have graven thee upon the palms of my hands" [beginning with E in Latin]; "in His side" the I: such a mark the wound of the lance imprinted, that is "the door of the Ark" which [was] "in the side," etc. in Genesis; and in John: "reach hither thy hand and thrust it into my side, and be not unbelieving" [a verse which begins with an I in Latin]; the O and U "in His feet": "thou hast put all things under his feet" [the Latin text begins with O]. So as you follow out [these links] you may say in fact: "My foot has held his steps" [the Latin begins with U]." A translation of Basevorn's text was published in Murphy, *Three Medieval Rhetorical Arts*, though I have given my own here in an effort to stress the mnemonic form of the advice.

99. In his *ars memorativa*, Thomas Bradwardine advises associating the number five with the five wounds which Christ suffered on the cross; see Appendix C.

100. Charland, *Artes praedicandi*, 311–312: "1) Walk as children of light [Eph. 5:8]; 2) Return, return, o Shulamite, return, return, that we may look upon thee [Cant. 6:12]; 3) To comfort your own soul is pleasing to God [Eccles. 30:24]; 4) Bring forth therefore fruits meet for repentance [Mt. 3:8]; 5) Loose thyself from the bands of thy neck, o captive daughter of Zion [Is. 52:2]; 6) Wash ye, make you clean [Is. 1:16]."

101. On Guido's solmization scheme and its development, including diagrams displaying how the full gamut was expressed in its syllables, see the exposition by K. Berger in Carruthers and Ziolkowski, eds., *The Medieval Craft of Memory*, 71–82. A number of medieval renditions of the Guidonian Hand are reproduced in Smits van Waesberghe, *Musikersiehung*. It is evident from these diagrams that the hand diagram was not always drawn in the same way, nor did the notes always occupy the same places. Indeed, a twentieth place on the back of the middle finger was added to later schemes, extending the nineteen places of the original diagram, which derived from its initial uses as a device to calculate the moveable feasts of the liturgical calendar.

102. Guido d'Arezzo, *Epistola de ignoto cantu*: "Habebis ergo argumentum ad inveniendum inauditum cantum facillimum et probatissimum ... Namque postquam hoc argumentum cepi pueris tradere, ante triduum quidam eorum potuerunt ignotos cantus leviter canere, quod aliis argumentis nec multis hebdomadibus poterat evenire"; Gerbert, *Scriptores ecclesiastici de musica sacra* (1794), vol. 2, 45. Translated by Strunk, revised McKinnon, 217.

103. Guido d'Arezzo, *Epistola de ignoto cantu*: "[P]ro unaquaque voce memoriae retinenda"; Gerbert, *Scriptores*, vol. 2, 45 (trans. Strunk, rev. McKinnon, 217). The whole letter is a very interesting account of the building and extending of a simple, rigid mnemonic to increasingly complex material. The scheme began with a particular melody and text (the hymn to John the Baptist and a

melody that Guido either composed or adapted in such a way that the initial syllables of the lines in the hymn matched their musical values) but was extended to signify all the notes of the gamut in every variety of combinations, independent of the text or melody of a particular chant. It worked so well, as the letter writer recognized, precisely because, unlike rote reiteration, it created informationally rich units. A significant attempt to apply this principle, and other mnemotechnic, to musical composition is Busse Berger, *Medieval Music and the Art of Memory*.

104. PL 177, 135–164. Only two items are listed under "undecim" (col. 164C) – compare the copious listings for all the other numbers, through "duodecim." There are no listings for numbers greater than twelve, or for one, evidently because "one" does not constitute a mnemonic "division."

105. Rouse and Rouse, *Preachers, Florilegia, and Sermons*, 69. A good example is Alanus's sermon "In adventu Domini," PL 210, 214–218, though many of the sermons contained in his "Art of Preaching" (which consists of examples rather than general principles, like those of Robert of Basevorn and Thomas Waleys) observe the same principle. Alanus also composed an alphabetically arranged index of distinctions.

106. *Inst. orat.*, XI. ii. 29: "If some things do not stick easily in the mind, it is quite useful to attach some marks [*notae*] to them, the recall of which will warn and jog the memory. No one surely will be so ill-endowed as not to remember what Symbol [*signum*] he has assigned to any given passage."

107. Bodleian Library, MS. Bodley 722. The textual pictures are indexed at the end of this manuscript of Holcot's commentaries, indicating that they were intended to be particularly valuable heuristics to users of the book. A full discussion is in Smalley, *English Friars*, 165–183; see also Saxl, "A Spiritual Encyclopaedia," 101–103. I will further discuss the function of marginal images in Chapter 7.

108. Peter of Ravenna, *Fenix* (Venice, 1491/2), c.iv.verso: "omnes enim lectiones meas Iuris canonici sine libro quotidie lego: ac si librum ante oculos haberem, textum et glossas memoriter pronuncio ut nec etiam minimam syllabam omittere uidear." (*Textum* in this context would refer to a cross-referential web of passages which a lecturer would concord as he commented on a passage of law, rather than to a "text" in the way we commonly use the word now.) He continues, "In locis autem meis quae collocauerim hic scribere statui et quae locis tradidi perpetuo teneo, in decem et nouem litteris alphabeti vigintamilia allegationum Iuris utriusque posui."

109. Peter of Ravenna, *Fenix*, b.iv.verso: "pro litteris alphabeti homines habeo et sic imagines vivas." The quotation which follows is also from this page. The need for vivid images to serve as mnemonic cues is a commonplace of mnemonic technique from antiquity onward, not depending solely, as we will see, on the *Rhetorica ad Herennium* for its dissemination.

110. The manuscript is mentioned by McCulloch, *Bestiaries*, 42, and in *Survival of the Gods* (exhibition catalogue, Brown University Art Department, 1987), no. 44. A color reproduction of two of its Bestiary pages is in the Pierpont

Morgan Library exhibition catalogue, *Early Children's Books and Their Illustration* (1957), 19 (illustration), 22.

111. Boncompagno, *Rhetorica novissima* (ed. Gaudenzi, 279): "Per illam siquidem imaginationem alphabeti, memorie naturalis beneficio preeunte, in XXX diebus quingentorum scholarium nomina memorie commendavi. Refero etiam, quod mirabilius videbatur, quia unumquemque nomine proprio, non omissa denominatione cognominis vel agnominis et specialis terre de qua erat, in conspectu omnium appellabam: unde cuncti et singuli admiratione stupebant." A translation by Sean Gallagher of the *memoria* section of Boncompagno's rhetoric is in Carruthers and Ziolkowski, eds., *The Medieval Craft of Memory*. On Boncompagno's work and personality ("[c]ompletely non-self-reflective"), see Witt, "Boncompagno and the Defense of Rhetoric."

112. Bischoff, "The Study of Foreign Languages," 232–233.

113. *Etym.*, I. 3. 2: "Vsus litterarum repertus propter memoriam rerum. Nam ne oblivione fugiant, litteris alligantur. In tanta enim rerum varietate nec disci audiendo poterant omnia, nec memoria contineri." See also I. 21. 1.

114. *Inst. orat.*, I. i. 25–26. On early training in ancient schools, see Marrou, *L'Histoire de l'éducation*, 211–214, 364–366. The learning of the alphabet in late medieval schools, which had changed little from ancient times, is discussed by Orme, *English Schools in the Middle Ages*, 60–63.

115. *Inst. orat.*, I. i. 25: "This is why teachers, even when they think they have sufficiently fixed the letters in a child's mind in the order in which they are commonly first written, next reverse this, or muddle it up in various ways, until the pupils come to recognize the letters by their shape and not by the order in which they come." In the cloister at Moissac, where novices were schooled, there is a capital which mixes up the order of the alphabet in just the way described here by Quintilian (AX, BV, and so on): see the discussion in Rutchick, *Sculptural Programs in the Moissac Cloister*.

116. *Inst. orat.*, I. i. 19: "initia litterarum sola memoria constant."

117. *Inst. orat.*, I. i. 37.

118. *Inst. orat.*, I. i. 36.

119. Marrou, *L'Histoire de l'éducation*, 366. The stress on syllables as a basic unit for teaching reading, and for organizing materials in monastically produced *artes lectoriae* is discussed by Paul Gehl, "Mystical Language Models"; this essay shows clearly some of the particular ways in which the pedagogy of grammar in antiquity was adapted to the Christian education of the monasteries.

120. Marrou, *L'Histoire de l'éducation*, 553, note 30.

121. Quintilian discusses punctuation in *Inst. orat.*, IX. iv. 122–125; the quotation is from section 125.

122. Quoted from *Inst. orat.*, IX. iv. 123. "Number" (rhythm) is analyzed in IX. iv. 52–57, where Quintilian distinguishes the numbers of prose from the more formal meters of verse, and defines prose-rhythm as informal but certainly present. The development of the prose cursus, a topic much discussed by literary historians, and used in administrative and legal writing especially, is probably a related mnemonic aid for the trained notary.

123. On the stability over time of the Latin Bible's *cola* and *commata* divisions see Berger, *L'Histoire de la Vulgate*, 317–318.
124. *Metalogicon*, I. 11. 49–50. "Memoria uero quasi mentis arca, firmaque et fidelis custodia perceptorum"; cf. "Et quia res percipit, earundem apud se deponit imagines, quare retentione et frequenti reuolutione quasi thesaurum memoriae sibi format" (IV. 9. 24–26). I use McGarry's translation here and in all subsequent quotations, with my changes indicated by square brackets.
125. *Metalogicon*, I. 20. 15–28. "Sunt et notae quae scripturarum distinguunt modos, ut deprehendatur quid in eis lucidum, quid obscurum, quid certum, quid dubium; et in hunc modum plurima. Pars haec tamen artis iam ex maxima parte in desuetudinem abiit, adeo quidem, ut studiosissimi litteram merito querantur, et fere lugeant rem utilissimam et tam ad res retinendas quam intelligendas efficacissimam, maiorum nostrorum inuidia aut negligentia artem dico deperisse notariam. Nec miretur quis tantam uim fuisse in notulis, cum et musici cantores paucis characteribus multas acutarum et grauium differentias indicent uocum. Et ob hoc quidem characteres illos, musicae claues dicunt. Si tamen tanta scientiae claus fuit in notulis, mirum est nostros licet plura scierint, non agnouisse maiores, aut tantae scientiae perditas esse claues."
126. *Metalogicon*, I. 20. 44–46: "et si totius haberi non potest, ad instructionem legendorum plurimum confert ipsius memoriter uel hanc tenuisse particulam."
127. See Caplan, "A Medieval Commentary," and especially Ward, *Ciceronian Rhetoric*, 188–192 (which deals specifically with the gloss on *Ad Her.* III. 20–21), and 226–237, on the manuscripts of the commentaries.
128. Caplan, "A Medieval Commentary," 265.
129. Leclercq, *Love of Learning*, 73.
130. Edited by Rossi, *Clavis universalis*, 286–289. I worked from the Huntington Library copy of the first edition of *Fenix*. The work (minus its preface) was translated from a French version into English by Robert Copland, a pupil of Wynkyn de Worde, and printed in London around 1545 (= *STC* 24112).
131. Rossi, *Clavis universalis*, 289.
132. In the form in which it came to be attached to later medieval Bibles, the fully alphabetized index became a sort of generalized dictionary of Biblical Hebrew, into which Jerome's original work was incorporated. It is described, and attributed to Stephen Langton, by Light, "Versions et révisions du texte biblique," 85–86. On Jerome's knowledge of Hebrew, his work on the compilations, and his astonishingly accurate concording memory, see *CHB*, vol. 2, 91–101 especially.
133. Jerome, Preface to *Liber interpretationis hebraicorum nominum* (CCSL 72, 59. 11–13): "et rei ipsius utilitate conmotus [*var.* nouitate conmotus], singula per ordinem scripturam uolumina percucurri, et uetus aedificium noua cura instaurans." If the variant reading, "excited by its novelty," is at all authentic, it suggests that Jerome thought this way of organizing Biblical glosses to be especially innovative as well as useful. His image of himself renewing an old building with a new editing method emphasizes his sense of innovation.

134. The Book of Durrow's glossaries are discussed in the facsimile edition, ed. Luce *et al.*, vol. 2, 7–14 and esp. at 10. A general discussion of alphabetical habits during the Middle Ages is Daly and Daly, "Some Techniques in Medieval Latin Lexicography."

135. Daly, *Alphabetization*, esp. 93–96; the ancients did know how to alphabetize absolutely, for examples of fully alphabetized lists survive. A common partial alphabetizing scheme used in the Middle Ages is by the first syllable of a word (e.g. ba- words, then be- words, then bi-, bo-, bu-). This most likely reflects early reading-recitation training, in which students proceeded from letters to syllables, before learning complete words; see the discussion below of a similarly aphabetized fourteenth-century index.

136. Quintilian, *Inst. orat.*, IV. v. 3.

137. First described in Thomson, "Grosseteste's Topical Concordance." Southern also discussed the making and purpose of the indices in *Robert Grosseteste*, 186–204; in particular Southern mined them for information about Grosseteste's sources and the many theological topics that concerned him. Southern calls the *Index* "a record of Grosseteste's reading" (191), but it is also his reference key to passages he had previously read and marked in many different books, which he could readily access again by using the index's subject-symbols and citations. One could think of it as a kind of prosthetic artifact made for his memory, extending and supporting the contents of his own mental library. As a prosthetic, others also evidently found it useful.

138. Hunt, "The Library of Robert Grosseteste," 132.

139. Hunt, "The Library of Robert Grosseteste," 121–122.

140. Thomson, "Grosseteste's Topical Concordance," 140.

141. Hunt, "The Library of Robert Grosseteste," 124, note 4.

142. Hunt, "The Library of Robert Grosseteste," 124. Another transcribed entry was printed by Thomson, together with a description of MS. Lyons 414, in his *Writings of Robert Grosseteste*, 122–124, and see also "Grosseteste's Topical Concordance."

143. Hunt, "The Library of Robert Grosseteste"; see also Hunt's "Manuscripts Containing the Indexing Symbols of Robert Grosseteste." To those which Hunt lists might be added Huntington Library MS. HM 26061, a Bible and missal of the mid thirteenth century, containing what appear to be indexing symbols, especially in the center margin of the book of Proverbs. It is not clear that these correspond to Grosseteste's system, however, and they might be those of a reader with his own version of notes, having shapes similar to some used by Grosseteste. See the reference to this MS. in Rouse and Rouse, *Preachers, Florilegia, and Sermons*, 18, note 34, and the description of it in the Huntington Library's *Guide to Medieval and Renaissance Manuscripts*.

144. Thomson, "Grosseteste's Topical Concordance," 144; cf. *Writings of Robert Grosseteste*, 124.

145. I have somewhat modified the translation of Hunt, "The Library of Robert Grosseteste," 127, from the Latin quoted in Callus, "The Oxford Career of Robert Grosseteste," 46: "Sed quando aliqua ymaginatio notabilis sibi

occurrebat ibi scripsit ne laberetur [*sic*] a memoria sua, sicud et multas cedulas scripsit que non omnes sunt autentice. Non enim est maioris autoritatis que dissute scripsit in margine libri phisicorum quam alie cedule quas scripsit, que omnia habentur Oxonie in libraria fratrum minorum, sicut oculis propriis vidi" (from MS. Vat. Palat. lat. 1805, fo. 10v).

146. Hunt, "The Library of Robert Grosseteste," 128–129.

147. Compare the typical entries transcribed by Hunt, "The Library of Robert Grosseteste," 124, with those transcribed by Thomson, "Grosseteste's Topical Concordance," 142, and *Writings of Robert Grosseteste*, 123.

148. There has been a suggestion made, amounting in some accounts now to a fact, that Grosseteste used parchment slips as well as margins to record notes; some scholars have speculated that these slips formed the basis of his concordance. The suggestion was based on William of Alnwick's reference to Grosseteste's having written marginal notes and "multas cedulas" (and on another manuscript reference to Grosseteste's *cedula*: "Hanc demonstracionem inveni Oxonie in quadam cedula domini Lincolniensis"; see Hunt, "The Library of Robert Grosseteste," 127). Latin *sceda* or *scida*, diminutive *scedula* or *cedula*, does indeed mean "a strip of papyrus" or "a small leaf or page" (Lewis and Short, s.v. *scida*). But, like Latin *pagina*, a word with which it is often associated (as in Martial, *Epigrams*, IV, 89), it carries the connotation of something composed or put together in haste and informally, the sort of thing one would write on the last little bit of a book. So, Latin *schedium* is "an impromptu poem or speech" (Lewis and Short, s.v. *schedium*). Quintilian refers rather contemptuously to scholars who toil away reading even worthless notations ("indignos lectione scidas," *Inst. orat.*, I. viii. 9). In other words, *cedula*, like Latin *pagina* and English *note*, can refer both to a kind of writing surface and to a genre of composition. It seems likely that William of Alnwick (and the writer of the marginal note mentioned by Hunt) was characterizing all of Grosseteste's marginalia as *cedulae*, that is "impromptu, disjointed memoranda of ideas," and not necessarily referring to actual little scraps of parchment. Indeed the parallelism of his reference tips the balance in favor of this interpretation ("what he wrote . . . in the margin of his *Physics* is of no greater authority than the other 'cedulae' which he wrote"). One must also wonder whether it is plausible that the library of the Friars Minor at Oxford had kept stacks of little parchment scraps having no authority as well as Grosseteste's books – for it is in that library that William Alnwick says he saw Grosseteste's marginal *cedulae*.

149. The text has been edited by Borgnet, vol. 5, 30–47.

150. Rouse and Rouse, *Preachers, Florilegia, and Sermons*, 20–21, talk briefly about the citational system used in this index, but not its alphabetizing scheme. The index is on fos. 318–322 of the manuscript.

151. The catalogue of Tichfield Abbey in Hampshire calls its cases *columpnae*; see Wilson, "The Medieval Library of Tichfield Abbey." A translation and sketch, reconstructed from the manuscript description, is given by Clark, *The Care of Books*, 77–79.

152. Thompson, *The Medieval Library*, 613–629. Medieval English pressmarks are illustrated in *Indices and Facsimiles of Ancient Manuscripts*, 1, esp. Plate 17; see also the account of pressmarks in Ker, *Medieval Libraries*, xviii–xix, and under individual entries.
153. Daly, *Alphabetization*, 18–26.

CHAPTER 4

1. Carruthers, *The Craft of Thought*, and Carruthers and Ziolkowski, eds., *The Medieval Craft of Memory*. On Boncompagno more particularly, see Carruthers, "Boncompagno at the Cutting Edge," and the bibliography recorded therein. On rhetoric at Oxford, see Camargo, "Between Grammar and Rhetoric," and *Medieval Rhetorics of Prose Composition*; Woods, "Teaching the Tropes in the Middle Ages" and "The Teaching of Poetic Composition"; and Lanham, "Writing Instruction."
2. See especially Bolzoni, *The Web of Images*. The thesis of Brian Vickers, *In Defense of Rhetoric*, that medieval rhetoric was so fragmented and diffuse that it had no influence on humanist grammarians of the fifteenth century and later, has been effectively challenged by the work of John O. Ward, J. J. Murphy, Kathy Eden, Martin Camargo, Marjorie C. Woods, Rita Copeland, and many others.
3. A history of the medieval teaching of these two ancient rhetoric textbooks is well demonstrated in Ward, *Ciceronian Rhetoric*; this study corrects a great many errors of fact and emphasis in older accounts of medieval rhetoric, such as that of C. S. Baldwin. The history of teaching rhetoric more generally between antiquity and early modern humanism is recounted by the essays and translated texts in Cox and Ward, *The Rhetoric of Cicero*. I discussed the medieval academic commentary traditions regarding *memoria* in the context of practical memory art between the eleventh and fifteenth centuries in "Rhetorical Memoria" and in "How to make a composition." Translations of a number of medieval works about memory craft, both practical and academic, which are discussed in *The Book of Memory*, can be found in Carruthers and Ziolkowski, eds., *The Medieval Craft of Memory*.
4. Carruthers, "Italy, *Ars memorativa*, and Fame's House." On the pre-twelfth-century dissemination of the *Rhetorica ad Herennium*, see the chapter by Taylor-Briggs in Cox and Ward, *Rhetoric of Cicero*.
5. The title, *Libellus de formatione arche*, has been adopted on good manuscript authority by its most recent editor, Patrice Sicard (CCCM 176). It was called *De arca Noe mystica* in PL, a title now superseded.
6. The text I have used is Traugott Lawler, *John of Garland's Parisiana poetria*. Lawler says that John of Garland's system was "applied only to what is said in the classroom" (237, note on lines 87–115), but this is not so, for lines 103–105 counsel paying attention to the page design in order to remember what one reads. John's treatise was also probably addressed to elementary students; see Lawler, xviii–xix.

7. Murphy, *Rhetoric in the Middle Ages*, 194–268.
8. In general, I quote Lawler's translation of the Latin text, but I have made changes which reflect the meaning of certain words in the context of memory advice. *Distinguo* means to "mark" or "set off" by a distinctive color or mark, as well as having the vaguer meaning "separate." It also means "punctuate." This phrase in this context is unambiguous advice to make mental *notae*, perhaps even in color, as is done in written texts. *Autentica* means "original" or "belonging to the sources," not "authentic" in our sense; see Chenu, *Introduction à St. Thomas*, 109–113.
9. *Differentias* is an alternative word for *distinctio*; see Lawler, 239, note to line 108.
10. The use of summary pictures and diagrams in monastic meditation is discussed in Carruthers, *The Craft of Thought*, esp. chapter 4.
11. Lawler places a comma in his text between "linguarum" and "sonorum," but I think the sense of the passage requires that it not be there; the phrase translates into English as "the sounds of languages," that is, familiar words associated mnemonically with strange ones by homophony, as Bradwardine in his art of memory uses English words to remember Latin (see Appendix C).
12. The standard study of the development of the Bestiary is McCullough, *Medieval French and Latin Bestiaries*, and see also W. Clark, *Medieval Book of Birds*.
13. See Morson, "The English Cistercians and the Bestiary," *Bulletin of John Ryland's Library* 39 (1956–7): 146–170; Morson especially discusses the use of material from the Bestiary in the writings of Aelred of Rielvaux and other English Cistercians.
14. Philippe de Thaon's Bestiary is discussed by McCullough, 47–56. On the patronage of Adeliza and other notable women aristocrats in Norman England, see the chapter by Crane on Anglo-Norman literature in *The Cambridge History of Medieval English Literature*.
15. Yates, *Art of Memory*, 118.
16. Host von Romberch, *Congestorium artificiose memorie*, Venice: Melchiorem Sessam (1533). The writing of the treatise is dated to 1513. Romberch was a Dominican friar from Cologne; the work is discussed by Yates, *Art of Memory*, 122–130, which reproduces some of the many schematic drawings in it.
17. Clark Hulse has suggested to me that this habit may help to explain why even in the sixteenth century the decoration of many books could be left incomplete; if readers were encouraged to supply a memory-image of their own for a text, they might not have objected as we now would to having books with missing decoration. Romberch's advice is aimed at an audience of readers wishing to retain written material. There is a brief chapter at the end on how to retain aurally presented material, but he begins by saying that he has little to offer on the subject beyond the fact that it is the speaker's duty to speak clearly and to use vivid gestures (advice going back to antiquity), and he observes that memorizing from a book is much easier because we can read the text several times in order to imprint it clearly.
18. I found this passage in Allen, "Langland's Reading," 352, where it is discussed in relation to an entirely different subject.

19. Nordenfalk suggests an Egyptian or at least Near Eastern source for the Eusebian layout. Using a grid to relate pictorial images is a lay-out found first in mosaics from the Antioch region. The chapter and verse grid format for the Bible goes back at least to the Masoretic text. All of this fragmentary evidence would point to a Near Eastern milieu for the beginnings of the mnemonic use of a grid. The little we can judge of Aristotle's systems suggests that he used linear schemes, but whether they constituted a true grid or not is hard to tell.

20. Obermann, *Bishop Thomas Bradwardine*, 10–22. The article on Bradwardine by Murdoch in the *Dictionary of Scientific Biography* does not mention this treatise at all. It is reported as a "doubtful" work by J. A. Weisheipl, "Repertorium Mertonense," 182. Weisheipl examined only the inferior version in Sloane 3744 (which he erroneously identifies as Sloane 377). The internal evidence of the text for date and provenance is strong, as I demonstrated in my 1992 edition of the text.

21. A much fuller discussion of the authorial and textual problems of this work, and a description of the manuscripts, is in my edition, Carruthers, "Thomas Bradwardine"; see also the preface to my translation of it in Carruthers and Ziolkowski, eds., *The Medieval Craft of Memory*, 205–206.

22. Yates mentions it, *Art of Memory*, 114, and Beryl Rowland treats it as in the Herennian tradition in "Bishop Bradwardine, the Artificial Memory, and the House of Fame."

23. Quintilian says that Metrodorus of Scepsis used the Zodiac as the basis for a mnemonic system of places (*Inst. orat.*, XI. ii. 22). Nordenfalk describes a Canon Tables, each one marked with a zodiacal sign, in a tenth-century manuscript: "A 10th-Century Gospel." There is no proof that these marks were being used as a mnemonic, but Nordenfalk comments that the use of the Zodiac as part of the decoration of Canon Tables was rare. Perhaps in this instance someone additionally marked the Canon Tables, which already organized Gospel references for easy collation and recollection, with these signs from some conventional mnemotechnique

24. In a number of studies, Sandler has analyzed illuminated devotional manuscripts made for the Bohun family during the fourteenth century, including at times and in places that Bradwardine also frequented: these are notably characterized by fanciful grotesques and drolleries in their margins. See Sandler, "The Word in the Text," "Political Imagery," and "The Writing Bear."

25. The Rutland Psalter (BL MS. Add. 62925) is dated *c.* 1260. Its use of marginal grotesques is "precociously early" in style; see Kauffmann, *Romanesque Painting*, no. 112. A facsimile of this psalter was prepared for the Roxburghe Club by Millar.

26. Albertus, *De bono*, IV. ii. a. 2. Resp. 11: "confusio generatur ex parte loci vel locati vel eius quod actu visibilem facit locum et locatum." See Appendix B for the whole text. Albertus's *Commentary on Aristotle's De memoria*, which also takes up the Herennian art of memory, is translated by J. Ziolkowski in Carruthers and Ziolkowski, eds., *The Medieval Craft of Memory*.

27. Albertus, *De bono*, IV. ii. a. 2. Resp. 11: "multas ingerit imagines, et ideo confrigunt se in anima et non manent, sicut undae multae confrigunt se in aqua."

28. Albertus, *De bono*, IV. ii. a. 2. Objection 16: "reponemus in memoria 'aegrotum in lecto, qui est defuncti figura et reum ponemus astare lecto, dextra poculum, sinistra tabulas tenentem et medicum astantem tenentem testiculos arietinos,' ut scilicet in poculo sit memoria veneni, quod propinavit et in tabulis memoria haereditatis sit, quas subscripsit, et in medico figura sit accusatoris et in testiculis figura testium consciorum et in ariete defensio contra reum in iudicio."

29. Caplan's text, 214–215, note b. No manuscripts known to us now seem to have the reading Albertus gives here; see the textual notes in F. Marx's *editio maior* of 1894.

30. Manuscripts of the E recension of *Rhetorica ad Herennium*, a twelfth-century edition based upon a rediscovered manuscript of the fourth or fifth century, omit altogether the reference to Agamemnon and Menelaus in *Ad Her.* III.21.34, and introduce the adjective *vagantem* for Iphigenia. But E manuscripts read *domum itionem* in the exemplary verse correctly, a reading which Albertus says that he knew but had rejected for an alternative – and wrong – reading, *domi ultionem*. On the E edition, see Caplan's introduction to the Loeb text, and F. Marx's preface to his *editio maior*, xii–xv. On the transmission of the *Rhetorica ad Herennium* in late antiquity up to the twelfth century, see the several essays of Taylor-Briggs.

31. This is suggested also by DiLorenzo, "The Collection Form and the Art of Memory," esp. 206–207.

32. Albertus, *Postilla in Isaiam*, 74. 70–76: "Unde in fabulis poetarum in Ovido magnus Iupiter, qui deus deorum confingitur, cum Phaethontem percutere deberet, qui caelum et terram et omnia quae in eis sunt, combusserat, iaculum post aurem accepit, ut patenter doceret, quod iudicum est prius diligenter audire et merita personarum et causarum ponderare et postea ferire feriendos."

33. Smalley, *English Friars*, 134. Yates suggested that these verbal pictures might be related to an art of memory; *Art of Memory*, 96–101.

34. Albertus Magnus, *Postilla in Isaiam*, 374. 17–22: "Duos pedes habet anima, intellectum scilicet et affectum. Qui quando aequales sunt, quod scilicet affectus adaequatur intellectui veritatis, homo bene ambulat. Si autem vel ambo vel alter curvus est, intellectus scilicet per errorum et affectus per libidinem, homo claudus est." Augustine wrote famously of how charity has two feet for running in the way of God; perhaps that is the trope which Albertus adapts here. See Augustine's commentary on Psalm 33:6, in which, discussing how people draw near to God by exercising their charity, he writes: "Pedes tui, caritas tua est. Duos pedes habeto, noli esse claudus. Qui sunt duo pedes? Duo praecepta dilectionis, Dei et proximi. Istis pedibus curre ad Deum, accede ad illum"; "Your feet are your charity. Make sure you have two feet; don't be lame. Two feet? Yes, the paired commandments of love, of

God and of neighbour. Run toward God on these feet, draw near to him" (*Enarr. in Ps.* 33. 10; CCSL 38, 289. 19–21; trans. Boulding). Cf. a sermon wrongly attributed to Augustine (no. 67. 5 on Matthew 8),: "per viam Christi quomodo debes currere? Si ambos pedes sanos habes feliciter curres. Qui sunt isti duo pedes? Si diligis Dominum et diligis proximum"; "in what way should you run along the way of Christ? If you have both feet healthy you will run happily. What are those two feet? When you love the Lord and you love your neighbour" (PL 39. 1874–1875).

35. Albertus Magnus, *Postilla in Isaiam*, 474. 76–78: "Propter hoc etiam Venus pingebatur, quod veste aliquantulum elevata crus revelavit, ut ad libidinem provocaret." See Smalley, *English Friars*, 115.

36. Yates, *Art of Memory*, 79. The Latin text of Albertus's commentary is in Borgnet, vol. 9, 97–118.

37. This gloss is discussed at length by Ward, *Ciceronian Rhetoric*, and Fredborg, "Commentaries by William of Champeaux."

38. William of Champeaux, trying to elucidate the *testiculos arietinos* in the original text, points out the evident pun on *testes* (testicles/witnesses) but then wonders why they are a ram's testicles, a matter not clarified in the *Ad Herennium*. He suggests it is because the aggressive nature of rams recalls the adversarial nature of the court proceeding. See Carruthers, "Rhetorical *memoria.*"

39. DiLorenzo, "The Collection Form and the Art of Memory."

40. The text of Alcuin's "Dialogue on Rhetoric and the Virtues" is in PL 101. 919–946; the brief discussion of memory is in col. 941. See also Howell, *Rhetoric of Alcuin and Charlemagne*, whose text and translation (136–139) I have quoted. Notice how Alcuin stresses practice in writing as one of the disciplines of memory, an emphasis one also finds in Quintilian's advice and others, like Martianus Capella, deriving from the same tradition. It is worth recalling, in this context, that Luria's subject, S., discovered that writing things down was useless to him in trying to forget anything. On the practical teaching of grammar and rhetoric from late antiquity through the twelfth century, see the essays in Lanham, *Latin Grammar and Rhetoric*. Many useful materials from these centuries can also be found in Irvine, *Textual Culture*.

41. There is no evidence to assume that Cicero was referring specifically to the art described in the *Rhetorica ad Herennium* when he said this. Yet evidently some "Method of Loci," as it is now rather grandly called by psychologists, was generally known.

42. Julius Victor, *Ars rhetorica*: "Ad [memoriam] obtinendam tradunt plerique locorum et simulacrorum quasdam observationes, quae mihi non videntur habere effectum"; Halm, 440, lines 15–17. A translation of his remarks about *memoria* is in Carruthers and Ziolkowski, eds., *The Medieval Craft of Memory*, 297–298.

43. Augustine, *Confessiones*, x. xvii; trans. Boulding.

44. Of early medieval references, Caplan (Loeb translation, xxxv) mentions only a letter of Servatus Lupus from the early ninth century, and comments that the

oldest extant manuscripts belong to the ninth and tenth centuries. Taylor-Briggs makes a strong case that the work was not taught after it was composed, nor even much known before a fourth century edition of it was made, possibly in North Africa, whence it came to Lombardy (Milan), perhaps with Augustine, at the time of Ambrose's reign as bishop. The work became strongly influential as a taught text only after the twelfth century – that is, wholly within a medieval and early modern ambit.

45. John of Salisbury, *Metalogicon*, I. 20. 28–33: "Seneca se artem comparandae memoriae traditurum facillime pollicetur: et utinam innotuisset mihi, sed quod eam tradiderit omnino non recolo. Tullius in rhetoricis operam dedisse [ei] uisus est; sed similibus mei multum non prodest."

46. Lines 2017–2019 in the edition of Faral, trans. M. F. Nims: "Tradit imaginibus peregrinis Tullius artem, / Qua meminisse decet; sed se docet et sibi soli / Subtilis subtile suum quasi solus adoret."

47. "[M]y own subtlety may be pleasing to me and not to [Cicero]. It is beneficial only to the one it suits, for enjoyment alone makes the power of memory strong. Therefore have no faith in these or other *notae* if they are difficult for you, or [less agreeable, *minus acceptae*]. But if you wish to proceed more securely, fashion your own signs for yourself, of whatever kind your own inclination suggests"; lines 2020–2025, trans. Nims, with my modifications.

48. Yates, *Art of Memory*, 50.

49. Martianus Capella, *De nuptiis*, V. 538–539; trans. Johnson. A translation, differing significantly in emphasis from Johnson's, is in Yates, *Art of Memory*, 51–52. Yates understood the references to memory places physically, whereas Johnson understood them solely as dead metaphors or abstractions. The best definition of *topos* by a modern scholar is that of Harry Caplan: "The *topos* is the head under which arguments fall, the place in the memory where the argument is to be looked for and found, ready for use" (*Of Eloquence*, 83). Cf. Cicero, *Topica*, II. 8: "It is easy to find things that are hidden if the hiding place is pointed out and marked; similarly if we wish to track down some argument we ought to know the places or topics: for that is the name given by Aristotle to the 'regions' [*quasi sedes*, "seats of a kind"] from which arguments are drawn"; trans. Hubbell, LCL.

50. Martianus Capella, *De nuptiis*, V. 539, lines 19–23: "nec uoce magna legenda sunt, sed murmure potius meditanda; et nocte magis quam interdiu maturius excitari memoriam manifestum est, cum et late silentium iuuat, nec foras sensibus auocatur intentio"; "[texts] are not read out in a loud voice, but are better meditated upon in a murmur, and it is plain that memory is more readily stimulated at night than during the day, when the silence on all sides also helps, nor is concentration distracted by sensations from outside"; trans. Johnson. Riché discusses the volume-level of early monastic students, *Education and Culture*, esp. 117–119, 465–466. The association of voice-level with different reading functions is discussed at length in Chapter 5, below.

51. On the iconoclastic issues for the Carolingian court (stemming in part from a famous letter of Pope Gregory I about the appropriateness of physical images

in churches), see Chazelle, "Pictures, Books, and the Illiterate," and Kessler, "Turning a Blind Eye." As Kessler succinctly says, "[m]edieval art theory distinguished pictures seen by physical sight from the mental images they were intended to evoke" (413). This crucial distinction is obscured by their use of such words as *imagines* and *pingere* for both, but Western scholars nonetheless consistently made it in their writings on the subject. A physical image can only start off a mental procedure, which includes forming the mental images or phantasms that in turn are essential to the machinery of thinking. The nature and use of mental imagining in monastic meditation from John Cassian onward is a major subject of my *Craft of Thought*.

52. Boncompagno's memory advice is translated by S. Gallagher in Carruthers and Ziolkowski, eds., *The Medieval Craft of Memory*. See also Carruthers, "Boncompagno at the Cutting-Edge of Rhetoric."

53. *Inst. orat.*, VI. ii. 31.

54. *Inst. orat.*, X. vii. 15.

55. I will return to this point in Chapter 7. The formative modern discussion of late medieval diagrams is that of Saxl, "A Spiritual Encyclopaedia." Saxl does not make any connection of these to the mnemonic technique of *imagines rerum*, however. I discussed these matters in much greater depth in *The Craft of Thought*, especially chapters 2–4, and the additional bibliography given there.

56. G. R. Evans, "Two Aspects of *Memoria*," 278.

57. On the curriculum at Padua, the influence of Boncompagno da Signa, and Albertus Magnus's possible studies there, see Siraisi, *Arts and Sciences at Padua*, esp. 37–43, 109–117. Albertus need not, of course, have been at Padua to study the recent translations of Aristotle; what is important is that he was their early, influential commentator and champion. About all we know of Albertus in Italy is that he says he was there, but he does not mention where he was and what he studied.

58. This history can be found in Ward, *Ciceronian Rhetoric*, and in my essay on the medieval transmission of Herennian and other ancient mnemotechnic in Cox and Ward, *The Rhetoric of Cicero*. The earliest extant full gloss on the *Ad Herennium* was compiled in the eleventh century by a "Magister Manegaldus"; it exists now in only one manuscript, in which the section on *memoria* is missing.

59. Thierry of Chartres, *Latin Rhetorical Commentaries*, 27, 307n. Fredborg's introduction sets forth the evidence of composition and date, and discusses both Thierry's sources and the influence of his commentaries on later writers.

60. Thierry of Chartres, *Latin Rhetorical Commentaries*, 306. 20–21: "Nota ad carmina poetarum in memoria retinenda verborum memoriam plus quam ad causas valere"; "Note that memory for words is more valuable for retaining the songs of poets in memory than for orational themes."

61. Thierry of Chartres, *Latin Rhetorical Commentaries*, 307. 31–36.

62. "*Intervalla*, id est locorum distenda … Confunditur aspectus ex re visa aspectui nimium appropinquata vel ab eo nimium remota"; Thierry of Chartres, *Latin*

Rhetorical Commentaries, 305. 70–72. In this gloss, Thierry shows he understood better than many later writers on the *Ad Herennium* what the *intervalla* were.

63. See D'Alverny, "Translations and Translators."

64. See Stump, *Dialectic and its Place in the Development of Logic*, and her introduction to her edition of Boethius's *De differentiis topicis*. Rossi, *Logic and the Art of Memory*, traces this ancient connection through the fourteenth and fifteenth centuries into the late seventeenth-century debates over the nature and possibility of universal and/or real language. See also Lewis, *Language, Mind, and Nature*, and "The Best Mnemonicall Expedient."

65. "[M]emoria dicendi est pars dyalectica sicut retorice"; Bodleian Library, MS. lat. class. d. 36, fo. 61, col. b. See also Carruthers in Cox and Ward, *The Rhetoric of Cicero*.

66. Yates, *Art of Memory*, 73. Yates underestimates the constant alliance of locational memory training with dialectic as well as rhetoric, and thus its strong identification with reasoned investigation and invention throughout the Middle Ages, not just after the thirteenth-century triad of Albertus, Aquinas, and Ramon Lull.

67. Caplan, Introduction to the Loeb *Rhetorica ad Herennium*, xxxv. Jean d'Antioche's "Rhétorique de Cicéron," from Musée Condé MS. 590, is described by Delisle.

68. On the spread of vernacular translations of Cicero in Italy during the late Middle Ages see Cox, "Ciceronian Rhetoric in Late Medieval Italy," which contains a descriptive *repertorium* of the earliest works. They include several "tratatelli" (little treatises) on memory arts, which circulated independently of comprehensive arts of rhetoric and oratory.

69. The roll of Dominicans is impressive. In addition to the thirteenth- and fourteenth-century writers mentioned in this chapter (Albertus Magnus, Thomas Aquinas, and Jacopa da Cessola) it includes Peter of Ravenna, the author of *Fenix*, who adapted the architectural mnemonic to a specifically Gothic setting. *Fenix* was first published in Venice in 1491, in an English translation finally in 1548, and it was one of the most widely published of the Renaissance treatises on *ars memorativa*. Peter began his life as a lay jurist, but became a Dominican friar. Johannes Host von Romberch, author of the *Congestorium* to which I have already alluded, was a German Dominican of the early sixteenth century. The three great authorities on the art of memory to which these Renaissance writers pay homage are Aristotle, Cicero, and Thomas Aquinas.

70. See the critical edition of *Fiore di rettorica* edited by Speroni 1994; the independence of the *memoria* section is discussed in xviii–xix, ccxli–ccxlii. Caplan makes the attribution to Bono Giamboni ("Introduction," xxxv). Rossi, *Logic and the Art of Memory*, 205, agrees that the vernacular translation which circulated as a preface to the *Ammaestramenti* was taken from the *Fiore di rettorica* of Bono Giamboni (see next note).

71. *Ammaestramenti degli antichi*: "Ma se l'uomo ha in se senno di saper bene in sulle cose vedere, e ancora in se senno e giustizia, cioè ferma volontà di volere le

cose bene disporre, e diritamente voler fare, sì fa bisogno di saper favellare . . .
che senza favella sarebbe la bontà sua come un tesoro riposto sotto terra . . .
Già abbiamo veduto della prima cosa, che al dicitore fa bisogno di sapere, cioè
come ha a imparare di favellare perfettamente in cioè, che a te ho mostrato
qual è buona, qual è composta, qual è ornata, e qual è ordinata favella . . . Or ti
voglio mostrare della seconda cosa, che fa bisogno al dicitore di sapere,
acciocchè perfettamente dica la sua dicería, cioè ome la sua dicería si reca a
memoria, acciocchè quando la dice, l'abbia bene a mente, perocchè niuno la
direbbe bene, se quando la dice, bene a mente non l'avesse." *Classici Italiani*
(Milan, 1808), 344–345; in this edition the appendix on *ars memorativa* is at
343–356. Compare Bono Giamboni, *Fiore di rettorica*, I. 12–15 and 82. 1–6.

CHAPTER 5

1. Often quoted, the sermon is found in Mynors, *Durham Cathedral
   Manuscripts*, no. 59; see David Diringer, *The Book Before Printing*, 206–207.
2. Jurgen Miethke, "Marsilius und Ockham: Publikum und Leser," esp.
   548–549; the composition of *III Dialogus* is discussed by Miethke in
   Ockhams Weg, 121–125.
3. On private book-collecting and ownership, see the chapter by Roberto Weiss
   in *The English Library Before 1700*, 112–135. One should remember, however,
   that some members of the lay aristocracy always owned a few books; see Riché,
   "Les Bibliothèques de trois aristocrats carolingiens," and *Education and
   Culture*, 184–265. A good earlier book discussing the matter of lay literacy in
   the later Middle Ages is Thompson, *The Literacy of the Laity in the Middle
   Ages*. One should therefore more accurately speak in terms of a late-medieval
   extension of private book ownership rather than its beginning, though the
   collecting of books simply to own them or to have a scholar's library, as
   Petrarch's was, is a late medieval phenomenon. Of book production and book
   selling at this time there are a large number of studies; Burrow, *Medieval
   Writers and Their Work*, provides a summary account as does De Hamel, *A
   History of Illuminated Manuscripts*. All considerations of this matter should,
   however, keep in mind the studies of Deanesly, such as "Vernacular Books,"
   which remind us that, while a few individuals owned many books, most, even
   those who might afford them, owned very few, if any.
4. *I Dial.* ii, 23 (1494 edn., fo. 14): "tu autem scis quod nullum habeo predicto-
   rum et forte illi de ordine nolunt mihi communicare predicta."
5. *III Dial.* i, prol. (1494 edn., fo. 181): "Ideo si tibi videtur de prefatis me
   nullatenus intromittam: maxime cum ad libros necessarios non valeam (vt
   estimo) peruenire. *Disc*: Timor non te retrahat memoratus."
6. *III Dial.* ii, prol. (1494 edn., fos. 229v–230): "*Magis*: Eorum perfecta cognitio,
   que tractanda commemoras ex libris sacre theologie vtriusque iuris canonici
   videlicet et ciuilis philosophie moralis et ex hystoriis romanorum atque
   imperatorum et summorum pontificum et aliarum gentium esset patentius
   extrahenda et solidius munienda. De quibus solummodo bibliam et decretum

cum quattuor libris decretalium spem habeo obtinendi. Quare ne forsitan opus imperfectum immo ridiculosum faciamus videtur consultius desistendum. *Disc*: Quis his diebus opus perfectum facere nequeamus cum de materia tam necessaria ... vtile erat penitus non silere vt alios copiam librorum habentes ad faciendum perfecta opera prouocemus."

7. Discussed by Miethke, *Ockhams Weg*, 121–122, and esp. notes 455 and 457. The chronicler reporting this event does not say that Albert saw a written copy of Ockham's work (as a nineteenth-century edition had it in error), but that Albert was persuaded to support Ludwig against the Clementine interdict because Ludwig supported his position ("innititur") with arguments drawn from a "dialogus" which Ockham had produced ("edidit") in the form of a student asking questions and a master responding ("sub forma discipuli querentis et magistri respondentis").

8. Many otherwise excellent, careful studies reflect such assumptions. For example, Richard and Mary Rouse have said that memory ceased to be emphasized after the twelfth century, and in an otherwise fine introduction to his edition of Bartolomaeus Anglicus's encyclopedia, R. J. Long refers to a thirteenth-century "scissors-and-paste" method of composing. Several scholars have supposed the widespread use of parchment slips; Antoine Dondaine pictures Thomas Aquinas pausing frequently in mid-composition to check quotations in his books; other scholars, analyzing the sources of florilegial compendia, have presumed it to be "self-evident" that a scholar compiling in a particular city must have had physically available to him where he was working copies of the works he cites, that he must be "quoting directly or paraphrasing" from a text physically before him, and that manuscript evidence, had it survived, could definitively tell us which written source it was. I mention these frequently made comments only to indicate how even the best of modern scholars have assumed that medieval ones worked from books exactly in our manner, though in much less convenient circumstances.

9. *Cambridge Medieval History* (short edition), 527. Roy Rosenstein has called attention to the crusader song of Jaufre Rudel, which clearly shows how this song was used to disseminate the Crusade; the relevant lines (29–34) are as follows: "Senes breu de pargamina / tramet lo vers que chantam / plan et en lenga romana / a N Hugon Brun per Fillol" ("Without a parchment document / I send the song we sing, / smoothly and in Romance language, / to Lord Hugh Brun, by Fillol").

10. Deferrari, "Augustine's Method of Composing," 103.

11. The circumstances surrounding the first making of eyeglasses were analyzed by Rosen, "The Invention of Eyeglasses." Friar Giordano announced that "it is not yet twenty years since the art of making eyeglasses was discovered ... I saw the one who first discovered and made them, and spoke with him "[*E disse il lettore: io vidi colui che prima la trovò e fece, e favellaigli*]." This sermon is XV in Delcorno's edition, preached in Santa Maria Novella, Wednesday, February 23, 1305 (1306).

12. Ward, *Cicero's Rhetorica*, 59–60, but especially "Quintilian and the Rhetorical Revolution." It is important to remember that the authors of most medieval

commentaries of the twelfth century were in fact mainly compilers of a pre-existing store; a number of studies have brought this out, but one might especially mention those of Beryl Smalley. After the eleventh century it was more usual for the glossator to sign his contribution, perhaps because – in the cases of both the Bible and the law – an ordinary gloss had been compiled from the mainly anonymous stock of glosses that existed before.

13. See Rouse and Rouse, "Statim invenire."

14. Occasionally, especially in late manuscripts, one or two individuals are shown with pens – these are the reporters, those "pencils" of the Middle Ages.

15. In *Familiares*, III, i, Petrarch recounts a conversation he had in Avignon with Richard de Bury, regarding the nature of "ultima Thule," and says of him that he was "not ignorant of letters"; the remark is patronizing, of course, but no more than that.

16. I, 27–29; 14–15. On Hugh of St. Victor's diagrammatic ladders, see my discussion of *De archa Noe*, in Chapter 7. Bury calls the books burned in the fire of the Alexandrine library "scrinia veritatis" (VII, 107; 59, lines 9–10), which he recalls "with a tearful pen" (VII, 106; 58, lines 8–9). Later, invoking the motif of *translatio studii*, he describes how learned Greece (especially Aristotle) transferred to its own treasuries all the ancient wisdom of Egypt (X, 160; 92, lines 3–4). I have used the translation of E. C. Thomas, slightly edited as indicated in brackets.

17. VIII, 126; 69, line 16: "paradisum mundi Parisius."

18. VIII, 128: "apertis thesauris et sacculorum corrigiis resolutis, pecuniam laeto corde dispersimus, atque libros impretiabiles luto redemimus et arena"; 71, lines 4–7.

19. This has been estimated at 1,500 books; the largest documented collections made by other men of Richard de Bury's time were on the order of 100 or so. Humphrey, Duke of Gloucester, a most avid collector of manuscripts a century later may have collected as many as 500; he gave Oxford about 300 of those. Only 4 surviving books have been identified as belonging to Richard de Bury, all returned to St. Albans after his death (whence he had bought them – perhaps extorted them – in the first place). See Wormald and Wright, *The English Library*, esp. 113–115.

20. IV, 58; 29–30: "Primum oportet volumen cum Ezechiele comedere, quo venter memoriae dulcescat intrinsecus ... Sic nostra natura in nostris famil-iaribus operante latenter, auditores accurrunt benevoli, sicut adamas trahit ferrum nequaquam invite. O virtus infinita librorum iacent Parisius vel Athenis simulque resonant in Britannia et in Roma! Quiescentes quippe moventur, dum ipsis loca sua tenentibus, auditorum intellectibus circum-quaque feruntur."

21. VIII, 134; 74–75: "A corpore sacrae legis divinae usque ad quaternum sophisma-tum hesternorum, nihil istos praeterire potuit scrutatores. Si in fonte fidei Christianae, curia sacrosancta Romana, sermo devotus insonuit, vel si pro novis causis quaestio ventilabatur extranea, si Parisiensis soliditas ... si Anglicana perspicacitas ... quicquam ad augmentum scientiae vel declarationem fidei

promulgabat, hoc statim nostris recens infundebatur auditibus nullo denigratum seminiverbio nulloque nugace corrumptum, sed de praelo purissimi torcularis in nostrae memoriae dolia defaecandum transibat." *Seminiverbio* is from the Vulgate of Acts 17, 18 (as Thomas's note indicates); *denigrare* is a synonym of *detergere*, "to wipe clean," as Du Cange notes, s.v.; *corrumpere* in the context of literary texts means "falsify" or "spoil" (Lewis and Short, s.v.). Anyone who has worked with medieval manuscripts will recognize the aptness of Bury's fears; I am reminded of Chaucer's warning to Adam, his scrivener, not to "wryten newe" his *Troilus*.

22. Much has ably been written on the content and methods of medieval *lectio* in both monastic and university settings; among the best studies are those of Smalley, *The Study of the Bible*; Evans, *Language and Logic of the Bible*; Clanchy, *Abelard*; de Lubac, *Exégèse médiévale*; Chenu, *Introduction à St. Thomas*; and Leclercq, *The Love of Learning*. In *Metalogicon*, I. 24, John of Salisbury defines the distinction very clearly, though his terminology for it is somewhat different from the more common one I have adopted here: "The word 'reading' [*legendi*] is equivocal. It may refer either to the activity of teaching and being taught, or to the occupation of studying written things by oneself [*ad scrutinium meditantis*; line 10]" (trans. McGarry, 65–66). He calls the former *praelectio*, following Quintilian (*Inst. orat.*, II. v. 4), and the latter *lectio*. He who aspires to philosophy, says John of Salisbury, must learn reading, organized study, and meditation, together with the exercise of good works ("apprehendat lectionem, doctrinam, et meditationem, cum exercitio boni operis"; I. 24. 1–2).

23. *Didascalicon*, III, 7–10; English trans. J. Taylor, 92–93.

24. This paraphrase–translation is of *De archa Noe*, II, v.

25. Frances Yates notes this reputation in her 1955 essay on "The Ciceronian Art of Memory"; the suggestion was adopted enthusiastically by Rossi, *Clavis universalis*, 292–294.

26. Petrarch's veneration for Augustine is discussed fully by Courcelle, *Les Confessions*, 329–351. The story of Petrarch's sortilege on the summit of Mont Ventoux is in *Familiares*, IV. I. There have been a number of discerning studies recently of this famous incident; see Greene, *The Light In Troy*, 104–111, and Kahn, "The Figure of the Reader."

27. Petrarch writes in the prologue: "So, little Book, I bid you flee the haunts of men and be content to stay with me." He may have begun *Secretum* at Vaucluse, but the main part was added in Milan, where Petrarch lived from 1353 to 1358; see H. Baron, *Petrarch's Secretum*.

28. *Secretum*, Dialogue Two; translated Draper (with my alterations), 97–100, 102. The Latin text is in Petrarca, *Prose*, 120–122, 126.

29. Petrucci, 38–57; see also Pellegrin and Billanovich, "Un Manuscrit de Cicéron annoté par Pétrarque" (BL MS. Harley 2493). Like most scribes, Petrarch used a different hand for glosses than for the main text.

30. *Penetralia* means "recess" or "interior" generally, but specifically "the innermost chamber of a shrine or temple" (Lewis and Short, s.v. *penetralium*), an

image that links up with that of memory as *scrinium*, and also with the use of the idealized Temple as a meditational device common in monastic meditational practice. Italian *penetrali* still carries the Latin meanings.

31. See Leclercq, 73ff.; as Leclercq demonstrates eloquently the model of rumination is at the core of monastic reading. *Ruminare* was used metaphorically to mean "meditate" in pagan writing also; the earliest citation in *Ox. Lat. Dict.* is third century BC (s.v. *rumino*). Quintilian, though he does not actually use the verb, says that meditation (by which he means memorizing) is like rechewing one's food (*Inst. orat.*, XI. ii. 41). See also West, "Rumination in Bede's Account of Caedmon."

32. *Moralia in Job*, I. 33: "In nobismetipsis namque debemus transformare quod legimus; ut cum per auditum se animus excitat, ad operandum quod audierit uita concurrat."

33. *Didascalicon*, V. 5: "cuius sententias quasi fructus quosdam dulcissimos legendo carpimus, tractando ruminamus"; Buttimer, 103, lines 26–27. Notice Hugh's use of the gerundive form of *tractare*, in a context similar to that in which Ockham also uses it. It is a scholastic use, "tracting" for the process of making "tracts" by mentally collating extracts during meditational composition (recall the account of Thomas Aquinas's composing habits – I have more to say about this whole matter in Chapter 6). On the genre called *tractatus*, see Kristeller, "The Scholar and His Public," in *Medieval Aspects of Renaissance Learning*, esp. 4–12.

34. *Regula Pastoralis*, III. 12.124–125. Gregory is commenting on two passages about stomach pains (*plaga uentris*), Prov. 20:27, 30. Gregory appears to have suffered from stomach troubles, as he apologized to his congregation at the start of one of his sermons on Luke (no. 21; PL 76. 1169).

35. *Didascalicon*, III. 11: "hoc etiam saepe replicare et de ventre memoriae ad palatum revocare necesse est"; Buttimer, 61, lines 1–2. Hugh cites Gregory, *Regula pastoralis*, III. xii, in this text.

36. Augustine, *Sermones*, 352. 1 (PL 39. 1550): "Unde cum sermonem ad vestram Charitatem non praepararemus, hinc nobis esse tractandum Domino imperante cognovimus. Volebamus enim hodierna die vos in ruminatione permittere . . . Praestet ergo Dominus ipse Deus noster, et nobis virium sufficientiam, et vobis utilem audientiam"; trans. Hill, vol. 10, 137. The lector's error and Augustine's consequent need to improvise his sermon was not a unique event for him: cf. the start of his Commentary on Psalm 138 (139), where again he says he is departing from what he had prepared to accommodate a lector's mistake (cited from note 1 to Hill's translation of Sermon 352). The commentaries on the Psalms began as sermons; see Boulding's preface to her translation of the *Enarrationes in Psalmis*.

37. *Ecclesiastical History*, IV, 24. West has discussed this passage and its context in the monastic traditions of *ruminatio* in "Rumination in Bede's Account of Caedmon."

38. See Darbishire (ed.), *The Early Lives of Milton*; my thanks to James Thorpe of the Huntington Library for bringing this material to my attention.

39. *Regula monachorum*, cap. 14 (PL 30. 365B): "Ad orationem nocte consurgenti non indigestio cibi ructum faciat, sed inanitas. Nam quidam vir inter pastores eximius: sicut fumus, inquit, fugat apes, sic indigesta ructatio avertit Spiritus sancti charismata. Ructus autem dicitur proprie digestio cibi, et concoctarum escarum in ventum efflatio. Quomodo ergo juxta qualitatem ciborum de stomacho ructus erumpit, et vel boni, vel mali odoris flatus indicium est, ita interioris hominis cogitationes verba proferunt, et *ex abundantia cordis os loquitur* (Lk. 6:45). Justus comedens replet animam suam. Cumque sacris doctrinis fuerit satiatus, de boni cordis thesauro profert ea quae bona sunt." This passage was incorrectly cited by West, 220, note 11.

40. The argument that medieval scatalogical imagery was subversive of high-culture piety, and/or expressed a carnivalesque "cultural unconscious," was made by Camille, *Images in the Margins*, and similarly understood as displaying late medieval class tensions by A. Taylor in his discussion of the Smithfield Decretals (BL Royal 10.E.iv), *Textual Situations*, 137–196. Both arguments are made in apparent unawareness of the monastic trope of reading as eating, meditation as digestion and elimination (including vomiting and shitting), and prayer as eructation – belching and farting. This trope is so shocking now that many scholars read right over it.

41. PL 30. 435C: "ut dum corpus saginatur cibo, saturetur anima lectione."

42. *Regula Benedicta*, cap. 38 (PL 66. 601–602): "Mensis fratrum edentium lectio deesse non debet."

43. There is debate over the date of the *Regula magistri*; the view of de Vogüé, its editor for the SC series, that it was contemporaneous with Benedict's Rule has been challenged by Dunn, *Emergence of Monasticism*, who argues for a date in the seventh century (see esp. 182–187).

44. *Regula magistri*, cap. 24: "ut nunquam desit carnali refectioni et aeca [= esca] divina, sicut dicit Scriptura, non in solo pane vivit homo sed in omni verbo domini, ut dupliciter Fratres reficiant, cum ore manducant et auribus saginantur."

45. PL 30. 435C–D: "Tunc uniuscujusque mens sobria intenta sit dulcedini verbi Dei, suspiret anxia, cum propheticus aut historicus sermo Dei saevitiam monstrat in pravos. Gaudio repleatur immenso, cum benignita Dei annuntiatur in bonos ... Non resonent verba, sed gemitus: non risus et cachinnus, sed lacrymae."

46. *Epist.* 52. 8: "Dicente te in ecclesia non clamor populi, sed gemitus suscitetur; lacrimae auditorum laudes tuae sint." See Riché, *Education and Culture*, 82–83.

47. The two accounts differ in one important particular, which the commentators noted. In Ezekiel, the prophet is presented with a roll and "written therein lamentations, and mourning, and woe"; he is commanded "Son of man, cause thy belly to eat, and fill thy bowels with this roll that I give thee. Then did I eat it; and it was in my mouth as honey for sweetness." At that moment, he receives his commission to prophecy. In Apocalypse, the angel tells the prophet that the little book will be sweet in the mouth but bitter in his belly; "And I took the

little book out of the angel's hand and ate it up; and it was in my mouth sweet as
honey: and as soon as I had eaten it, my belly was bitter."

48. *De claustro anime*, IV, 33 (PL 176. 1171D): "Librum ergo devoramus et
comedimus, dum verba Dei legimus. Multi enim legunt, et ab ipsa lectione
jejuni sunt … [alii] sanctum librum devorant, et comedunt, et jejuni non
sunt, quia praecepta vitae quae sensus capere potuit, memoria non amisit."

49. *Comm. in Hiez.*, I. 3b. 851–856, on Ez. 3:3 (CCSL 75): "quando uero assidua
meditatione in memoriae thesauro librum Domini condiderimus, impletur
spiritualiter uenter noster et saturantur uiscera ut habeamus, cum apostolo
Paulo, uiscera misericordiae, et impleatur ille uenter, de quo Hieremias
loquitur: *Ventrem meum, ventrem meum ego doleo: et sensus cordis mei con-
turbant me* (Jer. 4:19)." Jerome's commentary on Ezekiel, together with
Gregory the Great's sermons on Ezekiel, were – along with the great patristic
commentaries on the Psalms – the best-known and most frequently adapted
commentaries among Old Testament Biblical texts. Hrabanus Maurus commented on both Jerome and Gregory on Ezekiel: before him came Bede,
afterwards the Victorines, and many others. Even Abelard wrote an Ezekiel
commentary (a work that no longer exists). It is worth stressing this medieval
emphasis on Ezekiel, because it is not an obvious one, yet was profoundly
influential. On Ezekiel meditation more generally, see Lieb, *Visionary Mode*,
and Himmelfarb, "From Prophecy to Apocalypse."

50. "Ego autem, singula verba discutiens, audivi indignationem, audivi luctamen,
audivi tempestates sonoras, audivi murmur ac fremitum … Audivi rursum
regem in arce sedentem, audivi sceptrum tenentem, audivi prementem et
vinclis ac carcere frenantem"; Petrarch, *Prose*, 124.

51. "Sive enim id Virgilius ipse sensit, dum scriberet, sive ab omni tali consideratione remotissimus, maritimam his versibus et nil aliud describere voluit
tempestatem"; Petrarch, *Prose*, 124.

52. R. W. Southern has written of John of Salisbury "patiently picking over the
literary deposit of the past. The names of Lucan, Macrobius, Martianus
Capella, Ovid, Cicero, follow each other in his pages with a fine impartiality,
each in turn pointing a doctrine or adorning a sentence. Once the nectar had
been extracted, John of Salisbury passed on like a bee to another flower,
diligently, unemotionally, not stopping to consider whether it was a cowslip
or a clover, so long as it gave up its treasure"; *Medieval Humanism*, 126.
I would disagree with Southern's adverb "unemotionally" (for a memory
cannot be stored without an emotion), but otherwise he precisely describes
the attitude of a medieval scholar towards his sources. As he also writes of
twelfth-century authors, they looked backward to the past "only for the quite
practical purpose of equipping themselves to look forward" prudently. In this
passage from his *Secretum*, Petrarch, devoted textual scholar though he was,
shows himself, *as an interpreter of texts*, to share John of Salisbury's attitude.
Here again one can distinctly see the difference between the activities of *lectio*,
or textual commentation and scholarship, and *meditatio*, the application of
reading to moral life.

53. *Moralia in Job*, II, 1. 1–5: "Scriptura sacra mentis oculis quasi quoddam speculum opponitur, ut interna nostra facies in ipsa uideatur. Ibi etenim foeda ibi pulchra nostra cognoscimus. Ibi sentimus quantum proficimus, ibi a prouectu quam longe distamus." He is quoting *ad res* Augustine, *In Psalm. 103*, ser. 1, n. 4. On the activities of *lectio* and *meditatio* in monastic textual study, see Leclercq, esp. 15–17.

54. *De claustro anime*, IV, c. 33 (PL 176. 1172A): "Ventrem quippe doluit, qui mentis afflictionem sensit. Sed sciendum est quia, cum sermo Dei in ore cordis dulcis esse coeperit, hujus procul dubio contra semetipsum animus amarescit." From Gregory he quotes, "Librum devoramus cum verba vitae cum aviditate sumimus" (1171C). Hugh's meditation recalls the first part of one of Gregory's sermons on Ezekiel (x, 1–13).

55. Since the will acts from desire, a total loss of desire would also mean a loss of free will. This idea belongs in the category of essential Augustine, but it is best defined in *De trinitate*. The fullest literary expression of it is the whole *Divine Comedy*, but perhaps one moment especially captures it. At the end of *Purgatorio*, Dante finds himself able to do whatever he desires because his will is completely good; however, he has not, one should notice, been *purged* of desire. "Take henceforth thy pleasure for guide," Virgil tells him; "Free, upright and whole is thy will and it were a fault not to act on its bidding" (*Purgatorio*, 27. 131, 140–141).

56. For the texts from John of Salisbury, Isidore, and others, see above, 29–32, 139–140; Balogh, "Voces paginarum," lists several variants of this phrase, including "sonus litterarum" (Ambrose), "vox antiqua chartarum" (Cassiodorus); Paulus Diaconus wrote that "pagina canit" ("the page sings" or "chants"), perhaps an allusion to the murmur of memorative meditation.

57. See esp. the remarks of Hendrickson, "Ancient Reading"; Gavrilov, "Techniques of Reading"; McCartney, "Notes on Reading and Praying Audibly"; and Saenger, "Silent Reading."

58. Leclercq, 19; the phrase is from the Rule, c. 48. Benedict orders that the monks should pause in complete silence after the daily meal, although those who strongly desire to read may read to themselves in a way that does not disturb others: "sibi sic legat, ut alium non inquietet." See the comments of Riché on evidence for the use of the voice in monastic reading, *Education and Culture*, 465–466.

59. See Leclercq, *Love of Learning*, esp. chapter 2. Paul Gehl, "*Competens silentium*" provides an excellent discussion of monastic silence, and a useful bibliography. See also his essay "Mystical Language Models."

60. Saenger "Silent Reading", 396–398. The degrees of what passes for quiet are apparent in any library; see the judicious remarks of Hendrickson, "Ancient Reading," 194–195.

61. See Hugh of St. Victor, *De archa Noe*, IV, iv. 36, where the Bridegroom in the Canticles is said to call his Spouse "sono depresso uoce tenui," that is, in a whisper. This is the traditional voice of meditation, as befits this text's having become the great meditational text of monasticism. Interestingly, the Bible

itself does not so characterize the Bridegroom's voice. Perhaps the association was aided by the reference to God's voice calling the prophet Elijah, not in an earthquake or fire, but through a whispering, weak, breath of wind (1 Kings 19:12).

62. Translated by Maria Boulding from the CCSL edition of Verheijen. See in addition the comments of O'Donnell on this passage.

63. Boulding interprets the phrase *et aliter nunquam* as an independent clause, and starts a new sentence after *tacite*, thus: "It was never otherwise," *it* referring to the general reading situation. Other translators have understood the phrase in parallel with *tacite*, as modifying *legentem*.

64. The quoted words are from Hendrickson. Using this passage from the *Confessions* as the best evidence that the ancients normally read out loud (and silently only rarely if at all) goes back to Nietzsche (1885), as Balogh makes clear (85). Valuable evidence for the commonness of silent reading in antiquity was given by Knox, "Silent Reading in Antiquity" (1968), but the idea persisted that reading silently was highly unusual. Since I first wrote about this passage, the scholarly climate has shifted towards the interpretation I advance here. An important article by Gavrilov, "Techniques of Reading in Classical Antiquity," originally published in Russian in 1989 and then in English in 1997, marshals the considerable evidence that the ancients read silently as a matter of course when studying or meditating. Gavrilov's reading of this passage in Augustine supports mine with more evidence. We differ in that he sees Augustine's silence as the deference of a pupil to a master, and I understand it as recognizing and respecting a social convention. As Gavrilov concludes, reading silently and reading aloud were, in antiquity as now, interdependent modes that educated readers engaged in for the differing tasks to which each was better suited. Boulding's note on this passage accepts this interpretation, and her translation supports it.

65. The same contrast is made by Hugh of St. Victor (who knew Augustine very well, as many scholars have noted) in his characterization of *meditatio*: "Ea enim maxime est, quae animam a terrenorum actuum strepitu segregat, et in hac vita etiam aeternae quietis dulcedinum quodammodo praegustare facit" (*Didasc.*, III. 10; Buttimer, 59, lines 23–25). Notice also the metaphor of eating, *praegustare*, which is so commonly associated with meditation.

66. *Conf.*, IX. ix: "we arrived at the summit of our own minds; and this too we transcended, to touch that land of never-failing plenty where you pasture Israel for ever with the food of truth." Again, notice how strong the image of feeding ruminants is; of course Augustine is echoing the Bible here, but the physical activity of working the jaws that habitually accompanied ordinary *meditatio* pulls the literal conversation of mother and son together with the character of their discourse (as ruminative, recollective study) and with the Biblical grazing-motif.

67. See Chapter 2; here again I think it is interesting that Augustine thinks of memory (*mens* and *cor*) in terms of a physiological activity, even when it is the

path to true mystical rapture; it is through the *affectus*, that is, by way of sensory memory, that one ascends.

68. Isidore of Seville, *Sententiae*, III. 14. 9, a chapter entitled "De conlatione": "Acceptabilior est sensibus lectio tacita quam aperta; amplius enim intellectus instruitur quando uox legentis quiescit et sub silentio lingua mouetur. Nam clare legendo et corpus lassatur et uocis acumen obtunditur." *Silentium* has connotations of reverence as well as concentration; it is the state that prevailed when the auspices were being read (*Ox. Lat. Dict.*, s.v. *silentium*). As Isidore uses it here, with *sub*, it seems to be an independent state of being rather than describing a person's behavior.

69. *Ox. Lat. Dict.*, s.v. *rimo, rimor*; citations from Virgil (*Aen.*, VI, 599) and Juvenal (6, 551). Quintilian uses the word to mean "study thoroughly" in *Inst. orat.*, III. iv. 6, *cuncta rimanti*; we might translate this phrase into English as "thoroughly dissecting the matter." Interestingly here, Augustine uses the verb *rimor* to describe Ambrose's rumination of sacred text and the noun *silentium* (also used in connection with augury) to describe his own reverent and attentive notice of him. Saenger goes wide of the mark when he claims that the re-introduction of word divisions in early medieval scripts was motivated by a desire to read quickly; see "Silent Reading" and *Space Between Words*, esp. chapter 1.

70. Martianus Capella, *De nuptiis*, V. 539, lines 19–23 (ed. Dick, 269): "nec uoce magna legenda sunt, sed murmure potius meditanda; et nocte magis quam interdiu maturius excitari memoriam manifestum est, cum et late silentium iuuat, nec foras a sensibus auocatur intentio."

71. Cf. Fortunatianus on the same matter. That the activities requiring meditation were done best at night is apparent in the Latin word for them, *lucubratio*, "night-work"; *Ox. Lat. Dict.*, s.v.

72. Quintilian counsels at some length the need to practice achieving *silentium* in crowds, and cites the story of Demosthenes studying by the seashore in the roar of the breakers, to train himself not to be disturbed by crowd-noises ("meditans consuescebat contionum fremitus non expavescere," [studying] to accustom himself not to be frightened by the roar of the Assembly"); *Inst. orat.*, X. iii. 30.

73. This change is discussed by Yates, *Art of Memory*, 75–76, who finds it a curious medieval "misreading" of a classical concept; she is partly right, in that it is a particularly medieval change, though it is an obvious development in Christian hands of features already implicit in ancient teaching on memory. The *Ad Herennium* text is from Book III.19.31; Thomas Aquinas quoted is from *ST* II- II, Q. 49.

74. "Legebat quandoque in sacris libris, et quod animo semel iniecerat, indelebiliter scribebat in corde. Memoriam pro libris habebat, quia non frustra semel capiebat auditus, quod continua devotione ruminabat affectus. Hunc discendi legendique modum fructuosum dicebat, non per millenos evagari tractatus"; quoted by Balogh, 209, who also notes a change from Thomas's text when Bonaventure adapted it: "semel iniecerat, tenaciter imprimebat

memoriae, quia non frustra mentalis attentionis percipiebat auditu, quod continuae devitionis [*sic*] ruminabat affectus." Balogh thinks this remark is significant as expressing a disdain on Bonaventure's part for listening instead of writing. But Bonaventure is concerned to contrast Francis's mental attentiveness (concentration) with vain listening, a variation of the traditional *silentium/strepitus* opposition. His use of *ruminare* in the following clause bears out this interpretation.

75. *Didascalicon*, III. 9; ed. Buttimer, 58, line 25.

76. Cicero, *Brutus*, 12. 47.

77. *Inst. orat.*, II. iv. 22 and V. xiii. 57. See Aristotle, *Rhetoric*, I. 2. 21–22, and Cope, *Aristotle's Rhetoric*, 130–131.

78. PL III. 11D–13A: "[C]ogitabam, quid Tuae Sanctitati gratum et utile in scribendo conficere possem: quo haberes ob commemorationem in paucis breviter adnotatum quod ante in multorum codicum amplitudine et facunda oratorum locutione disertum copiose legisti … Haec enim omnia mihi sollicite tractanti venit in mentem ut juxta morem antiquorum qui de rerum naturis et nominum atque verborum etymologiis plura conscripsere, ipse tibi aliquod opusculum conderem in quo haberes scriptum non solum de rerum naturis et verborum proprietatibus, sed etiam de mystica earumdem rerum significatione ut continuatim positam invenires historicam et mysticam singularum expositionem."

79. The making of this complete line-by-line gloss of the Bible was a culminating labor of monastic scholarship, completed by Anselm of Laon and his many helpers by 1117. Like Smalley, G. R. Evans sees this as the labor that ended one phase of Biblical scholarship and helped to enable another, the general considerations of Biblical doctrine that we associate with the scholastics; see her *The Language and Logic of the Bible*, esp. chapters 1–3. On the development of the glossed Bible lay-out, see De Hamel, *Glossed Books of the Bible*, and L. Smith, *Masters of the Sacred Page*.

80. Isidore, *Sententiae*, III.14.7: "Lectio memoriae auxilio eget."

81. C. von Nolcken, "Some Alphabetical Compendia." On the genres of medieval florilegia, see Rouse and Rouse, *Preachers, Florilegia and Sermons*, esp. 3–42. See also their "Florilegia of Patristic Texts."

82. The opinion is that of Peter, Prior of Holy Trinity in Aldgate, with my emphasis added. It was first adduced by Hunt, "English Learning in the Twelfth Century," and subsequently by Smalley, *Study of the Bible*, 248, and von Nolcken "Some Alphabetical Compendia," 282. In such ways modern scholarship also depends on the florilegial reading of others.

83. B. Munk Olsen, "Les Classiques Latins dans les florilèges médiévaux," esp. 47–57.

84. Quoted by Munk Olsen, "Florilèges," 56. Cf. 52, note 2, in which the verses of Hadoard are quoted, explaining how, when he was in charge of the book-cases, he gathered together extracts of material he wished to recollect; having preserved and gradually built up this store, he will now pay out its image in the form of a book. Munk Olsen discusses the purposes of Carolingian florilegia which contain extracts from classical texts in "Les Florilèges d'auteurs classiques."

85. On vocalizing while writing, see Balogh, "Voces paginarum," 214–216; McCartney, "Notes on Reading," 184–187; and Skeat on ancient scribal dictation. The most famous ancient allusion is in Ovid, *Heroides* 18. 19–20, discussed in Chapter 6, below.
86. *Inst. orat.*, I. i. 36; trans. Russell.
87. Riché, 464. Though a great deal has been written recently on the subject of reading and ethics in the Middle Ages, the importance of pedagogical practices, especially at the elementary level, has not been sufficiently stressed. The work of Judson B. Allen, *Ethical Poetic*, and Minnis (for example in "Art and Ethics in John Gower") has focused on theoretical statements and advanced practices, chiefly in university or court settings; this, I think, is to start at the end of the matter not the beginning, although their work provides essential explorations of the issues. See also Stock, *Augustine the Reader*, and Illich, *Vineyard of the Text*, which have appeared since *The Book of Memory*, and which complement both my discussion here and that of Leclercq, *Love of Learning and the Desire for God.*
88. *Metalogicon*, I. 24: "Historias, poemata, percurrenda monebat, diligenter quidem et qui uelut nullis calcaribus urgebantur ad fugam; et ex singulis, aliquid reconditum in memoria diurnum debitum diligenti instantia exigebat"; (I. 24. 89–92). On the long pedagogical tradition of such memory work to build character and learn both reading and writing, see Orme, *English Schools*, chapter 3.
89. The quotation from Cassiodorus is given above, Chapter 1, note 66.
90. Trans. Clanchy, *The Letters of Abelard and Heloise*, 18–19. The quotation is *Pharsalia* 8. 94b–98a. A case against accepting Abelard's letters, including this one, as genuine was made by John Benton, "The Correspondence of Abelard and Heloise." For my purposes, the question of authentic authorship, while of interest, is not a dispositive one. What is important to my discussion is that this supreme ethical moment is narrated not as a private, but a public, one – designed to enrich the public memory. And it succeeded, for the story became a medieval "classic," helped along in part by its retelling in the *Roman de la Rose*. Since I first wrote this note, scholarly opinion has decisively come to accept Abelard's authorship: see Clanchy, *The Letters of Abelard and Heloise*, lviii–lxxxiv.
91. Southern, *Medieval Humanism*, 86–104, esp. 93–94. Southern also points out that Heloise's irony in choosing these words is lost on Abelard, for Pompey shows his moral greatness in not accepting his wife's offer, a crucial difference between Cornelia's fate and that of Heloise.
92. *Conf.*, VIII. xxix. Augustine elsewhere expresses disapproval of using Scripture for sortilege, though only because divine words shouldn't be asked to provide answers to mundane business affairs; still, he says, it would be better to consult Scripture than "demons"; *Epist.*, 55. 37.
93. Liddell and Scott, s.v. χαρακτερ; for an interesting discussion of the use of the word in rhetoric, see Hendrickson, "Characters of Style." On the memorial physiology of habit-building, see my discussion in Chapter 2, above.

94. Cicero, *Orator*, 36 (edited Hendricks, LCL); *Ox. Lat. Dict.*, s.v. *forma*.
95. A careful attempt to articulate the Exegetical school's position on the moral function of medieval literature, which starts from the premise that literature is properly part of ethics but ends up with conclusions quite opposite to those I argue here, is Allen, *Ethical Poetic*. On the importance of the rhetorically achieved negotiation of norm and occasion in ethics, see Trimpi, *Muses of One Mind*.
96. Huizinga was one of the first historians to emphasize the theatre or perform-ance aspect of late medieval culture (which he viewed, in *The Autumn of the Middle Ages*, as a sign of decadence); the concept of performance in terms of the oral character of vernacular literature has been developed especially by Paul Zumthor – see his *Essai*, and especially *La Poésie et la voix*.
97. A great deal has been written on the changing concept of the "individual" in medieval culture. See Hanning, *The Individual in the Twelfth Century Romance*; Benton, "Consciousness of Self"; Morrison, *The Mimetic Tradition of Reform*; and Bynum, "Did the Twelfth Century Discover the Individual?" (chapter 3 of *Jesus as Mother*). The term "subjectivity" I have taken from Patterson, *Negotiating the Past*, esp. 182–184.
98. See Carruthers, "Mystery of the Bed-Chamber," for a detailed working through of these themes in *Book of the Duchess*.
99. Lacan, *The Four Fundamental Concepts of Psychoanalysis*, 47; my thanks to my Illinois colleague, Ned Lukacher, for this citation.
100. Edited by F. J. Carmody, "Introduction," xxiii (my translation of the French).
101. Greene, "'Festina lente,'" 134. An excellent study of Erasmus's *Adagia*, proverbs, and early modern notions of intellectual property is Eden, *Friends Hold All Things in Common*.
102. Smalley, *The Study of the Bible*, 29 and note. The quote is from *Epistula* 36. 1: "ne me aestimas tantummodo dormitare, qui lectionem sine stilo somnum putas" ("for you do not think of me as asleep, you who believe that to read without [writing] with a pen is to sleep"). Jerome addresses Pope Damasus, asking to dedicate to him a translation of the Greek expositor Didymus, on the Holy Spirit, now lost.
103. Kristeller characterizes the culture of Renaissance humanism as basically "a lay culture," its religion "supported by laymen and secular clerics rather than by monks and friars" (*Medieval Aspects of Renaissance Learning*, 114), though he outlines certain important contributions of the religious orders in the final essay, with its extensive bibliography, of this same volume. The relationship between artificial memory books and these florilegial collections, especially in a lay context and in southern Europe, is well set out by Yates, *Art of Memory*, and Rossi, *Logic and the Art of Memory*. Since Kristeller wrote, the view of humanism as owing little to friars has been successfully challenged by, among others, Bolzoni: see especially her *The Web of Images*.
104. Cited by von Nolcken, "Some Alphabetical Compendia," 272, note 8, from the preface to John of Mirfield's *Florarium Bartholomei*.

105. This citation and the following paraphrase are from Bartolomeo da San Concordia, *Ammaestramenti degli antichi*, 1.

106. Dante, *Inferno*, V, 121–138; trans. Sinclair.

107. This assumption has come to characterize the exegetical school of medieval literary criticism, associated prominently with the name of D. W. Robertson. Though it is unfair to attribute to Robertson the original of it, he is perhaps its most expressive proponent. But such an authoritarian view assumes reliably authoritative texts, and medieval readers of written books could hardly afford to take for granted the correctness or completeness of their contents. Compare Richard de Bury's complaints about scribes as cloudy-headed word-scatterers, which is simply his version of a frequent, deeply held, and empirically based medieval bias.

108. *Piers Plowman, the B-Text*, Passus III. 338–343.

109. Text ed. Sommers (1910), vol. 3, 263: "And the queen saw that the knight did not dare to do more . and so she took him [Lancelot] by the chin and kissed him before Galehot for a long enough time . until the lady of Malehaut comprehended that she kissed him." Paget Toynbee transcribed and translated the text for the Dante Society a century ago, noting that the Lady of Malohaut's reaction is alluded to in *Paradiso* 16. 14–15. He transcribed the text from British Library MS. Lansdowne 757, which is punctuated exactly as the edition I have just quoted here. Early commentary on the *Paradiso* passage, cited by Toynbee, makes it clear that the Lady's instant discovery of the lovers' fault was understood by its readers to be an essential part of this famous scene; "Dante, and the Lancelot Romance," *Fifth Annual Report of the Dante Society* (1886), 41–74. Noakes, "The Double Misreading," reviews the criticism that understands reading to be a major theme in this scene, and gives a fine analysis of it of her own. Medieval readers familiar enough with the scene to understand Dante's allusion at all (and it was a famous scene) would have understood Francesca's reference to the exact *punto* that overcame them, for they memorized it in these divisions (recall Jerome's admonition to copyists to carefully preserve his *cola et commata*, essential, as Bishop Langton said, for remembering the text).

110. Ambrose, *Epist.*, VII. 37, 2 (*Sancti Ambrosi opera*, X. 2), written *c.* 395. The text is quoted by Balogh, 219. (In the Maurist's register of Ambrose's letters printed in the PL, this is no. 47.) Ambrose explains that he has sent a perfected codex to his correspondent, Bishop Sabinus, for his own copy-texts are not written "ad speciem," "to be looked at," but "ad necessitatem," "for use." He does not like to dictate always to a scribe, especially when he is doing what the Romans called "night-work," *lucubratio*, study, reading, and composition. I have freely translated the sentence that follows: "Nobis autem quibus curae est senilem sermonem familiari usu ad unguem distinguere et lento quodam figere gradu, aptius videtur propriam manum nostro affigere stilo, ut non tam deflare aliquid videamus, quam abscondere neque alterum scribentem erubescamus." *Senilis* here refers to the "ancients" or "elders" of the Church (Du Cange, s.v. *Senex*); *deflare* is a rare verb, usually glossed as

"blab," but with this citation from Ambrose being the only one given. It also means "blow about *or* around" – *Ox. Lat. Dict.* s.v. *deflo*; similarly Lewis and Short. Undoubtedly all sorts of textual study and meditational activities associated with it are implied by *distinguere ad unguem*, not just what we think of as punctuation, but, since the way one reads is by dividing, as Quintilian and so many others all said, punctuation is the basis. And it is clear that Ambrose is writing as an aid to his memory (it wouldn't have occurred to him to do otherwise), for not only is the activity of *distinguendum* the first step to memorizing, but the verbs *figere* and *affigere*, "to fix," the notions of order and habituation implied in the words *usus familiaris* and *gradus*, the time of day, and the contrast between scattering or idly "blowing" his studies "about" by dictating them to a scribe and hiding them away in storage, all suggest the memorial nature of Ambrose's activity.

CHAPTER 6

1. The medieval category of *intentio auctoris* developed as an essential part of understanding a text; see especially the commentaries translated in Minnis and Scott, *Medieval Literary Theory*, and in Huygens, *Accessus ad auctores*. We might think of it now as its "sense" (Latin *sententia*, medieval English *sentence*), an essential property of an artistic work which is yet not wholly circumscribed by its immediate historical context or its composer: indeed, in the commentaries called *accessus ad auctores*, the biography of the writer is treated quite separately from the *intentio auctoris* (and is often left out). Michael Baxandall explored the concept of an inherent intention in works of painting and architecture in *Patterns of Intention*; his analyses have fruitfully influenced mine. I have discussed it in relation to the late antique rhetorical concept of artistic *ductus*, and the related notion that a work was structured as a set of itineraries and routes, in *The Craft of Thought*, 77–94, 261–267, and at greater length in two essays, "Rhetorical *ductus*" and "Late Antique Rhetoric"; see also "The Poet as Master Builder."
2. Cited by Minnis, *Theory of Authorship*, 247, note 4, from Albertus's *Super epistolam ad Romanos*, cap. IV, lect. I.
3. As Minnis says, "The term *auctor* may profitably be regarded as an accolade bestowed upon a popular writer by those later scholars and writers who used extracts from his works as sententious statements or *auctoritates*, gave lectures on his works in the form of textual commentaries, or employed them as literary models"; *Theory of Authorship*, 10. The etymologies and distinctions are described in M. D. Chenu, "Auctor, actor, autor," from which all subsequent discussions of the matter, including mine, are derived. In addition, see Chenu's discussion of the matter in *Towards Understanding St. Thomas*, 130–132.
4. Jerome, "Commentary on Galatians," cited in Lewis and Short, s.v. *originalis*; see also s.v. *auctor*.
5. Petrarch, *Secretum*, II, trans. Draper, 102. The Latin reads: "Laudo hec, quibus abundare te video, poetice narrationis archana. Sive enim id Virgilius ipse sensit, dum scriberet, sive ab omni tali consideratione remotissimus, maritimam his

versibus et nil aliud describere voluit tempestatem; hoc tamen, quod de irarum impetu et rationis imperio dixisti, facete satis et proprie dictum puto"; Petrarca, *Opere*, 124, 126.

6. On the development of the *ars dictaminis*, considered crucial to the needs of increasing administrations both ecclesiastical and royal, see Haskins, *"Artes dictandi,"* and Murphy, *Rhetoric in the Middle Ages.* Training for notaries (that is, legal and administrative officials) at universities like Padua and Bologna included both *ars dictaminis* and the *ars notataria*; see Siraisi, *Arts and Sciences*, 33–65.

7. *Epistulae morales*, 84. All references are to this edition; the translations are my own. This particular commonplace was quoted intact by Macrobius in the preface to his *Saturnalia*, and it appears frequently in later medieval collections as well. A brief history of some of its citations, beginning in the seventh century, is in Rouse and Rouse, *Preachers, Florilegia and Sermons*, 115–117. Thomas of Ireland used it extensively in the preface to his florilegial collection, *Manipulus florum*; this collection was one of the most widely circulated and longest-lived of the florilegial collections for preachers, and is the subject of the Rouses' fine study.

8. In this same epistle, Seneca also counsels reading and writing together to blend one with the other, "so that what has been collected from our reading, our stylus may render in graphic form." For the Jerome reference see Chapter 5, note 102 above.

9. See Greene, *The Light in Troy*; this trope in particular is discussed, 72–80. Telfer, "Bees in Clement of Alexandria," considers the trope in early Christianity. See also the study of Erasmus's *Adagia* by Eden, *Friends Hold All Things in Common*, which importantly considers humanist ideas of intellectual property, based in Christian as well as pagan antiquity.

10. Greene, *The Light in Troy*, chapters 2 and 3.

11. A comprehensive study of this rich idea in Augustine is Stock, *Augustine the Reader*.

12. The late Latin formation *moderni* (always contrasted with *antiqui*) is discussed by Curtius, esp. 251–255. Southern has well analyzed the historical consciousness of twelfth-century scholars like John of Salisbury, in contrast to that of the Renaissance – see *Medieval Humanism*, 105–132. Southern notes that twelfth-century writers looked to the past "only for the quite practical purpose of equipping themselves to look forward" (126). A relationship between Froissard's "careless" attitude towards fact in his chronicle of the English and French wars and the scholastic definitions of memory found in Duns Scotus is the subject of Janet Coleman's essay on "Late Medieval *Memoria*." Coleman encounters a perennial problem of traditional intellectual history, however, because she cannot connect the formulations of a limited intellectual elite, represented by Scotus, to a general literary culture, represented by Froissard; that connection is to be found in rhetorical *memoria*. A more complete discussion of the historiographical problem is in Coleman, *Ancient and Medieval Memories*.

13. See L. Smith, *Masters of the Sacred Page*, for the development of visual page lay-out and commentary traditions. Smith suggests that the page format of a large-letter central text (in the script called *textualis*), with interlinear glosses plus layers of commentary written in generous margins – which for all its technical difficulties was adopted very rapidly for study books in Europe during the twelfth century – was first used for books of law (in the teaching of which commentary was vital), thence for Biblical material. Examples are illustrated in Smith's Figures 5 and 6. See also Gibson, *The Bible in the Latin West*, esp. her introductory survey of types and Plate 14.

14. The story is in Southern, *Life of Anselm*, 150–151; my quotations are from these pages.

15. Dondaine, *Les Secrétaires*, 17.

16. *OED*, s.v. *maker*; cf. *MED*, same heading. The word *writer* could be used, from a very early time, to mean author, but this was not its primary meaning until very recently (*OED*, s.v. *writer*). In Middle English, the primary mean-ing of *writer* was "one who writes, a penman." Chaucer's scribe Adam has been identified as Adam Pinkhurst, a member of the London Scriveners Company whom Chaucer employed over the course of two decades: see Mooney, "Chaucer's Scribe."

17. Marrou, *Histoire de l'éducation*, 230–231, 375, 522, note 13, and 553, note 30.

18. *Inst. orat.*, X. iii. 15.

19. Aristotle, *De anima*, III, 11. 434a 9–10; see Wolfson, esp. 91–93.

20. This was especially true of Thomas Aquinas; see Wolfson, 122.

21. Wolfson, 78, referring to *Metaphysics*, 6. 1027b 29–30, and *De anima*, III, 7. 431a 14–17: "when the object [of perception] is pleasant or painful, the soul makes a sort of affirmation or negation, and pursues or avoids the object. To feel pleasure or pain is to act with the sensitive mean towards what is good or bad as such. Both avoidance and appetite when actual are identical with this: the faculty of appetite and avoidance are not different, either from one another or from the faculty of sense-perception; but their being is different. To the thinking soul images serve as if they were contents of perception (and when it asserts or denies them to be good or bad it avoids or pursues them). That is why the soul never thinks without an image (*phantasmatos*)"; (trans. by J. A. Smith of the text ed. by Ross). The passage in the *Metaphysics* defines the combinative and separative functions of judgment.

22. D'Avray describes the contents of small, pocket-sized books (*vademecum*), which mendicant friars carried with them; these contain sermon models and other sermon aids. In one, the sermons are written out only as sets of rhyming headings to which Scriptural texts are attached. This is truly a model or outline of subject matters for a sermon, the *res* which an individual preacher would then be able to expand extempore; *The Preaching of the Friars*, 59–60.

23. *De memoria augenda*, s. 2b; I refer to the Huntington Library copy, published at Rome, *c.* 1493. Matheolus was greatly influenced by Hugh of St. Victor, as well as the standard trio of Thomas Aquinas, Cicero, and Aristotle.

24. *Heroides*, 18, 19–20: "talibus exiguo dictis mihi murmure verbis, / cetera cum charta dextra locuta mea est." Cited by Balogh, 214–216; see also McCartney, "Notes on Reading."
25. *Conf.*, X. ix. I have used the Latin text of Verheijen, CCSL 27.
26. The quoted words are from *Conf.*, X. xi.
27. Augustine took these etymologies from the Roman lexicographer, Varro; the frequentive intensifier *-ito* is added to the root in each case.
28. *Sermones.* 225; PL 38. 1097: "Et ego scio . . . nec ego comprehendo; sed cogitatio facit nos extendi, extensio dilatat nos, dilatatio nos capaces facit." This sermon was preached to the newly baptized (*infantes*) on Easter, *c.* 400–405.
29. *Conf.*, X. xvii.
30. Southern, *Life of Anselm by Eadmer*, x. Mackey, "*Inter nocturnas vigilias*: A Proof Postponed," gives an excellent analysis of the composition of the *Proslogion*, stressing its origin in prayerful emotion.
31. Southern, *Life of Anselm by Eadmer*, 29–30. I have given a part of the Latin text in parentheses because, while Southern's is an excellent English translation, it cannot entirely preserve the connotations of the original.
32. Murray, *Reason and Society in the Middle Ages*, esp. 6–14, 401–404.
33. Gui, c. 14, transl. Foster, 37. Cf. Tocco, c. 30 (*AASS*, March 1. 669F): "post brevem somnum in sua camera . . . in loco, quem sibi ad orandum elegerat, in oratione prostratus; ubi orando mereretur addiscere, quae oportuisset post orationem scribere vel dictare."
34. Tocco, c. 31 (*AASS*, March 1. 670B), trans. Foster, 70: "ut affectus orando mereretur ad divina ingredi, et intellectus huius merito intueri, quae altius intelligeret, quo affectus ardentius in id, quod luce caperet, amore flagraret." Thomas Aquinas is one of Murray's examples of an individual in whom "monastic" and "intellectual" cultures coexisted; *Reason and Society*, 340. Evidently, Anselm would be another.
35. Gui, c. 16, trans. Foster, 38.
36. Foster, 37. Recall that Quintilian suggests lying on one's back to stimulate invention. A posture associated with Augustine during meditational composition is seated, bowed over with his knees drawn up, and his head in his hand; see the plates in Courcelle, *Les Confessions*. A typical posture of composition in later medieval portraiture shows the composer sitting at a desk with his scribal pen and knife, staring into space before a *blank* sheet. I am indebted to Michael Camille for pointing this out to me.
37. The *forma tractatus/tractandi* is discussed particularly by Minnis, *Theory of Authorship*; see also Allen, *Ethical Poetic*, and Simpson, "Modes of Thought and Poetic Form in *Piers Plowman*."
38. *Ars rhetorica*, III, 13.
39. *Ars rhetorica*, c. 23 "De memoria" (Halm, *Rhetores latini minores*, 440).
40. *Inst. orat.*, VIII. vi. 64.
41. This and the preceding quotation are from *Inst. orat.*, X. iii. 2.
42. *Inst. orat.*, X. iii. 3. On the translation of Quintilian's phrase "sanctiore aerario conditae," see Russell's note in the new Loeb translation, 336.

43. *Inst. orat.*, X. iii. 25.
44. *Inst. orat.*, X. iii. 21.
45. *Inst. orat.*, X. iii. 17.
46. *Inst. orat.*, X. iii. 28.
47. *Inst. orat.*, X. iii. 31–32.
48. *Inst. orat.*, X. vi. 1.
49. *Inst. orat.*, X. vi. 5.
50. *Inst. orat.*, X. vii. 1–29; all quotations in this paragraph are from that chapter.
51. Quintilian uses the same phrase used also in the *Ad Herennium*, *imagines rerum*. It is thus apparent that he did not despise the making of such images; on the contrary, he regards them as most necessary, but as additional associations to stir the orator's memory not as a substitute for the heuristic of divisions marked in orderly sequences.
52. *Inst. orat.*, I. ii. 30.
53. *Inst. orat.*, VI. ii. 29; cf. X. vii. 15. See also IV. ii. 121ff., where Quintilian describes the usefulness of *imagines rerum* to engage the *intentio* of the audience as well. But this motive is always secondary to their necessity to the author.
54. *Inst. orat.*, X. vii. 32.
55. Cited by Rosen (30), from the 1839 edition of Giordano's sermons, 121. Modern editions of Giordano da Pisa's sermons are appearing with some regularity, beginning with Delcorno's 1974 edition of the Lenten sermons, and see especially Delcorno's 1975 study of him, *Giordano da Pisa*. His technique is discussed as typical of early fourteenth-century Pisan Dominican preaching by Bolzoni, *The Web of Images*, 1–40.
56. Cited by Rosen (31), from the 1839 edition of Giordano (60), vol. 386 in the series "Biblioteca scelta di opere italiane antiche e moderne." This passage was subsequently quoted in the biographical preface to Narducci's 1867 edition of Giordano's *Prediche inedite*, xx, note 1. All of these editions are described by Delcorno, xv–xvii.
57. On the editorial problems presented by a lack of author-corrected exemplars, see Delcorno's introduction to *Quaresimale Fiorentino*, esp. lxxii–lxxiv.
58. Deferrari, "Augustine's Composition," 108, citing Gregory of Nazianzus, *Oratio* 42. 26 ("Farewell Sermon"), PG 36. 492A (more recently ed. Bernardi, SC 384). The word Gregory uses, *graphides*, refers to incising with a stylus on wax tablets rather than writing with a reed pen or *kalamos*, which was used on papyrus: see Liddel and Scott, s.v. ΓΡΑΦΩ, and Thomas, *Literacy and Orality in Ancient Greece*, esp. 64–88.
59. Deferrari, "Augustine's Composition," 105; cf. PG 67. 741. Deferrari cites much evidence of similar practices, 101–106; in *De doctrina christiana*, IV. 62–63, Augustine recommends the practice of ex tempore composition of sermons but allows that some preachers may need to memorize and deliver what others have composed eloquently and wisely before.
60. *Sermones*, 225, 3 (PL 38. 1097): "ecce ego qui vobiscum loquor, antequam ad vos venirem, cogitavi ante quod vobis dicerem. Quando cogitavi quod vobis

dicerem, jam in corde meo verbum erat. Non enim vobis dicerem, nisi ante cogitarem." Augustine is preaching on the text "Verbum erat apud Deum" (Jn. 1:1) , so the word *verbum* is a pun in this sermon – moreover, on this occasion *verbum* is the *res* (subject) of his sermon, a paradox of the sort Augustine relished.

61. Examples occur throughout Giordano's sermons, especially when he spoke twice in a day. The reporter will note that Friar Giordano finished his sermon later, "but I was not there and so I didn't write down any more." Examples are in Delcorno's edition, 105, 284, and 418.

62. *Inst. orat.*, XI. ii. 47.

63. Cicero, *Brutus*, 139.

64. *De archa Noe*, I. i. 12–16: "In qua collatione, quia quedam specialiter placuisse fratribus scio, ea potissimum stilo commendare uolui, non tantum ideo quod ea digna scribi existimem, quam idcirco quod quibusdam prius inaudita et ob hoc quodammodo magis grata esse cognoui"; ed. Sicard, CCCM 176. All references are to this edition; the translation is that of "a Religious of CMSV." The treatise has a different title in the Patrologia Latina edition (PL 176. 618–680), *De arca Noe morali*; the accompanying ekphrastic picture-summary of the work, thought to be related but separate by the PL editors and titled *De arca Noe mystica* (PL 176. 681–702), is now considered properly to be a fifth book and is so presented by Sicard, with the heading *Libellus de formatione arche*.

65. Isidore, *Sententiae*, III. 14. In this same chapter Isidore also defines, as part of the same topic, the difference between reading aloud and silently, and the need for *memoria*. See Chapter 5 above.

66. The structurally exceptional phrase in *De archa Noe*, II. xvi. 7–8, is "per circunspectionem frondet et expandit ramos," which is an elision of two three-word phrases. It is worth paying attention to these internally rhyming figures of speech in medieval treatises, which often occur where one would expect an orientating summary or outline of what is to follow at the start of a major new section in a work (as here, between Books II and III).

67. *De archa Noe*, III. i. 3–4. Hugh had concluded, after the summary verses outlining the stages of the *arbor sapientiae* which he will develop next, that they all needed a break from such long-winded discourse: "Sed quia longius sermo processit, paululum respiremus" (II. xvi.11). Though this treatise was obviously written down, Hugh is careful to maintain the feel of an oral delivery, which makes the close connection of this meditation to the wholly verbal ekphrastic picture accompanying it particularly interesting. A similar twelfth-century treatise with an ekphrasis is the meditation on the Exodus Tabernacle by the Norbertine canon Adam of Dryburgh, composed around 1180. The ekphrasis is used as a device to organize a meditation on the life of the Church, much as Hugh of St. Victor uses Noah's Ark; see Carruthers, *The Craft of Thought*, 237–254. The Norbertines were closely connected to the Victorines.

68. *De archa Noe*, III. xvii. 43–49: "Sed iam, dum incidentium rationum exposi-tionem prosequimur, longius a proposito nostro digressi sumus. Vnde et de

hoc quoque ueniam postulamus, quia, ut uerum fatear, sepius in hoc tractatu scribendo plura inuenimus quam inuenta scriberemus. Neque enim uel in hoc meam insipientiam fateri erubesco. Nunc ergo ad propositum reuertentes de fabricatione arche sapientiae prosequamur."

69. Though related to oral composition theories of poetry, the characterization of oral style in sermons is somewhat different. On oral formulaic style in Greek poetry, see Parry and Lord. The theory as applicable to medieval poetry has been considerably modified – see Watts, *The Lyre and the Harp*; Curschmann, "Oral Poetry"; Brewer, "Orality and Literacy in Chaucer"; Foley, *The Theory of Oral Composition*; and Zumthor, *La Poésie et la voix dans la civilization médiévale*.

70. See Leclercq's essays "L'Art de la composition" and "Sur la caractère littéraire des Sermons de S. Bernard." Leclercq quotes Robert of Basevorn on Bernard: "Sciendum quod modus ejus sine modo … Hic semper devote, semper artificialiter procedit" (Charland, 247). Notice how, for Basevorn, Bernard's seeming artlessness ("modus ejus sine modo") is always the product of artfulness ("semper artificialiter"), that is, of his artful *memoria* which, when properly designed and adequately stored, allows for what one might call artfully planned-in-advance-spontaneity. That this ancient goal of oratory was not thought to be incompatible with monastic humility and silence is clear from a comment by an anonymous monk, who speaks of "Bernardus noster, monachorum Antonius et Tullius oratorum" (quoted by Leclercq, "L'Art de la composition," 153). Another twelfth-century composition that was formed through internal meditation and dialogue with his community is Anselm's *Monologion*, as he tells us in its preface.

71. Southern, *Life of Anselm*, 30.

72. Southern, *Life of Anselm*, 31.

73. The meaning of *livore carens* is discussed by Southern, *Life of Anselm*, 30, note 1. There have been a number of studies by Renaissance scholars of how modern notions of intellectual ownership and copyright came into being; one that takes proper account of the late medieval, humanist context within which those legal notions arose is Eden, *Friends Hold All Things in Common*.

74. Southern, *Life of Anselm*, 31. All the earliest copies of *Proslogion* include the two additions; see Southern, *St. Anselm and His Biographer*, 65.

75. Stock, *The Implications of Literacy*, 331–351.

76. Stock, *The Implications of Literacy*, 335.

77. Root, ed., *Troilus and Criseyde*, esp. lxx–lxxiii. A more recent discussion of the versions of this poem is the introduction by Windeatt to his edition of *Troilus and Criseyde*, who argues that the textual revisions are not authorial but scribal editing of Chaucer's foul papers, the state his *dictamen* might well have been left in. For a judicious overview of these matters with regard to Chaucer's texts, see Fisher, "Animadversions on the Text of Chaucer, 1988."

78. On the problems which such medieval practices present to modern editors seeking to produce an authoritative text (in the modern sense), see the editors' introduction to Kane and Donaldson, *The B-Text of Piers Plowman*, and also

Kane, "John M. Manly and Edith Rickert," in *Editing Chaucer*, and two essays by Donaldson, "Manuscripts R and F in the B-Tradition of *Piers Plowman*" and "The Psychology of Editors of Middle English Texts." For a consideration of the problem in terms of modern literary theory, see Patterson, *Negotiating the Past*, chapter 2.

79. Discussed by Pasquali, *Storia della tradizione*, esp. 437–449.

80. The situation of a literary text after the mid thirteenth century becomes ever more complicated as it achieves status as a proper author or Poet in a vernacular language which is just achieving respectability. The scribes can assume editorial powers in such cases, and the dialogue of readers with texts becomes quite complex. The role of commentaries in this process is critical.

81. De Hamel, *Glossed Books of the Bible*; my remarks on the actual page formatting of glossed books owes much to this study. More recently, see Smith, *Masters of the Sacred Page*; Gibson, *The Bible in the Latin West*; and Rouse, *Manuscripts and their Makers*.

82. G. R. Evans, *The Language and Logic of the Bible*, 46–47; this book and the earlier studies of the development of Biblical exegesis during the previous medieval centuries, especially by Smalley, *The Study of the Bible in the Middle Ages* and *The Gospels in the Schools*, show how their major scholarly project was to develop such a line-by-line complete commentary, and how Anselm of Laon was deliberately reductive and non-controversial in his project, as is suitable for a study and teaching book. Both books also clearly show how much more sophisticated advanced commentary had become during these same centuries.

83. De Hamel, *Glossed Books of the Bible*, 22. In order to recapture a somewhat similar understanding about the inclusive nature of a text, Jacques Derrida revived the format for his meditation, *Glas*.

84. De Hamel, *Glossed Books of the Bible*, 23. Peter of Poitiers's Biblical genealogy is discussed briefly in my next chapter.

85. De Hamel, *Glossed Books of the Bible*, 36–37.

86. De Hamel, *Glossed Books of the Bible*, 42–44.

87. The page lay-out and decoration of these books has been described well by De Hamel, *Glossed Books of the Bible*, esp. 24–27, 42–44, and 57–58.

88. The commentary sources in this manuscript are discussed in S. Kuttner and B. Smalley, "The 'Glossa Ordinaria' to the Gregorian Decretals." There are large illuminated initials at the start of each of the five books of Decretals, which makes this one of the earliest illuminated Decretals. The basic commentary is the standard beginning commentary put together by Bernard of Parma, and first promulgated in 1234, so this is quite an early copy.

89. De Hamel, *Glossed Books of the Bible*, 25.

90. This manuscript, in Latin, was written for a monastery in Bohemia in the late fourteenth century. Besides the Fulgentius/Bersuire, it also contains a poor text of Hugh of Fouilloy's treatise on the dove and the hawk (discussed in greater detail in Chapter 7).

91. Pasquali, *Storia della tradizione*, 446.

92. *Inst. orat.*, II. iv. 27–29.

93. *Metalogicon*, I. 24. 80–84: "Siquis autem ad splendorem sui operis alienum pannum assuerat, deprehensum redarguebat furtum; sed poenam saepissime non infligebat. Sic uero redargutum si hoc tamen meruerat inepta positio, ad exprimendam auctorum imaginem, modesta indulgentia conscendere iubebat." The image of patching with stolen cloth, as McGarry notes, is both from Horace, *Ars poetica*, 16, and from Mt. 9:16, "no man putteth a piece of new cloth unto an old garment."

94. Aldo Bernardo, whose translation I have used, translates *turba* as "mass" but Petrarch is using it specifically in the context of recollection, and in such a context *turba* refers not to mass as such but rather the unorganized, undesigned "crowding" of material that overwhelms memory; cf. Albertus Magnus on Tullius' rules.

95. *Familiares*, XXII, 2; trans. Aldo Bernardo, 213. On the notion of the authoring text in the early modern period, see Cave, *The Cornucopian Text*.

CHAPTER 7

1. Blum, *Die Antike Mnemotechnik*, esp. 1–17.

2. See Miedema, "The Term *Emblemata* in Alciati." An interesting set of late Middle English meditational emblem-poems was described in an essay by Thomas W. Ross, "Five Fifteenth-Century 'Emblem' Verses from Brit. Mus. Addit. MS. 37049." See also Hanning, "Poetic Emblems in Medieval Narrative Texts." Since this note was first written, a great deal more work has been done on Additional 37049, a Carthusian product intended for meditational use, and others like it, in the light of medieval meditational practices described in the first edition of *The Book of Memory* and subsequently in *The Craft of Thought*. The early modern emblem books have been much studied and reproduced in facsimile. Enenkel and Visser, *Mundus emblematicus*, contains essays by reliable scholars, and extensive current bibliography.

3. Mâle, *The Gothic Image*, esp. 390–396. The phrase *laicorum litteratura* is from the twelfth-century meditational treatise, *Gemma anima* by Honorius Augustodunensis. Discussing the uses of *pictura*, the author lists three: "first, because it is the reading-material of the laity; secondly, as the house is honored by such adornment; thirdly, that the life of those who lived before is recalled in memory" (PL 172. 586). The wide currency of such reasons for using pictures is discussed, with a number of excellent examples, in De Wit, *The Visual Experience of Fifteenth-Century English Readers*. Recent discussions of Gregory and Bishop Serenus include Duggan, "Was Art Really the 'Book of the Illiterate?'" and Chazelle, "Pictures, Books, and the Illiterate" and "'Not in Painting but in Writing.'" A broader context for the problem is provided by Frank, *The Memory of the Eyes*, and Kessler, "Gregory the Great and Image Theory," "Turning a Blind Eye," and *Spiritual Seeing*, esp. 104–148; see also Onians, "Abstraction and Imagination in Late Antiquity," especially on the ubiquitous use of verbal ekphrasis in late antique literature, and B. Newman,

"What Did It Mean to Say 'I Saw?'" on the role of human agency in garnering divine visions. Important discussions of the philosophical problems raised by painted and sculpted images in the Middle Ages, West and East, include Belting, *Likeness and Presence*, and Morrison, *The Mimetic Tradition of Reform* and *History as a Visual Art*.

4. "Sicut enim littere quodam modo fiunt uerborum figure et note, ita et pictura scriptarum rerum existunt similitudines et note"; Gilbert Crispin, *Disputatio Iudei et Christiani*, section 157 (ed. Abulafia and Evans, 52). See also Camille, "The Book of Signs," esp. 135–138.

5. On the matter of reading the decorative apparatus of medieval books, see especially the comments of Alexander, *The Decorated Letter*, Parkes, "The Concepts *Ordinatio* and *Compilatio*," and Camille, "The Book of Signs." On the role of ornament more generally, see the acute comments of Grabar, *The Mediation of Ornament*; Grabar focuses on Islamic art but his remarks have general relevance.

6. Gregory I, *Registrum epistularum*, XI. 10. 22–26: "Aliud est enim picturam adorare, aliud per picturae historiam quid sit adorandum addiscere. Nam quod legentibus scriptura, hoc idiotis praestat pictura cernentibus, quia in ipsa ignorantes uident quod sequi debeant, in ipsa legunt qui litteras nesciunt; unde praecipue gentibus pro lectione pictura est." Gregory expressed the same sentiment in an earlier letter (IX. 209, written July, 599) to Bishop Serenus regarding the same incident: "Idcirco enim pictura in ecclesiis adhibetur, ut hi qui litteras nesciunt saltem in parietibus uidendo legant, quae legere in codicibus non ualent" (lines 12–14): "For this reason painting should be used in churches, that those who do not know letters at least by looking at the walls may read those [things] which they are not able to read in books." Notice the use of the verb *legere* for both books and painting. The relationship of these two letters (and the issue of their genuineness) is discussed by Chazelle, "Not in Painting but in Writing."

7. See above, Chapter 2. The matter is also discussed at length in *The Craft of Thought*, especially chapters 2, 3, and 4. Kessler underscores the point in "Turning a Blind Eye"; the ambiguity created by consistently using the word *imago* for both physical and mental images throughout the Middle Ages has caused a great deal of problems for unwary historians. A similar ambiguity can attend the use of verbs like *pingo* and *describo* in verbal ekphrases, as demonstrated later in this chapter.

8. The modern edition is by Segré. The *Bestiaire* and its *Response* have been admirably discussed by Beer, *Beasts of Love*, who also translated the work, though I have made my own here. Sylvia Huot first drew my attention to Richard; she discusses his work in *From Song to Book*.

9. These commonplaces Richard could have found in Isidore; see Segré's introduction to his edition, vii–viii, and note 3.

10. Richard de Fournival, *Li Bestiaire d'amours*: "Ceste memoire si a .ij. portes, veir et oir, et a cascune de ces .ij. portes si a un cemin par ou i puet aler, che sont painture et parole"; 4.

11. Richard de Fournival, *Li Bestiaire d'amours*: "Car quant on voit painte une estoire, ou de Troies ou d'autre, on voit les fais des preudommes ki cha en ariere furent, ausi com s'il fussent present. Et tout ensi est il de parole. Car quant on ot .i. romans lire, on entent les aventures, ausi com on les veïst en present"; 5.

12. Richard de Fournival, *Li Bestiaire d'amours*: "Car il est bien apert k'il a parole, par che ke toute escripture si est faite pour parole monstrer et pour che ke on le lise; et quant on le list, si revient elle a nature de parole. Et d'autre part, k'il ait painture si est en apert par che ke lettre n'est mie, s'on ne le paint"; 5.

13. On *energeia/enargeia* in medieval meditative practice, see *The Craft of Thought*, 130–142. The figure is discussed by Aristotle, *Rhetoric*, III. 10–11, and by Quintilian, *Inst. orat.*, VIII. iii, especially (as *ornatus*). On Aristotle's use of the term, see both Kennedy's translation of the *Rhetoric* and S. Newman, "Aristotle's Notion of 'Bringing-Before-the-Eyes.'"

14. Richard de Fournival, *Li Bestiaire d'amours*: "Car je vous envoie en cest escrit et painture et parole, pour che ke, quant je ne serais presens, ke cis escris par sa painture et par sa parole me rendre a vostre memoire comme present"; 6–7. Beer translates *escris* as "composition," a word that does not capture how writing itself was thought to have *painture*, as a scribe was referred to as *pictor*, and the verb *describere* can mean both "write" and "describe."

15. Parkes, "The Concepts *Ordinatio* and *Compilatio*."

16. Dante Alighieri, *La vita nuova*: "In quella parte del libro de la mia memoria dinanzi a la quale poco si potrebbe leggere, si trova una rubrica la quale dice: Incipit vita nova. Sotto la quale rubrica io trovo scritte le parole le quali è mio intendimento d'assemplare in questo libello; e se non tutte almeno la loro sentenzia." Edited by M. Barbi for the Società Dantesca Italiana; translated by Charles Singleton, *An Essay on the Vita Nuova*, 26. I discussed this passage also in Carruthers, "*Ars inveniendi, ars memorativa*."

17. Singleton, *Essay on the Vita Nuova*, esp. 25–42.

18. DeWit discusses this poem, calling attention to its heavy visual emphasis, 24–28. The text is in *Minor Poems of John Lydgate*, ed. McCracken, 268–279. I discussed an anonymous poem composed about this same, the so-called "Long Charter of Christ," whose visual layout in CUL MS. ii. 3. 26 helps to demonstrate the ekphrasis and prosopopeia of the words, which invite the reader continually to remember and recollect the Passion, in *The Craft of Thought*, 102–103.

19. Similarly, in "The Second Nun's Tale," the figure of St. Paul appears in order to speak a text from Ephesians (*Canterbury Tales*, VIII. 200–216).

20. These examples are given by Alexander, "Scribes as Artists," 107–109. See also now his comprehensive study, *Medieval Illuminators and their Methods of Work*.

21. Nordenfalk, *Kanontäflen*, 46–54, and the same author's "Beginnings of Book Decoration," 9–15 (the quotation is from p. 10).

22. De Hamel, *Glossed Books of the Bible*, 60.

23. Nordenfalk, "Beginnings of Book Decoration," 12.

24. The excellent study prepared in connection with the 1996 exhibit of the Utrecht Psalter in the Catharijne Convent museum in Utrecht includes a lengthy analysis of the manuscript by van der Horst (van der Horst *et al.*, *The Utrecht Psalter*, 23–84). Important older studies include those of DeWald, *The Illustrations of the Utrecht Psalter*, and Dufrenne, *Les Illustrations du Psautier d'Utrecht*. Van der Horst comments on (81–83) and dismisses the idea that the Psalter images could be mnemotechnical, citing particularly Gibson-Wood, "The Utrecht Psalter and the Art of Memory," but also *The Book of Memory*. His comments make it clear that he has misunderstood the nature of *imagines rerum*, for he wrongly thinks that such advanced mnemonic craft was designed for beginners just learning to read, and scorns the idea that a complex manuscript like the Utrecht Psalter was composed for the use of novice readers in the cloister. But the uses he ascribes to them (82–83) are exactly those to which the method of *imagines rerum* is addressed – advanced scholarly study. Van der Horst also (81) wrongly characterizes Hugh of St. Victor's *Chronicle* Preface as being in the Herennian tradition of architectural mnemonic, with which it has no connection at all (see Chapter 4 above). See also my further comments on the Utrecht Psalter in *The Craft of Thought*, 203.

25. As described in Chapter 3 above, the murmur of study was a valued and much-remarked habit in antiquity as well as the Middle Ages.

26. I am indebted to William Noel's excellent discussion of the English manuscripts in van der Horst *et al.*, *The Utrecht Psalter*, 121–165. The Utrecht Psalter was in Christ Church, Canterbury, during the eleventh to twelfth centuries, and three copies of it made while it was there are extant: London, BL Harley MS. 603 (begun *c.* 1025 but composed in fits and starts until *c.* 1200, unfinished); Cambridge, Trinity College MS. R. 17. 1 (written *c.* 1155–1160, drawn during Thomas Becket's tenure as archbishop, complete); and Paris, BnF MS. lat. 8846 (*c.* 1200, unfinished in England but completed later in Spain); see also Kauffmann, *Romanesque Manuscripts*, 96–97. Jonathan Alexander comments on the copy in MS. Harley 603 (The Harley Psalter), and the difficult questions this poses, in *Medieval Illuminators and their Methods of Work*, 73–76; I am grateful to him for many stimulating and informative conversations.

27. DeWald, *The Utrecht Psalter*, 64–65; the illustrated page is fo. 82v (DeWald's Plate 129). Other examples are given by van der Horst *et al.*, *The Utrecht Psalter*, 55–73.

28. See the discussion by Morgan, *Early Gothic Manuscripts*, no. 162, vol. 2, 157–162, and the bibliography which Morgan supplies on this manuscript.

29. The pictures in Douce 104 are discussed by Scott, "Illustrations of *Piers Plowman* in Douce MS. 104," and again in her commentary in the facsimile volume, edited by Pearsall and Scott. She comments on the "idiosyncrasy" of the drawings. She and Pearsall both agree that the manuscript is a personal production, the work of either a single scribe-illuminator or two individuals working very closely together; in any case the illuminator, like the scribe, was an intelligent reader of the poem. Annotations in Douce 104 are by another

person, but one also working soon after the manuscript was made. The evidence for the manuscript's provenance is assessed by Kerby-Fulton and Despres, *Iconography and the Professional Reader.*

30. In her part of *Iconography and the Professional Reader*, Kerby-Fulton insists that some patron must have commissioned the manuscript; she is reluctant to consider the possibility that the scribe undertook to write it and illustrate it for himself. (She goes so far as to imagine – in order to reject – an owner "scribbling" and sketching such a book for himself without any competencies at all, a circumstance completely out of the question and never, to my knowledge, suggested.) Despres, rightly in my opinion, argues for the "personal" nature of this book's production as well as its conception. As she and Kerby-Fulton both emphasize, there are other books – ones far more elaborate and expensive than Douce 104 – which scribes are known to have made for their own use. Most notable from the late English Middle Ages is the encyclopedia book of James le Palmer, written and decorated by himself; this is fully discussed by Sandler, *Omne bonum.*

31. Frances Yates noticed how much Holcot's pictures were like *imagines rerum*: *The Art of Memory*, 96–101.

32. Transcribed by Smalley, *English Friars*, 172–178.

33. Smalley, *English Friars*, 112.

34. Smalley, *English Friars*, 118. These images are also discussed by Allen, *The Friar as Critic*, 51–52; his whole discussion is of interest (29–53), though he does not mention a mnemonic connection.

35. Transcribed by Smalley, *English Friars*, 173 from Bodley 722, fo. 21: "Hic dicendum est secundum Augustinum super Iohannem sermone 7: Qualem faciem habet dilectio, qualem formam, qualem staturam, quales manus, quales pedes habet, nemo potest dicere. Habet tamen pedes, quia ipsi ducunt ad ecclesiam. Unde ex ista imagine potest caritas sive dilectio describi sicut una regina in throno collocata, statura elevata, figura quadrata, Phebo maritata, prole vallata, melle cibata, cum facie quadriformi et veste auriformi, manus habens stillantes et porrectas, aures apertas et directas, oculos flammeos et uxorinos et pedes caprinos" (comment in reference to Hosea 6). The heavy use of internal rhyme is also characteristic of Holcot's pictures, and mnemonically effective, as counselled by Robert of Basevorn and other authors of arts of preaching (see Chapter 3 above).

36. Smalley, *English Friars*, 172, 179.

37. On how the *Rhetorica ad Herennium* was taught, see Ward, *Ciceronian Rhetoric*, and the essays in Cox and Ward, *The Rhetoric of Cicero.*

38. Smalley, *English Friars*, 173, transcribing from Bodley 722, fol. 30: "in fine capituli, super illam litteram *Noli letari*, ubi loquitur de idolatria, pono picturam antiquorum de idolatria." Yates also comments on this passage, *Art of Memory*, 99.

39. See Carlo de Clercq, "Hughes de Fouilloy."

40. Some scholars have believed the picture described in Hugh's *Libellus* must have been an actual object. Though both Sicard (in *Diagrammes médiévales*,

though he withdrew this opinion in his CCCM edition) and Zinn ("Exile and Hugh of St Victor") have held this opinion, the most forceful case is made by Rudolph, *Mystic Ark*. Rudolph maintains that the *Libellus* is not the description of an actual painting nor instructions for making a real object, but a gathering of materials for meditation that were initially guided by a real painting, which was painted on some large flat surface at St. Victor (perhaps a wall or the floor) and used by Hugh as the focus for a set of lectures, many of which became what Rudolph calls "The Moral Ark" (i.e. *De archa Noe*). But the lexical evidence remains strongly against such an interpretation. Latin *pictura*, at this time, refers as readily to verbal ekphrasis and imagined pictures as it does to actual painting, and absent any evidence other than Hugh's use of this word, the case for a complex mural painting having been made at St. Victor – let alone made as the focus for a set of lectures – is unproven, though it would certainly be remarkable if it had occurred. See my comments on the meditational genre of *pictura* in *The Craft of Thought*, esp. chapter 4 and also B. Newman, "What did it mean to say 'I saw?'" Hugh's *Libellus* is translated by J. Weiss in Carruthers and Ziolkowski (eds.), *The Medieval Craft of Memory*, 41–70.

41. Goy, *Die Uberlieferung*, 237; the first two rubrics are from Bodleian Library Laud Misc. 370 and Laud Misc. 409, both twelfth-century mss. from St. Albans, the third from BnF. lat. 10631, also of the twelfth century.

42. Smalley, *Study of the Bible*, 96; Smalley comments briefly, but cogently, on how "the roles of text and picture, that we are accustomed to, seem to be reversed in much of the twelfth-century educational literature. You begin with your picture. . ."; 95–96.

43. Rudolph argues that these gaps and inconsistencies are evidence that the *Libellus* is an uncorrected *reportatio*, made by an incompetent student, which somehow escaped Hugh's normally careful correction (yet, unchallenged, gave rise to many manuscript copies). This seems unlikely.

44. Hugh of St. Victor, *De formatione arche*, I. 1–25; trans. Weiss. The Latin text is that of Sicard, CCCM 176. All subsequent citations are to this translation and edition. Notice Hugh's two-language pun on the Greek letter *chi*, X, the first letter in the name *Christos* and also, in Latin, the number 10, written x, and so resembling *chi* in its visual form. Migne regarded the writing of *c* here as a simple error. But it is not. From the end of the Carolingian period, the final sigma of the *nomina sacra* was often written as a *c* in Latin script – χρς – (see Lindsay, *Notae latinae*, 396), though this apparent "c" is actually ς. The cabalistic principle that names and numerology are contained in the same forms may also have influenced Hugh here, perhaps another example of the interest in Jewish exegetical traditions that is associated by Beryl Smalley with St. Victor; see Smalley, *Study of the Bible*, 103–105, 149–172, 361–365.

45. Hugh's understanding of moralizing is very well described in his definition of the tropological genre of Biblical exegesis: "tropology . . . is the changing-direction word or the phrase folded-back, for truly we turn the word of a narrative concerning others to our own instruction when, having read of the deeds of others, we conform our lives to their example"; see Appendix A.

46. At one point, Hugh refers to the right limb (*cornus*) of the central cross as being on the north side, "dextero lateri, id est aquiloni" (II. 41) but in another he says he labels the left limb as on the north side, "in sinistro, 'latera aquilonis'" (IV. 19). The inconsistency could arise from a difference in Hugh's mental orientation towards his figure, that is whether he imagines himself looking towards it or out from it, an inconsistency that would arise more easily if one were working with a mental image than with an actual graph. Sicard attempted several drawings of the features described by Hugh; these are reproduced for his edition as CCCM volume 176 A. It is telling that he requires eleven plates to reproduce all the features that Hugh has put into his single picture. Zinn has reproduced a computer-generated version from Hugh's ekphrasis in "Exile and Hugh of St. Victor," though even it has had to be simplified and requires a zoom tool in order to be fully practical.

47. *De archa Noe*, I. v. 157–158. A diagram of the Ark, shown as a cut-off pyramid, accompanies some manuscripts of Peter of Poitiers's *Genealogia*. An example is Bodleian Library MS. Laud Misc. 151, fo. 1, a manuscript of the second quarter of the thirteenth century (a century after Hugh of St. Victor) in which the *Genealogia* precedes the texts of the Pentateuch and Peter Comestor's *Historia scholastica*. Two other diagrammatic drawings of the Ark as a curtailed pyramid are in a genealogical roll written about 1420–1430 in English (Bodleian Library, MS. Barlow 53); this roll is prefaced by a translation of Peter's preface, discussed later in this chapter. But the Ark took many forms throughout this period.

48. *Libellus de formatione arche*, I. 87–95. I discussed the issue of whether Hugh's picture was real or not in *The Craft of Thought*, 243–246; see also the introduction to Weiss's translation in Carruthers and Ziolkowski (eds.), *The Medieval Craft of Memory*. Though the evidence tends towards understanding Hugh's description as verbal ekphrasis (the meaning of Latin *descriptio* at this time), something rather like it was soon realized in varying forms in Gothic church architecture, for the exegetical conflation of the church (and church building) with Noah's Ark is patristic, found as early as Ambrose. Relevant matters are discussed in *The Craft of Thought*, 221–276, and see also Carruthers, "The Poet as Master-Builder."

49. *Libellus de formatione arche*, II. 67–69: "Post hec, singulis nominibus suas imagines superpono semiplenas a pectore sursum, quales nonnunquam in tabulis solent figurari, quas Graeci frequentiori usu 'iconas' uocant."

50. *Libellus de formatione arche*, II. 73–78. At this time, the Bible was considered to have 22 books in the Old Testament and 8 in the New, as Hugh of St. Victor describes them in *De archa Noe*, Book I. v. 16–19 (ed. Sicard, 24).

51. Something like these circles, represented as lunettes, can be seen in Hugh's history diagram, figure 5. Hanning has argued suggestively that the Creator-Majesty image was especially employed during the twelfth century as a model for human as well as divine creativity: "'*Ut enim faber ... sic creator.*'" Hanning's notes contain a bibliography of discussions of the Majesty image from the early Middle Ages onward. It seems to have peaked in popularity,

judging by its survival in manuscript painting, during the twelfth to thirteenth centuries; one should, however, be careful in relying too heavily upon such evidence for a true assessment of the relative popularity of a particular mnemonic device since mental composition and imaging, employing such *formae*, seem to have been a feature even of early monastic culture. A good example is the use, in Benedict's Rule, of the *scala Jacobis* (Jacob's ladder) to organize the stages of humility.

52. This work is now fully available in a splendid edition and translation by Willene Clark. On Hugh's life, see *Dictionnaire de spiritualité*, s.v. "Hughes de Fouilloy."

53. See the essays by Carlo de Clercq, "Le Rôle de l'image" and "Hugues de Fouilloy."

54. Those with complete cycles are Heiligenkreutz (a Cistercian monastery) MS. 226, British Library, MS. Sloane 278, St.-Omer MS. 94 (from the Cistercian abbey of Clairmarais), and Troyes MS. 177 (from Clairvaux itself). These manuscripts are all of the thirteenth century. Two other manuscripts of the twenty-one still extant have most of the cycle – Bodleian Library MS. Lyell 71, the one I have examined most fully and the subject of de Clercq's "Le Rôle de l'image," and Brussels, Bibliothèque Royale MS. II, 1076. On the Lyell manuscript itself, which was made in northern Italy around 1300, see de la Mare, *Lyell Manuscripts*, 211–216. I commented briefly in Chapter 4 above, and in *The Craft of Thought*, 84–101, on the significance of Bestiaries forming so common a feature of Cistercian libraries, given the order's strictures against using excessive and monstrous decoration and ornament in the cloister (where most reading occured), and especially representation of animals.

55. Hugh de Fouilloy, *Aviarium*, prol. 1: "Ego enim de clero, tu de militia. Ad conversionem venimus ut in regulari vita quasi in pertica sedeamus" (ed. and trans. Clark, 118–119).

56. I have described the image in MS. Lyell 71; MS. Sloane 278 has the same image, somewhat less finely executed, as is true generally of this manuscript, but with identical titles and lay-out.

57. Hugh de Fouilloy, *Aviarium*, prol. 1: "et qui rapere consueveras domesticas aves, nunc bonae operationis manu silvestres ad conversionem trahas, id est seculares". (ed. and trans. Clark, 118–119).

58. De Clercq, "Le Rôle de l'image," 24. In the Authorized Version (1611), where it is numbered Ps. 68:13, the word is rendered as "pots" ("Though ye have lain among the pots"); the New Revised Standard (1989) reads "sheepfolds" ("though they stay among the sheepfolds").

59. Hugh de Fouilloy, *Aviarium*, Prol. 1: "Desiderii tui, carissime, petitionibus satisfacere cupiens, columbam, cujus *pennae sunt deargentate et posteriora dorsi ejus in pallore auri* [Ps. 67:14] pingere et per picturam simplicium mentes aedificare decrevi, ut quod simplicium animus intelligibili oculo capere vix poterat, saltem carnali discernat: et quod vix concipere poterat auditus percipiat visus" (ed. and trans. Clark, 116–117; my change indicated in square brackets). Clark understands *simplicii* to mean "laity," but this is unlikely in

context: Hugh addresses the novices in monastic vocation, the "converted" in the sense developed by the twelfth-century monastic reform centered around the Cistercians (who thought of themselves as "the converted").

60. Hugh de Fouilloy, *Aviarium*, prol. 2: "Quod enim doctioribus innuit [s]criptura, hoc simplicibus pictura ... Ego autem plus laboro ut simplicibus placeam, quam ut doctioribus loquar, et quasi vasculo pleno latices infundam" (ed. Clark, 118, 120; my translation).

61. As Eugene Vance has remarked, "medieval sign theory necessarily involves a problematics of memory," *Mervelous Signals*, 304. Vance's study, especially chapter 3, is excellent on this relationship. A playful meditation by Umberto Eco upon the relationship of *artificialis memoria* and semiotics, published in English some twenty-two years after it was first written, is "An *Ars Oblivionalis*? Forget It!"

62. Isidore, *Sententiarum*, III, 14.3: "Multum prosunt in conlatione figurae. Res enim quae minus per se aduertuntur, per conparationem rerum facile capiuntur." I used the literal translation, "gathering," for the complex process denoted by *collatio*, Isidore's word, on the example of J. Taylor's translation of Hugh of St. Victor's *Didascalicon*.

63. See the description in the Huntington Library's *Guide to Medieval and Renaissance Manuscripts*.

64. This is especially true of Bodleian Library, MS. Lyell 2, a twelfth-century copy of a life of Jerome and of some of his Epistles, and of Harvard College MS. 27, a collection of saints' lives. Lyell 2 also contains marginal titles enclosed in geometric forms, though nothing so elaborate as HM 19915; Harvard College 27 contains a distinctive cryptogram of "NOTA" found also in HM 19915.

65. I have seen a much later manuscript in which the catchwords have been decorated in a basically similar way (Trinity College, Cambridge MS. O.9.1; see DeWit, 84). Catchwords, however, are for the use of scribes and binders; the phrases so decorated in HM 19915 are *tituli*, and so can only be for the use of readers needing to remember text.

66. *Histoire de la Vulgate*, 307; the discussion of *tituli* is in 307–315. The mnemonic utility of these *lectionis tituli*, "summary-phrases for reading," is clear from comments by Cassiodorus, quoted by Berger, 308.

67. Tying a string around one's finger as a mnemonic help is ancient; Quintilian mentions it in his discussion of *memoria*, *Inst. orat.*, XI. ii. 30. The many types of mnemonic images discussed by Host von Romberch include implements, animals, and birds, as well as architecture.

68. On marginal drolleries, see especially Randall, *Images in the Margins of Gothic Manuscripts*, and Camille, *In the Margins*. On the transmission and dissemination of the *Rhetorica ad Herennium*, see Ward, *Ciceronian Rhetoric*, and the essays in Cox and Ward, *The Rhetoric of Cicero*, especially those by Taylor-Briggs and Carruthers (on teaching memory arts).

69. This story is best-known to us through the version told in the beginning reading book which the Knight of LaTour-Landry made for his daughters. Randall collected a number of images which refer to this tale (misidentified as

"man defecating"): see esp. figures 530 and 581–584. In these latter figures, the eggs laid by the squire have been collected into a basket. A great deal has been published since the mid-1980s on *bas-de-page* images, including two fine studies of the Luttrell Psalter by Camille and Sandler.

70. The *mise-en-page* of this book is "altogether different . . . from any other known system of decoration of Canon Law texts" (Sandler, *Gothic Manuscripts*, no. 101). The book has now been studied in detail by Bovey, *The Smithfield Decretals*. Taylor, *Textual Situations*, devotes a chapter to it, suggesting various connections (some more persuasive than others) between its images and its themes.

71. The chief illustrations of this book are reproduced in Plummer, *The Hours of Catherine of Cleves*.

72. A well-known example is in the Book of Hours made for Engelbert of Nassau in the fifteenth century, Bodleian Library MS. Douce 219, fo. 16v. Another page (fo. 40r) has a border of pearl and ruby jewelry. Both pages are reproduced in Alexander, *The Master of Mary of Burgundy*. Recent illuminating studies of how such books were used include especially K. Smith, *Art, Identity and Devotion*, and Wieck, *Painted Prayers*.

73. See *The Craft of Thought*, 99–115 especially. Hair-pulling is featured in some of the Romanesque capitals of the abbey church at Vézelay; these are understood by Ambrose as images of violent disorder: see his *The Nave Sculptures of Vézelay*. Struggle, however, especially with demons, not only is associated with violence, but is part of the constant ascetic exercise of the athlete of God, as the life of St. Antony attests. It soon became an ascetic trope.

74. The manuscript, in four volumes (BL MS. Royal 1 D v–viii), is described by Maunde-Thompson, *A Catalogue of Ancient Manuscripts*, vol. 1. 17–20. Such drawings can be seen in vol. 2, fo. 148v, and vol. 4, fos. 5v, 76r. There are also simple flowers and leaves, and baskets of fruit on other pages of this codex. A facsimile, also edited by Maunde-Thompson, was published by the British Museum, 1879–1883.

75. *Commentary on Aristotle's De memoria*, ii, iii; ed. Borgnet, p. 110.

76. "That is the way of the cat; it wants the fish, but not the fishing," *Poetria nova*, 2028–2029 (trans. Nims). The saying is proverbial, recorded in W. W. Skeat's *Early English Proverbs* and Walther's *Lateinische Sprichwörter*, esp. numbers 2490–2491, 2495, 2504. A common form is "Cattus amat pisces, sed non vult tangere flumen," "A cat loves fish, but does not want to touch the river."

77. See, for example, BL MS. Royal 5 D x. (English, late thirteenth century), fo. 82v; in the left margin a hand pulls in a fish on a line opposite a text from Augustine, beginning "Nam gaudet et piscis." The drawing is later than the writing of the manuscript, evidently the work of a reader. This manuscript contains some of Robert Grosseteste's indexing symbols, and is mentioned in Hunt, "Manuscripts Containing Indexing Symbols." Sandler, "Gone Fishing," discusses how a single, complex *bas-de-page* scene of apes fishing and preparing their catch on the first folio of a Book of Hours serves to orient

readers to the whole book's essential tasks. A famous book using fish as one of its visual elements is the Book of Kells, of which I have more to say below.

78. *The Winchester Malory* (facsimile edition), ed. Ker, fo. 23.

79. Kauffmann, *Romanesque Painting*, 45.

80. Weitzmann, *Late Antique and Early Christian Book Illumination*, 112 and plate 41. See also *Cambridge Illuminations*, no. 1, where the grid lay-out of the pictures is described as "very unusual, especially for this early period" (47).

81. The Cuerden Psalter is also preceded by picture-pages in a rigid grid format. The first of the picture-pages in M 183 (fo. 9v) contains in one of the roundels reserved for saints an image which incorporates a common mnemonic of the Seven Deadly Sins, the acronym SALIGIA. This is written on two sword-like shafts which pierce the bosom of the Virgin, before whom a male figure kneels. The background is plain gold leaf, the undifferentiated sort of color suggested for memory places. It is an *imago rerum* for the Feast of the Seven Sorrows of the Virgin. I would like to thank Dr. William Voelkle of The Morgan Library for bringing this image to my attention.

82. Translated by Cahn, "The Allegorical Menorah," 118; see also Smalley, *Study of the Bible*, 214. Alberic of Trois-Fontaines, a Cistercian chronicler, recorded that Peter of Poitiers "pauperibus clericis consulens excogitavit arbores historiarum veteris Testamenti in pellibus depingere," MGH *Scriptores* XXIII. 886. The text of the *Genealogia* and its manuscripts are discussed in detail by Moore, *The Works of Peter of Poitiers*, 97–117.

83. On all of these manuscripts, see Pächt and Alexander, *Illustrated Manuscripts in the Bodleian Library*, nos. 377 (Laud misc. 151), 429 (Lat. th. b. 1 and c. 2), 883 (Barlow 53). The lay-out of the two companion rolls is also discussed briefly by Morgan, *Early Gothic Manuscripts*, vol. 2, 180. See also Cahn, "The Allegorical Menorah," on the connection of this popular lecture diagram also with Peter of Poitiers.

84. Moore, *The Works of Peter of Poitiers*, p. 99: "quasi in sacculo quodam memoriter tenere narrationes hystoriarum ... Quod et fastidientibus prolixitatem propter subiectam oculis habita [*sic*] memorie commendari et omnibus legentibus utilitatem conferre."

85. Geoffrey of Vinsauf, *Poetria nova*, 2013–2014. The translation is that of Nims though I have kept the Latin words, as indicated by my italics.

86. Host von Romberch distinguished clearly between *similitudo, figura,* and *forma,* which he defined as follows: "Forma dat esse specificum artificiato: poterit per inde abstracta rei species in loco imaginata." In other words, *forma* fulfills the function of a diagram. Romberch is much too late to serve as definite evidence for what the word meant to Geoffrey of Vinsauf, of course, but it is interesting to see that *forma* acquired so technical a meaning in later mnemonic practice.

87. The seminal discussion of later medieval diagrams is that of Saxl, "A Spiritual Encyclopedia of the Later Middle Ages"; a discussion in the general context of memorial use is Friedman, "Les Images mnémotechniques dans les manuscrits de l'époque gothique," 169–183, in Roy and Zumthor, *Jeux de mémoire*.

In the introduction to her study of the DeLisle Psalter, Sandler reproduces versions of some of the more elaborate mnemonic *formae* of the late Middle Ages; of particular interest is the independently produced "Tower of Wisdom," which utilizes an alphabet grid as its basic ordering structure. The fact that such an elaborate set of mnemonic *picturae* is Franciscan-sponsored is of interest because, we recall, one of the picture-making friars mentioned earlier in this chapter, John Ridevall, was a Franciscan.

88. It is reproduced by Faral, *Les Arts poétiques*, 87; see also Lawler, 40–41. Book IX of Isidore's *Etymologiae* has several of what Isidore calls *stemmata* which indicate complex degrees of kinship (and thus whom one cannot marry); most are in tree form, like modern genealogies, but one is in the form of partitioned concentric circles. Evidently such forms were later adapted to show kinship among other kinds of things as well; they still are, of course.

89. *OED*, s.v. *rote*. *MED*, s.v. *rote*, gives additional Middle English citations, but does not substantially change the meanings given by *OED*, and it does not, of course, give etymologies.

90. The phrase also occurs in the Prioress's Tale, where the "litel clergeon," just beginning his grammar-lessons, learns a hymn by listening, "And herkned ay the wordes and the noote, / Til he the firste vers koude al by rote" (VII. 1711–1712); and in the portrait of the Sergeant of Law, who knew all the statutes from the time of King William, and "every statut koude he pleyn by rote" (I, 327). In these two instances, the phrase simply means "by heart" or "habit," to use the commoner Middle English synonym.

91. In addition to her *Art of Memory*, see Yates's essays collected in *Lull and Bruno*; Hillgarth, *Ramón Lull and Lullism*; and Johnston. *The Evangelical Rhetoric of Ramón Lull* and *The Spiritual Logic of Ramón Lull*. On the affinities (and the important differences) between Lull's system and Francis Bacon's systems and other seventeenth-century efforts to create "real" languages and logics, see Rossi, *Logic and the Art of Memory*, and R. Lewis, *Language, Mind, and Nature*. Bolzoni, *The Gallery of Memory*, discusses similar post-medieval studies in the Italian academies of the fifteenth and sixteenth centuries.

92. On China, see Spence, *Memory Theater of Matteo Ricci*. On Mexico, see especially P. Watts, "Hieroglyphs of Conversion," demonstrating the importation by Franciscans of some of their familiar medieval mnemonic systems for missionary purposes. Ramón Lull's missionary aims, for which his "Great Art" was designed, clearly foreshadowed those of the sixteenth-century Spanish friars who desired to convert the Mexican Indians. But when such images were put to the new purpose of teaching alien speakers in alien cultures (Mexico and China), the initial purpose of these image schemes – that is, to serve the compositional needs of preachers already adept in their Bible and theology – was radically altered to serve instead the elementary learning requirements of a wholly catechumenal population.

93. Yates, *Art of Memory*, 176.

94. These roots in monastic disciplines are the focus of my *The Craft of Thought*, and demonstrated as well in the works collected in Carruthers and Ziolkowski

(eds.), *The Medieval Craft of Memory*. That Neoplatonism may be overrated as a major influence on twelfth-century art is the sobering conclusion of an essay by Kidson, "Panofsky, Suger and St. Denis." Kidson argues that Suger was no Neoplatonist, and not much of a dogmatic theologian at all, but wrote from a practical belief that aesthetic experience and knowledge are completely intertwined, an assumption that is evident as well in mnemonic pedagogy.

95. Saxl, "A Spiritual Encyclopedia," 83–84.

96. The history of these diagrams is fully discussed in Sandler's introduction to her study of them. Sandler has separately discussed the diagram called "The Tower of Wisdom" (*turris sapientiae*) in Carruthers and Ziolkowski (eds.), *The Medieval Craft of Memory*, 215–225. On the Cherub diagram, also see Carruthers, "Movement in the Mind's Eye," and the translation of *De sex alis* by B. Balint in Carruthers and Ziolkowski (eds.), *The Medieval Craft of Memory*, 83–102. Bolzoni has discussed the use of the Cherub device in a set of vernacular sermons by Bernardino da Siena in *The Web of Images*.

97. Jacques Guilmain, "The Geometry of the Cross-Carpet Pages in the Lindisfarne Gospels"; the quotation is from p. 52. On the keeping of such books as the Book of Kells, see Françoise Henry, 149–153.

98. Giraldus Cambrensis, *In topographia Hibernie*. The translation is from the text edited by James F. Dimock for the Rolls series. The recension Dimock edited is of one of the last of Giraldus's revisions; he produced at least five, the first composed between 1185, when he went to Ireland, and 1188, when it was read at Oxford. The account of the book is in a chapter now called "De libro miraculose conscripto" (II. 38). For the history of the text, and an edition of the first recension (which excludes the last sentence I have translated here), see O'Meara, "Giraldus Cambrensis in Topographia Hibernie."

99. For basic information and bibliography on the Book of Durrow (Trinity College Dublin MS. A. 4. 5) and the Book of Kells (Trinity College Dublin MS. A. 1. 6), see Alexander, *Insular Manuscripts*. Both manuscripts have been produced in facsimiles, the Book of Durrow edited by Luce *et al.*, and the Book of Kells edited by F. Henry.

100. De Hamel, *A History of Illuminated Manuscripts*, 101.

101. "Multa sunt alia que dici possent de his, que nos necessario in hoc loco preterire oportet" (CCCM 176, 151, 26–27).

102. A variant of the proverb about the cat who likes fish but not to fish has to do with cats who like full bellies but not catching mice. For example (one with some of the obscurity generic to proverbs): "Cattus amat pisces, sed non vult crura madere; / Isque adeo tumidus, si non vult carpere mures: / Nulla farina tamen quamvis aliud sit in urna"; "The cat likes fish but does not wish to get his legs wet; / And he is very full indeed, if he does not wish to catch mice: / no flour though, even if the other is in the storage-jar" (Walther 2491). The first part is clear – the second part seems to mean that the cat must be very satisfied to forgo catching mice in a flour container because it might also get some flour (on its feet?).

APPENDIX A

1. My translation from the edition of William M. Green, "De tribus maximis circumstantiis gestorum." This edition was based on the twelfth-century St Victor manuscript, with accompanying diagram (figure 3), which is now BnF MS. lat. 15009. Two typographical errors in that text have been corrected: *ornatem* (for *ornatam*), 490.24, and *pituit* (for *potuit*), 490.40. With permission of The University of Pennsylvania Press, I have used my own translation, previously published in Carruthers and Ziolkowski (eds.), *The Medieval Craft of Memory*.

2. Hugh uses such words as *distinctio, discretio, partitio* with both *rerum*, referring to the division and classification of subject matters, and *locorum*, referring to the mental locations imagined for the mnemotechnique he is describing. This lexicon shows how, from the beginning of scholastic method, locational "rhetorical memory" for composing an oration and "dialectical memory" for analyzing and composing an argument were intentionally closely allied.

3. Evidently a box-like structure rather than a point on a line, Hugh's mental locations have dimension.

4. Hugh confirms that his technique is intended to facilitate and ease recollection on the part of those for whom the individual Psalm texts are already known by rote, and thus can be visualized and divided according to the consciously held requirements of each practitioner, filling each cell-like "number" in the grid with the familiar incipits of Psalm verses. The mental grid described here has the textual numbers in order, but as read and sung for the liturgical offices the psalter did not, since the texts were ordered by different schemes. Complete beginners at this time memorized their Psalms through reciting the offices. As Hugh says, his method is for the more advanced students needing to support arguments in school disputations and like situations, and remains useful for senior scholars composing colloquies and sermons.

5. No English word captures the double and simultaneous meaning of Latin *ornatus* and *ornamentum*, "equipment, adornment." The marriage of function and beauty, use and delight, which this family of words achieves I have rendered into English alternately with words conveying usefulness and function, and words referring to decoration.

APPENDIX B

1. My translation is based on the Geyer edition of the works of Albertus Magnus, vol. 28. Albertus's comments on this same passage in the *Rhetorica ad Herennium* in his commentary on Aristotle's *De memoria et reminiscentia* have been translated into English by Ziolkowski, in Carruthers and Ziolkowski (eds.), *The Medieval Craft of Memory*, 118–152. Thomas Aquinas's commentary on Aristotle's treatise, now available in two different English translations (see Bibliography) is also especially pertinent; see *The Medieval Craft of Memory*, 153–188.

2. See Sorabji, *Aristotle on Memory*, 77–78, and Aristotle, *Nicomachean Ethics*, 1139b 15.

3. Albertus's concern in this first article is to define how rhetorical *memoria*, as it is discussed in the *Rhetorica ad Herennium*, can be fitted into Aristotle's philosophical discussion, especially in *De memoria et reminiscentia*, with its distinction between the psychological powers of memory and reminiscence. This requires Albertus to distinguish the trained habits of memory technique from the psychological faculties which Aristotle defined, and show how mnemotechnique requires the action of both faculties in its working. I have left the Latin word untranslated but in italics, in order to convey the fact that *memoria* is a term under discussion in this article, and not a word whose definition is settled.

4. The quotations are from *Ad Her.* III.16.28ff., as Albertus continues his effort to fit the rhetorician's understanding of *memoria* to that defined in Aristotle's psychological works. *Inductio* is probably understood technically here, referring to a kind of argumentation, discussed by both Cicero and Quintilian, which proceeds by analogy from a number of specific cases to infer a general principle or universal rule.

5. Albertus may be thinking here of Aristotle's definition of *memoria*, which includes the observation that a memory can be generated only after some time has past after the event we remember. But the idea that past time is part of the very definition of memory is familiar in the thirteenth century, and does not have to be related specifically to Aristotle – recall the common figure of Prudence with three eyes, looking to past, present, and future.

6. As shown in Chapter 4, the obscurity of this segment of the *Rhetorica ad Herennium* is not helped by the fact that Albertus was using a bad edition of it. The correct reading is, in part, "Aesopum et Cimbrum subornari ut ad Iphegeniam in Agamemnonem et Menelaum," "Aesop and Cimber being dressed as Agamemnon and Menelaus for [a drama of] *Iphigenia*." Albertus's text read something like "Aesopum et Cimbrum subornari ut vel vagantem Ephigeniam." Albertus does what he can with this senseless quotation – understanding *subornari* as "supply, prepare, equip," he has Aesop and Cimber being supplied or fitted-out as wandering Iphigenia (though he seems to reverse the order of the characters in the last clause of his explanation).

7. Again, Albertus has an altered text: *Ad Herennium* reads "egregie turpe, inhonestum, inusitatem, magnum, incredibile, ridiculum"; Albertus has "egregie aut honestum aut turpe in homines, tum inauditum, magnum, incredibile, periculosum."

8. In his response, Albertus reverses the order of the fourth and fifth of Tullius' precepts, as set forth in his first statement of them. This reversal seems to reflect Albertus's understanding that the rule regarding *intervalla*, which I discussed in Chapters 2 and 4, refers not to the viewer's imagined distance from the background but to the differentiation of one imagined location from others in its set (which is a possible meaning of *intervalla*, just not the one operative here). In later memory arts, such as Peter of Ravenna's *Fenix* and Robert Copland's

English version of it (1548), both imagined dimensons are given, roughly thirty feet for the imagined distance of the viewer and five or six feet for the distance between the imagined locations.

9. On Albertus's distinction between *vis formalis* and *vis imaginativa*, see Wolfson, "The Internal Senses," and Chapter 2 above. Basically, the "shaping-power" (*formalis*) is more simply passive than the "image-making-power" (*imaginativa*), though both are prior (and so "lower") to the "higher" functioning of memory and recollection.

APPENDIX C

1. I have translated the text which I edited from the three extant manuscripts. The manuscripts, authorship, and manuscript variants are all discussed in that edition. See also my introduction to this text in Carruthers and Ziolkowski (eds.), *The Medieval Craft of Memory*. Previously published in *The Medieval Craft of Memory*, the translation is printed here with permission of The University of Pennsylvania Press.

2. The linguistic legerdemain in this text is noteworthy. Not only are puns made readily across the three main languages of England (English, French, and Latin) but dialect variants also are pressed into service. Bradwardine exploits "the sounds of all languages" as John of Garland had also advised a century earlier. Just as Latin *qui* is sounded as *ky*, so this pun would require that *anguilla* be sounded as *angilla* to make a proper, if partial, homophony with *anglia*.

Bibliography

I REFERENCE WORKS

Bell, David N. *An Index of Authors and Works in Cistercian Libraries in Great Britain*. Kalamazoo, MI: Cistercian Publications, 1992.

Blaise, Albert. *Lexicon latinitatis medii aevii*. Corpus christianorum continuatio medievalis, 28. Turnhout: Brepols, 1975.

Cambridge Companion to the Bible. Edited by H. Kee *et al*. Cambridge: Cambridge University Press, 1997.

Dictionary of Medieval Latin from British Sources. Prepared by D. R. Howlett, R. E. Latham *et al*. London: Oxford University Press, 1975–.

Dictionnaire de spiritualité ascétique et mystique. Edited by Marcel Viller. Paris: G. Beauchesne, 1937–1995.

Dictionnaire de théologie catholique. Edited by A. Vacant and E. Mangenot. Paris: Lerouzey & Ané, 1909–1950.

Du Cange, Charles du Fresne (Sieur) *et al*. *Glossarium mediae et infimae latinitatis*. Originally published 1610–1688. Revised edition, 10 vols. in 5. Graz: Akademische Druck, 1954–1955.

Indices to Facsimiles of Ancient Manuscripts, First Series, 1903–1912. London: New Paleographical Society, 1914.

Lewis, C. T., and C. Short, *A Latin Dictionary*. Oxford: Clarendon Press, 1879.

Liddell, H. G., and R. Scott. *A Greek–English Lexicon*. Revised edition. Oxford: Clarendon Press, 1968.

Middle English Dictionary. Edited by H. Kurath, S. M. Kuhn, and R. Lewis. Ann Arbor: University of Michigan Press, 1957–2001. Online edition, *Middle English Dictionary Online*.

The New Grove Dictionary of Music and Musicians. London: Macmillan, 1980. Online edition, *Grove Online*.

Ochoa, Xaverius, and Aloisius Diez. *Indices titulorum et legum corpus juris civilis*. Rome: Commentarium pro Religiosus, 1965.

Indices canonium, titulorum et capitulorum corpus juris canonici. Rome: Commentarium pro Religiosus, 1964.

The Oxford English Dictionary on Historical Principles. Edited by J. H. A. Murray *et al*. Oxford: Clarendon Press, 1933. Online edition, *OED Online*.

The Oxford Latin Dictionary. Edited by P. G. W. Clare. New York: Oxford University Press, 1982.

Pollard, A. W., and G. R. Redgrave, compilers. *A Short-Title Catalogue of Books Printed in England, Scotland, and Ireland, 1475–1640.* Revised and enlarged edition. New York: Modern Language Association, 1972.

Previté-Orton, C. W. *The Shorter Cambridge Medieval History.* 2 vols. Cambridge: Cambridge University Press, 1952.

A Revised Medieval Latin Word List. Prepared by R. E. Latham. Oxford: Oxford University Press, 1965.

Skeat, Walter W. *Early English Proverbs.* Oxford: Clarendon Press, 1910.

Thesaurus linguae latinae. [Leipzig] Munich: Bayerische Akademie der Wissenschaften, 1900–.

Wallace, David, ed. *The Cambridge History of Medieval English Literature.* Cambridge: Cambridge University Press, 1999.

Walther, Hans. *Lateinische Sprichwörter und Sentenzen des Mittelalters.* 6 vols. Gottingen: Vandenhoeck & Ruprecht, 1962; new series, 1983.

Young, Morris N. *Bibliography of Memory.* Philadelphia: Chilton, 1961.

II CATALOGUES OF MANUSCRIPT COLLECTIONS AND EXHIBITIONS

Alexander, Jonathan J. G. *A Survey of Manuscripts Illuminated in the British Isles,* vol. I: *Insular Manuscripts, 6th–9th Centuries.* London: Harvey Miller, 1978.

Biblioteca Medicea Laurenziana. [Boccaccio:] *Mostra di manoscritti, documenti e edizioni.* 2 vols. An exhibition at the Biblioteca Medicea Laurenziana. Florence, 1975.

Binski, Paul, and Stella Panayotova. *The Cambridge Illuminations.* London: Harvey Miller, 2005.

Brown University Department of Art. *Survival of the Gods: Classical Mythology in Medieval Art.* Exhibition catalogue. Providence, RI: Brown University Press, 1987.

Butler, Pierce. *A Check List of Fifteenth Century Books in the Newberry Library and in Other Libraries of Chicago.* Chicago: The Newberry Library, 1933.

Cahn, Walter. *Romanesque Manuscripts: the Twelfth Century.* 2 vols. A Survey of Manuscripts Illuminated in France. London: Harvey Miller, 1996.

De la Mare, Albinia C. *Catalogue of the Collection of Medieval Manuscripts Bequeathed to the Bodleian Library, Oxford, by James P. R. Lyell.* Oxford: Clarendon Press, 1971.

De Ricci, Seymour. *A Census of Medieval and Renaissance Manuscripts in the United States and Canada.* New York: H. W. Wilson Co., 1935–1940. *Supplement.* Edited by W. H. Bond. New York, 1962.

Dutschke, C. W. *Guide to Medieval and Renaissance Manuscripts in the Huntington Library.* 2 vols. San Marino, CA: Huntington Library Publications, 1989.

James, M. R. *A Descriptive Catalogue of the Manuscripts in the Library of Corpus Christi College, Cambridge.* Cambridge: Cambridge University Press, 1912.

A Descriptive Catalogue of the McClean Collection of Manuscripts in the Fitzwilliam Museum, Cambridge. Cambridge: Cambridge University Press, 1912.

Catalogue of Manuscripts and Early Printed Books from the Libraries of William Morris, Richard Bennett, Bertram, Earl of Ashburnham, and other Sources, now Forming Portion of the Library of J. Pierpont Morgan. 4 vols. London: Chiswick Press, 1906–1907.

The Western Manuscripts in the Library of Trinity College, Cambridge. 4 vols. Cambridge: Cambridge University Press, 1900–1904.

John Rylands Library. *Catalogue of a Selection of Mediaeval Manuscripts and Jewelled Book-Covers Exhibited in the Main Library.* Third exhibition catalogue. Manchester: Manchester University Press, 1939.

Catalogue of an Exhibition of Mediaeval and other Manuscripts and Jewelled Book-Covers Arranged in the Main Library. Second exhibition catalogue. Manchester: Manchester University Press, 1924.

Catalogue of an Exhibition of Mediaeval and other Manuscripts and Jewelled Book-Covers Arranged in the Main Library. First exhibition catalogue. Manchester: Manchester University Press, 1910.

Kauffmann, C. M. *A Survey of Manuscripts Illuminated in the British Isles*, vol. III: *Romanesque Manuscripts, 1066–1190.* London: Harvey Miller, 1975.

Lowe, E. A. *Codices latini antiquiores: a Paleographical Guide to Latin Manuscripts Prior to the Ninth Century.* 12 vols. Oxford: Clarendon Press, 1933.

Maunde-Thompson, E. *A Catalogue of Ancient Manuscripts in the British Museum.* 2 vols. London: British Museum, 1881.

Morgan, Nigel. *A Survey of Manuscripts Illuminated in the British Isles*, vol. IV: *Early Gothic Manuscripts, 1190–1250.* 2 vols. London: Harvey Miller, 1975.

Mynors, R. A. B. *Durham Cathedral Manuscripts.* Oxford: Clarendon Press, for the Chapter of Durham Cathedral, 1939.

Pächt, Otto, and Jonathan J. G. Alexander. *Illuminated Manuscripts in the Bodleian Library, Oxford.* 3 vols. Oxford: Clarendon Press, 1966–1973.

Pierpont Morgan Library. *Early Children's Books and Their Illustration.* Exhibition catalogue. Boston: David Godine, 1975.

Saenger, Paul. *A Catalogue of the Pre-1500 Western Manuscript Books at the Newberry Library.* Chicago: University of Chicago Press, 1989.

Sandler, Lucy Freeman. *A Survey of Manuscripts Illuminated in the British Isles*, vol. V: *Gothic Manuscripts, 1285–1385.* 2 vols. London: Harvey Miller, 1986.

Scott, Kathleen L. *A Survey of Manuscripts Illuminated in the British Isles*, vol. VI: *Later Gothic Manuscripts, 1390–1490.* 2 vols. London: Harvey Miller, 1996.

Sherman, Claire Richter, and Peter M. Lukehart, eds. *Writing on Hands: Memory and Knowledge in Early Modern Europe.* Washington, DC: Folger Shakespeare Library, 2000.

Smits van Waesberghe, Joseph. *Musikerziehung: Lehre und Theorie des Musik in Mittelalter.* Musikgeschichte in Bildern, Bd. III/3. Leipzig: VEB Deutscher Verlag für Musik, 1969.

Temple, Elzbieta. *A Survey of Manuscripts Illuminated in the British Isles*, vol. II: *Anglo-Saxon Manuscripts, 900–1066.* London: Harvey Miller, 1976.

Wallace, David, ed. *The Cambridge History of Medieval English Literature.* Cambridge: Cambridge University Press, 1999.

III EDITIONS AND TRANSLATIONS

Abelard, Peter. *Historia calamitatum.* Edited by J. Monfrin. Paris: Vrin, 1959. Translated by M. T. Clanchy and B. Radice, *The Letters of Abelard and Eloise.* Revised edition. London: Penguin, 2003.

Alanus de Insulis (Alan of Lille). Sermon: "In adventu domino." PL 210, 214–218.

Albertus Magnus. *Opera omnia*, vol. IX: *Commentary on Aristotle's De memoria et reminiscentia.* Edited by August Borgnet. Paris: Ludovicum Vives, 1890. Translated by J. Ziolkowski in Carruthers and Ziolkowski (eds.), *The Medieval Craft of Memory*, q.v.

Opera omnia, vol. XXVIII: *De bono.* Edited by H. Kuhle, C. Feckes, B. Geyer, W. Kubel. Aschendorff: Monasterii Westfalorum, 1951.

Opera omnia, vol. V: *Mineralia. Liber de apprehensione.* Edited by August Borgnet. Paris: Ludovicum Vives, 1890.

Opera omnia, vol. XIX: *Postilla in Isaiam.* Edited by F. Siepmann. Aschendorff: Monasterii Westfalorum, 1952.

Alcuin. *De rhetorica et de virtutibus.* PL 101, 919–946. Translated by W. S. Howell, *The Rhetoric of Alcuin and Charlemagne.* Princeton: Princeton University Press, 1941.

Expositio in psalmos poenitentiales. PL 100, 596–639.

Ambrose. *Sancti Ambrosii opera*, pars X: *Epistulae et acta.* Edited by O. Faller and M. Zelzer. In 4 vols. CSEL 82. Vienna: Hoelder, 1968–1996.

Anselm. *Opera omnia.* Edited by F. S. Schmitt. 6 vols. Edinburgh: Nelson, 1946–1961.

Aristotle. *Aristotle's Constitution of Athens.* Edited by J. Sandys. 2nd edition. London: Macmillan, 1912.

The Art of Rhetoric. Edited and translated by J. H. Freese. Loeb Classical Library. Cambridge, MA: Harvard University Press, 1959. Also, translated with commentary by G. A. Kennedy. *Aristotle, On Rhetoric.* Oxford: Oxford University Press, 1991.

The Complete Works of Aristotle. Edited by J. Barnes. 2 vols. The Revised Oxford Translation. Princeton: Princeton University Press, 1984.

De anima. Edited by W. D. Ross. Oxford: Oxford University Press, 1956. Translated by J. A. Smith from Ross's edition, in *The Complete Works of Aristotle*, ed. Barnes, q.v. Also *On the Soul [De anima], Parva naturalia, On Breath.* Translated by W. S. Hett from the edition of Biehl (1897). Loeb Classical Library. Cambridge, MA: Harvard University Press, 1957.

De memoria et reminiscentia. See *On Memory* and *Parva naturalia.*

De motu animalium. Edited and translated with commentary and interpretative essays by Martha Nussbaum. Princeton: Princeton University Press, 1978.

Metaphysics. Edited and translated by H. Tredennick. 2 vols. Loeb Classical Library. Cambridge, MA: Harvard University Press, 1961–1962.

Nicomachean Ethics. Edited and translated by H. Rackham. Loeb Classical
Library. Cambridge, MA: Harvard University Press, 1934.
On Dreams and *On Divination in Dreams*. See *Parva naturalia*.
On Memory. Translated with interpretative essays and commentary by
R. Sorabji. Providence, RI: Brown University Press, 1972.
Parva naturalia. Edited and translated by W. D. Ross. Oxford: Clarendon
Press, 1955.
Posterior Analytics. Edited and translated by H. Tredennick. Loeb Classical
Library. Cambridge, MA: Harvard University Press, 1960.
Topica. Translated by W. S. Pickard-Cambridge. In *The Complete Works of
Aristotle*, ed. Barnes, q. v.
Arnaldus de Villanova. *Arnaldi de Villanova opera medica omnia*, vol. II: *Aphorismi
de gradibus*. Edited by M. McVaugh *et al*. Grenada: Universidad de
Barcelona, 1975.
Opera omnia. Basle, 1585.
Augustinus Aurelius. *Confessionum libri XIII*. Edited by L. Verheijen. CCSL 27.
Turnhout: Brepols, 1981. Also, edited with commentary by J. J. O'Donnell.
3 vols. Oxford Classical Texts. Oxford: Oxford University Press, 1992.
Translated by M. Boulding. Hyde Park, NY: New City Press, 1997. Also,
translated by William Watts, corrected by W. H. D. Rouse. 2 vols. Loeb
Classical Library. Cambridge, MA: Harvard University Press, 1960–1961.
De doctrina christiana. Edited by J. Martin. CCSL 32. Turnhout: Brepols, 1962.
Translated by E. Hill. *Teaching Christianity*. Hyde Park, NY: New City
Press, 1996. Also edited (Oxford Early Christian Texts, 1995) and translated
(Oxford World's Classics, 1997) by R. P. H. Green.
De magistro. Edited by K. D. Daur. CCSL 29. Turnhout: Brepols, 1970.
Translated by J. M. Colleran. Ancient Christian Writers, 9. Westminster,
MD: Newman Press, 1950. Also, translated (French), with notes, by
G. Madec. Rpt. Paris: Institut d'études augustiniennes, 1999.
De musica libri VI. Edited by M. Jacobsson. Acta Universitatis Stockholmiensis.
Studia Latina Stockholmiensia, 47. Stockholm: Almqvist & Wiksell, 2002.
De natura et origine animae. CSEL 60. Editum consilio et impensis Academiae
Caesareae Vinobonensis. Vienna, 1866.
Enarrationes in Psalmis. Edited by E. Dekkers and J. Fraipont. 3 vols. CCSL
38–40. Turnhout: Brepols, 1954–1984. Translated by M. Boulding, *Expositions
on the Psalms*. 6 vols. Hyde Park, NY: New City Press, 2000–2004.
Epistulae. Edited by K. D. Daur. 2 vols. CCSL 31–31A. Turnhout: Brepols,
2004. Translated by R. Teske, 4 vols. Hyde Park, NY: New City Press,
2001–2005.
Sermones. Translated by E. Hill. 11 vols. Hyde Park, NY: New City Press, 1990–.
Averroës. *Epitome of Parva naturalia*. Edited by A. L. Shields and H. Blumberg.
Cambridge, MA: Medieval Academy of America, 1949. Translated by
H. Blumberg. Cambridge, MA: Medieval Academy of America, 1961.
Avicenna (Latinus). *Liber de anima seu sextus de naturalibus*. Edited by S. Van Reit.
2 vols. Leiden: Brill, 1968–1972.

Bartholomaeus Anglicus. *De proprietatis rerum*. Edited by M. C. Seymour. 2 vols. London: Oxford University Press, 1975.

  On the Properties of Soul and Body. Edited by R. J. Long. Toronto Medieval Latin Texts, 9. Toronto: Pontifical Institute of Medieval Studies, 1979.

Bartolomeo da San Concordia. *Ammaestramenti degli antichi*. Classici Italiani. Milan, 1808.

Bede. *De arte metrica, et liber secundus, de schematibus et tropis. (Bedae opera didascalica, pars I)*. Edited by C. Kendall. CCSL 123 A. Turnhout: Brepols, 1975.

  Historia ecclesiastica gentis Anglorum. In *Bede: Opera historica*. Edited and translated by J. E. King. Loeb Classical Library. London: Heinemann, 1930.

[Bede.] *De loquela digitorum*. PL 90, 685–702.

Biblia sacra juxta vulgatam versionem. Edited by R. Weber *et al.* 2nd edition. Stuttgart: Deutsche Bibelgesellschaft, 1983. English of the Authorized Version (1611) provided for the convenience of readers.

Boccaccio, Giovanni. *Teseida*. Edited by S. Bataglia. Florence: Sansoni, 1938. Translated by B. M. McCoy. New York: Medieval Text Association, 1974.

Boethius. *The Consolation of Philosophy*. Edited by L. Bieler. CCSL 94. Turnhout: Brepols, 1984. Also, edited by H. F. Stewart, with the translation of "I T," revised. Loeb Classical Library. London: Heinemann, 1962.

  De differentiis topicis. Translated with commentary by E. Stump. Ithaca: Cornell University Press, 1978.

  In Ciceronis topica. Translated with commentary by E. Stump. Ithaca: Cornell University Press, 1988.

Boncompagno da Signa. *Rhetorica novissima*. In *Bibliotheca iuridica medii aevi*, vol. II: *Scripta anecdota glossatoria*. Edited by Augusto Gaudenzi. Bononiae [Bologna], 1892.

Bradwardine, Thomas. *De memoria artificiali adquirenda*. Edited by M. Carruthers. *Journal of Medieval Latin* 2 (1992): 25–43. Translated by M. Carruthers, appendix C.

Carruthers, Mary, and Jan M. Ziolkowski, eds. *The Medieval Craft of Memory: An Anthology of Texts and Pictures*. Philadelphia: University of Pennsylvania Press, 2002.

Cassiodorus Senator. *Institutiones*. Edited by R. A. B. Mynors. Oxford Classical Texts. London: Oxford University Press, 1937. Translated by L. W. Jones, *An Introduction to Divine and Human Readings*. New York: Columbia University Press, 1946.

Charland, T. M., ed. *Artes praedicandi*. Ottawa: Institut d'Études médiévales, 1936.

Chaucer, Geoffrey. *The Riverside Chaucer*. Edited by L. D. Benson *et al.* 3rd edition. Boston: Houghton, Mifflin, 1987.

  The Text of The Canterbury Tales. Edited by J. M. Manly and E. Rickert. 8 vols. Chicago: University of Chicago Press, 1940.

  Troilus and Criseyde. Edited by B. Windeatt. New York: Longmans, 1984. Also, edited by R. K. Root. Princeton: Princeton University Press, 1926.

Cicero, M. Tullius. *Brutus and Orator*. Edited and translated by G. L. Hendrickson and H. M. Hubbell. Loeb Classical Library. London: Heinemann, 1939.

De inventione, Topica, De optimo genere oratorum. Edited and translated by H. M. Hubbell. Loeb Classical Library. Cambridge, MA: Harvard University Press, 1949.

De oratore. Edited by A. S. Wilkins. Oxford Classical Texts. Oxford: Clarendon Press, 1902. Translated by J. M. May and J. Wisse, *Cicero, On the Ideal Orator*. Oxford: Oxford University Press, 2001.

Topica. Edited and translated, with commentary, by T. Reinhardt. Oxford Classical Monographs. Oxford: Oxford University Press, 2003.

[Cicero, M. Tullius.] *Rhetorica ad Herennium (Ad C. Herennium libri IV de ratione dicendi)*. Edited and translated by Harry Caplan. Loeb Classical Library. Cambridge, MA: Harvard University Press, 1954. Also the critical edition by G. Calboli, *Cornifici Rhetorica ad Herennium*. 2nd edition. Bologna: Patron, 1993.

Columella. *De re rustica*. Edited and translated by H. B. Ash. 3 vols. Loeb Classical Library. Cambridge, MA: Harvard University Press, 1948–1955.

Crispin, Gilbert. *The Works of Gilbert Crispin, Abbot of Westminster*. Edited by A. S. Abulafia and G. R. Evans. Auctores Britannici Medii Aevi, 8. Oxford: Oxford University Press, for The British Academy, 1986.

The Cyrurgie of Guy de Chauliac. Edited by M. Ogden. EETS, os 265. Oxford: Oxford University Press, 1971.

Dante Alighieri. *The Divine Comedy*. Edited by G. Petrocchi. 4 vols. Milan: Mondadori, 1966. Translation and commentary by C. Singleton. 6 vols. Princeton: Princeton University Press, 1975.

La vita nuova. Edited by M. Barbi. Florence: Bemporad, 1932. Italian text and English translation by D. S. Cervigni and E. Vasta. Notre Dame: Notre Dame University Press, 1995.

Darbishire, Helen, ed. *The Early Lives of Milton*. London: Constable, 1932.

Dissoi logoi [Dialexeis]. In H. Diels and W. Kranz, eds. *Die Fragmente der Vorsokratiker*. 2 vols. II: 405–416. Translated by R. K. Sprague, "Dissoi logoi or Dialexeis." *Mind* 77 (1968): 155–167.

Eadmer. *The Life of St. Anselm*. Edited and translated by R. W. Southern. London: Thomas Nelson, 1962.

Faccio, Anselmo. *Memoria artificiale di casi di conscienza*. Messina, per Pietro Brea, 1621.

Faral, Edmond. *Les Arts poétiques du XIIe et du XIIIe siècles*. 1924. Rpt. Paris: Champion, 1953.

Ferreolus. *Ferreoli episcopi regula ad monachos*. PL 66, 959–976.

Fortunatianus, Consultus [Chirius]. *Ars rhetorica*. Edited by L. Calboli Montefusco. Bologna: Patron, 1979.

Foster, Kenelm. *Biographical Documents for the Life of St. Thomas Aquinas*. Oxford: Blackfriars, 1949.

Geoffrey of Vinsauf. *Poetria nova*. Edited by E. Faral, *Les Arts poétiques du XIIe et du XIIIe siècles*, q.v. Translated by M. F. Nims. Toronto: Pontifical Institute for Medieval Studies, 1967.

Giamboni, Bono. *Fiore di rettorica*. Edited by G. Speroni. Testi: Dipartimento di scienza della letturatura e dell'arte medievale e moderna, 1. Pavia: Università di Pavia, 1994.

Giordano da Pisa [Giordano da Rivalto]. *Quaresimale Fiorentino, 1305–1306*. Edited by Carlo Delcorno. Florence: Sansoni, 1974.

Giraldus Cambrensis. *In topographia Hibernie*. In *Giraldus Cambrensis, opere*. Edited by J. F. Dimock. Rolls Series, vol. 5, no. 21. London: Longmans, 1867. Also, an earlier recension of this text, edited with commentary by J. J. O'Meara. *Proceedings of the Royal Irish Academy* 52. C (1949), 113–178. Translated by J. J. O'Meara, as *Gerald of Wales, The History and Topography of Ireland*. London: Penguin, 1982.

Gregory Nazianzus. *Discours 42–43*. Edited by J. Bernardi. SC 384. Paris: Cerf, 1992.

Gregory the Great. *Homiliae in Hiezechihelem prophetam*. Edited by M. Adriaen. CCSL 142. Turnhout: Brepols, 1971.

Moralia in Job. Edited by M. Adriaen. CCSL 143–143B. Turnhout: Brepols, 1969.

Registrum epistularum. Edited by D. Norberg. CCSL 140–140A. Turnhout: Brepols, 1982.

Regula pastoralis. Edited and translated by F. Rommel and C. Morel. SC 381–382. Paris: Cerf, 1992.

[Gregory the Great.] *Dialogues*. Edited by A. de Vogüé. 3 vols. SC 251, 260, 265. Paris: Cerf, 1978–1980. Translated by O. J. Zimmermann, *Dialogues*. The Fathers of the Church, 39. Washington: Catholic University of America Press, 1959.

Gui, Bernardo. *Life of St. Thomas Aquinas*. Latin text edited by D. Prümmer, q.v. Translated by Kenelm Foster, q.v.

Guido d'Arezzo. *Epistola de ignoto cantu (Letter to Brother Martin)*. Edited by M. Gerbert. *Scriptores ecclesiastici de musica sacra*. Vol. 2. San-Blaise, 1774, 42–46, 50. Partial translation in *Source Readings in Music History*. Edited by O. Strunck, revised by L. Treitler. New York: Norton, 1998, 214–218.

Guidotto da Bologno. *Il fiore di rettorica*. Edited by B. Gamba. Bologna: Masi, 1824.

Halm, Carolus, ed. *Rhetores latini minores*. Leipzig: Tuebner, 1863.

Havelock the Dane. Edited by W. W. Skeat. 2nd edition, revised by K. Sisam. Oxford: Clarendon Press, 1915.

Hawes, Stephen. *The Pastime of Pleasure*. Edited by William E. Mead. EETS, os 173. London: Oxford University Press, 1928.

Honorius Augustodunensis. *Gemma animae*. PL 172, 541–737.

Horace. *The Epistles*. Edited by A. S. Wilkins. London: Macmillan, 1939. Translated by S. P. Bovie. *Satires and Epistles*. Chicago: University of Chicago Press, 1959.

Hrabanus Maurus. *De universo libri xxii*. PL 111, 9–614.

Hugh of Fouilloy. *De avibus*. Edited and translated by W. B. Clark, *The Medieval Book of Birds: Hugh de Fouilloy's De avibus*. Binghamton, NY: MARTS, 1992. *De claustro anime*. PL 176, 1017–1182.

Hugh of St. Victor. *De archa Noe* (formerly *De arca Noe morali*). Edited by
   P. Sicard. CCSL 176. Turnhout: Brepols, 2001. Translated from the PL text
   (176. 618–680) by a Religious of C.M.S.V. *Hugh of St. Victor: Selected Spiritual
   Writings*. London: Faber and Faber, 1962.
   De institutione novitiorum. PL 176, 925–952.
   De tribus maximis circumstantiis gestorum. Edited by W. M. Green. *Speculum* 18
      (1943): 484–493. Translated M. Carruthers, appendix A.
   De unione corporis et anime. PL 177, 285–294.
   Didascalicon. Edited by C. H. Buttimer. Washington: Catholic University
      Press, 1939. Translated by J. Taylor. New York: Columbia University Press,
      1961.
   Libellus de formatione arche (formerly *De arca Noe mystica*). Edited by P. Sicard.
      CCSL 176, 176 A. Turnhout: Brepols, 2001. Translated by J. Weiss in
      Carruthers and Ziolkowski, *The Medieval Craft of Memory*, q.v.
   Libellus de modo dicendi et meditandi, De modo orandi, De meditando. PL 176.
      877–880, 977–987, 995–998.
Isidore of Seville. *Etymologiae.* Edited by W. M. Lindsay. 2 vols. Oxford Classical
   Texts. Oxford: Clarendon Press, 1911.
   Sententiae. Edited by P. Cazier. CCSL 111. Turnhout: Brepols, 1998.
   "Versus in bibliotheca." Edited by Charles Beeson, *Isidorstudien.* Quellen and
      Untersuchungen zur lateinischen Philologie des Mittelalters, 4.2. Munich:
      Oscar Beck, 1913.
Jean d'Antioche. "Rhetorique de Ciceron (Musée de Conde MS. 590)." Excerpts,
   edited by Leopold Delisle. *Notices et extraits* 36 (1899): 207–265.
Jerome. *Commentarii in Hiezechielem.* Edited by F. Glorie. CCSL 75. Turnhout:
   Brepols, 1964.
   Commentariorum in Esaiam Prophetam. Edited by M. Adriaen. CCSL 73.
      Turnhout: Brepols, 1963.
   Epistulae. Edited by I. Hilberg. CSEL 54. 1910. Reissued, Austrian Academy of
      Sciences, Vienna: 1996. Edited and translated (French) by J. Labourt. 8 vols.
      Paris: Les Belles Lettres, 1949–1963.
   Index rerum et sententiarum. PL 23, 767–804.
   Liber interpretationis hebraicorum nominum. Edited by P. de Lagarde. CCSL 72.
      Turnhout: Brepols, 1959.
   Prefaces to the Vulgate Bible. PL 28.
[Jerome.] *Regula monachorum ex scriptis Hieronymi collecta* and *Regula monacha-
   rum.* PL 30, 319–386; 391–426.
John of Garland. *Parisiana poetria.* Edited by Traugott Lawler. Yale Studies in
   English, 182. New Haven: Yale University Press, 1974.
John of Mirfeld. "Florarium Bartholomei." In *Johannes de Mirfeld of St.
   Bartholomew's, Smithfield: His Life and Works.* Edited and translated by
   P. H.-S. Hartley and H. R. Aldridge. Cambridge: Cambridge University
   Press, 1936.
John of Salisbury. *Metalogicon.* Edited by J. B. Hall and K. S. B. Keats-Rohan.
   CCCM 98. Turnhout: Brepols, 1991. Also, edited by Clement Webb.

Oxford: Oxford University Press, 1929. Translated by D. D. McGarry, 1955. Rpt. Gloucester, MA: Peter Smith, 1971.

Julius Victor. *Ars rhetorica*. Edited by C. Halm, q.v.

Langland, William. *The B-Text of Piers Plowman*. Edited by George Kane and E. Talbot Donaldson. London: Athlone Press, 1975. Also, edited by A. V. C. Schmidt, *The Vision of Piers Plowman*. London: Dent, 1987.
 Piers Plowman: An Edition of the C-Text. Edited by Derek Pearsall. Berkeley: University of California Press, 1978.

Latini, Brunetto. *Li Livres dou tresor*. Edited by F. J. Carmody. Berkeley: University of California Press, 1948. Also, edited by S. Baldwin and P. Barrette. Tempe: ACMRS, 2003.

Layamon. *Brut: Or the Chronicles of England*. Edited by G. L. Brook and R. F. Leslie. 2 vols. EETS, os 250, 277. Oxford: Oxford University Press, 1963, 1978.

Legrand, Jacques. *Archiloge sophie et Livre des bonnes meurs*. Edited by E. Beltran. Paris: Champion, 1986.

Le Livre de Lancelot del Lac. In *The Vulgate Versions of the Arthurian Romances*, vols. 3–5. Edited by H. O. Sommer. Washington: Carnegie Corp., 1910.

Lydgate, John. *Minor Poems*. Edited by H. N. McCracken. EETS, es 107. London: Oxford University Press, 1911.

Martial. *Epigrams*. Edited and translated by W. C. A. Ker and E. H. Warmington. 2 vols. Loeb Classical Library. London: Heinemann, 1920–1925.

Martianus Capella. *De nuptiis philologiae et mercurii*. In *Martianus Capella*. Edited by J. Willis. Leipzig: Teubner, 1983. Also edited by Adolphus Dick, 1925. Rpt. Stuttgart: Teubner, 1969. Translated with commentary by W. H. Stahl and R. Johnson, *Martianus Capella and the Seven Liberal Arts*. 2 vols. New York: Columbia University Press, 1977.

Matheolus Perusinus. *De memoria augenda*. Rome: Johann Besicker and Sigismund Mayer, 1493 [1494].

Murphy, James J., ed. *Three Medieval Rhetorical Arts*. Berkeley: University of California Press, 1971.

Ovid. *Heroides*. Edited and translated by G. Showerman, revised by G. P. Goold. 2nd edition. Loeb Classical Library. London: Heinemann, 1977.
 Metamorphoses. Edited and translated by F. J. Miller, revised by G. P. Goold. 2nd edition. 2 vols. Loeb Classical Library. London: Heinemann, 1984.

Paulinus of Nola. *Sancti Pontii Meropii Paulini Nolani opera*. Edited by G. de Hartel, revised and augmented by M. Kamptner. 2 vols. CSEL 29–30. Vienna: Austrian Academy of Sciences, 1999.

Pecock, Reginald. *The Donet*. Edited by E. V. Hitchcock. EETS, os 156. 1921. Rpt. New York: Kraus, 1971.

Peter of Poitiers. *Works*. Edited by P. S. Moore. Washington, DC: Catholic University of America Press, 1936.

Peter of Ravenna (Petrus Tommai). *Foenix domini petri ravenatis memoriae magistri*. Venice: Bernardinus de Choris de Cremona, 1491 [1492]. Translated from French to English by Robert Coplande, *The Art of Memory, Otherwise Called Phenix*. London [1548?].

Petrarca, Francesco. *Le familiari*. Edited by V. Rossi and U. Bosco. 4 vols. Florence: Sansoni, 1933–1942. Translated by A. Bernardo, *Letters on Familiar Matters*. 3 vols. Baltimore: Johns Hopkins University Press, 1975–1985.

Prose. Edited by G. Martelotti *et al.* Milan: Riccardi, 1955.

Rerum memorandarum libri. Edited by G. Billanovich. Florence: Sansoni, 1945.

Secretum. Edited by D. A. Carozza and H. J. Shey. New York: Peter Lang, 1989. Translated by W. H. Draper. London: Chatto and Windus, 1911. Also, translated by C. E. Quillen, *The Secret*. Boston: Bedford / St. Martin's, 2003.

Plato. *Collected Dialogues* [translated by various hands]. Edited by E. Hamilton and H. Cairns. Princeton: Princeton University Press, 1961.

Phaedrus. Translated by J. McDowell. Clarendon Plato Series. Oxford: Clarendon Press, 1973. Edited and translated by H. N. Fowler. Loeb Classical Library. London: Heinemann, 1914. See also "History and Criticism" in Hackforth, *Plato's Phaedrus*.

Theaetetus and Sophist. Edited and translated by H. N. Fowler. Loeb Classical Library. London: Heinemann, 1921.

Pliny [the Elder]. *Natural History*. Edited and translated by H. Rackham *et al.* 10 vols. Loeb Classical Library. Cambridge, MA: Harvard University Press, 1938–1962.

The Poetry of Cercamon and Jaufre Rudel. Edited by G. Wolf and R. Rosenstein. New York: Garland, 1983.

Prümmer, Dominicus, and M. H. Laurent, eds. *Fontes vitae S. Thomae Aquinatis notis historicis et criticis illustrati*. Toulouse: Revue Thomiste, Saint Maximim, 1911–1934.

Publicius, Jacobus. *Ars memoratiua Iacobi publicii florentini*. Venice: Ratdolt, 1482, 1485.

Quintilian, M. Fabius. *Institutio oratoria*. Edited by M. Winterbottom. 2 vols. Oxford Classical Texts. Oxford: Clarendon Press, 1970. Translated by D. A. Russell, *The Orator's Education*. 5 vols. Loeb Classical Library. Cambridge, MA: Harvard University Press, 2001.

Regula Benedicti (La Règle de Saint Benoît). Edited by A. de Vogüé. 6 vols. SC 181–186. Paris: Cerf, 1971–1972. Translated with commentary by T. Kardong, *Benedict's Rule*. Collegeville, MN: Liturgical Press, 1996.

Regula Magistri (La Règle du maître). Edited by A. de Vogüé. 3 vols. SC 105–107. Paris: Cerf, 1964.

Richard de Bury. *Philobiblon*. Edited and translated by E. C. Thomas. London: Kegan Paul, 1888.

Richard de Fournival. *Li Bestiaire d'amours*. Edited by Cesare Segré. Milan: Riccardi, 1957. Translated by J. Beer, *Beasts of Love: Richard De Fournival's Bestiaire D'Amour and a Woman's Response*. Toronto: University of Toronto Press, 2003.

Robert de Basevorn. *Forma praedicandi*. Latin text edited in Charland, q.v. Translated in James J. Murphy, ed., q.v.

The Romance of Sir Beves of Hamptoun. Edited by E. Kölbing. EETS, ES 46, 48, 65. 1885–1894. Rpt. New York: Kraus, 1973.

Romberch, J. Host von. *Congestorium artificiose memorie*. Venice: Melchiorum Sessam, 1533.

Seneca. *Epistulae morales*. Edited by L. D. Reynolds. Oxford Classical Texts. Oxford: Clarendon Press, 1965. Translated by R. M. Gummere. 3 vols. Loeb Classical Library. London: Heinemann, 1953–1962.

Shakespeare, William. *The Complete Plays and Poems*. Edited by W. A. Neilson and C. J. Hill. Cambridge: Houghton Mifflin Company, 1942.

Sigebert of Gembloux. *Liber de scriptoribus ecclesiasticis*. PL 160. 547–588.

Spenser, Edmund. *The Faerie Queene*. Edited by A. C. Hamilton. 3rd edition. New York: Longmans, 1977.

The Tale of Beryn. Edited by F. J. Furnivall and W. G. Stone. EETS, es 105. 1909. Rpt. New York: Kraus, 1973.

Thierry of Chartres. *The Latin Rhetorical Commentaries*. Edited by K. M. Fredborg. Toronto: Pontifical Institute of Medieval Studies, 1988.

Thomas Aquinas. *Catena aurea in quattuor Evangelia*. Edited by A. Guarienti. Turin: Marietti, 1953.

In decem libros ethicorum Aristotelis ad nicomachum expositio. Edited by A. Pirotta. Turin: Marietti, 1934.

Sentencia libri De anima. Edited by R.-A. Gautier, *Sancti Thomae de Aquino Opera omnia*, vol. 45. 1. Paris: Vrin, 1984. Also, *In Aristotelis librum De anima commentarium*. Edited by A. M. Pirotta. Turin: Marietti, 1959. Translated by K. Foster and S. Humphries, *Commentary on Aristotle's De anima*. London: Routledge, 1951. Also, translated (from Gautier's edition) by R. Pasnau, *A Commentary on Aristotle's De anima*. New Haven: Yale University Press, 1999.

Sentencia libri De sensu et sensato cuius secundus tractatus est De memoria et reminiscentia. Edited by R.-A. Gauthier, *Sancti Thomae de Aquino Opera omnia*, vol. 45. 2. Paris: Vrin, 1985. Also, *In Aristotelis libros de sensu et sensato, de memoria et reminiscentia commentarium*. Edited by R. M. Spiazzi. 2nd edition. Turin: Marietti, 1949. Translated by J. Burchill and M. Carruthers, in Carruthers and Ziolkowski, *The Medieval Craft of Memory*, q.v. Also, translated by K. White and E. M. Macierowski, *Commentaries on Aristotle's "On Sense and What is Sensed" and "On Memory and Recollection."* Washington, DC: Catholic University of America, 2005.

Summa theologica. Blackfriars edition (Latin and English). 61 vols. New York: McGraw-Hill, 1964–1981.

Thomas Waleys. *De modo componendi sermones*. Edited by Charland, q.v.

Tocco, Gulielmus de. *Life of St. Thomas Aquinas*. In *Acta sanctorum*, March, vol. I. Paris: Société Bollandists, 1648. Also edited by Prümmer, q.v. Translated by Foster, q.v.

Varro. *De lingua latina*. Edited and translated by R. G. Kent. 2 vols. Loeb Classical Library. London: Heinemann, 1938.

Virgil. *Works*. Edited and translated by H. R. Fairclough. 2 vols. Loeb Classical Library. London: Heinemann, 1932.

The Wakefield Pageants in the Towneley Cycle. Edited by A. C. Cawley. Manchester: Manchester University Press, 1958.

William of Ockham. *Dialogus de imperio et pontificia potestate.* In *Opera plurima*, vol. I. Lyons, 1494–1496. Rpt. London: Gregg Press, 1962.

Wyclif, John. *De veritate Sacrae Scripturae.* Edited by R. Buddensieg. 3 vols. Wyclif's Latin Works, 18. London: Teubner for The Wyclif Society, 1905–1907.

IV FACSIMILE EDITIONS OF MANUSCRIPTS

Gibson, M. T., and K. Froelich. *Biblia latina cum Glossa ordinaria: Facsimile Reprint of the editio princeps Published by Adolph Rusch of Strassburg 1480/81.* 4 vols. Turnhout: Brepols, 1992.

Henry, Françoise. *The Book of Kells.* New York: Knopf, 1974.

Herrad of Hohenbourg. *Hortus deliciarum.* Edited by Rosalie Green *et al.* 2 vols. London: Warburg Institute, 1979.

Ker, N. R. *The Winchester Malory.* EETS, SS 4. London: Oxford University Press, 1974.

Luce, A. A., P. Meyer, G. O. Simmons, and L. Bieler. *Evangelium quattuor codex Durmachensis.* 2 vols. Olten: Urs Graf Verlag, 1960.

Maunde-Thompson, E. *Codex Alexandrinus.* 4 vols. London: British Museum, 1879–1883.

Millar, E. G. *An Illuminated Manuscript of La Somme le Roy.* Oxford: Roxburghe Club, 1953.

The Rutland Psalter. Oxford: Roxburghe Club, 1937.

Pearsall, Derek, and Kathleen Scott. *Piers Plowman: A Facsimile of Bodleian Library, Oxford, MS Douce 104.* Cambridge: D. S. Brewer, 1992.

Sandler, Lucy Freeman. *The Psalter of Robert De Lisle.* London: Oxford University Press for Harvey Miller, 1983.

V HISTORY AND CRITICISM

Ahern, John. "Binding the Book: Hermeneutics and Manuscript Production in *Paradiso 33.*" *PMLA* 97 (1982): 800–809.

Alexander, J. J. G. *Medieval Illuminators and Their Methods of Work.* New Haven: Yale University Press, 1992.

The Decorated Letter. London: Thames and Hudson, 1978.

"Scribes as Artists: The Arabesque Initial in Twelfth-Century English Manuscripts." In M. B. Parkes and A. G. Watson, eds., *Medieval Scribes, Manuscripts and Libraries: Essays Presented to N. R. Ker*, pp. 87–116. London: Scolar Press, 1978.

The Master of Mary of Burgundy. New York: Braziller, 1970.

Alexander, J. J. G., and M. T. Gibson, eds. *Medieval Learning and Literature: Essays Presented to R. W. Hunt.* London: Oxford University Press, 1987.

Alford, John. "The Role of the Quotations in Piers Plowman." *Speculum* 52 (1977): 80–99.

Allen, Judson B. "Langland's Reading and Writing: *Detractor* and the Pardon Passus." *Speculum* 59 (1984): 342–362.

———. *The Ethical Poetic of the Later Middle Ages.* Toronto: University of Toronto Press, 1982.

———. *The Friar as Critic.* Nashville, TN: Vanderbilt University Press, 1971.

Althoff, Gerd, Johannes Fried, and Patrick J. Geary, eds. *Medieval Concepts of the Past: Ritual, Memory, Historiography.* Cambridge: Cambridge University Press, 2002.

Ambrose, Kirk. *The Nave Sculpture of Vézelay: The Art of Monastic Viewing.* Toronto: PIMS, 2006.

Amsler, Mark. "Affective Literacy: Gestures of Reading in the Later Middle Ages." *Essays in Medieval Studies* 18 (2001): 83–109 (eight figures).

Auerbach, Erich. *Literary Language and its Public in Late Latin Antiquity and in the Middle Ages.* Translated by R. Mannheim. Princeton: Princeton University Press, 1965.

Baddeley, Alan D. *The Psychology of Memory.* New York: Basic Books, 1976.

Baldwin, Charles S. *Medieval Rhetoric and Poetic to 1400.* 1928. Rpt. Gloucester, MA: Peter Smith, 1959.

Balogh, Josef. "'Voces paginarum': Beitrage zur Geschichte des lauten Lessens und Schreibens." *Philologus* 82 (1927): 84–109, 202–240.

Baron, Hans. *Petrarch's Secretum: Its Making and Its Meaning.* Cambridge, MA: Medieval Academy of America, 1985.

———. *From Petrarch to Leonardi Bruni.* Chicago: University of Chicago Press, 1968.

Baxandall, Michael. *Patterns of Intention.* New Haven: Yale University Press, 1985.

———. *Giotto and the Orators.* Oxford: Oxford University Press, 1971.

Belting, Hans. *Likeness and Presence: A History of the Image Before the Era of Art.* Chicago: University of Chicago Press, 1994.

Benson, Robert L., and Giles Constable, eds. *Renaissance and Renewal in the Twelfth Century.* Cambridge, MA: Harvard University Press, 1982.

Bent, Margaret. "Ciconia, Prosdocimus, and the Workings of Musical Grammar As Exemplified in *O Felix Templum* and *O Padua*." In P. Vendrix, ed., *Johannes Ciconia, musicien de la transition*, pp. 65–106. Turnhout: Brepols, 2003.

———. "The Grammar of Early Music: Preconditions for Analysis." In C. C. Judd, ed., *Tonal Structures in Early Music*, pp. 15–59. New York: Garland, 1998.

Benton, John F. "Consciousness of Self and Perceptions of Individuality." In R. Benson and G. Constable, eds., *Renaissance and Renewal in the Twelfth Century* (q.v.), pp. 263–295.

———. "Fraud, Fiction and Borrowing in the Correspondence of Abelard and Heloise." In *Pierre Abélard, Pierre le Vénérable*, pp. 469–511. Paris: CNRF, 1975

Berger, Samuel. *L'Histoire du Vulgate pendant les premiers siècles du Moyen Age.* 1893. Rpt. New York: Burt Franklin, 1959.

Berns, Jörg Jochen, and Wolfgang Neuber, eds. *Seelenmaschinen.* Vienna: Bölau, 2000.

Ars memorativa: Zur Kulturgeschichtlichen Bedeutung der Gedächtniskunst 1400–1750. Tübingen: Max Niermeyer Verlag, 1993.

Bischoff, Bernhard. "The Study of Foreign Languages in the Middle Ages." In B. Bischoff, *Mittelalterliche Studien*, vol. II, pp. 227–245. Stuttgart: Hiersemann, 1967.

Black, Max. *Models and Metaphors*. Ithaca: Cornell University Press, 1962.

Blum, Herwig. *Die Antike Mnemotechnik*. Spudasmata, 15. Hildesheim: Georg Olms, 1969.

Bolzoni, Lina. *The Web of Images: Vernacular Preaching from its Origins to St. Bernardino da Siena.* Translated by C. Preston and L. Chien from *La rete delle immagini* (Einaudi, 2002). Aldershot: Ashgate, 2004.

The Gallery of Memory: Literary and Iconographic Models in the Age of the Printing Press. Translated by J. Parzen from *La stanza della memoria* (Einaudi, 1995). Toronto: University of Toronto Press, 2001.

Bovey, Alixe. *The Smithfield Decretals: Tales From the Margins of a Fourteenth-Century Law Book.* London: British Library, 2008.

Bower, Gordon H. "A Selective Review of Organizational Factors in Memory." In E. Tulving and W. Donaldson, eds., *Organization of Memory*, pp. 93–137. New York: Academic Press, 1972.

Branca, Vittore. "Copisti per passione, tradizione caratterizzante, tradizione di memoria." In Raffaele Spongano, ed., *Studi e problemi di critica testuale*, pp. 69–83. Bologna: Commissione per i testi di lingua, 1961.

Brewer, Derek. "Orality and Literacy in Chaucer." In W. Erzgraber and S. Volk, eds., *Mundlichkeit und Schriftlichkeit im englischen Mittelalter*, pp. 85–119. Tubingen: Gunter Narr, 1987.

Bruns, Gerald L. *Inventions: Writing, Textuality, and Understanding in Literary History.* New Haven: Yale University Press, 1982.

Bundy, Murray Wright. *The Theory of Imagination in Classical and Medieval Thought.* University of Illinois Studies in Language and Literature, 12. Urbana, IL: University of Illinois Press, 1927.

Burnyeat, M. F. "Aquinas on 'Spiritual Change' in Perception." In D. Perler, ed., *Ancient and Medieval Theories of Intentionality*, pp. 129–153. Leiden: Brill, 2001.

"Dissoi logoi." In E. Craig, ed., *The Routledge Encyclopedia of Philosophy*. vol. 3, pp. 106–107. London: Routledge, 1998.

Burrow, John A. *Medieval Writers and Their Work*. Oxford: Oxford University Press, 1982.

Busse Berger, Anna Maria. *Medieval Music and the Art of Memory*. Berkeley: University of California Press, 2005.

Bynum, Caroline Walker. *Metamorphosis and Identity*. New York: Zone Books, 2001.

Jesus as Mother: Studies in the Spirituality of the High Middle Ages. Publications of the Center for Medieval and Renaissance Studies, UCLA, 16. Berkeley and Los Angeles: University of California Press, 1972.

Cadbury, H. J. "The Odor of the Spirit at Pentecost." *Journal of Biblical Literature* 47 (1928): 237–256.

Cahn, Walter. "The Allegorical Menorah." In J. F. Hamburger and A. S. Korteweg, eds., *Tributes in Honor of James M. Marrow: Studies in Painting and Manuscript Illumination of the Late Middle Ages and Northern Renaissance*, pp. 117–126. Turnhout: Harvey Miller, 2006.

Romanesque Bible Illumination. Ithaca: Cornell University Press, 1982.

Calboli Montefusco, Lucia. "Ductus and Color: The Right Way to Compose a Suitable Speech." *Rhetorica* 21 (2003): 113–131.

Callus, D. A. *Robert Grosseteste, Scholar and Bishop*. Oxford: Clarendon Press, 1955.

"The Oxford Career of Robert Grosseteste." *Oxoniensia* 10 (1945): 42–72.

Camargo, Martin. "Between Grammar and Rhetoric: Composition Teaching at Oxford and Bologna in the Late Middle Ages." In W. B. Horner and M. Leff, eds., *Rhetoric and Pedagogy: Its History, Philosophy, and Practice*, pp. 83–94. Mahwah, NJ: Erlbaum, 1995.

Medieval Rhetorics of Prose Composition: Five English Artes Dictandi and Their Tradition. Binghamton, NY: MRTS, 1995.

Ars dictaminis, ars dictandi. Typologie des sources. Turnhout: Brepols, 1991.

Camden, Carroll. "Memory, the Warder of the Brain." *Philological Quarterly* 18 (1939): 52–72.

Camille, Michael. *Image on the Edge: The Margins of Medieval Art*. Cambridge, MA: Harvard University Press, 1992.

"The Book of Signs: Writing and Visual Difference in Gothic Manuscript Illumination." *Word and Image* 1 (1985): 133–148.

"Seeing and Reading: Some Visual Implications of Medieval Literacy and Illiteracy." *Art History* 8 (1985): 26–49.

Caplan, Harry. *Of Eloquence: Collected Essays*. Edited by A. King and H. North. Ithaca: Cornell University Press, 1970.

Carr, David M. *Writing on the Tablet of the Heart: Origins of Scripture and Literature*. New York: Oxford University Press, 2005.

Carruthers, Mary. "How to Make a Composition: Memory-Craft in Antiquity and in the Middle Ages." In S. Radstone and W. Schwarz, eds., *Mapping Memory*. New York: Fordham University Press, 2007.

"Rhetorical Memoria in Commentary and Practice." In Cox and Ward, q.v., pp. 205–233.

"Sweetness." *Speculum* 81 (2006): 999–1013.

"*Ars inveniendi, ars memorativa*: Visualization and Composition in the Late Middle Ages." In *Il senso della memoria*, pp. 29–42. Atti Dei Convegni Lincei, 195. Rome: Accademia Nazionale dei Lincei, 2003.

"Late Antique Rhetoric, Early Monasticism, and the Revival of School Rhetoric." In C. D. Lanham, ed., *Latin Grammar and Rhetoric: Classical Theory and Medieval Practice*, pp. 239–257. London: Continuum, 2002.

"The Mystery of the Bedchamber: Mnemotechnic and Vision in Chaucer's *Book of the Duchess*." In J. M. Hill and D. Sinnreich-Levi, eds., *The Rhetorical Poetics of the Middle Ages*, pp. 67–87. New Jersey: Fairleigh-Dickinson University Press, 2000.

"Rhetorical Ductus, or, Moving Though a Composition." In M. Franko and A. Richards, eds., *Acting on the Past*, pp. 99–117. Hanover, NH: University Press of New England, 2000.

The Craft of Thought: Meditation, Rhetoric, and the Making of Images, 400–1200. Cambridge: Cambridge University Press, 1998.

"Boncompagno at the Cutting-Edge of Rhetoric: Rhetorical *Memoria* and the Craft of Memory." *Journal of Medieval Latin* 6 (1996): 44–64.

"The Poet As Master Builder: Composition and Locational Memory in the Middle Ages." *New Literary History* 24 (1993): 881–904.

"Italy, *Ars memorativa*, and Fame's House." *Studies in the Age of Chaucer*, Proceedings Series 2 (1987): 179–187.

Carty, Carolyn M. "Dream Images, *Memoria*, and the Heribert Shrine." In. E. Valdez del Alamo with C. S. Pendergast, eds., *Memory and the Medieval Tomb*, pp. 227–240 + 6 plates. Aldershot: Ashgate, 2000.

"The Role of Gunzo's Dream in the Building of Cluny III." *Gesta* 27 (1988): 113–123.

Cave, Terence. "The Mimesis of Reading in the Renaissance." In S. G. Nichols and J. D. Lyon, eds., *Mimesis*, q.v., pp. 149–165.

The Cornucopian Text: Problems of Writing in the French Renaissance. Oxford: Clarendon Press, 1979.

Caviness, Madeleine H. "Images of Divine Order and the Third Mode of Seeing." *Gesta* 22 (1983): 99–120.

Chalmers, David J. *The Conscious Mind: In Search of a Fundamental Theory.* Oxford: Oxford University Press, 1996.

Chaytor, H. J. *From Script to Print: An Introduction to Medieval Literature.* Cambridge, MA: Cambridge University Press, 1945.

Chazelle, Celia. "'Not in Painting but in Writing': Augustine and the Supremacy of the Word in the *Libri Carolini*." In E. English, ed., *Reading and Wisdom: The De Doctrina Christiana in the Middle Ages*, pp. 1–22. Notre Dame: University of Notre Dame Press, 1995.

"Pictures, Books, and the Illiterate: Pope Gregory I's Letters to Serenus of Marseilles." *Word and Image* 6 (1990): 138–153.

Chenu, M.-D. *Introduction à l'étude de St. Thomas d'Aquin.* 3rd edition. Paris: Vrin, 1974.

Nature, Man, and Society in the Twelfth Century. Edited and translated by L. Little and J. Taylor. Chicago: University of Chicago Press, 1968.

"Auctor, actor, autor." *Bulletin Du Cange* 3 (1927): 81–86.

Clanchy, M. T. *Abelard: A Medieval Life.* Oxford: Blackwell, 1997.

From Memory to Written Record, England 1066–1307. 2nd edition. Cambridge, MA: Harvard University Press, 1993.

Clark, Andy. *Being There: Puttting Brain, Body, and World Together Again.* Cambridge, MA: MIT Press, 1997.

Clark, Donald L. *Rhetoric in Greco-Roman Education.* New York: Columbia University Press, 1957.

Clark, Francis. *The Pseudo-Gregorian Dialogues.* 2 vols. Leiden: Brill, 1999.

Clark, John Willis. *The Care of Books*. Cambridge: Cambridge University Press, 1902.

Clarke, Edwin, and Kenneth Dewhurst. *An Illustrated History of Brain Function*. Berkeley: University of California, 1972.

Cogan, Marc. "Rodolphus Agricola and the Semantic Revolution in the History of Invention." *Rhetorica* 2 (1984): 163–194.

Coleman, Janet. *Ancient and Medieval Memories: The Reconstruction of the Past*. Cambridge: Cambridge University Press, 1992.

"Late Scholastic *Memoria et Reminiscentia*: Its Uses and Abuses." In P. Boitani and A. Torti, eds., *Intellectuals and Writers in Fourteenth Century Europe*, pp. 22–44. London: Boydell and Brewer, 1986.

Medieval Readers and Writers. London: Hutchinson, 1981.

Coleman, Joyce. *Public Reading and the Reading Public in Late Medieval England and France*. Cambridge: Cambridge University Press, 1996.

Colish, Marcia. *The Mirror of Language*. Revised edition. Lincoln: University of Nebraska Press, 1983.

Cope, Edward M. *An Introduction to Aristotle's Rhetoric*. London: Macmillan, 1867.

Copeland, Rita. *Rhetoric, Hermeneutics and Translation in the Middle Ages*. Cambridge: Cambridge University Press, 1991.

Cornford, F. M. *Plato's Theory of Knowledge*. 1934. Rpt. New York: Bobbs Merrill, 1957.

Courcelle, Pierre. *La Consolation de philosophie dans la tradition littéraire*. Paris: Études Augustiniennes, 1967.

Les Confessions de Saint Augustin dans la tradition littéraire. Paris: Études Augustiniennes, 1963.

Cox, Virginia. "Ciceronian Rhetoric in Late Medieval Italy." In Cox and Ward, eds., *The Rhetoric of Cicero*, q.v., 109–143.

Cox, Virginia, and John O. Ward, eds. *The Rhetoric of Cicero in Its Medieval and Early Renaissance Commentary Tradition*. Leiden: Brill, 2006.

Curschmann, Michael. "Imagined Exegesis: Text and Picture in the Exegetical Works of Rupert of Deutz, Honorius Augustodunensis, and Gerhoch of Reichersberg." *Traditio* 44 (1988): 145–169.

"Oral Poetry in Mediaeval English, French, and German Literature: Some Notes on Recent Research." *Speculum* 42 (1967): 36–51.

Curtius, Ernst R. *European Literature and the Latin Middle Ages*. Translated by W. R. Trask. 1953. Rpt. New York: Harper and Row, 1963.

D'Alverny, Marie-Thérèse. "Translations and Translators." In R. Benson and G. Constable, eds., *Renaissance and Renewal in the Twelfth Century*, q.v., pp. 421–462.

Daly, Lloyd W. *Contributions to a History of Alphabetization in Antiquity and the Middle Ages*. Brussels: Collection Latomus, 1967.

Daly, Lloyd W., and B. A. Daly, "Some Techniques in Medieval Latin Lexicography." *Speculum* 39 (1964): 229–239.

Davis, Charles T. "Education in Dante's Florence." *Speculum* 40 (1965): 415–435.

D'Avray, D. L. *The Preaching of the Friars.* Oxford: Clarendon Press, 1985.

De Clercq, Carlo. "Hugues de Fouilloy, imagier de ses propres oeuvres?" *Revue du Nord* 45 (1963): 31–42 + plates.

———. "Le Role de l'image dans un manuscrit médiéval (Bodl. Lyell 71)." *Gutenberg Jahrbuch* 37 (1962): 23–30.

De Hamel, C. F. R. *A History of Illuminated Manuscripts.* Boston: David Godine, 1986.

———. *Glossed Books of the Bible and the Origins of the Paris Booktrade.* London: Boydell and Brewer, 1984.

De Lubac, Henri. *Exégèse Médiévale.* 4 vols. Paris: Aubier, 1959–1964.

De Wald, E. T. *The Illustrations of the Utrecht Psalter.* Princeton: Princeton University Press, 1932.

De Wit, Pamela. "The Visual Experience of Fifteenth-Century English Readers." D. Phil. diss. Oxford University, 1977.

Deanesly, Margaret. "Vernacular Books in England in the Fourteenth and Fifteenth Centuries." *Modern Language Review* 15 (1920): 349–358.

Deferrari, R. J. "St. Augustine's Method of Composing and Delivering Sermons." *American Journal of Philology* 43 (1922): 97–123, 193–219.

Delaissé, L. M. J. "Towards a History of the Medieval Book." *Codicologia* 1 (1976): 75–83.

———. "The Importance of Books of Hours for the History of the Medieval Book." In U. McCracken, L. Randall, and R. Randall, eds., *Gatherings in Honor of Dorothy E. Miner,* q.v., pp. 203–225.

Delcorno, Carlo. *Giordano da Pisa e l'antica predicazione volgare.* Biblioteca di Lettere Italiane, 14. Florence: Olschki, 1975.

Delhaye, Phillippe. "L'Enseignement de la philosophie morale au XIIe siècle." *Medieval Studies* 11 (1949): 77–99.

Derolez, Albert. "The Genesis of Hildegard of Bingen's 'Liber divinorum operum.'" In J. P. Gumbert and M. J. M. de Haan, eds., *Litterae textuales: Essays Presented to G. I. Lieftinck,* vol. II, pp. 23–33. Amsterdam: Van Gendt, 1972.

Derrida, Jacques. "Plato's Pharmacy." In *Dissemination,* pp. 61–171. Translated by B. Johnson. Chicago: University of Chicago Press, 1981.

———. *Glas.* Paris: Galilee, 1974.

———. "White Mythology: Metaphor in the Text of Philosophy." Translated by F. C. T. Moore. *New Literary History* 6 (1974): 5–74.

DiLorenzo, Raymond D. "The Collection Form and the Art of Memory in the *Libellus super Ludo Schachorum* of Jacobus de Cessolis." *Mediaeval Studies* 35 (1973): 205–221.

Diringer, David. *The Book Before Printing: Ancient, Medieval, Oriental.* 1953. Rpt. New York: Dover Publications, 1982.

Dodwell, C. R. *The Canterbury School of Illumination.* Cambridge: Cambridge University Press, 1954.

Donaldson, F. Talbot. "The Psychology of Editors of Middle English Texts." In *Speaking of Chaucer,* pp. 102–118. New York: W. W. Norton, 1970.

"Manuscripts R and F in the B Tradition of Piers Plowman." *Transactions of the Connecticut Academy of Arts and Sciences* 39 (1955): 177–212.

Dondaine, Antoine. *Les Secrétaires de Saint Thomas.* 2 vols. Rome: Editori di S. Tommaso, 1956.

Draaisma, Douwe. *Metaphors of Memory: A History of Ideas about the Mind.* Translated by P. Vincent from *Metaforenmachine: een geschiedenis van het geheugen* (Groningen, 1995). Cambridge: Cambridge University Press, 2000.

Dubois, Jacques. "Comment les moines du Moyen Age chantaient et goûtaient les Saintes Écritures." In P. Riché and G. Lobrichon, eds., *Le Moyen Âge et la Bible*, q.v., pp. 261–298.

Dudai, Yadin. *Memory From A to Z: Keywords, Concepts and Beyond.* Oxford: Oxford University Press, 2002.

Dufresne, Suzy. *Les Illustrations du Psautier d'Utrecht.* Paris: Éditions Ophyrs, 1978.

"Les Copies anglaises du Psautier d'Utrecht." *Scriptorium* 18 (1964): 185–197.

Duggan, Lawrence. "Was Art Really the 'Book of the Illiterate?'" *Word & Image* 5 (1989): 227–251.

Dunn, Marilyn. *The Emergence of Monasticism: From the Desert Fathers to the Early Middle Ages.* Oxford: Blackwell, 2000.

Eco, Umberto. "An *Ars oblivionalis?* Forget It!" *PMLA* 103 (1988): 254–261.

Eden, Kathy. *Friends Hold All Things in Common: Tradition, Intellectual Property, and the* Adages *of Erasmus.* New Haven: Yale University Press, 2001.

Hermeneutics and the Rhetorical Tradition. New Haven: Yale University Press, 1997.

Eisenstein, Elizabeth. *The Printing Revolution in Early Modern Europe.* Cambridge: Cambridge University Press, 1983.

The Printing Press as an Agent of Change: Communications and Cultural Transformations in Early Modern Europe. 2 vols. Cambridge: Cambridge University Press, 1979.

Ellis, John. *The Theory of Literary Criticism: A Logical Analysis.* Berkeley and Los Angeles: University of California Press, 1974.

Enders, Jody. *The Medieval Theater of Cruelty: Rhetoric, Memory, Violence.* Ithaca: Cornell University Press, 1999.

Rhetoric and the Origins of Medieval Drama. Ithaca: Cornell University Press, 1992.

Enenkel, Karl, and Arnoud Visser, eds., *Mundus emblematicus: Studies in Neo-Latin Emblem Books.* Turnhout: Brepols, 2003.

Eskridge, James B. *The Influence of Cicero Upon Augustine in the Development of His Oratorical Theory for the Training of the Ecclesiastical Orator.* Menasha, WI: Banta, 1912.

Evans, G. R. *The Language and Logic of the Bible in the Earlier Middle Ages.* Cambridge: Cambridge University Press, 1984.

"Two Aspects of *Memoria* in Eleventh and Twelfth Century Writings." *Medievalia* 32 (1980): 263–278.

Evans, Michael. "Fictive Painting in Twelfth-Century Paris." In John Onians, ed., *Sight & Insight: Essays on Art and Culture in Honour of E. H. Gombrich at 85*, pp. 73–87. London: Phaidon, 1994.

"An Illustrated Fragment of Peraldus's *Summa* of Vice: Harleian MS 3244." *Journal of the Warburg and Courtauld Institutes* 45 (1982): 14–68 + Plates 1–9.

Farrell, Thomas B. *Norms of Rhetorical Culture*. New Haven: Yale University Press, 1993.

Feigenbaum, Edward A. "Information Processing and Memory." In D. A. Norman, ed., *Models of Human Memory*, pp. 451–468. New York: Academic Press, 1970.

Ferruolo, Stephen C. *The Origins of the University*. Stanford, CA: Stanford University Press, 1985.

Finnegan, Ruth. *Literacy and Orality*. Oxford: Oxford University Press, 1988.

Oral Poetry: Its Nature, Significance, and Social Content. Cambridge: Cambridge University Press, 1977.

Fisher, John. "Animadversions on the Text of Chaucer, 1988." *Speculum* 63 (1988): 779–793.

Fleming, Brian. "Thomas de Bradwardine." Ph.D. dissertation, Louvain, 1964.

Fodor, Jerry A. *The Language of Thought*. 1975. Rpt. Cambridge, MA: Harvard University Press, 1980.

Foley, J. M. *The Theory of Oral Composition*. Bloomington: Indiana University Press, 1988.

Fontaine, Jacques. *Isidore de Seville et la culture classique dans l'Espagne wisigothique*. 2 vols. Paris: Études augustiniennes, 1959.

Frank, Georgia. *The Memory of the Eyes: Pilgrims to Living Saints in Christian Late Antiquity*. Berkeley: University of California Press, 2000.

Freccero, John. *Dante: The Poetics of Conversion*. Edited by R. Jacoff. Cambridge, MA: Harvard University Press, 1986.

"The Fig Tree and the Laurel: Petrarch's Poetics." *Diacritics* 5 (1975): 34–40.

Friedman, John B. "Les images mnémotechniques dans les manuscrits de l'époque gothique." In B. Roy and P. Zumthor, eds., *Jeux de mémoire*, q.v., pp. 169–184.

Gallo, Ernest. "The Poetria nova of Geoffrey of Vinsauf." In J. J. Murphy, ed., *Medieval Eloquence*, q.v., pp. 68–84.

Gardner, Edmund G. "Imagination and Memory in the Psychology of Dante." In M. Williams and J. A. de Rothschild, eds., *A Miscellany of Studies in Romance Languages and Literatures Presented to Leon E. Kastner*, pp. 275–282. Cambridge: Heffer, 1932.

Gavrilov, A. K. "Techniques of Reading in Classical Antiquity, Translated With a Postscript by M. F. Burnyeat." *Classical Quarterly* 47 (1997): 56–76.

Geary, Patrick J. *Living With the Dead in the Middle Ages*. Ithaca: Cornell University Press, 1994.

Phantoms of Remembrance. Princeton: Princeton University Press, 1994.

Geertz, Clifford. *The Interpretation of Cultures*. New York: Basic Books, 1973.

Gehl, Paul F. *A Moral Art: Grammar, Society, and Culture in Trecento Florence*. Ithaca: Cornell University Press, 1993.

"*Competens silentium*: Varieties of Monastic Silence in the Medieval West." *Viator* 18 (1987): 125–160.

"Mystical Language Models in Monastic Educational Psychology." *Journal of Medieval and Renaissance Studies* 14 (1984): 219–243.

"Texts and Textures: Dirty Pictures and Other Things in Medieval Manuscripts." *Corona* (Montana State University) 3 (1983): 68–77.

Gibson, Margaret T. *The Bible in the Latin West*. Notre Dame: University of Notre Dame Press, 1993.

Goldschmidt, E. P. *The Printed Book of the Renaissance*. Cambridge: Cambridge University Press, 1950.

Gombrich, E. H. *Meditations on a Hobby Horse and Other Essays on the Theory of Art*. New York: Phaidon, 1963.

Goy, Rudolph. *Die Überlieferung der Werke Hugos von St. Viktor*. Stuttgart: Anton Hiersemann, 1976.

Grabar, Oleg. *The Mediation of Ornament*. Princeton: Princeton University Press, 1992.

Greene, Thomas M. "Erasmus's 'Festina lente': Vulnerabilities of the Humanist Text." In S. G. Nichols and J. D. Lyons, eds., *Mimesis*, q.v., pp. 132–148.

The Light In Troy: Imitation and Discovery in Renaissance Poetry. New Haven: Yale University Press, 1982.

Greimas, A. J. *On Meaning: Selected Writings in Semiotic Theory*. Translated by P. J. Perron and F. H. Collins. Theory and History of Literature, 38. Minneapolis: University of Minnesota Press, 1986.

Grmek, M. D., ed., *Western Medical Thought From Antiquity to the Middle Ages*. Translated by A. Shugaard from *Storia del pensiero medico occidentale I: Antichità e medioevo* (Laterzo, 1993). Cambridge, MA: Harvard University Press, 1998.

Guilmain, Jacques. "The Geometry of the Cross-Carpet Pages in the Lindisfarne Gospels." *Speculum* 62 (1987): 21–52.

Hackforth, R. *Plato's Phaedrus*. Cambridge: Cambridge University Press, 1952.

Hajdu, Helga. *Das Mnemotechnische Schrifttum des Mittelalters*. Vienna: Franz Leo, 1936.

Hajnal, St. "Universities and the Development of Writing in the XIIth–XIIIth Centuries." *Scriptorium* 6 (1952): 177–195.

Hamburger, Jeffrey F. *Nuns As Artists: The Visual Culture of a Medieval Convent*. Berkeley: University of California, 1997.

Hanning, Robert W. "Poetic Emblems in Medieval Narrative Texts." In L. Ebin, ed., *Vernacular Poetics in the Middle Ages*, pp. 1–32. Kalamazoo, MI: Medieval Institute Publications, 1984.

"'Ut enim faber … sic creator': Divine Creation as Context for Human Creativity in the Twelfth Century." In C. Davidson, ed., *Word, Picture, and Spectacle*, pp. 95–149. Kalamazoo, MI: Medieval Institute Publications, 1984.

The Individual in the Twelfth Century Romance. New Haven: Yale University Press, 1977.

Harris, William V. *Ancient Literacy*. Cambridge, MA: Harvard University Press, 1989.

Harrison, Julian. "The English Reception of Hugh of St. Victor's Chronicle." *Electronic British Library Journal* (2002): Article 1.

Harvey, E. Ruth. *The Inward Wits*. London: Warburg Institute, 1975.

Hasenohr, Geneviève. "Méditation méthodique et mnémonique: un témoignage figuré ancien (s. XIIIe–XIVe)." In R. LeJeune and J. Deckers, eds., *Clio et son regard: mélanges Jacques Stiennon*, pp. 365–382. Liège: Mardaga, 1982.

Haskins, Charles H. *Studies in Medieval Culture*. Oxford: Clarendon Press, 1929.

Havelock, Eric A. *The Literate Revolution in Greece and Its Cultural Consequences*. Princeton: Princeton University Press, 1982.

Hendrickson, G. L. "Ancient Reading." *Classical Journal* 25 (1929): 182–196.

"The Origin and Meaning of the Ancient Characters of Style." *American Journal of Philology* 26 (1905): 249–290.

Henry, Avril. "'The Pater Noster in a Table Y-Peynted' and Some Other Presentations of Doctrine in the Vernon Manuscript." In Derek Pearsall, ed., *Studies in the Vernon Manuscript*, pp. 89–113. Cambridge: D. S. Brewer, 1990.

Hillgarth, J. R. *Ramon Lull and Lullism in Fourteenth Century France*. Oxford: Clarendon Press, 1971.

Himmelfarb, Martha. "From Prophecy to Apocalypse: The Book of the Watchers and Tours of Heaven." In A. Green, ed., *Jewish Spirituality I: From the Bible Through the Middle Ages*, pp. 145–165. World Spirituality, 13. New York: Crossroad, 1987.

Holdsworth, Christopher. "Were the Sermons of St. Bernard on the Song of Songs Ever Preached?" In C. Muessig, ed., *Medieval Monastic Preaching*, pp. 295–318. Leiden: Brill, 1998.

Howell, Wilbur S. *Logic and Rhetoric in England, 1500–1700*. Princeton: Princeton University Press, 1956.

Hughes, Andrew. *Medieval Manuscripts for Mass and Office*. Toronto: University of Toronto Press, 1982.

Huizinga, Johan. *The Autumn of the Middle Ages*. Translated by R. J. Payton and U. Mammitzsch from *Herfsttij der Middeleeuwen* (Willink, 1921). Chicago: University of Chicago Press, 1996.

Hunt, R. W. "The Library of Robert Grosseteste." In D. A. Callus, ed., *Robert Grosseteste, Scholar and Bishop*, pp. 121–145. Oxford: Clarendon Press, 1955.

"Manuscripts Containing the Indexing Symbols of Robert Grosseteste." *Bodleian Library Record* 4 (1953): 241–255.

"English Learning in the Late Twelfth Century." *Transactions of the Royal Historical Society*, series 4, 19 (1936): 19–35.

Huot, Sylvia. *From Song to Book: The Poetics of Writing Old French Lyric and Lyrical Narrative Poetry*. Ithaca: Cornell University Press, 1987.

Hutchinson, D. "Doctrines of the Mean and the Debate Concerning Skills in Fourth-Century Medicine, Rhetoric, and Ethics." *Apeiron* 21 (1988): 17–52.

Huygens, R. B. C. *Accessus ad auctores*. Collection Latomus, 15. Brussels: Berchem, 1954.

Illich, Ivan. *In the Vineyard of the Text: A Commentary to Hugh's Didascalicon.* Chicago: University of Chicago Press, 1993.

Infeld, Leopold. *Quest: An Autobiography.* 2nd edition. New York: Chelsea Publishing, 1980.

Irvine, Martin. *The Making of Textual Culture.* Cambridge: Cambridge University Press, 1994.

"Grammatical Theory and the House of Fame." *Speculum* 60 (1985): 850–876.

Jacquart, Danielle. "Medical Scholasticism." In M. D. Grmek, ed., *Western Medical Thought From Antiquity to the Middle Ages,* q.v., pp. 197–240.

Jaeger, C. Stephen. *The Envy of Angels: Cathedral Schools and Social Ideals in Medieval Europe, 950–1200.* Philadelphia: University of Pennsylvania Press, 1994.

Jager, Eric. *The Book of the Heart.* Chicago: University of Chicago Press, 2000.

Johnston, Mark D. *The Evangelical Rhetoric of Ramon Llull: Lay Learning and Piety in the Christian West around 1300.* Oxford: Oxford University Press, 1996.

The Spiritual Logic of Ramon Llull. Oxford: Clarendon Press, 1987.

Kahn, Victoria. "The Figure of the Reader in Petrarch's *Secretum.*" *PMLA* 100 (1985): 154–166.

Kane, George. "John M. Manly and Edith Rickert." In P. G. Ruggiers, ed., *Editing Chaucer: The Great Tradition,* pp. 231–252. Norman, OK: Pilgrim Books, 1984.

Katzenellenbogen, Adolf. *Allegories of the Vices and Virtues in Medieval Art.* London: Warburg Institute, 1939.

Kelly, Douglas. "Obscurity and Memory: Sources for Invention in Medieval French Literature." In L. Ebin, ed., *Vernacular Poetics in the Middle Ages,* pp. 33–56. Kalamazoo, MI: Medieval Institute, 1984.

"Topical Invention in Medieval French Literature." In J. J. Murphy, ed., *Medieval Eloquence,* q.v., pp. 231–251.

Kennedy, George A. *Classical Rhetoric and Its Christian and Secular Tradition From Ancient to Modern Times.* 2nd edition. Chapel Hill: University of North Carolina Press, 1999.

A New History of Classical Rhetoric. Princeton: Princeton University Press, 1994.

Kenny, A. J. P. *Action, Emotion and Will.* 2nd edition. London: Routledge, 2003.

Aquinas on Mind. London: Routledge, 1993.

"Intellect and Imagination in Aquinas." In *Aquinas: A Collection of Critical Essays,* pp. 273–296. 1969. Rpt. Notre Dame: University of Notre Dame Press, 1976.

Ker, N. R. "The Beginnings of Salisbury Cathedral Library." In J. J. G. Alexander and M. T. Gibson, eds., *Medieval Learning and Literature,* q.v., pp. 23–49.

Medieval Libraries of Great Britain. 2nd edition. London: Royal Historical Society, 1964.

English Manuscripts in the Century After the Norman Conquest. Oxford: Oxford University Press, 1960.

Kerby-Fulton, Katherine, and Denise Despres. *Iconography and the Professional Reader: The Politics of Book Production in the Douce Piers Plowman.* Minneapolis: University of Minnesota, 1999.

Kessler, Herbert A. "Turning a Blind Eye: Medieval Art and the Dynamics of Contemplation." In A.-M. Bouché and J. Hamburger, eds., *The Mind's Eye*. pp. 413–439. Princeton: Princeton University Press, 2006.

"'*Hoc visibile imaginatum figurat illud invisibile verum*': Imagining God in Pictures of Christ." In K. Morrison, G. de Nie, and M. Mostert, eds., *Seeing the Invisible in Late Antiquity and the Early Middle Ages*, pp. 291–325. Turnhout: Brepols, 2005.

Spiritual Seeing: Picturing God's Invisibility in Medieval Art. Philadelphia: University of Pennsylvania Press, 2000.

Kidson, Peter. "Panofsky, Suger and St. Denis." *JWCI* 50 (1987): 1–17.

Knox, Bernard M. W. "Silent Reading in Antiquity." *Greek, Roman, and Byzantine Studies* 9 (1968): 421–435.

Kolve, V. A. *Chaucer and the Imagery of Narrative*. Stanford, CA: Stanford University Press, 1984.

Kristeller, Paul O. *Medieval Aspects of Renaissance Learning*. Durham: Duke University Press, 1974.

Küchler, Susanne, and Walter Melion. *Images of Memory: On Remembering and Representation*. Washington: Smithsonian Institution Press, 1991.

Kully, Rolf Max. "Cisiojanus: comment savoir le calendrier par coeur." In B. Roy and P. Zumthor, eds., *Jeux de mémoire*, q.v., pp. 149–156.

Kuttner, S., and B. Smalley. "The 'Glossa Ordinaria' to the Gregorian Decretals." *English Historical Review* 60 (1945): 97–105.

Lacan, Jacques. *The Four Fundamental Concepts of Psychoanalysis*. Edited by J. A. Miller and translated by A. Sheridan. London: Hogarth Press, 1977.

Lampe, G. W. H., ed. *The Cambridge History of the Bible*, vol. II: The West from the Fathers to the Reformation. Cambridge: Cambridge University Press, 1969.

Lanham, Carol Dana. *Latin Grammar and Rhetoric: From Classical Theory to Medieval Practice*. London and New York: Continuum, 2002.

"Writing Instruction From Late Antiquity to the Twelfth Century." In J. J. Murphy, ed., *A Short History of Writing Instruction*, q.v., pp. 79–121.

Larès, Micheline. "Les Traductions bibliques: l'exemple de la Grande-Bretagne." In P. Riché and G. Lobrichon, eds., *Le Moyen Âge et la Bible*, q.v., pp. 123–140.

Lawton, Lesley. "The Illustration of Late Medieval Secular Texts." In D. Pearsall, ed., *Manuscripts and Readers in Fifteenth-Century England*, pp. 41–69. Cambridge: D. S. Brewer, 1983.

Leclercq, Jean. "L'Art de la composition dans les sermons de S. Bernard." *Studi Medievali* 3rd series, 7 (1966): 128–153.

"Sur le caractère littéraire des sermons de S. Bernard." *Studi Medievali* 3rd series, 7 (1966): 701–744.

The Love of Learning and the Desire for God. Translated by C. Misrahi. 3rd edition. New York: Fordham University Press, 1982.

Lecoq, Danielle. La "*Mappemonde*" du De Arca Noe Mystica de Hughes de Saint-Victor (*1128–1129*). In M. Pelletier, ed., *Géographie du monde au Moyen Âge et à la Renaissance. Mémoires de la Section Géographie*, pp. 9–31. Paris: CTHS, 1989.

Lewis, Rhodri. *Language, Mind and Nature: Artificial Languages in England, Bacon to Locke*. Cambridge: Cambridge University Press, 2007.

———. "'The Best Mnemonicall Expedient': John Beale's Art of Memory and Its Uses." *Seventeenth Century* 20 (2005): 113–144.

Lieb, Michael. *The Visionary Mode: Biblical Prophecy, Hermeneutics, and Cultural Change*. Ithaca: Cornell University Press, 1991.

Light, Laura. "The New Thirteenth-Century Bible and the Challenge of Heresy." *Viator* 18 (1987): 275–288.

———. "Versions et revisions du texte biblique." In P. Riché and G. Lobrichon, eds., *Le Moyen Âge et la Bible*, q.v., pp. 55–93.

Lindsay, W. M. *Notae latinae*. Cambridge: Cambridge University Press, 1915.

Lokhorst, Gert-Jan, and Timo T. Kaitaro. "The Originality of Descartes' Theory About the Pineal Gland." *Journal for the History of the Neurosciences* 10 (2001): 6–18.

Lord, Albert B. *The Singer of Tales*. Cambridge, MA: Harvard University Press, 1960.

Luria, A. R. *The Neuropsychology of Memory*. Translated by B. Haigh. Washington, DC: Winston, 1976.

———. *The Mind of a Mnemonist*. Translated by L. Solotareff. New York: Basic Books, 1968.

McCartney, Eugene S. "Notes on Reading and Praying Audibly." *Classical Philology* 43 (1948): 184–187.

McCracken, U. E., L. M. C. Randall, and R. H. Randall, eds. *Gatherings in Honor of Dorothy E. Miner*. Baltimore: Walters Art Gallery, 1974.

McCulloch, Florence. *Medieval French and Latin Bestiaries*. Chapel Hill: University of North Carolina Press, 1960.

McKeon, Richard. "Literacy Criticism and the Concept of Imitation in Antiquity." In R. S. Crane, ed., *Critics and Criticism*, pp. 147–175. Chicago: University of Chicago Press, 1952.

———. "Rhetoric in the Middle Ages." In R. S. Crane, ed., *Critics and Criticism*, pp. 260–296. Chicago: University of Chicago Press, 1952.

Mackey, Louis H. "*Inter nocturnas vigilias*: A Proof Postponed." In L. A. Finke and M. B. Schichtman, eds., *Medieval Texts and Contemporary Readers*, pp. 69–99. Ithaca: Cornell University Press, 1987.

McKitterick, Rosamond. "Text and Image in the Carolingian World." In R. McKitterick, ed., *The Uses of Literacy in Early Medieval Europe*, pp. 297–318. Cambridge: Cambridge University Press, 1990.

Malcolm, Norman. *Memory and Mind*. Ithaca: Cornell University Press, 1977.

Mâle, Emile. *The Gothic Image*. Translated by D. Nussey. 1913. Rpt. New York: Harper, 1958.

Mandonnet, P. "Pierre Calo et la légende de S. Thomas." *Revue Thomiste* new series, 2 (1912): 508–516.

Marks, Richard, and Nigel Morgan. *The Golden Age of English Manuscript Painting*. London: Chatto and Windus, 1981.

Markus, R. A. "Augustine on Signs." *Phronesis* 2 (1957): 60–83.

Marrou, Henri I. *Histoire de l'éducation dans l'antiquité.* 6th edition. Paris: Seuil, 1965.

Saint Augustin et le fin de la culture antique. Paris: de Boccard, 1938.

Martz, Louis L. *The Poetry of Meditation.* New Haven: Yale University Press, 1954.

Matson, Wallace I., "Why Isn't the Mind–Body Problem Ancient?" In P. Feyerabend and G. Maxwell, eds., *Mind, Matter, and Method,* pp. 92–102. Minneapolis: University of Minnesota Press, 1966.

Matthews, Gareth B. "Augustine On Speaking from Memory." In R. A. Markus, ed., *Augustine: A Collection of Essays,* pp. 168–175. New York: Anchor Doubleday, 1972.

Mazzotta, Guiseppe. *Dante: Poet of the Desert.* Princeton: Princeton University Press, 1979.

Miedema, Hessel. "The Term *Emblemata* in Alciati." *JWCI* 31 (1968): 234–250.

Miethke, Jürgen. "Marsilius und Ockham: Publikum und Leser ihrer Politischen Schriften im Späteren Mittelalter." *Medioevo: Rivista di Storia della Filosofia Medievale* (Padua) 6 (1980): 543–567.

Ockhams Weg zur Sozialphilozophie. Berlin: de Gruyter, 1969.

Miller, George A. "Information and Memory." *Scientific American* (August, 1963): 42–46.

"The Magical Number Seven, Plus or Minus Two: Some Limits on Our Capacity for Processing Information." *Psychological Review* 63 (1956): 81–97.

Minnis, Alastair J. *Medieval Theory of Authorship.* 2nd edition. Philadelphia: University of Pennsylvania Press, 1988.

"Langland's Ymaginatif and Late Medieval Theories of Imagination." *Comparative Criticism* 3 (1981): 71–103.

"John Gower, *sapiens* in Ethics and Politics." *Medium Aevum* 49 (1980): 207–229.

Minnis, Alastair J., and A. B. Scott. *Medieval Literary Theory and Criticism c. 1100 – c. 1375: The Commentary-Tradition.* Revised edition. Oxford: Clarendon Press, 1991.

Mooney, Linne R. "Chaucer's Scribe." *Speculum* 81 (2006): 97–138.

Morrison, Karl. *History as a Visual Art in the Twelfth-century Renaissance.* Princeton: Princeton University Press, 1990.

I Am You: The Hermeneutics of Empathy in Western Literature, Theology, and Art. Princeton: Princeton University Press, 1988.

The Mimetic Tradition of Reform in the West. Princeton: Princeton University Press, 1982.

Morson, John. "The English Cistercians and the Bestiary." *Bulletin of John Rylands Library* 39 (1956–1957): 146–170.

Mundò, Anscari. "Bibliotheca, bible, et lecture de carême d'après S. Benôit." *Revue Bénédictine* 60 (1950): 65–92.

Munk Olsen, B[irger]. "Les Florilèges d'auteurs classiques." In *Les Genres littéraires dans les Sources Théologiques et Philosophiques Médiévales,* pp. 151–164. Louvain: Université Catholique de Louvain, Publications de l'Institut d'Études Médiévales, second series, 5 (1982).

"Les Classiques latins dans les florilèges médiévaux antérieurs au XIIIe siècle." *Revue d'Histoire des Textes* 9 (1979): 47–121.

Murphy, James J. "The Key Role of Habit in Roman Writing Instruction." In J. J. Murphy, ed., *A Short History of Writing Instruction*, q.v., pp. 35–78.

Rhetoric in the Middle Ages. Berkeley: University of California Press, 1974.

Medieval Rhetoric: A Select Bibliography. Toronto: University of Toronto Press, 1971.

ed. *A Short History of Writing Instruction.* 2nd edition. Mahwah, NJ: Erlbaum, 2001.

Medieval Eloquence. Berkeley: University of California Press, 1978.

Murray, Alexander. *Reason and Society in the Middle Ages.* Oxford: Clarendon Press, 1978.

Murrin, Michael. *The Veil of Allegory.* Chicago: University of Chicago Press, 1969.

Nagle, Thomas A. "What is it like to be a bat?" *Philosophical Review* 4 (1974): 435–450.

Nash, Ronald H. *The Light of the Mind: St. Augustine's Theory of Knowledge.* Lexington: University Press of Kentucky, 1969.

Nelson, Robert S., ed. *Seeing As Others Saw.* Cambridge: Cambridge University Press, 2000.

Newman, Barbara. "What Did It Mean to Say 'I Saw?': The Clash Between Theory and Practice in Medieval Visionary Culture." *Speculum* 80 (2005): 1–43.

Newman, Sara. "Aristotle's Notion of 'Bringing Before the Eyes': Its Contributions to Aristotelian and Contemporary Conceptualizations of Metaphor, Style, and Audience." *Rhetorica* 20 (2002): 1–23.

Nichols, Stephen G., and J. D. Lyons, eds. *Mimesis: From Mirror to Method, Augustine to Descartes.* Hanover, NH: University Press of New England, 1982.

Noakes, Susan. "The Double Misreading of Paolo and Francesca." *Philological Quarterly* 62 (1983): 221–239.

Nordenfalk, Carl. "A 10th-Century Gospel Book in the Walters Art Gallery." In U. McCracken, L. Randall, and R. Randall, eds., *Gatherings in Honor of Dorothy E. Miner*, q.v., pp. 139–170.

"The Beginning of Book Decoration." In O. Goetz, ed., *Essays in Honor of George Swarzenski*, pp. 9–20. Chicago: Regnery, 1951.

Die Spätantiken Kanontäfeln. 2 vols. Goteborg: O. Isacsons, 1938.

Nordenfalk, Carl, and André Grabar. *Early Medieval Painting.* New York: Skira, 1957.

Norman, Donald A. *Learning and Memory.* San Francisco, CA: Freeman, 1982.

Memory and Attention. New York: J. Wiley, 1969.

Norman, Donald A., ed. *Models of Human Memory.* New York: Academic Press, 1970.

Notopoulos, J. A. "Mnemosyne in Oral Literature." *Transactions of the American Philological Association* 69 (1938): 465–493.

Nussbaum, Martha C. *The Therapy of Desire: Theory and Practice in Hellenistic Ethics.* Princeton: Princeton University Press, 1994.

Obermann, Heiko. *Archbishop Thomas Bradwardine: A Fourteenth-Century Augustinian*. Utrecht: Kemink, 1958.

O'Donnell, James J. *Augustine: A New Biography*. New York: Ecco, 2005.

Cassiodorus. Berkeley: University of California Press, 1979.

Ong, Walter J. *Ramus, Method, and the Decay of Dialogue*. 1958. Rpt. Cambridge, MA: Harvard University Press, 1983.

Orality and Literacy. London: Methuen, 1982.

Onians, John. "Abstraction and Imagination in Late Antiquity." *Art History* 3 (1980): 1–24.

Orme, Nicholas. *Medieval Schools: From Roman Britain to Renaissance England*. New Haven: Yale University Press, 2006.

English Schools in the Middle Ages. London: Methuen, 1973.

Pächt, Otto. *The Rise of Pictorial Narrative in Twelfth-Century England*. Oxford: Clarendon Press, 1962.

Pack, R. A. "An *Ars memorativa* from the Late Middle Ages." *Archives d'histoire doctrinale et littéraire du Moyen Âge* 46 (1979): 221–265.

Parkes, M. B. "*Folia librorum quaerere*: Medieval Experience of the Problems of Hypertext and the Index." In C. Leonardi *et al.*, eds., *Fabula in tabula: una storia degli indici dal manoscritto al testo elettronico*, pp. 23–41 + 8 plates. Spoleto: Centro Italiano di studi sull'alto medioevo, 1995.

Pause and Effect: An Introduction to the History of Punctuation in the West. Berkeley: University of California Press, 1993.

"The Influence of the Concepts of *ordinatio* and *compilatio* on the Development of the Book." In J. J. G. Alexander and M. T. Gibson, eds., *Medieval Learning and Literature*, q.v., pp. 115–141.

"The Literacy of the Laity." In D. Daiches and A. Thorlby, eds., *Literature and Western Civilization*, vol. II: *The Medieval World*, pp. 555–577. London: Aldus, 1973.

Pasquale, Giorgio. *Storia della tradizione e critica del testo*. 2nd edition. Florence: le Monnier, 1952.

Patterson, Lee. *Negotiating the Past*. Madison, WI: University of Wisconsin Press, 1987.

Payne, Robert O. "Chaucer's Realization of Himself as Rhetor." In J. J. Murphy, ed., *Medieval Eloquence*, q.v., pp. 270–287.

The Key of Remembrance. New Haven: Yale University Press, 1963.

Pellegrin, E., and G. Billanovich. "Un Manuscrit de Ciceron annoté par Petrarque au British Museum [MS. Harley 2493]." *Scriptorium* 8 (1954): 115–117.

Petrucci, Armando. *La scrittura di Francesco Petrarca*. Vatican: Biblioteca Apostolica, 1967.

Plummer, John. *The Hours of Catherine of Cleves*. New York: Braziller [1966].

Randall, Lillian M. C. *Images in the Margins of Gothic Manuscripts*. Berkeley: University of California Press, 1966.

Reese, Gustav. *Music in the Middle Ages*. New York: Norton, 1940.

Reitman, Walter. "What Does It Take to Remember?" In D. A. Norman, ed., *Models of Human Memory*, q.v., pp. 469–509.

Richardson, John T. E. *Mental Imagery and Human Memory*. New York: St. Martins, 1980.

Riché, Pierre. "Le Rôle de la mémoire dans l'enseignement médiéval." In B. Roy and P. Zumthor, eds., *Jeux de mémoire*, q.v., pp. 133–148.

Éducation et culture dans l'occident barbare, vie–viiie siècles. Paris: Seuil, 1962. Translated by J. J. Contreni, *Education and Culture in the Barbarian West, Sixth Through Eighth Centuries*. Columbia: University of South Carolina Press, 1976.

"Les Bibliothèques de trois aristocrats laïcs carolingiens." *Le Moyen-âge* 66 (1963): 87–104.

Riché, Pierre, and Guy Lobrichon, eds. *Bible de tous les temps*, vol. iv: *Le Moyen Âge et la Bible*. Paris: Éditions Beauchesne, 1984.

Ricoeur, Paul. *History, Memory, Forgetting*. Translation by K. Blamey and D. Pellauer of *Mémoire, l'histoire, l'oubli* (Seuil, 2000). Chicago: University of Chicago Press, 2004.

Time and Narrative. 3 vols. Translation by K. McLaughlin and D. Pellauer of *Temps et récit* (Seuil, 1983–1985). Chicago: University of Chicago Press, 1984–1988.

The Rule of Metaphor. Translation by R. Czerny of *La métaphore vive* (Seuil, 1975). Toronto: University of Toronto Press, 1977.

Rivers, Kimberley. "The Fear of Divine Vengeance: Mnemonic Images as a Guide to Conscience in the Late Middle Ages." In A. Scott and C. Kosso, eds., *Fear and Its Representations in the Middle Ages and Renaissance*, pp. 66–91. Turnhout: Brepols, 2002.

"Memory and Medieval Preaching: Mnemonic Advice in the *Ars predicandi* of Francesc Eiximenis (c. 1327–1409)." *Viator* 30 (1999): 253–284.

Roberts, Colin H., and T. C. Skeat. *The Birth of the Codex*. Oxford: Oxford University Press for The British Academy, 1983.

Robinson, H. Wheeler. *The Bible in its Ancient and English Versions*. Oxford: Clarendon Press, 1940.

Roesner, Edward H. "Who 'Made' the Magnus Liber?" *Early Music History* 20 (2001): 227–266.

Rorty, Richard. "Is Derrida a Transcendental Philosopher?" *Yale Journal of Criticism* 2 (1988–1989): 207–217.

Philosophy and the Mirror of Nature. Princeton: Princeton University Press, 1979.

Rosen, Edward. "The Invention of Eyeglasses." *Journal of the History of Medicine and Allied Sciences* 9 (1956): 13–46, 183–218.

Ross, Thomas W. "Five Fifteenth-Century 'Emblem' Verses from Brit. Mus. Addit. MS. 37049." *Speculum* 31 (1957): 274–282.

Rossi, Paolo. *Clavis universalis: arti mnemoniche e logica combinatoria de Lullo a Leibniz*. Milan: Riccardi, 1960. Translated by S. Clucas, *Logic and the Art of Memory: The Quest for a Universal Language*. Chicago: University of Chicago Press, 2000.

Rouse, Richard. "La Concordance verbale des Écritures." In P. Riché and G. Lobrichon, eds., *Le Moyen Âge et la Bible*, q.v., pp. 115–122.

Rouse, Richard, and Mary A. Rouse. *Manuscripts and Their Makers: Commercial Book Producers in Medieval Paris, 1200–1500*. Turnhout: Harvey Miller, 2000.

"The *Florilegium Angelicum*: Its Origin, Context, and Influence." In J. Alexander and M. Gibson, eds., *Medieval Learning and Literature*, q.v., pp. 66–114.

"Florilegia of Patristic Texts." In *Les genres littéraires dans les sources théologiques et philosophiques médiévales*, pp. 165–180. Louvain: Université Catholique de Louvain, Publications de l'Institut d'Études Médiévales, second series 5 (1982).

"*Statim invenire*: Schools, Preachers, and New Attitudes to the Page." In R. Benson and G. Constable, eds., *Renaissance and Renewal in the Twelfth Century*, q.v., pp. 201–225.

Preachers, Florilegia, and Sermons. Toronto: Pontifical Institute, 1979.

Rowland, Beryl. "The Artificial Memory, Chaucer, and Modern Scholars." *Poetica* (Japan) 37 (1993): 1–14.

"Bishop Bradwardine, the Artificial Memory, and the House of Fame." In R. H. Robbins, ed., *Chaucer at Albany*, pp. 41–62. New York: Franklin, 1975.

Rowland, Christopher. "Imagining the Apocalypse." *New Testament Studies* 51 (2005): 303–327.

The Open Heaven: A Study of Apocalyptic in Judaism and Early Christianity. London: SPCK, 1982.

Rowlands, John. *Holbein: The Paintings of Hans Holbein the Younger*. Boston: David Godine, 1985.

Roy, Bruno, and Paul Zumthor, eds. *Jeux de mémoire*. Montreal: Les Presses de l'Université de Montreal, 1985.

Rudolph, Conrad. *First, I Find the Center Point: Reading the Text of Hugh of Saint Victor's The Mystic Ark. Transactions of the American Philosophical Society* (Philadelphia: American Philosophical Society) 94 4 (2004).

"Building-Miracles As Artistic Justification in the Early and Mid-Twelfth Century." In W. Kersten, ed., *Kunstgeschichte Richtung Radikale Historizität? Eine Zwischenbilanz*. Marburg: Jonas Verlag, 1995.

Rutchick, Leah. "Sculpture Programs in the Moissac Cloister: Benedictine Culture, Memory Systems, and Liturgical Performance." Ph.D. diss. University of Chicago, 1991.

Sacks, Oliver. *The Man Who Mistook His Wife for a Hat*. New York: Summit Books, 1985.

Saenger, Paul. *Space Between Words: The Origins of Silent Reading*. Stanford: Stanford University Press, 1997.

"Books of Hours and the Reading Habits of the Later Middle Ages." *Scrittura e Civiltà* 9 (1985): 239–269.

"Silent Reading: Its Impact on Late Medieval Script and Society." *Viator* 13 (1982): 367–414.

Sandler, Lucy Freeman. "Bared: The Writing Bear in the British Library Bohun Psalter." In S. L'Engle and G. Guest, eds., *Tributes to Jonathan J. G. Alexander*, pp. 269–280. London: Harvey Miller, 2006.

The Lichtenthal Psalter and the Manuscript Patronage of the Bohun Family. London: Harvey Miller, 2004.

"Political Imagery in the Bohun Manuscripts." In A. S. G. Edwards, ed., *Decoration and Illustration in Medieval English Manuscripts*, pp. 115–153. London: British Library, 2002.

"The Images of Words in English Gothic Psalters." In B. Cassidy and R. M. Wright, eds., *Studies in the Illustration of the Psalter*, pp. 67–86. St. Andrews Studies in the History of Art. Stamford: Shaun Tyas, 2000.

The Psalter of Robert De Lisle. London: Harvey Miller, 1983. Reissued 1999.

"The Word in the Text and the Image in the Margin: The Case of the Luttrell Psalter." *Journal of the Walters Art Gallery* 54 (1996): 87–99.

Sarton, George. *Introduction to the History of Science.* 3 vols. Washington, DC: Carnegie Institution, 1931.

Saxl, Fritz. "A Spiritual Encyclopaedia of the Later Middle Ages." *JWCI* 5 (1942): 82–137.

Schmitt, Jean Claude. *Le Corps, les rites, les rêves, le temps: essais d'anthropologie médiévale.* Paris: Gallimard, 2001.

Ghosts in the Middle Ages: The Living and the Dead in Medieval Society. Chicago: University of Chicago Press, 1998.

"Les Images classificatrices." *Bibliothèque de l'École des Chartes* 147 (1989): 311–341.

"Écriture et image: les avatars médiévaux du modèle Grégorien." In E. Baumgartner and C. Marchello-Nizia, eds., *Théories et pratiques de l'écriture au moyen âge*, pp. 119–151. Littérales. Paris X-Nanterre: Centre des Recherches du Département de français, 1988.

Scribner, Sylvia, and Michael Cole. *The Psychology of Literacy.* Cambridge, MA: Harvard University Press, 1981.

"Unpackaging Literacy." In M. F. Whiteman, ed., *Writing: The Nature, Development, and Teaching of Written Communication*, pp. 71–87. New Jersey: Erlbaum, 1981.

Seidel, Linda. *Legends in Limestone: Structure, Sculpture, and Site at St-Lazare of Autun.* Chicago: University of Chicago Press, 2000.

Shapiro, Meyer. "On the Aesthetic Attitude in Romanesque Art." In *Romanesque Art*, pp. 1–27. New York: Braziller, 1977.

Sherwin-White, A. N. *The Letters of Pliny: A Historical and Social Commentary.* Oxford: Clarendon Press, 1966.

Sicard, Patrice. *Diagrammes médiévaux et exégèse visuelle: le Libellus de formatione arche de Hugues de Saint-Victor.* Turnhout: Brepols, 1993.

Hugues de Saint-Victor et son école. Turnhout: Brepols, 1991.

Silverstein, Theodore. "Adelard, Aristotle, and the *De natura deorum.*" *Classical Philology* 46 (1951): 82–86.

Simpson, James. "Modes of Thought and Poetic Form in *Piers Plowman.*" *Medium Aevum* 55 (1986): 1–23.

Singer, Charles J., and R. A. Underwood. *A Short History of Medicine.* Oxford: Oxford University Press, 1962.

Singleton, Charles. *An Essay on the Vita nuova.* 1949. Rpt. Baltimore: Johns Hopkins University Press, 1977.

Siraisi, Nancy. *Medieval and Early Renaissance Medicine.* Chicago: University of Chicago Press, 1990.

Arts and Sciences at Padua. Toronto: Pontifical Institute, 1973.

Skeat, T. C. "The Use of Dictation in Ancient Book Production." *Proceedings of the British Academy* 42 (1956): 179–208.

The Codex Sinaiticus and the Codex Alexandrinus. Revised edition. London: British Museum, 1955.

Small, Jocelyn Penny. *Waxed Tablets of the Mind: Cognitive Studies of Memory and Literacy in Classical Antiquity.* London: Routledge, 1997.

Smalley, Beryl. *The Gospels in the Schools, c. 1100 – c. 1280.* London: Hambledon, 1985.

The Study of the Bible in the Middle Ages. 3rd edition. Oxford: Blackwell, 1984.

"The Bible and Eternity: John Wyclif's Dilemma." *JWCI* 27 (1964): 73–89.

English Friars and Antiquity in the Early Fourteenth Century. New York: Barnes and Noble, 1960.

Smith, Kathryn A. *Art, Identity and Devotion in Fourteenth-Century England: Three Women and Their Books of Hours.* London: The British Library, 2003.

Smith, Lesley J. *Masters of the Sacred Page: Manuscripts of Theology in the Latin West to 1274.* Notre Dame: University of Notre Dame Press, 2001.

Sorabji, Richard. *Emotion and Peace of Mind.* Oxford: Oxford University Press, 2000.

Southern, R. W. *Robert Grosseteste.* Oxford: Clarendon Press, 1986.

Medieval Humanism and Other Studies. Oxford: Blackwell, 1970.

St. Anselm and His Biographer. Cambridge: Cambridge University Press, 1963.

Spence, Jonathan. *The Memory Palace of Matteo Ricci.* New York: Viking, 1984.

Stock, Brian. *Augustine the Reader: Meditation, Self-Knowledge, and the Ethics of Interpretation.* Cambridge, MA: Harvard University Press, 1996.

"Medieval Literacy, Linguistic Theory, and Social Organization." *New Literary History* 16 (1984–1985): 13–29.

The Implications of Literacy: Written Language and Models of Interpretation in the Eleventh and Twelfth Centuries. Princeton: Princeton University Press, 1983.

Stump, Eleonore. *Dialectic and Its Place in the Development of Medieval Logic.* Ithaca: Cornell University Press, 1989.

Sutton, John. *Philosophy and Memory Traces.* Cambridge: Cambridge University Press, 1998.

Tatteo, Francesco. *Dialogo interiore e polemica ideologica nel "Secretum" del Petrarca.* Florence: Le Monnier, 1965.

Taylor, Andrew. *Textual Situations: Three Medieval Manuscripts and Their Readers.* Philadelphia: University of Pennsylvania Press, 2002.

Taylor-Briggs, Ruth. "Reading Between the Lines: The Textual History and Manuscript Transmission of Cicero's Rhetorical Works." In Cox and Ward, eds., *The Rhetoric of Cicero,* q.v., 77–108.

"Codices integri and the Transmission of the "Ad Herennium" in Late Antiquity." *Revue d'Histoire des Textes* 23 (1993): 113–142.

"Pre-History in the Ninth-Century Manuscripts of the "Ad Herennium." *Classica et Medievalia* 44 (1993): 181–254.

Telfer, W. "'Bees' in Clement of Alexandria." *Journal of Theological Studies* 28 (1926–1927): 167–178.

Testard, Maurice. *St. Augustine et Cicéron.* 2 vols. Paris: Études augustiniennes, 1958.

Thomas, Rosalind. *Literacy and Orality in Ancient Greece.* Cambridge: Cambridge University Press, 1992.

Thompson, J. W. *The Literacy of the Laity in the Middle Ages.* Berkeley: University of California Press, 1939.

Thompson, J. W., *et al. The Medieval Library.* Chicago: University of Chicago Press, 1939.

Thomson, S. Harrison. *Writings of Robert Grosseteste.* Cambridge: Cambridge University Press, 1940.

"Grosseteste's Topical Concordance of the Bible and the Fathers." *Speculum* 9 (1934): 139–144.

Thorndike, Lynn. *History of Magic and Experimental Science.* 8 vols. New York: Macmillan and Columbia University Press, 1923–1958.

Toynbee, Paget. *Dante, and the Lancelot Romance.* Fifth Annual Report of the Dante Society. Cambridge, MA: Dante Society, 1886.

Tracy, Theodore. *Physiological Theory and the Doctrine of the Mean in Plato and Aristotle.* Chicago: Loyola University Press, 1969.

Trapp, Damasus. "Augustinian Theology of the Fourteenth Century: Notes on Editions, Marginalia, Opinions, and Book-Lore." *Augustiniana* 6 (1956): 146–274.

Treitler, Leo. *With Voice and Pen: Coming to Know Medieval Song and How It Was Made.* Oxford: Oxford University Press, 2003.

Trimpi, Wesley. *Muses of One Mind.* Princeton: Princeton University Press, 1983.

Tselos, Dimitri. "English Manuscript Illustration and the Utrecht Psalter." *Art Bulletin* 41 (1959): 137–149.

Unger, Richard W. *The Art of Medieval Technology: Images of Noah the Shipbuilder.* New Brunswick, NJ: Rutgers University Press, 1991.

Van der Horst, Koert, William Noel, and Wilhelmina Wüstefeld. *The Utrecht Psalter in Medieval Art: Picturing the Psalms of David.* London: Harvey Miller, 1997.

Van Dijk, S. J. P. "An Advertisement Sheet of an Early Fourteenth-Century Writing Master at Oxford." *Scriptorium* 10 (1956): 47–64.

Vance, Eugene. *Mervelous Signals.* Omaha: University of Nebraska Press, 1986.

"Saint Augustine: Language as Temporality." In S. Nichols and J. Lyons, eds., *Mimesis,* q.v., pp. 20–35.

Vegetti, Mario. "Between Knowledge and Practice: Hellenistic Medicine." In M. D. Grmek, ed., *Western Medical Thought from Antiquity to the Middle Ages,* q.v., pp. 72–103.

Verkerk, Dorothy. *Early Medieval Bible Illumination and the Ashburnham Pentateuch.* Cambridge: Cambridge University Press, 2004.

Vickers, Brian, ed. *Occult and Scientific Mentalities in the Renaissance*. Cambridge: Cambridge University Press, 1984.

Vickers, Nancy J. "Petrarchan Lyric and the Strategies of Description." In S. Nichols and J. Lyons, eds., *Mimesis*, q.v., pp. 100–109.

Von Nolcken, Christina. "Some Alphabetical Compendia and How Preachers Used Them in Fourteenth-Century England." *Viator* 12 (1981): 271–288.

Walz, Angelus Maria. *San Tommaso D'Aquino: studi biografici sul dottore angelico*. Rome: Edizioni Liturgiche, 1945.

Ward, John O. *Ciceronian Rhetoric in Treatise, Scholion and Commentary*. Turnhout: Brepols, 1995.

"Quintilian and the Rhetorical Revolution of the Middle Ages." *Rhetorica* 13 (1995): 231–284.

"From Antiquity to the Renaissance: Glosses and Commentaries on Cicero's *Rhetorica*." In J. J. Murphy, ed., *Medieval Eloquence*, q.v., pp. 25–67.

"*Artificiosa eloquentia* in the Middle Ages." Ph.D. diss. University of Toronto, 1972. (Also see under Cox and Ward).

Watts, Ann C. *The Lyre and the Harp*. New Haven: Yale University Press, 1969.

Watts, Pauline Moffit. "Hieroglyphs of Conversion: Alien Discourses in Diego Valadés's 'Rhetorica Christiana.'" *Memorie Domenicane* 22 (1991): 403–433.

Weinrich, Harald. *Lethe: The Art and Critique of Forgetting*. Translated by S. Rendall from *Lethe: Kunst und Kritik des Vergessens* (Munich: C. H. Beck, 1997). Ithaca: Cornell University Press, 2004.

Weisheipl, J. A. "Repertorium mertonense." *Medieval Studies* 31 (1969): 174–224.

Weitzmann, Kurt. *Late Antique and Early Christian Book Illumination*. New York: Braziller, 1977.

Illustrations in Roll and Codex: A Study of the Origins and Method of Text and Illustrations. Rpt., with additions. Princeton: Princeton University Press, 1970.

West, Philip J. "Rumination in Bede's Account of Caedmon." *Monastic Studies* 12 (1976): 217–226.

Wieck, Roger. *Painted Prayers: The Book of Hours in Medieval and Renaissance Art*. New York: Braziller, 1997.

Wilkins, Ernest H. *Studies in the Life and Works of Petrarch*. Cambridge, MA: Medieval Academy of America, 1955.

Wilson, R. M. "The Medieval Library of Tichfield Abbey." *Proceedings of the Leeds Philosophical and Literary Society* 5 (1940): 150–177, 252–276.

Witt, Ronald G. "Boncompagno and the Defense of Rhetoric." *JMRS* 16 (1986): 1–31.

Wolfson, Harry A. "The Internal Senses." *Harvard Theological Review* 28 (1935): 69–133.

Woods, Marjorie C. "The Teaching of Poetic Composition in the Later Middle Ages." In J. J. Murphy, ed., *A Short History of Writing Instruction*, q.v., pp. 123–143.

"Teaching the Tropes in the Middle Ages: The Theory of Metaphoric Transference in Commentaries on the *Poetria nova*." In W. B. Horner and

M. Leff, eds., *Rhetoric and Pedagogy: Its History, Philosophy, and Practice.* pp. 73–82. Mahwah, NJ: Erlbaum, 1995.

"A Medieval Rhetoric Goes to School – And to the University: The Commentaries on the Poetria nova." *Rhetorica* 9 (1991): 55–65.

Wormald, Francis. "The Monastic Library." In U. McCracken, L. M. Randall, and R. Randall, eds., *Gatherings in Honor of Dorothy E. Miner*, q.v., pp. 93–109.

"The Survival of Anglo-Saxon Illumination After the Conquest." *Proceedings of the British Academy* 30 (1944): 127–149 + plates.

Wormald, Francis, and C. E. Wright, eds. *The English Library Before 1700.* London: Athlone, 1958.

Yapp, Brundson. *Birds in Medieval Manuscripts.* London: British Library, 1981.

"The Birds of English Medieval Manuscripts." *Journal of Medieval History* 5 (1979): 315–349.

Yates, Frances A. *Lull and Bruno: Collected Essays.* 2 vols. London: Routledge and Kegan Paul, 1982.

The Art of Memory. London: Routledge and Kegan Paul, 1966.

"The Ciceronian Art of Memory." In *Medioevo e rinascimento: studi in onore di Bruno Nardi*, pp. 871–903. Florence: Sansoni, 1955.

Ziegler, Joseph. *Dulcedo dei: ein Beitrag zur Theologie der Griechischen und Lateinischen Bibel.* Alttestamentliche Abhandlungen, XIII Band. 2 Heft. Muenster: Aschendorff, 1937.

Zinn, Grover A., Jr. "Exile, the Abbey of Saint-Victor at Paris and Hugh of Saint-Victor." In S. Hayes-Healy, ed., *Medieval Paradigms: Essays in Honor of Jeremy Duquesnay Adams.* vol. II, pp. 83–111. New York: Palgrave-Macmillan, 2005.

"Suger, Theology, and the Pseudo-Dionysian Tradition." In Paula Gerson, ed., *Abbot Suger and St-Denis: A Symposium*, pp. 33–40. New York: Metropolitan Museum, 1986.

"Hugh of St. Victor and the Art of Memory." *Viator* 5 (1974): 211–234.

Ziolkowski, Jan M. *Nota Bene: Reading Classics and Writing Melodies in the Early Middle Ages.* Turnhout: Brepols, 2007.

"Mnemotechnics and the Reception of the Aeneid in Late Antiquity and the Middle Ages." In C. Foss and P. E. Knox, eds., *Style and Tradition: Essays in Honor of Wendell Clausen*, pp. 160–175. Stuttgart: Teubner, 1998.

"Theories of Obscurity in the Latin Tradition." *Mediaevalia* 19 (1996): 101–170. ed. *Obscure Styles in Medieval Literature.* Mediaevalia 19 (1996).

Zumthor, Paul. *La Poésie et la voix dans la civilisation médiévale.* Essais et Conférences du Collège de France. Paris: Presses Universitaires de France, 1984.

Essai de poétique médiévale. Paris: Seuil, 1972.

Index of manuscripts

BRUSSELS
Bibliothèque Royale de Belgique
  KBR ms. II, 1076: 449
CAMBRIDGE, England
Corpus Christi College
  MS. 286: 166, 325
Fitzwilliam Museum
  MS. McClean 169: 163–164
St. John's College
  MS. L.1: 264
Trinity College
  MS. B.5.4: 267–268
  MS. O.9.1: 450, 451
  MS. R.17.1: 445
University Library
  MS. Gg. 1.1: 67, 244
  MS. Ii. 3.26: 444
CAMBRIDGE, Massachusetts
Harvard College
  MS. 27: 450
CHANTILLY
Musée Condé
  MS. 590: 419
CHICAGO
Newberry Library
  MS. 31.1: 269–271, 441
DUBLIN
Trinity College
  MS. A.1(58): 333–337
  MS. A.1.6: 454
  MS. A.4.5: 454
FLORENCE
Biblioteca Medicea Laurenziana
  MS. Acquisti e Doni 325: 271
HEILIGENKREUZ
Stiftsbibliotek
  MS. 226: 449
LONDON
British Library
  MS. Add. 37049: 442
  MS. Add. 62925: 170

MS. Arundel 83-II: 332
MS. Cotton Nero A.v: 159–160
MS. Harley 603: 282, 445
MS. Harley 4166: 163–164
MS. Royal 1.D.v–viii: 451
MS. Royal 5.D.x: 451–452
MS. Royal 10. E.iv: 315, 451
MS. Sloane 278: 449
MS. Sloane 3744: 163–164, 414
LYONS
Municipal Library
  MS. 414: 147, 149, 410
MILAN
Biblioteca Ambrosiana
  MS. R.50.supra: 191
NEW YORK
Pierpont Morgan Library
  MS. 917: 318, 451
  MS. 945: 318, 451
  MS. M 183: 327, 452
  MS. M 756: 285–287
  MS. M 832: 138, 407–408
  MS. M 860: 118–120
OXFORD
Bodleian Library
  MS. Auct. D 1.2: 404
  MS. Auct. E inf.6: 267–268
  MS. Barlow 53: 448, 452
  MS. Bodley 177: 331
  MS. Bodley 198: 146–147
  MS. Bodley 717: 280
  MS. Bodley 722: 292, 407
  MS. Douce 104: 288–291, 445–446
  MS. Douce 219: 451
  MS. Lat.class.d.36: 419
  MS. Lat.th.b.1: 328, 452
  MS. Lat.th.b.4: 269
  MS. Lat.th.c.2: 328, 452
  MS. Laud Misc. 151: 328, 448
  MS. Laud Misc. 370: 447
  MS. Laud Misc. 409: 447

MS. Lyell 2: 450
MS. Lyell 71: 449
New College
  MS. 112: 150–151
PARIS
Bibliothèque Nationale
  MS. lat. 8846: 445
  MS. lat. 10631: 447
  MS. lat. 15009: 455
  MS. N.A.L. 2334:
    51, 384
ROME
Vatican
  MS. lat.3256: 281
  MS. lat.9850: 5–6

SAINT-OMER
  MS. 94: 449
SAN MARINO, California
Huntington Library
  MS. EL 9 H4: 121
  MS. HM 148: 121
  MS. HM 1073: 145–146
  MS. HM 19915: 310–314, 450
  MS. HM 26052: 404
  MS. HM 26061: 410
TROYES
  MS. 177: 449
UTRECHT
University Library
  MS. 32: 282–285

General index

abacus 99
abbot, Bradwardine's image of 170–171
abbreviations 146–147
    Latin 141
    see also *littera inintelligibilis*; shorthand symbols
Abelard, Peter 178, 222–223, 227, 426, 431
abstractions, memorizing of 58
    Bradwardine on 168–169, 365
    Thomas Aquinas on 62–63, 72
accuracy
    of oral and written transmission 199–200
    see also inaccuracy
adaequatio, use of word in medieval philosophy
    28–29, 30–31, 140, 376
Adam (Chaucer's scrivener) 242–243,
    422–423, 436
Adam of Dryburgh, meditation on *Exodus* 439
Adelard of Bath 115
Adeliza of Louvain (Henry I's second wife)
    159, 413
Aelred of Rielvaux 413
Aeolus (description in *Aeneid*), Petrarch's
    interpretation 209–210, 211
Aeschylus, *Prometheus* 34
Aesop, *Fables*, as *bas-de-page* pictorial
    narrative 315
Aesopus (Roman actor), as mnemonic image
    175–176
"affection" (*affectio, affectus*) 296
    Aristotle's conception of 69, 85
    memory and 75–76, 85, 87, 217
Alan of Lille 134–135, 142, 407
    On the Six Wings (of the Cherub) 333
"Alanus" gloss (on *Rhetorica ad Herennium*)
    142–143, 154, 186–187, 189, 191
Alberic of Trois-Fontaines 452
Albert, Duke of Austria 197, 421
Albertus Magnus, St. 19, 99, 172–179, 186–187,
    204, 418
    commentary on Aristotle 173, 178, 190, 345,
      346, 348–349, 357–358, 359, 373–374, 391, 414

commentary on Isaiah 177–178, 415–416
commentary on *Rhetorica ad Herennium* /
    architectural mnemonic 155, 156, 172–177,
    178, 189, 192, 193, 345–346, 347–348,
    349–360, 456–457
consideration of "memory for words" and
    "memory for things" 174–176, 359–360
De anima 350
De bono 190, 345–360
definition of "author's intention" 235–236
distinguishes between "natural" and "artificial"
    memory 88, 348, 373–374
distinguishes between *vis formalis* and *vis
    imaginativa* 457
on ethics and memory 191–192
influence on Thomas Aquinas 62, 87
on memory as habit / attribute of prudence
    87–88, 345–360
on nature of recollection 22–23, 24, 29, 84, 191,
    323–324
quotations from pagan authors 177–178
see also alphabet(s); *locus*
Alcuin 47, 122, 126, 181, 383
    discussion of memory 179–180, 184, 416
Aldhelm, "De arca libraria" 384
Alexandrine Greece
    anatomists 59, 386–387
    bestiaries 138, 159, 183
    florilegia 217
    library 151–152, 422
    philosophy 64
algorisms 75, 170–171, 365–368
allegory, *allegoria* 55, 210
Allen, Judson B. 161
alphabet(s)
    Albertus Magnus's alphabetical ordering
      system 150, 151
    Aristotle recommends use of, in memory
      scheme 34, 129, 137, 143
    florilegia arranged alphabetically 220
    foreign/imaginary, use of 137–139

full alphabetization, use of 409, 410
human/animal figures in shape of 137, 160–161
John of Garland's alphabetical ordering of
    voces animantium 157
learning of 134, 138, 140–141, 408
mnemotechniques based on 34, 135–152, 157
partial alphabetization, use of 144–146, 150
used in design of concordances 143–150
see also Jerome; Peter of Ravenna; syllables
Ambrose, St. 117, 240, 258, 416–417, 451
    Aquinas's quotations from 6, 84
    habits of study 212–216, 233, 281, 429, 433–434
Ammon *see* Thammuz
anatomists, ancient, theory of memory 59, 64
Andrew of St. Victor 10
anger, experience of / guarding against 209–210
animals
    as manuscript decoration 161, 310–314
    mental faculties, compared with human
        62–63, 86
    mnemonic use 157–158, 159–162
    see also alphabet; bear; bestiaries; birds; coops;
        ram; Zodiac
Anselm, St. 242, 243, 250, 395, 437
    attitude to written works 263
    compositional methods 246–247, 248, 249,
        260–264
    genesis of work 263
    Monologion 263–264, 440
    motives for publication 261–262
    Proslogion 260–264
    response to criticism 262–263
Anselm of Laon 265, 429, 430, 441
Anthony, St. 14, 223
Antonius, Marcus (orator) 25–26, 32, 93, 257
Apocalypse *see* Revelations
Apostles, mnemonic in *Libellus de formatione
    arche* 299
apotheca, apothecarius 54, 385–386
Aquinas *see* Thomas Aquinas
Arabic commentaries on Aristotle *see* Aristotle;
    Averroës; Avicenna
arbor sapientiae see sapientia
arca
    arca sapientiae 51–55, 202–203, 259
    associated with books 53–54, 151–152
    association with medieval Scriptural study
        54–55
    memory as 40, 51–55, 101
    see also Ark of Noah; Ark of the Covenant
arch, as memory-place 118, 173–174
architectural mnemonic 16, 44, 51, 89–98, 274
    Chaucer's acquaintance with 384
    Dominican and humanist sponsorship of 155,
        193–194, 315

history, first–thirteenth century 153–155,
    188–189
medieval revival 156–159
modern use 94–98, 396
similarity to Hugh of St. Victor's mnemonic
    scheme 101
see also Albertus Magnus; Bradwardine;
    Cicero; John of Garland; Julius Victor;
    locus memory-images; Quintilian; *Rhetorica
    ad Herennium*
architecture, mnemonic usefulness of design/
    ornamentation 274
    see also building metaphors
Aristotle/Aristotelianism 15, 18–19, 165, 218, 276,
    388–389, 393
    analysis of *memoria* 18–19, 27, 56–57, 62–67,
        191, 375, 456
    Arabic/Hebrew commentaries 57, 64 (*see also*
        Averroës; Avicenna)
    artificial memory system 33–34, 90, 101, 109, 129
    conception of cogitative activity 244
    and distinction between "philosophical" and
        "rhetorical" concerns 29, 375–376
    and dream-images 73–74
    on *energeia* 444
    on forgetting xi, xii
    hylemorphism 15, 390
    idea of knowledge composed of experience
        constructed from many memories 40, 50–51,
        65, 83–84, 86, 134
    idea of memory as part of prudence 83–84
    influence on medieval thought 57, 71–72,
        393–394
    insistence on primacy of visual over other
        sensory modes 32, 122
    medieval study/commentaries 22–23, 25, 155,
        187, 189–190
    and nature of imagination 69, 244
    Physics, medieval annotation 148
    physiological theory 59, 60, 67, 386, 389
    and recollection process 58–59, 79–80, 94,
        191–192
    on sensory perception 436
    stress on emotional accompaniment of
        memory 76, 85, 387, 392
    topica and system of "places" 39–40, 190–191
    on two kinds of knowledge and memory
        ("singulars" and concepts) 58–59, 62–63
    use of bird/pigeon-hole metaphors 43, 381
    use of hunting metaphor 323
    use of seal-in-wax metaphor 24–25, 70–71, 372
    view of politics 28
    on "wonder" as memory component 176
    see also Albertus Magnus; alphabet; memory-
        images; soul; time

Ark of Noah, diagram of 448
  see also *De archa Noe*; *Libellus de formatione arche* (both Hugh of St. Victor); Noah
Ark of the Covenant 51
armarium 151, 382
Arnaldus de Villanova 61–62, 387–388
ars dictaminis 157, 237, 241, 435
ars memorativa, "art" of memory x, 155–156, 189–194, 396–397
  earliest references 172, 179–182, 186–187, 445–446
  efficacy xiv
  essential features 164, 178–179
  see also Albertus Magnus; Bradwardine; John of Garland; laity
ars notataria 142–143, 157
"art"
  medieval understanding of 50–51, 82
  of memory see *ars memorativa*
artes poeticae 50
artificial memory 396–397
  Albertus Magnus's discussion of 88
  Quintilian's skepticism concerning 92
  see also Aristotle; mnemonics; natural memory
Ashburnham Pentateuch 51, 384
associative nature of memory 76, 80–81, 91, 393
  Albertus Magnus on 22–23
  Aristotle on 80–81
  Petrarch on 76–78
  Quintilian on 135
  see also Thomas Aquinas
Atreus, sons of, mnemonic for 175–176, 188, 189, 351–352, 415, 456
Atticus, bishop of Constantinople 255–256
Aubrey, John 207
auctor
  author's intention 235–237, 434
  conceived in textual terms 235–237, 279
  etymology 236
  relationship with readers/commentators 268–269, 434
  see also authority/authorship
audience
  adaptation of speech or text to different kinds of 307–308, 330–331
  presence crucial to making of ethical action 225–226
auditory memory 19, 31, 97
  need to fix aural reception by association with visual 20–21, 31–32, 91
  see also hearing
Auerbach, Erich 239
Augustine, St., of Canterbury *see under* Gospels
Augustine, St., of Hippo x–xii, 11, 40, 58, 62, 93, 171, 183, 216, 229, 230, 250, 267–268, 315, 377, 415–416, 431

  and architectural mnemonic 181
  on charity 415–416
  citational style 124, 125
  City of God 177
  compositional habits 243, 245–246, 256, 437
  conception of memory 60, 375, 428–429
  Confessions 203, 212–216, 223, 238, 383, 428
  conversation with St. Monica 214
  description of Ambrose 212–216, 258, 428, 429
  on desire / free will 427
  Enarrationes in Psalmis 403, 404, 424
  Enchiridion 310–314
  extempore speaking 206, 424, 438–439
  on feats of memory 21–22
  intimate knowledge of Psalms 112, 123–124
  metaphors for memory 25, 41, 46–47
  and Neoplatonism 15, 375
  Petrarch's admiration for 203 (*see also* Petrarch, *Secretum*)
  on reading and meditation 276–277
  and relationship between inner truth and language 29–30
  scholarly citations from works 6, 146, 149, 210, 293, 427
  spiritual journey 239, 246
  and trinitarian nature of human soul 81
authenticity, documentary 38
authority/authorship, connections between *memoria* and 234
  "authorization" of text through public comment and response 234, 262–265, 271
  glossed book as model of authorship and textual authority 265–271
  modern *vs.* medieval notions 264
  relationship of medieval authors to their antecedents 237
  and vernacular texts 441
  see also *auctor*; *autor*; composition; plagiarism
autor (distinguished from *auctor*) 236
Averroës (Ibn Rushd) 69, 71, 192
  on direct knowledge of abstractions 64–67, 389
  interest in dreams 74
  on mental imagery and recollection 27, 75, 76, 87
  as source for Thomas Aquinas 62, 84
Avicenna (Ibn Sina) 62, 63, 68, 71, 388
  interest in dream-images 74–75
  and mental imagery 27, 244
  and sensory-consciousness process 57, 64, 69, 122, 389

Babylon, captivity in 300, 301
Bacon, Francis 45, 453
Baldwin, C. S. 412
Balogh, Josef 213, 429–430

Bartholomaeus Anglicus 64, 421
Bartolomeo da San Concordio 198
  Ammaestramenti degli antichi 194, 221,
    229–230, 291
Baxandall, Michael 434
bears, memory-images of 161–162
Becket, St. Thomas 267
Bede 125, 206–207, 403, 426
  De loquela digitorum (ascr.) 99
bees/honey, metaphor for scholarship/memory
  41–42, 44–45, 53–54, 237, 382
  academic analyses 238
  illustrated in "The Hours of Catherine of
    Cleves" 318
  Petrarch's use of 273
belching/farting *see* scatological imagery
Benedict, St., Rule of 31, 109, 125, 208, 212, 325,
  399, 427, 448–449
Benedictines 133, 171–172
Benton, John F. 431
Berger, Samuel 314
Bernard of Chartres 111, 188, 222, 272, 273, 447
Bernard of Clairvaux, St. 171–172, 198, 243, 440
Bernard of Parma 441
Bersuire, Pierre 269
  Ovide moralisée 177, 269
Berwick, battle of (1333), referenced by
  Bradwardine 169, 367–368
bestiaries 138, 171, 179, 304, 413
  in monastic libraries 137–138, 449
  possible mnemonic function 138, 159–160
  see also Richard de Fournival
Bible(s)
  citational conventions 124–128
  concordances 128–129, 144–149, 193
  divisional schemes/chaptering 118–123, 402,
    414 (*see also* Langton, Stephen)
  English (late) 121
  exegeses 384 (*see also* three modes of
    interpretation *below* thirteenth century)
  Exodus 302
  French (*c.* 1325) 145–146
  fundamentalist approaches 13, 371
  Geneva (1560) 122–123
  glosses 145–146 (see also *Glossa ordinaria*)
  Hosea 293
  institutionalization, through interpretation/
    adaptation 11
  Jerome's index and gloss of Hebrew names
    144–146
  King James version 102
  Lamentations 300
  Masoretic text 122
  memorizing 102–104, 112, 217
  metaphors for memory 33, 34, 40, 43

mnemonic value of presentation 118–122
monastic study 237
number of books in Old and New Testaments
  300, 448
"Paris" 102, 121
pocket versions 121, 402
Proverbs 116
textual authority 236
textualist interpretations 14
Thomas Aquinas's knowledge of 3, 6
three modes of interpretation 53, 55, 210–211,
  300, 343 (*see also* tropology)
see also Canon Tables; Daniel; Ezekiel;
  Gospels; Psalms; Revelations; Solomon
bins, memory as set of 30, 166
birds
  associated with memory 41–44, 158, 211, 308
  as manuscript decoration 323
  see also dove; Hugh de Fouilloy
Bischoff, Bernhard 139
Black, Max 18
Bloomfield, Leonard 37
Blum, Herwig 274
Boccaccio, Giovanni 272
  Teseida 20, 271
Boethius 84, 356, 379, 381–382, 395
  De consolatione philosophiae 146
  influence on teaching of dialectic 190
  use of bird metaphors 43
Bohun family 414
Bologna, university 154, 187
Bolzoni, Lina xii, 432
Bonaventure, St., of Bagnoregio 429–430
Boncompagno da Signa 138–139, 154, 184–185,
  187, 408, 418
Bono Giamboni 193–194, 229–230
book covers, decorated 47–49
Book of Life 301, 323
bookcases 42
  see also *arca*; *armorium*; *columna*
bookmarkers 128–129
books
  "eating the book," metaphor of 53–54, 201,
    208–209, 231, 425–426
  effect on *memoria* of increased use and
    availability 153, 195
  glossed *see separate main heading*
  lay-out, and memorial effectiveness 10, 17,
    240, 265, 268–269, 309, 452 (*see also*
    manuscripts)
  metaphors for 43–45, 47, 200–201
  as model for medieval *memoria* 240
  pocket-sized, carried by friars 436
  private collection/ownership 200–202,
    420, 422

books (cont.)
  subsidiary role with respect to *memoria* 9, 11,
    18, 137, 197, 240, 323
  see also *arca*; book covers; bookcases;
    codex; literature; manuscripts;
    marginalia; memory-as-book metaphor;
    texts
Books of Hours 49, 279, 318–323, 451–452
Bower, Gordon H. 378–379
Bradwardine, Thomas 138, 141, 159, 178–179, 184,
    193, 229, 328, 397, 414
  biography 163, 186
  De causa Dei 163
  De memoria artificiale see separate main heading
  mathematical works 163
  see also *locus*; memory-images; Zodiac
brain, and memory, ancient/medieval theory 59,
    61, 65, 69, 386
brevity, memorial principle of 98, 146, 214–215,
    309, 397
  Hugh of St. Victor on 98, 104–105, 343
  see also *divisio*
Bruno, Giordano 331
Bruns, Gerald L. 17, 375–376, 377
building metaphors 118, 217, 294, 409
  in Biblical exegeses 384
bull, as memory image *see* Zodiac
Bundy, Murray Wright 386
Burnyeat, Myles 70, 390
Buttimer, C. H. 398

Caedmon, Bede's account of 206–207
Calboli-Montefusco, Lucia 399
calculation, memory as 22
calendar, images of 159–160, 302, 324
  see also months
Callus, D. A. 146–147
Camillo, Giulio 331
canon law 127, 265
  see also Decretals
Canon Tables 174, 323, 414
  see also Eusebius
Canticles 427–428
Caplan, Harry 90, 175, 417
Carolingian
  florilegia 430 (*see also* Hrabanus Maurus)
  manuscripts 125, 403
  religious art 417–418
  scrinia 47
"carpet-pages" 333–335
Carruthers, Mary
  The Craft of Thought ix, 56, 294, 434,
    453–454
  (with Jan Ziolkowski), *The Medieval Craft of
    Memory* ix, 374, 453–454

Cassiodorus Senator 182–183, 227, 229,
    267–268, 380
  divisional scheme 122, 125
  system of "memory-places" 38–39, 222,
    223–224
cat, lazy, proverb of 324, 337, 451, 454
catalogues 151–152
  rhyming 99, 396
catena ("chain")
  as compositional structure 6, 259
  as image for items associatively grouped in
    memory 78, 143
  of marginal comments 240, 265–267
  see also Thomas Aquinas, *Catena aurea*
cathedral, Gothic, as form of literature 274–275
Catherine of Cleves, Book of Hours 318
Cato, M. Porcius "the Elder," *Distichs* 121, 222
Caxton, William 179
cedula 411
cella/cellula 40, 41–42, 45, 268
character, medieval notion of 224, 431
  memory considered prerequisite for 222, 226
charity
  Holcot's picture of 293
  metaphorical representation 415–416
Charlemagne, Alcuin's advice to 179–180, 184
Charmadas 110
Chaucer, Geoffrey 29, 59, 61, 239, 330, 384
  The Book of the Duchess 227
  The Franklin's Tale 223, 225
  The House of Fame 20, 211, 279–280
  The Legend of Good Women 264
  The Pardoner's Tale 49, 330–331
  The Prioress's Tale 453
  reworking and revision of texts 242–243
  The Second Nun's Tale 444
  The Summoner's Tale 23, 61, 207
  Troilus and Criseyde 264, 422–423, 440
  use of words and images associated with
    memory 40, 41, 49
  The Wife of Bath's Tale 235
Chenu, M. D. 6
"Cherub" (picture-diagram) 333, 454
chess game, allegorical treatment of 179
chi (Greek letter)
  chi-rho page in Book of Kells 337
  in Hugh of St. Victor's description of Ark
    diagram 295, 447
China xii–xiii, 453
Christ, genealogy of 328–329
Chronicle (Hugh of St. Victor) (especially
  Preface, "De tribus maximis circumstantiis
  gestorum") xiii–xiv, 100–106, 117–118, 129,
  143, 148, 172, 205–206, 259, 329, 339–344,
  396–397, 455

lay-out 117–118, 265–267, 329
manuscripts 100–101, 455
sources/influences 101, 401
target audience 100, 102–103, 121
on the three levels of Biblical exegesis 210
vocabulary 455
Chrysostom, St. John 6
"chunking" (neuropsychological term) 105, 397
Cicero, M. Tullius xiv, 21–22, 93, 117, 203, 218, 224, 225, 370
advice on composition and oratory 93, 115, 255, 257, 396
attribution of *Rhetorica ad Herennium* to 16, 394
De inventione 89, 398
De oratore (on architectural mnemonic) 25–26, 32, 89, 91–92, 180, 375–376
influence on Albertus Magnus 177
influence on other scholars 101, 107, 115, 142, 163, 183
influence on Thomas Aquinas 81–82, 84, 393
medieval study/commentaries 153–154, 412
Partitiones oratoriae 18
on prudence 81–82, 83, 84, 87–88, 191
Topica 33, 190, 379
use of seal-in-wax metaphor 25–26, 32
vernacular translations 419
Verrines 92
see also *locus*; memory-images
"Ciceronians" 155, 194
Cimber (Roman actor), mnemonic image of 175–176
Cistercians
art style 310
bestiaries in libraries of 159–160, 413, 449
citational conventions 118–131
in Carolingian manuscripts 125
modern *vs.* medieval 128
see also Bible; Jerome; Psalms
Clanchy, M. T. 36, 380
Clark, F. 382–383
Clark, J. W. 42
classification schemes 340–344
see also Grosseteste; indexing systems
clerks 201
codex
and metaphors for memory see seal-in-wax metaphor
mnemonic value of always using same codes 100, 117–118, 157, 310
see also Quintilian; wax tablets
Codex Alexandrinus 323, 451
coding theory 372–373
cogitatio, conceptions of 39, 68, 243–249, 250
of Anselm 246–247
of Augustine 245–246

of Quintilian 243, 248, 253
see also *vis cogitativa*
coins
as manuscript decoration 318–323
as metaphor for memory see *sacculus*; treasure-house
cola
as memorial unit 114, 121, 141
text divided into 102, 122, 310
Coleman, Janet 435
Coleridge, Samuel Taylor 4
collatio/collectio/colligere 42, 217
Augustine on 245–246
definitions 244–246, 250, 269
Hugh of St. Victor's understanding of 250, 258
Isidore's understanding of 258, 450
see also "gathering"
color(s)
as memory aid 10, 167, 168
symbolism see under *Libellus de formatione arche*
Columella, Junius Moderatus, *De re rustica* 42
columna
columnar format as mnemonic device 117–118, 157–159, 162–163
term used for bookcase 151–152
see also *intercolumnia*
Comestor, Peter, *Historia scholastica* 328
commata, division of text into 102, 121, 122, 141, 310
common memory see public memory
common sense see *sensus communis*
commonplace 40, 161, 227
moral nature of 218, 222
notion of memory-place as 224–226
compass, points of, symbolic significance 300–301, 448
composition 234, 379
aids to 106–110, 186, 251, 252
attempts to stimulate 243, 248–249
as collation of methods/sources 246
as complement to *divisio* 107–109, 110, 153, 234, 310, 332, 398
as essentially memorial activity 219, 237
imagines rerum as "sites" for 185, 186, 254
invention stage 241, 243–258
John of Garland's assumptions concerning 156–157
metaphors for 206–207, 217
methods, relationship with levels of style 251, 254–255
nature of *res* in process 235, 241
physical accompaniments 248, 437
post-invention stage 241
relationship of reading to 273

composition (cont.)
  revision stage (shaping of *res* into *dictamen*)
    241, 250, 252–253, 261
  "scissors-and-paste" method 198, 421
  scribal fair copy see *exemplar*
  stages of evolution 240–243, 244–246, 260–263
  see also Anselm; Augustine; Cicero; *dictamen*;
    Hugh of St. Victor; improvisation;
    Quintilian; Thomas Aquinas
concentration
  and composition 7, 247, 252
  and mnemonics 7–8, 9, 62, 75, 215, 216
concordances 143–152
  see also Bible; Dominicans
consuetudo see habit
cookbook, fifteenth-century 49
coops, memory as set of 38, 323
Cope, E. M. 379
"copiousness," definitional 30, 199–200, 226, 227
Copland, Robert 409, 456–457
copying, professional see scribes
copyright see plagiarism
Cornelia (wife of Pompey), as model for Heloise
    223, 225–226, 431
Cornford, F. M. 374
Cornificius 394
cosmology, of Hugh of St. Victor 294, 302
Courcelle, Pierre 112
cow, Bradwardine's pun on dialect pronunciation
    of 169
Crassus, M. Licinius, treatment in *De oratore* 93
creativity, nature of 1–4
Crispin, Gilbert, abbot of Westminster 275, 276
cross-referencing systems 135, 217
Crusades 198, 421
Cuerden Psalter 285–287, 452
cultural values see "modality"
Cyril of Alexandria 198

d'Arezzo, Guido see Guido d'Arezzo
D' Avray, D. L. 405
Damasus, Pope 228, 432
Daniel (Biblical character), dream of bear 161–162
Dante Alighieri 124, 228, 239, 249
  conception of memory 73, 371
  The Divine Comedy 427
  Inferno, Paolo/Francesca episode 230–233, 433
  Inferno, Shereshevski's memorizing of 96, 159
  Paradiso 73, 391
  use of memory-as-book metaphor 18, 33
  La vita nuova 278–279, 371
De archa Noe (Hugh of St. Victor) 53–55,
    202–203, 257–260, 263, 332, 333, 382,
    427–428, 439
  collatio 258

compositional structure 259
  digression on *arbor sapientiae* 258–260, 296, 439
  extempore nature 259–260
  genesis (in conversation) 257–258, 263
  inaccuracy of citation 115–116
  relationship with *Libellus de formatione arche*
    294, 296, 298
  title 385, 400–401
  see also *Libellus de formatione arche*
De Clercq, Carlo 303, 306, 307
De Hamel, C. F. R. 265, 336
De Lisle, Robert, Psalter of 332–333, 452–453
De memoria artificiale adquirenda (Bradwardine)
    163–172, 361–368, 406
  compared/contrasted with *Rhetorica ad
    Herennium* 156, 164–165, 166, 170
  discussion of memory for words ("memory by
    syllables" / *memoria orationis*) 151, 169–171,
    185–186, 315, 365–368
  examples of technique 169–170
  extreme nature of images 166–167, 168–172
  humor 169, 170, 171–172
  on *imagines* 166, 299, 327
  influences/sources 164–165
  on *loci* 164–166
  manuscripts 163–164, 190, 414
  and memory for things 166–167, 286–287,
    363–365
  university-level target audience 163
  use of bilingual puns 169, 171, 413, 457
De Wit, Pamela 444
death
  belief that sensory memory does not survive 73
  metaphors for 161–162
decoration (book/manuscript) 265, 309–337
  incomplete 413
  influence on/of mnemotechniques 309, 315
  as integral to text 303–304
  practical use 336
  scribe as book's decorator 280–281
  see also animals; manuscripts; marginalia;
    painted figures; *tituli*
decorum, principle of 29, 30
Decretals 208
  Bolognese manuscript (fifteenth century) 107
  citational style 127
  Gregorian 269, 441
  Smithfield, manuscript decoration 315, 451
Deferrari, R. J. 255, 256
Democritus 352
Demosthenes 429
Derrida, Jacques 17, 379
desire 230–231, 427
  relationship to *memoria* 211, 249
Despres, Denise 291

detail, mnemonic value of 77
diagrams, medieval 309, 324, 406, 418, 452–453, 454
  circular 307
  full-page drawings as 325–327
  function 332
  Hugh de Fouilloy's *De columba et accipitre* 294, 304
  Hugh of St. Victor's Ark-diagram 294–302, 307, 324–325
  indeterminacy of meaning 336–337
  open-endedness 336
  pictorial 293–294
  purpose 296–297
  tree 328, 329, 453
  wheel 303–304, 307, 329–331 (see also *rota Virgili*)
  see also education; medical theory of memory
dialectic 190–192, 419
Dialexeis (anon.) 32, 110, 274, 378
dicta et facta memorabilia / dictiones 9–10, 89
  role in formation of character / morality 223–224, 226
dictamen ("draft" stage of composition) 241, 258, 261, 264
  process of formation 250
  revisions 255, 264
  see also *ars dictaminis*
dictare, meaning of, in compositional process 242–243
Diderot, Denis 192
diet, relationship with memory 61, 315, 388
digestion–rumination metaphor
  Biblical grazing motif 215, 428
  for reading/meditation and composition 205–211, 238, 240, 272, 273, 424, 425, 428
  see also stomach–memory metaphor
digital mnemonic 99
DiLorenzo, Raymond D. 179
Diogenes Laertius 80
distancia (distance of viewer from background in memory-place) 166
  see also *intervallum*
distinctio(nes) 147, 158, 405
  collections 158–159
distinguere 413, 433–434
divisio (division of text into short segments for memorizing) 8, 125, 153, 183, 217, 328, 332, 398
  Hugh of St. Victor's advice on 98, 102, 104–105, 217, 234, 281
  Julius Victor on 109
  poor, in Dante's *Inferno* 231–232
  role of book decoration and punctuation 141, 281

as study trope 106–107
  value in composition of sermons 114–115, 131–133, 254, 405
  see also Bible; brevity; Quintilian
"domestication" *see* "familiarization"
Dominicans 419
  concordance 193, 405
  mnemonic schemes 128–129, 155, 161–162, 193, 315, 405
  pictured in Cuerden Psalter 285
Dondaine, Antoine 4, 7, 8, 421
dove(s) 305–307
  dove-cote 41
  see also Hugh de Fouilloy; Noah
Draaisma, Douwe 380
dream-images 73–75
"drolleries," in manuscript margins *see* marginalia
drunkenness, advice against 61, 180, 388
Du Cange, Charles du Fresne, Sieur 117
Duns Scotus, John 435
Durrow, Book of 47–49, 145, 333, 335, 410, 454
dwarfs, poor memory of 60, 387

Eadmer, *Life of Anselm* 242–243, 246–247, 250, 257, 260–263
Eadwine Psalter 282
"eating the book," metaphor *see* books
Eco, Umberto 450
education, medieval
  elementary reading texts 222, 431
  Hugh of St. Victor's aphorism on value 101, 325, 342–343
  Hugh of St. Victor's Ark, as organizing metaphor 54–55, 294
  learning of elementary mnemotechniques 138, 140–141, 221–222, 408
  memoria as basic practice of x, 1, 134, 184, 195, 196, 197–198
  moral component 89
  range of mnemotechniques 16–17
  role of diagrams 328, 332
  role of memorization 8, 112–113
  see also "rote" memory
Edward III of England 44, 163
Egypt, ancient 379–380
  see also Thammuz
eikōn(es) 19, 27
Einstein, Albert, qualities of genius 2–4
Eisenstein, Elizabeth L. 371–372
Eiximinis, Francesc 405
ekmageion 24–25
"embodiment" of knowledge, notion of 69, 72–73
emotional accompaniment of memory 387, 392
  as key to creativity 246–249

emotional accompaniment of memory (cont.)
and oratory 254
see also "affection"; Aristotle; memory-images;
oratory; reason and emotion
Engelbert of Nassau 451
epistemology 375–376
epistylion ("architrave"), Aristotle's use
of 43
Equitius, Abbot 46
Erasistratus of Ceos 59
Erasmus, Desiderius, *Adagia* 228
error
double meaning 324
elimination 107–109, 114, 398–399
see also forgetting; recollection, errors of
estimative power see *vis aestimativa*
Ethica, painted manuscript figure of 268
ethics/morality 16, 226
architectural metaphor 53–54
Hugh of St. Victor's "moralization" see under
Libellus de formatione arche
memory for things *vs.* memory for words *see
under* memory for things
public memory's role in development of
individual ethical behavior 229
reading and 211, 237
relationship with habit 85–86
well-trained memory as sign of moral virtue 1,
14–15, 172, 354–355
see also judgment, moral; literature, moral
function; prudence
Etsi cum Tullius see William of Champeaux
Eusebius, Canon Tables 118, 144, 162–163, 281,
324, 401, 414
Evan the Breton (Thomas Aquinas's secretary)
7–8, 370
Evans, Gillian R. 56, 187, 265, 430
ex tempore dicendi see improvisation
Exegetical critics 433
view of moral function of literature
224–225, 432
exemplar (scribal fair copy) 241–242, 255, 261,
263–264
eyeglasses, invention of 198, 421
Ezekiel (Biblical book/character) 20, 53–54, 209,
231, 275, 425–426
plans of Temple complex 303

fables, animal, as manuscript decoration *see*
Aesop; Renart
Faccio, Anselmo 396–397
"familiarization"/"domestication" (making one's
reading a part of oneself) 204–205, 273,
276–277
Ferreolus, Rule of 112

fields/gardens (garths)
associated with books/memory *see* bees;
"flowers of reading"
as memory-places (*loci*) 174, 356
filing-cabinet model, compared with medieval
metaphors 38
Fishacre, Richard, syllable index 150–151, 411
fishing
metaphor for recollection 78, 259, 323–324
scenes in manuscript margins 451–452
see also cat; hooks
fives
Bradwardine's sets of memory-places in
165–166, 184, 361–362, 406
division of text into 132
Flann (son of King Malochy of Ireland) 47–49
Fiore di rettorica 419
florilegia 30, 35, 105, 217–222, 432
compiled by regular clergy 229
defined 217–218
definitional "copiousness" of *see* "copiousness"
(intended) memorization 221
justification for use 221–222
ordering principles 220–221
purpose 220–221
reasons for compilation 219–220
target audience 220–221, 228–229
types of 220
vernacular, of Italian and French humanism
227–230
see also Bartolomeo da San Concordio; Latini,
Brunetto: *Trésor*; Petrarch: *Rerum
memorandarum libri*; Thomas of Ireland
Florilegium Duacense 221, 430
"flowers of reading" trope 30, 45, 220,
229–230, 333
Fodor, J. A. 26
"forest" (of disordered material) see *silva*
forgetting x, 78
difficulty in 95–96
selective xi–xii
two sorts of xi–xii
see also recollection, errors of
forma/ae 224, 329
forma tractatus/tractandi, distinction
between 250
Fortunatianus, Consultus 107, 214, 250, 399
memory advice 110–112, 115, 182–183, 307
forulus 42, 44
France/French
humanism 227–228
memorial *artes* 193–194
see also Bible; *Rhetorica ad Herennium*,
translations
Francis of Assisi, St. 14, 89, 217

Franciscans 193, 452–453
Fredborg, Karin 188
Froissart, Jean 435
Fulgentius 269
fundamentalism 13, 371

Galen 57, 59, 61, 64, 390, 394
Gardner, Edmund G. 73
"gathering," technique of 42, 105, 226, 309
  Hugh of St. Victor on 104, 130
  see also *collatio*
Gaunilo, critique appended to *Proslogion*
  262–263
Gavrilov, A. K. 428
Geary, Patrick x
Geertz, Clifford 17
Gehl, Paul F. 408
genealogical diagrams (by Hugh of St. Victor)
  294, 328
  see also Christ; Peter of Poitiers
Geoffrey of Vinsauf 452
  Documentum 156
  memory advice 182, 188, 324, 329, 337, 402–403
  metaphors for memory 41, 388
Gerald of Wales (Giraldus Cambrensis) 335, 454
gesture, rhetorical/mnemonic importance 122, 252
Giordano da Pisa 131, 198, 255, 256, 421, 438, 439
Gisze, George 49
Glossa ordinaria 219, 265, 430, 441
glossed books 240, 265–271
  lay-out 265–267
glosses
  different scripts for text and 267, 271, 423, 436
  organization/memorization 293
  stock of, "gloss potpourri" 198–199, 421–422
  see also Bible; *Glossa ordinaria*; glossed books
Gloucester, Humphrey, Duke of 422
God
  Augustine on way to (through memory) 239, 246
  as author 13
  as beyond human knowledge 73, 308
  Creator–Majesty image 302, 448–449
  eternity of 239
  see also gods, pagan
gods, pagan, moralized stories of 177
Gospels 333–335
  binding 47
  concordant passages 118
  of St. Augustine (of Canterbury) 166, 325–327
Göttweig, monastery of (Austria) 138
Gower, John, *Confessio amantis* 330
Gratian, Emperor 127
Greek(s)
  alphabet/language 137–138, 147
  Roman attitudes to 93, 180

tradition of memory 12, 20
  see also Alexandrine Greece; Aristotle
Green, William M. 100
Greene, Thomas M. 228, 239
Gregory I "the Great," Pope 46, 112, 205, 223, 383
  commentary on Ezekiel 426, 427
  Dialogues 382–383
  on function of *picturae* 226, 274, 275,
    417–418, 443
  Moralia in Job 53, 130
  on reading (text as mirror) 210–211, 231, 333
  use of eating/digestion metaphors 206, 424
Gregory IX, Pope 346
Gregory Nazianzus 255, 347, 438
Greimas, A. J. 16, 17, 371
grid format 325–327
  of John of Garland 156–158, 162–163
  for placement of *loci* 179
  see also Hugh of St. Victor; numbers
Grosseteste, Robert 146–149, 204, 267, 411,
  451–452
  scheme of referencing symbols 138, 410
Guda (nun) 280
Gui, Bernardo, "Life of St. Thomas Aquinas"
  3–4, 6, 8, 249, 252
Guido d'Arezzo 20, 21, 22, 133–134, 373, 406–407
Guidotto da Bologna 193–194
Guilmain, Jacques 333
Gutenberg, Johannes 37

habit/*habitus* 23, 203
  trained memory as (enabling moral judgment)
    81, 82, 85, 87–89
  see also associative nature of recollection; *hexis*
Hadoard see *Florilegium Duacense*
Haimon, Bishop 218–219, 220
Hajdu, Helga 99
hands, pointing, in manuscript margins 324
Hanning, Robert W. 448–449
Harvey, E. Ruth 386
Havelock, Eric 18
Havelock the Dane 49
Hawes, Stephen 136
  The Pastime of Pleasure 49–50
heads, as manuscript marginal marks 314, 324
hearing, sense of
  see also auditory memory
heart (*cor*), association with memory 59–60,
  386, 389
Hebrew, alphabet/language 137–138
  names in Bible, Jerome's gloss on see Jerome
Heloise, Abbess 222–223, 224–226, 431
Hendrickson, G. L. 213
Henry III of England 402
Henry, Françoise 337

Herbert of Bosham, glossed Psalter 267–268, 302
heresies, medieval, and fundamentalism 13
"hermeneutical"
  "dialogue," reading/composition as 211,
    230–232, 245
  distinguished from "heuristic" *see under*
    "heuristic"
Herophilus of Chalcedon 59
"heuristic"
  definition/etymology 23
  distinguished from "hermeneutical" 22, 23
  systems 135, 143, 150, 151–152, 217, 248, 296
hexis 85–86, 222, 224, 394
  see also habit
Hildegard of Bingen 370–371
Hillgarth, R. J. 331
historia, as one of the three levels of Biblical
  exegesis 55, 210
historical consciousness, medieval 239–240
history, relationship with memory 380
Holbein, Hans, portrait of George Gisze
  49, 384
Holcot, Robert 44, 113, 136, 292–293, 407, 446
  Moralitas 177
  pictures of Charity/Idolatry 293
Holmecultram Abbey (Cumberland) 310, 314
  Bestiary 159–160
Homer 24, 177, 217
homophony/puns 132–133, 153–154, 169, 171, 274,
    416, 438–439
  bilingual 162, 169, 171, 413, 447, 457
  visual 32, 175, 281–291, 314–315
  see also rebus
honey *see* bees
Honorius II, Pope 299
Honorius of Autun 442–443
hooks/hooking, as metaphor for recollection 78,
    268–269
  see also fishing
Horace (Q. Horatius Flaccus) 19, 177, 372
  Ars poetica 442
Hortensius, Q. 370
house, as memory-place 173–174, 184
Hrabanus Maurus 45, 138, 218–219, 220, 426
Hugh de Fouilloy (Hugo de Folieto) 209,
    210–211, 427
  biography 303–304
  De avibus 134, 303–309
  manuscript drawings 303–304
  "On the dove and the hawk" (treatise) 294,
    304–309, 333
  target audience 307–309, 449–450
  True and False Religious 331
  wheel treatises 303
Hugh of St. Cher 161–162, 405

Hugh of St. Victor 8–9, 122, 187, 218,
    379–380, 447
  advice on reading/meditation 223, 231, 273,
    285, 333–335, 428
  attribution of *De avibus* to 303
  Chronicle see separate main heading
  compared with later scholars 158, 164, 165, 183,
    283–285
  compositional habits/advice 115–116, 148,
    257–260 (see also *divisio*; "gathering")
  and connection between memory and moral
    character 89
  contemporary/later influence 200
  De archa Noe see separate main heading
  *De archa Noe mystica see Libellus de formatione
    arche* as main heading
  Didascalicon xiii, 50, 53, 100–101, 104–105,
    116–117, 121, 202, 206, 224, 228, 258, 401, 424
  *Libellus de formatione arche see separate main
    heading*
  on memory as basis of learning 101, 104,
    106, 134
  metaphors for memory 41, 46–47, 51, 116–117,
    135, 142, 162, 206
  on mnemonic value of textual lay-out / need
    always to use same codex 10, 100, 117,
    199, 268
  and need to impress the circumstances of
    memorization 76, 103, 157, 342–343
  on *notae* 135–136
  number grid system 100–106, 125–126, 156,
    160, 268, 340–341, 455
  Preface to *Chronicle see Chronicle* as main
    heading
  use of visual aids 158, 161
  see also brevity; *collatio*; *divisio*; education;
    locus; memory-images; *sophismata*
Hugo Rainerus 304, 307–308
Hugo "the Painter," pictured on manuscript 280
Hugutio of Pisa 236
Huizinga, Johan 432
Hulse, S. Clark 413
human figures, as manuscript decoration
    267–268
  see also alphabet; heads
humanism 432, 435
  and florilegia 227–230
  identification of architectural mnemonic with
    155, 315
humors, medical theory of 60
Hunt, R. W. 146, 147
hunting
  as metaphor for recollection 78, 201, 323–324
  scenes in manuscript margins 323
Huot, Sylvia 443

Ibn Rushd *see* Averroës
Ibn Sina *see* Avicenna
iconography 23–24, 296, 336–337
Idolatry, Holcot's picture of 293
"illiteracy," medieval understanding of 12, 307–309
see also laity; literacy
images
    dual meaning 443
    function, in medieval culture 62–63, 67–68,
        442–443
    see also diagrams; dream-images; memory-
        images; pictura(e); "word-pictures"
imagination
    ancient and medieval theories of 63–65, 67–68
    change in relative status of memory and 1–4
    "deliberative" 65, 244
    prophetic 74–75
    see also *vis imaginativa*
imagines rerum see memory for things
imitation, true *vs.* false 272–273
improvisation (*ex tempore dicendi*) 153–154, 206,
        255–257, 438
    fully stored and effectively designed memory
        essential for 253–254, 256–257
    in written composition 259–260
inaccuracy (of reproduction) 111–112, 113
    as conscious choice 113, 116
indexing systems 128–130, 147, 195
    fully alphabetized 409
individual, concept of, in medieval culture 432
    see also character
inductio and memory, Albertus Magnus's
        discussion of 456
Infeld, Leopold, on Einstein 2–3, 4
information
    dissemination, in Middle Ages 198, 200
    retrieval systems 378–379
initial letters
    decoration (in manuscripts) 121–122, 285–287,
        310, 441
    as mnemonic device 106, 127
Innocent III, Pope 134–135, 402
inspiration, Avicenna on 74–75
Insular Gospels 333–335
"intellectual memory" 62–63, 73
intellectual property *see* plagiarism
intentio (response), as component of memory-
        image 65, 85, 389
    see also *auctor*: author's intention; concentration
intentus (state of concentration) 215–216
    see also concentration
intercolumnia, as background places (in memory)
        118, 173–174
intervallum 90, 189, 456–457
    see also *distancia*

invention *see* composition
inventory, memory as 39, 180
    see also store-house model
investigatio, concept of 22–23
Isaiah (Biblical book/character) 300
    see also Albertus Magnus; Jerome; Thomas
        Aquinas
Isidore (monk), depicted as scribe 280
Isidore of Seville 114, 162, 181, 258, 308, 383, 443,
        450, 453
    Etymologiae 219
    on reading 47, 211–212, 214–215, 220, 429, 439
    and *voces animantium* 159, 160
    on writing and purpose of letters 133–134, 139,
        235–236, 275, 278, 378
    see also *collatio*; notae
Italy
    humanism 155, 227–228
    memorial *artes* 193–194
    see also *Rhetorica ad Herenniu*: translations
iteration *see* recitare; "rote" memory

Jacob's ladder, mnemonic trope of 31, 200,
        448–449
Jacobus Publicius 190
Jacopa da Cessola 179
James, M. R. 327
James of Venice 189–190
Japanese memory artist 94, 97
Jaufré Rudel 421
Jean d'Antioche 192
Jean de Meun 382
    Le Roman de la rose 431
Jerome, St. 145, 181–182, 208, 228, 236, 267–268,
        380–381, 402–403, 432
    commentary on Ezekiel 20, 53–54, 209, 426
    commentary on Isaiah 403
    division of Bible and citational style 122–123,
        124–125, 281, 402, 433
    Index and gloss of Hebrew names in the Bible
        144–146, 409
    metaphors for memory 39, 53–54, 59–60
    on reading and meditative composition 238
    translation of the Psalms 267, 282, 403
jewels, on book covers / in illuminations 47–49
John I of England 402
John XXII, Pope 196
John Damascene, St. 347
John of Garland 138, 162–163, 172, 178–179, 186,
        329–330, 412
    on architectural mnemonic / *Rhetorica ad
        Herennium* 156–159, 182
    compared with Bradwardine 163, 165,
        169, 457
    Parisiana poetria 156, 157, 163

John of Metz 332
John of Mirfield 315
  "Florarium Bartholomei" 229
John of Salisbury 32, 51, 211–212, 378, 423, 426, 435
  account of Bernard of Chartres 111, 222, 272
  and artificial memory schemes 134, 188
  on link between *notae* and *memoria* 142–143
  Metalogicon 142
Johnson, R. 417
judgment, moral 225
  role of memory in shaping 11, 85–86, 172, 219
Julian Antecessor 46
Julius Caesar, C. 84
  (alleged) prodigious memory 8, 93, 370
Julius Victor 111, 222, 398
  on composition 250–251
  disparages architectural mnemonic 107,
    180–181
justicia, as example of word imperfectly
  representing *res* 30–31
Juvenal (D. Iunius Iuvenalis) 84, 215

Kauffman, C. M. 325
Kells, Book of 47, 333, 335, 337, 451–452, 454
Kerby-Fulton, Katherine 291, 446
key-word system 144–149
Kidson, Peter 453–454
knowledge, pre-modern conceptions of 58–59,
    69, 71–72
  compared with modern theory 30
  and prudence 83
  see also Aristotle
Kristeller, Paul O. 432

Lacan, Jacques 227
ladder diagrams, of Hugh of St. Victor
    300–302, 336
  see also Jacob's ladder
laity
  growth in popularity of arts of memory among
    192–194
  literacy of 274, 420, 442–443
  manuscripts produced by 287–291
Lancelot romance, Dante and 232–233, 433
Langland, William 291
  see also *Piers Plowman*
Langton, Stephen 402–403, 409, 433
  chapter divisional scheme for Bible 121,
    122–123, 233
language
  relationship with Truth/reality 11
  sounds of, as memory aid 158–159, 169
  subsidiary role with respect to *memoria* 11
  theory 28–30, 37
Lateran Council, Fourth 193, 402

Latin
  knowledge of, as criterion for literacy 12
  rules of grammar, mnemonic for 99
  syntax (compared with English) 397
Latini, Brunetto 155
  Trésor 83, 193–194, 227–228, 229, 393
LaTour-Landry, Knight of 450–451
law, studies 12, 13
  see also canon law; Decretals; lawyers
Lawler, Traugott 412
lawyers
  memory aids for 99
  need for well-stocked memory 127, 137,
    192–193
  training in *ars notataria* 141, 157
  see also law
Layamon, *Brut* 49
Leclercq, Jean 17, 112, 129, 143, 424
lectio 205–206, 210–211, 423, 427
  difference between *meditatio* and 202, 213,
    228–229, 276
  listeners' response to 216
  see also reading
Legrand, Jacques 10
letters see *litterae*
Lévi-Strauss, Claude 37
Libellus de formatione arche (Hugh of St. Victor)
    155, 294–302, 307, 323, 324–325, 326–327,
    336, 446–447, 448
  absence of graphic realization 294, 303
  on division into "roomettes" 302
  elevation plan 297–298
  mnemonic advice 295
  (modern) attempts at realization 448
  moralizing content 295–297, 298,
    299–302, 447
  plan of whole structure 297–298
  (possible) visual basis 448
  representation of Biblical/Christian history
    298–300
  symbolic use of color 295, 297, 298, 299
  title 385, 400–401, 412, 439
  see also cosmology
libraries 200
  catalogues 99, 151–152
  as metaphor for memory 39, 42, 151–152, 180
  monastic *see* bestiaries; catalogues *above*
  private *see* books: private collection
  see also Alexandrine Greece
light, nature of 69–70
lignum (sapientiae/vitae) see *arbor*; Tree of
    Knowledge; Tree of Life
linea (line), as mnemonic ordering device
    162–163, 183–184
literacy 36, 371–372

distinction between "oral" and "literate"
cultures 11, 18, 19, 212
relationship between *memoria* and 11–12
see also "illiteracy"; laity; orality
literature
distinguished from literacy 11–12
institutionalization 11, 13
and *memoria* 10, 227
moral function 17, 210, 224–227, 432
"socialization" 11, 14, 262–263, 268–269
see also authority/authorship; books;
composition; reading; texts; vernacular;
writing
littera, as first mode of Biblical exegesis
205–206, 210
littera inintelligibilis (Thomas Aquinas's "short-
hand") 5, 146–147, 251
litterae
as category of signs 235–236, 278
function 139–140
symbolism (for Hugh of St. Victor) 295, 447
see also Isidore of Seville
Livy (T. Livius) 84
loculamenta 42, 44, 381
locus, loci (background places in architectural
mnemonic) 33, 37, 149, 416
Albertus Magnus on 173–174, 349–352, 356–359
Bradwardine's rules for 164–166, 361–362
Cicero on 91
essential features 97–98, 173–174, 178–179
Hugh of St. Victor's understanding of 342,
455 (*see also* Hugh of St. Victor: number grid)
placement 179
in *Rhetorica ad Herennium* 90
Thierry on 188–189, 445
logic, relationship to *memoria* 190–191, 378–379
Lombard, Peter 121
Biblical commentary 265–268
Long, R. J. 421
"Long Charter of Christ" (anon.) 444
Longinus 44
Louis XI of France 5
Lucan, *Pharsalia* 223, 225–226
Ludwig I, Emperor 197, 421
Lull, Ramón 331–332, 453
Luria, A. R., description of Russian mnemonist
see Shereshevski
Lydgate, John 279, 314–315

McKeon, Richard 375
Macrobius 84, 345, 435
Magna Carta 402
Maimonides 84
Malcolm, Norman 373
Mâle, Emile 274–275

male (leather strong-box), as metaphor for
memory 40, 49–51, 383
Malory, Thomas, *Morte d'Arthur*, Winchester
manuscript 324
manuscripts, mnemonic value of page lay-out/
decoration 10, 118–122, 164, 292, 314
see also books; decoration; laity; marginalia;
scribes; vernacular
maps
mappa mundi 301
mental 26
marginalia, manuscript 309–324
academic (*divisiones/discretiones*) 106–107
bas-de-page pictorial narratives 315
citations 125
connection between memory-images and 170,
267–268, 324
enclosed in images 310–314
florilegial 220, 274
grotesques and "drolleries" 170, 315, 414
mnemonic function 323
notae 135–136
Petrarch's use of 204
recurrent images 318–324
space left for reader's additions 269, 405, 413
written before main text 269–271
see also *catena*; Grosseteste, Robert; *tituli*
Marius Victorinus 183
Markus, R. A. 377
Marrou, Henri I. 17, 141
Marsh, Adam 146, 149
Marshal, William 402
Martial (M. Valerius Martialis) 42, 177
Martianus Capella 25, 33, 110, 135, 205, 379–380
memory advice 182–184, 185–186, 215, 416, 417
Martin of Braga 393
Matheolus of Perugia 59, 61–62, 190,
244–245, 436
Matson, Wallace I. 60
Mazzotta, Guiseppe 391
meadows *see* fields
medical theory of memory 60–68, 207, 386–387
diagrammatic representation 67–68
meditatio/meditation 202–203, 204, 206, 210–211,
213, 216, 228–229, 427
circumstances appropriate to 252
considered as memorial activity 53–54, 212
(dangers of) excess 61
etymology 244–245
pictorial representation 289–291
role in composition 241, 276
three-stage process 231
see also digestion–rumination metaphor; Hugh
of St. Victor; *lectio*; murmur of meditation;
reading

memoria orationis see themes, memory for
memory, centrality to medieval culture x, 1–2, 9,
  15, 153
  see also education
memory-as-book metaphor 10, 18, 33, 137,
  278–279
memory feats, prodigious 8, 14, 21–22, 76–77,
  94–98
  skepticism regarding 92
  see also mnemonists
memory for things (*memoria ad res*) / *imagines
  rerum* 110–116, 185–186, 234–235
  advice in *Dialexeis* 32, 274
  and book decoration 309
  description of technique in *Rhetoria ad
    Herennium* 91, 110, 174
  ethical superiority over memory for words
    92–93
  Fortunatianus on 110–118
  imagines rerum associated with Psalm texts
    282–287
  and manuscript illustration 282–285, 314
  Martianus Capella on 183, 185–186
  and plagiarism 272
  Quintilian on value of *imagines rerum* 185,
    309–310, 315
  Thierry's explanation of 188–189
  "word-pictures" as *imagines rerum* 292,
    309–310
  see also Albertus Magnus; *De memoria
    artificiale adquirenda*
memory for words (*memoria ad verba*) / *imagines
  verborum* 94–95, 110–116
  advice in *Dialexeis* 32, 274
  description of technique in *Rhetorica ad
    Herennium* 91, 110, 175–176
  Fortunatianus's advice on 110–118
  Martianus Capella on 183
  and plagiarism 272
  (recommended) reservation for extracts from
    poets 91
  reservations concerning image-making
    schemes 92–93
  Thierry's mistrust of 188–189
  Thomas Waleys's advice on 113–114
  see also Albertus Magnus; Bradwardine;
    Quintilian
memory-images / mental imagery 18–21, 37
  for abstractions *see* abstractions
  advice against using ready-made 180, 189,
    335–336, 353–354, 392
  Albertus Magnus on creation of 174, 351
  Aristotle's theories concerning 18–19, 27, 60,
    65, 79–80, 375
  Bestiary as source of *see* bestiaries

book decoration as source of 281–291
Bradwardine on 166, 327, 362
Cicero's rules for 32, 91–92
distinguished from other kinds of image 73–76
emotional component 75–76, 85, 87, 211
grouping 167–168, 179, 299
Holcot's use of 136, 293
Hugh de Fouilloy's use of 308–309
Hugh of St. Victor's use of pieces of text as 100,
  101–102, 117–118, 295
for numbers 170–171, 368
painture and 277
physical location 32
physiological theories of 59, 60–68, 70–72, 80,
  86, 389, 428–429
pictorial nature 21, 26–28, 31–32, 72, 91–92, 97,
  176–177, 279–280, 308, 417–418
and process of recollection 77–78
reading and 276–277
representational aspect 26–30
Rhetorica ad Herennium's advice concerning
  91, 164, 174–178, 188, 216, 315
Shereshevski's use of 95–97
significant features 75–76, 179
single, construction from multiple 244
spatial nature 80
temporal nature 76
variety 179, 184
"visualized homophony," as principle for
  forming 32, 91, 132 (*see also* homophony:
  visual)
vivid/unusual, mnemonic value 166–167,
  168–169, 176–177, 179, 189, 315, 337, 352–353,
  359–360, 362–363, 407 (*see also under*
  oratory)
see also habitus; memory for things; memory
  for words; Quintilian; synaesthesia; Thomas
  Aquinas; "word-pictures"
memory-places *see locus*
memory-storage 56–76
  see also locus; memory-images; seal-in-wax
    model; store-house model
mens, used to mean trained memory 53
  see also mind
Merton College, Oxford, Bradwardine at 163
Metrodorus Scepsis 32, 92, 93, 110, 414
Michael (monk), letter of Guido d'Arezzo to 133
Miethke, Jürgen 197
Miller, George A. 86, 105, 116
Milton, John 207
mind–body problem 60, 64–65, 387, 389
mind/mental activity, ancient and medieval
  theories concerning 60
  three-fold classification 64
  see also brain; *mens*; mind–body problem; soul

miniator 117
Minnis, Alastair J. 386
mirror *see* Gregory I (on reading); *Speculum theologiae*
mistakes *see* recollection: errors of
mnemonics 8–9, 15, 16, 99–100, 396
  attitudes to, from first to thirteenth century 153–155
  attitudes to, modern *vs.* medieval 134
  dissemination into general culture 129
  individually fashioned systems preferable to ready-made 80, 97, 98
  moral aspect *see under* ethics
  physiological basis *see under* memory-images
  see also alphabet; architectural mnemonic; *ars memorativa*; *divisio*; "heuristic" systems; numbers
mnemonists *see* Japanese memory artist; memory feats; Shereshevski
"modality" of medieval culture, *memoria* as 16
monasteries
  behavioral/educational traditions 56, 154–155, 399, 423, 453–454 (*see also* prayer; reading)
  rules 112, 125 (*see also* Benedict; *Regula magistri*)
  see also libraries
money-pouch metaphor see *sacculus*
Monica, St. 214
months of the year, mnemonic for 99
morality *see* ethics
Morton, John, Cardinal, rebus of 328, 333
mos 88
Munich, William of Ockham at Franciscan convent 196
Munk Olsen, B. 220
murmur of meditation 92, 110, 183, 205, 212, 331, 427–428, 445
  as accompaniment to composition 245
  see also voice-level; writing: vocalizing while
Murray, Alexander 247–248
music, representation in visual terms 20–21
  see also solmization

Nagle, Thomas A. 387
narratives, *bas-de-page* pictorial *see* marginalia
natural memory 110, 183
  relationship between artificial and 87–88, 97, 142, 164
negotia, Albertus Magnus's use of word 99
Neoplatonism 15, 64, 184–185, 377, 379–380, 381–382, 453–454
  Augustine and 15, 375
  influence on twelfth-century art 331
  rejection 71

Nepotianus 380–381
nidus 42
Nietzsche, Friedrich 428
night, memorizing easier at 110, 183, 215
Noah (Biblical character) 51–55
  dove released by 43, 305, 382
  see also Ark of Noah; *De archa Noe*; *Libellus de formatione arche* (both Hugh of St. Victor)
noise, as mnemonic enemy 95, 214, 249, 428
Nora, Pierre x
Norden, Eduard 213
Nordenfalk, Carl 281, 414
Norman, Donald A. 26, 86, 378–379
notae/notulae 110, 135–143, 184
  individually fashioned preferable to ready-made 136
  Isidore's definition 139–140, 142
  of John of Garland 158–159
  Martianus Capella's advice on 183
  mental 135–136
  nota imperative in manuscript margin 136, 161, 289, 310, 314
  Petrarch on 204
  Quintilian's advice on 92, 135
  Robert Grosseteste's system 146–148
  see also *notataria*
notaries, training of *see also* lawyers
notataria 140–143
  mnemonic value 142
Notopoulos, J. A. 379–380
numbers/numerical grid 122, 131, 407
  Bradwardine's use of memory-images for 170–171, 368
  imposed on Scripture 106, 122–123, 125–128, 414
  memory schemes based on 79–80, 100–106
  problems of 128
  and sermon divisions 131–133, 134–135, 256
  symbolic significance 300, 302
  see also fives; Hugh of St. Victor; *linea*; numerology; Psalms
numerology 124, 126
Nussbaum, Martha 375, 387

"oblivion" xii
"occasion," need to pay careful attention to, in memorizing 342–343
Ockham *see* William of Ockham
Ong, Walter 37
orality/oral culture 379–380
  oral transmission 12, 198–200, 201–202
  "oral" *vs.* "written" style, in composition 260, 440
  see also literacy

oratory
  ex tempore see improvisation
  faults of 257, 272
  florilegia as aid for 220
  methods of composition 185, 253
  need of vivid images 185, 186
  see also sermons
orchard metaphor 333
*The Orchard of Consolation see Speculum
  theologiae*
The Orchard of Syon 333
order, as key to memory schemes 8–9, 79–80,
  183–184, 185
  see also "scanning"; starting-point
Origen 58, 84, 144
originalis, synonym for *auctor* 236
originality 1, 2–3, 4
  of text (in medieval sense) 236, 262–263
ornatus/ornamentum, Hugh of St. Victor's use
  of 455
otter eating salmon image (Book of Kells) 337
"overloading" of memory 98
  see also brevity
Ovid 84, 177
  Heroides 245
Oxford
  Franciscan convent 146, 411
  University 154

Padua, University 187, 418
page *see* manuscripts (mnemonic value of page
  lay-out); *pagina*
pagina 117
  paginator 117
  see also *voces paginarum*
painting, mental 75, 91–92
  with words *see* "word-pictures"
  see also *painture*
painture 277–278, 279–280, 281, 291, 293,
  314, 444
papal power, William of Ockham's challenge
  to 197
paraphrase *see* inaccuracy
parchment slips, transcribing of fair copy onto
  242–243, 261–262, 411
Paris
  glossed books 265
  libraries 200
  University 154, 173, 187
Parkes, Malcolm B. 278
parole 277–278, 279–280, 291–292
Pasquali, Giorgio 271
passio, memorial phantasm as 85
  see also *pathos*
past *see* historical consciousness; time

"patch of new cloth on old garment," image
  of 272
pathos 85–87
patriarchs, mnemonic in *Libellus de formatione
  arche* 299
Pauline Epistles *see* Bible
Paulinus of Nola 47, 117, 124–125
Peacock, Reginald, *Donet* 405
Pearl poet 124
pedagogy, medieval *see* education
penetralia (recesses) 423–424
perception *see* senses
peristereon 42–43
perspective *see distancia*
Peter, Prior of Holy Trinity, Aldgate 430
Peter of Poitiers, *Genealogia* 265–267, 328–329,
  448, 452
Peter of Ravenna 137, 150, 190, 419
  Fenix 143, 407, 409, 456–457
  version of alphabetical mnemonic 127, 137–141,
    143–144, 145, 160, 161
Petrarch (Francesco Petrarca) 212, 216, 225,
  272–273, 423, 442
  accounts of remarkable memories 8,
    76–77, 370
  analysis of reading 203–205, 211
  compositional habits 264
  interpretation of Cave of the Winds passage in
    the *Aeneid* 209–210, 236–237
  library 420
  reputation as authority on memory training
    8, 203
  Rerum memorandarum libri 203, 217–218, 228
  and Richard de Bury 200, 422
  Secretum 203–204, 205, 209–210, 423, 426
  veneration for St. Augustine 203
phantasm *see* memory-images
Philippe de Thaon, Bestiary 159–160
Philo of Alexandria 51–53, 144
philosophy, relationship with rhetoric 28
physiological theory of memory *see* medical
  theory of memory; memory-images
"Physiologus" 160
pictura(e)/"picturing" 155, 160, 186, 274,
  291–293
  pictura (imperative?) in manuscript margin 136
  as synonymous with writing 308
  see also diagrams; Gregory I;
    memory-images: pictorial nature;
    painture; "word-pictures"
Piers Plowman (Langland) 49, 232, 404
  manuscript decorations 288–291, 445–446
  manuscript variations 264, 446
pigeon-hole metaphor 37–38, 42–44, 382
  see also dove

pilgrims' badges, as manuscript motif 323
plagiarism 271–273
   modern/medieval attitudes to 262–263, 273, 440
   as poor *memoria* 271–272, 273
Plato
   doctrine of recollection 18, 29
   Laws 25
   metaphors for memory 19, 24–25, 37–38,
      42–43, 372
   Phaedrus 18, 35–36, 139, 180, 211, 379–380, 381
   and relationship between writing and memory
      18, 35–36, 139, 375
   Republic, composition 251
   Theaetetus 24–25, 37–38, 42–43, 374
Platonism 40
   see also Neoplatonism
"*Plena et perfecta*" (gloss on *Rhetorica ad*
   Herennium) 187, 191
Pliny the Elder (C. Plinius Secundus) 93, 370
poetry
   composition 206
   oral style 440
   see also verses, mnemonic
polemical writing, composition of 197
Pompey the Great (Cn. Pompeius Magnus)
   223, 431
popes, listed in *Libellus de formatione arche* 299
Porphyry, *Isagoge* 395
prayer
   Aquinas's recourse to, during composition 3,
      248–249
   monastic 56, 247–248
preaching *see* sermons
pressmarks 412
Priscian 181–182
prose, rhythms 141, 408
prostitutes, Albertus Magnus's reference to 178
prostration *see* composition: physical
   accompaniments
Protagoras 218
prudence 81–84, 393
   Albertus Magnus's discussion of
      87–88, 345
   distinction between "know-how" and
      82–83, 88
   ethical character 82–83, 172, 237
   relationship with *memoria* 83–84, 87–89,
      191, 219
   three-eyed representation 238, 456
   see also Cicero; Thomas Aquinas
Psalms 121–122
   divisional schemes and citational conventions
      102, 123–127 (*see also* numbering *below*)
   glossed format 267–268
   images accompanying 282–287, 327

incipit (opening phrase), mnemonic
   importance 102, 103, 127
   memorizing xiii–xiv, 101–103, 106, 112, 123, 125,
      222, 285, 340
   (mis)quotation 116
   numbering 124–127, 403, 404
   vernacular translations 402
   verse divisions 125–126
Psalters 121–122, 208, 281–287
   picture-pages in 327
   as study books 282–283
   variant wordings 282
   see also Cuerden Psalter; Eadwine Psalter;
      Herbert of Bosham; Rutland Psalter;
      Utrecht Psalter
psychoanalysis 227, 372–373, 398
psychologists, cognitive, interest in memory 19,
   378–379
public memory 28, 229
   entry of literary work into 234 (*see also*
      literature: socialization)
public speaking *see* oratory
punctuation 141, 142, 232–233, 433–434
   manuscript decoration as subspecies of 280–281
   see also *cola*; *commata*; Quintilian
puns *see* homophony

Quintilian(us), M. Fabius 92–93, 180, 205, 218,
   325, 408, 411, 414
   advice to orators 44, 109, 185, 208, 416, 444
   and architectural mnemonic 89, 92–93, 143, 153
   and compositional process/methods 241, 243,
      248, 250, 251–255, 256–257, 260, 437
   defines *hexis* 86, 222, 394
   doubt about utility of memory for words
      92–93, 98
   on *florilegia* 221–222
   influence on medieval scholars 107, 110, 183, 324
   on learning the alphabet 140–141
   and memory-images 67, 78, 309–310, 392, 438
   metaphors for memory 25, 40, 47, 78, 324, 424
   on plagiarism 272, 273
   and principle of *divisio* 92, 104, 125, 141,
      146, 310
   on reading and meditation 92, 112, 276, 429
   recommends always using same codex (to aid
      memorizing) 92
   recommends learning outstanding literary
      texts by heart 111
   and use of *notae* and key-words 92, 135–136
"quotation," practice of 130–131, 233
   see also citational conventions

rabbits, in *bas-de-page* pictorial narrative 315
Rabelais, François 207

Rackham, H. 91, 396
ram, memory-images of 174, 178, 416
Ramus, Peter / Ramism 37, 192
Rand, E. K. 84
reading
    active agency of reader 209–211, 230–231,
        264–265, 337
    aloud 92, 112, 212, 214–215, 277, 291 (*see also*
        murmur; voice-level)
    analyses 202–212
    ancient reading habits 212–217
    as dialogue between two memories
        211–212 (*see also* "hermeneutical":
        "dialogue")
    as essentially visual act 20–21
    ethical nature 211, 226–227 (*see also under*
        ethics/morality)
    Greek and Latin verbs for 34
    incomplete 231–233
    learning 408
    mealtime 208–209, 258
    and memorizing 129, 136, 197–198, 201–202
    monastic 112, 208–209, 237
    reading-seduction of Paolo and Francesca in
        Dante's *Inferno* 230–233
    Richard de Bury's description of 44–45
    silent 212–217, 428
    see also Augustine; books;
        digestion–rumination metaphor;
        "familiarization"; Gregory I; Hugh of
        St. Victor; illiteracy; Isidore of Seville;
        Jerome; *lectio*; literacy; Petrarch; Quintilian;
        texts; voice-level
reason and emotion, in composition 247–248
rebus 274, 285–287, 309–310, 314–315, 328,
    333, 337
recitare/recitation
    distinction between *retinere* and 115, 235
    role in medieval education 110, 141, 399–400
    see also iteration; "rote" memory
recollection 75–81, 93, 97–98
    definitions 23–24, 29, 56, 79–81
    distinction between "rote" memory and
        22–23 (*see also* "rote" memory)
    errors of 77–78, 95, 335
    as foundation of moral training 87–89
    metaphors for 323–324
    technological models 380
    see also accuracy; Albertus Magnus; Aristotle;
        associative nature of memory; memory-
        images; order; Plato; *reminiscentia*; Thomas
        Aquinas
recordari 59–60, 214
Reginald (friar-companion of Thomas Aquinas)
    3, 5–6, 7–8, 249

Regula magistri 51, 112, 208–209, 425
Regula monachorum 207–208
"remember," medieval use of verb 160, 186
Remigius of Auxerre 6, 109
reminiscentia/reminiscence 56, 355, 391–392
    see also recollection
Renaissance commentators, responses to
    medieval culture 238, 239
Renart fables 315
reportatio (written-up draft composition) 255
representation theory 275–277, 372, 375
res
    definition 28
    of literary text 235, 236–237, 241, 252–253,
        260–261
    pictures as cues for 275, 308–309
    relationship between word and 28–31, 234–235
    see also composition; memory for things
        (*memoria ad res*)
Li response du Bestiaire (anon.) 277
retinere 115, 235
Revelations (Bible) 209, 300
rhetoric 13, 49–50
    Alcuin's dialogue with Charlemagne on
        memoria and 179–180
    "art" of memory dissociated from study of 172,
        180–181, 190
    ethics and 35–36, 50, 92–93, 218, 224–225
    handbooks of 122, 157
    medieval curriculum 186–187, 228, 237
    memoria as part of x, 8, 11, 15, 56, 107, 179,
        191–192, 257, 378–379, 380, 456
    relationship with philosophy *see under*
        philosophy
    Roman 93, 218, 228
    "topics" of 33
    see also oratory
Rhetorica ad Herennium xiii, 16–17, 21, 129, 254, 293
    authorship 394
    counsels against substituting memory schemes
        of others for one's own 97, 180
    description of architectural mnemonic 32, 79,
        89–93, 99–100, 101, 315, 331
    discussion of "memory for things" and
        "memory for words" 91, 98, 110
    and distinction between natural and artificial
        memory 88, 142
    Italian and French translations 192,
        193–194, 229
    manuscripts 175–176, 415
    medieval study/commentaries 153–155, 156–159,
        161, 178, 181–182, 186, 187, 191, 198–199, 409,
        412, 418 (*see also* Albertus Magnus; John of
        Garland; Thierry of Chartres; Thomas
        Aquinas)

metaphors for memory 25, 40, 47
on prudence 81
revival, in thirteenth century 154–155, 182,
  281–282, 416–417
on solitude 216
textual variants 456
see also "Alanus" gloss; *De memoria artificiale
  adquirenda*; *locus*; memory-images
rhyme, internal, use of 439, 446
rhythm *see* prose
Ricci, Matteo xii–xiii
Richard de Bury 292, 401, 422–423, 433
  on collecting and memorizing of books
    200–202
  use of bees and honey trope 44–45
  view of scribal copying 202
Richard de Fournival 277–278, 291, 292, 305
  Li Bestiaire d'amours 277–278, 443
Richard of St. Victor 303
Richardson, J. T. E. 26, 372, 373
Riché, Pierre 17, 111, 112, 399–400, 417
Ricoeur, Paul xi, 17, 28
Ridevall, John 292, 452–453
rimor, used for meditative reading 215, 429
Rivers, Kimberley 405
Robert of Basevorn 256, 440, 446
  discussion of quoting 130, 233
  and sermon division 131–133, 134, 158–159
Robertson, D. W. 433
Rolle, Richard, English psalter of 121–122
Romance of Sir Bevis of Hamptoun 49
Romberch, Johannes Host von,
  Congestorium artificiose memorie 161, 413,
    419, 450, 452
Rome, ancient, cultivation of memory 12
  see also Greece; rhetoric
room, as memory-place 135
Root, R. K. 264
Rorty, Richard 17
rosary 99
Rossi, Paolo 17, 89, 419
Rota Virgili 329–330
"rote" memory
  advice against 92–93, 113
  distinction between *memoria* and xii, 22–23,
    77, 103–104
  etymology 330–331, 374, 453
  role in medieval education 102–104, 111
  see also *recitare*
Rouse, Richard/Mary 17, 128–129, 134–135, 199,
  220, 403, 421
Rowland, Beryl 414
rubrics/*rubricator* 117, 278–279, 302, 307
  "pictorial" 281
Rudolph, Conrad 446–447

rumination *see* digestion–rumination metaphor
Rutland Psalter 170

sacculus (money-pouch), as metaphor for
  memory 40, 45–46, 329
  Hugh of St. Victor's use of 45, 101, 116–117, 329,
    339–340
  Richard de Bury's use of 200–201
Sacks, Oliver, *The Man Who Mistook His Wife for
  a Hat* 391–392
St. Albans abbey 281
St. Bartholomew's priory, Smithfield *see*
  Decretals: Smithfield
St. Mary's abbey, Holmecultram *see*
  Holmecultram
St. Victor, cathedral school of 100–101, 102–103,
  178, 283–285
saints
  (alleged) memory feats 14, 89
  lives of, in *bas-de-page* pictorial narratives 315
Sallust (C. Sallustius Crispus) 84
Sandler, L. F. 332, 414
Sandys, John Edwin 43
sapientia (wisdom, knowledge) 104
  arbor sapientiae 258–259, 439 (see also under *De
    archa Noe*)
  prudence as 81–82, 83, 219
  see also *arca sapientiae*
Saussure, Ferdinand de 37
Saxl, Fritz 332, 418
"scanning" (ability to move around memory
  instantly and securely) 8–9, 21–22, 79–80,
  90, 140–141
  see also order; starting-point; texts: backwards/
    forwards recollection
scatological imagery, use of 207–208, 425
Schmitt, Jean-Claude x
scholasticism 16–17, 89
Scott, Kathleen 445–446
Scotus Eriugena, John 331
scribere 242–243
scribes 255, 264, 422–423
  editorial powers 441
  as "painters" 280–281
  Thomas Aquinas's use of 5–6, 7
  unreliability 202
scrinium, as metaphor for memory 40, 46–49,
  423–424
  scrinarius 46
scripts, use of different, for text and commentary
  265–267, 271, 423, 436
  see also littera inintelligibilis; *textualis formata*
seal-in-wax model
  applied to moral character 89, 224
  basic to Thomas Aquinas's analysis 70

seal-in-wax model (cont.)
  of memory 16, 24–25, 32–33, 34, 60, 70, 90, 91,
    374, 378, 395
  see also wax tablets
secretorium 46–47
sedes, used for mental locations 33, 110
Seneca, L. Annaeus 42, 83, 84, 182, 238, 381, 435
  Quintilian and 93, 121–122, 180
  and trope of reader/author as bee 44,
    237–238
senses / sensory perception 69–70, 72–73
  errors of perception 95
  inward/interior, conception of 57–58, 64
  memory as final process of sensory perception
    97–98
  see also hearing; *sensus communis*; sight; smell;
    taste; touch
sensus communis 62, 63–65, 67–68, 74, 390
sententia, defined 114–115
sententialiter, remembering material 111, 114–115,
    116, 169, 400
Serenus of Marseilles, Bishop 274, 275,
    277, 443
sermons
  composition/publication 198, 255–257
  delivery 122
  extempore 206, 256–257
  numerical division 131, 256
  "oral" *vs.* "written" style 260
  "university" *vs.* "popular" 131
  see also Thomas of Waleys
Servatus Lupus 416–417
Seven Deadly Sins, depictions of 288–289,
    328, 452
"seven plus or minus two," rule of 105, 164
sexuality
  in metaphors for reading 382
  in mnemonic images 168, 171–172
Shakespeare, William 217
Shereshevski ("S.," Russian mnemonist) 16,
    94–98, 104, 122, 159, 291–292, 396, 416
short-hand symbols 141
  see also abbreviations; *notae*
Sicard, Patrice 400–401, 448
Sigebert of Gembloux 373
sight/visual sense
  primacy 19, 122, 274, 373
  Thomas Aquinas on special nature of 69–70
  see also memory-images: pictorial nature
signa 184–185
  see also *notae*
signs/signification theory 25, 29–31, 308, 450
silence 427
  silent reading *see under* reading
  silentium 215, 282, 429

silva (forest, disordered material) 252
  as metaphor for untrained memory 39, 78, 324
  of Scripture 205
Silverstein, Theodore 115, 400
Simonides 25–26, 110, 183, 250, 327
Simplicius, Augustine's description of 21–22, 40
Singleton, Charles 279
sins *see* Seven Deadly Sins
Skeat, Walter 49
sleep *see* dream-images
Smalley, Beryl 113, 177, 292–293, 294, 421–422
  on the Bible 14
smell, sense of 69
Smith, L. 436
Smithfield Decretals *see* Decretals
Smits van Waesberghe, Joseph 406
Socrates (Greek church historian) 255–256
Socrates (philosopher) 24, 35–36, 37–38,
    379–380
solitude
  synonymous with *sollicitudo* for Thomas
    Aquinas 216, 429
solmization 133–134, 406–407
Solomon (Biblical character) 300
Sommercote, Robert de, Cardinal 277
sophismata 116–117, 218, 401
Sorabji, Richard 19, 34, 72, 76, 79, 375
sortilege, using books for 203, 431
soul
  Aristotelian analysis 60, 63–64, 65, 85, 436
  Augustinian analysis 81
  Neoplatonist view 381–382
sound, nature of 388–389
  see also auditory memory; hearing; noise
Southern, R. W. 223, 426, 435
spatial memory *see under* memory-images
Speculum theologiae 332–333
Spenser, Edmund 46
"squire who laid eggs" fable 315, 450–451
starting-point, mnemonic requirement of 77,
    79, 109
Statius, P. Papinius 271
Stock, Brian 14, 17, 263, 371
stomach–memory metaphor 206, 207–208, 388
  see also diet; digestion–rumination metaphor
Stone, Lawrence 15
store-house model, of memory 16, 37–55, 101,
    180, 237–238, 318–323
  importance of structure 39
  see also *apotheca*; *thesaurus*
strepitus (loud noise, confusion) *see* noise
string tied round finger, as memory aid 314, 450
structuralism 37
Suger, Abbot of St.-Denis 453–454
Swift, Jonathan 45

syllables
  as basic unit for teaching reading 408
  indexing by 150–151, 410
  "memory for" (Bradwardine) 169–170, 365–368
syllogism, mnemonic 99, 396
synaesthesia 97, 291–292, 315, 396

Tacitus, P. Cornelius 93
Tale of Beryn 49
taste, sense of 69, 97
Taylor-Briggs, Ruth 416–417
Terence (P. Terentius Afer) 84
texts
  ancient/medieval attitudes to 239–240
  backwards/forwards recollection xiii, 21–22,
    113, 168
  distinguished from books 9
  etymology of term 14
  see also accuracy; authority/authorship; books;
    composition; *divisio*; glosses; manuscripts;
    reading; *res* (of literary text); writing
textualis formata 267
textualism 13
"textualization" 11, 14
  see also "familiarization"
textus/textum 14
Thammuz (Ammon) 35–36, 95–96
"theatre" aspect of medieval culture *see* audience
themes, memory for (*memoria orationis*) 169,
  185–186, 315
Theodectes, prodigious memory of 92
thesaurus 37, 40–41, 101, 200–201
  see also store-house model; treasure-house/
    treasury, memory as
Theuth (Thoth) 35–36
Thierry of Chartres 398, 418
  commentary on *Rhetorica ad Herennium*
    187–189, 447
  contemporary/later influence 189
thing(s) *see imagines rerum*; memory for things;
  res; word *verbum*: representational
  relationship with thing
Thomas Aquinas, St. 2–4, 9, 244, 276, 382, 437
  analysis of mental imagery 69–73
  and Aristotelianism 15, 83–84, 190, 374, 375,
    389, 390, 394, 455
  Catena aurea 3, 6, 113
  commends architectural mnemonic 155, 192,
    193, 203
  commentary on Isaiah 5–6
  commentary on Psalms 10
  commentary on *Rhetorica ad Herennium*
    82–83, 216, 429
  compositional habits 4–8, 242, 245, 246,
    248–249, 251, 252, 261, 421

concept of "intellectual memory" 62–63,
  73, 388
contemporaries' admiration for 14, 217
on memory as habit / condition for prudence
  81–84, 86–87, 88, 191–192
memory training advice 9, 62, 216
on nature of recollection 80, 81, 191, 393
range of sources 6, 84, 177
Summa contra gentiles 5, 146–147, 251
Summa theologiae 5–6, 7, 67, 72, 251
understanding of knowledge/perception/
  memory 60, 62–63, 69–73
  see also littera inintelligibilis; sight
Thomas of Celano 3, 217, 429–430
Thomas of Ireland, *Manipulus florum* 435
Thomas Waleys 182, 235
  advice on preparation of sermons 113–115, 131, 256
  and citation 126, 130, 405
Thomson, S. Harrison 147–148
Thoth *see* Theuth
Tichfield Abbey, Hampshire, medieval library
  of 411
time, and memory 54, 74, 83–84,
  238–240, 377
  see also historical consciousness; "occasion"
tituli (summary phrases on manuscripts)
  109, 450
  enclosed in images 310–314, 450
topos, topica 33–34, 38–39
  defined 417
  relationship with mnemonic "places"/topics
    79, 222, 395
touch, sense of 69, 97
  "tactile memory" 19
"Tower of Wisdom" 454
Towneley plays 49
tractare, tractandum 136, 424
  see also *forma tractatus/tractandi*
Tracy, Theodore 85–86, 387, 390, 394
treasure-house/treasury, memory as 37–38, 107,
  142, 252, 339
  see also thesaurus
tree diagrams see *arbor sapientiae*; diagrams; Tree
  of . . .
Tree of Jesse 328
Tree of Life 301, 323, 333
Tree of Vices and Virtues 333
triads 79
Trimpi, Wesley, *Muses of One Mind* 17,
  375–376
tropology 210, 343, 447
Tully/Tullius see *Rhetorica ad Herennium*:
  authorship of
turba ("crowding"), as mnemonic enemy 249,
  269, 273

Uccelli, Pietro 5
umbra 162
unicorn, as memory-image for "one" 170
universities, medieval 156, 186–187, 192–193, 199,
    247–248, 269, 399–400, 423, 446
Urban IV, Pope 3
Urban VIII, Pope 45
Utrecht Psalter 282–285, 404, 445

Valerius Maximus 84, 228
van der Horst, Koert 445
Vance, Eugene 450
Varro (Reatinus), M. Terentius 59, 84, 437
Vatican library 45
Vegetius 84
Venus, Albertus Magnus's comment on 178
vermis 68
vernacular
    authority of texts 441
    memorial *artes* 193
    performance and 432
    sermons 193
    texts, decoration 287
    texts, marginalia/glosses 264–265, 271
    translations into 328, 402, 419
    works of devotion 333
verses, mnemonic 99
vessel of memory 323
vestigia (footprints, tracks), as metaphor for
    recollection *see* hunting
vices 300–302
    see also Seven Deadly Sins
Vickers, Brian 412
Villedieu, Alexandre de, *Doctrinale* 99
violence, in memory-images 168,
        171–172, 451
Virgil (P. Vergilius Maro) 21–22, 43, 84, 177, 215,
    217, 225, 381
    Aeneid 111, 188, 209–210, 211, 236–237, 381
    Augusteus manuscript 281
    Georgics 41, 42, 44–45, 47
    "Wheel of" *see Rota Virgili*
virtues
    as *habitus* 85–86
    Hugh of St. Victor's depiction of 300–302
    Thomas Aquinas's discussion of 81–84
vis aestimativa 62, 65, 244
vis cogitativa 62, 244, 245, 250
vis formalis 67–68, 244, 457
vis imaginativa 62, 73–74, 244, 457
visual sense *see* sight
Vitruvius (M. Vitruvius Pollio) 177
voces 291–292
    paginarum 211–212, 427
    see also *voces animantium*

voces animantium 138, 304
    mnemonic function 158–159, 160
voice-level, association with different reading
    functions 214–215, 278, 417, 427–428, 439
    see also murmur of meditation
Von Nolcken, Christina 220

Ward, John O. 199, 412
Watts, Isaac 45
wax tablets 24–25, 117, 374
    use in composition 242, 251–252, 253,
        260–261
    writing on, to aid memorizing 110, 141, 195, 215
    see also codex; seal-in-wax model
Weinrich, Harald xi–xii
West, Philip J. 206–207
wheel-diagrams *see* diagrams; *Rota Virgili*
wheels, moving 331
will *see* desire
William of Alnwick 148, 411
William of Champeaux 178, 187, 416
William of Moerbeke 71, 85, 375
William of Ockham 196–198, 199, 203, 219, 315
    contemporary influence 197
    Dialogus 113, 127, 196–197, 421
    use of *tractandum* 424
William of Shoreham 330
wisdom see *sapientia*
wise men (Magi), *thesauri* of 41
Wittgenstein, Ludwig 26
Wolfson, H. A. 57–58, 65, 386
women, images of, to stimulate memory 137
Wood of Life (*lignum vitae*) *see* Tree of Life
"word-pictures" 281–309
word/*verbum*
    Augustine's notion of "inner word"
        29–30, 377
    representational relationship with thing 28–31
    sound (*parole*) called to mind by visual shape
        (*painture*) of 278
    unfamiliar, method of storing in memory
        157–159
    see also memory for words; *parole*;
        "word-pictures"
wrestling, in marginal images 323
writing
    as fundamental to human society/
        language 36
    introduction into oral culture 380
    likened to picturing 26–27
    practice in, as discipline of memory 195
    relationship to composing 241–242
    relationship to memory 9–10, 18, 34–36,
        139–140, 251–252
    relationship to thought 123

as social product 36–37
teaching of 195
vocalizing while 243, 431
"writer," early usage 436
see also Isidore of Seville; *scribere*; scribes;
   scripts
Wyclif, John 11, 376
Wynkyn de Worde 409

Yates, Frances 17, 92, 160, 182, 192, 331–332, 417,
   419, 423, 429
   and architectural mnemonic 89, 93, 154, 178, 181

Zeno (the Stoic) 40
Zinn, G. A. 396–397
Zodiac 138, 159–160, 302, 324, 414
   Bradwardine's use of 159, 167–168, 364

CAMBRIDGE STUDIES IN MEDIEVAL LITERATURE

1. Robin Kirkpatrick *Dante's Inferno: Difficulty and Dead Poetry*
2. Jeremy Tambling *Dante and Difference: Writing in the "Commedia"*
3. Simon Gaunt *Troubadours and Irony*
4. Wendy Scase *"Piers Plowman" and the New Anticlericalism*
5. Joseph Duggan *The "Cantar De Mio Cid": Poetic Creation in its Economic and Social Contexts*
6. Roderick Beaton *The Medieval Greek Romance*
7. Kathryn Kerby-Fulton *Reformist Apocalypticism and "Piers Plowman"*
8. Alison Morgan *Dante & the Medieval Other World*
9. Eckehard Simon (ed.) *The Theatre of Medieval Europe: New Research in Early Drama*
10. Mary Carruthers *The Book of Memory: A Study of Memory in Medieval Culture*
11. Rita Copeland *Rhetoric, Hermeneutics and Translation in the Middle Ages: Academic Traditions and Vernacular Texts*
12. Donald Maddox *The Arthurian Romances of Chrétien de Troyes: Once and Future Fictions*
13. Nicholas Watson *Richard Rolle and the Invention of Authority*
14. Steven F. Kruger *Dreaming in the Middle Ages*
15. Barbara Nolan *Chaucer and the Tradition of the "Roman Antique"*
16. Sylvia Huot *The "Romance of the Rose" and its Medieval Readers: Interpretations, Reception, Manuscript Transmission*
17. Carol M. Meale (ed.) *Women and Literature in Britain, 1150–1500*
18. Henry Ansgar Kelly *Ideas and Forms of Tragedy from Aristotle to the Middle Ages*
19. Martin Irvine *The Making of Textual Culture: Grammatica and Literary Theory, 350–1100*
20. Larry Scanlon *Narrative, Authority and Power: The Medieval Exemplum and the Chaucerian Tradition*
21. Erik Kooper *Medieval Dutch Literature in its European Context*
22. Steven Botterill *Dante and the Mystical Tradition: Bernard of Clairvaux in the "Commedia"*
23. Peter Biller and Anne Hudson (eds) *Heresy and Literacy, 1000–1530*
24. Christopher Baswell *Virgil in Medieval England: Figuring the "Aeneid" from the Twelfth Century to Chaucer*
25. James Simpson *Sciences and Self in Medieval Poetry: Alan of Lille's "Anticlaudianus" and John Gower's "Confessio Amantis"*
26. Joyce Coleman *Public Reading and the Reading Public in Late Medieval England and France*
27. Suzanne Reynolds *Medieval Reading: Grammar, Rhetoric and the Classical Text*
28. Charlotte Brewer *Editing "Piers Plowman": The Evolution of the Text*
29. Walter Haug *Vernacular Literary Theory in the Middle Ages: The German Tradition in its European Context*

30. Sarah Spence *Texts and the Self in the Twelfth Century*
31. Edwin Craun *Lies, Slander and Obscenity in Medieval English Literature: Pastoral Rhetoric and the Deviant Speaker*
32. Patricia E. Grieve *"Floire and Blancheflor" and the European Romance*
33. Huw Pryce (ed.) *Literacy in Medieval Celtic Societies*
34. Mary Carruthers *The Craft of Thought: Meditation, Rhetoric, and the Making of Images, 400–1200*
35. Beate Schmolke-Hasselman *The Evolution of Arthurian Romance: The Verse Tradition from Chrétien to Froissart*
36. Siân Echard *Arthurian Narrative in the Latin Tradition*
37. Fiona Somerset *Clerical Discourse and Lay Audience in Late Medieval England*
38. Florence Percival *Chaucer's Legendary Good Women*
39. Christopher Cannon *The Making of Chaucer's English: A Study of Words*
40. Rosalind Brown-Grant *Christine de Pizan and the Moral Defence of Women: Reading Beyond Gender*
41. Richard Newhauser *The Early History of Greed: The Sin of Avarice in Early Medieval Thought and Literature*
42. Margaret Clunies Ross *Old Icelandic Literature and Society*
43. Donald Maddox *Fictions of Identity in Medieval France*
44. Rita Copeland *Pedagogy, Intellectuals, and Dissent in the Later Middle Ages: Lollardy and Ideas of Learning*
45. Kantik Ghosh *The Wycliffite Heresy: Authority and the Interpretation of Texts*
46. Mary C. Erler *Women, Reading, and Piety in Late Medieval England*
47. D. H. Green *The Beginnings of Medieval Romance: Fact and Fiction 1150–1220*
48. J. A. Burrow *Gestures and Looks in Medieval Narrative*
49. Ardis Butterfield *Poetry and Music in Medieval France: From Jean Renart to Guillaume de Machaut*
50. Emily Steiner *Documentary Culture and the Making of Medieval English Literature*
51. William E. Burgwinkle *Sodomy, Masculinity, and Law in Medieval Literature*
52. Nick Havely *Dante and the Franciscans: Poverty and the Papacy in the "Commedia"*
53. Siegfried Wenzel *Latin Sermon Collections from Later Medieval England*
54. Ananya Jahanara Kabir and Deanne Williams (eds) *Postcolonial Approaches to the European Middle Ages: Translating Cultures*
55. Mark Miller *Philosophical Chaucer: Love, Sex, and Agency in the "Canterbury Tales"*
56. Simon Gilson *Dante and Renaissance Florence*
57. Ralph Hanna *London Literature, 1300–1380*
58. Maura Nolan *John Lydgate and the Making of Public Culture*
59. Nicolette Zeeman *Piers Plowman and the Medieval Discourse of Desire*
60. Anthony Bale *The Jew in the Medieval Book: English Antisemitisms 1300–1500*
61. Robert J. Meyer-Lee *Poets and Power from Chaucer to Wyatt*
62. Isabel Davis *Writing Masculinity in the Later Middle Ages*

63. John M. Fyler *Language and the Declining World in Chaucer, Dante and Jean de Meun*
64. Matthew Giancarlo *Parliament and Literature in Late Medieval England*
65. D. H. Green *Women Readers in the Middle Ages*
66. Mary Dove *The First English Bible: The Text and Context of the Wycliffite Versions*
67. Jenni Nuttall *The Creation of Lancastrian Kingship: Literature, Language and Politics in Late Medieval England*
68. Laura Ashe *Fiction and History in England, 1066–1200*
69. J. A. Burrow *The Poetry of Praise*
70. Mary Carruthers *The Book of Memory, Second Edition*